GUEST OF THE EMPEROR

The Story of Dick Darden

To Senator Faircloth,
Best wishes.
Jim Darden
Sept. 17, 2014

by James B. Darden, III

GUESTS OF THE EMPEROR
The Story of Dick Darden

The Greenhouse Press
Clinton, North Carolina, USA

ISBN # 0-9615912-1-8

Cover designed by Joseph Johnson II, on a Macintosh Computer

DEDICATION

I take great pride in dedicating this book to the following four individuals:

James B. (Dick) Darden, Jr.—My father, a man who was wounded in the defense of American territory and spent all but sixteen days of World War II in Japanese prisoner of war camps. He has given his all for his country and for the people close to him.

Ralph Holewinski—A man who served his country by taking his pride in his homeland to the ultimate limits. He stood face to face with death on more than one occasion, was severely wounded in the defense of his country, and served forty-five months in an enemy prison camp.

Col. Arthur A. Poindexter—A man who charged a Japanese landing craft armed with hand grenades and who successfully led his men in an attack of enemy ground forces while being vastly outnumbered. He endured forty-five months in enemy prisons, and he personifies a professional military man of the highest caliber.

James H. (Jim) Cox—A member of the Navy boat crew on Wake Island who served during the final battle as a machine gunner under the command of Lt. Arthur Poindexter. Jim Cox remained at his machine gun position throughout the entire fifteen day Battle of Wake Island He was captured and spent forty-five months in a Japanese prisoner of war camp.

SPECIAL ACKNOWLEDGEMENT

Dozens of books, interviews, pamphlets, magazine articles, and other sources of information have been used in the compilation of the factual and historical data in this book. (see the bibliography) It has been my sincere effort to be truthful, factual, and accurate regarding the information herein.

However, the true picture has been difficult to derive because virtually every participant and source of information tells the story in a slightly different manner. In addition, recollections of the events have become clouded and/or embellished during the interceding forty-seven years, and inter-service rivalries have shaped various accounts of the action which took place during World War II and on Wake Island.

I have, therefore, chosen to use THE DEFENSE OF WAKE, by Lt. Col. R. D. Heinl, Jr., U.S.M.C., as the final authority for the information concerning Wake Island. In preparing this monograph, published by the Marine Corps in 1947, Col. Heinl interviewed many of the participants soon after the war when their recollection of events was at its best. This publication is corroborated by the actual participants in virtually all instances.

I have relied heavily on Col. Heinl's work for the chronology of events that occurred on Wake Island. It has been used to establish the sequence of historical events, derive factual and historical data, authenticate information acquired through personal interviews, and settle disputes or disagreements which have arisen. THE DEFENSE OF WAKE is considered by this author as the final word concerning the time period prior to and during the Battle of Wake Island.

MY SINCERE THANKS TO EVERYONE WHO HAS MADE THIS BOOK POSSIBLE, ESPECIALLY THE FOLLOWING:

To my Dad, the many interviews and complete support that he has given have been invaluable, and without them this book would not have been possible.

To my Wife, Mary Nell, who has endured my many hours at the word processor, my travels, my expenditures, all the while allowing the book to happen.

To Michael Rhode, Archivist at the Institute of Pathology, Walter Reed Medical Center, Washington, who freely gave his time and efforts to dig POW photos from deep within vaults, a professional who has my great respect.

To Kathy Lloyd, Naval Archives, Washington, D.C., whose interest in our project was very much appreciated, and whose keen knowledge of war records added immensely to this book, particularly the records of POW's and war trials.

To Charles Haberlein, Naval History, Washington Navy Yard, whose expert knowledge of the whereabouts of Naval historical photos led to many of the photos in this book, which otherwise I would not have been able to locate.

To William Jordan, Director of Admissions at Sampson Community College, without whose help at the computer I would be years away from finishing this book.

To Susan Nance Sautter, Marsha Williams, and Brig. Gen. Joseph Nagel, who read and re-read my manuscripts to help correct and improve my feeble attempts at writing.

To Joseph Johnson II for converting my TRS-80 files to Macintosh files so it could be sent to the publisher.

To Carolyn and David Johnson for laying out the book.

To Mark Rushing for photographic assistance.

To Jerry Morgan for acting as publishing agent for *Guests of the Emperor* .

GUESTS OF THE EMPEROR
The Story Of Dick Darden

Table of Contents

PART 1—FROM THE BEGINNING TO WAKE ISLAND

PART 2—THE SIEGE OF WAKE ISLAND

PART 1
FROM THE BEGINNING TO WAKE ISLAND

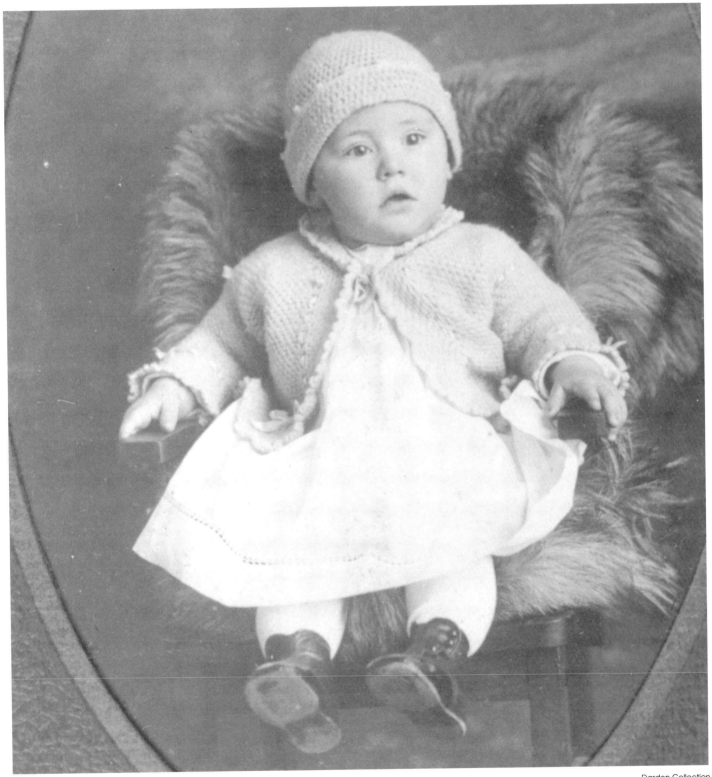

Dick Darden at one year old, 1921.

Chapter 1
THE EARLY YEARS

James Bizzell Darden Jr. was born in Clinton, North Carolina, on January 29, 1920, the son of James B. Darden and Eva Bell Williamson Darden. Dick, as he would be called, grew up in a typical small southern town, nestled in the rich farming country of the sandy coastal plain of The Old North State.

Dick was descended from Stephen Durden, who sailed to the tidewater area of Virginia from England in 1681. Five generations later, just after the Revolutionary War, William Darden moved from Virginia to Sampson County, North Carolina. Several of the Dardens migrated southward and westward during the ensueing years. A few, including Dick's forefathers, remained on the rich lands of their small farms in this remote area and endured the toil and turmoil of the nineteenth century. They were poor, and they had few, if any, slaves, to help them farm the soil.

Dick's grandfather was an exception. He was Dr. James Hicks Darden, a prominent physician. Dr. Darden had been a surgeon in the Confederate Army. He was only 26 years old when the war started in 1861, but he had already finished medical school in Philadelphia and begun to practice medicine. He enlisted in the Confederate Army on February 4, 1863, and became the Assistant Surgeon for the infantry in Regiment 38. Dr. Darden was hospitalized in Richmond, Virginia, on July 10, 1864 with "febris remut," or, recurring fever. Sixteen days later, on July 26, he was furloughed for thirty days. Dr. Darden returned to the army at the end of his furlough. Less than nine months later, on April 9, 1865, Dr. Darden and the Confederate Army surrendered at Appomattox Court House, Virginia, with General Robert E. Lee.

After the war ended Dr. Darden returned to the rural Piney Grove area of northern Sampson County. The countryside had been devastated by the Yankee army. A large segment of Sherman's army, some 60,000 strong, had marched through the northern end of the county in March, engaging General Johnston's 30,000 Confederates at Bentonville, just a few miles from the Darden homeplace.

The bloody encounter at Bentonville was the largest battle of the war fought in North Carolina, but in the end the Yankees overpowered the outnumbered Rebels. Johnston withdrew under the cover of darkness and retreated northward. At Bennett Place, just outside Durham, Johnston learned of Lee's surrender at Appomatox and surrendered his army to the Federals.

James Hicks Darden and the boys of the Conferderate Army, haggard and beaten, trickled back southward to their homes. The vast majority had been poor dirt farmers before the war, far poorer than the modern stereotype of the rich plantation owners like those portrayed in Gone With The Wind. Even though they had been soundly beaten, the returning Conferderate boys were intensely proud and intent upon retaining their small farms and meager lifestyle.

The returning men found their home county in virtual ruins. It was too late to plant a spring crop, so food became a scarce commodity. Most Southerners had put their heart and soul into the Conferderate cause, not to mention most of their money. When they returned their Confederate money was worthless. The few who had been affluent enough to own slaves before the war had lost the labor of the Colored folks who had worked the farms with them. For several years the Yankees occupied the area, which was in economic chaos.

Holding on to their meager land and possessions became a struggle for Southern whites. Dr. Darden was a physician and fared better than most. Large numbers of less fortunate Southerners lost what they had and were forced to move on to new lands farther south or west. Many went to Georgia, Alabama, and Texas, while others moved to the relatively undeveloped lands of Tennessee and Arkansas. Some banded together to try to save whatever they could by any means necessary.

The political, social, and economic circumstances in the South during the early part of the twentieth century, during Dick Darden's youth in the 1920's and 1930's, were spawned during the bleak years that followed the War Between the States. Perhaps we can better understand the conditions that existed in Sampson County and influenced young Dick by learning of the friends and relatives of his father and grandfather and the decades prior to his birth. Dick was born only fifty-five years after the war ended, and many of those

Dick's Parents, Eva Bell Williamson & James Bizzell Darden

Darden Collection

Jim Darden holding Dick with Aunt Mary Bell and Aunt Maggie Fitzgerald, summer 1920.

who actually participated in the Confederate cause were still alive when he was a youngster.

Just before the war had ended a group of Confederates known as Wheeler's Scouts had come into Sampson County. This unit had kept tabs on Sherman's army as it moved northward from Savannah and Columbia. They reported the whereabouts and movements of the enemy force to Confederates army regulars in the area. It was said that when Wheeler and his men encountered Federal advance scouts they killed them, never taking prisoners. When the war ended a number of Wheeler's men blended into the population, remaining in the county rather than returning to their homes and the possibility of reprisals.

After the war it was said that many Southerners, particularly the more militant factions such as the Wheeler's Scouts, never fully accepted the surrender. They formed the nucleus of the white opposition to the carpetbaggers, blacks, and scallawags who united under the Republican banner during Reconstruction. Many from the old Conferderate ranks banded together as Democrats in what they felt was their only alternative to being overrun and chased from their land. Some of the Scouts felt than a different approach was required in order to survive the chaotic times of the 1870's. They formed an organization called the Ku Klux Klan.

Dr. Darden's first cousin and neighbor, George Washington Hargrove, was said to have joined the Klan. It was said that the Blacks had become "unruly" in certain areas. In fact, they outnumbered whites in several parts of the county, and had begun to take power with the help of the Federals and Republicans. The KKK vowed not to let this happen, feeling that everything they owned, along with their families and their culture, was at stake. They felt that the struggle to retain their families, land, and culture legitimized the

use of any methods necessary to keep the Blacks in line. The Klan attempted to use the tactic of intimidation to prevent Blacks from assembling and organizing their quest for power.

During this period of hatred and resentment between the races an incident occured in which a Black man was killed. It was said that George Hargrove was a member of the guilty group. Sinced he was the only single man involved in the incident he agreed to take the blame. He became a fugitive from the Federal authorities and sometime during the 1870's he suddenly vanished from Sampson County.

George W. Hargrove was being sought by Federal agents in connection with the Klan incident. Not even his family knew where he had gone or what had happened to him. George's two sisters, Sudie and Lizzie, neither of whom ever married, remained on the family land, teaching school and trying to cling to their family legacy.

It was later learned that George Hargrove had moved to Texas. There he started a new life, marrying and fathering two boys named Edward and Benjamin Franklin Hargrove. In 1888, when his oldest son was three years old and the youngest only ten months, a mysterious visitor from North Carolina came to see their father. Later it was thought that the visitor was a cousin, Tom Hargrove, from North Carolina. George Hargrove sat and talked with the stranger all day and all night. The next morning the stranger was gone.

Apparently the authorities had learned George's whereabouts. He had been tipped off by the man from North Carolina. George Hargrove told his family that he was going to work at the nearby sawmill. He walked away from the house and out of sight, never to be seen again by his family in Texas. Once again George Washington Hargrove had vanished, leaving his wife and two son behind, never to see them again.

Such as the atmosphere during the social and economic upheaval of the Reconstruction period before the turn of the century. Dr. James H. Darden married Sarah Elizabeth Bradshaw and settled down to practice medicine and raise a family. He and Sarah had eight children, one of whom was James Bizzell Darden.

Dr. Darden's practice included much of the northern end of the county, so he traveled extensively by horse and buggy to serve his patients throughout the rural farmland. After venturing out on late night calls it is said that Dr. Darden was often observed asleep and slumped over in his buggy being pulled down dirt roads in the black of night by his trusty horse, which had been trained to return home through the night without supervision. Dr. Darden practiced medicine until his death in 1905.

Dr. Darden's son James was born in 1878. He was given the middle name Bizzell. Bizzell was a prominent name in the county, since there were four Bizzell brothers near Clinton, all of whom had become medical doctors. Jim Darden became a well known barber in Clinton during the teens and twenties, and he also served as the town's fire chief.

Times were hard for Jim's family. His first wife, Nina Peterson Darden, died in 1915. The next year Jim Darden married Eva Belle Williamson Draughon, who had lost her first husband, Buck. The couple moved into her wood frame house on McKoy Street within sight of the court house square. It was on that square

3

Dick Darden displaying his string of fish after a day at the river with his father.

that Jim operated his barber shop. Eva Bell bore Jim a son four years later in the house on McKoy Street, a son who would carry his name. James B. Darden Jr. would become known as "Dick."

Jim Darden and Nina Peterson had had one daughter, Dick's older half-sister, Frances. Eva Bell and Buck Draughon had two children, Jenny and Buck Jr. This provided Dick with another half-sister and a half-brother. So, Dick Darden came into the world as the fourth child in the family. Four years later, in 1924, another son, Henry Franklin Darden, was born, giving Dick a younger brother. Dick's only full sibling, Henry, became known as "Pete."

When Dick Darden was only a year old in 1921, events were unfolding on the opposite side of the earth which would have a profound effect on the young lad. For centuries there had been a credo in Japan known as HAKKO ICHIU, which espoused the ideology that the destiny of Japan was to bring the entire orient and Pacific hemisphere under its control. Some Japanese, thinking on an even grander scale, believed that Japan would eventually rule the entire earth.

Japan's ideas of expansionism and HAKKO ICHIU had been little more than a smouldering coal for centuries because the island country had been isolated from the occident by its rulers from 1603 until 1853. Only then, when Commodore Mathew C. Perry visited Japan, was it reopened to the outside world. Japanese rulers had excluded foreigners and effectively stifled any expansionist aspirations.

In 1921 a Japanese fascist named Ikki Kita wrote a book which revived the ancient philosophy of HAKKO ICHIU, which means "the way of the warrior." Kita's ideology was called KODO-

HA. Superficially it called for the uniting of brothers of Asian blood, from India to Hawaii, to rise up and crush the "white devils" who were practicing colonialism in Asia. This included the Americans and Europeans who had a foothold in India, Indochina, Malaysia, and throughout the Pacific. The ideology of Kita was strikingly similar to another radical racist, Adolph Hitler, who was active at the same time in Europe.

Kita's 1921 book caused a groundswell of fanaticism that opposed Asian colonialism by western powers. The tactics of KODA-HA called for oppression, terror, and assasination to be used by the Japanese to take over Asia for themselves and force the Europeans out. The followers of Kita believed that the Japanese people were a master race and were destined to rule all of their Asian brothers, whom they regarded as inferior underlings.

Americans did not fail to take note of the militant fever in Japan. As early as 1921 Marine Lt. Col. Earl H. "Pete" Ellis cautioned that a Japanese attack against American forces in the Pacific could occur at Pearl Harbor. He even suggested that it might come early on a Sunday morning.

The Japanese did, indeed, see western colonialism running rampant in Asia during the early 1900's. The British were in Burma, Borneo, and Malaya. The French were in Indochina, later to become the quagmire of Vietnam, and the Dutch were in the East Indies, later to be known as Indonesia. Not to be outdone, the United States had laid claim to the islands of Wake, Midway, and Guam, and maintained a strong presence in the Philippines. As the Japanese watched the ever increasing expansion of western colonialism, they began to feel more and more crowded by the Caucasians.

HAKKO ICHIU portrayed the white men as devils. And, in actual fact, the westerners who brought colonialism to Asia often

Dick and his friend after taking part in a wedding in 1926

4

Darden Collection

Dick's third grade school picture in 1929.

did little to improve their image. They exploited millions of natives, often paying them only pennies a day for backbreaking labor. White men and their governments became wealthy by extracting resources from the orient. The white men often thought of the natives as less than human, evoking the backlash of resentment that gave the followers of HAKKO ICHUI a motive for the initiation of violence.

Japan's ideas of expansionism were heightened by a steadily deteriorating world situation during the Depression of the 1920's. The tiny island country was wrought with economic problems. Most of the people lived as poor peasants, densely crowded together on the limited amount of usable land. The only hope for the bulging population appeared to many to be the usurping of more land and raw materials. The economic problems ultimately led to upheaval, assassinations, uprisings, and finally a takeover by the military zealots who ascribed to the philosophy of HAKKO ICHIU. The Japanese people began to feel that the military was their only salvation from the bad times and corrupt leaders. Even the Emperor, the God of the people, became powerless to control the Japanese military.

By the time Dick Darden was born in 1920 many Southerners had lost their land and left the county, while others had found it necessary to move into town to find work. Jim Darden was among this group, moving into Clinton where Dick was born. The trauma of the Civil War was still affecting many other North Carolinians, including George Washington Hargrove. At about the time of Dick's birth, George returned to see his family in Sampson County. He had been gone for nearly 50 years, and his only surviving sister, Sudie, did not recognize him. He had a long white beard and wore tattered clothes. Though he tried in earnest to convince her of his identity she would not believe him.

George began to tell the story of his travels around the world that had occurred during his long absence. For over a week he lived with neighbors Jim and Frank Bell near his sister Sudie's home, and every night neighbors and relatives would come over to visit and listen to the unbelievable stories.

The next Sunday afternoon a large crowd assembled at Poplar Grove church where George agreed to tell his story to the entire community. For an entire afternoon he talked, telling of travels to the far corners of the earth. Sister Sudie sat in the back row of the church, listening quietly to the stories but still skeptical about the identity of the man who claimed to be her brother.

Many of their relatives had been convinced that the man was actually George Hargrove, but Sudie had still not been convinced. George told the crowd of events that had happened during his youth in Sampson County. He also revealed the amazing extent of his travels all over the world. First George had crossed the United States, moving from Kentucky, then across the midwest, and finally searching for the wild west. From the west coast he ventured on to Texas and New Orleans, where he boarded a ship for New York.

In New York he joined an expedition to the arctic, and was received during the quest by Admiral Perry. All but seventeen men died during the dangerous journey to the north. George was one of those who lived to return. Soon thereafter he joined another geographical expedition, this time to Africa to join Henry Morton Stanley of Livingston and Stanley fame. After landing in Cairo, George and the party ventured over 2000 miles up the Nile. They finally found Stanley, who was returning from an excursion farther into the interior of the continent.

Darden Collection

Dick and his younger brother, Pete, playing with their rabbits and chickens in 1931.

George returned to the United States in 1890. The following year he joined an archeological expedition to Egypt, Arabia, and Palestine for the Smithsonian Institute. For the next nine years he traveled, visiting the Great Pyramids, the temple of Urr in Chaldee, and the sixty-mile-long walls of Babylon. He and his group collected ancient relics from Nineveh and returned them to Washington in 1900. Soon after returning he was off again, this time to China. George was there in 1901 when the Boxer Rebellion erupted. He returned from China in 1910 and went to work in Arizona and New Mexico.

A few years later the wanderlust struck him again, so he began making his way toward his original homeplace in North Carolina. George walked from St. Petersburg, Florida, through Georgia, South Carolina, and finally North Carolina. When he arrived in Sampson County his tattered appearance certainly attested to the fact that he was a worn out old man who was returning from a long, hard journey.

When the long afternoon at Poplar Grove Church concluded, Sudie had heard George relate enough of the tidbits of fact about his childhood in Sampson. He knew too many things about the past to be an imposter. Finally she was convinced. She accepted George as her brother and took him home with her. George lived at Sudie's home on the old Hargrove plantation for the next two years.

After having a disagreement with his sister over his claim to part of the family land, George left his family in Sampson County again. He would never return to North Carolina, moving on to start his life over again, this time as a poor old man in Savannah, Georgia. The effects of the War Between the States lingered, repeatedly fragmenting George's family and following him to his death.

So, too, was young Dick Darden affected in many ways by the crushing defeat that had occured only fifty-five years before his birth. Consequently, he knew hard times as a youth during the 1920's. While his family was struggling through the Depression there was no extra money for frivolities. Everyone worked long hard hours and did whatever they could to survive the stark economic times. Time for recreation was limited, usually consisting of the five mile walk out to Coharie Creek for an afternoon of fishing. The times toughened many young American boys in the 1920's. The spartan lifestyle endured by many young people in the decade of the twenties would prove to be preparatory for even tougher times ahead.

In 1926 a new Emperor was crowned in Japan. On Christmas Day of that year Emperor Hirohito became the 124th Emperor of Japan. He was said to be a direct descendant of Emperor Jimmu, the first Emperor of Japan. Jimmu was a direct descendant of the god of storm and the goddess of the sun. These gods were spawned by the gods who had given birth to the Japanese islands themselves. Hirohito, therefore, was of godly origin and was thought of as a divine entity. The Japanese people believed this and worshipped Hirohito, believing that their greatest possible act on earth would be to die for their heavenly leader.

Chapter 2
THE THIRTIES

Darden Collection

Jim Darden (second from rear chair) in his barber shop. The shop in downtown Clinton had five barbers.

1931

In 1931, when Dick was eleven years old, the KODA-HA fanatics had risen to a ruling position in the Japanese military by using the tactics of terror and assasination. In September of that year, a clique within the Japanese Imperial Army, the Kwantung Army, seized control of the government. Korea had been ceded to Japan at the end of the Russo-Japanese War in 1905. The Kwantung Army had gone farther west and had seized Manchuria without orders or permission from the Japanese government. The military zealots in the Kwangtung Army knew that the vast natural wealth of Manchuria would be an important asset to Japan in her future quest for expansion.

Members of this extremist faction in Japan conducted a bloody reign of terror in order to seize and maintain control of the government. On February 9, 1932, Japanese Finance Minister Junnosuke Inouye was shot to death as he walked down a Tokyo sidewalk. On May 15th of that year the 75-year old incumbent Prime Minister of Japan, Tsuyoshi Inukai, was shot to death in his home. Both of these men made the fatal mistake of publically opposing the expansionism of the Kwantung Army.

By the early 1930's the Depression was straining the incomes of nearly all businessmen in Clinton, and Jim Darden was no different. Though he had one of the largest barber shops in town, boasting five chairs and barbers, it was difficult to make any money after expenses. Dick, soon be a teenager, began hanging out in the barber shop, frequently spending his time lounging on a bench by the street just outside the front door. He needed to earn some money, so Eva Bell took $12.00 of her tatting money and bought him a reel-type push grass mower. Dick began mowing grass, making an occasional nickel or dime for his efforts.

Even though Jim had several good barbers working for him, business began to sag in the barbershop. He had his brother, Frank, Cleve and Herman Bunch, along with Beautancus Dixon working there. At one time Jim had enjoyed the services of Irving Bell, who was a pretty good barber, too. But Irving had gone across the street and, along with Slim Register, opened up his own shop, known as the Model Barber Shop. So, as the number of paying customers dwindled, the competition increased.

In the late 1920's a haircut cost fifteen cents and a shave cost only a dime. Even so, most men couldn't spare that much money. Jim provided everything for the other four barbers in the shop, even the chair. In return he got about half of the money that they made. In better days it had been a pretty good business. The shop was open from 7:00 a.m. until 7:00 p.m. on weekdays, and 7:00 a.m. until 11:00 p.m. on Saturdays. The late hours were necessary on Saturday so that many of the local men could come into town and take their Saturday bath in the tubs that Jim provided in the back room.

The story of Dick's uncle Frank Darden is interesting. Uncle Frank had been involved in a train accident several years earlier. He had fallen between two boxcars and one of them had rolled over his legs. Both legs were crushed and mangled. One had to be taken off at the knee joint, and the other was amputated just below the knee.

Uncle Frank was a pitiful sight walking around on his nubs. A special pair of boots had to be made for him. They were round on the bottoms, somewhat like elephant feet. After a while Uncle Frank developed thick calluses on the bottoms of the stumps of his legs and he could get around pretty well.

Jim took Uncle Frank on at the barber shop. Frank got the fifth chair, located at the back of the shop. Jim built a platform in the shape of a horseshoe around the back of the chair. It was built to the correct height for Uncle Frank to cut hair, which he did for many years. He could walk around the platform and reach any point on a man's head.

Uncle Frank became a pretty good barber and developed a large clientele. Amazingly, he could walk around the platform on his stumps and cut hair on Saturdays from 7 a.m. until 11 p.m. just like the other barbers. Many years after his death, people would still tell the tale of the barber with no legs who cut hair on the horseshoe-shaped platform in Clinton.

1932

In 1932 Joseph Grew was named the American ambassador to Japan. It soon became apparent to him that the Japanese military intended to take over much of Asia. Grew warned officials in Washington that the Japanese were about to engage in regional conflicts in order to expand their empire.

Jim Darden lost his barber shop during the trying times of the Great Depression. Men simply did not have enough money to pay for haircuts, so they allowed their hair grow down to their shoulders and then let a family member cut it. After a long Saturday at the barber shop Jim Darden would come home near midnight with eight or nine dollars and a handful of change to show for his sixteen hours behind the chair. Then he had to pay the rent and other overhead from his meager earnings. On weekdays business was even slower. It became impossible to provide for his family of seven on the money he earned barbering, and Jim was forced to close the barber shop.

Jim went to work as a guard at the local prison unit. There he earned $43.00 per month. In an effort to save precious food and money, Jim would remain at the prison on week nights so he would allowed to eat his meals in the prison kitchen. Since he did not have an automobile, he would walk the three miles into town to be with his family and children on weekends. He gave Eva Bell the money that he earned, holding out only enough to buy a wooden box of Black Moriah chewing tobacco plus fifty cents for spending money.

1933

Joseph Grew's warnings of Japanese expansion soon became a reality. The Japanese army invaded Manchuria and their quest to conquer Asia. Calling for unity between the Asian "brothers" while decrying the white colonial dogs, Japan continued to conquer and marched into northern China in 1933.

Jim Darden spent most of his days guarding a chain gang that the prison sent out to cut underbrush from ditchbanks on the roads around Clinton. He stood at one end of the group of toiling men with a shotgun while another guard stood at the other end. Even though the life of a prisoner was stern, many of the men knew that during the Depression things could be worse. One prisoner in particular would serve his time and be released, only to go straight downtown and commit a petty crime so that he could go back to the prison. The cycle happened over and over again. As hard as life in prison was, it provided a roof over each man's head and three meals a day. Some preferred the prison life to any other alternative that they had during the Depression.

Somehow Eva Bell stretched Jim's salary and the small amount that she made sewing, tatting, and embroidering, into a meager living. In the fall of the year just before school started, Dick, like most children, was taken to the mercantile store where he got two suits of school clothes. These two sets of clothes had to last the entire year. One suit was worn while the other was being washed.

When the knees or seats of the pants wore through, as they commonly did near the end of the school year, large patches were sewn over the holes. If a hole came in a patch, a smaller patch was sewn over it. During the springtime it was not uncommon to see kids with patches three deep on their knees and rumps.

Almost all of the school children wore cheap canvas tennis shoes which cost about $1.50 a pair. The kids wore the cloth shoes every day except Sunday, so after being worn through a few mud puddles they began to smell pretty high. By Christmas they had an outright stink about them. When thirty-five kids were inside a closed classroom at school, sometimes such an aroma would arise from the shoes that teachers had to raise windows in the dead of winter just to get a breath of fresh air.

Most kids also had a suit of clothes only to be worn on Sundays or special occasions. In the fall of 1933 Eva Bell had earned enough sewing money to buy Dick a nice new $5.00 Sunday suit. The first Sunday Dick wore the new suit she told him, in no uncertain terms, not to soil the new clothes or mess them up in any way.

After the family had come home from church, Dick walked two doors up the street to see a friend, David Turner. The Turner family was about to drive their Hutmobile out into the country to see their Uncle Rice Matthis and invited Dick along. Eva Bell gave him permission to go, as long as he did not mess up his new Sunday suit.

8

Uncle Frank Darden, also known as "Shorty", holds
Dick in 1922.

Dick was excited as he hopped into the car that had four doors and
a cloth top.

When they got to the farm Mr. Rice asked the boys if they
would like to ride his mules. Dick jumped at the chance, giving no
thought to his new outfit. He rode one of the poor beasts bareback
all afternoon. When he got off he noticed that he had worn holes in
both cheeks of the seat of the new pair of pants. Dick knew that he
was in serious trouble. He feared the worst, but Eva Belle only
chewed him out when he got home. She washed the Sunday suit and
applied two patches, making sure that the suit was ready for the
following Sunday.

1934

Wake Island is a tiny speck of coral in the middle of the
Pacific Ocean. In 1934 American military planners placed it under
the jurisdiction of the United States Navy because they were
concerned about military movements in the Pacific by Japan. The
Navy wanted a base within reach by airplane of the Marshall Islands
which had been mandated to the Japanese at the end of World War
I. An American base on Wake would allow reconnaissance planes
to observe the construction of Japanese bases and the movement of
Japanese ships in the region. The U. S. Navy began to consider a base
on Wake for the placement of patrol planes.

The Japanese simultaneously began to develop an interest
in Wake Island. They realized that its crucial location could offer
them a convenient point from which to attack the forward perimeter
of the American defenses in the Pacific, namely Midway, Johnston,
and then the juiciest prize short of the mainland of the United

States—Hawaii.

In Clinton Dick had reached the age of fourteen and began
to help his family as much as possible through the tough times of the
depression. Events in the Pacific were of no concern to him. Earning
a few pennies for food or clothing was foremost on his mind. Had
it not been for his Uncle Henry, Dick's early teenage years would
have been bleak. Uncle Henry Darden owned half interest in a
mercantile store downtown and a house just a couple of blocks away
on Sampson Street. He helped to keep shoes and overalls on Dick
at a time when many kids had no shoes and were wearing clothes
with patches on top of patches.

One of Dick's best friends was Henry Vann, Jr. Henry's
father was married to Aunt Madge. Uncle Henry had become quite
successful in the farming business. He owned a large amount of land
and several businesses in town, including the two local movie
theaters, a Ford dealership, a tractor company, and various other
enterprises. He would later become a state senator.

On Saturdays Dick would help Henry Jr. distribute flyers
advertising the movies showing at the State and Gem theaters. The
two would take one of Uncle Henry's Fords and ride all over the
county to Roseboro, Salemburg, Garland, and even over into
neighboring Duplin County to Kenansville. While Henry was
posting the advertisements in local businesses Dick would go to
every house in the area and slip a flyer inside the screen door. The
theaters in Clinton were the only ones between Wilmington and
Fayetteville, so the boys helped to draw patrons from all over the
region into Clinton businesses.

In 1934 a scientific discovery was made in Italy that would
change the course of world history and eventually save Dick
Darden's life. Dr. Enrico Fermi was a professor of physics at the
University of Rome. The Italian scientist, then only thirty-three
years old, was doing research which involved the nucleii of atoms.
At his lab in Rome he bombarded various chemical elements with
neutrons. When he bombarded uranium 235 his results led him to
believe that he had made a new element. In fact, he had split the
nucleus of an atom.

Fermi's discovery was the basis for later research which
would lead to unimaginable changes and advancements, including
the ability of man to kill huge numbers of his own kind with but a
single weapon in his arsenal. The atomic age had begun.

1935

It was the advent of the airplane that jolted Wake Island out
of centuries of slumber as a pristine speck of white coral sand.
Aviation caused the island to be transformed for human habitation.
In 1935 Pan American Airways implemented plans for the first
trans-Pacific air travel for commercial customers. This was to be
accomplished by crisscrossing the vast ocean with long-range
propeller-driven seaplanes known as Pan American Clippers.

These Martin 130 "Clippers" were huge aircraft for their
day, great boat planes which would leave the west coast of the
United States and hopscotch their way from one island base to
another. Even though the big flying boats had a tremendous range
they were unable to cross the 4200 miles between San Francisco and
Wake Island without refueling. The Pan Am schedule called for
them to make the 3000 mile flight to Hawaii on the first day, and then
fly 1100 miles on to Midway Island on the second day.

Sampson Street, one of the narrow, tree-lined streets in Clinton in the 1930's.

On the third day of the five day journey the Clippers would complete the next leg of the trip, flying just over one thousand miles and landing on Wake Island, little more than a pinpoint of land rising out of the sea in the middle of the huge Pacific Ocean. Wake Island lay just under 2000 miles from Tokyo and the Japanese mainland.

On the fourth day the Clippers would cover another 1300 miles, landing on the island of Guam in the Marianas. From Guam the big planes embarked upon the final leg of the flight to Manila. Each leg of the flight took one day. The Clippers would take off soon after daybreak, spend the day traversing the long expanse of ocean, and land at a desolate island outpost for refueling.

On May 5, 1935, the freighter SS NORTH HAVEN arrived at the remote and uninhabited place called Wake Island and began to offload supplies and equipment belonging to Pan Am's construction company. The captain of the NORTH HAVEN was aware of the treacherous reef encircling the three islets collectively known as Wake Island. He could he could not venture too close to shore. To further complicate matters, he could not anchor the ship due to the great depth of the ocean just offshore. This presented a number of problems to the men who were offloading the construction equipment.

It was decided that the materials would go ashore on the south side of Wake Island. The winds and ocean current came from the northeast, so the south side was the calmer leeward side of the island. The vessel "lay to" on the leeward side of the atoll in order to take advantage of the calmer surf. Materials would be taken ashore on a small dock and distributed to the three small islets that made up the atoll. There were no roads, no buildings, and virtually no evidence of mankind. There was only sand, coral, salt water, and scrubby gnarled undergrowth.

Peale Island was the islet on the northwest corner of Wake atoll. It was chosen for the Pan Am seaplane base. Soon after unloading the equipment from the NORTH HAVEN the men on the construction team went to work reshaping the island. The work crew had orders to move forward with the construction of the airbase without delay, so construction began immediately. On August 9, barely two months after the initial landing of the construction company, the first Pan Am Clipper successfully landed on the lagoon between Wilkes and Peale Islands.

At the same time the air base was being built construction began on a modern hotel that would provide overnight accommodations for the Pan Am travelers who stopped on the island. Also under construction near the hotel were a number of other buildings and facilities, including hydroponic vegetable gardens, a rainwater catchment, and an animal farm.

In November of 1935 Pan Am began mail service, without passengers, along the route of the China Clippers. Soon the big

Dick with jack fish he caught in the Coharie River, 1933.

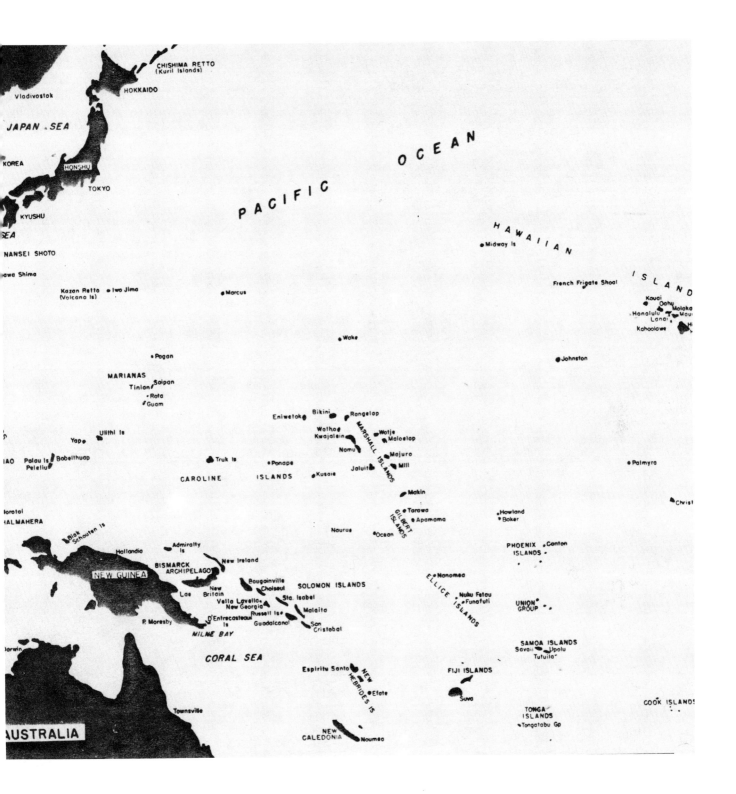

The Western Pacific Ocean

seaplanes would carry 30 passengers and five crewmen who would spend the nights in hotels, dubbed Pan American Hotels, which had been constructed for them at each of the island stops. The five-day excursions were to begin in late 1936 with service between San Francisco and Manila.

Wake Island was strategically positioned to become one of the stops on the route that crossed the Pacific. This speck on the map was the property of the United States, which had designated it to be a bird sanctuary. Pan American had been given permission by the American government to hire a private construction firm to build the clipper base.

The building of the Pan Am base on Wake was initially a very difficult operation since there were no docks or port facilities on the island. Supply ships could not cross the jagged reef, and even if that were possible, they could not venture into the lagoon in the center of the atoll. Not only was it too shallow for ocean-going ships, but it was also filled with sharp coral heads which would wreak havoc on the bottom of a vessel.

The offloading of construction materials, therefore, became a dangerous and painstaking ordeal for the first permanent settlement on Wake Island. The North Haven had to lie offshore while smaller boats, called lighters, ferried materials to the small pier-like dock on Wilkes Island. A miniature railroad was built, beginning on the ocean-side dock, to carry supplies across the island to the lagoon.

On the lagoon side of Wilkes Island another pier was built allowing small boats to carry the materials across the calmer waters of the lagoon to other parts of the atoll. The railroad engine, scarcely larger than an automobile, pulled small flatcars across the island while barrels could be rolled on the rails by hand. Bulldozers came ashore on small barges and were used to pull sleds of supplies to various points on the island.

When completed, the Wake Island hotel was nestled in a forest of low, gnarled ironwood trees on Peale Island. The handsome building boasted forty-five well furnished rooms where, considering the remoteness of the site, the Pan Am travelers and crews found comfortable overnight accomodations.

There were several small buildings near the hotel for the maintenance of the base, and there was a dock on the lagoon side of Peale Island. This pier extended a considerable distance out into the lagoon, and a floating dock at its end was used to moor the Clippers when they arrived. The big boat-planes would glide down over Wake's lagoon, skim across the emerald green waters, and then tie up at the dock. Passengers and crew would deplane and walk down the long dock to the hotel complex. Maintenance crews would refuel the plane and have it ready for the travelers to depart the following morning on the next leg of the voyage.

1936

As the calendar turned to the year 1936 Dick Darden was beginning to make a name for himself as a boxer. The tall, rangy fifteen-year-old joined the Clinton High boxing team and, despite being only a ninth grader, went undefeated during the 1935-1936

The North Haven arrives at Wake Island, May 1935

A bulldozer pulls materials on a sled across the rough, rocky coral beaches of Wake Island, May 1935

season. There were only a few teams in the eastern part of the state. The Clinton boys fought matches in Fayetteville, Warsaw, and Penderlea. Each fight was scheduled for three 3-minute rounds. Dick fought in the 150 pound weight class

The fighting was much simpler in Clinton in early 1936 than in other parts of the world. On February 26 over 1500 troops seized the Japanese government in Tokyo. Finance Minister Korekiyo Takahashi, who had resisted the increasingly huge budget demands of the military, was shot to death at his home. Former Prime Minister Makoto Saito, a moderate who was not an intense supporter of the military, was also shot to death. This turbulent political climate in Japan was the precursor of the upheaval that was soon to follow.

In October of 1936 Pan American Airways began commercial air service from San Francisco to Manila via the trans-Pacific route. Wake Island, for the first time in history, became accessible to commercial air travelers. Each week two Clippers would swoop down onto Wake Island, one going westbound toward the Orient and the other headed toward Hawaii and the United States. The number of Pan Am employees increased as more people were needed to service the planes and passengers. The growing number of Pan Am employees on the island included several natives of Guam called "Chamarros," who were well accustomed to the remoteness and harshness of island life.

Conditions on Wake continued to improve as construction progressed. The Pan American hotel was made as comfortable as conditions allowed for the travelers. Since there was no fresh water on Wake, a system of catch basins was built to capture the tropical rains. A tiny garden was planted to provide a small quantity of fresh vegetables. As one of a few recreational activities, Pan Am provided the travelers with air rifles so they could shoot at the multitudes of rats on the island.

By the fall of 1936 Dick was sixteen years old, enrolling for his second year at Clinton High School as a tenth grader. CHS had an unusually large enrollment that year, boasting 279 students in grades 8-11. The twelfth grade had not yet been added. Ads in the school newspaper, THE MIRROR, explained that the Model Barber Shop in Clinton had seven registered barbers, along with showers and tub baths. Dick's mother, Mrs. J. B. Darden, and Mrs. C. C. Tart visited the ninth grade home room on October 21 as grade mothers.

The Gem Theatre in Clinton advertised that it would award the football squad a free movie pass with each victory. Dick was a starter on the varsity football team as a ninth grader. The first game of the season was with Warsaw on the Dark Horses' home field, and the young Clinton team put up a valiant fight before being beaten 6-0. Dick gained a good bit of experience, as did his teamates Harold Cook, James Furman Honeycutt, and Turner Holland.

A week later the Dark Horses played Rich Square and the results were considerably better. The "invincible" team from Rich Square was given fits by James Furman Honeycutt, who intercepted three passes and led Clinton to a 13-0 victory. The following Friday, Dick and his teammates visited the Green Waves of Dunn, only to be whipped 20-0. The powerful Dunn team scored its twelfth consecutive victory. Despite the sound trouncing at the hands of the Green Wave, the Dark Horses came back the following week to post a victory over Erwin, evening their record at 2-2.

The Clinton football team improved steadily during the fall

Materials from the North Haven are taken ashore on a crude dock built on Wilkes Island, May 1935.

of 1936, posting a 6-2-2 record for the year. As the season wound down the Dark Horses gained strength and confidence, downing Erwin again and closing out the year with a 46-0 victory over Roseboro. The Clinton team scored over 100 points that year while holding its opponents to only 33. James Furman continued to intercept passes, and Nick Waller, Bobby Hargrove, Lewis Talton, and Bill Packer came on strong for the Horses. Good things were in store in the years to come for the young, green boys from Clinton.

The State and the Gem were the only two movie houses in the hundred miles of farmland between Wilmington and Fayetteville, so they drew good crowds from a large area covering several counties. In late November, 1936, the State showed "Ladies in Love," starring Janet Gaynor, Loretta Young, Don Ameche, and Simon Simone. This was followed in early December by "Dimples," featuring Shirley Temple. The Gem countered in November with "Shipmates Forever," with Dick Powell and Ruby Keeler. This was called "the sweetest picture ever made," and children between the ages of 6 and 14 were admitted at half price for only five cents.

With football season over, the movies became more popular than ever for Dick and his friends. On December 14th the Gem Theater played "The Charge of the Light Brigade," starring Errol Flynn and Olivia deHavilland. Admission was ten cents for all. On Christmas Eve the Gem screened "The Big Show," with Gene Autry, and on Christmas day showed "Piccadilly Jim," with Robert Montgomery and Madge Evans.

Young Dick was tall but did not play basketball. He eagerly looked forward to the spring and baseball season. His buddies on the basketball team went to Lumberton in mid-December

for a tournament and "acquitted themselves in a very commendable manner" according to THE MIRROR, coming in third out of sixteen teams. Purcel Jones was a rawboned young player, well over six feet tall, who added strength to the Dark Horse basketball team in 1936. The boys opened up with victories over Lillington, Plain View, and Turkey.

1937

In January of 1937 Dick, by then over six feet tall, turned seventeen, and was becoming one of the best athletes at Clinton High. His long brown hair was combed straight back and in the student council photo he proudly wore his Clinton High School letter sweater with the big "C" on the front. The all-white school consisted of 262 students in the last four grades, not including graduate students. Some graduates came back to school for additional courses or to compete an extra year on the athletic teams.

On January 21 the State Theater featured Barbara Stanwyck and Joel McCrae in "Banjo On My Knee." Cook Machine Company advertised their machine shop and blacksmith, and Reynolds Drug Store offered home deliveries for telephone orders. Their telephone number was 333-1.

The Southern Tavern, a small bar and dance hall located where the creek crossed Beamon Street, had a swimming pool filled by a continuously running artesian well. Dick occasionally worked at the tavern, and the experience proved to be an education different from any he had received before. Downstairs the bar did a brisk business serving beer and soft drinks to a local clientele. Upstairs there were several "tourist" rooms. These served the needs of out-of-town guests and provided the setting for goings-on that were new to the young lad of seventeen. The rooms provided a convenient spot for some of the good old boys from over in Goldsboro, about thirty-five miles to the north, to bring their girlfriends.

A buzzer had been installed so that patrons upstairs in the rooms could call downstairs for service. Dick provided the room service, taking food and beverage orders. More than once he encountered naked customers walking to the restroom down the hall. Occasionally he would enter the rooms and take orders from naked couples who impudently instructed him to bring another Coke so they could mix another drink.

On February 5th the Gem Theater featured a stage vaudeville act called the "Rhythm Girls Revue," staring "Hot Dog Johnson," the Ace of the Black Face Comedians. Pep, Spice, and Ginger were the names of the girls in the show. A Lebanese immigrant named G. Kaleel (Americanized from Kahlil) had settled in Clinton and opened a fruit stand called the Carolina Fruit Palace. His telephone number was 419-1. A debate was going on in the community concerning the advantages and disadvantages of a ninth month added to the school year and a twelfth grade added to the high school.

Late in February "Born to Dance" came to the Gem Theater, starring Eleanor Powell and James Stewart. Soon afterwards the Gem showed "Tarzan Escapes" with Johnny Weissmuller and Maureen O'Sullivan, followed by "Camille" with Robert Taylor and Greta Garbo. The State Theater countered with "Green Light" starring Errol Flynn, and "Daniel Boone" with Flash Gordon.

Typhus fever was becoming a common disease in Sampson County, so Mr. Cliff Wood, the coach and biology teacher at Clinton High, discussed the disease at the February meeting of the Boys Hi-Y.

During March Mr. Wood, the baseball coach, held the season's first baseball practice. Dick had been waiting for this day all winter. Coach Wood informed the boys on the team that he had just spent the tidy sum of $75.00 for new uniforms, balls, and other equipment for the team. The season started well for the Dark Horses, who won their first three games by outscoring their opponents 43-4.

April saw the Horses lose two games to cross-county rivals Roseboro and Salemburg, but they still maintained a respectable 7-2 record. Harold Cook, John Flake, James Furman Honeycutt, Purcel Jones and Dick Darden were singled out for leading the charge. Harold Cook and Nick Waller were the star pitchers. Cook was also the county champion in the 100 yard dash at the county track meet.

Clark Gable and Myrna Loy were starring at the Gem Theater in "Men In White" late in April of 1937. The school year was winding down for young Dick. May brought an exciting baseball game for Dick and his teammates when they traveled to Durham to play the Duke University freshman team. The Clinton boys held their own against the older college men, losing by only one run in a high scoring game that ended with the score 14-13. Just a few days later the Clinton High class of 1937 graduated, and Dick looked forward to his summer vacation.

But, suddenly, in May of 1937, anticipation turned to grief

A small boat on barge is pulled by a bulldozer and pushed by hand through the shallow water of Wilkes Channel into the lagoon, May 1935

15

Pan Am travelers shoot rats for recreation near the pier on the Wake Island lagoon with air rifles.

Railroad cars loaded with food for the construction workers are pulled by a small locomotive.

1935-36 Clinton High School Boxing team, Dick is in the back row, just left of coach Cliff Wood.

for young Dick Darden. On Sunday morning, the 5th of May, just as the family was awakening to a new spring day, everyone heard Eva Bell scream from her bed. Jim Darden was home for the weekend from his work at the prison camp. By the time Dick had rushed to his bedside he could tell that something was terribly wrong with his Father. Dick did not know that the paralysis which quickly rendered his father's body motionless was caused by a massive stroke. Every effort was made to comfort the dying man, but within two hours he was in a coma, never to regain consciousness.

The next morning Jim Darden died. He was only fifty-eight years old. The family grieved, but Dick had heard his father say that he would rather die quickly than lie in bed for a prolonged period in a useless state. Jim had gone quickly out of Dick's life. But, Dick was glad that his father had realized his wish and had not suffered for a long period of time.

With the death of Jim Darden, Dick and his family lost not only a father, but also Jim's support at a time when they were having a great deal of difficulty making ends meet. Dick's mother soon told each of the children that they would have to make a contribution to the support of the family, so Dick took on a variety of odd jobs. He made enough money mowing grass that summer with the old push mower to buy his clothes for the fall school term.

Eva Bell Darden also knew that she would have to support her family in a monetary way. She had a talent for sewing, so she took a job at Isaac Hurwitz's clothing store. She was a clerk, who sold clothes to customers and then did the alterations. She made $20.00 a week, less than half of the income that the family had

enjoyed before Jim died. While in the clothing store she became good friends with Mr. Hurwitz's wife Freda, and learned that the Hurwitzes were originally German Jews. They had come to America to escape the Nazis in their homeland.

In June of 1937 the U. S. Marine Corps formed a unit of fighter aircraft which would later be named VMF-211. This Marine air unit was first stationed at the San Diego Naval Air Station in California. The first planes used by these Marine pilots were Grumman F-3F biplanes.

On July 7, 1937, Japanese and Chinese forces clashed at the Marco Polo Bridge near Peking, and full scale war erupted shortly afterwards. The Chinese, under Generalissimo Chiang Kai-Shek, lost battle after battle and city after city to the superior Japanese forces. The Japanese seized the city of Nanking and slaughtered tens of thousands of innocent civilians. About 20,000 men were murdered with bayonets, machine guns, or by burning with gasoline, and nearly the same number of women were raped, killed, and mutilated. By late 1937 the Japanese forces had taken control of a huge portion of northern China.

The 1937 school year began in late September at Clinton High. Dick was in the tenth grade, just two years short of graduating. It was time for football and Dick was itching to get started. In the first game of the fall Clinton played Goldsboro and was whipped 19-6. Dick suffered a "slight sunstroke" during the game and Snooky Chesnutt broke his collarbone. Dick soon rejoined his teammates Pete Lovell, Richard Kaleel, Bobby Hargrove, Charles Tart, Thomas Turlington, and Nick Waller.

17

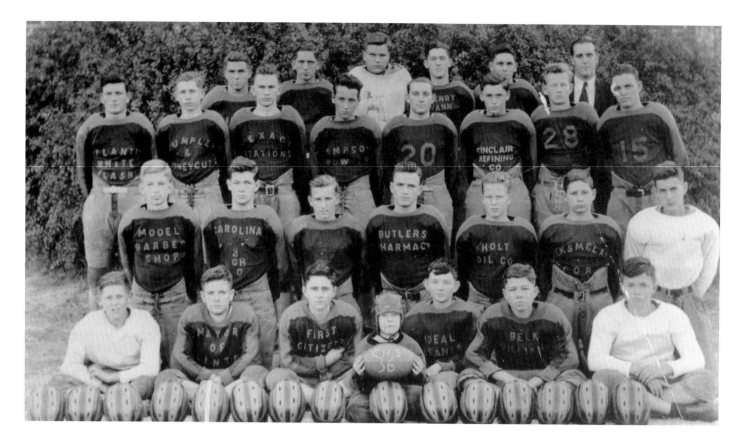

1936 Clinton High football squad, Dick in the backrow, third from right with "Henry Vann" jersey.

During October, 1937, Henry Fonda and Bettie Davis starred in "That Certain Woman" at the State Theater. The Dark Horses went up against a larger and more experienced team from Erwin. The younger Clinton boys took their worst beating in several years, losing 36-0. Henry Lee Turlington and Sumner Eakes were among several players who were saluted for a good effort in the losing cause. All of the city schools scheduled fire drills late in October. Fire Chief Herman Bunch, who was operating the barber shop opened by Jim Darden, reported that it took seventy-three seconds for Clinton High to be cleared, while the "colored" school on McKoy Street was cleared in fifty-nine seconds.

Finally, in late October, the Clinton gridders got on track, edging the team from Selma 7-6. This was followed the next week by a 7-0 victory over Warsaw. A big announcement was made on October 18 that the W. P. A. would build a new football stadium for Clinton High. It would seat 500 people and would be surrounded by a seven-foot-high board fence. The work would be completed by March, but there would be no showers or dressing rooms built during the initial phase of construction. The City Cafe advertised in THE MIRROR that their chicken dinners were thirty-five cents.

The football team was ready to take on another larger team, the Fayetteville Bulldogs. During the initial period the Horses drew first blood and led 7-0. On the ensuing kickoff the Fayetteville runner fumbled and John Avery Peterson recovered for Clinton. On the next play, Dick took the ball for a sixty-five yard run only to be tackled on the three yard line. Dick took the next handoff and drove the ball over for the score. Clinton led 14-0. Fayetteville scored late

in the game, but the Horses held on for a solid 14-7 victory.

On the following Friday night the confident Clinton team took its fourth straight victory, a close 7-6 win over Wallace. Things were going well for Dick as winter approached. The Horses played their final game of the season in late November, topping the Roseboro team 12-7. Dick was now captain of the team, and scored the winning touchdown in the fourth quarter. Several other Clinton players were described as "superlatives" after the victory, including Turner Holland, Henry Lee Turlington, and Sumner Eakes. James Cagney and Evelyn Daw were at the Gem Theater that weekend in "Something To Sing About," and "Double or Nothing" was playing at the State with Bing Crosby, Martha Raye, and Andy Devine.

The Clinton players were rewarded the next Saturday with a trip to the Duke-Carolina football game in Durham. The Turlington brothers, Henry Lee and Thomas, along with James Furman Honeycutt, Morris Bell, and a large group of boys and girls from Clinton High enjoyed the game. As Dick neared his eighteenth birthday, he was enjoying several aspects of his high school life, especially his status as captain of the victorious football team. He was also looking forward to spring on the baseball diamond. Dick was becoming a strapping young man, excelling at football, baseball, and boxing.

In December, 1937, the annual football dance was held. Members of the football team were awarded their prestigious letters, and a program was presented by the coach from N. C. State College. Afterwards, the boys and their guests enjoyed refreshments and danced to the music of the Cliff Stevens Orchestra. The year was

18

A Pan Am Clipper leaves San Francisco on a flight to the orient

Dick with brother Pete in 1936, Dick's football jersey bore the name of Henry Vann, his uncle, who owned a local tractor and Ford dealership.

winding down for Dick, but it had been a memorable one he would not forget.

Dick had little concern for events in Japan and China, but he was beginning to hear bits and pieces of news stories which gave him his first notions of unrest in other parts of the world. Conflicts on the other side of the earth were exploding, and young men there were not enjoying a carefree childhood such as Dick's. Many young Japanese boys had, by the age of eighteen, been thrust into war, indoctrinated to believe that their greatest achievement would be to die on the battlefield for their government and Emperor.

Tensions between Japan and the United States were severely strained on December 12, 1937, when Japanese planes sunk an American gunboat, the PANAY, on the Yangtze River in China. Though he was only a teenager in 1937, Dick began to sense the threatening world situation. During that year, Japan signed a pact with Germany and Italy in which she agreed to help topple the democratic and communist governments of England, Russia, and the United States. The three countries united against the Allied powers and became known as the Rome-Berlin-Tokyo Axis.

Chapter 3
1938—WAR CLOUDS BUILD

The four engined Hawaii Clipper ties up at the docks on Wake Island. This was the third stop in as many days for the big passenger plane on its five day voyage to Manilla

In January, 1938, the United States Navy got a 20% increase in appropriations from Congress which enabled it to develop a two-ocean navy. President Roosevelt asked for a voluntary embargo on American companies selling goods to Japan that could be used in the war effort. Congress listened to recommendations from the Navy that Wake Island be fortified and voted to spend twenty million dollars to build a naval air base there. This action converted Wake Island from a stop-over base for the Pan Am Clippers to a strategic forward defense base for the United States military.

The American military strategists were well aware of the worsening world situation as war looked more and more probable. Each of the foreign adversaries of the United States was given a code name corresponding to a color, and strategies were developed to deal with any aggressor which might threaten American soil or interests.

Japan was given the code name "Orange," and it headed the list of possible troublemakers in the Pacific theater.

When all of the strategies were brought together into a plan for dealing with a possible war in the Pacific, the color coding lent itself to the name of the overall blueprint. The war plan was called "Rainbow 5." The Rainbow 5 plan called for using several of the American island outposts as our outer defense perimeter. These included Wake, along with Samoa, Palmyra, Johnston, and Midway islands. As war appeared ready to break out in several areas around the globe, Wake Island became increasingly important in America's defensive plans.

Rainbow 5 called for American naval forces to be ready to venture beyond the defensive perimeter and capture the Japanese-held Marshall Islands, and then forge a shipping lane that would allow supplies and materials to flow westward to the Philippines.

The need evolved for forward naval bases, including submarine facilities and refueling bases for aircraft going to and from critical points west of Wake Island. The planners in Washington began to look upon Wake as five square miles of very important coral sand.

By 1938 Japan was posing a serious threat to America's defense perimeter. On Truk in the Caroline Islands, just over 1100 miles from Wake, and at several bases in the Marshall Islands, barely 600 miles away, the Japanese Imperial Navy had positioned its Fourth Fleet. The fleet was small and had no aircraft carriers, since Japanese strategists felt that Wake would offer little resistance and could be taken in a day. On Kwajalein Atoll in the Marshalls the Japanese had land-based bombers which could be over Wake Island in less than six hours.

The Clinton High boxing team was back in action in February, 1938, and was coached by Jim Hubbard. Jim was a former boxer at the school who had graduated from the university at Chapel Hill and returned to town. Dick was undefeated in the heavyweight class. He scored a T.K.O. in an exhibition bout during the pugs' match with Warsaw. Several "colored bouts" were scheduled afterwards. "Socko" Chesnutt, fighting for the Clinton colored school, beat "Tiger" Warren, and "Lightning" Chesnutt, also from Clinton, whipped "Brown Streak" Coley from Goldsboro.

If the boxing matches or basketball games were not the best entertainment in town in the early part of 1938, surely the movies were. "Judge Priest" came to the State Theater, starring Will Rogers and Stepin Fetchit. This was followed by "True Confession" with Carole Lombard, Fred MacMurray, and John Barrymore. Mossette Butler, a former student at Clinton High, was getting his big chance in the theater in New York City. Mossette had been chosen for a minor role in Erskine Caldwell's play "Journeyman" which opened on January 29th at the Fulton Theater.

T. P. L. Motor Company was advertising its new 1938 Chevys as having comfort and safety for a low price. The public was invited to come downtown and see one, or call 452-1 for more information. Money was so tight that the Dardens had not entertained the thought of getting an automobile. To help with expenses Dick's younger brother, Pete, went to work parttime at Uncle Henry Vann's theater. "Big Broadcast of 1938" was showing in late March and starred Martha Raye, Dorothy Lamour, and W. C. Fields.

The long awaited baseball season began in April as the Clinton team christened the new stadium by splitting a double header with Kinston. Goldmon Lovell was manager of the Capitol Market where he advertised free home deliveries of groceries. The official dedication of the new high school stadium was held in early May and the mayor, several other dignitaries, and the W.P.A. engineer made speeches. They praised the city and the school for building the new $14,000.00 complex.

A college baseball game was planned as the first event on the new ball field. The University of North Carolina edged North Carolina State College in an exciting game which drew a big crowd and christened the new Clinton athletic stadium.

Edwards Military Institute was the next victim of the

A coral roadway bisects the Pan Am compound on Wake Island. The hotel complex is visible on the left and the anchor of the LIBELLE is on display near the small building on the right.

21

Air travelers watch the flightless rails as they walk the grounds of the Pan Am Hotel on Wake.

Clinton baseball team. With the bases loaded Hamp Whitfield made a diving catch of a sure grand slam homer to save the victory. Nick Waller pitched a nifty five-hitter with Sumner Eakes behind the plate. Bette Davis and Henry Fonda came to the State Theater in May in the movie "Jezebel." The cost of admission was ten cents for children and fifteen cents for adults.

The baseball team finished its season with an 8-6 record. Sumner Eakes led the team with a .314 batting average, followed by star shortstop James Furman Honeycutt at .300. On May 23rd commencement exercises were held at the high school. When the graduating class of 1938 received their diplomas, Dick had only one year left in high school, the eleventh grade.

A week after the seniors had graduated the State Theater showed "Rebecca of Sunnybrook Farm," starring Shirley Temple. As summer arrived and the pace of life seemed to slow down, Dick found several lawns to mow so he could earn money to buy his school clothes for the much awaited fall school term. Local businesses were offering special incentives in order to compete for the limited business there was to be had. Goldmon Lovell continued to offer free home deliveries of groceries. Orders could be called in to telephone number 292-6.

Nine miles down the road west of Clinton was the hamlet of Roseboro. Among the 1938 graduates of Roseboro High School was a strapping young man named Rufus Geddie Herring. Young Geddie planned to attend Davidson College in the fall but had no particular major in mind. He would probably go into economics or business, but he had no specific career in mind for the future, and he was just looking forward to going away to school.

Even though Geddie Herring and Dick Darden lived only a few miles apart, during that day and time, such a distance clearly separated people. Automobiles were scarce, and if the two young men knew each other, it was only because they were both well known as athletes. Even so, the paths of the two would later cross in a way that neither could imagine in 1938.

Neither of these young men had any real conception of what war actually meant. Now and then they heard tidbits of information that made them aware of the rumbling war machines of the Germans and Japanese. But war? They gave it little thought. When Dick returned to C.H.S. in the fall for his last year of high school, Geddie Herring was leaving for college. The last thing on the boys' minds was world conflict. That was left to the older generation.

The fall school term at Clinton High finally arrived, beginning in September with Dick immensely proud to have reached his final year. Dick had purposely planned his eleventh grade schedule so that he would fall just short of graduating after the customary eleven years in school and he could return in the fall and play football. This would make him what was known as a "post-graduate" the following year.

Dick took a limited schedule of shorthand, typing, bookkeeping, and business law, all in the commercial business program. He would have to pass two out of the four courses to be eligible to play on the sports teams. At the beginning of the 1938-1939 school term the student population at Clinton High had grown to 280 pupils.

Four additional typewriters had been ordered due to the unexpected increase in interest in commercial courses.

Dick was the subject of the "Who's Who" column in the first MIRROR of the year. He was described as "a good looking, tall, brown haired, brown eyed fellow. His whole appearance gives you a mysterious air. You just can't figure him out. He wears a solid expression like a plotting Indian. He gets around quietly and quickly, and he is always where you least expect him. He says very little but his grin means a lot. The football team could never get along without him."

During the fall of 1938 in laboratories at the Kaiser Wilhelm Institute in Berlin, scientists Otto Hahn and Fritz Strassmann repeated the experiments that had been carried out by Enrico Fermi in Italy. They confirmed that the bombardment of uranium atoms with neutrons had resulted in the splitting of atoms and the release of extraordinary amounts of energy. It had become clear to them that the potential existed for a bomb of a staggering, unprecedented magnitude.

The Germans were trying to find a "final solution" that would purge their population of the Jews. Ironically, they had applied adequate pressure to cause Lise Meitner, a Jewish scientist and colleague of Hahn and Strassmann, to leave Germany. However, before leaving she had made Danish physicist Neils Bohr aware of the findings of the two German scientists.

Also in 1938, Rear Admiral A. J. Hepburn reported the results of a survey on America's needs for additional strategic naval bases to the United States Congress. Wake Island was given a high priority by the Hepburn Report, which recommended that $7.5 million dollars be spent to develop a base on the remote atoll. It suggested that Wake Island should become an air base for long range reconnaissance planes, and also serve as refueling base for planes making the long voyage from Hawaii to the Far East. The Hepburn Report stated: "The immediate continuous operations of patrol planes from Wake would be vital at the outbreak of war in the Pacific."

Margaret Morrison won the 1938 Miss Clinton pageant, with Lucky Johnson a close runnerup. The football team began practice with Dick more anxious to get onto the field than ever. One reason for his enthusiasm was that his younger brother, Pete, had made the team for the first time. The team was a veteran group and was expected to do well during the fall campaign.

Dick and James Furman Honeycutt were elected co-captains of the team. But, James Furman broke his collarbone, leaving Dick as the team leader on the field. James Furman appeared in the team pictures in street clothes with his arm in a sling. He had been counted on heavily and would be missed.

In the first game the boys got a setback when they visited Morehead City. They fought hard, but were beaten 13-0 on a field "five feet deep in mud." To make matters worse, they had a tire to blowout on the bus coming home. After a three hour wait the tire was repaired, and they continued on the hundred mile trek toward home. Just before they got to Kenansville the bus ran out of gas. Several of the boys walked three miles into town to get fuel. The team finally made it home at 5:00 a.m.

While Dick was battling on the football field, a much more ominous type of fighting was being conducted elsewhere during October of 1938. Chinese leader Chiang Kai-Shek had temporarily joined forces with Mao Tse-Tung, a communist guerilla leader, when their troops fled from the advancing Japanese army and made their way deeper into China's interior. Despite heavy loses the Chinese leaders steadfastly refused to quit fighting against the Japanese invaders.

The rumblings of war around the world had led to uneasiness in North Carolina. In October, thirty-nine counties in the eastern part of the state staged a huge aircraft detection drill. Zones were created, each eight miles square. During designated times any aircraft which crossed a zone would be reported by telephone to the Army at Fort Bragg. The purpose of the exercise was to test the efficiency of the Army Air Corps and the Antiaircraft Defense Corps. The exercise also allowed the military leaders to see the reaction of citizens in case of real war.

With the military exercises going on nearby, international tensions had reached around the world and come home for Dick Darden. Even so, world conflict was still far from an urgent problem for the eighteen year old high school senior. Dick's greatest worry was whether the football team could whip Selma. Thanks to a two-touchdown performance by Richard Kaleel the Dark Horses were successful by a score of 18-6 in their first home game of the season.

The victorious Dark Horse team was treated the following day to a trip to Durham to see the Duke play Georgia Tech in a college football game. The newspaper advertised Isaac Hurwitz's clothing store in downtown Clinton, where Dick's mother still worked. Just down the street was Flake's Esso Station, which offered N. C. tested gasoline at eighteen cents per gallon.

In November, 1938, Dick made his first appearance on the school honor roll in the company of perennial intellects McPhail Herring and Snooky Chesnutt. Football season was winding down when it was time for the annual game to be played with Clinton's arch rival—Warsaw. The visitors from thirteen miles to the east came into town and stung the Dark Horses by a 31-6 score.

On Friday night, November 11, the football team and cheerleaders had their football party at the community building. There was lots of dancing, and punch and cakes were served. The kids were pumping nickels in the piccolo when it came time to end the party and go home. They reluctantly called it a night after much insistence from the adult chaperones.

The final football game of the season came on the twenty-second of November when the Dark Horses met in-county rival Roseboro. Since he was captain of the team, Dick wanted to close out his career with a victory. That is exactly what the team did, trouncing the visitors 21-0. Henry Lee Turlington and Turner Holland were also seniors playing their last game for Clinton, as were postgraduates John Flake and Irving Bell.

While the swirling porridge of world politics and power struggles was coming to a boil both in Europe and in Asia in 1938, Dick was leading the carefree life of a popular and outstanding high school senior. He was president of the Hi-Y Club his last year at CHS, and the club was responsible for the school assembly program in November. After Dick made the opening remarks several of the members of the club gave short talks. Hamp Whitfield spoke on "Good Sportsmanship," and David Turner spoke on the students' code of ethics. Henry Lee Turlington talked about school spirit. After Dick made closing remarks, the assembly adjourned.

In early December Clintonians turned out in large numbers

The Pan Am pier reaches out into the Wake Island lagoon to greet air travelers from the Clipper

to attend a program that was put on by Jewish members of the community to raise money to rescue Jewish children from oppression in Nazi Germany. Talented locals entertained the crowd with their singing, dancing, and comedy routines. Mrs. Beaver Barwick, Mrs. Jim Ayers, and Polly Pool represented the Clinton Study Club with a skit entitled "Meet Me On The Corner." The Clinton Lions Club sponsored an act that was an imitation of a Negro preacher.

Most of the local civic clubs supported the program, having heard stories of the ruthless Nazis and their treatment of innocent Jewish citizens in Germany. The Rotary Club sponsored a masculine dress show with Principal B. E. Lohr, Algernon Butler, and Fes Turlington modeling the latest designs to the delight of the audience. The program was a big success and the newspaper headlines proclaimed "Clinton Helps Cramp Hitler's Style."

Germany and Japan were not the only world powers whose governments had been taken over by power-hungry tyrants. In Italy Benito Mussolini was dictator of the Fascist government. Enrico Fermi was still conducting his research in nuclear physics, but was beginning to feel the tension created by the Italian government. He decided to flee his country, leaving Italy and moving to the United States.

Fermi would become an important cog in the machinery which would allow the United States to be the world's first nation to master nuclear energy and build atomic weapons. Had he remained in Italy and contributed his work to the Axis powers, world history might have been written differently. Also in 1938, Enrico Fermi was recognized for his amazing work on the splitting of the atom when he was awarded the Nobel Prize in physics for outstanding research in the field of nuclear energy.

1939

When the calendar was turned over to 1939, Dick Darden faced five months and one baseball season before graduation from Clinton High, and then a very uncertain future. He was a big, strong boy, weighing nearly 200 pounds. He was uncommonly tall, standing well over six feet in height. Dick had little time to relax after football season, for early in January the boxing team began workouts. Dick would fight in the 175+ class, the heaviest weight division. Joe Kaleel and Bobby Hargrove were back from the 1938 team. David Turner and post-graduate John Flake helped to round out a pretty tough bunch of fighters.

Entertainment during the early part of the year consisted primarily of going to the movies and watching the basketball team. Purcel Jones was one of the star basketballers. He scored a team-high six points in Clinton's 18-14 victory over Newton Grove, and in several games he managed to score in double figures.

The list of senior superlatives came out at Clinton High in February, and Dick was named as having the voice of the ideal boy. Henry Lee Turlington was considered as having the ideal appearance. The girl with ideal hair was Baby Doll Smith, and the girl with the ideal appearance was Gloria Reynolds.

In January, 1939, scientist Neils Bohr came to the

United States. He shared his knowledge of the splitting of the atom, gained from the German researcher Lise Meitner, with scientists at Princeton University. Bohr even published a report on the new phenomenon. Both the Germans and the Americans were aware of the cataclysmic military potential of an atom bomb.

In early 1939 the United States Congress debated the issue of building up the American military presence on Guam. Guam was located in the Mariana Island some 1400 miles west of Wake and was, therefore, the closest American base to the Japanese homeland. It was clearly a provocative geographical location, evidenced by Japan's positioning of several military bases on islands nearby. Realizing this, and not wanting a direct confrontation with Japan, Congress voted on February 23, 1939, not to fortify the American base on Guam. It became apparent that Guam would be conceded to the Japanese if war was to break out. America's first line of defense across the Pacific would be drawn farther to the east.

The CHS boxing team had a match in February with Burgaw, a team which earlier in the season had dealt the Clinton pugs their only loss of the year in a close 4 1/2 to 3 1/2 decision. The second match was a hard-fought battle which ended in a 4-4 tie. Purcel Jones and Tracy Robinson led the basketball team to a 23-16 win over Clement to establish the Horses as the best team in the county.

The final boxing match of the year was held in March, when the Clinton boys facing their stiffest competition of the season. The team from Warsaw was not able to fill the heavy weight class with a man to fight Dick, who was described as the "local ace." So,

an exhibition bout was scheduled in the heavy weight bracket with Dick fighting John Avery Peterson, a Clinton High graduate who was fighting for N. C. State College in Raleigh. Dick knocked Peterson senseless and was on the verge of a knockout, but he was unable to put the older boxer on the canvas. Two local Negro fighters, Faison and Stinson, finished out the card with an exhibition fight described as a "battle royal."

As the boxing season ended the baseball season began, and the Clinton team's first game was in late March with Wilmington. The team bus left just after noon and headed down highway 60 toward the "land of seafood." About half way through the fifty-seven mile journey, a tire blew out on the bus and had to be repaired. Coach Wood telephoned ahead to alert the opponents of the delay. Meanwhile, the Dark Horses took to the woods to change into their uniforms while the tire received a patch. Soon the bus was rolling again with the team hoping to whip the larger school for a victory in the first game of the year.

Victory was to elude the boys from Clinton this day, as they were defeated in a close 2-1 contest. Dick scored Clinton's only run. After the game the team dressed, ate some eclairs at the Sally Ann Bakery in Wilmington and headed toward home. Somewhere between Delway and Taylors Bridge another blowout occured, and again the team was on the side of the road. Fes Turlington walked down the road to Delway where he found a telephone and called home for help. Meanwhile, the team built a fire on the shoulder of the road to stay warm. Dick and Hamp Whitfield flagged down a passing motorist who agreed to take them back to town. Just before

Pan Am travelers enroute to the orient enjoy dinner in the dining room of the hotel.

midnight the remainder of the team finally arrived back home in Clinton.

Things began to look up for the baseball team after the Wilmington game, and the team won five of its next six games. Dick went 3-for-3 in a 9-2 win over Ingold. Then came a 37-2 shellacking of the team from Garland. This put the Dark Horses one game behind a team from the Herring community for the conference lead. The team finished a strong season, and soon it was May and time for the class of 1939 to graduate.

A football scholarship was offered to Dick by Wake Forest College which he accepted shortly after graduation. Late in the summer he packed his clothes and headed off to college to be a Demon Deacon. He looked forward to playing college football at Wake, which was located a few miles north of Raleigh. Before long, however, Dick became homesick and a bit frustrated by college life. He returned home to Clinton disillusioned with the college and the brand of football played there. He decided to look for work in Clinton.

Dick took a job delivering milk for Charlie Kerr, who had a small dairy business. Early each morning Charlie delivered milk to each of his residential customers around town while Dick delivered to all of the business customers. Just after lunch Dick would drive his milk truck to Fayetteville some forty miles away and pick up a load of milk from Pemberton's Dairy. Then he would return to Clinton and prepare the milk for his deliveries early the next morning.

Dick continued to work at the dairy through the fall of 1939. He knew that delivering milk was not going to be his lifelong career. But, having turned down the football scholarship, Dick no longer had the option of going into athletics. It seemed that almost every day he was seeing young men drafted into the military. Dick did not know which way to turn and making career plans was becoming a real dilemma for the nineteen year old, especially since war with the Nazis and Japanese was beginning to appear as a real possibility. The greatest concern for most young men was the potential for war with the Nazis in Germany. Few, including Dick, felt that Japan posed much of a threat.

Far from Clinton, N.C., in the cold expanses of northern Michigan, another young man was ready to venture out into the unsteady world. His name was Ralph Holewinski. Ralph was one of twelve children. His father was a dairy farmer in Gaylord, Michigan, who also grew seed potatoes for other farmers in Michigan's potato country.

By the age of twelve Ralph was helping out on the family farm during the rough times of the early 1930's. He was attending school at St. Mary's, which was three miles from the Holewinski's farm. There were no school buses, so each day the children would make the long walk to class, sometimes through the freezing cold of the northern Michigan winters.

After graduation from high school Ralph Holewinski worked on his family's farm and helped them through tough times until his eighteenth birthday. He decided to join the Marine Corps, so he took a Greyhound bus down south to Chicago and enlisted on May 15, 1939. Ralph thought he wanted to be a seagoing Marine so he could see the world, but he was first sent to California for boot camp. One day while he was in basic training in San Diego he saw the aircraft carrier ENTERPRISE moored in the harbor. Young Holewinski was awestruck at the sight of the immense ship. More than ever he wanted to be a Leatherneck. After boot camp he was assigned to the 15th Marines in an anti-aircraft artillery unit.

In September Hitler's fury boiled over in Europe and the continent became embroiled in war. German forces invaded Poland and the world seemed to be heading for all out war. Dick began to sense real danger in the air.

With world tensions strained by the Nazi invasion of Poland, the United States began to bolster its armed forces. Each day Ralph Holewinski saw more and more young Marine recruits pouring into San Diego. In fact, so many reported that there were not enough uniforms for them all and many of the young recruits were drilling in their civilian street clothes and dress shoes.

Late in 1939 another member of the 1st Defense Battalion received a promotion. Charles Holmes was a young Marine corporal from Spur, Texas. He was promoted to buck sergeant. He, like Holewinski and Darden, was spawned during the hard times of the Depression. Holmes had worked since he was a young boy farming cotton and grain on his family's spread in west Texas. He had joined the Marine Corps in 1934 and after over four years of hard work he was proud of his new rank.

Holmes had received extensive training at Fort Monroe, Virginia, in antiaircraft artillery. He had hoped to enter college and become an engineer after serving in the Marines, so he jumped at the chance to go to the artillery school. For 43 weeks he took courses in electrical engineering, physics, algebra, trigonometry, and mechanical drawing. Holmes wanted to learn as much as possible to enable him to get into a good engineering college after his stint in the service. The Marines wanted him to use their newest and most sophisticated devices for aiming anti-aircraft guns and knocking enemy planes out of the sky.

After months of grueling classroom work, the Marines sent Holmes to Parris Island, South Carolina, where he became part of an antiaircraft battery. The unit had .50 cal. machine guns and 3" antiaircraft guns along with powerful searchlights. The unit trained across the river at Hilton Head. Later to become a luxury resort, Hilton Head was, at that time, a jungle rife with snakes, alligators, and teeming with insects. Holmes and his unit erected their tents near the old lighthouse and practiced firing their 3" guns nearby.

A very brave, or naively confident, Marine gunner named Al Munch pulled a canvas target on a short tow rope behind a Grumman "Duck" airplane over Hilton Head. He apparently had great faith in the marksmanship of Holmes and his men, since they fired away at the target with their powerful 3" guns as Munch pulled it through the air just a few feet behind his cockpit. The anti-aircraft unit got pretty good with their cannon and managed never to shoot Munch down, but Charles Holmes gained great respect for his bravery.

On October 11, 1939, a letter was sent to President Roosevelt from physicist Albert Einstein. Einstein had become privy to the reports of Enrico Fermi's experiments and realized the magnitude of the conclusions. In the letter to the President, Einstein suggested "quick action" on the part of the United States. If it were possible to build a bomb of unprecedented proportions with the new technology, persisted Einstein, America should be at the forefront of experimentation in nuclear physics.

The letter from Einstein, and discussions with others,

The 1938 Clinton High School football squad. Co-captain James Furman Honeycutt has a sling on his shoulder and co-captain Dick Darden is on his left.

convinced President Roosevelt that world history could be changed with this new atomic technology. The President realized that if the Nazis developed atomic weapons first they could rule the world. In a decision of immense foresight and wisdom, Roosevelt authorized the initiation of research to explore the potential of atomic energy. The race for nuclear weapons with Germany had begun. The United States gathered the finest available scientists from throughout America and the free world to begin the massive project.

In October, 1939, President Roosevelt ordered the U.S. Pacific fleet to move its base of operations from San Diego, California, to Hawaii. Also during 1939 the Marine Corps devised the concept of the "Defense Battalion." These fighting units were to be comprised of just under one thousand men, and their primary purpose was to defend small island outposts on the perimeters of America's defenses. Wake Island, Johnston Island, and Palmyra were being considered for such a defense battalion.

The Marines also planned to place defense battalions on Midway Island, Samoa, and the other island outposts which constituted America's outer defensive shield in the huge Pacific Ocean. Midway was already being transformed into a forward base by the Marines of the 3rd Defense Battalion. Units of the 1st Defense Battalion would install defensive positions on Palmyra and Johnston Islands. The 7th Defense Battalion would work on Pago Pago and American Samoa. There would also be a defense battalion stationed in Iceland. These defense forces, in theory, would dig in along the beaches of the islands and be able to repel an enemy assault from the sea.

The basic organizational plans for the defense battalions called for two types of heavy armaments. In theory, each defense battalion was a modified artillery unit. It would consist of 3" anti-aircraft batteries to protect against aerial assaults, and 5" seacoast artillery batteries, or large cannons. These big guns were expected to defend against enemy ships. The 5" guns were the largest weapons that were planned for the outpost on Wake Island. These were naval guns that had been designed for use in the broadside batteries of pre-WW I American battleships.

In addition, there would be .30 caliber and .50 caliber machine guns. Eighteen pedestal-mounted .50 cal. machine guns would provide anti-aircraft support and thirty M1917 water-cooled .30 cal. machine guns would be used for beach defense in case enemy landing craft were able to make their way to the beaches and initiate an amphibious landing. There would also be several large 60" searchlights in case the enemy launched a night landing. No infantry unit would be assigned to the defense battalion because the enemy, at least in theory, was not supposed to be allowed to land on the heavily fortified islands.

1940

Dark and ominous clouds of war were building worldwide in early 1940. Hitler's German armies rolled over the Netherlands and France, and appeared to be poised to subject Britain to the same Blitzkrieg tactics. Dick could feel the tension. He was still delivering milk but knew that he soon would be drafted into the Army. Being a foot soldier in the Army infantry didn't seem to be

Dick proudly sports his letter sweater as he poses with members of the graduating class of 1939

a good idea to a young man who provided a 6'3" target, so he went to Wilmington to enlist in the U. S. Navy.

The news reports mentioned the Japanese adventurism, but Dick didn't give it much thought. After all, Japan was a world away. His greatest worry was what was happening to England, our closest ally in Europe. Hitler was bombing Great Britain, and there seemed little doubt that war was coming.

The Navy recruiter in Wilmington, having filled his quota of recruits for the month, proclaimed that Dick had failed his physical examination because he was colorblind. He turned Dick down, telling him to go home and eat carrots for a month. Then he could return a month later when the recruiter had a new quota to fill and would probably pass the eye test. Dick left Wilmington dejected and even more confused about what he should do with his future.

Not to be outdone by the Navy recruiter, and still worrying about the Army draft, Dick and a friend, Kenny Smith, went to Raleigh in a car borrowed from Ted Boney, Dick's first cousin. The two decided to try to enlist in the Navy through the recruiting office there. Hundreds of young men were trying to enter the Navy. Many, like Dick, thought it would be a better alternative than being drafted

into the Army and becoming a foot soldier. It was not surprising that Dick's physical in Raleigh found no sign of color blindness. He was sworn in as a Seaman Apprentice on June 12, 1940. Dick Darden was in the United States Navy.

Development of the naval air base on Wake Island progressed steadily between 1935 and 1940. The Pan American Airways hotel was a fine facility with forty rooms to accommodate the passengers on the Clippers. The facility tried to grow some of its own food rather than going to the great expense of importing everything. A hydroponic vegetable garden was established.

In 1940 two typhoons ripped into Wake Island. Although there was damage to the Pan Am facility, none of the buildings was destroyed and construction proceeded soon after the storms abated. Ships continued to arrive off the south shore of the island, and small boats were essential for ferrying materials to shore. The USS WRIGHT was one of the ships that visited Wake, bringing supplies and materials for the development of the facilities.

There had been reports that the islands had been completely flooded by ocean waters during storms in the past, but this did not occur during the post-1935 period while the island was inhab-

28

ited. Some thought that this explained the fact that there was no fresh water on any of the three islands. However, the prevalence of porous coral sand, which would not hold water beneath the surface of the atoll, and the relatively low rainfall were probably better explanations.

Darden Collection

1939 Clinton High School baseball team: Front Row: Tracy Robinson, Fes Turlington, Sumner Eakes, Purcell Jones, Dick Darden, Hamp Whitfield.

National Archives

The Pan Am Hotel, March 5, 1940, uses the knarled, scrubby native vegatation in its landscape.

Chapter 4
THE UNITED STATES NAVY

After a few final weeks at home, Dick Darden reported for basic training at the Naval Training Station in Norfolk, Virginia. He spent eight tough weeks in July and August of 1940 becoming a top notch sailor. Norfolk was hot, really hot, and humid during the summertime. Dick's pay was $21.00 a month. He took out a life insurance policy worth $2500.00 through the Veterans Administration just in case the family might need help with his burial expenses. This cost Dick $4.53 each month, so every two weeks when he visited the paymaster he received between seven and eight dollars in cash for his services

Apprentice Seaman Dick Darden began to think perhaps he had mistakenly joined the Army instead of the Navy because his basic training seemed to be one continual marching exercise. Although the training was tough and uncomfortable, he learned to take orders and accept supervision. Becoming mentally tough would prove to be a salvation during the upheaval that the next five years would bring. Though he didn't know it, only his willpower and fate would deliver him through the next five years alive.

On August 1, 1940, Ambassador Grew warned that the Japanese considered the situation in Europe to be in their favor. They knew that white Americans would be distracted from the Far East by the events in their European homelands. To compound the problem for the United States, the British, French, and Dutch would not be able to defend their colonies in the Far East while waging war with the Germans on their home soil.

It was during August, 1940, that American military forces broke the Japanese diplomatic code. This allowed them

to monitor Japanese communications and become aware of the Japanese intentions for war in Asia. A new Japanese government was formed with Yosuke Matsuoka as the powerful Foreign Minister and Lt. General Hideki Tojo as the Minister of War. On September 27, 1940, Matsuoka signed the Axis Pact aligning Japan with Germany and Italy. The sides were clearly chosen. Of the Axis alliance members, Japan had the greatest potential for expansion in Asia. However, General Tojo, the leader of the Kodo-Ha faction, saw his dream of HAKKO ICHIU being realized by Europeans and not by the Japanese. The Caucasion race from Europe and America seemed to be taking over the world. This directly opposed Tojo's plan for Japanese rule over much of the earth. Japan maintained its alliance with the strange bedfellows Germany and Italy, but began to plot its own destiny in Asia.

The Navy allowed Dick a ten day leave after basic training, so he came home to Clinton looking every bit the part of a skinned-head recruit. This would be his last time at home before the furor of World War II would explode. Before he would see Clinton again he

Darden Collection

Dick poses with his neice during his first leave in September, 1940

would pay a huge price for his freedom and he would suffer more indignities at the hands of the Japanese than any human being should ever be forced to endure.

The return to Norfolk in the fall of 1940 was the beginning of an odyssey that would take Dick Darden around the world. He had no idea where he was going or what his duty assignment would be. The Navy didn't offer recruits a choice in 1940, so he didn't know what job would be given him upon his return to Norfolk. He only knew that Hitler was on a rampage in Europe, having conquered nearly all of America's allies except England, and the Japanese now seemed to be inching closer to war with the United States in the Pacific.

Ralph Holewinski's unit became the nucleus for the 1st and 2nd Marine Defense Battalions. Most of the men in the unit who had served aboard ships drew assignments on the large 5" guns. Holewinski was promoted to Corporal and assigned to a machine gun company. He was extremely proud of getting his second stripe, especially since he got the promotion in about half the time that it took most men to move up in rank. He also enjoyed the privileges afforded to a corporal. There would be no more walking guard duty or fire watches, no more cleaning the barracks prior to the weekly field day, and most importantly, there would be a raise in pay from $18.00 to $54.00 a month.

In addition to the new pay rate, Holewinski drew another $3.00 per month in sharpshooters pay. At a time when a glass of beer was only ten cents, the new pay grade placed Holewinski in pretty good company. He was especially proud of the red stripe that he wore on his dress blue trousers, another advantage of the promotion.

The USS HELENA would be Dick Darden's first seagoing assignment. She was a light cruiser, one of the most modern, measuring over 550 feet in length with a 55 foot beam. The HELENA mounted 6" guns and much of the latest equipment. She was a sleek fighting machine, one of America's newest ships, and was said to be virtually unsinkable. Soon after Seaman Darden's arrival, the HELENA was off to sea.

The HELENA steamed southward and Dick Darden tasted the life of a seaman for the first time. He was assigned to fire control on the ship, but most of his duties involved deck work. His first tour of duty at sea took him to the Caribbean, steaming to several islands off Florida and Cuba and visiting several ports. For a twenty year old boy from a small southern town, it was quite an adventure. The HELENA steamed on toward Guantanamo, stopping in several ports for just a day or two. The sailors were granted shore leave on several occasions.

The HELENA arrived at the Panama Canal, docking at its eastern end. The ship remained in port for a week, and the crewmen were allowed to go ashore and enjoy the tropical atmosphere. Then the HELENA cleared through the canal, after which she again dropped anchor. The stay at the western end of the canal also lasted for one week.

In addition to their normal duties, the sailors stood four-hour watches on the ship. They tried to get as much sleep as possible during the remaining time, but this was difficult due to frequent drills. General quarters were sounded at anytime during the day or night, and the men went through the routine of simulating the firing of their guns. They did it so many times they could do it in their sleep. They practiced again and again and again, passing the powder, passing the ammunition, loading and locking the guns. They began to function like robots at their battle stations.

From Panama the HELENA steamed northward and reached San Diego and Long Beach, California, late in the fall of 1940. It was in southern California that Dick Darden was transferred from the USS HELENA to the USS CINCINNATI. The CINCINNATI was a light cruiser like the HELENA, but she was not a new and modern ship. The CINCINNATI was of World War I vintage.

The CINCINNATI had put in for repairs at Mare Island Navy Yard in Vallejo, California. She was 550' long and built much differently from the HELENA. Dick could go below decks on the CINCINNATI and see nearly the entire bowels of the ship. The lower deck was open almost from one end to the other, and there were few, if any, watertight compartments. Dick wondered what would happen if she were to spring a leak below decks.

One of Dick's first assignments was to help refit the entire ship from hammocks to bunk beds. Next he was assigned to help refinish and paint the ship from the waterline down. First the men had to remove the old paint from the sides of the ship. This they did with chipping hammers while suspended down the side of the ship on wooden stages with ropes. One man would chip with his hammer and chisel, and then another would come behind him and brush the metal smooth with a wire brush. The old paint on the ships hull was about one inch thick.

Once Dick was working at the CINCINNATI's stern when he hit the side of the ship with his chipping hammer and the head of the tool went right through a hole in the hull of the old cruiser. The steel skin of the ship was old and rusty. There were many holes, some several inches deep, that penetrated almost through the steel plating of the ship below the water line. The men were instructed to repair the holes by putting grease, similar to heavy axle grease, in the holes and simply paint over them.

After the steel hull had been stripped bare and sanded, a thick coat of an anti-corrosive material, almost like wax, was applied. Then another thick layer of anti-fouling paint, designed to withstand the harsh salty rigors of sea duty, was applied. Finally came two layers of Navy gray finishing paint.

The USS HONOLULU, another light cruiser, was moored farther up the Pacific coast. Several men aboard her would later play major roles in Dick Darden's story. On October 21, 1940, Fireman 1st Class Jim Cox was transferred to the HONOLULU at Bremerton, Washington. Cox was a young Navy man only two months removed from civilian life in his home state of Michigan. The HONOLULU was the flagship of Cruiser Battle Force 8. It was commanded by Admiral Husband E. Kimmel, who was destined to become a central figure in the fate of the men at Pearl Harbor and on Wake Island.

In November of 1940 Ralph Holewinski went back home to Michigan on leave. He gave up a good job coaching machine gunners, but it was well worth the sacrifice to see his family again in Gaylord. For a month the young Marine enjoyed his family, but each day he read in the newspapers of the worsening conditions around the globe. The entire world seemed to be about to boil over.

When Holewinski's leave came to an end, his family drove him to the train station for the long journey back to

The USS HELENA

California. Along the way Ralph asked that they stop at his parish house. Even though it was nearly midnight he was met at the door by Father Francis Kaminski. The two talked for a short time, after which the priest gave the young soldier his blessing.

When the family reached the station Ralph boarded the midnight train for San Diego. He reassured his mother, telling her not to worry about him. He reminded her that he only had two and a half years left in his hitch, and then he would return home. The train pulled out of the station, heading first to Chicago. There he ran into a fellow Marine who was also a member of the First Marine Battalion. Since both were returning to their unit in San Diego, they agreed to travel together.

When the train stopped in Omaha, Nebraska, an elderly lady asked the two Marines if they would carry her bags into the station. Ralph and his buddy were happy to oblige. After they had gotten the lady situated inside, she gave each of them a hefty $1 tip along with a big smile and "thank you." The two Marines were in uniform, so they wondered if she had mistaken them for bell hops or porters. At any rate, they were glad to get the nice tips.

There seemed to be quite a lot of activity on the train as it prepared to leave Omaha. Ralph and his buddy learned that Nebraska was about to play in the Rose Bowl, so there was a large group of Cornhusker fans boarding the train for the trip to the game. The two Marines decided to check out the bumper crop of young female fans and sat down with two that

they would chitchat with on the long ride to California.

Ralph Holewinski was treated royally by the Nebraska fans all the way to California and he never had the opportunity to spend the $1 tip that he earned in Omaha. The trip westward went by too quickly as Holewinski enjoyed the merriment and fun being had by the Rose Bowl bound Nebraskans. When the train reached Los Angeles the newly made friends from Nebraska left the train to follow their football team to Pasadena. Reality set in again as the train carrying the two Marines continued down the California coast toward San Diego.

Soon after being painted and repaired, the CINCINNATI left port and put out to sea destined for Manila in the Philippine Islands and ultimately Hawaii. Dick Darden's spirits were running high with the excitement of a tour of duty to such exotic places.

Dick's assigned job aboard ship was "Fire Control," which involved coordinating the range finders on the big guns. He would peer through telescopic sights on the guns and determine the distance and direction that a target was from the ship. Then he would radio this information to officers below deck in the plotting room. They would compute the distance, wind velocity and angle, water currents, and the speed of the ship, before radioing back a setting. The gun would then be adjusted to the prescribed setting and fired.

While enroute to the Philippines, the CINCINNATI put into Guam. By this time Seaman Darden was assigned to

32

The USS CINCINNATI visits Portland, Oregon during the 1930's

the annunciator, a device located just aft the captain of the ship on the bridge. This instrument would ring up the speed that the Captain wanted for the ship. Dick would stand behind the annunciator with a lever in each hand. His left hand controlled the two huge engines and screws on the port side of the ship, and his right hand controlled the two on the starboard side. As the Captain barked orders, Dick would repeat the order out loud to insure the accuracy of the conveyance and then slide the arms of the annunciator to the correct positions. This would register below deck in the engine room and the order would be carried out there.

The ship had to maneuver through a 100' wide channel to get to the dock area on Guam. As the CINCINNATI began to leave Guam and exit through the dangerously narrow channel, Dick Darden was manning the annunciator. The ship carefully moving through the channel when the engine room suddenly indicated that the ship's rudder had jammed in a position fully extended toward one side. This would surely have run the ship aground had the Captain not been alert. He looked at Dick and said, "Son, if you ever got an order right in your life, get this one."

The Captain then began spitting out orders which Dick successfully relayed on the annunciator to the engine room. One of Dick's arms would thrust forward and the other would fly back, causing the two giant propellors on one side to push and turn the ship slightly. Moments later the order would come for him to reverse the positions of the arms of the annunciator, causing the opposite screws to engage and push the ship back slightly in the other direction. The captain

skillfully zigzagged the 550' long ship out of the 100' wide channel, never touching the dangerous sides of the waterway. Once out in open waters the rudder was repaired.

Between Guam and the Philippines the CINCINNATI encountered a full-blown typhoon. Dick was operating the annunciator on the bridge of the ship when the first news of the storm came over the radio. It was about 6:00 a.m., and the radio message indicated that the ship was about a half day away from the storm and headed directly toward it. Dick knew first-hand the condition of the hull of the old ship, and he wondered if she would be able to hold up under the strain of such a storm. He would soon find out.

By noon the ship was in the typhoon, and Dick was still at the annunciator. The Captain barked orders for speed and direction which Dick rang up on the annunciator. The Captain held the bow of the ship directly into the wind so that the huge waves would break perpendicular to the line that the CINCINNATI was traveling. Her bow would rise several stories out of the water and then crash down through the next wave. As the waves would break over the bow of the ship, the water would rush all the way to the base of the bridge beneath Dick.

The CINCINNATI was tossed about in the ocean like a cork for twenty-four hours as it struggled through the typhoon. The ship would sometimes wallow from side to side when it would get off line with the waves. When this happened the two great propellers on one side would be completely exposed. As they rotated in vain above the water Dick would hear them making an eerie "wush, wush, wush"

33

sound. The screws would make four or five full revolutions before the ship would roll back and the sea would cover them with water again. Then the other side would rise up out of the water and do the same thing.

Of course no one could go on deck during the fury of the storm. The violence of the typhoon had washed away anything on deck not secured beforehand, and had torn away some things that had been. Most of the radar equipment, which had been held in place by large metal cables, was gone. Three of the life boats had been torn free and disappeared into the frothy ocean, and the one which remained was dangling over the side of the ship, still bound by a lone cable. With each motion of the ship it would banged loudly into the side of the vessel.

Men moved from below deck to the bridge through a stairwell that had been built into a hollow metal tube that acted as a support for the bridge. When Dick's shift on the bridge was over he was replaced by another seaman and he descended through the tubular stairwell to his quarters below decks.

Dick was exhausted when he jumped into his newly installed bunk, but the violent lurching of the ship made sleep impossible. Had the old hammocks still been in place he could have swung with the movements of the ship and probably dozed off. This, however, was not possible in the bunk because he had to hold onto the sides to keep from being thrown onto the steel deck below. Dick asked one of his buddies to take a cloth strap and cinch him into the bunk tightly. Two straps were put on him, one at his chest and the other at his knees. This secured him into the bunk, and the tired seaman went right to sleep.

The CINCINNATI spent several days in Manila docked at Cavite Navy Yard and then several more days in Manila harbor. After a week had passed, the seamen had attended to their duties on ship so well they were issued passes for shore liberty. They enjoyed the exotic sights, nightlife, and the pretty girls in this new and strange country. The young seaman from rural North Carolina enjoyed the sights and sounds of this colorful, extravagant, yet seemingly bizarre part of the world. Soon it was time for the ship to move on to its next port of call, Pearl Harbor. The CINCINNATI weighed anchor and put to sea. Everyone was anxious to see Hawaii.

Between the Philippines and Hawaii Dick fell victim to urethral colic, an illness similar to small kidney stones. Dick would later remember this as the most painful thing that ever happened to him, even more excruciating than the bloodletting that would occur at the hands of the Japanese.

The illness proved to be serious enough that he was transferred at sea to the USS RELIEF, a hospital ship transporting its cargo of men to the Mare Island Naval Station at Vallejo, California. Dick was admitted to the hospital at Mare Island, located some distance up the bay between San Francisco and Oakland. The illness turned out to be serious, and Dick remained in the hospital for six weeks before he was able to return to active duty.

After being released from the hospital, Darden was assigned to the YN-53 in San Pedro, near Long Beach in southern California. The YN-53 was a wooden fishing vessel purchased from its owner by the Navy for military use. The men aboard her would prepare the YN-53 for laying submarine nets in Pearl Harbor and Honolulu Bay.

Late in 1940 the seven crewmen on the YN-53 went to work renovating the old fishing boat. First, there were several layers of tar on the deck which had to be removed. Each day two or three of the sailors worked with scrapers, while others came behind them with wire brushes. They cleaned, chipped, scraped, and sanded the deck until it was so clean they could lie down on it in their dress whites and not get dirty. Civilian workers were brought in to speed up the job. They used steam hoses to clean out the filthy holds where fish had been stored. Finally the ship was in top shape, ready to serve in the U. S. Navy.

While Dick spent the Christmas of 1940 in California, men were busy at work in Hawaii loading ships and barges with supplies for Wake Island. Work was about to begin in earnest. The United States would soon transform the sleepy atoll into a military installation that would become part of its forward defense perimeter against Japan.

A consortium of private construction firms, collectively known as Contractors Pacific Naval Air Bases, had won the contract to build the Wake Island facility. The primary contractor in this consortium was the Morrison-Knudsen Company. During the peak of the construction effort, over 1200 civilian laborers would be on the island, and the contractor estimated that construction of the base on Wake Island would take over three years to complete.

Darden Collection

Seaman Dick Darden

34

Upon completion of the facility on Wake, there would be several bases packed onto the small atoll. The island would be a defensive position supporting the First Defense Battalion of the U. S. Marine Corps. In addition, there would be two air bases: a seaplane base which would be located near the lagoon to provide the landing area for the big flying boats, and an air base with a runway that would support fighters and bombers. The refueling of long range planes destined for the Far East was a primary consideration. There would also be a submarine base which would use the safe waters of the calm lagoon for servicing American U-boats.

In December, 1940, the U. S. Navy began to implement the recommendations of the Hepburn Report by taking

advance detachment would begin construction of a naval air station on Peale Island, while the runway and support facilities for the airport would be on Wake.

The work was feverish as the stevedores and civilian workers loaded ton after ton aboard the ships. About eighty workers would accompany this initial shipment of materials and launch the project, but soon there would be over 1200 civilians on Wake. The men would be required to build roads, buildings, a water tower, the air strip, concrete bunkers, barracks, houses, and every imaginable segment of the small city that would soon evolve on Wake. They were competent men who were up to the task. Many of these tough construc-

U. S. Navy

The USS. WILLIAM WARD BURROWS in 1940

the first steps toward building a naval air base on Wake Island. Eighty men and 2000 tons of equipment were loaded aboard the U.S.S. WILLIAM WARD BURROWS, a transport ship moored at Honolulu.

This pioneer party took thousands of pieces of equipment and types of supplies aboard the BURROWS. From heavy equipment to food service machinery, anything that would be required to maintain a large group of workers and engage in heavy construction was loaded on the ship. This

tion workers had been involved in major projects around the world, including the great dam projects in the western United States.

The BURROWS would tow a 100' barge loaded with heavy equipment. Huge bulldozers, cranes, tractors, road scrapers, and many other pieces of equipment would be needed to complete the job. A 50' tugboat, the PIONEER, would escort the BURROWS on its journey. On December 26, 1940, the ships sailed out of Honolulu harbor bound for Wake Island.

Chapter 5
1941: THE PACIFIC ODYSSEY BEGINS

On January 9, 1941, the BURROWS and PIONEER reached their destination—Wake Island. Since there were no port facilities and sailing into the lagoon was impossible, the ships had to lay-to off the south beach of Wilkes Island. The first contingent of civilian workers, about eighty men in all, went ashore the next day and began to unload the construction materials onto Wake's sandy beaches.

Almost simultaneously the crew of the YN-53 in California took the round-bottomed "purse seiner" out to sea with the Hawaiian Islands as their destination. It took ten days to make the journey, and the boat bobbed and rolled during the entire trip. All of the men aboard, including the old salts who were seasoned to ocean life, were seasick most of the time. There was a Chief Boatswains Mate on the ship who had been in the Navy for twenty-eight years and never "flashed his hash," but he became violently seasick before the California coast faded over the horizon.

Another young North Carolinian was already in Hawaii in January, 1941. Lt. Henry Gorham Webb was a Marine fighter pilot from Oxford, N.C. Webb had been nicknamed "Spider" by his fellow pilots for obvious reasons. Spider Webb's squadron arrived at Ewa airbase in January flying the outdated Grumman F3F biplane fighters. The Marine pilots spent most of their time training to provide an combat air patrol for the USS YORKTOWN. They would go up over the aircraft carrier and practice defending it against incoming aircraft. Sometimes they would reverse roles, practicing attack maneuvers against the ship.

While stationed in Hawaii in 1941, Spider Webb's air unit was alerted that they could be assigned at any time to defend any of the outlying islands in America's outer defensive perimeter in the Pacific. These included Midway, Palmyra, Johnston, and Wake islands. The fighter squadron could be ordered at any moment, without any communications to family back home in the States, to move out into the Pacific to one of the defensive bases.

The pilots in Webb's squadron had an emergency packet always ready so they could leave on short notice without any preparation time. This packet included a sleeping roll, tooth brush, and other essential overnight gear. The packet had to be small enough to fit into the cockpit of the plane with the pilot. The Grumman fighters could operate off the decks of aircraft carriers or from the airstrips of tiny Pacific islands.

The Japanese were also formulating war plans and by early 1941 they were thinking in terms of war on a grand scale. As the year progressed the Japanese strategy evolved into plans for all out war in the Pacific. The plan did not espouse a slow island-by-island expansion by the Nipponese forces. The Japanese were preparing to strike swiftly and overrun numerous targets all over the Pacific. They were scheming to launch military strikes against Pearl Harbor, Wake Island, Guam, the Solomon Islands, New Guinea, the Celebes, Borneo, Java, Sumatra, the Malay Peninsula, Indochina, the Philippines, China, Korea, and Manchuria.

There was nothing timid about the Japanese or their ambitions in Asia and across the Pacific. Even though Admiral Yamamoto did register mild opposition to the plan, citing the differential between Japan and the United States in size and industrial potential, the Imperial Supreme War Council approved the war plan. Each of the military leaders went to work to prepare for the glorious onslaught, which they eagerly scheduled to begin early in December, 1941.

The YN-53 was not the only U. S. Navy ship bound for the central Pacific during the early days of 1941. On a Saturday in February the commander of the First Defense Battalion, Col. Bohn, announced that he would not conduct the normal Saturday inspection; instead, he ordered his company commanders to have their men pack in preparation for leaving the mainland. Ralph Holewinski and each of the non-com's would be allowed only one seabag and one foot locker. Other personal property would be shipped home. Gun sheds were emptied. The battalion was about to ship out for the Hawaiian Islands.

The First Defense Battalion went aboard the USS ENTERPRISE, which was docked at North Island in San Diego harbor. Holewinski marveled at what a beautiful ship she was. This was be the first time the great aircraft carrier had been used as a transport. Over 1000 Marines and all of their equipment—guns, trucks, caterpillars, searchlights, and much more—were loaded aboard the ship. On the flight deck there were eighteen Army aircraft from Selfridge Field, Michigan, marking the first time that Army planes were put aboard an aircraft carrier.

The ENTERPRISE put to sea that night. The next morning the Marines had roll call and not one man was missing. The new commander of the battalion was Major James P. S. Devereux. He asked the ship's captain who was in command of the Marines when they were at sea on a Navy vessel. The captain replied that they were under his command as long as they were on his ship. At that, Major Devereux turned to his men, who were still standing in ranks on the ship's deck, and told them, "Today is Sunday. There will be no work for you today." It was his custom to give his men Sunday off. It appeared that the wiley Major Devereux had decided against yielding his command to the Navy captain, retaining command of his men even while at sea on a Navy ship.

After a week at sea the ENTERPRISE arrived in the vicinity of Pearl Harbor. When the ship was within sight of land, the Army pilots were instructed to take their planes ashore. They were quite excited since they had never flown off the deck of a carrier before. They got into their aircraft with noticeable grins on their faces. Since they had been getting advice all week about the spills and thrills of taking off from carriers, they were confident they could do it. Each of the eighteen planes lifted off the deck of the ENTERPRISE and landed safely on Oahu.

Ralph Holewinski and the Marines of the First Defense Battalion spent only one week in Hawaii. They never had time to visit the city of Honolulu. Holewinski and eight other machine gunners were ordered to pack their gear. They were taken to the docks at Pearl Harbor and boarded the supply ship USS ANTARES. Once aboard, the men learned they had been assigned to a 5" artillery group. There were twenty men and three officers in the group, one of them the feisty Major Devereux. They were heading for a place called Johnston Island.

After several days at sea the ship slowed to a snail's pace. Word was passed to the men to look for a water tower on the horizon. A few minutes later a sailor who had climbed the mast and was acting as a lookout shouted that he had sighted land. Johnston Island came into view. As the ship neared the small patch of sand she dropped anchor.

The next morning Holewinski was among a party of men who formed a work detail and went ashore. There were 150-200 civilians on the island employed by a contractor who was building an air base. Later in the day the men from the Antares were invited to eat in the civilian mess hall. They welcomed this opportunity since the food on the ship had been poor, both in quality and quantity. Holewinski enjoyed his first hearty meal since leaving Hawaii.

Holewinski and his Marine buddies spent five days on Johnston Island. They went ashore each day and worked in the grit and hot sun digging gun emplacements into the island. When they had completed the gun positions, they went back aboard the ship which promptly hoisted its anchor and headed out to sea again. This time they were heading toward the southwest and the destination was another tiny speck of coral in the central Pacific, Palmyra Island.

After nearly a week at sea the ANTARES reached its destination. The weather along the way had been extremely rough and all but a few of the men aboard the ship were seasick throughout the voyage. This discomfort, along with the poor quality of food in the mess hall, accounted for the fact that there were few good appetites during the trip. The beautiful group of islands known as Palmyra was a welcome sight to all aboard. There the Marines went ashore carrying the rest of their equipment with them.

The Marines pitched their tents in a grove of palm trees on Palmyra. Problems with their housing cropped up immediately. At high tide water came into the tents to a depth of about eight inches. There were about 150 civilians on Palmyra and they came to the aid of the six Marines and five sailors who would be calling the island home. They erected a wooden building that would serve as barracks for the men. Soon the accommodations became more comfortable and the men even built a handball court and a boxing ring.

Major Devereux remained on the island for about two weeks to supervise the installation of more defensive positions and give them his final approval. At low tide there were over fifty small islands that made up Palmyra. The sailors' job was to ferry the Marines to their work assignments on the various islands.

Occasionally Major Devereux would want to check a position on a nearby island, but he would have to ford knee-deep water to get there. The Major would always wear a full summer dress uniform, and disliked taking his shoes off or getting his trousers wet. So, he would order Holewinski to ferry him across, piggyback style. Since Holewinski would be dressed in his work clothes, usually nothing more than shorts and a sun helmet, he would not mind venturing into the shallow waters with the commander on his back.

Palmyra was made up mostly of coral rocks covered by a thin layer of sand. Shoe leather did not last long in the wet conditions on the island and on the jagged coral, so Holewinski wore sneakers most of the time. Duty on Palmyra fell into a routine: The men were up at 6:00 a.m. and worked all day in 90-100 degree heat on their defensive positions. The island was within 200 miles of the equator, so the heat and humidity were sweltering.

At the end of each day the men would take a swim to clean up. Then they would enjoy a game of handball or watch movies. The supply ships that serviced the island and an occasional destroyer would bring new movies or trade used ones with the men. Even so, most of the movies were seen several times by almost every man.

The men on Palmyra enjoyed the luxury of having Sundays off. In this free time they would go fishing or hike to nearby islands through the shallow water that barely covered the coral bottom. The waters around the island were teeming with sea life. Sea bass and red snappers weighing 20-30 pounds were plentiful, as were yellow tails. There were also manta rays, sharks, eels, and the deadly poisonous coral snakes.

One Sunday two sailors went out fishing and caught two sea turtles. They brought the turtles back and took several hundred pounds of good meat from them. The turtle meat was served in the mess hall to civilians and military men alike. Everyone thought they were eating veal cutlets, and the turtle dinner was a big hit. The sailors dried the two huge shells and made souvenirs of them. Both shells measured over three feet in height.

After reporting for duty at Pearl Harbor, Dick and the men aboard the YN-53 were assigned to duty laying submarine nets in and around Honolulu Harbor and Pearl Harbor. In March of 1941 the motor in the vessel knocked off, requiring extensive work and a time-consuming overhaul. It had to be torn completely down. Men had to use winches to lift the motor's heads out of the bowels of the boat.

While the YN-53 was being repaired, a similar vessel moored next to it was assigned double duty to get the heavy workload done. The sailors on that boat became understandably chagrinned as they watched Dick and his mates lounge about and enjoy the Hawaiian weather on their lame vessel. After the engine had been repaired, the YN-53 went out to sea on a trial run. On the first day the engine blew up again, and the boat had to be towed back into Pearl Harbor for another complete overhaul.

The YN-53 was effectively crippled. Beginning late in the spring of 1941, Dick was stationed on a helpless boat that bobbed up and down in Honolulu Harbor waiting for repairs. The boat was ordered moved into a yacht basin near Alamoana Boulevard where a private contractor would again work on the blown engine. The crew of the YN-53 was given no further orders except to remain with their boat.

The YN-53 sat idle from March until September, 1941. The men were assigned to wait with their ship until repairs had been made and then to continue their duties. In other words, for six months Dick Darden was assigned to enjoy the tropical paradise of Hawaii with no duties to perform. To make matters even better, he had been promoted to Seaman Second Class and he enjoyed the good life in the tropics as much as he could at his new pay grade of $36.00 per month. After life insurance had been taken out, he received almost fifteen dollars in cash every two weeks.

The crew of the YN-53 had nothing to do but sit on their boat and wait for the never-ending repairs to be completed. They sat on the boat or up on the docks, occasionally walking the half mile of dirt road out to Alamoana Boulevard. There they could turn left and go into Honolulu, turn right and go to Waikiki Beach, or walk across the street to a bar where they hung around and drank beer daily.

There were seven men on the boat, but no cook. The Navy allowed each man $1.00 a day for food. It was difficult to find three square meals a day in town and stay within the budget. One day the Lieutenant in command of the YN-53 came aboard and gathered his crew together. "We need a cook," he said. "Is there any one of you who has any experience cooking?" All were silent. No one wanted to volunteer for extra duty. Then the Lieutenant offered that if someone in the crew would cook, he would not have to stand watch on the boat.

Still no takers.

Dick thought hard about the watch duty that he disliked so much. Finally he stepped forward. "I'll give it a try," he responded. Everyone else breathed a sigh of relief. Dick had very little experience in the kitchen. After his father died Dick had to take on additional responsibilities at home, and cooking was occasionally one of them. He felt that a little experience was better than none, so he began his new duties in the galley of the YN-53. The men pooled their money together and Dick went ashore to buy groceries.

When Dick returned he had an assortment of foods. He started with scrambled eggs and didn't do too bad a job. The crew came back for more, so he began to gain confidence in the galley. Soon he was cooking roasts, baking hams, and making meatloaf. For six months Dick Darden would be the chef of the YN-53. It meant three good meals a day and no watch duty. It also helped to break the monotony.

Boredom became a real problem in paradise. There wasn't much the crew of the YN-53 could do to pass the time and stay within their budgets. One day Dick decided to go into Honolulu with thirty-five cents in his pocket to spend. He wasn't too crazy about the idea of walking the three miles into the city, so he spent a quarter to ride the bus. When he arrived downtown he had only ten cents left. He began walking around in hopes of finding something to do for the dime in his pocket.

First Dick went to the YMCA. Then he began walking down Baratania Street into the outskirts of the city. He found himself in a rather rough section of town filled with slums and cheap bars. The neighborhood even smelled bad, so Dick kept on walking. He noticed that most of the people were oriental looking natives or derelicts. He saw a theater which advertised all movies at ten cents. It appeared to be

the perfect way for Dick to spend his last dime. He plopped down the coin and went inside.

As Dick went inside the rickety theater, an odor hit him that almost nauseated him on the spot. It was the smell of human body odor. The theater was full of oriental workers who had not bathed in some time. Dick started to leave, but he knew that he had left his last dime at the box office. He became determined to stay and enjoy the movie. When the feature came on the screen it was a foreign language movie. "Oh hell," thought Dick, who had just spent his last dime on a movie that he could not even understand.

Before long Dick left the theater and began finding his way back to the YN-53, a distance of several miles. He didn't want to walk the entire distance, but he didn't have the twenty-five cents needed to ride the bus. As he stood at the bus stop he pondered his dilemma. How could he hitch a ride with no money in his bell bottoms?

Soon the answer presented itself. A nice looking young fellow happened along and stood waiting for the bus near Dick. The two began talking and had struck up a friendly conversation when the bus came into view. When it stopped and opened its door Dick hopped aboard in front of his new friend. When the attendant asked for his quarter, he motioned to the fellow behind him and said, "I don't have any money. He will take care of it."

Dick's new acquaintance had a puzzled look on his face, as if he didn't know what to do. He was faced with the choice of having a poor service man put off the bus or pay his fare. After a few moments of confusion the man put down the double fare and soon Dick began his free ride back to the yacht basin.

The crew of the YN-53 found one nighttime activity that

National Archives

The USS ENTERPRISE leaves Pearl Harbor February 12, 1943. Her deck was covered with one and two wing fighters. The two great hotels on Waikiki Beach can be seen in the background.

would be a costly error for the First Defense Battalion on Wake.

In June a group of 300 Marines in the First Defense Battalion were ordered to go to Midway Island. These men would relieve a similar group from the Third Defense Battalion. Among the men going to Midway was Sgt. Charles Holmes and his anti-aircraft unit. The fresh Marines were giving their counterparts some time off for "R & R." After about six weeks the two groups rotated again, Holmes and his men going back to Pearl Harbor.

In July of 1941 Japanese forces seized Indochina from the French. The Japanese had first pressured the French, who were fully occupied with the Nazi threat to their homeland, to allow them to place military bases in the French colonies. The Japanese moved quickly to occupy bases in Cam Rahn Bay, Da Nang, and Saigon in what would later be known as Vietnam.

President Roosevelt responded to the Japanese moves by placing an embargo on oil and other vital materials going to Japan. This was an effort to reduce their ability to wage war and to curtail their expansionism. All Japanese assets in the United States were frozen and trade between the two countries was cut off. Washington was sending a clear message to the Japanese leaders: End your aggressive and belligerent behavior. But the war machine was already fully engaged, and the warriors of Nippon were spreading toward several fronts outside of mainland Japan.

In August of 1941 the Japanese replaced Foreign Minister Matsuoka with Admiral Teijiro Toyoda. At that time the Chinese, both in China and in the United States, were intensely opposed to Japanese intervention in their country. They constantly appealed to Washington for assistance in the fight against Japan. American leaders knew that increased pressure on Japan by the United States, especially in the form of military assistance to China, might result in a military response by the Japanese against America. At the same time, to sit idly by and not respond would be tantamount to abandoning the Chinese. Washington found itself in the midst of a difficult dilemma.

During the first week of August Major Lewis A. Bohn, along with 177 officers and men of the First Defense Battalion, both Marines and sailors, embarked from Honolulu on the U.S.S. REGULUS. This would be the advance group for the defense battalion which would follow. Weapons and equipment for the new camp on Wake were loaded aboard the transport. In a matter of days she was ready to venture westward into the Pacific.

On August 8, 1941, the REGULUS, loaded with young American fighting men who would become the first defenders of Wake Island, sailed out of Pearl Harbor. Included was a young Marine officer named Lt. Arthur A. Poindexter. Poindexter had been a football player at the University of Kansas before joining the Marine Corps. He would be in command of a unit of .30 caliber machine guns on Wake.

Also aboard were several Navy men, including Fireman 1st Class Jim Cox. On Wake Island Cox would be temporarily assigned to a small boat crew responsible for ferrying men and materials from one island to another. He was attached to the First Fleet Marine Force of the First Marine Defense Battalion and was ordered to remain on Wake until completion of the naval air station then under construction.

The REGULUS towed two barges filled with miscellaneous supplies. The strain of pulling the barges slowed the REGULUS substantially, causing the trip from Pearl Harbor to Wake to take twelve days. The 178 Marines onboard the REGULUS reached their destination on August 19. The civilian work crews had sufficiently transformed the island for the Marines to begin to installing the 3" guns, 5" guns, and machine guns that would give the United States a stronger defense in the central Pacific.

The REGULUS made landfall at Wake on August 19 and immediately began unloading the men and supplies, using the same method of "lightering" cargo to shore that previous supply ships had used. By the time the REGULUS left Wake eight days later, the Marines had built a tent city at the end of the south fork of Wake Island, near the channel between Wake and Wilkes and across the lagoon from the far fancier accommodations of the civilian work force. The military camp would be known as Camp 1 and the civilian camp would be called Camp 2. Preparations for the defense of Wake Island were underway.

The objectives of the two groups of men on the island were clear. The task given of the civilian contractors was the construction of the buildings, barracks, roads, bunkers, and the airport on Wake. They also had the responsibility for dredging the channels to provide an entrance to the lagoon, and blowing out the coral heads that made boat travel in the lagoon dangerous. The Marines, on the other hand,

National Archives

Two great hotels on Waikiki Beach in 1940: The Royal Hawaiian and the Mauna Loa.

had only one objective. They were to assume the posture of a Marine Defense Battalion, installing their weapons and being prepared to defend Wake Island against any attempt by the enemy to take control.

While American activities on Wake were moving forward at a furious pace in August of 1941, the Japanese were not idle. Training and preparation for the Pearl Harbor attack had already begun. Early in August the elite of the Japanese Army and Navy met in Tokyo to formulate plans for taking control of Asia. With maps and table-top models they debated strategies until firm plans for waging war on several fronts had been drawn. The Japanese war lords were readying their country for the ultimate conquest.

Late in the summer of 1941 a fresh contingent of Marines was ordered to replace the unit occupying Palmyra Island. This was good news for Ralph Holewinski. He had spent five long months on the island doing heavy construction work just 200 miles from the equator. When the new troops arrived, "Ski" and his buddies boarded the ship for the trip back to Pearl Harbor for some well deserved time for R & R. Once they arrived in Honolulu they were rewarded with several weeks of liberty.

Boredom had become unbearable during the idle six months that Dick had spent in Honolulu with the crippled YN-53. Finally he put in for a transfer, hoping to escape the monotonous situation. He had heard that duty in China was more exciting, so he asked to be reassigned there. The word around Honolulu was that duty in China was great. Rumor had it that the work there was easy for sailors. In the American city of Pearl Harbor, Dick's meager wages were stretched pretty thin. He had heard that a little bit would go a long way in China, and sailors there could live like kings.

The Lieutenant in charge of the unit denied several of Dick's requests to be transferred, saying that he had only seven men and couldn't afford to lose even one of them. Dick submitted several subsequent requests only to have them denied as well. He decided to be persistent, and he continued to request a transfer every few days.

Finally, in September of 1941, orders came down for two seamen to be transferred to Wake Island. Seaman Darden and Seaman Andrew Fuller were selected to become members of a boat crew on Wake Island, a remote atoll in the central Pacific. Wake was little more than a speck on the map somewhere between Midway and Guam that Dick Darden knew very little about. The two sailors accepted the opportunity, however, figuring that the assignment on Wake would at least get them halfway to China. They figured that Wake would be a good place to re-apply for duty farther to the west.

The two seamen had no way of knowing that the winds of war were rising and that this move would eventually land them in the eye of the storm. They had no idea they were beginning a journey that would lead them directly into a wartime enemy's homeland where they would be thrust into the humiliation and agony of forced slave labor.

National Archives

Sailors enter the Royal Hawaiian Hotel on Waikiki Beach.

On September 3, 1941, Japanese military leaders decided to continue negotiations with President Roosevelt until November. If the embargo was not lifted by then, they would use force against the colonial powers in their region. Three days later, on September 6, Emperor Hirohito went to Tokyo's old imperial palace to meet with a group of military and civilian leaders. They discussed a policy for dealing with the encroachment of foreign powers in the hemisphere, particularly the embargo of critical raw materials and oil into Japan.

It was during September of 1941 that the Japanese leaders made their fateful decision to go ahead with plans to seize virtually all territories in the Pacific, stopping just short of Burma, Australia, Hawaii, and the Aleutian Islands. They had already taken control of major portions of mainland China and Indochina. During the fall of 1941 the preparations for these conquests took shape and war plans were refined. For the Japanese this would be a four-pronged attack:

1. Lt. General Tomoyuki Yamashita and the 25th Imperial Japanese Army would move down the Malay Peninsula and capture the British stronghold at Singapore.

2. General Hitoshi Imamura, with the 16th Army and naval forces would take the Dutch East Indies.

3. Lt. General Masaharu Homma and the 14th Army would take control of the Philippines.

4. Lt. General Shojiro Iida and the 15th Army would move from Thailand to Burma.

The war in Europe was beginning to sound very ominous to Dick as he lounged about Pearl Harbor in late summer, 1941. However, he had little fear of problems with the Japanese in the Pacific. If he had, he would never have considered any kind of transfer that would have taken him farther to the west. Even though the Japanese were obviously expansionists who were rattling their samurai swords in China, it was inconceivable that they would be fool enough to pick a fight with a power like the United States.

In the back of his mind Dick's greatest fear was that some small incident, perhaps the sinking of an American ship or the assassination of a prominent American in Japan, would trigger some type of confrontation between the two countries. But, considering the world situation as a whole, Dick felt that he was in just about the safest place for an American military man to be—thousands of miles away from Europe. The very idea that the Japanese might attack Hawaii was so preposterous that it had never crossed Dick's mind.

It was the first week in September, 1941. Seamen Darden and Fuller left Honolulu for the long journey over 2000 miles of open Pacific Ocean. When Wake Island appeared in the distance, it resembled a tiny V-shaped land mass, a speck of land in the seemingly endless vastness of the Pacific. Wake Island was actually the tip of an ancient volcanic mountain which rose several thousand feet out of the depths of the Pacific, but with its coral-encrusted tip barely rising above the surface of the water.

Wake Island represented a burr in the mitten of the Imperial Japanese Empire since the only American military base closer to Japan was on Guam. Wake provided the United States with the opportunity to have bombers within striking distance of the largest Japanese base in the Marshall Islands, Kwajalein, located only 625 miles to the south. Equally irritating to the Japanese was Wake's proximity to their base at Taongi, a scant 425 miles over the open ocean. The Japanese war lords felt, to say the least, that Wake Island in American hands was a threat to their plans to dominate the Pacific theater.

Wake seemed to be in a no man's land in the Pacific. The Japanese master plan would accept no advancement of American positions west of Hawaii. Conversely, America's defense policy had been formulated with an entire chain of islands, from Midway and Wake to the Marshalls and Carolines, to be a link with U.S. bases in the Philippines. Clearly, the war plans of these two empires over-lapped, and Wake Island was believed to be crucial to both sides.

The American workers on Wake had made substantial progress toward the completion of an air base. The runways were nearly completed and plans called for reconnaissance planes and long range bombers to use Wake. Plans also called for a dozen fighters to be based there for the protection of the island. In order to fuel the thirsty aircraft, several large steel fuel storage tanks were built near the Wilkes channel.

Tanker ships would "lay to" just off the south beach since it was too deep to anchor. Then large hoses would be floated ashore and connected to the storage tanks. Petroleum fuel, the life blood of the planes and equipment on the island, was pumped into the tanks. So much was needed on the island that 55 gallon metal barrels were used for additional storage space. Fuel was moved about the islands by tanker trucks.

Darden Collection

Dick enjoying the sights of Honolulu, spring and summer

Darden Collection

Dick cheek to cheek with a Hawaiian beauty.

43

Chapter 6
WAKE ISLAND – ENTERING THE TEMPEST

The floor of the Pacific Ocean is actually covered with many hundreds of mountains that remain as evidence of ancient volcanic activity. The tops of most of these lie beneath the surface of the ocean, completely obscured from human sight by the vast ocean. Several hundred, however, protrude through the surface of the water, thus creating a sprinkling of small islands across the Pacific between North America and Asia. Some of these are habitable by human beings, while others are too small or lack essential elements such as fresh water.

Wake Island is such a speck of land on the Pacific surface. Its mean height above sea level is only twelve feet and it is thought to have been completely flooded by typhoons during its recent history. A coral reef encircles the island and acts as a barrier to shipping, preventing the entry of all but the smallest boats into the shallow lagoon in the center of the three islands.

The islands form an atoll, a ring of coral surrounding a lagoon. The entire land mass of the three is just over three square miles, or about 2600 acres. Wake is actually all that remains of the eroded peak or rim of an ancient volcanic mountain whose upper edge protrudes above the ocean's surface today. The highest elevation on the entire island is just over eighteen feet.

The actual coordinates for Wake Island on a map of the Pacific are 19 16' N., 166 37' E. From the point of the wishbone on the eastern end (Peacock Point) to the farthest point on the tips of the open end (Toki Point on Peale Island, Kuku Point on Wilkes Island) is a distance of only 4 1/2 miles. On the open end of the island the distance across the lagoon between Toki Point and Kuku Point is 1 1/3 miles. Objects on one side of this open end can be clearly seen from the other side without the aid of binoculars. From the ocean side of Peale Island to the ocean side of Wilkes Island is only 2 1/4 miles.

Wake Island is one of the most isolated islands in the world inhabited by humans. It is located virtually in the center of the Pacific. The island rests over 2000 miles west of Hawaii, and over 1200 miles east of Guam. It is over 1000 miles southwest of Midway Island, and over 500 miles north of Eniwetok, Kwajalein, Wotje, and Roi-Namur in the Marshall Islands. Wake is simply the only land mass in a huge area of the immense Pacific Ocean.

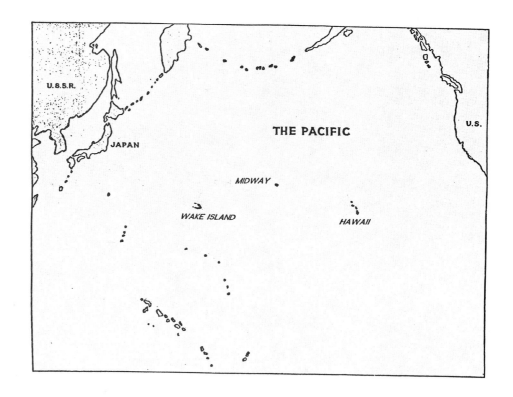

The Pacific Ocean

Wake Island

Wake Island falls in the same latitude as the Hawaiian Islands. A straight line can be drawn through the island of Hawaii, Wake Island, and the northernmost island of the Philippines. Wake falls approximately halfway between Midway Island and Saipan in the Marianas. The nearest group of islands to Wake is the Marshall Islands. Pokaakku atoll in the Marshalls lies only 304 miles south of Wake. Of greater interest to the Americans on Wake was the chain of atolls in the Marshalls known as Kwajalein, since the Japanese had several bases there. The air base on Kwajalein Atoll was only 639 miles to the south and posed a direct threat to the Americans on Wake.

Three small islands are collectively known as Wake Island. The largest of the three islands is named Wake, and is positioned at the point of the "V". It was upon this largest island that an air strip was being constructed. At the end of each of the arms of Wake Island's "V" is a narrow inlet, across from which is another slender finger-like island. Peale Island is the northerly extension of Wake Island's "V", while Wilkes Island extends the island's south side. These two smaller islands, each less than one mile long, are separated from the larger island by narrow channels.

The total linear distance around the three islands, from the tip at Toki Point on Peale Island to the tip at Kuku Point on Wilkes Island, is only about nine miles. In the center of the three islands, in the crater of the ancient volcano, is a shallow lagoon. Its beautiful crystal clear blue waters can be dangerously deceptive. The bottom of the lagoon is encrusted with coral and has many long spears called "coral heads" which point toward the surface of the water. Many come very near the surface and have sharp, jagged, rocky points that are well within the draft of virtually any ship which might seek a safe haven in these relatively calm waters.

The coral heads in the Wake Island lagoon were capable of ripping huge gashes in the hulls of any ships which might seek protection from the ocean waves by venturing into the placid waters of the lagoon. Despite the dangers that lurked in the lagoon, it was a beautiful body of water, having a distinctive pale blue color which contrasted markedly with the dark blue of the deep ocean just beyond the reef. From the surface of the lagoon the bottom was so clearly visible that it seemed as if the water did not exist.

A coral reef almost completely encircled the island, even the open end between Peale and Wilkes. Waves constantly crashed over the shallow reef making a deafening roar. This was a clear indication to the skippers of approaching ships that they could not bring their vessels into the lagoon. At several points around the perimeter of the island the reef was very close to the beach, sometimes less than one hundred feet offshore. At other places the reef was well over a half mile offshore.

The reef varied from being hidden under the waves in waist deep water to being clearly visible and protruding above the waves. Where the reef was very close to the shore it rose out of the surf high enough to hide several men. Only one small break existed in the reef just outside the channel between Wake and Wilkes Islands. This channel provided the only possibility for ocean-going ships to enter the lagoon; however, it was barely 100 feet wide.

The channel between Wake and Peale Islands, spanned by two bridges, was over 150 feet wide at its narrowest point. The reef outside this channel, however, denied its use to shipping. Only shallow draft boats, such as the lighters used by the Navy crews, could navigate either of the channels and enter the lagoon safely. Work was underway to dredge the Wilkes channel and prepare the lagoon for future use as a submarine base. This presented multiple problems, however, since the lagoon itself varied from very deep to dangerously shallow.

Even though there were only three square miles of land comprising the islands, the length of the coastline to be defended was another matter. On the inside of the island, along the lagoon, there were about eight miles to be patrolled. More importantly, on the other side of the three islands there were approximately twelve miles of coastline facing the ocean. This presented a real problem for the defenders since their ranks would be stretched uncomfortably thin if they attempted to stop an enemy attack anywhere along these twenty miles of coastline.

The weather on Wake Island was typically warm and sunny, not unlike the weather in the Hawaiian Islands. The air was always balmy over Wake. The temperature varied little from season to season, rarely falling below 68 degrees and not exceeding 95.

The warm winds which constantly swept across Wake Island came generally from the northeast, causing a heavy surf

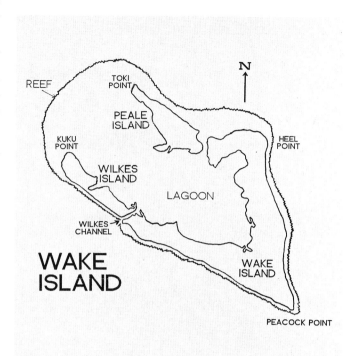

Wake Island

National Archives

An aerial view of Wake Island appraching from the Northeast. The road around the island is visible as is the Pan Am complex on Peale Island on the right.

46

An aerial photo of Wake Island taken over Heel Point on Wake. Across the bridge on Peale Island is the Pan Am Base

to pound continually against the north side. This created a lee side on the south exposure of the island, making that side much more favorable to approaching ships. The waves were much calmer on the south beach when compared to the northern coastline. When the tropical sun set, the trade winds caused cool night temperatures which could make the men uncomfortably cool if a modest amount of clothing was not donned over the daytime garb. Wake Island was relatively dry when compared to other islands in the south Pacific. It would normally get only about thirty-three inches of rainfall annually.

In several locations the white coral sand of the beaches was covered with coral rocks of varying sizes. In some places the beach was made up almost entirely of rocks the size of bowling balls. Elsewhere the sand was spotted with boulder-size rocks, some as large as trucks. Many of these coral boulders had jagged edges and presented dangerous obstacles. The white strand of beach varied in width from just over 50 feet to nearly 500 feet.

The land mass of Wake Island was a rather forbidding place, with no large trees growing in its coral sand. Some observers accused Wake of being little more than a reef with a few patches of scrubby undergrowth. There were no coconut palms growing here, but several areas were covered with thick tropical shrubs and trees, often thorny, which offered the only vegetation on the island. This was amazing since the island had no fresh water. Most of this tough undergrowth was short gnarled trees known as "ironwood" which grew to a maximum height of ten to twenty feet.

All three of the islands had substantial areas covered with low brushy vegetation. Although it seemed unlikely in this spartan environment, numerous species of plants had adapted to the sand-and-coral soil, to the constant coating of brine from the salt spray of the ocean, and to the brackish ground water of this windswept landscape. In fact, some plants actually flourished on Wake. Morning Glory, IPOMOEA GRANDIFLORA, is quite common on all three islands. The spreading habit of the vine earned it the name "octopus." Woody plants in the maritime forest of the island include a shrub called "Desert Magnolia," SCAEVOLA FRUTESCENS, and a dwarf tree called Buka or Ceodes, PISONIA GRANDIS.

The south leg of Wake had the most dense vegetation, especially in the area around the airstrip. The flora on this part of the island would prove to be adequate, even though low and scrubby, for the concealment of a large number of assault troops. While the trees were not tall, they could be particularly thick. In some places the thick jungle-like entanglement was difficult for a man to walk through.

While the vegetation on the gritty coral atoll had little to offer, the animal life was another matter. The ocean waters just off the gleaming white beaches and beyond the reef dropped immediately off to a depth of several thousand feet and teemed with fish and other ocean life. The water was crystal clear, and fish could be seen a hundred feet below the surface. The water around the reef was another matter as the constant wave action breaking there created a continual frothy turbulence.

In the clear waters around Wake Island many species of marine life could be found. Dozens of species of exotic fish lived in the lagoon. Many were small, multi-colored tropical fish. The lagoon at Wake Island was said to harbor one of the best collections of tropical fish in the world. Octopus were also common in the lagoon and on the reef that encircled the atoll.

Many edible species of fish lived in the ocean just beyond the reef. Yellow-Fin Tuna and King Mackerel were plentiful. Spotted Rays and Giant Rays seemed to fly through the clear waters with their huge wing-like fins. Sharks and barracuda were present in large numbers, presenting an everpresent danger to anyone who might be caught off guard while swimming in Wake Island waters.

On the island many species of insects and other animals provided an interesting and extensive fauna. Mosquitos were not a problem on Wake during the months Dick spent there, probably because the brisk trade winds were blowing almost all of the time. A particularly voracious species of rats were rampant on Wake Island, sometimes walking strangely on their hind legs and appearing unafraid of their new human cohabitors. They were thought to have been marooned on the island long ago when they escaped from an ancient fishing boat. Small land crabs were abundant on the islands.

Thousands of birds used this lonely speck of land in the center of the Pacific as their nesting place. The coral sand of Wake was the only piece of solid ground for hundreds of miles that would support the birds' eggs. Among the avian population of Wake were Terns, Boatswains, Boobies, Frigates, Plovers, Curlews, and the flightless Rail.

While oriental fishermen might have seen Wake Island earlier, the first known sighting of the tiny atoll was on October 2, 1586 (1568?), when Spanish explorer Alvaro de Mendana discovered it. Mendana was an adventurer, sailing between Mexico and the Philippines in search of treasure. His two ships, the LOS REYES and the TODOS SANTOS, were low on water and supplies, and he hoped to find provisions on the island. He was frustrated, however, when he found no fresh water on Wake, and little else besides sand, coral, scrubby undergrowth, multitudes of birds, and the unusual variety of rats that could stand on their hind legs. He named the islands Lamira, Discierta, and San Francisco, and his stay there was brief.

The coral isle lay uninhabited and virtually forgotten for over 200 years after Mendana discovered it. Japanese fishing boats and Spanish treasure ships stopped occasionally. Various names were given the island by these transient visitors, including Discierta, Spanish for "desert island."

In 1796 the island was visited by a British merchant ship, the schooner PRINCE WILLIAM HENRY, captained by Samuel Wake. He, too, found the island to be rather inhospitable, but he did leave it his name.

Captain Wake noted the island on his map and indicated the presence of a dangerous coral reef, which lay from one hundred feet to just over one half mile off of the white sand beaches. He also noted that there was a narrow entrance some 100 to 150 feet wide through the reef. He noted that this opening was located between Wake and Wilkes Islands, but that even the lagoon posed a danger for ships since coral heads rose from the bottom almost to the surface, and that they could rip the bottom of a vessel which might be seeking the safety of the lagoon's smooth waters. Captain Wake compared the continuous breaking of waves on the reef to the roaring of cannons.

In December of 1840 the U.S.S. VINCENNES became the first American ship to visit Wake Island. Commodore Charles Wilkes was a U. S. Navy officer exploring and mapping the islands of the Pacific. He surveyed the island and gave his name to the small island on the southwestern tip of the tiny archipelago. Also on the VINCENNES was a naturalist named Titian Peale who collected animal life from the atoll. From these three men were derived the names of Wake, Wilkes, and Peale Islands which would collectively become known as Wake Island.

A tense drama unfolded in this remote corner of the Pacific in 1866 when a German ship, the bark LIBELLE, ran aground on the reef at Wake Island while on a voyage from Honolulu to Hong Kong. The ship broke into pieces on the reef during a storm, but after three anxious days the crew and passengers of the LIBELLE were able to make their way ashore. With them, it was said, they took valuables worth over a quarter of a million dollars. The "treasure" was said to be in coins and flasks of quicksilver (mercury).

After three weeks the shipwrecked party had exhausted the food and fresh water from the ship and realized that Wake had none to offer. They hid the valuables on the island and went about rigging sails for two small boats, barely more than skiffs and measuring only twenty feet long, which were salvaged from the LIBELLE. These two boats set sail for Guam, a distance of nearly 1400 miles over open sea.

Eighteen days later one of the boats safely landed on Guam. This 22' longboat carried a passenger of considerable international fame, the noted opera singer Mme. Anna Bishop. The second boat never arrived. A party returned to Wake from Guam and recovered the valuables. The LIBELLE's captain and seven others on the missing boat were never heard from again. The anchor of the LIBELLE was salvaged in 1935 and used to adorn the entrance of the Pan American hotel on Peale Island.

Around the turn of the century a number of ships stopped at Wake, including several American ships carrying troops to the Philippines during the Spanish-American war in 1898. In January of 1899 Navy Commander Edward D. Taussig visited Wake Island on his gunboat, the U.S.S. BENNINGTON. On January 17, under the administration of President William McKinley, Taussig's men raised the American flag, saluted with a cannon volley, and officially claimed the island for the United States of America.

Commander Taussig claimed the island because

the United States planned to lay a cable from Midway Island to Guam, and Wake was being considered as a cable station. The island's lack of fresh water, and the possibility of flooding due to its low topography, caused concern. Taussig was reluctant to recommend that the station be put on Wake, and he suggested laying the cable directly from Midway to Guam. It was laid bypassing Wake entirely.

Believing that Wake was unsuitable for an outpost, Commander Taussig promptly sailed away. Centuries after the first human set foot on the island, Wake was claimed as a bona fide territory of the United States of America.

In 1906 John J. Pershing, then a U. S. Army Captain, stopped on Wake and left an American flag. As was the custom of the day, a cache of supplies was left in remote locations to be used by victims of emergencies such as shipwrecks. This humanitarian effort went for naught, however, as Japanese fishermen probably absconded with the emergency supplies.

Fishermen continued to make an occasional stop at Wake Island. They fished the rich waters around the atoll and some came ashore to collect the colorful and valuable bird feathers. However, the island was still unable to supply food and water to its visitors and had little to offer passing ships. Wake Island gained little attention until Pan American World Airways came in 1935 to establish a permanent base for its commercial airplanes. Before that time Wake Island had never supported a permanent settlement of inhabitants from any country, and had remained virtually untouched and unchanged for hundreds, perhaps thousands, of years.

Wake was of no strategic value to any of the combatants in World War I. It was accessible only by ship and had no water or provisions to offer sailors who used the shipping lanes between the Hawaiian Islands and the Orient. Most ships could store an adequate supply of provisions for such a trip, and did not need to stop on an uninhabited, inhospitable desert island in the middle of the Pacific.

The only noteworthy visitors during the 1920's were two scientific and geographical expeditions which briefly visited Wake in 1922 and 1923. The 1923 visit was a scientific study of the island sponsored by Yale University and the Bishop Museum in Honolulu, Hawaii. During the 1923 visit scientists charted the islands and gathered scientific data.

Wake Island remained uninhabited well into the twentieth century. Even into the early 1930's it continued to be nothing more than a desolate desert island. Well into the third decade of the twentieth century Wake was covered by dense pristine maritime forest which had been sculpted not by man, but by the continuous wind and salt spray. The remainder of the island was open undisturbed sand and coral.

These expanses of sand and beach provided a perfect nesting place for thousands of birds. Wake was the only solid ground in several thousand square miles of the open Pacific, so birds came from far and wide to use Wake for nesting. Terns sometimes hovered in layers over the island, waiting for a chance to drop onto an open space and lay their eggs. When men arrived later they sometimes found it difficult to walk because the ground was covered with eggs.

By the time Dick Darden got his orders for Wake, the island was being transformed into a military base. The civilian contractors constantly graded the road with their big equipment, keeping the 30 feet wide thoroughfare in excellent condition. The glistening white road stretched nearly five miles around the horseshoe end of Wake Island, connecting the contractor's village at Camp 2 with the Marines at Camp 1. The road was made of hard packed coral sand and was wide enough for two vehicles to pass without running into the underbrush.

A fifty foot tall water tank was constructed at the Marines' tent city, Camp 1. In this tank much of the supply of precious fresh water was stored. Rainwater had to be collected in cisterns or salt water had to be processed through an evaporator in order to provide potable water for the men on the island. The top of the tank also served as an observation post to watch for enemy ships or planes, since the island had no radar. From the top of the tower a lookout was able to scan the seas for a distance of nine miles offshore.

Much of the dense vegetation on the south leg of Wake Island had been bulldozed and the area had been excavated to build a runway. An air strip was built to accommodate both long-distance bombers and cargo planes, as well as the short-range fighter aircraft that were planned for the island. The runway was gleeming white and was made of hard packed coral much like the roadway. It measured 200 feet wide and 5000 feet long.

Chapter 7
THE BOAT CREW

An aerial view of Wake Island shows Camp 1, the Marine fuel tanks in the center, and the docks on the lagoon side of the island where the boat crew was based.

By the time Dick reached Wake Island in September, 1941, he had attained the rank of Seaman 1st Class, and was earning $54.00 per month. He and the other Navy seamen were responsible for operating two 26' motor boats and one 50' motor launch as ferries. They carried men and materials across the inlets between the islands, and they brought men and materials ashore from ships offshore. The ferries ran daily, and each sailor was assigned to the ferry service one out of each three days. On the other two days the men had free time. On a few occasions Marine officers requested fishing trips when one of the boats was not being used elsewhere.

The men assigned to the boat crews included Boatswains Mate 2nd Class Kirby Ludwig, the senior enlisted man in charge of Dick's boat. Other young Navy men assigned to the Wake Island boat crews with Dick Darden included Jim Cox, Ted Roberson, Andrew Fuller, McPherson Plecker, Clarence Wolfe, George Wolney and John Thorsen.

The men in the Navy detachment were assigned to Camp 1, the Marine camp located near the boat channel between Wake and Wilkes Islands. Dick and five other seamen bunked together in one tent. The tents were built over a wooden framework for support and had a wooden deck for the floor. They also had screens on the sides which allowed the island breeze to cool the men after the long hot days working in the tropical heat.

The Marine defense force on the island numbered about 422 men. The Marines were preparing Wake to be a refueling station for aircraft destined for the Philippines and other islands farther to the west. Seaman Darden was one of twelve sailors assigned to assist the Marines in their preparations on Wake. Navy men were needed because the Marines needed ferry services to help them transport men, supplies, and equipment across the inlets from Wake Island to Wilkes Island.

Dick worked on the boats nearly every day, rarely getting free time for himself. Most of his "off" days were consumed with fishing trips in the clear waters just off the beaches and coral reefs surrounding Wake Island. The fishing trips helped the Marine officers break the boredom of life on the remote island, but they also provided some food for the men. Late in the fall of 1941 food supplies nearly ran out, and the fish brought back from these recreational sorties became welcome food for the men.

The motor boats were small vessels used in the thundering surf and ocean swells around Wake. They had air-tight canisters under the seats and were virtually impossible to sink. From his arrival in September until the first week in December, Dick was out in the boats almost daily.

The Marines carried much of their catch ashore and the men gladly ate the local fish. Once food supplies were so low that

Dick ate rice and chopped beef tongue for lunch. As supplies dwindled, the fishing expeditions became more and more important for some of the men as their source of food. Supply ships had not visited the island recently to bring the large coolers full of fresh food, so nearly everything was eaten out of cans.

The fishing excursions brought back sharks, some of which measured eight feet in length. The Marines skinned the sharks and cut them into long side steaks. These were then cut into square chunks. On some occasions there would be 400-500 pounds of "shark steaks" in the coolers.

When Dick was assigned the duty of taking Marines out fishing he wore a white Navy cap, cut-off white Navy trousers, canvas shoes, usually no shirt, and a razor sharp hunting knife on his belt. He did not wear a good uniform because when he returned he was usually covered with slime and grime from the fish he cut up for bait for the Marine fishermen. This, along with the normal grime, grease and brine associated with boating, made him a nasty sight when he returned to the docks.

Some of the sharks in the tropical waters around Wake Island were monsters, many measuring 15' to 20' long. When Dick skippered the motor boats off the reef, occasionally a big shark would come almost close enough for Dick to reach out and touch the dorsal fin. The big beasts seemed almost as long as the 26 foot boat, and as they rolled over and looked at the men with their beady eyes everyone aboard knew they wouldn't last ten seconds if they went overboard.

Dick's skin became baked to a dark brown hue as he worked the long hours on the boats in the tropical sun. Rarely did Dick have a day off. Occasionally there would be no men or materials to move on the two smaller boats, so the sailors would be on standby to carry Marines out fishing. Dick was either on duty hauling materials or was responsible for a fishing excursion nearly every day. While on the fishing trips Dick operated the tiller, cut bait, and managed the boat while the Marines did the fishing.

When Dick took the small boat off the south shore of Wake the current would quickly carry the small bobbing craft toward open waters. He would continually have to power the boat back toward the island against the strong ocean current. Just off shore the water was clear and teeming with thousands of fish which could be seen moving about at great depths around the reef. Just beyond the reef the bottom disappeared to a depth of several thousand feet.

There was a shortage of fishing equipment, so Dick often improvised tackle for the Marines. Several hooks and heavy bolts were tied into a line and dropped overboard without the benefit of a rod and reel. The first fish caught would be cut into strips to provide bait. The men would drop the hooks into the schools of swarming fish and frequently pull in "rock cod" weighing 20-25 pounds with their gloved hands on the bare lines.

One day two Marine officers ordered Dick to take them fishing even though a typhoon was approaching the island. Dick took the twenty-six foot boat because it had built-in ballasts and would not sink. The two Marines did not know that the boat would not sink if it turned over, and Dick did not volunteer the information. Against his better judgement Dick met the two Marines at the dock and prepared to go fishing.

The three men headed seaward in the small craft, quickly encountering 30 foot swells. Dick decided they should get their money's worth, so he kept the boat on the high seas long enough for both Marines to get thoroughly seasick. Soon the ill-advised trip became scary for all on board, and they were ready to head back toward land. As the big waves crashed around them, Dick navigated the small boat back through the turbulent channel to safety.

Chapter 8

Early in October of 1941 the U.S.S. WILLIAM WARD BURROWS left Pearl Harbor carrying a contingent of Marines and other military men along with much of the weaponry for the defense of Wake Island. The BURROWS was an old ocean liner that had been converted into a troop transport. The bridge of the old ship leaked so badly that men standing watch during rain storms had to wear ponchos.

Aboard the Burrows was the small, thin, mustachioed man who commanded the 1st Defense Battalion, Major James Patrick Sinnot Devereux. Devereux would, for a time, become the highest ranking officer on the island. "Jimmy," as he was known to his friends, was only 5'5" tall and was very slight of stature, but was a veteran of eighteen years in the Marine Corps. He was an excellent leader and military strategist who did not waste words.

Prior to his arrival at Wake Island Major Devereux had been executive officer of the First Defense Battalion. When he arrived on October 15 he relieved Major Bohn as the detachment commander.

James P. S. Devereux had been born on February 20, 1903, in Cabana, Cuba, the son of an U. S. Army doctor. Devereux followed in his father's military footsteps, enlisting in the Marines in 1923 at the age of 20. He became an officer within two years.

Major Devereux went on to serve his country around the world, including assignments in the Philippines, China, and Nicaragua. He had been decorated on several occasions and had the reputation of an officer who was thorough in his preparations and conducted himself in a very professional manner. He was described as little, wiry, taciturn, able, and efficient. Major Devereux was a no-nonsense sort of officer who insisted that rules and regulations be followed to the letter.

In October President Roosevelt met with Dr. Vannevar Bush, coordinator for the nuclear energy research project, for a report on the progress of the scientists. Estimates were discussed for the requirements to produce atomic bombs. The consensus of those in the meeting was that it was urgent for the United States to develop the first atomic weapon. Experimentation and development was to proceed with all possible speed.

Also aboard the WILLIAM WARD BURROWS was Aerographer 1st Class Walter Cook, who had been assigned to Wake Island to set up a weather station. With air traffic rapidly increasing at the landing strip on Wake, meteorological information was becoming more and more crucial to safe air travel. No sophisticated satellite systems existed at that time, so planes taking off from Honolulu flew blindly into the elements over the Pacific with no weather data from points in between. Walter Cook and his weather team were responsible for collecting such data and radioing it back to Pearl Harbor.

On the day before the BURROWS reached Wake, Cook was standing watch on the bridge when Major Devereux came up and introduced himself. Until that time Cook had not known who his commanding officer would be on Wake. Major Devereux had been checking over the personnel rosters and knew that Cook had been assigned to the weather station. The men discussed the aerographer's assignment, and Cook learned that neither he nor Major Devereux knew the extent of the construction on Wake or where the weather station would be located. Both would have to become familiar with the circumstances once they were ashore.

When Major Devereux arrived on Wake Island on October 15, the Navy boat crews were in charge of the small boats which took the Major and all other personnel ashore. Devereux took command of all military personnel on the island. Of immediate interest to him was the state of readiness of the men on the island. After his arrival he toured the defensive positions to determine how he would make further preparations for the defense of Wake.

Major Devereux noted that the civilian work crews were nearing completion on several reinforced concrete ammunition magazines just north of Peacock Point. These concrete domes, reinforced with steel, were partially underground. They would hold the ammunition and be among the most secure areas on the island. He also noticed that a Navy hospital and seaplane ramp were being built on Peale Island.

Little construction had been done on Wilkes Island, except the building of several large tanks for fuel storage. That was the area where tanker ships would lie offshore and pump fuel onto the island through large hoses that were floated on the surf. Ammunition magazines had not yet been built on Wilkes. A new channel was being cut through the island in hopes of allowing deep water access to the lagoon area. The new channel was about midway down the island and was being cut from the lagoon side.

Major Devereux made spot inspections at the docks,

Maj. James P.S. Devereux, Senior Marine Officer on Wake Island

This battery of 5-inch guns aboard the aircraft carrier, USS ENTERPRISE, is similar to the largest artillery weapons on Wake Island. Wake's 5-inch guns were take from World War I cruisers.

ometimes reprimanding the Navy men for offenses such as failing to have ll the ropes coiled in the same direction. As Dick returned from a fishing rip one day such an inspection was in progress. When the Major spotted he half-clad Seaman he became livid and chewed Dick out. He suggested hat Dick "get in the proper uniform of the day." This would include a long leeve jumper top and full length trousers. Some of the enlisted men began o refer to Major J. P. S. Devereux as "Just Plain Shit" Devereux. When he chips were down in the coming days, however, the Major's stern liscipline would prove its value many times over.

Dick was not issued a weapon while serving on Wake Island. His nly means of defense was his slingshot. During his childhood in Clinton,

Dick was an expert marksman with his slingshot. Its handle was covered with notches for birds killed by its projectiles. He decided to fashion a similar weapon from a forked branch of one of the scrubby trees on Wake. After carving a new slingshot Dick began to kill large numbers of the atoll's prolific avian population using chunks of coral rock for ammunition.

Dick marveled at the many species of birds on the island that he had as targets. These included terns, frigates, peewees, pirate birds and bosun birds. Dick began to hunt the birds along the beaches and in the scrubby undergrowth. He especially enjoyed hunting one type of bird the men on the island called "gooney birds."

Dick killed hundreds of the feathery targets. He became so skilled with his slingshot that he could knock a 20-25 pound bird out of the scrubby trees with one shot.

Soon the sport caught on and many of the men were passing time by shooting birds. Gooney birds were a favorite target, as were the Frigates, which had an eight foot wingspan extending from their two-pound bodies. These Frigate birds would wait until the gooney birds returned from fishing and peck them on the head until they regurgitated the day's catch. The Frigates would then catch the fish before they hit the water, snatching their dinner right out of thin air.

The sport of sling-shooting birds became a niusance because the rotting corpses of the birds lay everywhere. The flies and rats began to enjoy the many dead birds that littered the island. Major Devereux called a halt to the sport by ordering that "anyone caught shooting a gooney bird, in any form or fashion, will be punished."

Even the ever-present rat population became the target of hunters on Wake Island. Hunting the pesky rodents was introduced as a recreational activity by someone on the Pan Am staff. When travelers stopped over for a night in the Pan Am Hotel, they found little to do for amusement on the island. Air rifles were provided for guests to hunt the obnoxious creatures.

Though meager for the circumstances, the weaponry held by the Marines on Wake Island would prove later to pack a wicked sting. The Marines were dug into the coral and sand of Wake with a coastal defense that included .30 and .50 caliber machine guns along with 3" anti-aircraft guns and 5" coastal guns. These larger guns were taken from World War I ships which had become obsolete. Unfortunately, several of the big guns lacked the critical range finders and fire control equipment necessary for fighting a serious battle.

There were six of the 5" guns on Wake, one pair strategically positioned to protect each of the three corners of the island's triangular "V" shape. Battery A at Peacock Point on Wake Island, Battery L at Kuku Point on Wilkes Island, and Battery B at Toki Point on Peale Island each had two of the 5" guns. Twelve of the 3" anti-aircraft batteries were spread more widely around the islands. Sgt. Charles Holmes was assigned to Battery E, the 3" anti-aircraft battery at Peacock Point. He was in charge of the fancy gadgetry that would aim the 3" guns at any enemy planes that might intrude into the air space over Wake Island.

When ships carrying men and supplies approached the island it was the job of the Navy men on the 50' motor launch to go out and ferry them to the island. This could be a tricky operation with a fast 10-knot current running from north to south and a stiff breeze blowing. Also, since Wake atoll was perched atop the peak of an ancient volcano, the ocean floor fell away so quickly just offshore that it was impossible for ships to anchor. The ships had to "lie to" just offshore and fight the current until the unloading was completed.

Chapter 9
CIVILIANS ON WAKE ISLAND

An aerial view of th closed end of Wake Island showing the civilian camp in the foreground and the area for the proposed air strip on the far side.

The civilian contractor's work force on the island was substantial, ultimately numbering over 1200 men. They were under the direction of a former Washington State College football player named Dan Teters, who had a reputation of being firm but fair with his men. Under his competent leadership the civilian laborers worked wonders on Wake, constructing roads, buildings, and the airstrip. They had all types of heavy equipment, including cranes, tractors and bulldozers.

The civilians lived in a small city they had built near the bridge between Wake and Peale Islands. This civilian camp was referred to as Camp 2. The civilian workers were craftsmen from virtually every trade in the construction industry: carpenters, plumbers, electricians, and welders. Many were highly skilled, having been involved in the great construction projects in earlier years at Boulder Dam and Bonneville.

These men signed on with the company in California,

agreeing to work for a year on Wake. In return they made good money, considerably more than the Marines and Navy men there. Some of the civilians were earning eight to ten times as much as the servicemen who were laboring just across the lagoon. While the military men were quartered in tents, the civilians were housed in much more comfortable wooden buildings.

The civilians had an outdoor movie theater which showed movies six nights a week. They also had a general store, a barber shop, an ice cream parlor, and a swimming area in the lagoon. Their small city was the envy of the Marines with one small exception. The Marines had ice boxes full of cold beer waiting for them after work, a luxury not afforded to the civilians. No alcohol was provided for them. In fact it was said that some signed up for the project on Wake Island in order to separate themselves from the evil liquid.

Even with all of the "luxuries" afforded to them, the plight of the civilian laborers was not enviable. Construction work on Wake was extremely tough, both for the Marines and the civilians.

A considerable number of civilians found it to be too demanding and broke their contracts, taking supply ships back to civilization.

When the true test came on Wake Island, a number of the civilians proved to be tough men and excellent fighters. Although many of the 1200 civilians would, when the fighting began, scurry into the bush to avoid the battle altogether, a substantial number would report for duty and fight side by side with the Marines. Many of the military men would later remember certain civilians as fellow defenders of the island.

The unarmed civilians were completely vulnerable to the enemy. Most had little or no military background, and few military skills. If captured, they did not know if they would be treated as prisoners of war or simple criminals. If they were captured by the enemy and considered to be subversives, there was little doubt that they would be executed. They had heard of Japanese atrocities in China and knew that Japanese punishment could be doled out as fast as the flash of a Samurai sword. Even so, they lent their labor and heavy equipment to the cause, digging out bunkers and moving guns, equipment, and ammunition.

The civilian workers also provided invaluable assistance as mechanics. They would make a great contribution to the maintenance of the American planes on Wake, helping to keep the tiny air force in remarkable condition considering the battering that it endured. The civilians passed ammunition, cooked the food and fed the men. They would provide much of the backup support that allowed the Marines to fight so valiantly. Even so, their contributions were to be largely overlooked by military historians.

Civilian chief Dan Teters' wife, Florence, spent a good bit of time with her husband on the island, leaving only five weeks before the hostilities began. She found herself one of only two or three women on a small tropical island with over 1600 men. The other women were employed by Pan Am at the seaplane terminal on Peale Island. From all reports Mrs. Teters was a good looking woman and a gracious hostess as well.

When a naval vessel arrived at Wake Island, Major Devereux would don his best uniform and be ferried out to the ship to pay a courtesy call on the captain. The motor launch would make its way through the treacherous channel, navigate the better part of a mile out to the ship, come along side and let the Major off. The meeting with the Captain could take from an hour to a half day after which the two officers would sometimes go ashore to the officer's club for drinks.

On one such occasion Major Devereux invited the Captain ashore. The two men boarded the motor launch with the Captain dressed in his clean white uniform. As the motor launch cleared the channel and neared the dock the seaman handling the boat attempted a difficult maneuver. The idea was to approach the dock at a relatively fast speed and, at the last moment, swing the bow around and gunn the motor in reverse, thus nuzzling the stern right up to the dock.

It was an impressive maneuver when executed to perfection. This time, however, when the gears were to be changed they failed to engage, grinding loudly as the Machinist's Mate struggled to force them. The boat slid toward the dock and with a loud "wham" it crashed into the wooden pilings. Both Major Devereux and the immaculate Captain were thrown on the deck, rolling around in the bilges in their dress uniforms. Devereux shot up off the deck and

threatened to give the young seaman a general court martial.

Soon after Walter Cook arrived at Wake in October on the WILLIAM WARD BURROWS, he and several of his Navy buddies were busy constructing a wooden building that would become the weather station. Cook drew up plans for a one story building that would measure 24' x 28' and contain various gadgets and instruments to record the current weather conditions and predict upcoming meteorological events. Planes were having to fly into unknown atmospheric conditions as they neared Wake Island. The weathermen in this new station could advise them by radioing the weather information to them before they arrived. Cook built an outside stairway which led up to the flat roof where wind masts, antennas, and a thermoscreen would assist him in the collection of weather data.

Cook went to Lt. Commander Elmer B. Greey's office to order the materials for the construction of the station. Greey, the ranking officer who supervised the civilian construction office, decided that the weather station would be located just across the road from the civilian hospital. Commander Greey fully cooperated with Cook in his effort to make the weather station operational as quickly as possible.

In his hurry to get the weather station in operation as soon as possible, Cook circumvented some of the procedures for requisitioning materials. He felt that his orders called for him to expedite the process, because two additional weathermen were on the way to staff the office, and he was expected to begin sending weather information back to Pearl Harbor shortly.

Cook was assigned two civilian carpenters who went right to work on the new facility. A bunk room would be at one end of the building so that the weathermen could be housed very close to their station and would not have to bunk with the civilians in Camp 2 some distance away. Cook accepted this decision with some reluctance because the civilian food was superb and available in unlimited quantities. If he remained with the Marines across the island at Camp 1 he would subsist on food which left a great deal to be desired.

Walter Cook and his crew of Navy weathermen continued to enjoy mess at the contractor's camp for a while. The cooks there were regular hotel chefs who offered a wide variety of food in a "family style," all-you-can-eat format. Plus, there were always at least two desserts. In five days the weather station was complete, and the men moved tables, desks, counters, shelving, and all the necessary gear into the building. Operations began immediately.

One of the toughest jobs facing the men on Wake during this period was the refueling of the B-17 "Flying Fortresses" that were stopping regularly on their way to the Philippines. The big bombers were being moved to the East and needed to be refueled somewhere in the mid-Pacific. There were no Army personnel on Wake to take care of the job, so it fell to the Marines.

It took 3000 gallons of petroleum to refuel one of the B-17's. There was only one tanker truck available to refuel planes. When there was more than one plane on Wake for refueling, or when time was of the essence, Marines were called upon to pump fuel into the tanks from 50 gallon drums with hand pumps. Sometimes the timing of the arrivals required that this go on all night. Needless to say, the Marines did not relish the pumping duties after a hard day of preparing their defensive positions.

The fact that two American submarines, USS TRITON and

USS TAMBOR, were operating in the area of Wake Island was top secret. Even though no one was supposed to know about them, they did make contact with the island occasionally to bring messages to Major Devereux from Pearl Harbor. The submarines would only approach the island under the dark of night. They would signal the island with small blue lights, which would be seen by the lookouts on the water tower. The Navy men and their small boats then had to venture out into the black ocean and try to locate the submarines without getting lost in the stiff current.

The swift ocean current plus the blackout of the island made it difficult to find the U-boats, especially on moonless nights. The current would move the two boats around so much that the motor launch could go to a spot where the submarine had just been sighted and find nothing but black ocean.

Once the submarine had been located, the small boats would have to take messages ashore to Major Devereux and then venture out again to deliver his reply. Sometimes other materials would be traded. The submarine might be willing to swap ice cream from its electrically powered coolers for the latest movies or magazines that the PBY's had brought to Wake. Movies would usually be viewed aboard the sub and then returned a few nights later.

Jim Cox made two trips out to find submarines off Wake Island. On the second of these he was the engineer of the boat that picked up Chief Thompson from the sub. The Chief had come down with appendicitis and Cox's boat was on an emergency mission to bring the man ashore for medical attention. The 50' motor launch had a terrible time finding the submarine that night as it bobbed up and down on the eight foot ocean swells.

The sub showed the blue light at one end of the island and the motor launch headed into the pitch black ocean in pursuit. The boats passed in the night as the strong Pacific current moved the sub swiftly past the island, and suddenly Cox saw the blue light several miles away at the other end of the island. Off the went go again only to pass each other a second time as the sub tried to move back to its original position.

The motor launch had its running lights on, so the submarine knew the location of the smaller boat. On the third try the sub turned on enough lights for Cox to see it, and the two boats made their rendezvous. Cox was expecting a dying man in serious condition and was prepared to take the man on board with a "stokes litter." To his surprise Chief Thompson actually jumped off the sub onto the motor launch and sat up the entire ride back to shore. An appendectomy was successfully performed on the Chief by Dr. Kahn, the Navy doctor. The submarine, however, was never able to come back and pick him up.

Fri JAN. 16 - 42 · THE WILMINGTON NEWS, WILMINGTON. N. C.

MARINES ON WAKE ISLAND GET FUEL FOR THEIR PLANES

Chapter 10
NOVEMBER 1941 –
COMMANDER CUNNINGHAM ARRIVES

Commander Winfield Scott Cunningham
Commander Cunningham was the Senior Officer on Wake Island

To begin military operations against their enemies based on the Pacific islands, Japan had assembled a specially trained force of amphibious assault troops under the command of Vice Admiral Nariyoshi Inouye. This force was part of the Fourth Imperial Fleet based at Truk, located due west of the Marshall Islands toward the Philippines. In November of 1941 the plans for the Japanese attack on Pearl Harbor were in motion. Immediately after the Pearl Harbor attack Admiral Inouye was to occupy Guam, Midway, and Wake Islands.

On November 1, 1941, the U.S.S. CASTOR arrived in the vicinity of Wake transporting additional Marines from Pearl Harbor. An attempt to land the troops was made, but rough seas caused the attempt to be aborted. The CASTOR sailed around the island several times, but stormy weather and huge ground swells prevented the ship from getting close enough to the island to offload its men and supplies.

On November 2 the seas calmed sufficiently for the lighter boats from the island to approach the ship and begin ferrying the troops ashore. Two Texans, Sgt. Charles Holmes and Private Wiley Sloman, were among the 198 enlisted men and 15 officers who were taken ashore on Wake that day. Holmes found that the 3" guns and equipment he was to man were already on the island in boxes. He and his fellow Marines began to assemble the guns and mold the materials and the island into a defensive fortress. This influx of manpower brought the military population of Wake island to nearly 400 men.

Soon after Wiley Sloman reached shore he was given a jack hammer to dig holes in the coral island for tent posts. To his surprise, putting up a tent on the sandy island was no easy matter. Hard coral rock lay just underneath a thin top layer of sand. After a long day working with the jack hammer Sloman had not finished setting all of the posts for his tent, so he slept on his cot under the stars his first night on Wake. After working on the jack hammer all day his cot seemed to jump from side to side all night.

By the second night Sloman's tent was up and he had moved inside. Each tent housed five men. Each man carried a 1903 Springfield rifle, which had been the standard shoulder arm of the American military for thirty years. This reliable bolt action rifle had a five-shot magazine and used 30-06 ammunition. It was patterned after the 1898 German Mauser rifle, an equally impressive fire arm.

Even though the Marines on Wake had been promised the new M-1 semi-automatic carbine, most were very happy to stick with their trusty and time proven Springfield. Regardless of his specialty, each Marine was a foot soldier first. Each man lived with his rifle. He cleaned it, cared for it, and took it everywhere with him. Each man knew the serial number of his rifle by heart, and no one bothered another man's rifle.

Under general conditions ammunition for the rifles was issued very sparingly, if at all. As soon as Sloman and his buddies had erected their tent on Wake they were issued a full case of 30-06 ammunition. Sloman had never seen ammunition issued in such quantity before, so he knew right away someone that something could happen on Wake. Everyone immediately understood that the situation on Wake must be serious, or they would not have issued so much ammunition to the five men in the tent.

Japanese Admiral Osami Nagano was the Chief of the Naval General Staff of the Imperial Japanese Navy. On November 3, 1941, the day following the arrival of the CASTOR on Wake, Admiral Nagano gave his approval to a plan which called for Japan to initiate its quest to conquer and rule all of Asia.

On November 5 the Japanese Naval Ministry issued detailed orders for the fleet commanders in the Imperial Japanese Navy, outlining their roles in the hostilities that were about to be initiated against the United States, Great Britain, and the Netherlands. Admiral Inouye's orders contained only a short, but profound, reference to Wake Island. He was ordered to "defend the South Seas Islands, patrol, maintain surface communications, capture Wake." He went about planning the takeover operation.

On November 8 the USS WRIGHT reached Wake Island carrying more American men and personnel. Among those on the Wright was Marine Corporal Ralph Holewinski, who had been assigned to the Marine First Defense Battalion to help defend island outposts. His original assignment with this group had been in February when he was among the first Marines to be assigned to the Marine contingent on Johnston Island.

By mid-November Walter Cook and the Navy crew at the weather station had all their equipment in full operation. They were submitting regular reports which were being radioed to Pearl Harbor and preparing weather maps which provided information on local and regional forecasts. Cook also conducted briefings in the weather station for pilots who stopped at Wake for refueling.

Walter Cook was one of only three meterological specialists at the weather station, so they really had their work cut out for them. The three men maintained round-the-clock watches in order to have current weather data ready anytime an incoming pilot might need it. Air traffic coming through the landing strip on Wake Island was steadily increasing. B17's and twin-engined PBY's were coming through enroute to Guam and the Philippines.

On November 20, Thanksgiving Day, 1941, the USS WRIGHT again left Pearl Harbor bound for Wake Island. The aircraft tender was being used as a transport ship. It was brimming with men, supplies, and equipment that were to further transform Wake into one of a string of forward defense positions across the increasingly unsure waters of the mid-Pacific.

Aboard the WRIGHT was a group of about fifty Marines who would provide support for the incoming squadron of fighter planes. This group included Lt. Robert J. "Strawberry" Conderman, from New Bern, North Carolina. Lt. Conderman would command the unit of Marines who would maintain the planes of the air unit, VMF-211.

Wiley Sloman and the other Marines in his unit began readying the big 5" guns on Wilkes Island. The men worked every day from sun up until sun down at their gun position. They had to set up the gun and then install and calibrate the range finders so the guns would fire properly and safely. They worked on Armistice Day and Thanksgiving day as well, all the while realizing the urgency of becoming well prepared as soon as possible. No one anticipated an outbreak of hostilities soon, but the officers who were coordinating

The USS CASTOR

59

the effort wanted to take no chances.

Finally the big 5" cannons were ready to fire. They were "bag and projectile" guns. This meant that the fifty-pound projectile was put into the barrel first, followed by a silk bag of powder. Silk was used because it burned completely up when the gun was fired, leaving no ash or residue in the barrel which might impede the rapid insertion of the next round. After the projectile and powder had been put into the breech, a percussion cap was placed into the firing lock and the breech was closed. The cannon was ready to fire.

Wiley Sloman's unit on Wilkes Island was called Battery L. Once this unit had installed its gun it was time to test fire it for accuracy. There were no targets to shoot at, so Battery L fired their cannon out into the ocean. They became quite good at firing the gun, able to reload, close the breech, calibrate the distance to a target, aim, and fire at ten second intervals. After a short time they became satisfied that they could hit a target if one presented itself.

Once the 5" gun was ready for action the men in the detachment at Battery L began sandbagging the position, erecting an observation tower, and thinking about getting back to Hawaii. Sloman's group had been told that they were on Wake temporarily to install the guns and get them ready to fire. A detachment of Marines was in training at Pearl Harbor and would be out in about thirty days to relieve Sloman's unit.

On November 25, 1941, U. S. intelligence was aware that a large Japanese convoy was moving through the China Sea toward southeast Asia. Japan and the United States now seemed far apart in the negotiations aimed at avoiding war. The next day the fleet, known as Kido Butai, steamed out of Hitokappu Bay in the Kurile Islands destined for Pearl Harbor. It was using an infrequently traveled route in the north Pacific in an effort to elude any contact by American reconnaisance forces. Captain Mitsuo Fuchida, commander of the air strike force, watched from the carrier AKAGI as the task force slipped out of port and cheers of "Banzai" rose from the crew on her deck.

On November 27 Admiral H. R. Stark, Chief of Naval Operations in Washington, sent a message to Pearl Harbor warning that a Japanese military strike was imminent. But American intelligence did not know of the movement of the Kido Butai fleet, and everyone expected the Japanese strike to be in Asia.

While in Hawaii, Henry Webb and his unit, known as VMF-2ll, were introduced to the more modern single-winged Grumman F4F-3, a great improvement over the old F4F biplanes that they had been using. They practiced flying the newer Wildcats off of the decks of carriers and practiced firing the .30 cal. machine guns that had been installed in the planes' wings. A tow plane was used to pull a cloth sleeve, which was used for target practice. The Wildcats would dive on the sleeve and fire their machine guns into it. Each pilot used a different color of bullets, so the sleeve could be examined later and the accuracy of each pilot could be determined.

A. Y. Fish

The transport USS WRIGHT arrived at Wake Island November 8, 1941, with another group of Marines which included Ralph Holewinski. The Royal Hawaiian and Mauna Loa Hotels can be seen in the background

During the war games the flyers were stationed temporarily on Maui, where they slept in tents along the runway by their planes. They practiced hitting various targets with their Wildcats, using the machine guns and 100 pound bombs which could be mounted under the belly of each aircrft. They even attacked Pearl Harbor, where they practiced knocking out anti-aircraft positions. These exercises simultaneously gave gunners on the ground at Pearl Harbor practice firing at incoming planes. The exercises were meant to simulate war without using live ammunition.

On November 27, 1941, Henry Webb's squadron of F4F-3 Grumman Wildcat fighter planes were at the Marine air base at Ewa, Hawaii. That night orders were posted indicating that twelve pilots in Webb's unit were to bring their overnight gear (sleeping packets) and be ready to take off at 7:30 the next morning. They were not given their destination because the Marine Corps did not want them to contact their families and divulge any of their plans. There were twenty-four planes in the squadron, twelve of which had been selected to fly out the next morning. Henry Webb was one of those selected. He initialed the order sheet to indicate that he had received his assignment.

At 7:30 the next morning, November 28, the twelve Wildcats took off from Ewa and landed on Ford Island, in the center of Pearl Harbor. They waited there while the ENTERPRISE, already underway and outside the harbor, could get out into open water and maneuver into the wind for a landing. When notified that the ENTERPRISE was in position, the Wildcats prepared to take off.

An explosive charge, similar to a shot gun shell, was fired

60

Grumman Wildcats flying in formation

Grumman Aircraft

to spin the propeller and crank the engine of each plane. One of the twelve planes refused to crank, even after repeated attempts. So, only eleven planes were able to take off. By 10:00 that morning the eleven Wildcats had flown out to sea and landed on the deck of the ENTERPRISE. A Navy Wildcat already on board was ordered to join the unit, and the twelfth Marine pilot was ferried out to the carrier.

The mission of the Marine squadron was so secret that the pilots thought they were on another training exercise and carried only their sleeping bag and toilet articles with them. The eleven Marine planes and the Navy Wildcat were repainted aboard ship with camouflage colors which included a good bit of blue. This made the Wildcats more difficult to see as they flew over the ocean. Once all twelve planes had matching combat colors they were given new numbers, which were painted just behind the wing of each plane.

The ENTERPRISE, with the squadron of fighter aircraft aboard, was part of the task force commanded by Vice Admiral William "Bull" Halsey. In addition to the ENTERPRISE, Halsey's fleet included three cruisers and nine destroyers. Halsey knew the extreme importance of delivering the planes to the vulnerable installation on Wake, and he had his men ready for battle at a moments notice from their first day at sea.

Soon after landing on the ENTERPRISE the pilots of VMF-211 were briefed by Admiral Halsey on the importance of their mission. They were told they were going to Wake Island and were given information about the tiny atoll. None of them had ever been to Wake Island before.

Major Paul Putnam, the commanding officer in charge of the VMF-211 squadron, could sense the importance of the mission

as he wrote a letter while at sea enroute to Wake. "I feel a bit like the fatted calf being groomed for whatever it is that happens to fatted calves......," he wrote, and then went on to say, "The Admiral seems to be most determined to maintain secrecy regarding the position and activity of this force. There has been a continuous inner air patrol during daylight, and a full squadron has made a long search to the front and flanks each morning and evening. They are armed to the teeth and the orders are to attack any Japanese vessel or aircraft on sight in order to prevent the discovery of this force." Clearly, the Navy was ready to take drastic measures to insure that VMF-211 reached Wake Island without being detected by the Japanese.

The pilots of VFM-211 were not as concerned as Putnam about the upcoming assignment, and they felt no great sense of urgency about getting to Wake Island. Henry Webb and his friends knew that things were brewing with the Japanese in the Pacific, and they knew that they were going as fighting men to one of America's outermost defensive positions. Neither they, nor their high command, felt that an attack from the Japanese was imminent. They knew that the Japanese had bases to the west in the Carolines and to the south in the Marshalls, but they did not consider Wake Island to be a dangerous assignment.

On the morning of November 29, 1941, the USS WRIGHT approached the south beach of Wake Island. With it, in addition to the Marine support unit for the fighter squadron, came Commander Winfield Scott Cunningham. Commander Cunningham was a naval officer and the highest ranking man on Wake Island. He therefore became the commanding officer on Wake Island. Commander Cunningham had been sent to Wake primarily to oversee the installation of the new naval air station.

One runway on the airstrip at Wake was complete and warplanes were enroute to the island, so Commander Cunningham was responsible for making the Navy's new air station operational. His rank, however, created something of an awkward situation since it placed him in command of the entire defense force. With little or no experience in commanding Marine ground forces, Commander Cunningham would come to depend heavily on Major Devereux.

Major Devereux, the commander of Wake's entire defense force before the arrival of Commander Cunningham, now reported directly to Cunningham, who was his superior officer. Major Devereux continued, however, to direct the tactical military operations of the Marine contingent on the island, and would receive much of the credit for supervising the defense of Wake Island.

Major Devereux came out to the USS WRIGHT on a lighter to greet the new personnel. On board the ship he met Commander Cunningham, Commander Campbell Keene, Lt. Conderman, and Major Walter L. J. Bayler. Commander Keene would be an assistant to Cmdr. Cunningham, and Major Bayler was to install a radio system which would allow ground-to-air communications between the island and the squadron of fighter planes that were expected on the island in a few days.

Aboard the WRIGHT was a young yeoman by the name of Glenn Tripp who would be an administrative assistant to Commander Cunningham. Also arriving on the WRIGHT was Staff Sgt. Tom Kennedy, a member of the advance party that would prepare for the fighter planes enroute to the island on the Enterprise.

The Navy seamen came out in the small boats and ferried the men to shore. There was no ocean-side dock for off-loading men or supplies due to the steep dropoff of the ocean floor just beyond the beach, so the small boats had to make their way through a narrow channel which had been dug between Wake and Wilkes Islands. Due to the tides, the ten-knot ocean current, and the steady northeast trade winds, there was brisk white-water current rushing through the channel. This made it necessary to attach lines between the small boats and tractors on shore which would pull the bobbing craft through the turbulently spraying waters to the relative calm of the lagoon.

Once the boats gained the security of these green tropical waters they proceeded to a dock where the men went ashore. Soon thereafter Major Devereux and his executive officer, Major George H. Potter, Jr., drove Commander Cunningham around to show the new commanding officer the extent of their construction and fortification operations on the island. Commander Cunningham's office was set up in the same building with Dan Teters, the construction boss, and Commander Greey, the military liaison working with the civilian construction company. Yeoman Tripp began attending to the daily operations of Cunningham's office, which was located on Peale Island near the civilian camp on the north shore of the island.

The defensive fortifications on Wake began to take shape and were entirely manned by the Marines. Dick and all of his buddies in the Navy boat crew, as well as the six Army men on the island, were completely unarmed. They did not even have helmets. Both of these small "non-Marine" groups had special functions. The Navy operated the small boats, while the Army group, commanded by Captain Henry S. Wilson, set up a radio station. In addition to this, none of the 1200 civilians were armed.

Dick and the sailors manning the small boats were assigned the task of bringing the supplies and materials ashore from the WRIGHT. The ticklish job of winching the materials over the sides of the WRIGHT onto the lighters consumed the sailor's attention. The heavy materials were carefully, and dangerously, taken over the reef, pulled through the rushing waters of the channel, and taken ashore by cranes at the docks. The docks were located in the relatively calm lagoon waters on the inside of the island.

Walter Cook took the pickup truck that had been assigned to the weather station and proceeded down the coral road toward the Marine camp to pick up some of the supplies. He was following a road scraper that was maintaining the gravel road. He decided to pass

the slower machine, but just as he did his front tire hit a large piece of coral rock that had been turned up by the scraper's blade.

When the Cook's front tire hit the rock the truck was knocked into the air and instantly the turned over. Cook was momentarily knocked unconscious and when he regained his senses he was being taken to the hospital. Dr. Kahn diagnosed a painful slipped disc in Cook's back and put him to bed. This slowed the progress in the weather station a bit, but in a couple of days Cook was back at work, hobbling around on crutches and tending to the weather equipment.

A few days later Major Devereux dropped by the weather station on an inspection. He was surprised at the progress that Cook had made in completing the building and questioned him about the procurement of the materials so quickly. Apparently he was a bit miffed that the Navy aerographers were bunking in such nice quarters while his Marines were in tents. He also inquired about the circumstances of Cook's accident with the truck.

Cook had drawn some attention upon himself by doing so much so quickly. The fact that he had not gone through all of the proper channels concerned Major Devereux and Commander Keene. This was because the Marine defense bases were considerably over budget and every move was being scrutinized by auditors. In fact, an auditor from the Department of the Budget, a Mr. Heavenor, was on the island examining budgets and spending at that very time.

Construction was not going quite as smoothly at Camp 1 where Sgt. Tom Kennedy, the aviation specialist, was putting up his tent. He quickly found hard coral that was covered by a thin veneer of beach sand. He was unable to drive the tent posts into the hard coral rock, so he was forced to borrow a jack hammer to get the posts firmly driven into the ground.

During November of 1941 the defenders of Wake Island were well aware that hostilities could erupt and that they could be caught in the fury. Pearl Harbor issued a warning that read "International situation indicates you should be on alert." Major Devereux even requested permission to divert the efforts of the civilian laborers to the defensive needs of the military. His request was denied.

The defenders on Wake continued to enhance the island's fortifications with all of the resourses available to them. Ammunition was issued to the gun positions. Hostilities around the world were beginning to paint an ominous picture for American fighting men everywhere. But, none of the men in the Pacific could appreciate the full gravity of their situation. They were unaware that war clouds looming over them were blacker than ever, and that the enemy was on the brink of initiating the most horrible war in history. Realizing that danger was in the air, Major Devereux and Commander Cunningham pushed the men on Wake to ready themselves for whatever December, 1941, might bring.

Chapter 11
DECEMBER 1941 – INTO THE EYE OF THE STORM

National Archives

Aerial photo of Peale Island showing the Pan Am Complex and pier. One seaplane is moored at the end of the dock, while seven more wait in the lagoon.

On December 2, 1941, Admiral Kimmel, Commander of the Pacific Fleet at Pearl Harbor, was aware that a Japanese fleet had left port, moving into unknown waters and maintaining radio silence since November 16th. The location of the fleet was unknown to the American strategists in Pearl Harbor and Washington.

December 3 marked the arrival of twelve of the huge PBY flying boats (PSY-5's) on the lagoon at Wake Island. The planes would spend only three days at Wake, flying long range reconnaissance missions each day, covering large expanses of the central Pacific Ocean. The men on Wake did not know the mission of these planes, but they knew that the big planes were called the "eyes of the fleet." They suspected that the PBY's were looking for Japanese ships or planes in the sea lanes toward Hawaii to the east or toward the Marshall Islands to the south.

One of the primary missions of the PBY's was to provide reconnaissance in anticipation of the arrival of American fighter aircraft that would be stationed at the airstrip on Wake Island. But they would also be on the lookout for any large group of Japanese ships. American intelligence had, by this time, learned that a large Japanese fleet had left Japan, but its whereabouts were still unknown. The PBY's from Wake did not locate the enemy ships, which were far to the north and out of their range. The Japanese fleet heading for Pearl Harbor was on an obscure, seldom traveled, course so that it would avoid contact with any vessel which might report its location.

Another Japanese military movement was occurring on December 3 that would have a more direct bearing on the fate of the men on Wake Island than the Pearl Harbor attack fleet. Arriving at the Japanese base on the twin islands of Roi and Namur, part of the Kwajalein Atoll of the Marshall Islands less than 700 miles from Wake Island, was an assault force from Admiral Inouye's Imperial Japanese Fourth Fleet based at Truk. This force was under the command of Rear Admiral Sadamichi Kajioka, and it included 450 amphibious troops who were preparing to attack the American forces on Wake Island.

On December 4 the defensive complexion of Wake Island changed markedly with the arrival of the squadron of fighter aircraft. Marine Fighter Squadron 211, officially called Marfitron 211, or VMF-211 (heavier-than-air Marine fighter) took off from the decks of the carrier ENTERPRISE, then two hundred miles from Wake. One of the Navy PBY's that had arrived on Wake the previous day was sent out to meet the fighters and lead them to their new home on Wake.

After five days at sea the pilots of VMF-211 were happy to get into the air. Their Wildcats were much faster than the lead plane, so the smaller planes overran the lumbering PBY time after time, only to circle around and fall in behind her. Then Wake came into

view, and what a beautiful sight it was. The wishbone island and blue lagoon were clearly visible as the pilots circled the island and then landed on the glistening white airstrip. Less than two hours after the planes had taken off from the ENTERPRISE they all touched down safely on the newly completed runway on Wake Island.

Major Paul Putnam was the commanding officer of the twelve Grumman F4F-3 warplanes of VMF-211. The stubby one-man "Wildcats" and their courageous pilots would gain the respect of every man on Wake Island for their heroic efforts during the defense of the island.

In addition to Major Putnam, the other pilots were Captain Henry "Baron" or "Hammering Hank" Elrod, Captain Frank "Duke" Tharin, Captain Herbert Frueler, 2nd Lt. Henry Gorham "Spider" Webb, 2nd Lt. Robert J. "Strawberry" Conderman, Lt. Carl R. Davidson, 2nd Lt. Frank J. Holden, 2nd Lt. David D. Kliewer, 1st Lt. George A. Graves, 2nd Lt. John F. Kinney, Sgt. William J. Hamilton, and Sgt. Robert O. Arthur.

Many of the island's 1600 inhabitants were on hand at the air strip for the arrival of the fighters. The cheering men watched as the fighters touched down on the coral surface. The chunky little planes were a welcome addition to the island's defenses since Wake had no radar and the planes would provide eyes in the air for the defenders. Even though the Wildcats were not the Marines' most up-to-date warplanes, their arrival brought a new level of confidence to the men on Wake Island.

With the arrival of VMF-211 the Marines' defenses on the island were at their highest point. The defensive forces on the

U. S. Navy

Grumman F4F-3 Wildcats and VF-3 "Felix the Cat" fighters, along with Douglas "Dauntless" and "Devastator" fighters

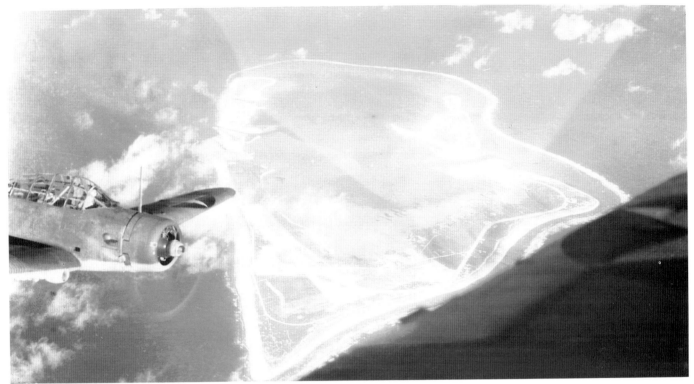

The View of Wake Island from an American plane through light cloud cover

ground were as prepared as they could be with the armaments they had on hand, and the newly arrived air wing gave the defenders of Wake Island a much stronger presence for warding off an enemy attack.

While the F4F-3 Wildcats were more modern than the biplanes flown earlier in the year by VMF-211, and they certainly raised the firepower of the defenders to a new level, in actuality the rugged little planes were nearly obsolete and presented several serious disadvantages for their Marine pilots. The Wildcats were soon to be replaced by the newer F4F-4's, into which had been built a number of significant improvements.

Unlike the more modern F4F-4 fighters, the F4F-3's did not have armor plating to protect the pilot, and they required the pilot to sit just above and forward of the fuel tanks. To make matters even more precarious, the tanks were not self-sealing, a feature that most of the newer fighter planes of the day had incorporated into their design.

Another major problem with the Wildcats on Wake was that their bomb racks did not match the bombs that had been shipped to Wake for them, and special homemade racks would have to be improvised if the 100 pound explosives were to be secured beneath the wings of the F4F-3's. Furthermore, no spare parts for the planes had arrived. No protective revetments, or earthen enclosures, had been constructed to shield the planes from enemy attack, and all fuel storage was in tanks above ground. At this stage of the game the air defenses on Wake made a juicy target for enemy aircraft.

The problems were not limited to the airplanes on Wake Island. Perhaps the biggest question was the inexperience of the pilots with this version of the Wildcat. Most of the pilots who brought the Wildcats to Wake Island had very little experience flying them.

The Wildcats did have retractable landing gear, but the wheels had to be raised and lowered with a hand crank that was operated by the pilot inside the cockpit. A wounded pilot who could not vigorously crank down his landing gear would have no wheels upon which to land his plane. Despite these drawbacks the twelve Wildcats were a prized addition to the defensive arsenal on Wake Island.

Major Putnam went right to work organizing his men into a formidable fighting unit. Putnam was a competent leader who had been decorated for his heroism over Nicaragua in 1931 where he had fought against the guerillas under General Augusto Sandino. Over fifty years later it would be the memory of Sandino which would inspire Communist insurgents, called Sandinistas, who would take over that country.

Major Putnam knew that most of the young pilots had very limited air time in the F4F-3's, so he put together a patrol schedule that allowed the men to fly the planes on surveillance missions while simultaneously familiarizing themselves with the capabilities of the new aircraft. There would be patrols at dawn and dusk. Four planes would go up on each patrol. They would venture out at least fifty miles from base and circle the island.

One of the most important abilities that the pilots had to develop was being a good navigator. The planes had no electronic homing device to assist in finding their way back to Wake from points far out over the ocean. Without such equipment the pilots had to relocate the tiny speck on the ocean by sight on the return flight. This was sometimes complicated by heavy cloud cover. The pilots became excellent navigators. None of the VMF-211 pilots on Wake were ever lost because of navigational errors over the Pacific.

On December 6, 1941, the squadron of PBY's left Wake, heading eastward toward Midway Island. Major Devereux decided that it was time to test the defense battalion, so on the morning of December 6 he called the first general quarters drill. Every military man on the island went to his battle station, and the exercise went smoothly enough to satisfy the difficult-to-please Major. All of the defense preparations were crystallizing, and the months of deployment by the defensive forces on Wake were nearly complete.

Major Devereux had put guns in as many strategic positions around the island as possible. He had decided that, rather than try to defend the entire twenty mile coast of the three small islands, he would concentrate his limited resources at strategic spots along the coastline.

The 5" guns were in place and ready for action at Peacock Point, the eastern point of the island's wishbone formation, and at Toki Point and Kuku Point, the two tips of the open end of the "V". Each of the batteries of 5" guns was protected by .50-caliber anti-aircraft guns. Four 3" anti-aircraft guns were also positioned at each of these locations. Thirty caliber machine guns were scattered along the beaches to stop any frontal assault by the enemy. The airfield was protected by .50-caliber anti-aircraft machine guns as well as .30-caliber machine guns.

Two sections of the 30 cal. machine guns, four guns in all, and ammunition would be loaded on the beds of two 6 x 6 cargo trucks. These trucks would be part of the Defense Force Mobile Reserve, a collection of Navy, Marine, and civilian personnel who were charged with the responsibility of moving around the island during any conflict to hot spots where the stationary emplacements were not adequate. The force was commanded by Marine Lt. Arthur A. Poindexter. In addition to the two machine gun trucks, there were additional riflemen and machine gun sections on the ground who were assigned to the Mobile Reserve.

So pleased was Major Devereux with the weeks of hard work and rigorous preparations by his men that he gave them the rest of the weekend off. Many of the Marines rested for the first time in quite a while, while others swam in the lagoon or fished on the Navy boats. The defenders of Wake Island breathed a collective sigh of relief, feeling that the island was as well prepared as possible with the limited manpower and the obsolete weaponry that had been afforded them.

While most of the Wake Island defenders rested, it turned out to be a busy weekend for Dick. In addition to playing a baseball game on Saturday, he also had to pull boat duty throughout the weekend. It was the first chance that many of the Marines had gotten to take advantage of the offshore fishing, so the Navy boats were busy all weekend. Dick ferried men from island to island and out to sea fishing. While the Marines got a much needed break, there would be little rest for any of the Navy men this weekend. The sentries were posted on top of the water tower and a skeleton crew manned each gun emplacement. Most of the rest of the Marine battalion took a well-deserved rest. While some read books and others slept, some had enough energy left to enjoy less sedentary activities. One such activity was the pickup baseball game, during which Dick met Marine Sgt. Tom Kennedy.

Everything was in limited quantities on the island, including athletic equipment. There were just enough baseball gloves for one team, so when the men chose up sides and started the game the team in the field got the gloves. When the side changed and the fielding team came in to bat, they had to give up the gloves to the team that was heading out into the field. Dick and Sgt. Kennedy were playing second base for the opposing teams, so they exchanged gloves twice each inning.

Tom Kennedy was a Marine radioman attached to the squadron of fighters at the air strip. It was his job to keep the communications system open between the flyers in the air and the command center on the ground. He had spare transmitters and receivers, along with spare parts for the radios themselves. Kennedy was also trained to be a rear seat gunner for larger planes. The Wildcats were one-seaters, so Kennedy never went aloft while he was on Wake Island.

Despite the fact that the guns had been well placed and camouflaged, Wake Island was not as well prepared as it would have been if a full complement of men and equipment for the First Defense Battalion were in place. Many of the guns did not have crews, while others did not have the proper range-finding and fire control equipment. Several of the larger guns had to be aimed by sighting through the breech. The airstrip was extremely vulnerable to an air attack due to the lack of revetments and prominent fuel storage tanks.

In order to adequately man all of the big guns and defensive positions on Wake, a full Defense Battalion would be required. On paper this called for 43 officers and 939 men. Wake's Marine contingent had only 15 officers and 373 men, fewer than half the required number. This would stretch the defenders precariously thin along the 20 miles of shoreline, and mean that only half of the twelve 3" guns on the island would be active. More men were urgently needed for a proper defense of the island.

Much of the hardware used by the Marines on Wake was obsolete. Many of the guns were of World War I vintage, surplus from mass-produced stockpiles of armaments over twenty years old. The basic weapon carried by the Marines on Wake was the M1903 bolt-action Springfield rifle, not the M1 semi-automatic field piece that was standard issue of the day. A few of the defenders carried Thompson sub-machine guns, and others carried .45 cal. semi-automatic pistols.

The general appearance of the Wake Island defenders was that of a World War I "doughboy," right down to the dishpan helmet that was characteristic of the American fighting man in the early part of the century.

With no radar on the island, advance warning of an enemy air raid would have to be provided from visual sighting by sentries atop the water towers. With no air-raid sirens, the Marines would signal the approach of incoming aircraft by firing their weapons three times. Clearly, many of the procedures used by the Marines on Wake were crude, and the capabilities of the defense forces were limited.

Good news greeted Dick on Sunday, December 6. The men were told that the following day they were to begin eating their noon meals

One of the last peace time views of Pearl Harbor shows pairs of American warships filling the harbor with Ford Island in the Center

at Camp 2, the civilian facility. This news was especially well received by the men who had just had a Sunday lunch of rice and ox tongue. All of the Marines got the same meal that day and were anxious to enjoy the finer food in the civilian camp. The Marines were fed on a stateside ration chart which budgeted $.42 per day per man for food. The cooks had problems serving food of adequate quality in reasonable amounts at that price. The mess sargent had been changed several times, and the military men were still complaining because of the low standards.   T h i n g s were considerably better in the civilian camp. There the daily food appropriation was $2.00 per man per day. Excellent food could be provided at that price, and even expensive vegetables could be brought in. Fresh bread was also baked daily for the civilian work force. Everyone was looking forward to getting into the good vittles at Camp 2 on Monday.

December 7, 1941, was a peaceful Saturday on Wake

Island. Since the island is across the international date line from Hawaii, it is one day ahead of the calendar at Pearl Harbor where it was December 6. The Pan American Clipper PHILIPPINE, piloted by Captain John H. Hamilton, landed on the lagoon that Saturday afternoon. She was bound for Manilla, but would spend the night on Wake, allowing her passengers and crew to rest the night in the Pan Am Hotel. They would take off early the next morning for another stop on Guam before arriving in the Philippines.

None of the American forces on December 6 at Pearl Harbor had any idea that a potentially devastating Japanese military force was steaming toward them. Japanese pilots of fighter planes were being given their final briefings on board an armada of Japanese aircraft carriers several hundred miles north of Hawaii. Japanese Vice Admiral Nagumo commanded the fleet from the bridge of his flagship, the AKAGI. Admiral Yamamoto sent a message to Admiral Inouye indicating that "The Divine Wind blows tomorrow." Thousands of American servicemen would soon feel the sting of "The Divine Wind."

Saturday, December 6, 1941, was a normal day in Honolulu, with business as usual for the military personnel stationed there. On Wake Island it was December 7, another day of ferry service for seaman Dick Darden. Marines relaxed on Wake, unaware that bombs were being loaded onto racks beneath the wings of Japanese twin-engine Mitsubishi bombers that would soon race toward them with the deadly cargo. Everyone on Wake was aware that for several years the Japanese had been building up a substantial military presence 600 miles to the south in the Marshall Islands. But there was no indication on Wake Island on December 7 that this powder keg was on the verge of exploding.

Pan Am employees on Peale Island attended to the twenty passengers who arrived on the clipper. Civilian workers prepared for another week of hard work, their newly transformed island soon to be changed again by the warriors of the Mikado.

The total defensive forces on Wake Island, including the Marines, Navy, and Army personnel, remained at less than half the number that was considered adequate for protecting the atoll from an invading enemy force. On December 7 there were 449 Marines, 76 Navy men, and six Army men on Wake Island. The Marine defense force led by Major Devereux consisted of fifteen Marine officers and 373 enlisted men on the ground, and ten Marine officers and 49 enlisted men in the aviation squadron. To make matters even worse, nearly 20 percent of the military men on the island, including Dick Darden and the sailors, had no arms with which to fight.

The civilian population of 1146 men, along with approximately 70 Pan American employees, brought the entire population of the island to just over 1680 men. There were 465 men in the fighting forces on Wake. Dick and everyone on the island had confidence in the defenders of the island, but they were unaware that such great danger was looming near them. The Japanese war machine in the Marshalls was, like a great Samurai warrior with his sword raised, about to come crashing down on the island and cut it away from the protection of the American homeland.

Among the men defending Wake Island were several who would come to play important roles in the months and years that were about to unfold in Dick Darden's life. This group included Navy Yeoman 3C Glenn Tripp, Marine Corporal Ralph Holewinski, Navy Fireman 1C Jim Cox, and Navy Aerographer 1C Walter Cook.

Jim Cox was the Duty Boat Engineer from 7:00 a.m. on December 7th until 7:00 a.m. on Monday, December 8th. He, along with Seamen Wolney and Fuller, was on duty in the boat crew tent at the docks near the channel between Wake and Wilkes Islands during the early morning hours of Sunday, December 8. At the same time the Japanese were launching their planes from the decks of their aircraft carriers and the vicious attack on Pearl Harbor was beginning.

PART 2—THE SEIGE OF WAKE ISLAND

Chapter 12
THE ATTACK ON PEARL HARBOR

This scene from a captured Japanese newsreel shows a Japanese warplane taking off from a carrier bound for Pearl Harbor.

The world would long remember the devastating attack that was unleashed by the Japanese upon the American military installation at Pearl Harbor on December 7, 1941. Swarms of planes rose from the decks of several Japanese aircraft carriers, including the SORYU and HIRYU, that had crept undetected to a position less than 200 miles north of the Hawaiian Islands. Upon reaching Pearl Harbor just after dawn that Sunday morning more than 350 planes released their deadly explosives onto the sleepy, unsuspecting fleet and civilian population.

The American military forces in the Pacific suffered tremendous losses during the attack on Pearl Harbor. Hundreds of ships and planes were damaged or destroyed. More importantly, a staggering price was paid in the lives of American servicemen. The Army forces in Hawaii reported 215 killed, 360 wounded, and 22 missing in action. Far greater were the Navy losses. There were 2036 Navy personnel reported killed in action or fatally wounded,

and another 759 men were wounded. The Japanese attack on Pearl Harbor and Hawaii had cost the United States over 2250 lives and left more than 1100 wounded.

The Japanese military strategists had crippled the American fleet with a masterfully planned surprise attack that was carried out with surgical accuracy. America's feeling of invincibility in the Pacific went up in smoke over Pearl Harbor early on that Sunday morning. Suddenly, America was on the defensive and confusion existed at Pearl Harbor, our strongest base in the Pacific.

There were reports of sabotage by enemy operatives in Hawaii. After the attack the FBI took a large number of suspected enemy agents into custody, including more than 360 Japanese, almost 100 Germans, and over a dozen Italians. Rumors abounded that these enemy agents had made an organized effort to glut the roads coming into Pearl Harbor with cars in an effort to stymy the American response during and after the attack.

Other rumors suggested that the enemy had poisoned drinking water and cut directional markers in sugar cane fields for the incoming Japanese planes to see from the air. While none of these rumors were ever substantiated, they did illustrate the disarray of the unsuspecting American forces after the surprise raid by the Japanese.

The Japanese had, indeed, scored an immense victory with their successful attack on Pearl Harbor. The following days brought word from Singapore that the British warships PRINCE OF WALES and REPULSE had been sunk. Reports from the Philippines were also bleak, indicating that Japanese attacks there had been successful. Throughout the Pacific it seemed the enemy was defeating the Americans and their allies.

Dick Darden found himself far out in the no-man's-land of the mid-Pacific, but it was a stroke of luck that he had not remained on the USS HELENA. The sleek new cruiser, which had only been in service for two years, was in Pearl Harbor on December 7 and was heavily damaged during the attack. A torpedo dropped by one of the attacking planes had passed under the OGLALA and struck the HELENA on her starboard side. The explosion that followed ripped a hole in her side below the armor belt, flooding the Number 1 engine room and Number 2 boiler room.

Even though she was seriously damaged, the HELENA did not sink. She soon entered a drydock where temporary repairs to her piping and wiring were made. She later sailed at half power to Mare Island Navy Yard in California for permanent repairs. The HELENA had been knocked down, but not out. She would return to fight again.

Wake Island is across the international date line from Hawaii, so Sunday, December 7, at Pearl Harbor was Monday, December 8, on Wake. That Monday morning began as a normal work day for Dick and the sailors in the Navy boat crew. The bugler sounded reveille at 6:00 a.m., and the weary men rolled out of their tents and had breakfast. As dawn broke over Wake atoll the Pan Am Clipper skimmed across the lagoon, its four engines straining to pull the big plane into the air. It vanished into the cloudy western sky with Guam and then Manila as its destinations.

Several of the Navy seamen gathered at the docks to begin another day of ferry service. Dick was among the group which had assembled to discuss the day's assignments. They had no idea what was occurring 2000 miles to the east at Pearl Harbor. There was no reason for undue concern, so the men prepared to begin another normal work day.

At 6:30 a.m. men all over Wake Island were preparing to report to their work stations. They were completely unaware of the catastrophe that had occurred at Pearl Harbor. Even though Wake was one day ahead of Hawaii on the calendar, Pearl Harbor was 2 1/2 hours ahead by the clock. At 6:30 a.m. on Wake it was 9:00 a.m. at Pearl, and the second wave of Japanese bombers had just finished raining death and destruction on the American fleet.

Henry Webb was piloting one of the four Wildcats assigned to the dawn patrol on December 8. At daybreak he had roared down the runway and lifted off into the crisp morning air over Wake. Major Putnam was the senior pilot on the dawn patrol

U.S. Navy

The forward magazine of the USS Shaw explodes during the Pearl Harbor attack.

The small boat in the foreground rescues a sailor from the water as the USS West Virginia billows smoke in the background.

that morning. The four planes planned to remain aloft until 8:00, when they would be replaced by four fresh planes. Everything seemed routine to the pilots, except that the radios were malfunctioning. They were unable to communicate by radio with the radio unit on the ground as they normally did. Little did they know that, while they patrolled the skies over Wake Island, Japanese warplanes were bombing and killing Americans at Pearl Harbor.

Just before 7:00 Walter Cook was lying awake on his bunk in the weather station when he heard coral pebbles striking his window. He went to the window and saw that the radioman from the Navy radio station on the beach about 100 feet away was trying to get his attention. Cook could tell that something was up, so he quickly made his way down to the radio unit. The radio was tuned to the Navy network and a broadcast was coming from Pearl Harbor.

The men listened to the live report as it described a massive bombing raid on the American military facilities at Pearl Harbor. The attack was in progress as the men listened to the broadcast. The man reporting the news of the onslaught seemed frantic, and in an unusual departure from procedures of the day the message was uncoded. The report was delivered by the announcer with a sense of alarm, as if portending the heavy damages that had been inflicted.

Everyone in the radio station knew what the broadcast meant. The United States of America was at war with the people of Japan. The men on Wake Island knew the fury of the war

would almost surely turn toward them very soon; after all, Wake Island was geographically between the attacking forces at Pearl Harbor and the Japanese homeland. Cook left the radio unit and went directly to the supply depot to request timber and thick plywood with which to build a shelter just behind his new weather station.

Yeoman Glenn Tripp was in Commander Cunningham's office when 3rd Class Radioman John B. L. Anderson came in with the message about the raid on Pearl Harbor. Cunningham immediately had Tripp call Major Devereux on the phone and request that he come to the office. Devereux arrived at the office shortly to discuss the matter with Cunningham. Cunningham knew the implications of the attack on Pearl Harbor and instructed Major Devereux to get his troops ready for action at once. Dan Teters and Lt. Cmdr. Greey were also there, and after discussing the Pearl Harbor raid, Teters called the civilian leaders together and made them aware of the situation and its implications.

Major Devereux knew there was a major Japanese naval force attacking American bases in Hawaii. The men on Wake knew that this Japanese force must have a large group of aircraft carriers in order to provide enough air power for the Pearl Harbor raid, and, they deducted, this enemy force must be located between Wake atoll and the strength of the American fleet at Pearl Harbor. Suddenly, everyone on Wake understood how far out on a limb they actually were.

Minutes later Devereux was back in his command center on Wake. He assembled his officers and briefed them with the skimpy details he had. The attack on Pearl Harbor was actually in progress at that point and the reports were scanty, but he knew for sure was that a Japanese force was bombing an American base which was nearly 2000 miles east of Wake Island. He also knew that the Wake defenders were in a very precarious position.

Soon after the Marines on the ground learned of the Pearl Harbor attack they attempted to radio the news to the four Wildcats aloft on the dawn patrol. To their dismay they were unable to get through to the pilots, including Henry Webb, using the normally-reliable ground-to-air radio system. The frequency was being jammed, apparently by the Japanese, in an effort to curtail communications on Wake and keep segments of the defense force from going on alert status. It was speculated later that a Japanese submarine operating near the island had acted in harmony with the Pearl Harbor attack and jammed the radio frequency used by the pilots to communicate with the airstrip.

While the four wildcats in the morning patrol searched the heavens for unwelcome visitors, the airstrip became a center of intense activity. The pilots on the ground knew that they were easily within flying range of the enemy bases at Kwajalein, and chances were good that the Japanese would soon come calling at Wake. VMF-211 immediately went about organizing plans for their response to an enemy attack. The absence of radar complicated the effort immeasurably, since no advance notice would be forthcoming to warn the men of incoming aircraft except visual sightings from the observation posts.

The fighters remaining on the ground were refueled and fitted with bombs and belts of 50 cal. machine gun ammunition. Marines all over the island moved quickly to their positions, manning their guns and digging in. All of the Marines in the vicinity of the twelve sailors were in full preparation for battle, mounting guns and moving ammunition into position.

Shortly after 7:00 a.m. the island was alerted concerning the enemy action at Pearl Harbor. Cmdr. Campbell Keene rushed to the docks and gave the boat crews assembled there the startling news. "There's fire in the galley, and that's no shit!" he shouted. "Fire in the galley" was an old Navy phrase which meant the sailors were to take Cmdr. Keene's words very seriously. The expletive was not needed to give his message impact. Keene told the men what he knew of the scanty information that had come over the radio about the attack at Pearl Harbor.

Dick knew how dangerous his situation was, out on a limb on this speck of coral in the middle of the now hostile Pacific Ocean. The enemy was on a rampage much closer to home than Wake, at a base that had been considered secure. A major enemy force was active to the east, and Admiral Inouye had an impressive arsenal at his disposal to the west at Truk and south in the Marshalls within striking distance of Wake Island. The mood of the men quickly changed from a sense of security to one of great concern.

Immediately the sailors on the boat crew, like all military personnel on Wake Island, scurried to prepare the island for battle. Commander Keene instructed the men to mount a .30 cal. machine gun on the bow of the 50' motor launch. The sailors encountered problems immediately as they set about their task. First, there were no holes in the wooden deck of the launch and no drills that could accomplish the task. Secondly, Dick and most of the sailors had never fired a machine gun and did not know exactly how the gun needed to be positioned on the boat. After getting assistance from those who were familiar with machine guns and by improvising with the available tools they accomplished the task. The motor launch

was armed and ready.

This machine gun, plus their sling shots, would be the only weapons available to the Navy personnel on December 8, 1941. Major Devereux had ordered his field music bugler to sound "Call to Arms." When this signal echoed across Camp 1, the Marines scrambled to their gun positions all over the island. Wake Island went on full alert.

Sgt. Charles Holmes went straight to his 3" antiaircraft gun at the Peacock Point battery. His gun was one of the few with the ability to fire horizontally at ships or vertically at aircraft. It was also one of the few on the island with the sophisticated range-finding equipment that Holmes had trained on for so long. Knowing that this was the real thing, Holmes studied his equipment and the ammunition.

The sophisticated data computer on Holmes' 3" gun would read the height of aircraft above the island. He would take this all-important information and then set the fuses on the anti-aircraft shells in hopes that they would arrive at the plane at the moment of detonation. If Holmes and the machine were accurate the gun would score a kill. If this could be accomplished then perhaps the planes would not kill the defenders. If an attack came, Holmes knew that his job could determine life or death for the defenders on the island.

Wiley Sloman was still in the mess tent having breakfast when Lt. McAlister notified the men of the situation at Pearl Harbor. Shortly afterwards the general alarm was sounded. Sloman's unit had already left to go to the gun position on Wilkes Island, so he quickly wrapped his last hot cake around a sausage and was eating it as he went out the door. He went straight to his tent, where he put on several bandoliers of .30 cal. ammunition and his dishpan helmet.

There was still a bit of confusion in the camp, and possibly some question about the situation being a practice exercise or the real thing. The bugler was incorrectly sounding "fire call." As Sloman ran into the street he saw platoon Sargent Bedell, who was yelling, "Get your bucket, get your bucket." That seemed consistent with the field music being played, so Sloman ran back into his tent, threw down his rifle, and grabbed his fire bucket.

As Sloman ran back into the street he realized that the bugler was sounding "general alarm." Sgt. Bedell was yelling, "Get your gun, get your gun." Back into the tent went Sloman, picking up his rifle and ammunition, but hanging on to the fire bucket in case of further confusion outside. When he emerged from the tent this time, he was prepared to fight either a fire or a war.

"Have you got your damn mind made up yet?" questioned Sloman. Sgt. Bedell was a bit aggravated by Sloman's language, but there was no time to argue. Sloman threw the fire bucket back into the tent and hurried toward his gun unit. In the confusion he had forgotten his helmet, leaving it in the tent. Wiley Sloman would enter the war bare-headed.

In order to make their way to the 5" gun position on Wilkes, the Marines in Sloman's unit first had to walk several hundred yards from Camp 1 to the Wilkes channel. There they crossed the narrow waterway by ferry, and there would normally be a truck on the other side. The truck would carry them about a mile along the coral roadway to their position at the tip of the island. This morning there was no truck to be seen, so the men began covering the distance on foot.

Since the unit was entering an uninhabited area, and the

news of Pearl Harbor was fresh on their minds, they realized that enemy troops could have landed during the night and be in wait for them. For this reason they sent out forward observers, and Sloman was assigned to the point on the right flank. The idea was for the point men to be sacrificed if an ambush were to occur, but the main body of the sixty-man unit would not be surprised. This morning the Marines found Wilkes Island empty.

When the men reached their gun they went about making it ready for action. Sloman was in charge of fire control, which involved relaying information from the man on the observation tower to the gunners. They would take Sloman's estimates of direction and distance to a target and compute range and elevation figures used to aim the big gun. Regardless of their individual specialties, each Marine always kept his rifle within reach. Each man knew, even if his assignment was with an artillery unit, that he was a soldier first and foremost.

Even though the men had been preparing the 5" position for weeks, they realized now that the enemy was real and they were not as well prepared as they needed to be. The foxholes and dugouts around the gun were inadequate, so Wiley Sloman was assigned to begin digging in. He immediately began digging into the sand and rock soil, opening holes large enough to protect a man and using the excavated materials to fill sandbags. These were placed around the gun to further fortify it against attack. He dug a hole for himself near the 5" gun, and then went a few feet outside the pit to the base of the 16' observation tower where he began digging a hole for Lt. McAlister.

The Pan Am Philippine Clipper had been airborne for only

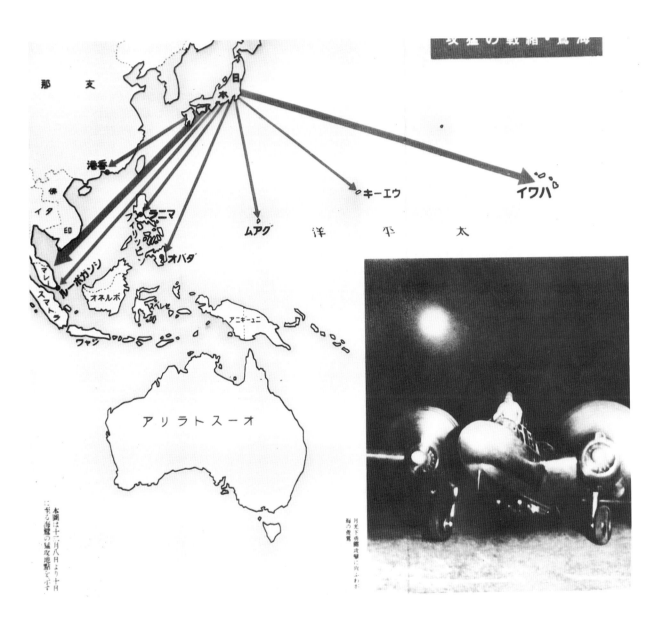

The Japanese caption on the chart reads,"This chart shows points attacked by our Navy Eagles, 8-10 December. Left to right: Hong Kong, Kotta Bharu, Singapore, Manila,Devao,Guam,Wake ,Hawaii." The caption on the insert'a Mitsubishi G3M bomber' reads,"One of the Raging Eagles or our Navy leaving for a moonlight attack."

ten minutes on its journey toward Guam when a radio message went out making it aware of the attack at Pearl Harbor. The Clipper was recalled to Wake, and it immediately turned back. The defenders were painfully aware of their lack of radar to alert them of incoming aircraft, and the men were understandably on edge. As the Clipper approached the island from the west, several gunners drew a bead on it in the sights of their anti-aircraft guns.

Wake's anti-aircraft guns were ordered to remain silent as the large four-engine Martin 130 "Clipper" came through the clouds and into full view. In a stroke of luck the big flying boat had still been within radio range when Commander Cunningham sent the message alerting it of the Pearl Harbor raid and calling it back to Wake. If the Clipper and her passengers had flown westward toward Guam they would have been heading almost straight into the jaws of the Japanese dragon. After circling the island, it glided down onto the lagoon and tied up at the Pan Am dock.

Admiral Inouye did, indeed, have an impressive force in the Marshalls. He commanded the 24th Air Flotilla, which was comprised of two air attack squadrons. One of these was comprised of shore based bombers and was based at Roi, some 720 miles from Wake. The other was made up of large four-engined patrol bombers, thought to be Kawanishi 97 aircraft that were similar to the big American PBY flying boats. These were based in Majuro, about 840

miles south of Wake and well within range.

Since Admiral Inouye had been given the responsibility of capturing Wake Island, along with Guam, Makin, and Tarawa, he initiated several operations on the morning of December 8 simultaneously with the attack on Pearl Harbor. Several of his targets were known to be lightly fortified and were expected to fall quickly and easily. Wake, on the other hand, was thought by the Japanese to have 1000 troops and 600 civilian laborers defending the island. Even though this presented a somewhat greater challenge than some of the other Pacific islands, the Japanese anticipated that they could overrun the island in a one-day operation.

Shortly after 7:30 a.m. the Marines had readied all of the gun positions. A truck carried a full allowance of ammunition to each position. A few light arms and dishpan helmets remained in the Marine storeroom, so they were issued to a handful of the Navy and Army men. Dick Darden was not one of the lucky few to be issued a weapon.

Henry Webb and the remainder of the dawn patrol landed as scheduled at 8:00 a.m. They were completely unaware of the Pearl Harbor attack. The first man who ran out to the planes told Webb. When Major Putnam learned of the attack he saw to it that the next four-plane patrol took off immediately. He immediately proceeded to coordinate VMF-211's defense of the skies over Wake.

Chapter 13
DAY 1—THE SIEGE BEGINS

When the alarm sounded on Monday morning, December 8, 1941, all twelve sailors in the Wake Island boat crew were busy securing the area around the docks near the Wilkes channel. It took most of the morning for the sailors to mount a machine gun on the motor launch.

The minute that the pilots on the dawn patrol were advised of the Pearl Harbor raid they began to prepare for an enemy attack. The assignments were posted for the pilots who would fly the upcoming patrols, and while on the ground several pilots received additional duties. They felt they would probably be hit by the enemy

soon, and that the Japanese might even have aircraft carriers in the vicinity which could launch a significant number of warplanes toward Wake. Major Putnam began formulating plans for responding to every conceivable type of enemy threat with the resources he had available.

Henry Webb was assigned to fly the noon patrol. In the meantime, Major Putnam ordered him to survey the area immediately around the airstrip and locate sites for slip trenches. These ditches would be dug for the pilots to jump into in case of a sudden surprise attack. Webb found several good locations nearby, and began trying

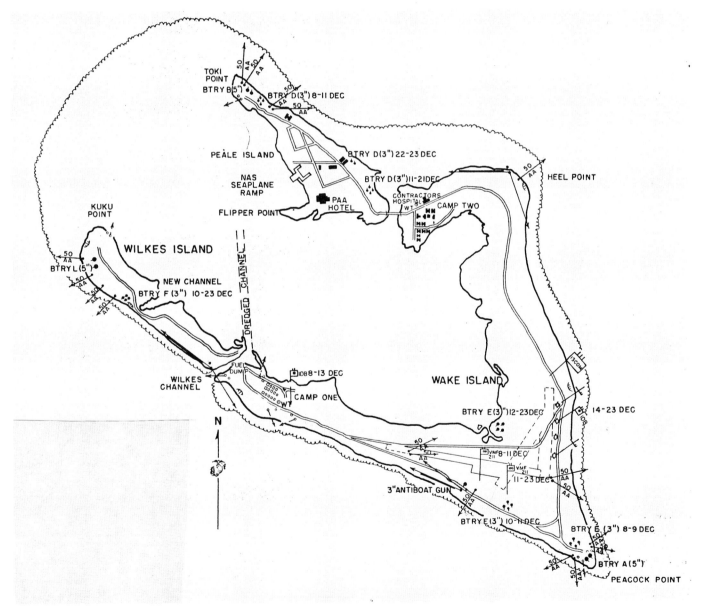

Wake Island's defenses at the time of the attack on Pearl Harbor

to dig holes in the sand. The coral under the sand was solid rock, far too hard for him to penetrate with his shovel. Webb called over to the contractor's camp and asked for some jackhammers. He continued to study the area along the edges of the runway while he waited for the power equipment to arrive.

Between 9:00 and 10:00 the morning patrol of Wildcats returned and was quickly attended by the ground crews. As one patrol landed another took its place, speeding out over the ocean to look for any signs of the enemy. While the patrol planes were scouting the seas around Wake from an elevation of 12,000 feet they encountered heavy clouds. These clouds obscured a formation of 36 Japanese bombers which sped past the Wildcats toward Wake.

The Marines on Wake, unaware of the enemy warplanes that were speeding toward them, scrambled to get ammunition to all gun positions and dig into the island as best they could. They knew that their position was a dangerous one, since all the reports from Pearl Harbor were gloomy. Little help could be expected from the Pacific fleet, which, from all accounts, seemed to have been virtually wiped out. Foxholes and gun positions were secured and sandbags were used to fortify many of the emplacements. The Marines camouflaged their positions as best they could. The reality of the situation began to sink in for the defenders of Wake Island.

The young men on Wake, many just out of high school, were optimistic and confident as they waited to see if the enemy intended to pay them a visit. Most of these young Marines had never seen the carnage of war, so the events of this day thusfar had all of the earmarks of an adventure. They waited nervously in their foxholes with guns at the ready, waiting for the Japanese to play their hand.

Even with the islands in full preparation for battle, there was no fear in the hearts of the defenders. After all, they had anti-aircraft guns to complement their anti-ship coastal guns. Even though sparsely deployed, there were numerous machine guns ready for action. In addition, there was a convoy enroute to Wake with relief supplies. In the convoy was the carrier USS ENTERPRISE, which would provide additional air support in the event of a conflict. The situation seemed well in hand on Wake.

Late in the morning a tropical rain squall brought heavy black clouds, lightning, and thunder over Wake Island. A torrential downpour ensued, drenching the island. Sheets of rain fell on the Marines, and even the lookouts on the water tower could see only a short distance into the storm. With no radar to alert the defenders of Wake against incoming aircraft, the island lay naked and vulnerable, especially with the weather limiting the visibility of the lookouts.

Capt. Henry Wilson was an Army radioman who had been sent to Wake to set up a communications station which would help direct Army bombers flying between Hawaii and points west of Wake. His equipment was mounted on a truck parked in an open area near the airfield. After hearing of the attack on Pearl Harbor, Wilson realized that a similar raid on Wake was possible, so he moved his radio truck into a wooded area where it was partially concealed under the scrubby thicket of undergrowth. This would prove to be a very wise move.

At about 11:45 several of the sailors left the docks in a panel truck in search of a noon meal. They were hungry after such a furious morning of hard work, and they understood that the civilians in Camp 2 were preparing food for them. Dick Darden was seated near the front of the truck's bed just behind the cab, while several of his buddies were sitting behind him near the back door. The back door of the truck was the only exit from its rear compartment. It was to stop first at the nearby air strip, pick up the mail, and deliver it to the Pan Am Clipper moored in the lagoon.

Tom Kennedy was working in one of the communications tents along the runway at the air strip. It was nearly lunchtime and he well remembered the ox tongue and rice meal that had been served by the Marine cooks on the previous day. Kennedy and several of his buddies were looking forward to having lunch in the civilian mess hall, having heard of the extensive menu and good food served there. Then word came down that the civilians were going to bring lunch to the men working at the air strip. That was okay with Kennedy and his buddies, who hoped they would not get another meal of ox tongue.

John Blandy was also a Marine who was working at the air strip that day. He was in another radio tent where a shortwave receiver was tuned to a news report from Pearl Harbor. Blandy and several Marines were listening to the latest reports of the damage that resulted from the Japanese raid that morning. The men were listening with keen ears because the transmission was garbled with static and they were trying to pick facts and figures out of the noise. One of the men had a wife and family living in an apartment very near the front gate to the Pearl Harbor base. Understandably, he was listening with the greatest concern.

The schedule that Major Putnam was employing for his squadron of twelve fighters called for four of the planes to be in the air at all times searching for any sign of the enemy. The other eight aircraft would be on the ground, with four sitting idle and cold, and the other four warming up, ready for action at a moments notice. The truck with the Navy men inside pulled up between the two groups, with the four cold planes sitting on the edge of the runway and perpendicular to it, while the other four were a few feet away warming up in a line that faced down the runway ready for takeoff.

No more precarious spot could have been found for the truck if trouble were to come, for the enemy would surely hit the fighter planes first, since they represented the island's first line of defense. The sides of the panel truck had an open slit down the length of both sides which allowed the occupants to see outside. As the driver stopped the truck and hopped out to get the mail, the men inside could see that planes were parked on both sides of them. It was 11:55 a.m. as Dick sat waiting for the mail bag and a hot lunch.

The rain squall ended just a few minutes before noon, but clouds from the storm remained over the island and limited visibility. The sentries on the water towers strained their eyes at the glimmers of sunlight as they shot between the clouds, still unable to see anything in the heavens that did not look unfriendly.

The patrol planes from Wake searched the cloudy skies in vain, still failing to spot the three "V" formations of Japanese Mitsubishi G3M2 "Bettys." Each "V" was comprised of a dozen of the twin engine bombers, each one carrying over 1700 pounds of high explosives that were bound for Wake Island. The bombers continued on their way undetected, bringing their calling cards from Roi and Namur Islands on Kwajalein Atoll in the Marshall Islands. The thirty-six planes were from the Air Attack Force No. 1 of the Japanese Navy's Twenty-Fourth Air Flotilla. Now they would have the chance to catch Wake Atoll by surprise.

The wily leader of the Japanese air attack squadron noticed the cloud bank over the southern part of Wake. The twin-tailed bombers were at 7000 feet, over a mile above the island, when they began their descent. When they reached a point about two miles from the island the leader signaled for his men to cut their engines and begin gliding toward the target. The three V-shaped formations dropped silently to the cloud bank with their engines idling quietly.

There had been no hint that Wake was in imminent danger. The four planes in the air had reported no sightings, and none of the islands' lookout positions had reported anything out of the ordinary. The sky was partly cloudy, and a cloud bank was moving over the air field. Even though men were scurrying about all over the three square miles of Wake Island making preparations for whatever the Japanese might throw at them, there was no indication yet that any such events would happen. Wake Island did not have radar, having gotten a garbage truck instead. It was nearly noon. Henry Webb was in the flight tent along the runway getting his last instructions before taking off with the noon patrol. His Wildcat had been serviced and stood ready about 100 yards away. He carefully studied the large board which held all of the scheduling information for the pilots. The jackhammers had never arrived, so no protective trenches had been dug along the airstrip. Webb tossed his parachute over his shoulder and was about to step out through the door of the tent.

Suddenly, just before 12:00 noon, a formation of airplanes appeared out of the clouds at high speed almost directly over the airstrip. The planes were at low altitude, only 2000 feet over the island, as they roared toward the row of cold Wildcats. The first reaction of some of the men was joyous, for they thought the planes from the ENTERPRISE were arriving. "Here comes the help," quipped one of the men in the back of the truck with Dick. "Look at all those planes."

Jim Cox and several of the Navy boatmen had been working near the docks when they heard the planes coming. They had finished their morning tasks and were walking the 100 yard distance toward Camp 1 where they would take their lunch break. They immediately recognized the aircraft as Japanese warplanes and scrambled for cover. There was little protection to be had where Cox was, so he and the men simply laid down in the sand. The bombers were in two formations, one heading for the civilians at Camp 2 and the other screaming directly over Cox heading for the airstrip and the eight Wildcats parked on the apron.

A split second later some of the men with Dick in the panel truck parked on the runway spotted the orange balls under the wings of the incoming aircraft and someone yelled "Hell, those aren't ours, those are Japs!" The wily Japanese pilots had eluded the four scout planes in the air and used the low cloud bank and rain squall as cover to catch the island completely off guard. Thirty-six enemy planes, loaded to the gills with high explosives, were heading straight for the heart of the Wake Island defenses—the fighter planes on the airstrip.

One civilian worker, unaccustomed to seeing military planes in attack formation and unaware of the severity of the moment, remarked that the wheels were falling off the incoming planes. What he had actually witnessed was a cluster of bombs being released from the attacking plane. In a few short moments he would be painfully aware that something much more horrible than airplane wheels was plummeting toward Wake atoll.

Marine Corporal Ralph Holewinski was in charge of two .30 cal. machine gun positions on the beach. He and six other Marines had the responsibility of defending a two mile stretch of beach immediately to the east of Cox's position. Holewinski saw the enemy

bombers come out of the clouds and yelled to his men to take cover. They ran to the exposed coral reef at the water's edge and watched as the bombs were dropped over the air strip.

One of Tom Kennedy's buddies at the air strip stepped out of his tent when he heard the incoming planes and exclaimed, "Jiminy cricket, look at all those airplanes! They must be B-17's!" "B-17's hell!" emphatically shouted another. The Marines in the tent knew instantly what he meant. Everyone dashed out of the tent and ran away from the openness of the air field toward the protection of the nearby underbrush.

Just as Henry Webb was about to step out of the tent and toward his airplane he heard someone shout, "They are not our planes." He peered out through the unfastened flap on the door and saw two formations of Japanese bombers crossing the beach and heading directly toward the runway. The eighteen two-man 'Bettys' were coming in low, probably not more than 1500 feet up.

The enemy planes were heading straight for the Wildcats parked on the apron of the runway. There was no chance for Henry Webb to get to his plane, much less to get it airborne. Realizing that, he threw down his parachute and began running toward a small sandy knoll about fifty yards away. The knoll had a few scrubby trees that he hoped would conceal him if he could reach them.

Panic, chaos, and all hell broke out instantly. The planes came in for their first pass over the airstrip, strafing and bombing the eight idle Wildcats parked on the edge of the runway about 100 yards apart. With their machine guns spewing out a shower of lethal projectiles that ripped through everything in their path, the planes passed low over the parked planes, perforating practically everything.

The raid had been well planned by the Japanese strategists. Each "V" of twelve bombers went to work without delay, heading straight to a predetermined target. As 100 pound fragmentation bombs and 20mm incendiary machine gun bullets made the island throb and burn, the men on the ground frantically scattered about the air field. Some headed for battle stations, ready to do battle with the marauders. Others dove for any available safety as the deadly projectiles rained down onto the island.

The sailors in the truck realized instantly that they were in an area where everything was about to be obliterated, so they threw open the back door to the panel truck and bolted for the exit. As they piled out onto the runway a Japanese fighter plane roared just above their heads, machine gunning the truck and the parked planes. The man who came out the back door of the truck just one step behind Dick was 3rd Class Boatswains Mate George J. Wolney. He was hit instantly by four or five rounds and fell on the airstrip like a sack of grain. Miraculously, he was not killed.

The truck was perforated with holes from the .50 cal. machine gun slugs. Everybody was scared and running for cover as fast as they could. Somehow Dick avoided the hail of bullets. He glanced over his shoulder and saw Wolney fall, thinking surely that the blood spattered man was dead. It was easy to see that the planes on the runway and the maintenance areas along the sides were prime targets. Dick began sprinting across the runway and away from the area being bombed to the only cover available, the scrubby undergrowth between the air strip and the beach. An incoming plane was spewing a shower of hot metal straight at Dick, so he ran a zigzag pattern and danced through the the deadly bullets.

As the Japanese gunner did his best to catch Dick in his

sights, Dick looked up at the plane which was so close that for a split second he could see right through the blister that was mounted on the side of the twin-engine bomber. He peered directly into the eyes of the Japanese machinegunner who was intensely staring back as he unleashed several bursts of machine gun fire. Each burst cut a furrow in the coral sand that just missed Dick.

Several times as Dick made his way toward the treeline he ran through a line of machine gun bullets that danced across the runway, kicking up coral and barely missing him. He dove head first into the thicket, happy to have some cover from the marauders above. Dick crouched in the coral sand next to a Marine officer who had also found the protection of the trees just moments earlier. The two men huddled close together as the attack continued a few feet away. Dick had somehow missed being hit, but as he glanced down he noticed several bullet holes in the legs of his bell bottom trousers.

Tom Kennedy was not as lucky. He was sprinting across the open area when he saw a bomb released from under the wing of an approaching plane that seemed to be coming directly toward him. He was running faster than he thought possible when he heard the blast a short distance behind him. Shrapnel cut deeply into his left knee, but he kept running. Kennedy was running at right angles to the lines of machine gun bullets that were spewing out of the planes and dancing through the coral sand.

Plane after plane roared over Kennedy. A machine gun bullet caught him firmly in the right arm and another piece of shrapnel pierced his shoulder. Still he kept running toward the trees. Another bullet just grazed him, taking skin off of his hip.

John Blandy heard the shouting outside his tent and stepped out to see an enemy plane coming straight at him down the runway in a strafing run. Unlike Kennedy, who tried to run across the lines of incoming bullets, Blandy instantly decided that his best chance to survive the moment was to fall between two of the lines. Blandy did exactly that, diving between two rows of bullets that were digging a trench toward him at 200 miles per hour. Blandy lay unhurt as the deadly projectiles raced past him.

Henry Webb was not as lucky. Before he could reach the top of the scrubby knoll one of the planes passed over him spewing out a spray of lethal projectiles. In a second, several bullets ripped into his body. One tore into his right shoe, severing two and a half toes from his foot. Another bullet went through his stomach, and yet another lodged in his spine. Henry Webb fell forward into the sand, badly wounded and in shock. As he lay in the sand his head was positioned so that he could see back toward the runway. His memory was indelibly marked with a picture of billowing smoke and huge fires that were erupting everywhere from the exploding planes and fuel tanks. He also noticed a stream of blood flowing from his shoe just before blacking out.

At least Henry Webb was still alive. Three of John Blandy's buddies came running out of their tent right behind him. Each ran in a different direction, trying to avoid the hail of bullets coming across

Burt Silverman
American Heritage

The airport began to erupt into flames all around Dick Darden.

the sand toward them. As the plane roared over all three of them were cut down, shot to death by the pilot of the attacking 'Betty.'

A Marine named Martin was on the observation tower above Wiley Sloman's 5" gun positon on Wilkes Island. He was standing lookout duty, and his job was to warn everyone below of any approaching ships or planes. Suddenly explosions were heard in the direction of the airstrip. Sloman, who had just finished digging Lt. McAlister's foxhole and was placing sand bags around its top, thought the civilian contractors were dynamiting again. All of a sudden Martin started yelling, "They're bombing the airport, they're bombing the airport."

As Sloman stepped out of McAlister's foxhole to investigate, he looked up and was met by a formation of planes coming directly at him. They screamed over the surf and right at him, low enough that he felt he could hit them with a rock. Rather than diving back into Lt. McAlister's foxhole, Sloman instinctively ran for his own where his weapon was waiting.

The machine guns on the plane were roaring and the bullets were kicking up coral all around Sloman. He dove through the hail of bullets into his foxhole and onto three Marines already seeking refuge there. Miraculously, he was not hit. He looked down to find

78

several bleeding cuts, however, from the sharp-edged coral chunks that were flying everywhere. The jagged coral had ripped his skin in several places and the cuts immediately began to "sting like hell."

Dick raised his head to scan the air field, but he could not believe what was happening just across the runway. The area was under full attack and a number of bodies lay on the runway. The precious fighter planes were exploding and burning. The fuel tanks were exploding, making the runway an inferno. A 25,000 gallon tank filled with high-octane aviation fuel erupted on the edge of the airstrip. After the initial deafening roar the belly of the huge tank seemed to purge itself of its remaining contents, sending a small wave of burning fuel toward the runway.

The runway had been cut a few inches lower than the surrounding sand. When the wave of aviation fuel got to the runway it spilled over the small ridge and began moving out onto the hard surface. The burning fuel rushed onward and covered several of the men who were lying on the runway. Some were motionless bodies, but others were screaming for help and unable to move as they were engulfed.

Hundreds of fifty-gallon metal drums had been used to store aviation fuel and were lining the far side of the runway. As the inferno became hotter the petroleum-laden drums began exploding everywhere. The attack was still in progress and the planes were dropping more bombs in the area adjacent to the runway, causing more of the fuel barrels to explode. There were bone-jarring explosions all around Dick and the Marine officer, the concussions of which shook their very souls. The acrid fumes of the bombs, the choking dust from the explosions, and the thick black smoke from the aviation fuel filled the men's lungs.

The Marine pilots were housed in a row of tents along the opposite side of the runway. Lt. Robert J. Conderman, a Marine fighter pilot, ran from his tent toward the line of parked planes, which were being warmed up. Just as he scrambled up the side and into the cockpit an enemy plane roared over him and showered him with machine gun fire. Conderman fell down onto the hardpacked coral surface mortally wounded.

Lt. Conderman was a fellow North Carolinian, known to his buddies as "Strawberry" because of his flaming red hair. He was from New Bern, less that 100 miles from Clinton. Neither he nor any of the seven other pilots on the ground were able to make it into the air to return fire against the waves of incoming planes. So completely did the Japanese surprise the Marine pilots on Wake that seven of their Wildcats were destroyed, blown out from under them and burned before they could get off the ground and into the fight.

Soon the area was an inferno as the Marine's bombs and machine gun bullets began exploding in and around the planes from the heat. Men were scattering everywhere. Dick clung tightly to the officer who had scrambled into the thicket just before him. The Marine was lying between Dick and the runway. The Japanese planes turned and headed back toward the air strip for another bombing run. This time their objective was to make sure the planes on the ground could not retaliate, while at the same time to avoid damaging the airstrip itself.

The Japanese had plans to use the landing strip later for their own planes. The 'Bettys' began unleashing their fragmentation bombs along the edges of the runway, further igniting the fuel storage area. The destruction caused by the bombing along the airstrip was complete, but the runway itself was spared.

Dick and the Marine officer lay as close to the ground as they could, hoping that the thicket would conceal them from the trigger happy raiders. They didn't realize that their hiding place, in the fringe area just off the runway, was exactly what the bombers were trying to destroy while leaving the runway intact. They heard a string of bombs, boom, boom, boom, getting closer and louder. A second later, just a few feet from where Dick Darden and the officer lay on the sand, a bomb struck producing a tremendous explosion.

The blast caused an enormous concussion, blowing sand, coral, and shrapnel in every direction. The force of the blast lifted both men over two feet off the ground, but luckily for Dick the officer was between him and the explosion. A spray of projectiles from the fragmentation bomb cut through the air in every direction. As the two men fell back into the sand Dick felt something hit his leg, as if he had been kicked in the back of the thigh.

A few moments later Dick shook his head, dazed by the blast and not sure what had happened. As he looked up to get his bearings he realized that blood was everywhere. The officer's body, which had shielded Dick from most of the blast, had been torn apart by the shrapnel. The Marine had died instantly and lay in a bloody mass just out of reach. As Dick began to regain his senses he noticed that some of the blood was his own.

A sharp piece of shrapnel had opened up the back of Dick's left leg to the bone just above the knee. The leg lay open and he could see that all of the muscles and blood vessels had been severed, and blood was spurting into the air. The fragment of hot metal had gone to the thigh bone, actually carving a groove into it that Dick saw as he peered into the wound. He knew that he would bleed to death if he didn't close the wound, so he instinctively pulled the bleeding tissue back together, not concerned about the sand, coral, twigs, and leaves left inside.

Unable to get to his feet, Dick dragged himself through the sand a few feet farther into the undergrowth, hoping to get out of sight of the Japanese pilots who were finishing up their short but devastating visit to Wake. The Jap pilots were smiling broadly and as they regrouped to leave Wake. They wagged their wings up and down to show how pleased they were with their first victory of the war.

Dick was covered with blood from the waist down. His injured leg was immovable, more stunned than painful. It felt as if a baseball line drive had hit him in the back of the leg. Within a few minutes a Pharmacists Mate stumbled by, dazed and looking for protection in the scrub. Seeing the bloody sailor he mumbled, "Are you hurt?" "What the hell does it look like?" retorted Dick as he lay in a pool of ever-thickening blood.

"What can we do about it?" asked the Pharmacists Mate. "You're supposed to know the answer to that," responded Darden as he lay bleeding to death with a trained medic looking at him. "I've got to stop this bleeding. Give me your belt," Dick instructed. The medic removed his belt, and the two made a tourniquet just above the wound, from which a steady stream of blood was pouring. The tourniquet was just below Dick's crotch since the leg had been split open from there down to the back of his knee.

The medic left, still dazed and not knowing exactly what to do in the chaotic, burning, exploding world around him. Dick tightened the tourniquet and elevated the leg into a bush in an attempt to slow the bleeding. He thought, "Well, my time has come right here and now." He could feel himself getting weaker by the minute as he watched blood continue to be pumped from his body, unable to stop it with the tourniquet.

After three or four minutes Dick felt his grip on the twisted belt begin to weaken rapidly. The massive loss of blood was causing him to lose his strength, and he was beginning to slip away. What was he to do? Without enough energy to walk or even crawl to the hospital, which was nearly two miles away—if it still existed after the furious bombing—he wondered if he would simply lie there in the sand and bleed to death. He could see blood pumping out into an ever-widening pool beneath him. He became confused and delirious and was about to give up.

As Dick lay helpless in the scrubby brush, two figures ran by. One yelled "Is anybody hurt over here?" "Yes, over here," Dick strained in all of the voice he could still muster. A hand parted the branches of the bush and a figure peered into the thicket. It was Captain Elrod and Captain Tharin, two of the ace pilots who had survived the bombing. "Hey Frank, here's one with his ass shot off!" shouted Elrod. That was the last thing Dick remembered before blacking out.

Ralph Holewinski and several other Marines had been on the beach at their machine gun position when the raid began. They took cover under a large piece of exposed coral reef at the water's edge. The rocky projection seemed to be their best protection in the open, exposed area of beach and dunes. They would move from one side of the large stone formation to the other as the planes moved across their position, always seeking protection on the side away from the oncoming aircraft.

Holewinski and his Marine buddies listened as the bombs thundered down, staying under the protection of the reef until the raid was over. Holewinski could see that the airfield, only a few hundred yards away, had been badly hit. When the planes disappeared the men immediately ran toward the columns of black smoke which rose from several scorching fires in the aviation fuel depot. When they got to the air strip they were shocked as they stared at the awesome sight. Dead and wounded men lay all over the area. They saw the Marine pilot who had been climbing into his cockpit, now lying on the ground and riddled by machine gun bullets that had come from the strafing planes. He was one of many in the aviation unit who had died in the ten minute raid.

Holewinski and his buddies saw a wounded sailor being moved. He was wearing a white uniform which was red with blood from the waist down. Major Bayler, a Marine radio specialist, had arrived at the air strip and noticed Holewinski and his buddies. Bayler approached the Marines and reacted as cool as a cucumber amidst the chaotic circumstances of the moment. He ordered Holewinski and the Marines to leave the area immediately and to return to their position on the beach.

Superficially Major Bayler was ordering the men to return to their positions so that the island could regain its full defensive posture, but Holewinski got the distinct impression that the Major didn't want the men to see any more of the scene on the airstrip. The destruction was so great that it might demoralize the men.

Holewinski and his buddies were too stunned by what they saw to be demoralized. As they realized the extent of the damage they became angry at the enemy who had done this. They returned to the beach and found that a string of bombs had been coming directly toward their machine gun. The last bomb had fallen about twenty feet from their gun and had left a crater that was 20 feet deep and 40 feet wide. Two civilians named Bryan and Gay came by the position and suggested that a bunker be made in the hole that the Japanese had excavated for them. They set about getting the materials and equipment to do just that.

When he regained consciousness, Dick Darden was in a field aid station, which had been quickly thrown together in an open area on the opposite side of the runway. Elrod and Tharin had apparently carried him there and several hours had passed. It was mid-afternoon and someone was administering a tetanus shot, which they told him was the last one on the island. Dick's wounded leg was throbbing, but at least it had stopped bleeding. He thought that was only appropriate, since common sense told him that there couldn't be much blood left inside to ooze out.

The doctors had not had time to work on the wound, since many other men with more severe wounds were lying nearby waiting for the attention of the only two doctors in their part of the world. Dr. Kahn, the Navy doctor, and Dr. Shank, the civilian doctor, finally looked at the wound, but only had time to wrap it tightly with gauze. They would have to attend to it later. Dick was laid back down among the wounded where he would wait while the doctors administered to the gravely wounded.

The devastation around the field aid station could not be believed. All eight planes on the ground had been damaged or destroyed. They had sat like plump ducklings, fully loaded with fuel, bombs, and belts of machine gun bullets, for the Japanese pilots to feast upon. Huge bomb craters pock-marked the entire area around the air strip. Twenty-three of the fifty-five men in the Marine Aviation Squadron had been killed or lay dying. Another dozen were wounded. Nearly all of the mechanics and ground crew who provided support for the aircraft were dead or wounded.

The attack had lasted only twelve minutes but had devastated VMF-211. The bodies of the maimed men, living and dead, had strewn the airstrip, cut to pieces by the machine gun bullets and the flying shrapnel. All around Dick in the hospital lay bodies with digits or parts of arms or legs blown off, while others moaned from throbbing compound fractures.

Camp 1, which had been the tent city where the Marines and Navy boat crew were housed, was in ruins. The rows of tents, along with the officer's club and other buildings, were completely destroyed. Strewn all over this section of the island were the personal belongings of the Marines, including their clothes, laundry, toilet articles, mementos from home, shoes, and anything else that they had stored in their tents.

The explosion that ripped apart the officer's club had thrown beer and whiskey bottles, cards and poker chips, and food stuffs to every corner of the area. Men picking through the rubble looking for their belongings found bottles of liquor unbroken and with contents still intact despite the considerable distance they had been airborne from the blast site. Marines were busy digging foxholes into the sandy atoll which would be their home for the next twelve days.

The Pan American facilities on Peale had been hit hard, with few structures still standing. The Pan Am hotel had been leveled, and ten Pan Am employees lay dead. All of these were Chamorros, natives of Guam, who had been civilian employees of the airline. Several of the remaining buildings at the seaplane base were on fire.

Amazingly, the Philippine Clipper, which had been a huge target as it sat in the lagoon during the attack, received only a few bullet holes in its fuselage. The Clipper, which had been moored at the end of the Pan Am dock, had sustained a few bullet holes in its hide from the Jap machine gunners, but apparently had not sustained any serious damage.

The manager of the Pan Am base decided to evacuate all of his personnel to Midway Island. At about 1:00 p.m., barely an hour after the nightmarish raid had begun, the Clipper was boarded by the maximum number of passengers that it could safely carry. These included all of the original passengers plus many of the Pan Am employees. With its huge engines roaring at full strength the Clipper skimmed across the lagoon trying to become airborne. Twice the heavily loaded plane failed to take off and nearly hit the beach on the opposite side of the lagoon.

Finally, on its third attempt, the big airplane sluggishly rose just above the surface of the water. It barely cleared Wilkes Island across the lagoon, struggling to become airborne and gain altitude with its heavy cargo. The Clipper then disappeared into the sky north of the atoll.

The civilian camp had also sustained tremendous damage. A number of the buildings in the compound had been destroyed, and as many as fifty workers had been killed. Most of the remaining civilian workers had fled into the scrubby forests of the island to hide from the Japanese.

Eight of the twelve Wildcats had been damaged or destroyed in the raid, and VMF-211 would experience one additional bit of bad luck on December 8. As Captain Elrod was bringing his plane in from the morning patrol he had to land on an air field that was strewn with debris and parts of destroyed planes. He brought his Wildcat down on the runway, but was unable to avoid a collision with a piece of debris. His propeller was bent and the engine of his plane was badly damaged. The air unit on Wake was reduced once more, now with only three planes operational.

Later in the afternoon an attempt was made to move the wounded men into a small wooden building that was being used as a hospital. It was located in Camp 2 several miles away. Dick and seven or eight other badly wounded men were loaded onto the back of a large flatbed truck, which began to move along the coral road toward the civilian camp. Each bump resulted in excruciating pain. The wound still had not been attended except to be bound more tightly with gauze.

The truck bounced along the road toward the hospital. The driver of the truck suddenly yelled "Here they come again!" Everyone strained to look skyward, and sure enough, a formation of winged objects approached in the distance. Some of the men on the truck were unconscious, others too badly wounded to move themselves. Dick and Edward E. Johnson, a wounded Marine, were together on the truck. They knew that men on a truck would be sitting ducks for the Japanese pilots if they strafed the island again. The two men looked at each other, realizing the imminent danger.

"Are you going to lay up here?" asked Johnson, whose arm had been nearly blown off at the shoulder. "Hell no," responded Dick. "Not if I can get off of here." Both men began dragging themselves, Johnson with one arm and Dick on his elbows, toward the edge of the flatbed. Then both men toppled over the side, endured the pain of hitting the ground, and crawled under the steel bed and rear axle of the truck, the only protection they could reach.

The truck driver had already bolted from the cab of the truck, scrambling to find a hiding place in the scrubby underbrush. He did not offer to help any of the men precariously stranded behind him and he never returned. Though seconds seemed like hours for the anxious men, they soon realized that the formation of incoming objects was only a flock of gooney birds, gliding over the island in a perfect "V" and, from a distance, closely resembling a squadron of Japanese planes. With no radar there would be no warning of incoming planes during the next fourteen days, and several times the birds caused quite a scare.

Finally someone came down the road. They lifted the wounded men back aboard the truck and drove them along the road that curved around the closed end of Wake Island to Camp 2 and the hospital. It consisted of a small four-room wooden hut with a screened porch which extended out about twelve feet on all four sides. A hall down the center of the small wooden building separated two rooms on either side.

Three of the rooms were filled with beds, and the other was being used as an operating room. Dr. Lawton S. Shank, the civilian doctor, and Dr. Lt. (jg) Gustav Kahn, the military doctor, had their hands full as most of the beds were already full of men with serious injuries.

Dick knew several of the wounded men who lay near him in the hospital. Kirby Ludwig had been with Dick on the boat crew. Henry Webb, the pilot who was known to his friends as "Spider," and Sgt. Tom Kennedy, with whom Dick had traded baseball gloves just two days before, were in a nearby room. Kennedy's arm was severely wounded and had been placed in a straight splint until surgery could be performed to set it.

Walter Cook and the other weathermen spent the afternoon earnestly digging in the sand behind their weather station. They prepared a large hole for a bunker and then used the timbers and plywood to build a roof to shelter the dug out area. This was covered with coral sand in hopes that it would conceal the men and provide protection during the next bombing raid from anything other than a direct hit.

"Strawberry" Conderman was in the hospital with Dick and was still clinging to life. When the enemy plane raked the side of his parked Wildcat with machinegun fire, Conderman had been hit several times. Both legs had severe wounds. One had already been lost and the other was barely attached at the knee as the doctors worked feverishly to save the young pilot. He had lost a tremendous amount of blood and there was little hope that he would live through the night. The doctors did everything they could for him with the few supplies available.

Next on the operating table was Spider Webb. Webb had awoken in the hospital sometime after dark, having been in and out of consciousness for more than ten hours. Dick had heard the doctors say they didn't think Webb would make it. All Webb could remember of the events after the bombing was a ride on the flatbed truck to the hospital. Bouncing around on the coral roadway had been so painful that it had momentarily brought him back to reality.

Everything else that occured during the afternoon and evening was a blur to Spider Webb. He would clearly remember waking only once more during the night, as he felt the doctors working on his gaping wounds without the benefit of anesthesia. Not long after the doctors finished doing all they could for Webb, Strawberry Conderman died.

By the time the doctors began to work on Dick's leg, it was 11:00 p.m. and there were virtually no supplies left. All of the sutures, all of the disinfectant, all of the anesthetic, and nearly all of the other supplies had been exausted. Dick was carried into the operating room. As the doctors unwrapped the tight gauze bandage, the extent of the wound became apparent. There would be nothing to numb the pain as they opened the gaping hole in his leg.

The leg would first have to be cleaned of the debris that had been bound in it. Dick was lying on his belly on a metal operating table, his arms dangling down on either side, as the doctors began working on the backside of his leg. They told him to hold onto a steel bar that functioned as a cross support and was attached horizontally between the table legs. He grabbed the bar with both hands, and gritted his teeth for what was about to happen. The table was too short for Dick's lanky frame. His head and upper chest hung off the end of the table so that the entire wounded leg could be firmly supported on the other end.

Dr. Kahn looked at Dick. "I've got to clean it out before I can start sewing it up," he warned the young sailor. He turned to a corpsman. "Do we have anything to clean it out with?" he asked. The answer was a firm, "no." The doctor picked up a small metal pan and handed it to the corpman, instructing him to get one box of table salt and dissolve it in hot water. He told the corpman to stir the solution with his hand, and use water as hot as his hand could stand. As the corpman prepared the brine the doctor opened the wound and began picking out stems, leaves, chunks of coral and sandy grit.

The doctor took a handful of cotton and dipped it into the salty solution. "Darden, this is going to hurt," he warned again. As the severed muscles and tendons were swabbed with the salty mix Dick Darden experienced the most painful moments of his life. He would remember the horrid, but life-saving, solution as "liquid fire."

Dick tightened his grip on the metal bar and, as the doctors worked on Dick's mangled limb and pain shot through the gaping wound, he bent the steel bar that supported the metal table nearly double. Dick wanted to scream, but he did not dare stop the doctors, for to stop this modest effort at disinfecting the wound would almost surely bring an agonizing death from gangrene.

Dr. Kahn reattached the severed muscles and tendons with a suture needle and cotton twine. There was simply nothing else left with which to work. After every two or three stitches he would dip the cotton in the bloody brine and swab out more blood and grit. Each time he did this he reignited the fire in Dick's throbbing leg.

Chlorine was the only material that the doctors had to further disinfect the leg wound. Yellow chlorine tablets had been used to sterilize the drinking water on the island. The doctor told a corpman to dissolve a chlorine tablet in hot water and pour this over Dick's bandaged leg periodically. This would be the only further precaution that was available to fight off infection in the mending limb.

As the doctor reattached the tissue with cotton stitches and closed the leg there was no guarantee that infection had not been left deep in the leg. They could only do their best and hope. Miraculously, the leg would heal during the next few months and Dick Darden would walk normally again, bearing only an ugly indented scar down the back of his left thigh as evidence of the ordeal.

Glenn Tripp was in the hospital on the night of the first raid to visit his wounded buddies when he heard two wounded men trying to raise each other's spirits by joking about their severe wounds. One of the men had had his right leg blown off, and the other had lost his left leg. One quipped to the other, "Well, I guess now we could wear one pair of shoes between us."

Jim Cox had been hit in the leg by bomb shrapnel during the first air raid, but his wounds were not serious enough to go into the hospital. He remained at Camp 1 where he served as a lookout and carried ammunition to the guns. He also helped to take much of the remaining supply of canned food out of buildings and load it onto trucks. It was then distributed to various places in the bush and hidden so that a lucky Jap bomb could not wipe out the entire food supply.

Cox, like all the Navy boatmen, had not been issued a weapon, not even a 1903 Springfield rifle, before the battle. After he was assigned to Lt. Poindexter's unit he was given a BAR (Browning Automatic Rifle), but one of the Marines needed the weapon more than he, so again he found himself defenseless. Then he managed to get one of the Springfields and a .45 automatic pistol. The old Springfield was a bolt action WWI model which fired 30-06 ammunition (.30" diameter, developed in 1906).

Between December 8 and December 23, Cox and several buddies were assigned by Lt. Poindexter to a .30 cal. machine gun position overlooking the beach near the boat channel that separated Wake and Wilkes Islands. Most of the sailors from the Navy boat crew did not know how to fire a machine gun. They were quickly taught the basics, how to load the guns and pull the trigger. The sailors also took turns standing watch on top of the nearby water tower, the highest point on the island.

Lt. Poindexter, who commanded the mobile reserve unit, also had several riflemen dug into the dunes just behind the beach in this area. Cox remained in this general area between the boat channel and Camp 1 throughout the battle. This was the area, along with the entire western end of Wake Island between the air strip and the channel, that Lt. Poindexter was charged with defending. Cox's only movement during the battle was to move his machine gun on a couple of occasions a short distance in an attempt to confuse the Japanese aircraft.

The .30 cal. machine gun at Cox's position was mounted on a tripod which was very low to the ground. Unlike the .50 cal. machine guns, which could be elevated and fired at airplanes, Cox's .30 cal. machine gun was intended to be fired horizontally across the beach in hopes of repelling enemy troops landing in an invasion attempt. The men firing the .30 cal. guns had to sit or kneel behind them, but could not get underneath them or point them upward. This was a severe limitation when trying to fire at incoming planes. During the air raids the men left their useless .30 cal. guns and ran for cover.

Initially there was little cover near Cox's position, only an embankment near the boat channel. Knowing the danger of their position, the men began digging into the sand embankment. They made a roof out of 1/4" sheet metal and then filled sand bags to put over the top and secure the sides. They believed the bunker would protect them from strafing attacks, but they knew that it would not stop a direct hit from a bomb. The bunker was open toward the lagoon on the inside of the island. The small enclosure was only large enough for two men, so Jim Cox and Andrew Fuller called it home. At no time during any of the Japanese assaults did Cox ever see any indication that any of the enemy were trying to land from the lagoon side.

Lt. Poindexter spent most of his daylight hours with Major Devereux at his command post near Camp 1. At night he would move down to the south beach between the air strip and Camp 1 with his

President Franklin D. Roosevelt declares war on the Empire of Japan. World War II becomes a global battle.

men. It was in this area that he spent the night.

The first day of the battle had been costly for all the different groups of people stationed on Wake Island. The Marine air wing had been devastated. The fragmentation bombs and machine gun bullets from the marauding planes had killed 23 officers and men of the VMF-211 unit and wounded eleven more. This meant that over 50% of the aviation personnel were casualties during the first ten minutes of the war on Wake Island.

It was clear that the major objective of the Japanese had been to reduce the Wake defenders' ability to wage war in the air. They had succeeded, reducing most of the fighter aircraft to heaps of rubble. The bombers had heavily damaged the civilian camp, as well as the Pan Am facility. Many of Pan Am's Chammoro employees had been killed or wounded. In all, there were 88 people, military, civilian, and Chammoro, killed in action at Wake Island on December 8, 1941.

Having successfully destroyed most of Wake's air force, the enemy began to target the artillery positions for destruction. Wake was in what the Japanese considered to be the "softening up" stage. Any position on the island that had the ability to fight back against the enemy would be targeted for elimination during a bombing attack. Anti-aircraft positions, 5" seacoast guns, storage facilities for fuel, explosives, and ammunition were sought out by the air raids.

After the noon raid Wiley Sloman and his artillery unit on Wilkes Island started digging in earnest. They spent the remainder of the day making their foxholes larger and adding sandbags. A running watch had been initiated, which called for each man to be on watch for an hour and then off for an hour. This meant the maximum duration of sleep was only one hour between watches. The men would soon tire of their new wartime schedule. The situation began to feel all too real, and the men began to accept the fact that they were at war with a shrewd enemy who was going to try to kill them.

Chapter 14
DAY 2—THE BOMBING OF THE HOSPITAL

The sunrise on December 9th shed light on a sad scene in the small wooden hospital. The entire building was crammed with cots upon which lay dead, dying, and wounded men. Dick Darden was fortunate compared to many. Mangled, barely breathing bodies lay all around him. Darden lay in the outer corner of the screened porch, just outside the small room that was used as an operating room. The porch area was covered by a tin roof. During the attack on the previous day the building had been hit by machine gun fire and the tin was perforated with bullet holes which allowed ribbons of sunlight to stream down onto the wounded men. All of Dick's bloody clothes had been removed, and he was stark naked with only a sheet covering his bandaged body.

Reveille came early on the morning of December 9. Before daybreak the defenders got the call to general quarters and before 5:00 a.m. the Marines were moving about in the pre-dawn darkness, digging in deeper for whatever the day would bring. The men assigned to the lookout positions were at their posts, and all telephone circuits were open to the command posts. All gun positions were manned and ready where men were available. The island still slumbered in the early morning darkness, but the defenders were positioned with their guns and ready for action.

The four remaining Wildcats warmed up at the airstrip, waiting for first light to begin the morning patrol. At 5:45 they took off, each searching a sector of the heavens over 60 miles long. The four planes scanned the skies around Wake, particularly to the south where the enemy was be expected to approach the island.

At 7:30 a.m., after nearly two hours in the air, the morning patrol landed and was refueled. No enemy planes had been sighted, so the island was notified to go from "Condition 1," a full alert, to "Condition 2," which kept only half the defenders at their guns.

Lt. John Kinney and Sgt. William Hamilton had worked most of the night cannibalizing the damaged aircraft for parts, and they were able to bring one additional Wildcat out of the junk pile and back into working order. It was decided to keep two planes in the air on patrol. This served two purposes: first, the patrol would be a lookout, warning the island by radio if approaching planes were sighted; and secondly, the Wildcats would engage the enemy planes, thus helping in a small way to stymy an attack. Though the bravery of the Marine pilots would be proven on many occasions, the overwhelming numerical odds in favor of the Japanese would prove to be too much for the tiny air force on Wake.

On the same day the Japanese struck Pearl Harbor they also hit over two dozen other targets throughout the Pacific theater. These included American installations in the Philippines, on Guam, and on Midway Island. Asian cities which immediately felt the wrath of the Emperor's forces were Shanghai, Singapore, Bangkok, and Hong Kong. Also hard hit by the rampaging Japanese forces were the islands of Tarawa and Makin in the Gilbert Islands, Java, Borneo, Sumatra, Timor, and Celebes. Mainland strikes also included Burma and Malaya.

Life for the Marines on Wake soon became a bone-tiring ordeal of working at hard labor all day and much, if not all, of the nights. Sleep became a rare and much-desired commodity. It came in short segments, an hour here, two hours there. Sleep came in sandy, gritty foxholes which were often infested with dozens of the pesky Wake Island rats.

On the morning of December 9 Walter Cook, along with H. L. Miller and Jack Hernandez, were in their weather station at 9:30 listening to a rebroadcast of President Roosevelt's Declaration of War speech over a short wave radio. They had posted the fourth member of their team, Floyd Dixon, outside as lookout.

The wounded men in the hospital were living through a tremendous amount of tension which complicated their physical maladies. Several were very near death and all were concerned primarily with their own individual battles to survive. They were unable to offer any assistance to the men defending the island and they gave little thought to the possibility of another bombing raid. The wounded men had no reason to expect another attack by the bombers, but they were about to get yet another taste of the Tokyo Express in action.

Holewinski and the Marines on the beach began construction of a super bunker in the huge bomb crater. Three civilians, Paul Gay, Bob Bryan, and Eric Lehtola, joined their ranks and had enough pull in the civilian camp to provide a dragline, which was used to scoop an even larger hole in the coral and even square up the walls of the hole from the hard, rocky material. The coral was so firm and rocklike that the walls inside the bunker did not have to be covered. The finished hole measured 10' deep and 20' square.

The two civilians were even able to procure several loads of wood and timbers. Large 8"x8" and 10"x10" timbers supported a wooden roof which was covered with sand, making a space large enough for all ten men at the position to lie down and sleep at the same time. The top of the bunker was at ground level, thus making it virtually invisible from the air. The bunker was a great improvement over the rat-infested holes that the men had been living in since Camp 1 and their tents had been bombed out.

A big plus in the bunker was the fact that the pesky rats could be excluded when the men carefully sealed the entrance with a blanket, and further protected themselves from the most determined of the varmits with rat traps near the opening. Most of the rats that persisted and made it into the bunker were caught in the traps. The rats were much less of a problem than they had been after the men began using the bunker.

Wake Island was of lesser importance in the Japanese war strategy than most of their other objectives immediately after Pearl Harbor. After all, only a small garrison of U. S. Marines was defending Wake, and the tiny speck was 2000 miles from the Japanese homeland. The warlords expected the Battle of Wake

Island to be little more than a mopping up operation which would take no more than a day to complete. But the fact that Wake represented a strategic refueling site for Allied planes had ranked it a high enough priority to be attacked on the first day of the war.

The Japanese invasion plans called for a "softening up" period on Wake during which the island would be attacked daily with aerial bombings. The Japanese bombers would leave at dawn from the Marshall Islands, some 600 miles to the southeast, and reach Wake about mid-day. The noon bombing became known as the "Tokyo Express," and the men on Wake grew to dread the daily carnage that resulted from it. The Japanese would vary the timing of the daily raids just enough to insure that the weary defenders would never get more than an hour or two of uninterrupted sleep.

Men tended to stay close to their bunkers or foxholes for protection from incoming planes. This was especially true as the morning progressed, since the Tokyo Express could be expected anytime after 11:00 a.m. When that hour arrived nearly all of the defenders would be in their position and ready for battle.

Civilians Bryan and Gay worked very hard and made a great contribution in getting the bunker finished, so the Marines promised them a rifle if one could be found. They were eager to join the Marines on the beach, but in the end this decision would cost them dearly.

Spider Webb regained consciousness just before noon in the hospital. He was still in critical condition as he began to look around the room and gather his thoughts. A wounded man was on a cot just next to him. On a table nearby sat a metal pitcher of water. One of Webb's first sensations was a desire for water. He had not taken any in nearly twenty-four hours and he had lost a great deal of his body fluids. This had made him terribly thirsty, but he could not move to reach for the pitcher and get a drink. He lay on his cot and stared at the pitcher.

Lt. Kliewer and Sgt. Hamilton were on patrol in their Wildcats late in the morning when they spotted a formation of twenty-seven 'Bettys,' the twin-engine Japanese bombers, heading straight for Wake. The Marines flew their Wildcats directly into the midst of the deadly group without hesitation, and remained in the furious fight until they were so near Wake that they were in danger of being shot down by their fellow Marines on the ground.

The aerial dogfight sped toward Wake at 160 knots. Lt. Kliewer and Sgt. Hamilton went after one of the bombers with their machine guns blaring. Despite intense return fire coming from the Jap machine gun in the bomber's back top turret, the two Wildcats held their position and pumped fire into the enemy plane. The bomber went into a flaming spin toward the ocean far below just as the Wildcats realized that Marine antiaircraft shells were exploding near them. The blazing bomber screamed back down to earth and exploded into the ocean.

The two Marines flew their Wildcats to a higher altitude to avoid the American anti-aircraft fire from below. Flak from the 3" guns was filling the skies around the Japanese bombers, exploding in black puffs and spraying hot shrapnel in all directions. At 11:45 Japanese planes were in full view over Wake Island, again intent upon wreaking havoc upon the defenders below. The Japanese pilots realized the deadly accuracy of the Marine anti-aircraft gunners like Charles Holmes, so in subsequent raids they executed their attacks from an altitude of 13,000 feet.

The planes were still able to drop their deadly bombs on the island even though they were over two miles above the anti-aircraft guns. The distance between the two adversaries was extended to the point that the accuracy of each was tested to the limit. The Japanese pilots expected the Marine gunners on the ground would have considerable difficulty hitting targets at such altitudes, and the bombadiers on the planes missed many of their targets, most of their bombs falling harmlessly on the island or into the lagoon. Some, however, found their marks with grim consequences.

This attack started out considerably different from the day before when the planes caught the defenders by surprise as they came in low over the island on their strafing and bombing runs. This time lookouts spotted the incoming planes and the island was notified on the telephone system. The three-shot warning signal was heard at numerous places on the three islands.

The vicious bombing attack began just minutes before noon on December 9. The twenty-six remaining Jap planes rained 500 pound bombs on Wake Island. It quickly became apparent that one of the day's targets was Peacock Point, one of the strongest defensive positions on the island, and the one which guarded the southern approach to Wake Island. Bombs fell very near the 3" gun position at Battery E and the 5" guns at Battery A. Both positions sustained damage.

One formation of bombers had its sights on Camp 1, the civilian complex on the north side of the island. Glenn Tripp was standing lookout duty on the top of the water tower and was one of the first to see the bombers coming toward the island. Dick Mayhew, another yeoman, was on the tower with Tripp.

The planes came out of the clouds and were on top of the civilians before they knew it. Tripp and Mayhew instantly sprang to the siren and began to crank wildly in order to warn the island, and as hell broke loose the events began to happen in microseconds, or so it seemed to Tripp. Everything seemed to be happening at once. The civilian buildings all around the water tower, barracks, machine shops, and storage buildings seemed to be exploding and burning. By this time the planes had descended to an altitude low enough to strafe the area around the precarious lookout post atop the water tower.

The machine guns of the attacking planes began to tear into the island. Tripp and Mayhew ran around to the opposite side of the water tank each time a plane came at them, hoping to avoid the deadly spray of machine gun bullets. Then they would sprint back to the other side as the plane passed just over their heads hoping to avoid being machine gunned by the tail gunner.

Walter Cook was in the weather station when he heard a lookout shout, "Here they come!" Everyone in the station scrambled through the back door and out toward the bomb shelter. As Cook looked back over his shoulder a twin-engine bomber was screaming directly toward him. Just as he dove into the shelter and one of his fellow weathermen slammed the sandbagged doorway, the spray of machinegun bullets raked over the sand-covered roof.

Three 100 pound bombs hit within eight feet of the weather station. All the sides were blown in and the building was demolished. Every bunk was riddled with bullet holes, as were the weathermen's shoes and clothing, and the floor of the building. The Japanese had apparently seen the weather station on their reconnaissance photos and targeted the building during this raid. They had successfully shut it down.

The enemy seemed to be hitting every target that they did not consider essential for their own later use. They avoided hitting the water tower, power plant, warehouses, and the dredges used for clearing the coral heads out of the PBY landing area in the lagoon.

Even though the Japanese pilots kept their planes at a high

altitude in hopes of avoiding the antiaircraft fire, their strategy backfired. Since the 3" anti-aircraft guns were much more effective when their targets were not coming in low and fast, Marines like Charles Holmes had their first chance to use their range-finding equipment on the tight enemy formations. The Leathernecks zeroed in on the Japanese raiders, shooting one down and causing four others to head for home trailing smoke.

Most of the men lying in the hospital were unable to move due to the severity of their wounds. Even if they did, where would they go? As the bombs began to fall, the island throbbed under the blasts. Although this time the island did have a warning that planes were approaching, and the lookout fired three shots and sounded the siren to announce the raid, the men in the hospital were caught by surprise and were defenseless.

Several of the Japanese bombers came in low enough to strafe the island on their first run. Dick looked up at the tin roof above him and realized that he had no protection from the incoming bullets. Only a sheet covered his naked body, so he pulled it over his face in token resistance to the planes. A Jap plane flew directly over the hospital with machine guns roaring. As Dick lay inside the building below it sounded as if a handful of rocks had been thrown onto the tin roof.

Looking through the sheet Dick noticed that light suddenly came into the small room. He slowly pulled the sheet back to see the source of the light rays. The tin roof had, in an instant, been perforated by the spray of bullets and now bright rays of sunlight shown through, bringing eerie columns of illumination down onto the wounded men.

Spider Webb again stared at the pitcher of cool water from his cot in an adjacent room of the hospital. He thought about how badly he wanted to enjoy its contents, but he was still unable to move. As the enemy plane passed just above the building and sprayed it with machine gun fire, one of the bullets pierced the metal pitcher cleanly. Webb watched as water streamed out of the hole and onto the floor. Then he glanced at the patient on the cot beside him. He had been hit by another bullet and died instantly.

Tom Kennedy was looking at the tin ceiling when machine gun bullets riddled through it just above him. Cots all around him started jumping up and down as the slugs pierced bed and bodies. A piece of sheet metal roofing came down on top of Kennedy, who shielded himself with his good arm causing the heavy metal to fall onto Chick Lanning who lay on the next cot. Both Lanning and Kennedy lived through the attack and could tell that the building was burning. Just then Commander Keene shouted that the building was on fire and that everyone should get out. Keene helped Kennedy to his feet and out of the building.

The planes came back toward the rickety hospital, this time to drop the bombs that clung to their bellies. The enemy had pinpointed the defenseless building for obliteration. Suddenly bombs began blasting around Dick as if hell itself had opened its doors. Three more powerful bombs blasted craters in the earth within twenty feet of the building. Then the wooden shanty took two direct hits. The first blast inside the hospital was on the opposite side of the building, rocking everything inside violently. The second explosion was just five cots away from Dick Darden.

The blast blew bodies apart and collapsed the remains of the roof and walls onto the men. Across the aisle from Darden lay Boatswains Mate Kirby Ludwig. He and Dick were momentarily unconscious from the concussion of the blast. Miraculously Dick had

not even been scratched by the flying shrapnel and timbers, but he awoke to hear a crackling sound which was unmistakable. The building was on fire and the men were pinned under the splintered wooden beams. Peering through the smoke, he could see that Ludwig was still alive.

"Boats, are you still there?" Dick shouted. "Yes," was the reply. "This place is on fire! We've got to get out of here or we're going to burn to death. Are you coming?" Dick asked. "I can't move," Ludwig said in a pleading tone. "It's got me pinned down, and I can't move." He had been wounded during the first raid in both legs, having both knees blown out. Both of his legs were tightly splinted straight, and he could move neither. "Well, I'm the same way," Dick responded as he tried in vain to push the wooden beams off.

Once again death appeared imminent for Dick Darden. The building was burning down around the men who lay pinned beneath the splintered ceiling rafters and sheet metal. They frantically attempted to claw their way out from under the rubble. The men had only bedsheets over their naked bodies for protection as the bombing raid continued.

Just as the helpless men were about to be engulfed in flames, a civilian worker named Owen G. Thomas appeared. He was straining to lift the burning debris, trying to find any men who might have lived through the blast. Thomas was over sixty years old and could have joined many of his fellow civilians who were hiding in the relatively safe underbrush. Instead he chose to help the frantic men who were about to die in the hellish inferno. At great risk to himself, Thomas began pushing aside pieces of the fiery rubble.

"Is anybody in there?" he yelled. "Yes, please help us!" Dick screamed in reply. Thomas saved the men by forcing his way into the burning building, much of which had already fallen in, and pulling off the timbers that were pinning the two wounded men down. Dick managed to pull himself upright and got to his feet, wrapping a sheet around his naked body.

Dick began to limp heavily as he dragged his mangled leg behind him and made his way out of the burning timbers. With each step he could feel the cotton stitches in his tearing, sending hot rays through his leg. The sutures were less than a day old, and he knew that the burning and stinging deep inside the leg meant they were being pulled out. But, he thought, it would be better to make it out of here a cripple than stay inside and burn to death.

Both of Ludwig's wounded legs were braced stiff. Somehow he managed to get on his feet and began walking like a robot behind Dick. The two men made their way out of the burning building as quickly as they could, each step causing the stitches to tear and the fiery pain to race through his body.

Both of the sheet-shrouded men reached the safety of a recreation field adjacent to the hospital. As they lay on the ground and began to assess the damage to their wounds, Dick could not help but think that they must have looked like two crippled Hindu's. The stunned men lay on the field and watched the building burn down. Several men did not come out alive.

Dr. Kahn and Dr. Shank were also trying to save the wounded men inside the hospital who had survived the blast. In addition to the men, they also wanted to save the precious medical supplies that were inside the burning building. They tried to enter the door on one side of the building but were forced back by the intense heat. They ran around to the other side and began to help pull the men out.

A pickup truck had been parked just outside the hospital when the attack occurred. As Thomas had helped Dick out of the hospital, the two had passed the truck and noticed that the blast had blown the truck's door open. A man who had been inside the hospital had been blown out, striking the open truck door while he was still airborne.

Dick hoped that he had died instantly from the blast in the hospital, for if not, the man had died a ghastly death. When his body had been blown through the air from the building, he had struck the door and it had impaled him. Part of the truck door had entered his chest and was sticking out through his back. The dead body still hung on the open door.

One of the men who had been in the hospital with Dick was George Wolney. He was the member of the boat crew who had bounded out of the panel truck on the airstrip just behind Dick during the first air raid. He had survived being hit several times by .50 cal. machine gun fire and had been brought from the airstrip to the makeshift hospital. However, on this second day of the war Wolney was not as lucky. He died when the burning hospital building caved in on top of him.

Spider Webb was in one of the rooms which had not completely fallen in. Even though he received no additional injuries, he was unable to move and could tell that the building was on fire. Webb lay helpless as the fire came closer. Then two men came in and placed him on a stretcher. They took him outside and pushed him underneath a truck for safety as smoke billowed out of the remains of the hospital. He was left there for about three hours while men fought the fire and removed the few remaining survivors.

The Japanese bomber pilots were well disciplined, flying in tight "V" bombing formations over the island. This might have been deemed a virtue by their squadron leader, but was actually a blessing for the Wake defenders. This lack of originality on the part of the flyers gave the anti-aircraft guns better targets, and the Marines took advantage of the opportunity. Five bombers trailed smoke as they left Wake. One was seen disintegrating in the air and falling into the sea. The fate of the others was not known. Whether the others were able to successfully negotiate the 600 mile flight over the ocean back to Roi is not known.

Major Putnam later said that, while the first raid was "well conceived and skillfully executed," those which followed were exceedingly well disciplined and therefore predictable. The time and method of attack required little guesswork, so the Wake defenders were prepared to fire their limited resources toward the enemy with great efficiency. Putnam indicated that the enemy "never, after the first day, got through unopposed."

The two doctors, Dr. Kahn and Dr. Shank, continued to work diligently on the wounded men. They now had no hospital, so Commander Cunningham ordered that two of the four concrete ammunition magazines at the end of the runway be used as hospitals. Dr. Shank would operate one for the civilians, and Lt. Kahn would use the other to care for the military wounded. These were heavily fortified dome-shaped concrete buildings, partially buried underground and made of steel-reinforced concrete. The four magazines had been built in a straight line perpendicular to the end of the runway along the eastern shore of Wake Island.

ウェーキ島を占領

開戦と共に、わが航空部隊が猛爆のウェーキ島めざして二十二日夜半、精鋭陸戦隊は、荒れ狂ふ南海の怒濤を冒して果敢な敵前上陸を敢行し翌日これを占領、その名も大鳥島と改称す。

An attacking Japanese plane takes this photograph during a bombing run on the civilian camp (Camp 2) on the north shore of Wake Island.

The first bunker, located on the north end of the row and called bunker #10, was converted into a Navy/civilian hospital and was operated by Dr. Shank. Dr. Kahn, along with Dick and about a dozen other wounded men, were moved into the other hospital magazine at the south end, which was known as the Marine hospital. It was located nearest to Peacock Point. Dick and the other wounded men were placed on cots inside the magazine, which would be their home for the next sixteen days, the entire duration of the battle for Wake Island.

The two bunkers in the center would later be used for military purposes. One would become a command post for Major Devereux (bunker #12), and the other would be a communications center (bunker #11). Captain Wilson began moving his radio equipment into the communications igloo right away. With Major Bayler's help he set up the radio, the only one still in operation on the island.

Commander Cunningham ordered that the ammunition in bunkers #10 and #13, the end "igloos," be stored in open but camouflaged positions so that the concrete and steel domes could be safely used as hospitals. Each of these "underground wards" allowed space for 21 cots to be tightly squeezed together. These magazines had a base measurement of 20' x 40' with a maximum height of 15' in the center of the domed roof.

The doctors knew that Dick's leg wound was severe. They knew that it would lose a good bit of fluid and much of the tissue that had been damaged too severely to heal. The shrapnel that had opened up Dick's leg had been red hot, so it had burned much of the tissue as it tore through the muscle. This tissue would have to come out of the wound, so the doctors had placed a drainage tube in the the leg when they closed the wound. The tube protruded through the bandages that bound the leg tightly together. In the days that followed the leg began to pass off liquids and rotten flesh which produced an awful odor.

There was no medication for the men to use on their wounds, so Dr. Kahn gave Dick several chlorine tablets of the type used to purify the island's water supply. These were to be melted down in water and then poured over the dressing several times a day. Dick kept the gauze wet with the chlorine solution at all times, hoping to keep out the gangrene and other disease germs that he knew could bring a deadly infection.

Spider Webb was on the cot beside Dick in the bunker hospital. The doctors still did not know if he would live or die. All they could do was change his bandages and give him some red pills for pain. The pills were a strong narcotic and they gave Webb a euphoric feeling, as if he was floating in air. For over a week he was in a semi-conscious state, floating about on the drugs and feeling little pain. He had no idea what was going on around him, and he would only remember the "lovely" feeling he got from the little red pills.

Major Devereux moved into another of the magazines and transformed it into his command post. The only radio left on the island was also moved into this bunker. It was felt that these concrete igloos were the most bomb proof buildings on the island. Nothing short of a direct hit would destroy them. When completed, bulldozers had virtually covered the entire building with sand, leaving only a ventilation shaft protruding through the roof and sand above.

The command post and all of the gun positions were wired together with a telephone system. This system operated like a party line, with calls from any location being amplified over speakers at all of the locations. Even messages from the fighter planes far offshore came over the speaker. The hospital had one of these speakers, so Dick and the other wounded men could listen to all communications sent back and forth on the island. In addition, Spider Webb's flying buddies

would come into the hospital each night and fill him in on the day's activities. Dick heard a firsthand blow-by-blow account of the battle in the sky over Wake Island.

Major Devereux realized the Japanese had not only bombed the island this day, but they had also photographed Wake so they could unleash their fury on the remaining military targets during the next air raid. In a stroke of brilliance, Devereux outfoxed the enemy by staying one step ahead of them. He ordered that the 3" anti-aircraft guns be moved and dummy guns be built in their places. The guns weighed several tons, and their movement presented the Marines with a grueling task.

While they would work in the tropical heat all day digging into the coral atoll and preparing for battle, they would then face a sleepless night at heavy labor moving the guns, sometimes less than 100 yards down the beach, and sometimes several hundred yards across the island. The anti-aircraft guns had to be jacked up off the ground, have wheels placed underneath them, and then lowered onto the wheels. They were pulled about by trucks. When the new locations were reached, the guns were jacked up, the wheels removed, and the guns then lowered meticulously into their new position.

Then there was more work for the weary Marines. The guns had to be camouflaged, sand bags had to be filled to protect the sites, and tons of ammunition had to be hauled to the new location. Sandbags were in short supply, so they could not be left at the old location. Thousands of pounds of sand had to be loaded by hand onto the trucks and taken to the new position, there to be offloaded and positioned around the 3" gun. Sleep became a rare commodity, stolen at any point during the long days and nights when the opportunity presented itself. Often the men would finish a long night of moving the guns just in time to go to battle stations at 5:00 a.m.

On December 9th, Wake Island time, Admiral Kimmel and Vice Admiral William Pye were at Pearl Harbor still assessing the destruction from the Japanese attack. Admiral Kimmel was Commander of the Pacific Fleet (CINCPAC), and Vice Admiral Pye, who had been in command of the battleship CALIFORNIA until it was sunk at Pearl Harbor, was his assistant. Admiral Kimmel was sent a new war plan from Washington which changed the mission of the Pacific Fleet. The new objective was defensive, meant to keep the Japanese out of the western hemisphere. Protection was to be given to America's line of defensive island outposts, which included Hawaii along with Wake, Johnston, and Palmyra Islands.

All of the islands needed reinforcements, but few could be offered by the American forces at Pearl Harbor. American strategists in Washington and Pearl Harbor felt strongly that another confrontation with the Japanese fleet, whose whereabouts was still unknown, could be a catastrophe to American forces in the Pacific. This was to be avoided at all costs until our forces were reinforced and up to the task.

A new plan, certainly more conservative and posing less danger to our Pacific forces, was about to be devised by Admiral Kimmel. A naval force would be formed to relieve Wake Island. Task Force 14 would be centered around the aircraft carrier SARATOGA, accompanied by three cruisers, along with an oiler, a transport, and several destroyers.

On December 9 the Japanese were already in action. Admiral Kajioka's invasion force steamed out of the Japanese base on Roi-Namur in the Marshall Islands bound for Wake Island. The Japanese strategy was to send 450 men ashore on the south side of the island. They had correctly surmised that the northern coast of the island would have heavier seas and therefore be less suitable for the amphibious landing. A force of 300 would go ashore on Wake Island and secure the air field. The remaining 150 would attack Wilkes Island. Should more men be needed, the crews of the two destroyers would be ordered to go ashore as infantrymen.

Walter Cook's weather station had been completely destroyed. Only the dugout shelter behind it remained. Pieces of charts, books, and reports were everywhere in the area of the splintered building. The weathermen decided to move their shelter to a new location in case the site was bombed again. Before they moved they were ordered to leave nothing of value in the remains of their station, so they burned the code books and outgoing weather reports. They would have little use for them now and wanted to make sure that they could not fall into enemy hands.

The Army radio personnel were moving their station into the command post where Commander Cunningham had his office, so the weathermen decided to put their dugout in a grove of ironwood trees in the same general area. This would allow them to use the radio to communicate with Pearl Harbor if need be without traveling great distances.

Using a truck that had not been hit during the raid, Cook and company collected usable lumber and supplies from the destroyed building and moved it to a new location deep in the underbrush, about 100 yards off the road. Food, especially that in tin cans, was stashed in the new dugout and under brush and small trees in the area. Tin cans

of food were especially valued since that was the only way they could be sure to have food that was not rancid for an extended period of time. Once opened even the tin cans of food had to be eaten completely due to the ants which would soon take over any leftover morsels.

Immediately they began digging the new shelter with their shovels. As before, they dug a large hole, erected a framework of timbers, and covered the frame with a plywood roof which was covered with a thick layer of sand. The men stored a load of supplies under cover and then returned the truck for more. So that enemy planes would not be alerted that there had been movement into the new site, they swept the truck's tracks away in the sand.

The new shelter was finished soon after dark. The men brought their gear in and lay down for the night. The shelter was well concealed, with the entrance below ground level for blast protection. The men felt that only a direct or very close hit would finish them off.

At airfields on Kwajalein the Japanese pilots boasted of their victories over Wake. With broad smiles they described the heroic deeds they had provided for their Emperor. Even while they talked their planes were being readied for another visit to the beleaguered outpost. Bombs were fixed under their wings and belts of machine gun shells were loaded into the planes. The pilots were soon be off again for Wake Island.

Holmes Collection

This recent photo shows the entrance to the concrete igloo hospital bunker, now covered vegetation growing in the sand.

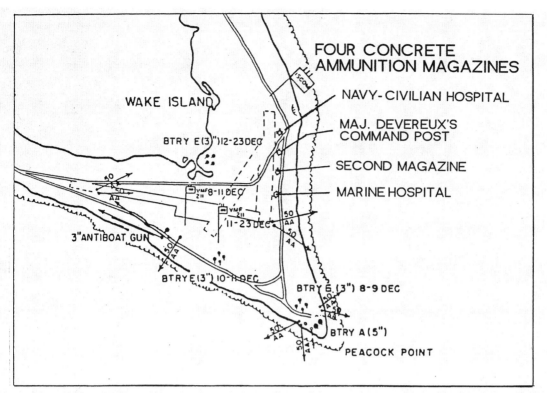

Position of the four concrete ammunition magazines near the end of the runway.

Smiling Japanese pilots on Kwajalein describe successful bombing runs over Wake Island. The caption reads, "This is the way I knocked him down." A just returned fly-boy tells his comrades-in-arms how he did it.

Chapter 15
DAY THREE – THE DEFENSE DIGS IN

The weary men on Wake Island began to settle into a wartime way of life, wrought with sleeplessness, daily bombings, and an awareness that the bombers could bring fire and death to the atoll at any time. The bombers continued to take off from their bases in the Marshall Islands over 600 miles away at daybreak, and would arrive for the daily bombing run on Wake at about noon.

The antiaircraft gunners on Wake developed a pretty good sense for anticipating the arrival of the bombers on their daily bombing raid to the island. However, the lack of radar on the ground created a situation in which they had very little time to respond to the incoming planes. Charles Holmes and his buddies on the 3" guns were able to communicate by radio with the Wildcats on patrol, which would often be able to alert them that enemy aircraft were approaching.

Occasionally the Marine pilots could even tell the gunners the altitude of the Japanese planes, thus giving them a small amount of preparation time which proved to be quite effective. The gunners could set the fuses on their 3" antiaircraft shells and lob the deadly explosives right into the laps of the incoming pilots.

The majority of the civilian labor force on the island had nothing to do but wait and hope that the next plane did not drop high explosives in their area. They hid themselves in the brush and throughout the island. There was an area called the "aggregate pile" where a large mound of coral chunks had been collected. These were to be crushed into the fine coral gravel used to construct the roads. For some reason a wood-reinforced tunnel had been built into the center of the aggregate pile and it looked very much like a mine shaft.

It was reported that a group of civilians were holed up in the tunnel in the aggregate pile, completely demoralized and afraid to come out at any time. It was said that they did not even come out to relieve themselves and that they remained in the tunnel for the duration of the battle. Some of the civilians, however, reacted in an entirely different manner. An estimated ten percent of the civilians actively contributed to the defense of the island.

Some of the civilians even tried to enlist with Major Bayler, who was a qualified recruiter. It was reported that over 180 men contacted the Major and tried to join up. However, there were no weapons for these men, and no time to train them, so none were inducted. They continued to assist in the defense nonetheless. They helped to dig bunkers with their equipment, they helped to carry ammunition to the gun positions, and they helped to serve the food. The intentions of these courageous men were good, but the Marines knew how precarious their plight would be if they were caught unarmed in an all out battle.

About mid-morning Walter Cook left the weathermen's dugout to report the condition of the weather station to Commander Cunningham in the command post. The "Tokyo Express" was a bit early on December 10, with twenty-six bombers appearing in the sky above the island at 10:45 in the morning. Cook was caught offguard in the command post, but it turned out to be a safe place to ride out the bombing raid.

During the bombing Cook watched as Commander Cunningham twice ventured outside the blast door of the bunker to count the number and types of enemy planes that were involved in the raid. From his vantage point on Peale he could see that the planes had picked the Peacock Point area on Wake and the storage buildings on Wilkes as their targets. The Japs already realized the accuracy of the anti-aircraft battery at Peacock Point, where Charles Holmes and his buddies had gotten a clear shot at them the previous day. They hit Peacock hard, trying to destroy the 3" guns that were a thorn in their side.

Capt. Henry Elrod was on patrol over Wake that morning and intercepted the formation of bombers before it reached its target. Elrod shot down two of the bombers before they could release their of bombs, but the rest made it through, and it was obvious that they had, indeed, targeted the gun emplacements for destruction. The bombers flew directly over a number of the dummy wooden guns, bombing and destroying several of them. Devereux's decision to move the guns had paid off. If the real 3" guns had been in the same positions as the day before, several would have sustained direct hits, many men would have been killed, and the island would have lost much of its defensive punch.

The bombers hit Wilkes Island harder than the previous two days, and this time they were looking for specific targets. One juicy target for the enemy pilots was a building used by the civilian contractors on Wilkes. The contractors had been busy cutting a new channel through Wilkes to provide a better entrance for ships to the lagoon. It was cut almost completely through the island, with only a narrow neck of land left on the ocean side. There was just enough of a land bridge left to provide a roadway connecting the two parts of the island.

The only way to cut the channel through the hard coral island was to blast it with dynamite. Dan Teters' men had stored 3000 cases of explosives in their building. The building had been sunk into the ground and had only a few feet above ground level. While it was somewhat protected, its construction might have tipped the enemy pilots that something was being protected inside.

First, the attacking planes raked Wilkes Island with machine gun fire. Then they went after the two 5" gun positions near Kuku Point. Wiley Sloman's gun sustained considerable damage. One of the scopes used for aiming the gun was damaged, and some of the gun's stored ammunition exploded.

Then several of the bombers attacking Wilkes Island went after the contractor's building, scoring a direct hit on the cache of dynamite—all 125 tons of it. With a massive roar, all of it detonated in one spectacular explosion. The entire island shook, and Wilkes was devastated. Since the building was situated down in the ground, most of the concussion blew upward. Thanks to this, Wiley Sloman, who was at his position about 200 yards away, was not killed. The blast was so powerful, however, that everyone in the area was severely shaken. It felt as if a huge hand had taken Sloman, picked him up, and given him a violent shaking.

When the dynamite exploded it blew all of the leaves off the trees throughout Wilkes Island. Many of the trees were burned and the vegetation virtually disappeared from the sandy islet. Several gun positions were damaged, but somehow only one Marine was killed. The vegetation on the island, including trees, shrubs, and vines, was almost completely denuded by the blast. One of the enemy planes also bombed the unmanned 3" gun position near Sloman's 5" gun. The 3" anti-aircraft shells stored with the gun began to explode one by one.

Everyone in the hospital could hear and feel a stick of bombs as they began to shake the island. First at a distance the men heard the CRUNCH, CRUNCH, CRUNCH of the bombs, each one nearer than the last. Men peered at the concrete ceiling of the bunker, never knowing if the line of bombs would cross over the

hospital and drop 500 pounds of terror in their laps. On this day the throbs of the blasts came ever nearer, each bomb shaking the building with increasing violence as the line came closer. The men had only their bedsheets for protection.

In the horrifying seconds of the last few blasts Dick dove from his cot onto the concrete floor of the bunker, responding to the natural reaction to seek cover when, in fact, the only additional cover this move afforded him was the canvas of his hospital cot. The final bomb in the stick exploded barely fifteen feet short of the bunker. The bomb's blast sent debris and bits of coral flying high in the air. As they rained down on the roof of the hospital, it sounded to the men inside as if a hail storm was pounding the roof.

Spider Webb lay on the cot next to Dick and he remained there even through the final explosion, knowing the futility of

Grumman

Wake's only aerial defense: The stubby, one-seat Grumman F4F-3 fighter. The Wildcats had one 1200 horsepower Pratt and Whitney engine making them capable of speeds up to 300 miles per hour.

scrambling for cover. "What in hell are you doing on the floor Darden,?" he questioned as he looked down at Dick. The men looked at each other with a petrified stare, still not entirely sure they had been spared from the carnage of a direct hit.

During this raid the civilians had suffered the heaviest loss of life, with over fifty of their ranks slain by the bombing. Many had seen friends slaughtered and large numbers of the maddened workers began to cry for revenge. Again Major Bayler regrettably had to turn down several of them when they requested to join the Marines. But, this would not deter the civilians from making their contribution. Many fought with the Marines and, at great risk, did what they could to support the defense effort.

After the bombers had finished their grisly work and disappeared into the sky toward the Marshalls, the men on Wake began the daily chores of attending to the dead and wounded, making necessary repairs to gun emplacements and equipment that had been damaged, and moving the guns to new locations. Marines knew that a few well-placed bombs could wipe out their entire stockpile of food, so they hid food, ammunition, tools, water, and other supplies throughout the island, mostly in the sand under scrubby undergrowth.

Later in the day Wiley Sloman was working to repair the damage to his position, adding even more sandbags to his foxhole. No one would go in the direction of the unmanned 3" gun because it was still burning and the ammunition was still exploding hours after the air raid. Suddenly one of the shells exploded and several fragment of shrapnel whistled close to Sloman's ear. The 3" shells continued to go off for the rest of the day and into the night. Luckily, in this game of Russian roulette, no Marines were wounded.

The wounded men in the hospital knew that the Tokyo Express would deliver its destruction around noon each day, but they were powerless to do anything for their own defense. They could only lie and listen. The men could hear the drone of the squadron of bombers as they approached, getting louder and louder. The bunkers were well concealed under the sand and coral, but many times the earth shook violently as the bombs hit near the hospital.

Even though the timing of the bombing strikes was predictable, the men could not relax when they were over. At night the Japanese would sometimes send a lone flying boat, similar to our PBY's, to Wake with a 1000 pound bomb under each wing. The bombadiers were not as accurate at night and usually there was relatively little damage from these raids, but they served the purpose of keeping the men on alert and denying the weary men the sleep they needed so badly. When the 1000 pound bombs fell to earth the entire atoll would shake. The blasts would produce craters large enough to drive two-ton trucks down into and out of sight.

Major Devereux did a fine job of outwitting the Jap raiders. He was fully intent upon stopping them no matter what ploy they might throw at him. He had the 50' lighter moored in a position so that it would block the channel between Wilkes and Wake Islands.

National Archives

The graveyard of F4F-3 Wildcats on Wake after the Japanese attack is used for spare parts. The caption reads, "Wake is Humbled."

It was loaded with heavy concrete so that would stop a good sized boat which might try to shoot the channel and land a ground force on the inside of the island. In addition to that he had an explosive charge wired inside the boat so that it could be sunk on a moments notice, adding to his ability to block the channel.

Majors Devereux and Potter were also concerned that the enemy might try to land planes on the airstrip, perhaps even gliding in under the cover of darkness, to plant part of an invasion force at a vital spot within the island's defenses. To avert this they parked pieces of heavy equipment on the runway at night that would wreck any such landing attempt. After all, the Japanese had carefully bombed only the perimeters of the airstrip, destroying the American planes, fuel, and support services, but preserving the runway for their own later use.

If the Japanese were somehow able to overrun the island, Major Devereux planned to deny them any use of the airstrip. He had explosive charges planted every 200 feet along the landing strip and wired them together so that if the enemy were to take the island he could issue one final defiant order to destroy the air field.

At the airstrip men were busy at work trying to get another plane ready to fly by cannibalizing damaged planes for spare parts. Four Wildcats were operational, and hopes were high for getting another in the air before the Tokyo Express arrived the next day. Two of the fighters were aloft at all times during daylight hours, with the other two on the landing strip at the ready.

At night Jim Cox and his buddies would leave their dugout bunker and go to the airstrip, just a few hundred yards away, and help the makeshift crew of mechanics repair the bruised and battered Wildcats. Many of the skilled mechanics had been killed or wounded in the first bombing raid, but the remaining men worked miracles in making the small one-seat fighters air worthy again. When a part was needed to repair one of the planes, the men would search through the graveyard of mangled wrecks and scavenge a part that appeared to work. If there were enough men pulling that duty, Cox and his friends would load machine gun belts for the airmen.

Rear Admiral Sadamichi Kajioka's fleet was about 100 miles south of Wake, steaming toward the atoll in anticipation of an invasion and takeover of the island on the following day. His task force consisted of his flagship cruiser YUBARI, cruisers TATSUTA, and TENRYU, along with destroyers MUTSUKI, KISARAGI, OITE, HAYATE, MOCHIZUKI, and YAYOI. The landing force of 450 men would be put ashore in what the Japanese thought would be a one-day operation to bring Wake Island into their empire.

Most of these assault troops were aboard the transports KONGO MARU and KONRYU MARU, along with two converted destroyers, APD32 and APD33. Two Japanese submarines prowled about 75 miles ahead of the main force to look out for U. S. Navy ships. They were also on the lookout for torpedo boats, for which they seemed to have the utmost respect. The reconnaissance ships apparently failed to spot the American submarine TRITON, which fired four torpedoes at an enemy ship, probably one of the Japanese task force. All four missed. The invasion force planned to be just off Wake's beaches several hours before daybreak on December 11.

The Japanese infantry troops were armed with the Arisaka 98 bolt action rifle. The officers carried Samurai swords, often family heirlooms that were hundreds of years old. A variety of light ordnance was thought to be carried by the troops, including knee mortars and small cannons. Some of the assault troops also carried light machine guns.

In Pearl Harbor the transport TANGIER began loading ammunition for the voyage to relieve the defenders on Wake Island. Marines were ordered to prepare for immediate embarkation on the TANGIER as soon as the task force was complete. However, the backbone of the task force being formed was the SARATOGA, and the big carrier was still enroute to Pearl from San Diego. "SARA" had to deviate from the quickest route in order to avoid Japanese submarines that were reported to be prowling the area. This diversion would delay her arrival at Pearl Harbor until December 14.

Admiral Kimmel, at Pearl Harbor, was not aware of the imminent invasion planned by the Japanese for Wake Island. He was formulating his own plan for the reinforcement of Wake on December 10 (Wake time), but he had fewer than 200 Marines that he could space for a relief expedition to Wake.

Admiral Kimmel established Task Force 14 for the relief of Wake Island. This force would consist of the carrier SARATOGA, which was heading toward Pearl Harbor from San Diego, heavy cruisers ASTORIA, MINNEAPOLIS, and SAN FRANCISCO, along with nine destroyers. This task force was commanded by Rear Adm. Frank Jack Fletcher, skipper of the SAN FRANCISCO.

Rear Adm. Aubrey W. Fitch, skipper of the SARATOGA, had on his flight deck eighteen FA2 Brewster Buffalo fighters intended to reinforce the squadron of F4F-3's already on Wake. Though old and relatively sluggish, these fighter planes would be a welcome addition to Major Putnam's air unit on Wake.

The cruiser SAN FRANCISCO carried 200 Marines who were itching to help their fellow Leathernecks on Wake. The troops involved in the relief effort for Wake Island were Marines of the Third and Fourth Defense Battalions, along with the remainder of the men from the First Defense Battalion. Some of these men had just arrived at Pearl Harbor on December 1 after being shipped in from Guantanamo Bay in Cuba. The SAN FRANCISCO had quietly passed through the Panama Canal and across the Pacific to Hawaii.

Some of the Marines were aboard the TANGIER, which was actually a seaplane tender that was being used as a troop transport. On the deck of the TANGIER was the radar equipment which was so critically needed by the defenders of Wake Island.

The task force would also include the oiler NECHES. The NECHES, while being entirely necessary to the success of the mission, was fully loaded and was the slowest ship in the Task Force. It was the weak link in the chain, and might ultimately prove to be the undoing of the mission. The task force could move no faster than the NECHES, which at full power could muster only ten knots.

While Task Force 14 was sent on the relief mission to Wake, an attempt was made to divert the attention of the Japanese away from Wake Island. Task Force 11, which included the aircraft carrier LEXINGTON, was ordered to strike at enemy facilities at Jaluit in the Marshall Islands some 800 miles south of Wake. Task Force 11 was commanded by Rear Adm. Wilson Brown and included, in addition to the LEXINGTON, the cruisers CHICAGO, INDIANAPOLIS, and PORTLAND, along with several destroyers and the oiler NEOSHO.

Another formidable naval force, Task Force 8, commanded by Vice Admiral William "Bull" Halsey and including the carrier ENTERPRISE, would be in a area west of Johnston Island. This force would have several cruisers which would be escorted by destroyers. Task Force 8 would guard the Hawaiian Islands from an approach by enemy ships while supporting the relief effort. The stage was set for the relief of Wake Island.

Early the next morning, December 11, 1941, the Japanese troops planned to demonstrate their loyalty to the Emperor by storming the beaches of Wake Island. So confident were the Emperor's warriors of victory that they had already planned to rename Wake Island Otori Shima, which means "Island of the Birds."

Japanese Admiral Inouye was assigned the duty of capturing several islands for the Emperor's forces in the Pacific. He was to secure Wake Island and Guam from the United States, and Tarawa and Makin Islands from the British. Inouye sprang into action immediately upon hearing of the victorious Japanese raid on Pearl Harbor. On December 10 his forces landed successfully on Guam, Makin, and Tarawa, taking all three with only light resistance. Only Wake remained, and the Japanese rulers in Tokyo made their instructions to Inouye clear. He was to take Wake Island on December 11 without delay.

Now that the hostilities had begun on Wake Island, Commander Cunningham began to realize just how shorthanded his defensive forces really were. He felt that he needed soldiers more than administrative assistants, so he reassigned Glenn Tripp to a battle position. Tripp was taken by the motor launch to join the crew of one of the 5" guns on Wilkes Island. Tripp was placed under Capt. Wesley Platt's command, and the gun captain at this position was Wally Tipton. He was immediately put to work handling ammunition for the 5" gun.

Corporal Holewinski was looking for any protection that the island might afford him near his machine gun position on the south beach. The reef protruded out of the water and was very near the shoreline in front of Holewinski's gun. He found that he could walk out to the reef and actually crawl up underneath parts of it, remaining dry but enjoying its protection. He was glad to have an assignment near the rocky coral covering since it offered some degree of protection and did not seem to be a target of the bombers. Holewinski slept on the exposed reef during the first days of the war. Each of the defenders on the beach carried a bolt-action Springfield rifle. During one of the first nights of the battle, Holewinski put his rifle over his shoulder and left the beach to get supplies. Camp 1 had not yet been bombed extensively and burned, so he headed down the beach road toward the Marine supply area on a motorcycle with a sidecar. He left the rifle in the sidecar and went in to Camp to get the supplies.

When "Skee," as Holewinski was called by his friends, returned with his supplies the rifle was gone. Even so, he was not terribly worried, figuring that if he ever needed a rifle he would be able to get his hands on one. Holewinski never found his rifle, but figured that it had been stolen by one of the many civilians who were hiding in the underbrush that covered much of the island.

The civilians were scared and they had no weapons, so they were arming themselves if they could get their hands on a gun. If a Marine was lucky enough to have a BAR (Browning Automatic Rifle) he would keep it with him at all times. The BAR was a 20-shot semi-automatic rifle that was far superior to the single-shot Springfield bolt action repeater, which held only five shells. In fact, some of the Marines with a BAR would not even hang around to socialize in groups where most of the men had Springfields. They knew that if they laid down their BAR for just a minute and left it unattended some one might switch weapons with them.

Chapter 16
DAY FOUR—THE FIRST INVASION

US Marine Corps

A cartoonist shows the great three-headed Axis serpent rising from the sea over the defenders of Wake Island.

At about 3:00 a.m. on Thursday, December 11, the Japanese attack force sighted Wake Island, and almost simultaneously Marine lookouts, peering out into the black ocean, spotted the enemy vessels. Several sightings were reported to Major Devereux, including one by Major Wesley Platt on Wilkes Island. Devereux went down to the beach to see for himself. After a short time scanning the dark ocean with his binoculars, he was also able to spot the enemy.

Major Devereux could make several disturbing observations about the fleet. First, all of the ships were Japanese. Second, there were cruisers mixed in with the destroyers. Devereux knew at once that he was outgunned.

The enemy ships were still over five miles offshore. While Wake was only barely visible on the horizon they were preparing to begin two phases of their invasion attempt. First, they were gradually moving toward Wake's south shore where the ships would make several runs back and forth parallel to the beach. While doing this they could bombard the island with their heavy guns. This would "soften up" the island sufficiently so that the second phase of the

operation, the landing of the assault troops, could proceed. The amphibious troops were boarding small boats in the darkness despite dangerously high waves and howling winds.

As Major Devereux quietly ordered the island to battle stations, he made another brilliant tactical decision that would prove to be a pivotal one in the battle that was about to ensue. He knew there were certainly guns on the ships that were larger than his 5" guns. The cruisers almost surely carried 6" guns that were superior in both range and size of projectile to Wake's largest weapon. This meant that the Japanese could remain offshore and devastate Wake with the big guns while sitting comfortably out of range of the Marines' 5" artillery.

Major Devereux correctly surmised that his only chance at an even fight with the larger Jap guns was to coax the enemy fleet into range of the 5" guns before playing his hand. He ordered all guns to remain silent until he gave the order to fire. Also, the decision was made not to use the searchlights, which were positioned on the south beach. These lights, capable of producing a beam with a million candle power, could illuminate the ships and allow the defenders to make better use of their fire power. However, the lights would also give away the locations of several gun positions which were located nearby and take away the defenders' element of surprise.

Major Devereux ordered Major Putnam at the airfield not to send his planes aloft until after he had begun firing. The entire island was to appear asleep until the enemy ships ventured closer to the beach, hoping to lure the warships into range. The Wake defenders anxiously watched and waited.

As the early morning hours elapsed at an excruciatingly slow pace, the Marines watched the approaching ships without firing a shot. By 5:00 a.m. there was enough light for Devereux to see the ships clearly. There were three cruisers, six destroyers, and four troop transports filled with men ready to swarm ashore on Wake's south beach. Devereux was sure the guns on the ships had greater range than his own. Using the telephone system that had been strung across the island he cautioned his men once again not to fire until he gave the command.

A lookout tower was perched atop a tool box next to Wiley Sloman's foxhole near Kuku Point on Wilkes Island. The lookout could climb up eight feet, where he could clearly see out onto the ocean or back across the lagoon. When Sloman took lookout duty he climbed up the steps to the top of the tower. He stood face to face with the Japanese ships. They continued to close on the island, getting closer and closer as they passed back and forth off the south shore.

As Dick lay in the hospital bunker he heard over the telephone speaker the gun captains on the south beach reporting the movements of the enemy ships. The gun crews had the Japs in their sights and could hardly wait for the chance to retaliate for the bombings of the past three days. They pleaded with Major Devereux, but he steadfastly insisted that the gun positions "Hold your fire." The men begged and cursed, but they obeyed their orders.

96

Wiley Sloman continued to observe the enemy, reporting the movements of the ships to the men below. As the ships made their turns near the end of Wilkes Island they turned broadside to Sloman's 5" gun, presenting themselves clearly to the rangefinders. Marine gun sights followed the ships, the gunners cursing aloud at the order not to open fire. Sloman guessed that the Jap pilots responsible for the huge dynamite explosion must have reported to their commanders that everything on Wilkes was destroyed because the ship were now baring themselves to the Marine guns, seemingly unafraid of anything left on the island.

The cruiser YUBARI, with Admiral Kajioka on her bridge, was beginning to pass very close to the southern coast of Wake Island. The Yubari executed a 180 degree turn and made yet another pass, closer than the last, parallel to the beach on the southern side of Wake Island. The Marines manning the 5" guns followed the ship in their sights as their trigger fingers became more and more itchy. By half past five all the Japanese ships were inching closer to Wake behind the YUBARI, and in the midst of the run down the beach the YUBARI opened fire.

Dick listened intently as the Japanese naval guns pounded away at the deceivingly dormant island. He could feel the blasts as the projectiles found Wake and made the entire island tremble. Dick could hear the shells landing outside the bunker with the dreaded CRUNCH, CRUNCH, CRUNCH. Everyone in the hospital wondered if a shell being loaded into a cannon several miles offshore had his name on it, soon to greet him face to face.

As shells began crashing down around the Marine gun crews they could not understand Major Devereux's reluctance to allow them to retaliate. Some of the 6" projectiles began to find their marks, as oil tanks exploded and turned into infernos on Wilkes Island. Then two more cruisers, the TATSUTA and the TENRYU, joined the column and began shelling the southern end of Wake Island. Only a reissuance of the order to hold fire stopped the Marines from blasting away with their seacoast guns at the unwanted visitors. The ships were being tracked in the sights of the 5" battery on Peacock Point, waiting only for the order to open fire.

Cpl. Ralph Holewinski and several of his Marine buddies were at their machine gun position about midway down the south beach of Wake. They had been sharing the protection of the coral reef at the water line with the rats, but from their position they had a bird's eye view of the ships maneuvering offshore. A call came in on the telephone from the command center ordering three men to go immediately to the 5" gun at Peacock Point to serve as ammunition carriers. Holewinski and two other Marines took off running down the two miles of beach to the point.

When the four Marines had made their way well down the expanse of beach they noticed muzzle flashes from the Japanese ships. They knew that high explosives were coming toward them, but they had no coral reef to protect them. They dove for protection into the nearest sand dune and listened as the salvo of shells whistled past them and exploded beyond them on the island.

The Marines began running again toward Peacock Point. Batteries on Peale, Wilkes, and Wake were now aimed directly at the Japanese ships. As more warships moved into position behind the YUBARI, by then less than four miles offshore, she turned toward the island again to make another run down the beach. Enemy ships were closing on Wilkes and Wake Islands, several pounding the islands with 6" shells.

Battery commanders were openly questioning Devereux's order to hold their fire. They grew more anxious by the second as they held the Japanese in their sights at nearly point blank range, having to endure the enemy's explosive shells that were landing all about them. By this time the ships, barely three miles offshore, were clearly visible in dawn's light. Shells rained onto the beaches and gunners begged their commander for the order to return fire.

When the ships fired their big guns at the island it seemed that they were belching fire directly into Wiley Sloman's face. They were so close that it took almost no time for the projectiles to reach the island. They were firing at the island at point blank range. The shells were crashing into the water on both sides of Wilkes, and Sloman was becoming extremely tense. What could Major Devereux be thinking?

It was just after 6:00 a.m. when the YUBARI passed within three miles of the south beach. The Japanese flagship executed a 180 degree turn toward the island, inching closer and pounding the island all the while. Marine Gunner Clarence McKinstry was in charge of a 3" gun at Battery F on Wilkes Island. His voice came over the telephone system as he called Commander Cunningham's headquarters, informing the Commander of the proximity of the enemy and pleading for the command to fight back. McKinstry's patience was growing increasingly thin, and finally he blurted out, "Dammit, Commander, I can see the whites of their eyes."

At 6:15 Major Devereux made the decision to open fire. He calmly picked up his telephone and gave the order to everyone on the island—"Commence firing." Though his strategy had not been understood by the chagrined gun crews, they had followed orders to the last moment and the enemy ships lay exposed before them at nearly point blank range.

The pent-up fury of the Marine's guns exploded all over the island within moments after the order had been given. The Marines' 5" guns instantly roared into action. The first salvo from Wake's south beach flew beyond the YUBARI, crashing harmlessly into the ocean and sending water high into the air. The cruiser turned to retreat, surprised by the intensity of the Marines' guns and immediately realizing that she had been lured much too near the American guns.

Both sides traded volleys of cannon fire as the second salvo also failed to find its target. Battery A's 5" guns at Peacock Point were reloaded and immediately cut loose again. With this salvo the American guns found their mark, hitting the YUBARI "between the wind and the water." Admiral Kajioka's ship felt the 5" shell crash into her about midship just above the waterline.

The YUBARI was just over three miles from shore. Smoke spewed from the cruiser as she began to retreat. When the YUBARI reached four miles offshore she was hit again, another bulls-eye near midship. A destroyer quickly moved between the Marine guns on Wake and the Yubari, laying down a smokescreen to help hide Admiral Kajioka's stricken flagship.

Holewinski and Marine Private Glenn E. Grubb made another dash toward Peacock. While most of the gunners in the 3" and 5" positions were in pits below ground level, Holewinski and the Marines on the beach could clearly see the action. Suddenly a spectacular sight occurred when one of the enemy destroyers took a direct hit, probably in the ammunition magazine.

Bristling with artillery guns, the Japanese cruiser Yubari was the flagship of Admiral Kajioka's invasion fleet.

Sloman and his mates at Battery L on Wilkes Island had fired their first salvo, missing the HAYATE long. They quickly reloaded the 5" cannon, adjusted the gun to compensate for the discrepancy, and fired the second salvo. Their marksmanship was perfect, and the projectile smashed into the center of the ship. A huge explosion ripped the middle of the ship as it separated into two pieces, the two halves moving instantly away from each other.

As Lt. John McAlister and his crew at Battery L, and the Marines down the beach in Holewinski's group, watched in disbelief, the two halves of the ship began sinking instantly. The two halves of the ship first lurched apart and then sank toward each other as if they were trying to rejoin. Both halves of the ship disappeared beneath the surface of the ocean in seconds. The men watched the incredible event in amazement. The projectile must have scored a direct hit on the ship's magazine, they surmised, for the explosion that parted the two halves of the ship was massive.

Both Sloman, on the watch tower at Kuku Point, and Holewinski, standing on the south beach near the center of Wake Island, watched the monstrous explosion and then the spectacular sinking. Both watched white foam cover the spot which, just moments before, had been occupied by a warship. There was no sign of survivors.

Suddenly another enemy shell from another ship came whistling over Holewinskij's head. The Marines dove for the cover

of a sand dune as the reality of war instantly set in. Seven enemy ships were assembled just off Kuku Point, with the lead vessel just under three miles offshore.

The HAYATE was sunk at ten minutes before seven in the morning. Everyone who watched the spectacle agreed that the ship dissappeared beneath the waves just seconds after the explosion ripped her apart. The men in Battery L cheered their marksmanship, and suddenly the fear and tension that had gripped them as they watched the enemy approach was gone, replaced by joy and confidence. The men had to be restrained in their euphoria and reminded that a battle was still in progress.

Wiley Sloman and all of the men in Battery L had been extremely scared and tense before they had been given the order to commence fire. As soon as they watched their second salvo destroy the Japanese warship they instantly felt the nervousness disappear, and confidence consumed them. Suddenly there was no tension, and nothing could have distracted the men from their assigned jobs. They began firing the big guns with confidence and fine tuned precision, again and again, at the fleeing Japanese ships. Just as quickly as the enemy ship had disappeared, the defenders of Wake became conquerers. They all felt it, and they fought like it.

The shelling from the Marine batteries was met with equally intense fire from the ships, thought to be cruisers with larger 8" guns, farther out to sea. Shells were exploding in the surf less than

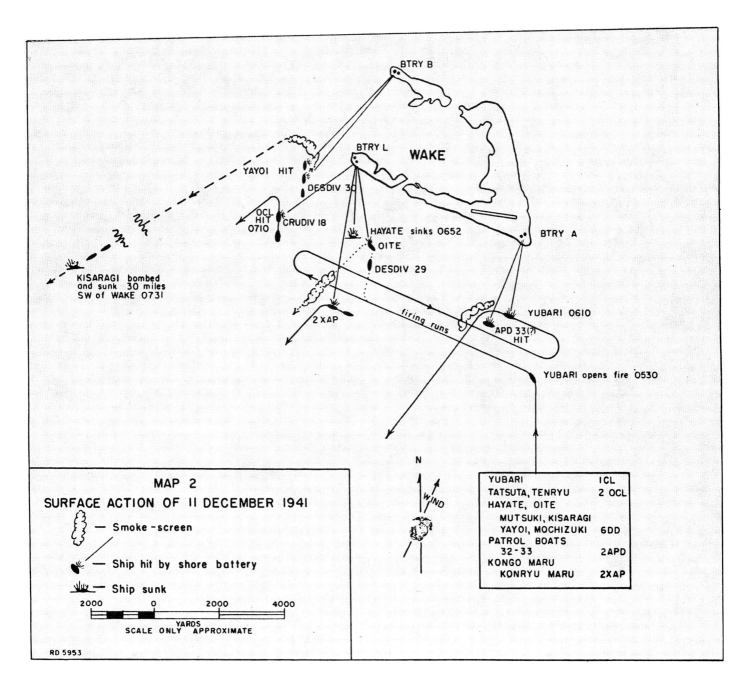

BTRY B

YAYOI HIT

DESDIV 30

WAKE

BTRY L

OCL
HIT
0710   CRUDIV 18

HAYATE sinks 0652

OITE

BTRY A

DESDIV 29

KISARAGI bombed
and sunk 30 miles
SW of WAKE 0731

2 XAP

firing runs

YUBARI 0610

APD 33(?)
HIT

YUBARI opens fire 0530

N

WIND

MAP 2

SURFACE ACTION OF 11 DECEMBER 1941

— Smoke-screen

— Ship hit by shore battery

— Ship sunk

2000   0   2000   4000
YARDS
SCALE ONLY APPROXIMATE

RD 5953

YUBARI	1CL
TATSUTA, TENRYU	2 OCL
HAYATE, OITE	
MUTSUKI, KISARAGI	
YAYOI, MOCHIZUKI	6DD
PATROL BOATS	
32-33	2APD
KONGO MARU	
KONRYU MARU	2XAP

Heinl

100 yards in front of Sloman's position as well as in the lagoon behind him. The Marine artillerymen knew that this meant the Japanese had the coordinates for straddling the island. There was concern among the men with Sloman because they knew that all the enemy had to do was adjust to coordinates between the two settings and they could drop projectiles right on the island.

Any artillery instructor would have told his students to split the difference when they were straddling a target. Sloman was very uneasy, expecting artillery rounds to begin arriving any second. For unknown reasons this never happened. Not one Japanese round fell on Wilkes Island the entire day.

Battery B, the 5" position at Toki Point on Peale

Island, got its chance to join the fight when several enemy destroyers steamed toward the north off the open end of the atoll. As the distance between the big gun and the lead destroyer narrowed the two adversaries began firing at each other. The first destroyer, thought to be the YAYOI, began shelling Peale. Her fire was accurate enough to do considerable damage to several gun positions.

While the more distant ships fired toward the island, the enemy destroyers began laying down smoke screens and retreating. As they scrambled to get out of range of the Marines' 5" guns, another ship, thought to be a troop ship, was hit and damaged. All of the ships off Kuku Point managed to get beyond the range of the shore batteries behind the smoke screens.

One of the two 5" guns at Battery B was put out of action,

99

so both crews began to furiously feed the one gun that remained operable. Their persistence in the face of a furious shelling paid off as they saw one of their 5" shells crash into the stern of the YAYOI. The ship was in flames as another destroyer laid down a smoke screen which allowed the YAYOI to retreat. By 7:00 the entire fleet was in retreat, sailing away from Wake Island to Kwajalein to lick their wounds and regroup. Many a Japanese sailor was left to the swift current and hungry sharks in the inhospitable waters off Wake Island that day.

The 5" guns on Peale and Wilkes opened up on the destroyers that had found themselves much too close to the island, so close in fact that the .30 cal. machine gunners had to be ordered not to open fire. After the HAYATE had been hit and had turned away from the island the Marine guns began firing on the destroyer OITE, which was next in line. Smoke was seen rising from the OITE as a 5" shell found its mark. All over the three islands the guns continued to belch forth their deadly projectiles in the face of heavy incoming fire from the enemy ships.

As the Japanese ships at both ends of Wake Island scrambled to zigzag their way out of the deadly range of the shore batteries, the Marines continued to fire from batteries on Wake, Wilkes, and Peale Islands. Shells from the Wilkes battery chased the retreating ships, finding their mark again on a troop transport, either the KONGO MARU or the KONRYU MARU, just over five miles away. The transports also made an immediate turn seaward after receiving the Marine greeting.

In less than an hour the initial phase of the battle was over. Shortly after 7:00 a.m. the joyous Marines and sailors were claiming an amazing victory. They had beaten back an enemy force decisively, sinking one ship, damaging several others, and stopping the Japanese landing force before it ever hit the beaches. There was jubilation on the ground, but the battle was still being waged in the air.

The four Marine pilots aloft in their Wildcats had searched the seas and skies around Wake, especially on its southern exposure beyond the enemy fleet and toward the Marshall Islands. They had been on the lookout for either a carrier-based air squadron or a coordinated landbased air attack in support of the invasion attempt. Having found neither, they flew back toward Wake to join in the fighting. By the time the F4F-3 fighters arrived in the vicinity of Wake the artillery battle was over and the ships were limping away in retreat.

The Wildcats spotted the retreating ships about fifteen miles from the island. They threw themselves at the enemy, braving intense anti-aircraft fire to dive straight at the ships and drop their 100 pound bombs as they flew right into the teeth of the enemy defenses, all the while blazing away with their own 50 caliber machine guns. The Leatherneck pilots risked their lives to get a parting shot at the enemy, hoping to deal the death blow to one of the damaged ships as it limped away in retreat.

Capt. Henry Elrod and Capt. Frank Tharin went after the two light cruisers, the TENRYU and the TATSUTA. They damaged both ships with their bombing and strafing runs, and each of their planes sustained damage from the ship's anti-aircraft fire. When their bombs and machine gun ammunition were exhausted they raced back to their base at the air strip where they would have more bombs mounted under their wings before speeding back out to sea

to do battle with the retreating ships.

The Wildcats were in a dead sprint, going to and from the ships in an attempt to ferry as many bombs as possible from Wake to the retreating ships before they limped out of range. Captain Freuler attacked one of the transports, the KONGO MARU, dropping a 100 pound bomb on her stern. A gasoline fire erupted and began burning out of control.

With the ships in retreat and the battle apparently over, Elrod and Tharin informed Major Putnam they wanted to go after a Japanese cruiser. They knew that the juicy target was just over the horizon. Their planes were being refueled and reloaded with 100 pound bombs and belts of .50 cal. machine gun bullets. Permission was granted for the mission and off went the two Wildcats into the sky over Wake Island.

Moments later the chit-chat between pilots could be heard in the command center as they dove on the enemy ship. Only one bomb found its mark. Back they screamed toward Wake, yearning for another belly full of fire to throw at the fleeing ships. In all, Elrod and Tharin went after the ships four times, waiting in their cockpits during each stop on the airstrip while the ground crews rearmed them. They dropped sixteen bombs, scoring eight direct hits. Capt. Herbert Freuler also flew out on sorties against the retreating ships.

In addition to the damage that Elrod and Tharin had caused on the cruisers, Captain Elrod dropped a 100 pound bomb squarely on the deck of the destroyer KISARAGI, which was loaded with depth charges. When Elrod's bomb detonated on the ship's deck it set the cruiser on fire. The wounded vessel tried to move to the south with her sister ships, burning as she went.

Eventually the fire ignited the explosives and there was a massive explosion on the KISARAGI. By this time Lt. John Kinney had relieved one of the other pilots, and as he approached the stricken ship on a bombing run of his own he watched the huge explosion. At a point approximately thirty miles south of Wake Island the ship simply dropped out of sight in a huge fireball. Captain Elrod's sinking of the Japanese cruiser gave him the distinction of being the first pilot of the war to sink an enemy warship.

The pilots flew a total of ten sorties against the Japanese ships. In all, the tiny air force, comprised of only four single-engine fighters, scored hits with the bombs on two cruisers, one destroyer, and two transports. The planes dropped twenty 100 pound bombs and fired an estimated 20,000 rounds of .50 cal. machine gun ammunition at the enemy ships. None of the planes was shot down, though all suffered flak damage from the anti-aircraft shells exploding all around them..

Captain Elrod's plane was the most seriously damaged, and he almost crashed into the ocean as his plane limped home with a severed fuel line. He was unable to make it to the runway and crash landed the Wildcat on the beach, destroying the plane but making it out of the wreckage unhurt. As he was pulled out of the plane he apologized for the damage to it, apparently feeling as if he had let his fellow Marines down.

Captain Freuler had also been stung by the enemy anti-aircraft flak. The oil cooler on his engine was damaged and one cylinder had been pierced by an enemy bullet. He was able to coax his ailing engine back to the airstrip and land the plane, but his engine was a total loss.

By the time that Ralph Holewinski and his buddies reached

Burt Silverman
American Heritage

The few remaining American fighters courageously chase the retreating Japanese War ships.

Peacock Point, the enemy ships were out of range and the Marines' guns had become quiet. There was no need for ammo carriers, so Holewinski and his buddies were told to go back to their machine gun positions down the beach. They did so, but not before noticing that the 5" gun position was enjoying much better food rations than they were at their beach position. They saw stacks of Cokes and piles of other goodies. One of the Marines told them they had better hurry back to their gun or they would miss breakfast.

This puzzled Holewinski since no one had been serving meals to the men in his position since the first attack on December 8. He had been living on such foods as cranberries and orange marmalade eaten from tin cans. He advised the officer at the 5" gun that he and his men were not being fed.

On this day, December 11, 1941, the Marines and sailors on Wake Island had scored a truly amazing victory over an enemy force that substantially outnumbered them. No Marines were killed in the air or on the ground, and fewer than a half dozen sustained injuries. In fact, not a single one of the 1200 civilians or the more than 400 defenders on Wake was killed despite the furious shelling from the ships.

At the same time, the Japanese admitted to the loss of 500 men, and postwar estimates by American intelligence placed the number nearer to 700. The actual loss of Japanese men in this action has been estimated by some as high as 5000, probably due to the fact that several of the enemy ships were sunk or severely damaged with

staggering troop losses. In all, the American forces had sunk two Japanese destroyers, the HAYATE and the KISARAGI. Three cruisers, the YUBARI, TATSUTA, and TENRYU, two destroyers, the OITE and YAYOI, and two transports, the KONGO MARU and Patrol Craft 33, had retreated on Kwajalein with damages from Wake's coastal guns and tiny air force.

The Japanese fleet had expected a quick takeover at Wake Island. Instead, it steamed back to the Marshall Islands in defeat. The Japanese base on Kwajalein Island would be ready when the ships arrived to begin immediate repairs, and the landing force would be bolstered. With the mettle of the Marines on Wake Island now evident to the enemy, there would be no taking them for granted again.

Masatake Okumiya, Commander of the Japanese Imperial Navy, would later state, "Considering the power accumulated for the invasion of Wake Island, and the meager forces of the defenders, it was one of the most humiliating defeats the Japanese Navy had ever suffered." The victory at Wake Island on December 11, 1941, was just the tonic needed by the American people to help their deflated morale rebound from the defeat at Pearl Harbor three days before. Just as "Remember the Alamo" and "Remember the Maine" had become rallying cries in previous wars, during the early part of World War II, "Remember Wake Island" was the rallying cry heard from Americans all around the world.

After the landing attempt on December 11 it was realized

Capt, Henry Elrod is pulled from the wreckage of the F4F-3 that he crash landed on the beach at Wake.

that the senior man on the beach was Corporal Holewinski, so it was decided that an officer would be assigned to that machine gun position. Lt. Robert Hanna took command of the Marines on the beach. Lt. Hanna was not a .30 cal. machine gun officer, but he began to make the adjustment and everyone liked him right away. One of his first decisions was to make a phone call and get the food wagon to stop with lunch. The men began getting cooked meat and fresh bread twice a day. Some had not eaten at all in the three days since December 8.

When Lt. Hanna took command of Ski's position, he made several changes that pleased the men. Prior to his arrival there was no organized watch duty, so each man had to be awake and alert all the time. Sleep became a precious commodity, but a precarious risk. Hanna ordered the men to observe four-hour watches so that each man was on for four hours and then off for four hours. This allowed the men to get at least four hours of sleep knowing that some one was on duty watching for the enemy.

Less than three hours after the early morning battle on December 11, at 10:00 a.m., the two remaining Wildcats, piloted by Lt. Davidson and Lt. Kinney, were back up on patrol. They soon realized that the Japanese were not yet ready to stop fighting when they sighted thirty enemy bombers heading toward the atoll to pound it yet again. This time the formations of bombers were approaching the island from the northeast, apparently having circled the target to confuse the defenders who expected them to come from the south.

The Wildcats were spewing a hail of bullets from their machine guns as they dove into the midst of the enemy planes. Two of the bombers, hit by Lt. Davidson's accurate fire, plummeted toward earth and crashed into the sea nearly three miles below. Lt. Kinney hit another bomber and smoke began billowing from its engine as it turned back toward the Marshall Islands. When the planes came within range of the island's anti-aircraft guns, another one was sent crashing into the ocean and several others began to trail smoke.

The remaining enemy planes went on about their business, plastering the island with their explosives. On the ground below, the bombs blasted out craters but did little serious damage to the gun positions. Marine Gunner John Hamas and Navy Boatswain's Mate Kirby Ludwig were trying to get more ammunition to the 5" battery on Wilkes Island. Hamas drove a truck loaded with the explosives onto the 50' barge, and Ludwig piloted the boat slowly across the channel. Both were painfully aware that if any of the bombs, which were falling perilously close, were to score a direct hit on the barge and its truck loaded with explosives, they would be blown to smithereens. The barge labored across the channel through the midst of the attack and reached the other side, successfully replenishing ammunition to the gun battery.

Later in the day, after 5:00 in the afternoon, the tired Marines were beginning an evening of hard labor moving the 3" guns to new locations. Suddenly three red flares and a smoke bomb

"SEMPER FIDELIS"

7 JAP WARSHIPS
1 CRUISER
4 DESTROYERS
1 SUBMARINE
1 GUNBOAT
9 JAP PLANES

WAKE

JERRY DOYLE

U. S. Navy

By sundown on the 11th the relief force in Hawaii was well into the loading process, preparing to ship men and supplies to the beleaguered defenders of Wake Island. Late that night the supplies continued to be gathered, even though there was a blackout in effect which made the task unusually difficult. In addition to this, the effort was further stymied when a temporary hold was put on the operation and the men were ordered to return to their defensive positions in the vicinity of Pearl Harbor.

It was on the night of December 11 that the first burials took place on Wake Island. A dragline was provided by Dan Teter's civilian corps, and it proceeded to scoop out a large trench in the coral sand. More than forty American bodies, both civilian and military, were placed in a common grave. This did not account for all of the fallen defenders on Wake. Some had been buried by fellow Marines where they had fallen. Other bodies were yet to be found in the dense underbrush of the island.

The bodies of the dead had been stored in large refrigerated coolers until they could be buried. The corpses were wrapped in sheets and laid side by side in the trench, which was located near the east end of the runway just north of Peacock Point. A prayer was said, and then a firing squad issued a final salute to the dead. After a bulldozer covered the bodies the area was camouflaged and offered little evidence to the enemy that Wake Island had swallowed up so many young American men.

At a later date a more suitable gravesite would be provided for the men who fell in the defense of the island. Even though a search was conducted for this first grave, it would not be located again. The first lads to die on Wake Island remain in the common grave to this day. They, like many other civilians, Pan Am employees, and soldiers, both Japanese and American, remain today in unmarked graves. Many hundreds of men who would perish here during the war, and they remain in graves of coral sand with no tombstone, nothing to mark their graves except Wake Atoll itself.

On the evening of the 11th an event was to occur which would be misinterpreted by millions of people around the world, and which was used to bolster the sagging egos of Americans everywhere. Having been soundly whipped at Pearl Harbor, patriotic Americans wanted to hear some good news. Everything they heard was bad, and many residents of the west coast were afraid that an enemy invasion might be launched on the mainland of the United States. The fact that the men on Wake Island had beaten back the Japanese invasion force fell on welcome ears throughout the United States. The defenders on Wake offered the United States its only news of young American warriors who were standing up and beating back the Japanese onslaught.

were sighted over the ocean about two miles offshore and northeast of Toki Point. In less than half an hour the signal was seen three times. The defenders would never know the source of the flares. Some would guess that Japanese submarines were operating in the area, while others believed that survivors of the battle had been left adrift at sea by the retreating Japanese fleet. Indeed, untold numbers of Japanese troops had been thrown into the shark-infested waters when their warships and transports had been sunk, or their landing craft had capsized in the heavy seas.

Soon after the gun batteries on Wake saw the mysterious flares, darkness covered the island and the process of moving the 3" guns began. Work began at 5:45 p.m. and proceeded until the guns were displaced, sandbagged, camouflaged, and ready to fire. The tired military and civilian men finished the job at 4:45 a.m., just fifteen minutes before they would be called to general quarters to begin the next day.

TO THE GLORY OF A SCAR SPANGLED BANNER

Cartoons lauded the courage and bravery of the Wake defenders.

When Commander Cunningham radioed Pearl Harbor that night his words were coded and scrambled so that the Japanese could not unravel the message. Part of his message read "SEND US STOP NOW IS THE TIME FOR ALL GOOD MEN TO COME TO THE AID OF THEIR PARTY STOP CUNNINGHAM MORE JAPS...." In what was to become one of the most popular myths of the entire war, the message was "depadded" and left to read "SEND US MORE JAPS."

In reality "more Japs" was the last thing the men on Wake wanted. They wanted good men to be sent to aid in the defense of the island, because they knew that more Japs were going to be coming their way. But by the time the media back home was finished, the legend of the Wake defenders was magnified to portray a tough bunch of Marines who not only had beat hell out of the Japs, but who were taunting Emperor Hirohito to send on some more. "SEND US MORE JAPS" and "REMEMBER WAKE ISLAND" became two of the most famous slogans of the war.

Soon after the attack on Pearl Harbor, President Roosevelt

ordered that funds be released for a huge construction project that would provide the facilities for the production of the atom bomb. Perhaps the President's feelings about the urgency of the ultimate weapon were galvanized by the Japanese attack and the entry of the United States into the war. For whatever reason, the President decided to fund the immense project and go forward with a serious effort to convert theory into reality, to make the first atomic bomb.

Gen. Leslie Groves, fresh from the Pentagon construction project, was assigned the responsibility of building the facilities. Three remote sites, all away from public view and populated areas, were selected for the complex project. They were Los Alamos, New Mexico; Oak Ridge, Tennessee; and Hanford, Washington. What would become known as the "Manhattan Project" was off and running.

Each of the three sites conducted its own experimentation and pursued different objectives. At Oak Ridge thousands of workers would attempt to produce small quantities of the rare but essential isotope of uranium, U-235, from U-238, the common form of naturally occurring uranium. This material would provide one of the fissionable forms of uranium that would fuel the atomic bomb.

At Hanford another huge complex of buildings and workers would attempt to produce a new element, plutonium, from uranium. This substance would also be a fissionable material that could form the core of an atomic bomb. Each of the sites was immersed in secrecy so most employees and local citizens had no idea why the work was going on or what the final product would be.

The atomic bombs themselves were to be assembled in Los Alamos under the direction of physicist Julius Robert Oppenheimer. Oppenheimer was an unlikely choice to head this segment of the project, having previously had leanings toward anti-war pacifism and communism. He accepted his assignment, however, and went about his work diligently.

As World War II began, the United States was making a concerted effort to develop nuclear weapons. The President and his staff seemed to fully understand the importance of being first to develop the bomb. Even though no nuclear weapon had ever been produced, tested, or used in warfare, and the technology still existed only in theoretical form, the United States was now fully committed to the production of an atomic weapon.

Chapter 17
DAY FIVE—VICTORY!! SPIRITS ARE HIGH

The victory of December 11 had elevated the spirits of the men defending Wake Island and morale was high. But after a long night of toiling in the sand and grit of Wake atoll to move the guns to new positions, the sweaty, tired men were ready to rest. When the job was completed just before 5:00 a.m. on Friday, December 12, the men settled down to what, for some, would be the first sleep in over twenty-four hours.

The Tokyo Express was not expected until noon, so the defenders hoped to catch a few hours of undisturbed solitude. But the Japs had decided to keep the pressure on the Wake defenders. At 5:00 a.m. two enemy patrol planes flew over Wake. Both of these were four-engine Kawanishi patrol bombers, similar to the American PBY flying boats. The raiders were part of the Japanese No. 3 Air Attack Force based on the island of Majuro in the Marshalls.

The bombers rousted the weary men out of their slumber by strafing with their machine guns and dropping their bombs as they crossed the atoll. Their arrival sent the weary defenders scrambling,

but there were no casualties from the attack. Both Wake and Peale Islands were hit, with much of the attack focused on the area immediately around the airstrip.

When the attack began, Capt. Frank Tharin had just taken off on the morning patrol and was flying alone in one of the few remaining Wildcats. Upon seeing the attackers he immediately flew into them, fixing his sights on the tail of one of the bombers. He didn't let go until he had cut the plane to pieces with his .50 cal. machine guns. The plane crashed into the ocean just off the coast.

The defenders on Wake began to fall into a routine which would continue for the next ten days. It called for the men to endure the uncomfortable life in the foxholes and defensive fortifications. Days became virtually indistinguishable as the men toiled almost non-stop. The daily bombings came almost like clockwork, after which the men would lick their wounds, bury their dead where they had fallen, and prepare to stay alive through the next raid.

Life in the shelters and foxholes was anything but pleasant. The Wake Island rats came out in profusion, crawling over the men

This captured photograph shows a large Japanese four-engine flying boat, an "Emily," and a smaller fighter, Mitsubishi "Rufe," on Kwajalein.

in their foxholes. Rare moments of sleep were sometimes interrupted by a rat scampering across one's face. Dead birds littered the island, killed by the concussion of the bombs. Others wobbled around as if intoxicated.

When the men were not moving the big guns, digging into the coral atoll for more protection, or trying to steal a few moments of sleep, there was plenty of additional work to occupy them. Damage to the guns and fortifications needed to be repaired. Dead men had to be buried, and the wounded were taken to the hospital bunker. Much of the time, however, the defenders of Wake were waiting—waiting for the next bombing, and hoping to live through it. Diarrhea became a problem, striking many of the men and further draining their strength.

The crew of the 5" gun on Wilkes where Tipton and Tripp had been assigned was now stabilized, so Tripp was reassigned to a patrol unit back on Wake Island. Several of the other Navy men, including Mayhew, Reynolds, and Manning, were also assigned to the same position. They were on the beach side of the road, about halfway between Peacock Point and the first bunker hospital.

The group of Navy men knew how perilous their position was, especially during the daily bombing raids. So they decided to build a bunker of their own. The small crude bunker was made from coral rocks piled up around a hole in the ground to offer them a small degree of protection. The sailors then lined the inside with mattresses that they were able to find in the ruins of Camp #1.

Each day the 3" anti-aircraft guns would fire at the Japanese planes during the air raid. The gun crews knew the Japs had photographed their position and would surely zero in on them during the raid the following day. Tripp was on the crew which helped them move the guns, usually about 100' to 150' from the original position. Dummy guns were built out of wood and left in the same positions that real guns had occupied. Sure enough, on several occasions the move saved the guns from being obliterated by the bombers, which blasted the dummy gun.

Shortwave radios provided the only entertainment on the island, allowing a few men to listen to music from Hawaii or California. From newscasts they learned how proud America was of them, but they also heard themselves being quoted as saying, "Send Us More Japs." This was hardly the case.

To the surprise and delight of the Wake Island defenders, "More Japs" was not the order of the day on December 12. The defenders braced for the anticipated attack, but it did not materialize. Several of the men used the unexpected and undisturbed time to work on projects that were needed for the continued defense of the island.

One such problem involved the oxygen used by the Marine pilots, a commodity that was crucial to flights into the thin air above 12,000 feet. The supply of oxygen was stored in bottles aboard the Grumman fighters and and it had been nearly exhausted. In order to continue to pursue enemy planes to high altitudes the pilots needed more oxygen in their bottles. The pilots would be severely handicapped if they ran out of the precious gas and had to remain at low altitudes when they were attempting to engage the enemy.

The only remaining supply of oxygen on the island was in tanks used by welders. A method would have to be devised to transfer the invaluable gas from one tank to another, an especially dangerous procedure due to the highly flammable nature of oxygen gas. Thanks to Captain Frueler the task was accomplished and the two Wildcats that could still fly were able to remain in service.

On December 12 Lt. Kinney and Sgt. Hamilton cannibalized enough parts from the graveyard of wrecked and burned Wildcats to patch together another fighter and put one more plane back into service. This gave Major Putnam three aircraft capable of flight. That evening two of the fighters went up for patrol. The third plane, piloted by Lt. Kliewer, was slow to crank, and so was about fifteen minutes late in getting into the air.

When he finally became airborne Kliewer raced after the other two planes, which were piloted by Lt. Kinney and Sgt. Hamilton. Before he could catch them, at a point about twenty-five miles from Wake, he spotted an object on the ocean below. Upon closer inspection Kliewer saw that the object was a submarine, and not a friendly one at that. The submarine was on the surface, thus providing Kliewer a good target.

Lt. Kliewer climbed to almost two miles above the ocean's surface and then, with the sun at his back to hide his approach, he dove at the sub. Kliewer's Wildcat came within twenty feet of the vessel before he released his bombs. He was almost blown out of the air himself when the bombs detonated, as the explosion sent metal fragments screaming back at him, piercing the thin skin of his plane's fuselage. By the time he could circle back around, only an oil slick remained. Thus the tiny air force on Wake Island was credited with sinking the first full size Japanese submarine of World War II.

Chapter 18
DAY SIX——THE ENEMY REARMS

US Marine Corps

A Grumman Wildcat, refueled, rearmed, and ready for action, is pushed out of its revetment and toward the air strip. This photo is on Palmyra.

Though Lt. Kliewer had not seen the submarine actually sink on the 12th, events of the following day indicated that such had probably been the case. The daily bombing raid by the Japanese planes originated at a base in the Marshall Islands, over 600 miles from Wake. It was difficult to find a pinpoint such as Wake Island in the middle of the Pacific Ocean. In order for the Japanese bombers to find the island it was thought that a submarine was operating near the island, sending a radio message which provided a homing signal to the planes.

Lt. Kinney agreed with this theory. He later said "Wake was a hard place to find. It was small and there were

usually a lot a scattered clouds around. If they (enemy bombers) had come in at night, it would have been possible for them to hit by accurate celestial navigation. But they were making five- and six-hundred-mile flights over water with no landmarks, by dead reckoning alone, and they always seemed to hit the island on the head just about the same time each day."

"Moreover," he continued, "we heard a lot of funny radio signals. We never had any radio direction-finding equipment, and therefore couldn't take any bearing on these strange signals, but I am convinced that the sub was leading them in."

The defenders on Wake maintained radio silence during the battle so they would not provide such a radio signal to lure the enemy to them. With the Marine radio blacked out on Wake it was a wonder that our own Wildcats never became lost over the ocean and unable to find their way back to the landing strip. Some thought it a miracle that the navigational skills of the pilots were so good that, on every one of their flights, some many miles over the horizon and completely out of sight of the atoll, they found the speck of coral they called home.

With no beacon to lure the bombers to their target there was no midday bombing raid on December 13. This caused the men to wait anxiously for some time after the normal 12:00 hour, waiting for the usual destruction to fall from the skies and the resulting carnage on the ground to occur. But none came that afternoon or evening. There was a small amount of satisfaction in getting the raid over with at midday. This meant that the men could spend their afternoon hours with the normal tension removed. This day they were kept guessing. It is probable that the absence of the bombing run on the 13th was due to Lt. Kliewer's sinking of the Japanese submarine.

On December 13 Admiral Kajioka brought his task force into the Japanese base at Kwajalein in the Marshall Islands. The force had been soundly defeated by the defenders of Wake Island and the Japanese naval hierarchy set out to determine how this could have happened. They certainly had not expected to be stung so severely by the American shore batteries, nor did they anticipate a vicious counterattack by the Marine pilots. The Japanese searched for ways to avoid these problems, along with others that they had encountered, such as the rough seas and adverse weather. Then they determined that they had gone about the task with insufficient men and materials. Having made these assessments the enemy leaders decided to have another go at the island, this time amassing a larger force to do the job.

The Japanese decided to pound the island with daily bombings in an attempt to eliminate the first two factors, the artillery and the remaining warplanes. They also decided that their invasion force was too small for the chore, so they went about the task of bolstering the fleet with more ships and the landing force with more men.

In assessing the damage caused by the first invasion attempt, the Japanese found that they could repair all of the ships that had been damaged. Nothing could bring back the two destroyers that Wake's defenders had sunk, but all of the remaining vessels with damages hurried to Kwajalein where men were waiting to start immediate repairs. Within ten days the ships in the Fourth Fleet of the Imperial Japanese Navy would be patched up and ready again for sea duty.

The Japanese admirals were now fully aware that the Marines on Wake would not be a pushover, having gained an extraordinary amount of respect for the American leathernecks. They realized that a larger and stronger fleet and landing force would be needed to take the island. As workmen got busy repairing the damaged ships the officers began planning the second offensive and assembling the

Wreckage of Grumman Wildcat on Wake.

force that would carry it out.

This force was larger in men, ships, and armaments, and was being assembled at Roi-Namur. Since the destroyers KISARAGI and HAYATE had been sunk, the fleet found itself shorthanded. The Japanese added three destroyers, the ASANAGI, the YUNAGI, and the sleek new OBORO, in their place. They also added the mine layer TSUGARU, the transport TENYO MARU, and a float-plane tender, the KIYOKAWA. This new invasion force would be considerably beefier than the last.

Instead of planning to use 450 men to assault the beaches of Wake Island, as the Japanese Admirals had for the December 11 attempt, this new force would have over 2000 men. The Maizuru Second Special Landing Force was summoned to Roi-Namur from Saipan in the Marianas in order to increase the size of the landing force. The first fleet had barely a dozen ships, but the second would boast well over two dozen. There would be more transports, more destroyers, more support ships, and more submarines. The respect that the Japanese had for the Wake defenders was quite apparent in their preparations for the second assault on the island.

Rear Admiral Hiroaki Abe would bring his carriers SORYU and HIRYU, both of which had been involved in the attack on Pearl Harbor less than a week before, to support the new invasion force. This would provide an ominous advantage to the Japanese forces, for with carriers they would be able to launch air attacks at the island from short distances and re-arm frequently, avoiding the 600 mile trip from the Marshall Islands. The aircraft carriers were home for over 100 of Japan's best fighter aircraft. Clearly, the defenders of Wake Island were no longer taken lightly.

American forces at Pearl Harbor were also busy on December 13 (December 12 East Latitude Time) making preparations for the relief effort for Wake Island. The relief force got orders to prepare to leave, and even though the orders were not explicit about the destination, the men knew that the force was assembling to go to the aid of the defenders on Wake Island. Marines, along with their gear and large quantities of ammunition, were loaded on the USS TANGIER.

The much needed radar equipment was brought aboard, along with fire control equipment that was necessary to accurately fire the 3" and 5" guns. Several of the large guns on Wake lacked this equipment and had to be aimed through the breach during the battle of December 11. Over 20,000 3" and 5" shells were loaded.

In addition to the supplies so desperately needed by the larger weapons, the TANGIER also took on ammunition for the smaller arms. Over 3,000,000 rounds of machine gun ammunition went on board. Ammunition for the rifles and side arms were loaded, along with hand grenades, mines, and other materials. The American leaders, like their Japanese counterparts, were taking the anticipated battle for Wake Island very seriously.

The dwindling air force on Wake suffered yet another setback on the evening of the 13th. Captain Freuler was taking off in one of the three remaining Wildcats for the evening patrol. As he roared down the coral strip the plane veered off course and narrowly missed a group of men standing beside the runway. It ground to a halt in the scrubby undergrowth adjacent to the runway, but luckily Captain Freuler climbed out of the wreak unscathed.

The much needed fighter plane was a total loss, and the Wake air unit was thereby reduced again to a total of two planes that were capable of becoming airborne. It, like the nine other incapacitated fighters, was put into service as a dummy to draw enemy fire. The ploy seemed to work, and the wrecked planes continued to be bombed and fired upon for the duration of the seige.

The small motor launch was still operational and was being used by the Navy men at the channel to move supplies across to the unit under Capt. Platt's command on Wilkes Island. Jim Cox would be assigned this duty during the daytime when he was not digging in at his dugout and preparing for the next air raid.

The lull in the daily bombings that occurred on December 13 was welcomed by the men who were dug into the gritty atoll. Many used this reprieve to bathe, something that most of them had not been able to do since the beginning of hostilities. Since there was no fresh water available for such purposes, most of the men bathed in the calm clear salt waters of the Lagoon.

Chapter 19
DAY SEVEN—MORE BOMBS

Day seven of the battle for Wake Island was the exact opposite of the previous day. Day six had seen no destruction rain down from the heavens. Sunday, December 14, was not to be so calm. Three Japanese long-range bombers, the large Kawanishi four-engine flying boats based at Wotje, appeared over the island at 3:30 in the morning. They dropped their bombs on Wake Island in the area around the airstrip, but failed to hit any strategic targets and did not kill any of the defenders. What they did accomplish was to deprive the

The precious engine of the burning plane appeared to be undamaged, so it was disassembled and pulled away. As one end of the fuselage burned, the other was being stripped and pulled away to safety so that it could fly again in another Wildcat. Lt. Kinney, assisted by Sgt. Hamilton and Navy Machinist's Mate First Class Jim Hesson, somehow managed to miraculously separate the engine from the burning aircraft. Even so, for the moment the air force on Wake consisted of one final Wildcat. The airmen went to work trying to find the

Dr.Diosdado M. Yap
Bataan Magazine

Japanese Ki-21 "Sally" bombers prepare for a night mission.

weary men below of another peaceful night of sleep.

The peace was broken again at midday when the largest formation of enemy bombers yet, thirty in all, attacked the atoll at 11:00 a.m. These were the twin-engine bombers that the defenders were accustomed to seeing on the "Tokyo Express" runs at noon. Military targets were singled out for destruction, and one of the remaining Wildcats took a bomb in its revetment, its tail section burning out of control. Men immediately scrambled to scavenge usable parts.

parts of an airworthy plane in which to install the salvaged engine.

Three "V" formations crossed the island, each one dropping bombs that blasted out craters in the coral and shook the entire atoll. Men lay flat in their foxholes and crouched in their bunkers as the earth shook. The toll was higher than it had been during the early morning raid. This time three men died. Anti-aircraft fire hit two of the attacking bombers and sent them crashing into the sea off the coast.

Jim Cox and Andrew Fuller had taken cover in their small bunker near Camp 1 when the Jap bombers hit a fuel tank at the dock just a short distance away. The tanks exploded into an inferno with a deafening roar as bombs landed very near the bunker. One blast was so great and so close that it almost covered the two men with sand. Cox had agreed with all of the men in foxholes in the area that after an air raid they would "get the hell out of their holes and check everyone" to make sure no one was covered up or hurt, so within moments after the blast several men were on the spot helping them crawl out of the hole. As Cox was pulled from his sandy hole he noticed "a hell of a crater" just a few feet away.

The raid, however, was not a total loss for the defenders. Even though they had lost one of their two remaining planes, the 3" antiaircraft crews had been able to shoot down two of the enemy planes.

There were 25-30 patients in the concrete bunker hospital. The men had nothing to do but talk and wait. People were constantly coming in and going out of the hospital. Many came to visit wounded friends. They brought the latest news of what was happening outside on the island during the seige. This often led to rumors and speculation about what was actually happening. The daily bombing was a predictable part of an otherwise very boring situation.

The hospital was well concealed by a heavy covering of sand and coral rocks. However, the large metal doors were visible and one day the bunkers became the target of one of the enemy bombers. Several large bombs exploded in the immediate vicinity of the hospital, but none of the four bunkers took a direct hit. One bomb detonated so near the bunker that Tom Kennedy thought it had blown the heavy metal doors off of their hinges.

Dick and the other wounded men in the hospital had, by that time, become accustomed to the midday bombings. They came to expect the noon pounding and even took preventative measures to thwart any unnecessary injuries. Several precautions would be observed by Dr. Kahn each day when the three warning shots were fired to signal incoming planes.

First, the heavy metal doors were closed and secured. Then each man would be given a wooden tongue depressor. He would place it in his mouth and clench his teeth tightly on it. Then the lights would be turned out and the nervous men would lie quietly with ears perked to determine how close the day's bombing run would come to them. The anxious men would pray that their bunker would not take a direct hit.

At Lt. Hanna's position on the south beach there was little to do but wait for the next air raid. The bunker was complete and it became home for Hanna's machine gunners. They began to lead a very monotonous life, spending most of their time near the relative safety of the bunker. There was little to do but talk for hours as they waited for the midday destruction to arrive. Then they would take cover in the shelter and sweat out the bombing.

The sun was intensely hot on Wake Island in December. The bunker offered not only protection but also shade to the Marines. One of the men would have to stand watch outside the bunker at all times until the incoming planes were spotted. He would usually lie in the tropical sun just outside the entrance until the warning shots were issued. Then everyone would scramble for safety underground.

On December 14 the SARATOGA finally reached Hawaiian waters after the trip from California. Over 500 Marines boarded the USS TANGIER before the transport shifted to a berth at the upper end of Pearl Harbor before heading out to sea. The relief effort was about to begin. Help was on the way for the defenders of Wake Island.

Chapter 20
Day Eight—
The SARATOGA Reaches Pearl Harbor

On the morning of December 15 Major Putnam was patroling above Wake in his Wildcat when he spotted an object several miles offshore. When he went down to investigate he found a submarine, but this one appeared to have Dutch markings so he did not attack. At any rate, the submarine dove immediately, not to be seen again.

Upon reporting his find to Commander Cunningham, Putnam was told that no Dutch ships were known to be in the area of Wake Island, and even if they had been they would not have been bobbing on the surface during daylight hours and tempting the Japanese to attack by air. Cunningham's cautious apprehension about the sub's Dutch markings were probably well based, for without a beacon to guide their flight the planes of the Tokyo Express did not make their customary run at noon on December 15.

More underground fortifications were being constructed by the defenders on December 15. At Peacock Point two new shelters, deeper than most of the previous ones, were bulldozed out and covered with three feet of coral. These were to be used by the 5" gun crews at Battery A. Smaller personnel shelters were also completed near the air field for the remaining men in VMF-211.

Even though the bombers from Roi did not appear on December 15, the day would not pass without destruction from above. At 5:30 p.m. a plane was sighted as it moved among the clouds off the eastern shore of Wake. Just as darkness began to settle over the island at 6:00 several of the big Kawanishi flying boats from Wotje, possibly as many as half a dozen, roared in over the island. The boat planes dropped their bombs, mostly over Battery D on Peale island, and they made a low run over the island in order to strafe the target with machine gun fire.

After darkness had fallen on this day, December 14th in Hawaii, the aircraft carrier SARATOGA arrived just outside Pearl Harbor. Since the submarine nets had been closed for the night, she could not enter. The huge flattop, with her planes at the ready for the relief effort, waited for the next morning when she could enter the harbor to refuel and make final preparations to sail for Wake.

The Japanese were preparing their strike force on December 15 for another assault on Wake Island. Admiral Inouye was reinforcing his armada to be a much more formidable force than the one defeated on December 11. He had added the crack assault troops from the Maizuru Second Special Landing Force on Saipan.

A huge advantage would favor the Japanese if they were to attack Wake a second time. This was because the carrier task force fresh from the victory at Pearl Harbor had been diverted to the Wake Island operation. This carrier task force boasted the two carriers SORYU and HIRYU, six cruisers, which included the AOBA, FURUTAKA, KAKO, KINUGASE, TONE, and CHIKUMA, and six destroyers. It would stand at some distance away from the island and offer air support. This potent task force was commanded by Admiral Hiroaki Abe, and it added greatly to the strength of the assault task force.

It was clear that the Japanese meant business with this invasion attempt. Admiral Kajioka was replaced by Admiral Abe as overall commander of the task force, but he retained command of the all important amphibious landing force. It was planned that several of the ships carrying 6" guns would remain off the coast of Wake, out of range of the defenders' 5" guns, while fighters from the two carriers would drop wave after wave of bombs on the atoll to systematically eliminate any resistance prior to the landing of the invasion troops.

The attack was planned for the early morning of December 23, and would commence under the cover of darkness so that the 5" and 3" guns on Wake could not be used against the landing craft. Over 1000 special Japanese amphibious assault troops would hit the south beach of Wake in their landing craft and overrun the Marine positions. The invasion plan, though larger in scale, was very similar to the plan used by Admiral Kajioka for the previous attack.

Late in the day on December 15 the last of the remaining classified documents on Wake were destroyed. All codes, ciphers, and other materials that might be of significance to the enemy were taken by Major Bayler and Captain Tharin and placed in one of the petroleum storage drums. They were covered with gasoline and set on fire.

Chapter 21
DAY NINE –
CAPT. THARIN DOWNS ANOTHER JAP PBY

U. S. MARINES STILL RETAIN WAKE ISLAND

Two More Attacks by Japanese Beaten Off; 2 Bombers Downed
1941

WASHINGTON, Dec. 15. (AP)—In a communique the navy department announced that two additional bombing attacks had been launched against the U. S. marine defenders on Wake island Sunday and that two of the attacking bombers had been shot down.

The communique said the first attack was a light one, but that the second was undertaken in great force. No damages of any consequence were inflicted.

The report added that "the marines continue to resist the enemy."

The communique further stated, "Japanese submarines are known to be operating in the Hawaii area with vigorous attacks being made against them by U. S. naval units. This communique is based on reports received up until noon today."

The navy announced Saturday it was unable to communicate with Guam either by cable or radio and said the Japanese probably had captured the island.

Darden Collection

The ninth day of the battle brought another savage air raid from the Japanese planes. Just after 1:00 p.m. twenty-three planes appeared over Wake. The attacking planes were over three miles high before they descended upon the island and its inhabitants. Half of the raiders attacked the airport area, while the remainder concentrated on Camp 2. There were no casualties.

Lt. Kinney and Lt. Kliewer were up in their Wildcats on patrol. They immediately engaged the enemy formation, but did not shoot down any of the incoming planes. Instead, the patrol planes radioed back to the anti-aircraft batteries on the ground the exact altitude of the attacking planes. This allowed the guns to accurately direct their fire at the enemy. The anti-aircraft shells from the batteries below were on the mark, scoring one kill and sending several planes back toward the Marshall Islands trailing smoke.

The bombing, however, was not yet finished. Just before 6:00 p.m. as dusk settled upon Wake atoll a single flying boat attacked Wake, strafing the island with machine gun fire and dropping four heavy bombs on Peale Island. The big seaplane bomber, perhaps displaying a bit of foolish bravery, made a wide turn and passed low over the airport, strafing it with machine gun fire. Capt. Tharin was airborne in one of the Wildcats conducting the twilight patrol. He was contacted on the radio and told of the marauder over the island.

Before the seaplane could get out of sight of Wake Island "Duke" roared down on top of her, ripping the plane with machine gun fire. One of her engines began to spew flames, and the big bomber was forced to make an emergency landing at sea. She was on fire, but Duke wanted to finish her off, so he returned to the airstrip to get a pair of bombs. When these had been attached beneath his wings he took off again in the direction of the ditched bomber. Tharin would not get a chance to sink the plane, though, because just as he neared the spot he saw her sink beneath the waves. The crew was never seen again.

The USS TAMBOR, one of the two American submarines operating near Wake Island, developed mechanical problems on December 16, and was ordered to return to Pearl Harbor. This meant that if enemy ships approached the island there would be no torpedoes from the TAMBOR to harass them.

To add to the discomfort experienced by the tired Wake Island defenders, there was a night bombing raid on the December 16. Those who were asleep were rudely awakened and most spent the remainder of the night peering into the black sky, having to remain on alert for fear of another bombing attack. There would be precious little sleep for the defenders of Wake this night.

At twilight on December 15 (December 16 on Wake) parts of the American relief force steamed out of Pearl Harbor bound for Wake with much needed men, supplies, and additional fire power. The transport TANGIER carried ammunition, supplies, and about 200 Marines. Though this force of fighting men was admittedly small, the Leathernecks were anxious to tangle with the Japs and intervene on behalf of their buddies who were holding out so valiantly at Wake. The oiler NECHES, loaded with the rich cargo of energy that would be needed by the fleet if it were to engage an enemy armada, crept slowly along with the TANGIER.

The sluggish tanker, easily the slowest ship in the group, would impede the progress of the entire force. A temporary escort of four destroyers accompanied the initial group leaving Pearl Harbor. The carrier SARATOGA was still refueling and would leave Pearl the following day and rendezvous with the remainder of the relief fleet.

Even though Admiral Kimmel had been ordered by Washington to take a defensive posture toward the Japanese, there is little doubt that he planned to follow through in the rescue of Wake Island's defenders with his relief force, even if it meant a confrontation with the enemy. The fleet was at sea and headed toward Wake.

The strategy to be employed by the relief force had been spelled out. The primary objective was to anchor to the buoys just off Wilkes channel and resupply the defenders with men, ammunition, materials, and aircraft. After offloading these supplies the ships would take on the wounded men, including Dick Darden, and some of the civilian work force.

As soon as the SARATOGA was within range of the island the squadron of Brewster Buffaloes on her deck were to fly off of the carrier and land on Wake, where they would bolster the nearly depleted ranks of VFM-211. For her own protection, the SARATOGA was to remain out of sight of the island and out of the flyways used by the bombers coming from the Marshalls.

The relief strategy seemed sound and the effort was underway. The men, supplies, and aircraft were on ships and were steaming toward Wake Island. As Dick lay in the concrete dome hospital little did he know that an American force was coming to take him to safety. Neither did he know that a strong enemy force was also preparing to visit Wake, bent upon killing the American defenders and taking the outpost for the Emperor. Dick's biggest concern was keeping his butchered leg from becoming infected and killing him before the enemy ever got their chance.

The men on Wake had no knowledge of the activity at Pearl Harbor to relieve them. They could only hope and speculate that help was coming. In the hospital, Spider Webb was still alive on the cot next to Dick and was beginning to improve to a small degree. He had been on the strong opiates for several days and have actually felt very little pain. He would later remember only the "lovely" feeling of floating around in a drug-induced stupor.

Even during the bombing raids, Webb cared little about his situation. While most of the patients gripped their cots and prayed in mortal fear to be spared by the bombers, Webb felt as if he was floating on a water bed and could not care less what the bombers did.

The doctors realized that Webb was becoming dependent on the highly addictive drugs, so they began to wean him from them. As he came down from the high, he realized that he was in a hospital with other wounded men. He gradually began to feel better and eat normally. The man on the cot on the other side of Webb was Marine Master Sergeant Andrew J. Paskiewicz. He had been a mechanic and, like Spider and Dick, had been wounded on the first day of the war.

Spider noticed that Paskiewitz constantly dipped Copenhagen snuff out of small, disk-shaped cans. Some of his friends would get the snuff at the contractor's mess and bring it to him when they visited during the evenings. Spider also noticed that Paskiewitz never spit. He wondered where all of the tobacco juice went, knowing that to swallow it would cause most men to become extremely sick to their stomachs. Paskiewitz continued to dip all day long, never getting sick or spitting.

The day to day grind was becoming extremely tiring and nerve-wracking for Wiley Sloman and the men at Battery L. The battery was standing running watches, with two hours on and then two hours off. This went on all day and all night, and meant that the maximum amount of sleep was for a two hour duration. The men were becoming irritable from the lack of rest. Since they had to work all day in the hot gritty sand fortifying their position, exhaustion was beginning to set in.

The only opportunity that Sloman had to bathe was during one of his two hour rest breaks after dark. He and his buddies could walk over to the nearby lagoon and rinse off in the briny water. There was no soap, but that didn't matter. It wouldn't lather in the salt water anyway.

Chapter 22
DAY TEN—SHIPS OFFSHORE?

The USS TANGIER, part of the relief force carrying men and supplies to beleaguered Wake Island.

Early on the morning of Wednesday, December 17, the defenders of Wake Island had some anxious and unexplainable moments. At about 2:00 a.m. the lookouts on Wilkes Island reported seeing several ships, possibly as many as a dozen, through a heavy drizzle just off the coast. So strongly did they feel they had seen ships on the dark waters that they called Major Devereux to alert him. Then other lookouts confirmed seeing ships as they strained to peer through the raw weather onto the blackened ocean.

Everyone felt that an invasion was imminent, so the entire defense force was ordered to report to their battle stations. Wake Island was on full alert, and for an hour the men peered into the darkness, straining to see a target. Everyone fully expected to see landing craft hit the beaches at any time and Japanese soldiers swarm onto the island. But, none would present themselves this night. At dawn there were no vessels of any kind on the seas around Wake atoll. No one would ever be able to explain what several lookouts had seen in the early morning hours. All that the men had to show for their efforts was another sleepless night.

At 6:00 a.m. the morning patrol lifted off to scan the seas

around Wake. Due to the miracles accomplished by Lt. Kinney and his men there were now four planes available for service. This was nothing less than an amazing feat, considering the state of the bombed and burned graveyard of planes from which the parts had been salvaged. In addition, many of the tools had been damaged or destroyed in the initial raid and were unusable. The removal of parts from the junked planes and the reassembly of the parts on the other planes was often being carried out with repaired tools or crude homemade replacements.

Major Putnam would later have the highest praise for Lt. Kinney, Sgt. Hamilton, Aviation Machinist's Mate Hesson, and the other men who solved the puzzles of matching parts until the airplanes would fly. Putnam said, "These three, with the assistance of the civilian workmen, did a truly remarkable and almost magical job. With almost no tools and a complete lack of normal equipment they performed all types of repair and replacement work."

"They changed engines and propellers from one airplane to another," Putnam continued, "and even completely built up new engines and propellers from scrap parts salvaged from wrecks. They replaced minor parts and assemblies, and repaired damage to fuselage and wings and landing gear; all this in spite of the fact that they were working with new types with which they had had no previous experience and were without instruction manuals of any kind." The efforts of these mechanics in transforming wrecks and heaps of bent and burned debris into operational warplanes was nothing short of extraordinary.

Later in the day the Tokyo Express paid its daily visit to pound the island. Just after 1:00 p.m. twenty-seven enemy bombers, in V-shaped formations over three miles above the ocean, approached Wake. When the bombs began to fall a diesel oil storage tank on Wilkes Island was set ablaze resulting in a column of smoke that rose thousands of feet into the heavens for the rest of the day, and most of the remaining tents and supply areas in Camp 1 were destroyed. One of the evaporators used to purify water was also damaged.

The Marine anti-aircraft guns shot down one of the enemy planes, but there were no casualties on the ground during this raid. The men hoped that this would be all the excitement for the day since they were weary to the bone from days of hard work, apprehension about the bombing raids, and the chronic lack of sleep. But the midday raid was not all that the Japanese had planned for the defenders of Wake Island on December 17.

Just minutes before six o'clock the largest attack to date by the big Kawanishi 97 flying boats from Wotje began. Eight of the huge patrol bombers flew over the island dropping their bombs and strafing selected targets. Despite the increased number of attacking planes, there was no major damage done as the island slipped into darkness.

By this time the relief task force had rendezvoused and the full complement of ships was steaming westward toward Wake. The only impediment to an expeditious voyage was the oiler NECHES, which toiled along at a top speed of about ten knots. The men of the relief force were eager but tense as they found themselves in a veritable no man's land west of Hawaii.

Only two weeks before this date the Americans had felt comfortable sailing these waters, feeling as if they were playing in their own backyard in the central Pacific. Now, with major enemy forces having ventured close enough to devastate Pearl Harbor, and with the whereabouts of that force still unknown, lookouts on the relief ships kept a close eye on the seas around them. The relative safety of Hawaii faded from view.

On December 17 the defenders on Wake were requested to advise Pearl Harbor on the status of the construction project on the island. It seemed to those receiving the transmission that there was confusion back at headquarters about the state of affairs on Wake. Commander Cunningham's reply informed those who made the request that half of the trucks and equipment used in the construction project had been destroyed during the enemy bombings; most of the fuel and explosives had been blown up; the machine shops, supply buildings, and warehouses had been burned to the ground; and that generally there was a war in progress on a daily basis amid which constructing an airport was difficult.

Pearl Harbor was informed that daytime construction was difficult because the noise of the bulldozers and heavy equipment obscured the sounds of incoming planes and made their detection very difficult. Nighttime construction was even more difficult since the island was blacked out. Cunningham indicated that the morale of the civilian work force was bad. Most of the civilians were, in fact, trying to hide in the scrubby forests and save their lives. Often it was difficult to get a crew together for a work detail, and before work had begun many of the civilians had melted back into the relative protection of the underbrush.

In Walter Cook's sand-covered shelter, the men were showing the effects of their strained lifestyle. They remained in or near the shelter most of the day to protect themselves from the Japanese raiders from the sky. At night they worked with the Marines moving their big guns and the oil and gas drums. Moving one of the guns involved more than jacking up the heavy piece of equipment and moving it to a new location. Cook and his friends would have to move several hundred sand bags and restack them around the new position. Despite the all-night work details the men felt that it was well worth the effort, since usually the next day the bombers would destroy the old gun site and miss the new positions.

Chapter 23
DAY ELEVEN—
ADMIRAL PYE UNSURE ABOUT RELIEF

On December 18 Admiral Kimmel was relieved of his duties as Commander of the Pacific Fleet at Pearl Harbor. Admiral Chester A. Nimitz was named to succeed him as Commander in Chief, Pacific Allied Command. The timing of this appointment could not have been worse for the men on Wake Island, for Admiral Nimitz was in Washington, D.C. and could not reach Hawaii to take full command until December 25, Christmas day, at the earliest.

Vice Admiral William S. Pye was given the unenviable duty of being the interim commander of the fleet until Admiral Nimitz could reach Pearl Harbor. His job was virtually impossible, because if he sent the relief force to Wake and the enemy destroyed it, he would be remembered for a huge blunder on nearly the same scale as Pearl Harbor. On the other hand, if he did not send the fleet, he would be accused of abandoning the boys on Wake.

Admiral Pye had several options, but he would have to make a hasty decision in picking a plan of action. Pye could send the relief force directly into the waters around Wake, which might be already occupied by enemy warships, and invite a major battle. He could approach Wake and attack the enemy with the planes from the carrier, SARATOGA. He could send the transports to Wake unprotected to evacuate the men. Or, he could do the safest thing for the Pacific Fleet and order the entire task force to turn back and return to Pearl Harbor.

The relief force was already bound for Wake. Plans were made, then changed, and then changed again. Pye was known as a good strategist , but he was also known to be very conservative. He was committed to do whatever could be done to relieve the defenders on Wake Island. At the same time, however, he realized full well that to send the relief fleet headlong into a battle might result in another catastrophe. On the heels of the catastrophe that American forces had just sustained at Pearl Harbor, such a defeat might truly jeopardize the entire American fleet in the Pacific.

Whereas Admiral Kimmel had favored an aggressive action to save the defenders of Wake, Admiral Pye was much more conservative and held the preservation of the existing American strength as his major objective until Admiral Nimitz arrived. As the American relief fleet moved closer to Wake, the decision to use it was becoming more unlikely.

The relief force continued to steam toward Wake, and the Marines on the ships began to get restless. Those who were 5" gun specialists practiced on the 5" gun on the TANGIER. The anti-aircraft specialists set up their guns on the TANGIER and practiced drills constantly, both to polish their skills and to work off nervous energy. Some of the Marines received instruction on the new radar equipment which they would deliver to Wake.

The delicate radar equipment, along with some of the other men, supplies, and ammunition, would have to be taken ashore on the lighters operated by the Navy boat crew. There was concern about the danger involved in sitting offshore during enemy bombing raids while the offloading process was taking place. It was decided that the .50 cal. machine guns would be lowered onto the barges in fully operational condition so they would be ready for action in the event of a simultaneous enemy attack. If the TANGIER got into serious trouble in such an attack she would beach herself in order to be certain that she would not sink and the materials would make it ashore.

There was no bombing raid on December 18. As the men anticipated the "V" formations of bombers, they were surprised to see only a single Japanese plane flying at a very high altitude nearly five miles above the atoll. The enemy plane was far above the range of the anti-aircraft guns, and even above the Wildcats on patrol that day.

The plane made no attempt to drop explosives on the island, but probably accomplished another objective which was just as important to the Japanese. If it was photographing the island it would give the enemy a detailed picture of every target which remained intact on the ground and would allow them to plan the next phase of their Wake Island siege.

Chapter 24
Day Twelve—The Tokyo Express Arrives Again

About December 19 a civilian worker came into the hospital late in the morning to visit one of the wounded men. He only stayed long enough to pass pleasantries and then he turned to leave the bunker. "You had better stay in here, it's almost time for the Tokyo Express," warned Dr. Kahn. "Oh, no, I'm all right," replied the man as he walked out through the hospital's metal doors, apparently unconcerned about the bombing that normally occurred about this time of day. It was a few minutes before eleven o'clock, and he ignored the obvious danger, feeling that there was plenty of time for him to reach his safe spot before the midday raid arrived.

Just moments after the man cleared the doors everyone inside could hear the explosions beginning somewhere down the island. The bombing raid had begun with twenty-seven enemy planes arriving over the island. There were three "V" formations, each composed of the usual nine planes. They struck near the hospital this morning, some concentrating on the air field and others on Camp 1. Since the hospital was located just across the road from the end of the airfield, this attack came very close to Dick and his wounded friends. Since the Japanese had selected the aviation area for their target, the civilian had walked right into a vicious bombing attack.

Less than five minutes after leaving the hospital, the civilian worker was rushed back into the concrete dome with a serious arm injury. A piece of shrapnel had nearly severed his hand, and only a small piece of tissue connected the bloody, dangling extremity to his nub of an arm. The doctors fixed him up as best they could and placed him three cots away from Dick. There were no tetanus shots remaining, as

Dick had received the last one on December 8.

The remainder of Camp 1, along with the Pan Am building, were destroyed during the attack. Anti-aircraft crews were successful in hitting four enemy planes. The crew of one of the stricken planes parachuted before the plane crashed into the sea. They landed in the sea and were not seen again.

Within a couple of days the civilian with the hand injury contracted lockjaw. Saliva would accumulate in his throat and he could not move his jaws to spit it out. He would reach into his mouth with his good hand and pull out long tags of saliva and mucous. The scene was gruesome, and there was nothing that the doctors could do for him. Dick and everyone in the hospital would have to listen to the chilling sounds of the man wheezing and gurgling to get his breathe all night long.

Finally the man died a slow, horrible death, or so it seemed. After having been pronounced dead he was rolled into a sheet and taken just outside the hospital bunker where the body was laid out of the way in the sand.

The strain of twelve days of battle was more evident than ever on the defenders of Wake Island. The men virtually lived in their gun pits or underground in protected areas to avoid the enemy raids. Their irregular eating habits combined with the never-ending tension to cause an epidemic of gastric disorders. Nerves were frayed and everyone was weary. No one had enjoyed the liberty of a good night's sleep since the siege had begun on December 8. The men could only hope that reinforcements were on the way.

Chapter 25
Day Thirteen—
Japanese Invasion Fleet Leaves Roi

At 7:00 a.m. on the morning of Saturday, December 20 a message came over the radio from Midway that a Navy PBY from Pearl Harbor was on its way to Wake Island. The men quickly heard the news and perceived it to be a good sign. Was this the relief force?

The weather on Wake was ugly this Saturday morning, and a hard rain fell from the thick cloud cover. Radio silence would normally be maintained, but the PBY radioed ahead for weather reports. The Japanese were almost surely monitoring the messages, so the PBY pilot was giving away his position to any enemy plane which might be in the vicinity and was eager to send an American plane into the Pacific.

Without incident the PBY splashed down in the lagoon at about 3:30 that afternoon. The two ensigns who piloted the plane were shocked as they got a firsthand look at the devastation on Wake. The neat ensigns, clad in their clean Navy whites, provided a striking contrast to the Wake defenders, most of whom had not been able to bath or shave for nearly two weeks. Wake's defenders were conserving their dwindling supply of fresh water by washing their clothes and sponge bathing themselves in the salt water of the lagoon.

The Ensigns were driven by Commander Cunningham in his pickup truck from Peale Island to the command post on Wake. There one of the pilots, Ensign Murphy, exchanged messages with Major Devereux and Commander Cunningham. The big chuckle that night that visitors brought into the hospital was how aghast the pilots had been at the devastation on Wake. No one back at Pearl Harbor had apparently envisioned the extent to which Wake was being pummeled by the bombings. The two ensigns had certainly not been prepared for what they saw.

One message indicated, much to the delight of Major Devereux and Commander Cunningham, that a relief force was enroute to Wake, and would arrive on December 24. Spirits soared as they learned that the TANGIER, with her Marines, and the SARATOGA, with her deck covered with American warplanes, were steaming toward them. The message contained specific instructions about the conduct of the relief effort. Nearly all of the civilians would be evacuated. A complete list of men and materials onboard the Tangier gave Cunningham and Devereux every reason to be optimistic with such a favorable turn of events.

A more ominous force was also steaming toward Wake on December 20. Admiral Kajioka left Roi in the Marshall Islands, again aboard his flagship YUBARI, with a reinforced fleet that had but one objective—to destroy the American presence on Wake atoll. Vice Admiral Inouye decided at his headquarters in Truk that he would take no chances this time. He ordered a powerful group of cruisers, which included the AOBA, FURUTAKA, KINUGASA, TONE, CHIKUMA, and KAKO to join the assault force. The original assault force of 450 men had swollen to over 2000. These troops were in several transports, protected by a swarm of destroyers.

The PBY was scheduled to return to Midway the next morning, and Major Bayler was ordered to be aboard. He had originally been ordered to continue to Midway by the earliest possible means so that he could set up a communications center there. For the rest of the afternoon and evening he worked feverishly to collect letters and messages that men all over the island were writing for him to carry back, in hopes that they would reach loved ones back home.

Major Bayler decided to send telegrams only to the families of the wounded, and he took a brief message from many of the men in the hospital. Chick Lanning and Spider Webb were among those giving him a brief message to be sent back. Originally it was planned that Mr. Hevenor, the Bureau of the Budget auditor who had missed his flight out of Wake on the first day of hostilities, would be aboard the PBY when it left the next day. However, he was told that a Navy regulation required any passenger on a Navy plane to have a parachute. Mr. Hevenor had none and there was not one available on the island. Hevenor would miss his last chance to be evacuated by friendly forces from Wake Island.

Meanwhile, the Wake Island that Major Bayler was leaving had begun to experience shortages of several precious commodities. Ammunition was running low at some of the gun emplacements for both the machine guns and the larger weapons. Medical supplies were in extremely short supply and food supplies were beginning to dwindle. Not the least of the Marines' worries were the civilians, some of whom began to come out of hiding in the bushes and take what they needed for survival.

In Washington, Admiral Harold Stark, Chief of Naval Operations, let Admiral Pye know that he thought of Wake Island as a liability. Indeed, another major loss to the Japanese at this critical point, less than two weeks after the attack on Pearl Harbor, could very well result in a greater loss of American men, equipment, ships, and ability to defend the west coast than Wake Island and her defenders represented in their entirety. It was a very tough decision that weighed on Admiral Pye, who would make the final decision.

Chapter 26
Day Fourteen—Carrier Planes Hit Wake

At about 7:00 on the morning of December 21 the PBY left Wake atoll bound for Midway Island. Major Bayler was aboard, carrying the messages from many Wake defenders which he would transmit to loved ones back in the States. Major Bayler would become known as "The Last Man Off Wake Island." As the PBY rose above Wake and headed for Midway it left behind a group of optimistic defenders who were confident that a force of Marines and warplanes were on the way to help them kick the Jap raiders in the teeth and keep Wake Atoll firmly in American hands.

In less than two hours the mood turned much more somber on Wake Island. Just before 9:00 a.m. enemy planes unleashed yet another air attack. Twenty-nine Japanese Navy attack bombers and eighteen fighter aircraft bombed and machine-gunned several targets, including most of the remaining gun positions.

Only one Wildcat remained in good enough condition to fly that morning. Major Putnam sped to the airstrip through enemy fire in his truck hoping to pursue the waves of planes. He was nearly hit several times, but he made it to the parked plane and managed to get it airborne near the end of the raid. This was the last of the worn out, shot up, cannibalized F4F-3's. It sputtered and gasped, not able to charge into combat. Major Putnam guided the wounded Wildcat back home to the coral runway, unable to engage the enemy.

While the damage wrought by the attacking planes was relatively little, the raid brought on an ominous change in the battle for the defenders of Wake Island. The attacking Japanese planes were not the normal long range bombers. They were Japanese Navy planes which operated from the decks of aircraft carriers. The Japanese carrier force was only 250 miles northwest of Wake, poised to offer massive air support if needed.

Commander Cunningham sent an urgent message to Pearl informing Admiral Pye of this new turn in the battle. There had to be at least one enemy aircraft carrier nearing the island. To make matters worse, Cunningham knew that carriers do not travel alone. A large enemy force was heading his way, and Cunningham knew what this meant. The immediate need for the relief force became more critical.

The carrier planes were unmistakable compared to the larger bombers that had stalked the Wake defenders for nearly two weeks. These planes were smaller, sleeker, faster, and roared in over the island at lower altitudes. Their attacks were conducted at high speeds and at close quarters. There was little or no time for the antiaircraft guns to react, and they were virtually ineffective against this new type of enemy. The dive bombers, on the other hand, were potent. They scored

The Japanese carrier HIRYU , part of the task force that attacked Pearl Harbor two weeks before, brought its deadly warplanes into the vicinity of Wake Island

hits on several positions, killing at least one Marine and damaging the guns at Toki Point on the northern tip of Peale Island.

The carrier-based planes were, in fact, operating from the decks of the Japanese carriers HIRYU and SORYU, two of the ships that had been instrumental in the surprise attack just two weeks before at Pearl Harbor. Wake Island was now getting a dose of the same treatment that had just laid waste to much of the American Pacific fleet in Hawaii.

Commander Cunningham did not know how near the relief force was to Wake, but, by this time he was painfully aware that the enemy fleet was within striking distance by air. What he didn't know was that over 100 enemy planes stood ready on the decks of the carriers within range of Wake Island.

The island's defenses against air attack were the lowest they had been. Charles Holmes' 3" gun position near Peacock Point was one of the few still in working order. Most of the guns had been damaged by the bombings, had never had proper range-finding equipment, or had never even had a complement of men for the gun crew. As the time for the final shootout drew near, Holmes' gun would be the only one on the island which had come through the bombings unscathed, was fully manned, and still had all operating equipment in full working order.

The worst fears of the Wake defenders were about to be realized. As the enemy carrier force operated in the waters north of Wake and began to accelerate the aerial bombardment of the beleaguered atoll, ships carrying the amphibious invasion force steamed out of the Japanese base at Roi and Namur Islands in the Kwajalein Atoll. The assault fleet steamed out of Roi at 9:00 a.m. on the 21st, heading almost due north toward its objective.

Most of these ships had participated in the failed attempt to take the island on December 8, and many still bore scars of that encounter. The invasion fleet would join the naval forces for the final assault on the atoll. Admiral Kajioka knew what another failure would mean.

The Japanese began to increase the pressure even more on the Wake defenders. Both the Navy planes, operating from the carriers some 200 miles north of the island, and the land-based planes from the Marshall Islands began to unleash their coordinated wrath upon strategic points on Wake, Wilkes, and Peale Islands. Wake's warplanes, artillery batteries, and machine gun positions were targeted. They were prioritized in that order of importance.

Just after noon another air raid began. This one was carried out by thirty-three twin-engine bombers which arrived from their base on Roi. They hit Peale Island especially hard. Fewer and fewer of the big guns remained operational. The men continued with the excruciatingly arduous task of moving the remaining 3" guns to new locations after each raid.

The Japanese planes were at an extremely high altitude, over 19,000 feet during the noon attack. This posed numerous problems for Charles Holmes. He had to use projectiles with twenty-one second fuses because of the altitude of the targets. This meant that the guns could not be fired until the planes were almost directly overhead and had already released some of their bombs. In order to fire at such targets, Holmes' 3" gun at Peacock Point had to be fired at maximum elevation, pointed almost straight up. Even so, the 3" guns that remained operational continued to belch out their deadly projectiles, filling the heavens over Wake with puffs of smoke from the explosions of lethal flak.

The attacking planes were at such an altitude that the accuracy of their bombing was somewhat impaired. Many of the bombs fell harmlessly into the lagoon, while others fell on non-target areas of the island. Some of the bombs did, however, find critical targets and draw blood.

During the bombing raids there was nothing Wiley Sloman could do but hide in his foxhole. The 5" gun could not be used to fire upward at the airplanes and his 1903 Springfield rifle was useless against aircraft. He was absolutely defenseless if one of the Jap bombardiers got lucky. Sloman had become so physically exhausted that during the bombing raids he would crawl into his hole and take a nap. It was one of the few opportunities that he got to rest. Only a blast in his immediate area would wake him.

Several men were killed by the second raid on December 21, and a number of wounded men were taken to the hospital. Battery D on Peale island was issuing heavy fire on the incoming planes when a bomb fell directly into the gun pit, killing Platoon Sgt. Johnalson E. Wright. "Big Wright," as the burly veteran was known, had been an inspiring leader for many of the younger Marines. The bomb's direct hit had also crippled the anti-aircraft defense of that segment of Peale Island.

With the loss of Battery D the already thin air defenses became practically nonexistent. Of the original twelve 3" anti-aircraft guns, only one battery remained. Little help could be expected from VMF-211. Despite the courageous efforts of the pilots and ground crews, only two planes remained in flying condition.

The need for the relief force to arrive and reinforce the defenders on Wake was rapidly becoming critical. At 8:00 p.m. on December 21 the relief force was 627 miles east of Wake Island. The task force was maintaining a strict radio silence so it would not give away its position to the enemy naval forces that were known to be in the area. However, as updates of the conditions on the island were radioed to headquarters at Pearl Harbor they were being relayed to the relief force.

Men worked long grueling hours that night preparing the airstrip with revetments for the planes they knew were on the decks of the relief carrier SARATOGA. They prayed that the relief force was steaming their way since it was their only hope against the enemy that was surely closing in. Admiral Fletcher on the ASTORIA, however, was still over 600 miles away at 10:00 that night.

Fletcher was fully aware of the dive bomber attacks being conducted by the Japanese carriers since he was monitoring the messages being sent from Commander Cunningham to Pearl. But, for the moment he was preoccupied with the slow process of refueling his destroyers. His ships had adequate fuel to reach Wake, but not enough for a prolonged naval battle in which extensive maneuvering at sea would require excessive fuel consumption.

The oiler NECHES had slowed the entire relief force to a snail's pace. The slow pace of the fleet angered the Marines and pilots who were anxious to get into the fray with their beleaguered comrades on Wake. Admiral Fletcher would have to bring his carrier within 200 miles of Wake before the Brewster Buffaloes could leave the ship enroute to the airstrip on the atoll.

During the night the aviation mechanics at the Wake air strip, headed by Lt. Kinney and Sgt. Hamilton, completed another puzzle, piecing together yet another cannibalized Wildcat. Now two planes were capable of lifting off the airstrip to do battle with the waves of enemy fighters and bombers.

On the 21st the TRITON, one of the two friendly submarines operating in the waters off Wake, was ordered to proceed toward the south and out of the general area so that it would not mistake the relief force for the enemy and attack friendly ships.

Japanese war art depicts the battle in the sky. A swarm of Japanese planes watch as an American plane, in flames, screams toward the ocean

Chapter 27
DAY FIFTEEN—THE ENEMY IS POISED

On the morning of December 22 Task Force 14 was just over 500 miles east of Wake Island. Admiral Fletcher was still trying to refuel his eight destroyers, but the task was being hampered by steadily worsening weather conditions and rough seas. In fact, it took all day to refuel half of the thirsty destroyers. Fletcher did not want to take a chance of engaging the enemy in a naval battle with his ships low on fuel. Should they find themselves in a chase or retreat it would be disastrous to run out of fuel. He decided to endure the problems of refueling at sea in order to avoid the risk of running low in battle.

In order for the ships to refuel they were required to slow down to a speed of six knots and be oriented into the wind. This made matters even worse, since the wind was coming from the northeast and to head the ships in that direction meant they would actually be moving away from Wake. At the end of the day, with four ships still to be refueled, Fletcher's ships were actually farther away from Wake than they had been earlier in the day.

Lt. Carl Davidson went up in one of the two remaining Wildcats for the noon patrol. The second fighter, showing less desire to become airborne than her pilot, refused to crank for over an hour. Finally the motor sputtered, the prop reluctantly churning into action, and Capt. Herbert C. Frueler took her aloft. Lt. Davidson radioed that he had found two formations of enemy planes, a total of thirty-nine planes, approaching Wake from the north at 12,000 feet.

The carrier-based planes included Aichi-99 dive bombers (Vals), Nakajima B5N Type 97 Carrier Attack Bombers (Kates), and six of the new Zero fighters (Zekes). The Zero was a sleek Japanese combat warplane far superior to the stubby F4F-3 Wildcats. This was the first time Zeroes had been encountered by the Marines in the skies over Wake.

Even though Davidson and Frueler were facing a new and superior warplane, the Marine pilots did not hesitate to engage the enemy. The two Wildcats were battered by fifteen days of combat. They were "kluged," or assembled from parts, by Lt. Kinney and Sgt. Hamilton. Lt. Davidson was in Wildcat #9, which was using the propeller from another plane and had the engine from #10, which had been destroyed earlier. Captain Frueler was in Wildcat #8, which had engine cylinders, pistons, magnetos, and a canopy from several destroyed aircraft.   The two pilots dove into the enemy formations in a heroic effort to ward off as many of the attackers as possible. Captain Frueler began tailing one of the Kates, firing at the plane with his machine guns while the rear gunner in the enemy bomber returned his fire. He continued to spray the plane, which had No. B1-315 emblazoned on its tail, with machine gun fire. He saw it begin trailing smoke just before it crashed into the ocean. He then directed his fire at a nearby Zero, causing it to explode into a fireball and, like the bomber, fall over two miles into the sea.

The force of the explosion from the Zero knocked Frueler's plane out of control and ripped its skin with fragments of hot metal. Both Frueler and Davidson suddenly found Zeros close on their tails

with machine guns blazing. To remain in the fray would almost certainly be a fight to the death, considering the numerical and aerodynamic superiority of the enemy in the air.

Frueler could not shake his pursuer and was suddenly hit in the back and shoulder by the zero's machine gun fire. He went into a steep dive toward the sea below in a last ditch effort to escape the fire from the enemy fighter. The maneuver worked, and Frueler's plane limped along just a few feet above the ocean toward the airstrip. He reached the island but was too weak to crank down the landing gear. He crash landed his Wildcat on her belly, narrowly avoiding being killed. The plane was destroyed.

When Captain Frueler last saw the other Wildcat, Lt. Davidson was firing on a Jap bomber but had a Zero close on his tail. Frueler had looked away while trying to save his own plane and he never saw Lt. Davidson again. Lt. Carl Davidson did not return to Wake Island and was never heard from again, presumably shot down at sea as he fought the Japanese Zero.

With the loss of Lt. Davidson and the crash of Captain Frueler, the Wake Island air defenses ceased to exist. Thus ended the heroic exploits of twelve planes and pilots of VMF-211. The twelve pilots had fought with great courage and valor during the fifteen day siege of Wake Island. They gained the respect of every man who watched them from below.

According to a post-war analysis of Japanese casualty reports, the bomber that Captain Frueler shot down was, indeed, the "Kate," Nakajima B5N bomber No. B1-315. The plane was piloted by Noboru Kani, who had flown the plane from the deck of the Japanese carrier SORYU to Pearl Harbor fifteen days earlier. Kani was officially credited with dropping the bomb on the USS ARIZONA at Pearl Harbor that sunk her and entombed over 1000 American sailors in her hull.

Later in the day the Japanese planes bombed and strafed Wake Island, this time with thirty-three land-based "Bettys" from the Marshall Islands. This was the sixteenth bombing attack on Wake in fifteen days. Nearly all conspicuous buildings and detectable targets had been reduced to rubble. Had it not been for Major Devereux's decision to move the 3" guns between raids, the island's antiaircraft defenses would probably have long since been demolished.

After Captain Frueler was taken to the hospital the remainder of the aviation unit, under the command of Major Putnam, reported to Major Devereux to fight as infantrymen. One of the pilots, Lt. Kinney, was ordered to the hospital, though he objected vigorously. He was put to bed immediately, completely exhausted and suffering from a serious case of diarrhea.

Wake's gallant aviators, VMF-211, had fought a courageous and amazing battle over Wake Island, but their planes had been reduced to so many piles of twisted rubble and none remained operational. The defenders of Wake were left with no air support to hurl against the forces that were massing against them.

The advance vessels of the invasion fleet neared Wake Island led by three submarines. These three ships, RO-60, RO-61, and RO-62, acted as forward observers, on the lookout for torpedo boats that were much dreaded by the Japanese. Close behind the submarines was a group of ships that formed a surface scouting force. The Japanese invasion plan was about to be put into effect. The enemy began to close in on the island.

Admiral Kajioka well remembered the sting leveled against his forces by the seacoast 5" guns on December 11. In order to minimize the effectiveness of these guns, he planned to invade the island in the middle of the night. To further surprise his adversaries he would not order a naval bombardment prior to landing his troops. There would be no light show to announce the arrival of these assault troops.

The men on Wake were fully aware that an invasion was imminent. Their defensive guns had been greatly reduced by over two weeks of daily bombing and strafing. But on December 22 they positioned themselves for one last stand. They prayed for the relief force to reach them in time, but time was running out and they knew it.

More than twenty Japanese ships were positioned in the vicinity of Wake Island on the evening of December 22, ranging from 30 to 200 miles offshore. The troop transports carrying Admiral Kajioka and his assault force were in place, as were the carriers with their decks covered with fighter planes.

The invasion force near Wake Island on December 22nd was over three times the magnitude of the one that had come for the previous attempt on December 11th. Fifteen hundred men were available to storm the beaches if needed. Of these, one thousand were members of the Maizuru Special Naval Landing Force. This unit had been brought to full strength for the landing on Wake when its reinforcements from Saipan had arrived on Roi.

The Japanese reconnaissance ships had not reported any American surface ships in the vicinity of Wake. The invasion was, therefore, proceeding as planned without resistance at sea. The Japanese had considered American naval resistance as probable, so they had positioned a significant portion of their fleet, Cruiser Division Six, just east of Wake in an attempt to intercept any American fleet which might attempt to intercede during the invasion. This Japanese force included four heavy cruisers and would have been a significant obstacle if the relief force decided to make a run for the island.

The Japanese landing plans called for four to six landing craft to carry fifty men each to the beach. Then the remainder of the assault troops, aboard two larger ships designated Patrol Craft 32 and Patrol Craft 33, would hit the beaches. These ships would run themselves aground in an area near the middle of Wake Island's south beach just below the airport.

Japanese assault troops planned to come ashore at several points, including Wilkes Island, Camp 1 on Wake, the airstrip area, and possibly just west of Peacock Point. Once ashore they would regroup, organize themselves, and then fan out to overrun their objectives.

Meanwhile, Admiral Fletcher was still lumbering along some five hundred miles east of Wake, with his superiors still indecisive about what to do. Admiral Pye was troubled by several

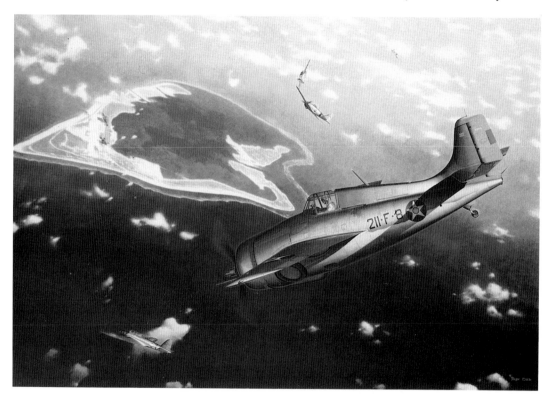

Capt. Herbert Frueler, flying on of the last two patched up Wildcats, engages and destroyers the Japanese "Kate" bomber, piloted by Noboru Kani, the pilot credited with sinking the USS ARIZONA at Pearl Harbor.

Gene Monihan

unknowns. How large was the enemy carrier force that was nearing Wake? Where was the force that had devastated Pearl Harbor just over two weeks before? Would a relief effort at Wake result in a major sea battle, and if so, would American forces be dealt another crippling blow?

Pye decided to protect the allied Pacific fleet at all costs. To be defeated again so soon after Pearl Harbor would render the entire west coast of the continental United States vulnerable to the Empire of Japan. Admiral Pye was a well-respected, but conservative, naval leader. He went about making plans to maximize the protection of American's overall interests in the Pacific.

On Wake everyone knew that the enemy was near. Every preparation that could be made with the island's now meager resources was being made. The gun positions were given ammunition and hand grenades. Nearly all of the American defenders of Wake Island were dug in, waiting in their foxholes for the enemy. One exception was Lt. Poindexter who, along with his group of about two dozen Marines and Navy men, supported by several civilian volunteers, were ready with the two trucks in the mobile reserve unit.

Major Putnam gathered his flyers and support personnel, fewer than twenty in all, and reported to Major Devereux. They would be infantrymen where the fight was expected to be the hottest, on the south beach. Devereux radioed a message to Pearl Harbor that an enemy attack was imminent. It was simply a matter of when and where the Japanese warriors would swarm onto the beaches. The fifteen hundred troops in the bowels of Admiral Kajioka's ships were ready to storm ashore and invade the island the instant he gave the order.

Admiral Stark in Washington was no more eager to risk a direct confrontation with a major Japanese force at sea than Admiral Pye, and he told him so. However, he did not rule out an evacuation of the men on Wake. The decision to, and the responsibility for, relief of Wake Island was squarely on Admiral Pye's shoulders. The Marines begged for orders that would allow them to confront the enemy and help their fellow leathernecks on Wake. But the agonizing decision could not be made. First it was,"yes", then it changed to,"no."

The American leaders at Pearl Harbor knew the situation on Wake was deteriorating rapidly. Again the circumstances and options were heard. A full relief effort at Wake might develop into a direct confrontation with a strong enemy fleet. This could result in another crushing defeat which might endanger the entire remainder of the American Pacific Fleet. The loss of this fleet could conceivably cost the United States the Hawaiian islands and all of the American bases there.

A compromise was considered. It called for the relief force not to engage the enemy, but to send the TANGIER on a dangerous run to Wake to deliver the additional Marines and simultaneously to send the Brewster Buffaloes from the SARATOGA to provide additional air support.

Admiral Pye wisely decided against the compromise idea. He did not know that Japanese Cruiser Division Six was stationed east of Wake. But he decided not to run the TANGIER to the island alone, almost surely saving the lives of the two hundred Marines aboard her. To have made that run would have sent the lightly armed

A Japanese "Kate" bomber during a bombing raid over Wake Island.
Gene Monihan

transcript directly toward the heavily armed Japanese cruisers, which lay waiting between the relief force and the island.

When the sun set on December 22 Admiral Pye had not yet decided which course of action to pursue. But there was no doubt in Admiral Kajioka's mind about the course of action that he would take. His objectives were crystal clear. So bent was he upon taking Wake Island this time that he was fully prepared to run two of his destroyers ashore on the island and have their crews join in the fighting if they were needed to turn the tide of the battle.

Admiral Kajioka was within thirty miles of Wake Island at 10:00 p.m. on the night of December 22, 1941. His fleet continued to move cautiously forward at about eight knots. The invasion force finally arrived in the immediate vicinity of Wake atoll, less than ten miles from Wake's south beach.

The weather was turning rough, certainly not favoring a landing by sea in small craft. Kayoshi Ibushi, a correspondent who was with the Imperial Japanese Naval Information Section docu-

menting the battle, wrote that "the storm came down upon the ship...and terrific wind whistled over the mast. The angry waves tossed the ships around as if they were toys."

There was no turning back for Admiral Kajioka, regardless of the weather. The invasion would continue as planned. The troops of the Maizuru Second Naval Landing Force prepared for battle. In full battle gear they were prepared to board the landing craft. This unit had three companies of riflemen. Each company was designated by number, but was commonly known by the last name of the company commander. The three commanders were named Uchida, Takano, and Itaya. These three men prepared their troops. The stage had been set and the battle for Wake Island was about to begin.

Then lookouts on the ships saw a blinking light through the storm. The faint outline of the island could be seen. The advance of the ships was slowed and the order was given to "Charge." The troops went to their landing craft and boarded, about to be dropped into the sea and sent out into the black raging ocean toward Wake Island in search of their destiny and the ultimate glory.

Lt., Carl Davidson was last seen with a Zero close on his tail. Davidson disappeared from Capt. Frueler's view and was never seen again.

Gene Monihan

126

Wake's South Beach braces for an invasion by the enemy.

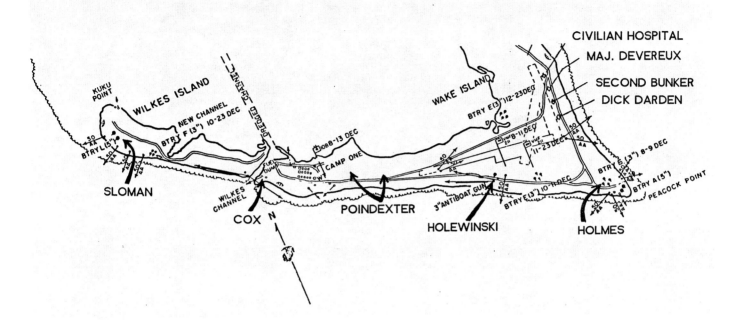

Ready for the Japanese: Wiley Sloman is at the 5" inch gun on Wilkes Island, Jim Cox is at his machine gun near the Wilkes Channel, Arthur Poindexter commands his Mobile Reserve on Wake's beach road. Ralph Holewinski is about to move from his machine gun to the 3" inch gun on the beach near the airport. Charles Holmes mans his 3" anti-aircraft gun near Peacock Point, and Dick Darden waits anxiously in the igloo hospital.

PART 3—THE BATTLE FOR WAKE ISLAND

Chapter 28
THE FINAL ASSAULT

The second invasion attempted by the Japanese on Wake Island began during the early morning hours of December 23, 1941. Between sundown and midnight on December 22 the Japanese invasion force had made its final preparations for the assault on Wake's south beach. Over one thousand men and essential materials were loaded onto landing craft as the Emperor's warriors prepared to take possession of the American territory by force. The night was especially black due to heavy cloud cover and rain squalls over the island. Strong gusts of wind made the seas heavy and the general conditions were especially raw and uncomfortable.

The first signs of the enemy came just before 1:00 a.m. Lookouts noticed a series of bright flashes over the horizon north of Peale Island. Those on the island who had experienced fleet maneuvers suggested that a battle was in progress several miles offshore. There was concern about the American fleet bringing reinforcements. Could they have been engaged by enemy warships? With the relief ships several hundred miles away, and Admiral Kajioka's plan stressing that no bombardment of the island was to occur, the unexplained flashes became something of a mystery.

It would later be assumed that a detached part of the Japanese fleet had opened fire on Peale Island. Since no shells landed in the vicinity of Peale at that time, it was thought that the bombardment must have simply missed its target. The ships from which the flashes originated could very well have been off course due to navigational errors during the inclement weather. Having not been able to get a visual fix on their target, the Japanese gunners' deadly projectiles apparently fell harmlessly into the turbulent ocean.

Reports came in to Major Devereux's command post around 1:00 a.m. that enemy landing craft were approaching Toki Point on Peale Island. The wounded men in the hospital could listen to the telephone messages coming over the open line that connected all of the defense positions. Everyone in the hospital was awake and aware that something was about to happen. Messengers were sent into the bunker periodically to make Dr. Kahn and Dr. Shank aware of the situation outside, finally advising the doctors to prepare for an impending battle. Lt. Poindexter, in addition to being in charge of numerous machine gun positions scattered over all three islands, was in command of a small mobile reserve force. This consisted of two sections (pairs) of .30 cal. machine guns, one section loaded in each of the two trucks. The .30 cal. machine guns were mounted in the beds of the trucks, which also contained ammunition and hand grenades. The Mobile Reserve unit was positioned near the burned out remains of Camp 1, along with several of the other 30 cal. machine gun sections.

In addition to a few trained Marine machine gunners, Lt. Poindexter's unlikely team consisted of some of the sailors, Marine cooks, supply clerks, and members of the motor transport group. A half dozen civilians rounded out the group, which numbered fewer than three dozen men. Each gun crew included a gunner and several ammunition handlers. The rest of the group were riflemen.

When Lt. Poindexter heard reports that the enemy was landing on Peale Island at about 1:00 a.m., he mobilized the two machine gun trucks of his Mobile Reserve unit and quickly telephoned Major Devereux, telling him that the Mobile Reserve was heading toward the sighting on Peale Island. He then sped away on the road just north of the air strip to what he believed to be the beginning of the battle.

The two machine gun trucks reached the intersection of the two roads at the east end of the runway just a few hundred yards north of the bunker hospital in which Dick and the other wounded men strained to hear the messages coming over the telephone hookup. At the intersection the trucks encountered a Marine who flagged them down. He was carrying a message from Major Devereux which instructed Lt. Poindexter to stand by.

Poindexter was soon ordered to join Devereux at the nearby command post bunker, which had been set up in one of the concrete ammunition igloos between the hospital bunkers near the east end of the runway. He quickly obeyed his orders, leaving his two loaded trucks and heading for the command post just a few minutes after 1:00 a.m. When he reached the concrete bunker, Major Devereux told him there had been some confusion about the actual landing area, and that lookouts at Peacock Point on the south beach had just reported sighting an enemy destroyer. It was approximately 1:15 a.m. He instructed Poindexter to "just stand by and let's see what's going on."

Devereux still expected, and correctly so, that the enemy would land on the south beach. When he called back to the unit at Toki Point, he was told that there were many lights in the water, but no landing yet. As reports came in from various positions on the south beach, it became apparent to Major Devereux that his prediction had been correct and that the attack was coming from the south.

Devereux ordered Lt. Poindexter to proceed back along the road that lay just north of the air strip and set up a defensive position near the confluence of the two roads at the west end of the air strip. Poindexter quickly preceded accordingly, arriving at that location just prior to 1:30 a.m. There he set up the two machine gun sections across the beach road and waited for further instructions. The wait would be a short one.

The defenders of Wake were dug in for the fight they knew was coming. While Wake measured less than five miles in length, the wishbone configuration of the island provided over twenty miles of coastline to defend. Barely two hundred Marine, Navy and

Holmes Collection

One of the 2 1/2 ton 6 x 6 cargo trucks of the type used to transport the personnel that comprized the mobile reserve shown here mounted with a machine gun and search light.

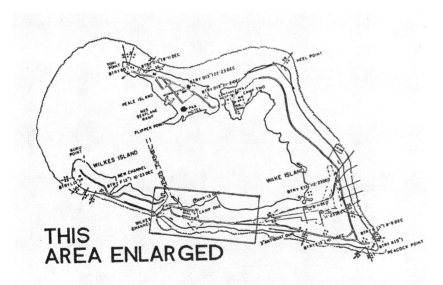

THIS
AREA ENLARGED

The following sketches of the battle areas on Wake's south beach (inset) near Camp #1 were drawn by Col. Arthur Poindexter, and all troop positions were drawn according to his instructions.

civilian defenders were about to attempt to turn back over a thousand Japanese warriors who were hell-bent upon overrunning the island and presenting it to their Emperor.

As December 23 began, the Wake defenders dug in deeper, knowing that the enemy lurked just out of sight in the darkness of the Pacific. The Marines crouched in their sandy foxholes and prepared themselves behind guns pointed out toward the black frothy surf. As the wind and roar of the waves breaking on the reef began to play tricks with their senses, the defenders anxiously waited.

Lt. Hanna's men had about one mile of beach to defend with their .30 cal. machine gun. The bunker that Holewinski, the Marines, Gay and Bryan had constructed came in very handy. The wooden shell that had been covered with sand now offered a small degree of protection to the men. It was located about halfway between the beach and the tree line, and about halfway between Camp 1 and Peacock Point.

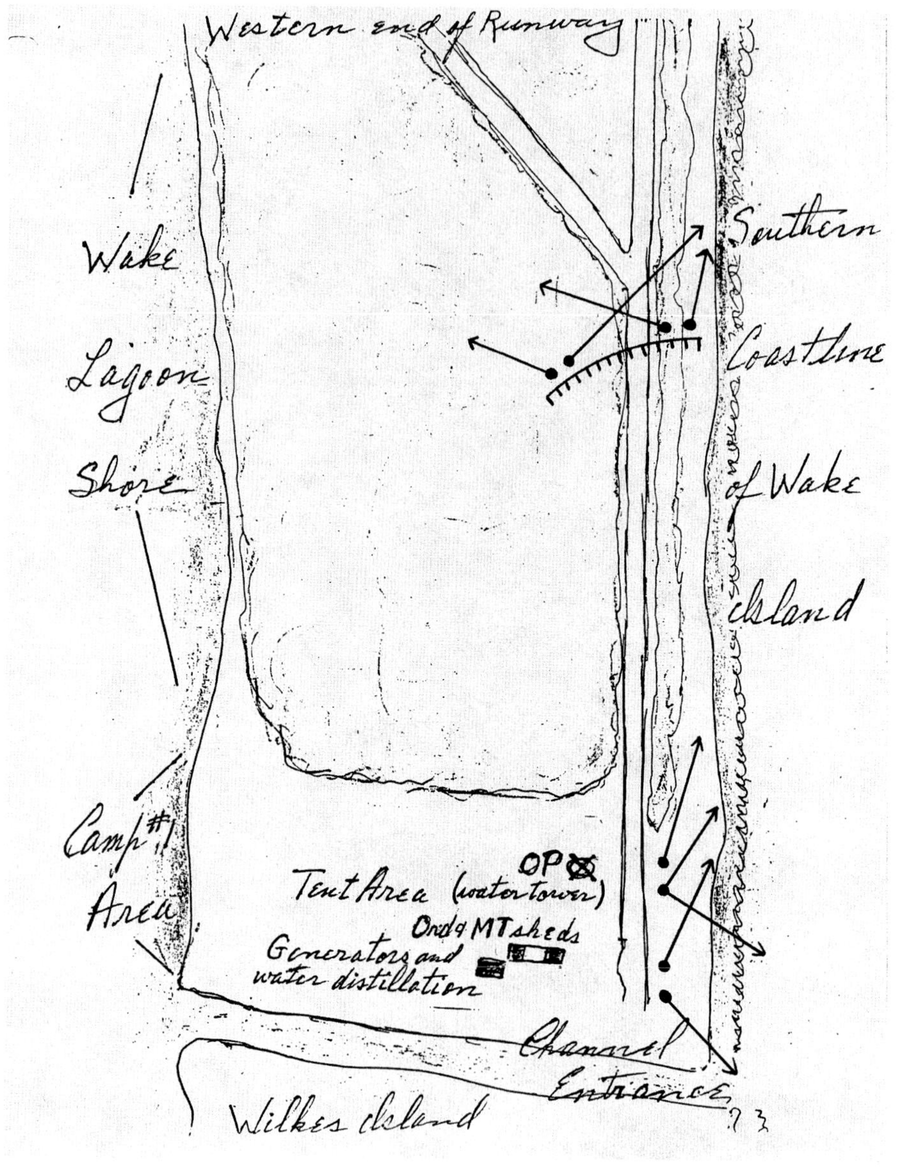

The Japanese armada of about thirty ships lay just offshore, and by this time they nearly surrounded the tiny island. Even though they were only a short distance offshore, they were invisible to the defenders in the darkness. Several lay less than five miles off the south beach, and would have been clearly visible to the Marine lookouts had it not been for the pitch blackness of the night.

There was only one large caliber weapon along the central part of Wake's south beach that could be used against incoming enemy ships. That was the 3" anti-aircraft gun near the beach in front of Lt. Hanna's machine gun positions. But that gun, which had no crew, was the only artillery protecting the west end of the airstrip. Lt. Hanna had been in command of the .50 cal. machine guns near the airstrip. He also directed Corporal Holewinski and his .30 cal. machine gun crew, along with several other machine guns which were emplaced on the beach side of the airstrip.

When Hanna and Holewinski discovered that ships were offshore, they realized that an anti-boat gun might be needed. Seeing the need for a crew on the 3" gun, Hanna ordered Holewinski and several other machine gunners to join him. They ran to the 3" gun and made the gun ready to open fire. Six other men under Hanna's command left the bunker for their machine gun nests elsewhere in the vicinity.

Holewinski had been given a brief introduction to similar 3" guns when he had helped to establish the Defense Battalion on Palmyra Island. While he was trying to briefly familiarize himself with the gun, a sergeant brought two wooden boxes of hand grenades. Skee and the two civilians began checking out the grenades, still feeling that they would probably not have to fire the 3" gun.

As the minutes melted quickly away and the men waited nervously by their guns, it became increasingly apparent that enemy ships were just offshore. This could only mean that an enemy assault force was near the island. The men at Hanna's position became very

Western end of Runway

Wake

Lagoon

Shore

Camp #1 Area

Tent Area (water tower)

OP

Ord⁹ MT sheds

Generators and water distillation

Southern

Coastline

of Wake

Island

Channel Entrance

Wilkes Island

Arthur Poindexter

Poindexter's Sketch #1 – Lt. Poindexter's Mobile Reserve sets up in position across the beach road near the end of the runway

130

serious about their proficiency with the 3" gun, knowing that they could expect a true test of their abilities very shortly.

Just before 1:00 a.m. a trigger-happy Japanese anti-aircraft gunner aboard one of the ships in the invasion force had begun firing wildly into the sky, thinking that he had seen American planes. Suddenly fire was directed toward the imaginary targets from several ships in the fleet, which lay barely five miles offshore. With this fire show the defenders of Wake Island experienced their first visual confirmation that the enemy was near.

By 1:00 a.m. the Japanese sailors of the Special Naval Landing Forces, sometimes referred to as Imperial Japanese Marines to the chagrin of many of the United States Marines, were crowded into landing craft that bobbed like corks on the rough seas. Unknown numbers of the Emperor's warriors, in full assault gear with heavy packs on their backs, fell or were thrown into the black brine, never to be seen again. Hundreds of additional troops were jammed aboard two troop transport ships called Patrol Craft. These two vessels were just offshore, and their captains planned to ram their ships aground on the south beach and allow the soldiers to come down the sides and into the battle.

Lt. Poindexter had finished positioning his machine gunners across the beach road near the end of the airstrip. One section of two .30 cal. guns on the beach side of the road was trained on the beach and surf back toward Peacock Point. The other section across the road was aimed at the end of the runway. Poindexter was preparing his men to engage the enemy if they landed on the south beach and attempted to take the airstrip or move west along the beach road toward Camp 1. The machine guns were ready for the approaching enemy.

The belts of machine gun ammunition had been loaded with three types of cartridges. First, there were regular projectiles known as "ball ammo," then there were armor piercing bullets which had metal alloy jackets on the slugs. Finally there were shells called tracers. Tracers did not have the striking power of the other two types because they were hollowed out and filled with a pyrotechnic chemical which would leave a tail like a comet when they flew through the air. This allowed the gunner to actually watch his bullets travel to the target, thereby assessing the accuracy of his aim.

While Lt. Poindexter was positioning his guns, the assault by Japanese troops from the sea was beginning just a short distance away. As the landing force neared the island, the Marines on Peale Island reported sightings of lights in the water just offshore. The battle was about to begin.

Jim Cox was under Lt. Poindexter's command in a machine gun nest on the beach side of Camp 1, at the west end of Wake Island and just across the channel from Wilkes. He sat poised behind his gun, peering out into the blackness of the ocean. He realized that if the attack came on the south beach he very well might be one of the first to engage the enemy. Cox was on the razor's edge this night and could feel the tension as he readied himself and his weapon.

Suddenly Cox thought he saw an unusual movement on the dark ocean just off the beach and a short distance to his left. He cut loose with his .30 cal. machine gun and watched as it spewed tracer rounds into the blackness. The ear-shattering sound of the machine gun drowned out the sounds of the surf for a moment, and the fire brightened the immediate area. Cox never had a clear view of an enemy landing craft, but as he watched the tracers ricocheting left and right he knew he was hitting something.

Lt. Poindexter heard the gun erupt from his position about a mile to the east near the air strip. He immediately jumped into one of the trucks and headed in the direction of the roaring gun, leaving Sgt. "Q. T." Wade in charge of the Mobile Reserve unit. Poindexter was afraid that the anxious sailors were overly eager to fire at an as yet unseen enemy. He knew his supply of ammunition was very low, and he wanted none of it wasted. He also knew that his men were nervous, scared, and angry, and that such a combination of emotions could cause men to see almost anything in the blackness of this night.

As Lt. Poindexter approached, Cox was firing the gun on an invisible enemy. Poindexter angrily shouted, "You goddam sailors are firing at shadows." He was afraid that the inexperienced gunner was needlessly wasting the priceless ammunition into the ocean. Poindexter took the gun himself and fired several bursts at the target that Cox insisted was there. He, too, witnessed the tracers as they ricocheted at oblique angles through the dark night. However, he was still unable to see the enemy. It appeared to Poindexter that even if the shells were striking an enemy landing craft they were simply being deflected without penetrating.

Cox was convinced that the enemy was in the surf in front of him. But, Lt. Poindexter disagreed, and he was so concerned that the limited supply of .30 cal. ammunition was being wasted that he instructed Cox to cease fire. He wanted all of the guns to be as well prepared as possible for the imminent battle. The men suspended their fire as ordered. But Jim Cox was sure that his tracers had glanced off of something in the black waters just a few hundred feet away beyond the reef.

The Japanese landing craft had armor plating in the shape of a rounded shield toward the stern and above the gunwales of the craft for the protection of the coxswain, who navigated the boat while peering through a slit in the protective metal. Because of the reef, no landing craft ever made it to the beach immediately in front of Cox's gun, so he was never able to confirm his target in the shadows. But he was sure that the tracer bullets were being deflected by something just offshore. As he would soon learn, two enemy landing craft had run aground just a short distance to his left.

Lt. Poindexter moved about checking on his other machine gun sections in the area. Within minutes Lt. Poindexter spotted one of the enemy landing craft hung on the reef just off the beach. The Japanese boat would ram into the coral reef, which was about thirty feet out in the surf. His objective was to run aground and then lower a ramp in the prow of the craft over which the troops could quickly proceed ashore. However, if he did not make it over the reef he would retreat, rev his engines, and ram it again.

The landing craft could not drop their ramp even a few feet outside the reef because the ocean floor dropped off sharply. Since Wake was the peak of an ancient volcano the ocean bottom followed the same line as the side of a mountain. The water instantly deepened just outside the reef. A short distance beyond the reef the water was several hundred feet deep. For assault troops, especially those with heavy backpacks, off-loading beyond the reef would be suicide.

Lt. Poindexter was with one of the machine gun sections on the beach when he spotted the landing craft. He and his gunners could see that the enemy boats were searching for spots in the reef over which they could navigate. Poindexter ordered the machine gunners to open fire on the craft. They did at once, but again the

Marines on the south beach man machine guns and the 3-inch gun as the Japanese ships beach themselves and troops come ashore.

tracers began to ricochet off of the target. The night was still too black for the Marines to tell exactly what the enemy craft was doing.

Poindexter did not know if the armor piercing bullets were penetrating the target, but the wildly ricocheting tracers led him to believe that his machine guns were not effective. Again he feared that precious ammunition was being wasted. He quickly changed his battle plan to one that was considerably more daring and dangerous.

First, Poindexter ordered the machine guns to hold their fire. Then he ordered several of his men, including Navy 1st Class Boatswains Mate James E. Barnes, Marine Sgt. Gerald Carr, and civilian R. R. Rutledge, to follow him out onto the beach and challenge the enemy. This tactic would be extremely dangerous, but a well thrown hand grenade into the midst of the tightly packed Japanese in the boat would be much more effective than engaging them in combat after they had a chance to spread out on the beach.

Poindexter felt that he had the element of surprise on his side, but that this would not be the case if the numerically superior Japanese forces were allowed to leave their landing craft and reorganize on the island. Poindexter and his men disregarded the fact that, if the front of the boat fell open and the unit of enemy troops confronted them face to face, it would mean certain death.

Each man grabbed several hand grenades and then ran out into the shallow surf on the beach side of the reef, dodging the chunks of coral rock that protruded up out of the water. As they neared the reef they could see that the ramps were still up on the landing craft, which were apparently still trying to maneuver over

the rocky edifice or were stuck on top of it.

Poindexter and his men began lobbing their hand grenades into the stranded boats. They could not tell if the landing craft were still full of Japanese troops, or if they had already discharged their assault force. They knew that at any moment the ramp could fall forward and they could find themselves face to face with a special landing force that was trained to penetrate a beachhead and kill everything in its path.

The Marines could not hurl the heavy hand grenades quite far enough to reach the landing craft, and they watched as their efforts fell short. They ran back onto the beach and gathered up more grenades, immediately racing back to the front. By wading farther out into the surf they were able to hit the enemy boat with their second salvo. Poindexter even reached the coral head at the very edge of the reef and threw his grenades at the boat from point blank range.

The ramps had not yet come down as Poindexter and his men sprinted back to the safety of their positions on the beach. At least some of their grenades had fallen into the boats, but they would never know if the craft were fully loaded with the enemy, or if their grenades detonated harmlessly in empty shells.

Lt. Poindexter was concerned about the whereabouts of the Japanese assault force from the landing craft, if they had indeed come ashore. He was even more concerned about the men of the Mobile Reserve who had stayed behind near the air strip. Poindexter left Gunnery Sergeant John Cemeris in charge of his machine gun positions near Camp 1 and headed back up the beach road in his truck toward the Mobile Reserve position. He probably passed within a few feet of the enemy troops who had just left their landing craft and were assembling in the scrubby trees just across the beach road.

On Wilkes Island, just across the boat channel from Jim Cox's position, Captain Platt was having the same problems. He could not see the enemy. Gunnery Sargeant Clarence McKinstry could not see the landing force from his .50 cal. machine gun on Wilkes, but he thought that he could hear a motor through the roar of the waves that broke continuously on the beach and a bit farther out on the reef. Captain Platt ordered that a damaged searchlight be turned on. It only managed to operate for a few seconds, but this was more than enough to confirm that landing craft were approaching.

When it became apparent that the Japanese were landing on Wilkes Island, Captain Platt passed the word that two Japs were to be captured and taken alive. He wanted two of the enemy soldiers for questioning. The word came to Wiley Sloman's 5" gun position, "Save me two prisoners."

Just after 2:00 a.m. the first landing craft were sighted as they came ashore on Wilkes Island. The brief illumination by the searchlight had shown the defenders that, without any doubt, an enemy invasion was in progress. The landing was directly in front of Battery F, the 3" anti-aircraft gun position on the beach side of the road about 250 yards west of the new channel. Two .50 cal. machine guns, gun 9 and gun 10, began

firing at the enemy troops as they came ashore.

The seventy Marines on Wilkes found themselves engaged in combat with one hundred assault troops of the Takano Unit of the Special Naval Landing Force. These troops, like all of the Japanese in the landing forces, were "picked men" who were presumably chosen because they were trained in amphibious landings. Battery F's 3" guns began firing at one of the landing craft.

Since Wiley Sloman's 5" gun was useless against a beach assault, his artillery unit was ordered to move to the south shore and engage the enemy. Sloman grabbed his Springfield, and the unit moved out. The Marines from Battery L arrived just as the enemy landing craft hit the beach. It was there that Sloman got his first taste of combat.

Two Marines ran out toward the landing craft from their positions about 150 yards to the east. They intended to use the same tactics that Lt. Poindexter had used minutes earlier on Wake. They would throw hand grenades into the barges, each filled with a full complement of fifty enemy troops.

The two Marines had just thrown their first grenade when they caught the full fury of the onrushing enemy. Sgt. Henry Bedell, Sloman's platoon sargeant and a veteran with nineteen years of service to the Corps, caught a belly full of machine gun fire. He was killed and the other Marine was wounded.

A large number of the enemy rushed toward Battery F and

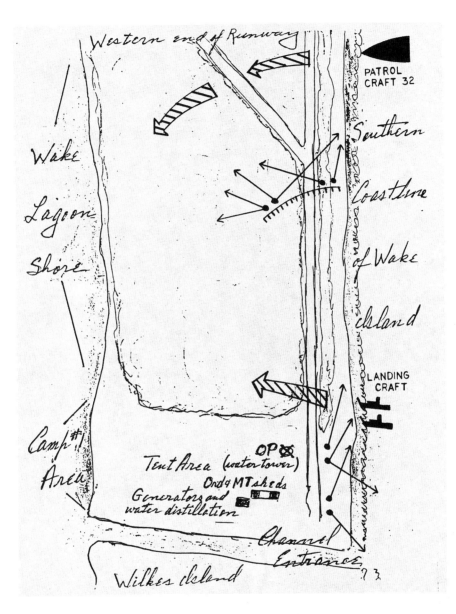

Poindexter Sketch #2

Position of the Mobile Reserve and movement of enemy troops between 2:00 a. M. and 3:00 A.M. December 23, 1941. The Jap assault force beached two landing craft near Camp 1 and two large Patrol Craft near the air field on the south beach. Enemy troops crossed the beach and beach road and began to organize in the scrub brush west oft the airfield attempted to overrun the position. Fierce hand-to-hand combat broke out all around the 3" guns. Gunner McKinstry realized very quickly that his men were vastly outnumbered and that they would have to retreat or be wiped out. They fell back toward the east and joined the Marines there. When Japanese riflemen pursued them they were met with intense fire from the Marine positions. The enemy then fell back to the 3" guns they had just captured. McKinstry had stripped the guns of their firing locks so they could not be used again.

The Japanese swarmed ashore on both Wilkes and Wake Islands. As Devereux expected, they were hitting the south beach. Two of the Japanese destroyers, also known as Patrol Craft, were serving as troop transports and had headed straight for the middle of the south beach on Wake. They were preparing to ground themselves, coming over the reef and grinding onto the beach. Hundreds of troops prepared to spill over their sides and hit the beaches moments later.

About one hundred enemy troops were in the company that came ashore on Wilkes Island to do battle with Captain Platt's defensive unit. The remainder of the Takano Company joined the other two companies in assaulting the south beach. On the two transports heading for the beach on Wake Island were the Uchida Company and the Itaya Company.

Wake Island had eight miles of lagoon shoreline and twelve miles of ocean front, any of which could have been the target of the landing craft. Since the defenders were spread so thinly throughout the island there were long expanses of beach, several hundred yards in many places, without defensive positions. Despite Major Devereux's best efforts to place his gun positions at all strategic locations along the south beach, much of the shoreline lay unprotected.

Judging from the large number of assault troops who were ashore the next morning, many had come across the beach without having to face the defenders. Two landing craft were even able to unloaded combat troops very close to Jim Cox's machine gun position near Camp 1 without being seen. Several units, however, were unfortunate enough to crash over the reef and directly into the teeth of the defense.

By, or before, 2:30 a.m. the men all over Wake Island were aware that an amphibious attack was in progress. Lookouts at Peacock Point sighted the two patrol craft, each brimming with enemy troops, as they headed in a westward direction and then turned toward the island's south beach. They began to approach the south shore of Wake near the middle of the island, one ship in front of the other. If they landed in the center of the long expanse of beach they would be just a short distance south of the vital airstrip.

The ships steamed directly toward the beach at approximately twelve knots. The troops had already deployed their ropes and Jacob's ladders so they could come down the sides of the boats as soon as they were beached. Charles Holmes' anti-aircraft battery at Peacock Point had one 3" gun which had been damaged and could not be used for vertical fire. They decided that it was safe for horizontal fire, so they prepared to use it as an anti-boat gun against the landing boats, which were rapidly coming into range.

Before 3:00 a.m. the two Japanese troop transports were speeding toward the south beach. There was just enough light on the black ocean for Hanna and Holewinski to make out the shape of the first ship. Hanna's decision to man the 3" gun had been a good one, because they realized they would have to use the gun to protect a large expanse of the south beach. The ships appeared to be heading straight toward the island as if to beach themselves less than a mile from Hanna's 3" gun emplacement.

Hanna, Holewinski, and three civilians immediately began firing the anti-aircraft gun, which was improvised for use as an anti-boat gun, at the Patrol Craft. The craft was about to become grounded on the reef where it would be a huge stationary target at a range of less than five hundred yards. The first two high velocity 3" rounds missed, but the third hit the Patrol Craft amidships in the area of the bridge, causing tremendous damage. Two of the enemy seamen were killed and seven were wounded, including the captain of the ship and the navigator. Hanna's 3" gun continued to fire on the ship as hoards of troops in the Uchida and Itaya companies came down the opposite side. The ship caught fire and provided pyrotechnic display which illuminated the entire central portion of the south beach.

Since the gun had no sights or range finding equipment, Hanna and Holewinski were bore sighting. They would peer through the open breech to aim the gun, then load the projectile and set the fuses. The civilians were quarreling over who would pull the lanyard that fired the gun, so Hanna told Holewinski just to sight the target through the barrel and load the gun.

Jim Cox remained on the beach at one of Poindexter's machine gun positions that formed the line protecting Camp 1. He had a clear view of the first troop ship as it approached the beach and ground up onto the reef with a loud crunching sound. He could not see any soldiers coming down the port side of the vessel, but he directed fire toward the ship with his .30 cal. machine gun. From his position Cox never did see any enemy sailors of the Special Naval Landing Force make it to the beach from the port side of the ship. But, after the ship was beached, Holewinski could see from the 3" gun position that the Japanese were coming over the side.

The fire on the first grounded ship illuminated the area enough that Hanna and Holewinski could see a clear silhouette of the second troop ship, Patrol Craft 32, as it headed toward the beach behind the first. It turned and came toward them, providing the 3" gun with another excellent target. Hanna again bore-sighted the weapon while Holewinski cranked the wheels to traverse the barrel toward the ship. The gun was loaded as the ship made its run toward the beach. One of the civilians, Paul Gay, Bob Bryan, or Eric Lehtola, pulled the lanyard to fire the weapon. Bulls-eye!! Cox and Holewinski both saw the second ship explode as it headed toward the beach. It was engulfed by flames as it crashed over the reef.

Hanna's battery fired over a dozen shells at the two ships as they made their approach to the south beach of Wake Island. Fire from the 3" gun caused extensive damage to the ships, leaving both on fire and clearly visible to the defenders all along the beach. Since they could see no other targets within range on the ocean, and as gunfire around the position became more and more intense, Hanna and his men took cover under the metal platform at the base of the gun. They abandoned the 3" weapon in favor of their small arms and hand grenades. The fight was coming toward them.

During the early morning hours of the battle a total of twenty-six men fell back to Hanna's gun and became involved in the defense of the position. Only one American, Pfc. Alexander B.

Venable Jr., would come through the fight at Hanna's gun without being killed or wounded. Ironically, Venable would die within a few days after the battle ended with a severe case of dysentery.

Fighting on the island had become so intense that the firing of weapons caused the underbrush to begin burning. Bullets were constantly whistling through the air. Hanna was fighting from under one side of the 3" gun, and Holewinski and the two civilians were firing from under the opposite side. All through the night the men saw movement in the coral dunes and underbrush around the position. The burning vegetation, constant gunfire, and movement of men as they ran back and forth around the gun made the situation very confusing for Ralph Holewinski.

Holewinski fired his 1903 Springfield bolt-action rifle at any movement that did not appear to be friendly. The commotion around the position became intense. Soldiers ran through the brush and sand dunes nearby, but Skee could not tell who they were. He shouted at the men, demanding that they identify themselves. When the troops responded in English, Skee and the civilians held their fire. When they heard Japanese chatter they opened fire with everything they had.

There was speculation later as to whether any Japs ever came ashore on the lagoon side of Wake Island. The reef at the open end of Wake was shallow enough that any boat that drew more than a couple of feet of water could not cross over it. However, rubber life rafts could make it across, since they could be walked over the reef. Several Marines told Poindexter that they saw life rafts on the lagoon side of the island the next day. A landing by the enemy along the lagoon shore has never been substantiated, although it could well have taken place.

Before 3:00 a.m. on the morning of December 23, 1941, the defenders all over Wake's three islands were aware that the final battle for Wake Island had begun in earnest. Several hundred enemy soldiers had come ashore off the two transports beached on the reef just to the west of Hanna's gun. They had crossed the beach road, hence the commotion that had confused Holewinski.

Most of the enemy were massing and organizing across the road near the runway, actually to the rear of Hanna's position. Patrol Craft 33 was nearest Hanna's gun. While some of the enemy troops from PC 33 remained in the area to offer resistance to the small group of defenders at Hanna's gun, others began moving into the central part of the island and taking positions at the airstrip. The enemy from Patrol Craft 32, a short distance farther down the beach, split into two groups. One of these groups moved east along the airstrip, while the other group encountered Poindexter's small contingent of machine gunners positioned just a short distance away astride the beach road.

At Hanna's gun the ammunition was already very limited. The civilian named Gay had a Colt .45 automatic pistol. The other, named Bryan, had no firearms but still had the two cases of hand grenades. Whenever he heard Japanese voices he would throw a grenade in their direction. Several times the Japanese picked up the grenades and threw them back into the gun pit. Luckily for Ski, Hanna, and the two civilians, none of the returned grenades exploded. All those thrown back by the Japs must have been inoperative duds.

By 3:00 a.m. on the morning of December 23, 1941, the Japanese had beached several landing craft on the south shore of Wake. These contained hundreds of amphibious assault troops of the Special Naval Landing Force whose orders were to take the island at all costs. The Japanese troops had gone into the scrub forests and were organizing their fighting units in preparation for assaulting the Marine positions.

The Japanese warriors had been thoroughly indoctrinated from their very birth to believe that they were on a personal mission for the Son of Heaven, their beloved Emperor Hirohito. A considerable number of the enemy were ashore in the scrub areas of the south beach, causing large areas of the island to become "no man's land."

As the Japanese troops came ashore on Wake Island they truly believed that the greatest and most honorable thing that could happen to them this day would be to die in battle for Hirohito. They were bent upon killing the enemy and being victorious, whatever the personal costs might be. They had swarmed onto the beaches with the zeal of fanatics, but few had engaged their enemy. Most of the hordes had quickly crossed the beach and found their way into the safety of the scrubby forests.

Much of the communication between the Marines and their commanders, Devereaux and Cunningham, came over the speakers throughout the island network. The men in the hospital listened as the battle progressed, helpless to stand or move about, much less to fight and defend their corner of the island. As the savage fighting continued one American position after another went silent or had to fall back before the enemy onslaught.

As Major Devereux attempted to coordinate his troops the telephone lines on the island were being cut by the enemy. He began to lose communications, which led him to believe that more of his units had been overrun than was actually the case. Early in the battle the line to Camp 1 and much of the general area around the airstrip went dead, indicting that the enemy had crossed the road and held portions of the south beach. However, another of the above-ground communications lines was located north of the airstrip, and it continued to connect the command center with Capt. Platt on Wilkes.

Realizing that the Japanese troops were on the move on several fronts, Major Devereux decided about 3:00 a.m. to set up a defensive line just south of the command bunkers and the hospital. He ordered Major Potter to take all available men in the vicinity, mostly clerical personnel and telephone operators, and defend a line scarcely 100 yards south of the command center toward Peacock Point. The enemy had pushed to within six hundred feet of Dick Darden and the hospital bunker.

Just before the communication lines to Camp 1 went silent, Lt. Poindexter had given Major Devereux a brief report of the situation there, so Devereux probably believed the position was still securely in American hands. By 3:00 Lt. Poindexter had returned to his men at the position near the end of the runway. He did not know that this position was extremely precarious due to the large number of enemy troops massing nearby.

Sgt. Wade had been left in command of the Mobile Reserve when Lt. Poindexter went back to Camp 1. When the Lieutenant returned he received a report on the circumstances there from Wade. "They are all around us, Sir," advised Wade. "They are on our left flank and maybe our rear." Poindexter quickly saw how dangerous it would be to remain in no-man's land near the runway. He decided on a retrograde movement, hoping that he could get his men safely

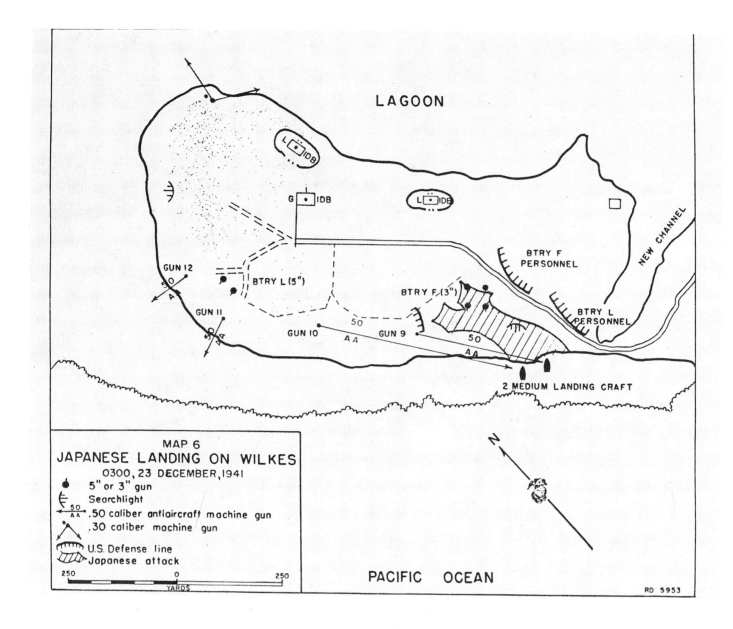

LAGOON

L · IDB

G · IDB

L · IDB

NEW CHANNEL

BTRY F
PERSONNEL

GUN 12

30

BTRY L (5")

BTRY F (3")

BTRY L
PERSONNEL

GUN 11

50

GUN 10
AA

GUN 9

50
AA

2 MEDIUM LANDING CRAFT

N

MAP 6
JAPANESE LANDING ON WILKES
0300, 23 DECEMBER, 1941
● 5" or 3" gun
Ɛ Searchlight
50 .50 caliber antiaircraft machine gun
AA
.30 caliber machine gun
U.S. Defense line
Japanese attack

250   0   250
YARDS

PACIFIC OCEAN

RO 5953

back to the protection of the machine guns at Camp 1. The withdrawal began immediately.

The break in communications with Camp 1 occurred just a few minutes later. Soon after the line went dead a very excited civilian entered the command post and indicated that he had just made his way there from the Camp 1 area. He excitedly reported that the enemy troops were overrunning Camp 1 and were bayoneting the Marines and sailors who were manning the machine guns of Poindexter's mobile reserve. This probably caused Major Devereux to assume that the Camp 1 position was lost, when actually it was still securely held by Poindexter's men.

Just after 3:00 a.m. Commander Cunningham received a message from Admiral Pye at Pearl Harbor. Cunningham was informed that there were no American Naval forces in the vicinity of Wake Island; furthermore, no relief forces would be in the area for at least twenty-four hours. There was no chance of immediate relief for the defenders on Wake. The enemy invasion force would have to be dealt with using only the men and materials already on the island.

The fighting on Wake's south beach became furious hand-to-hand combat as the bloodbath intensified. Major Putnam's unit, which had been fighting near the beach road since the battle began, was pushed back toward the 3" gun where Hanna and Holewinski were holding out. Putnam's men formed a semi-circular skirmish line on the north side of the battery, toward the airstrip.

As the onslaught of Japanese troops continued toward the defenders, the fighting in front of Hanna's gun was bloody savagery at close quarters. The Japanese, probably members of the Uchida company that had landed on one of the beached patrol craft, had come across the beach, crossed the road, and regrouped in the scrubby forest between Hanna's gun and the airstrip. They could then attack Hanna from a position north of the 3" gun, having circled behind the original line of fire. They were trying to literally push the Americans into the sea.

By 4:00 a.m. the Japs were steadily attacking Putnam, pushing him and his men back very close to Hanna's gun pit. Various

136

tactics were used by the enemy, ranging from the "creeping infiltration" of individual soldiers into the American lines to "screaming rushes" by groups of charging soldiers. Putnam, Hanna, Holewinski, and all of the men at Hanna's gun fought with their backs to the sea, repelling charge after charge by the Japs. By this time Putnam's line was a rough circle of men just outside the gun pit.

Major Putnam received a gunshot wound to the face. Nevertheless, he continued courageously to lead his men against the steadily attacking Japanese troops. He ordered his men to dig in and take a stand, saying resolutely, "This is as far as we go!"

Someone in Putnam's skirmish line had a Thompson submachine gun. Skee heard it firing in its distinctive ear shattering bursts. The skirmish line was about twenty feet in front of Holewinski. It was close enough that he could hear the flyers talking to each other, but it was still too dark to see them since they were apparently just outside the pit. The burning underbrush just beyond them silhouetted considerable movement of men through the scrubby forest.

The fighting at Major Putnam's line was brutal, bloody, hand-to-hand combat. The flyers showed a degree of courage and valor on the ground comparable with their previous exploits in the skies over Wake. They stood their ground despite the enemy's overwhelming numerical advantage. They literally met the enemy face to face. As Major Putnam fired his .45 cal. pistol into one charging Japanese soldier, the helmets of the two men crashed into each other.

Finally only five men, including Capt. Frank Tharin, remained in Putnam's unit. They had been pushed back into Hanna's gun pit, where only Hanna, Holewinski, and one civilian were left alive. The situation appeared extremely bleak when Putnam declared that his Marines would make their final stand here. In addition to the Marines who made such a valiant stand at Hanna's gun, there were several civilians who died in its defense.

At 4:00 a.m. the fight on Wilkes Island was a standoff. The enemy soldiers were still holding the 3" gun position at Battery F, but they had been unable to take any additional territory. McAlister and McKinstry had positioned riflemen in the remaining undergrowth, and these Marines were stymieing the advance of the Japanese troops.

Captain Platt had lost all contact with Major Devereux since the telephone line had apparently been severed by the Japanese troops. Platt also wanted to maintain contact with his men so he could control the course of the battle on Wilkes, but without communications lines this became impossible. His only hope of staying in touch with his men and coordinating the fighting was to leave his command post and join the men on the beach.

Platt left the command post at 4:30 a.m. After thirty minutes of crawling through the underbrush and over the rocky coral of the beach, he could see that most of the hundred enemy troops were, for the moment, congregated in the vicinity of the 3" gun at Battery F.

The telephone wires which were lying exposed on the

Poindexter Sketch #3

The position of the Mobile Reserve at 3:00 AM December 23, 1941. Lt. Poindexter's riflemen and machine gunners defend the beach road as Japanese mass and organize in the scrubby forest.

ground throughout the island had, at this point in the battle, been so extensively damaged that Cunningham and Devereux were increasingly out of touch with the battle's progress. These lines were vital to the two men, for without communications they had no way of directing their troops. When communications were lost with a unit it was not known if the telephone wires had simply been cut, or if the enemy had overrun the position. One by one the links with the combat units throughout the islands continued to go silent.

Across the channel on Wake Island near Camp 1, Lt. Poindexter was moving his men back toward the safety of the machine gun line he had set up across the island. Each of his two squads still had approximately ten men, and they were hopscotching their way down the beach road. One section of machine guns, supported by several riflemen, would cover the second as it moved as far back as possible, usually about 100 yards, and set up a new position. Then the second squad would open fire and cover the first as it made a similar move.

Poindexter's leapfrog tactics had become quite dangerous because the three small groups of men were meeting considerable resistance from the enemy, which was massing just across the road in far superior numbers. His two sections had managed to reach a position about halfway back to Camp 1 and the friendly machine guns. They were continually taking fire from small arms and mortars, resulting in several casualties.

One of the machine gunners, PFC Charles E. Tramposh, was hit and seriously wounded when a mortar round landed near him. A piece of shrapnel the size of a half dollar went through his abdomen, opening up a very messy wound when the fragment exited his belly.

The enemy continued to advance despite stiff resistance from the defenders. At about half past four Corporal Winford J. McAnally reported to Major Devereux that his .50 cal. machine gun position, located on the road about halfway between Peacock Point and the bunkers, was about to be rushed by a large force of Japanese soldiers. Indeed, wave after wave of Nippon warriors came through the undergrowth and coral sand at McAnally only to be cut to ribbons and repelled.

The enemy force rushed the .50 cal. gun time after time until bodies covered the ground immediately in front of the position. The defenders could hear them coming and would wait until the last second before opening fire. This important defensive position was the last resistance between the charging Japanese troops and the bunkers housing the hospitals and Major Devereux's command post.

Charles Holmes and the other Marines at Peacock Point nervously waited for the enemy soldiers moving toward them. Snipers began firing into the 3" and 5" gun pits from nearby undergrowth. Sgt. Raymond Gragg took a group of his artillerymen out on patrol where they became infantrymen and killed several of the enemy riflemen who had taken positions in the scrubby foliage.

Just over a half mile from McAnally was Lt. Kliewer's position. The former fighter pilot and three of his men were trying to defend a position along the airstrip. They had been given orders to place explosive charges along the runway and to detonate them if defeat appeared imminent. This would deny the enemy use of the landing facilities in the event that they were to overrun the island.

These Marines had been ordered not to blow up the airstrip until the very last moment so that, in the now unlikely event that relief planes might approach the island, they would have an airstrip on which to land with their reinforcements. But, if the enemy tried to land planes on the strip, or if the Japs were about to take the island, Kliewer was to destroy the runway.

Lt. Kliewer had been tempted several times during the night to detonate the explosives on the runway because he was under constant attack. The four men in his position had been in virtually uninterrupted combat since the beginning of the battle. Patrol Craft 32 was beached almost directly in front of Kliewer's position, and a large number of enemy troops had come ashore and headed inland almost directly at Kliewer. Amazingly, he and his men had repelled numerous charges by enemy troops, often battling them hand to hand. This small band of Marines were armed with only two machine guns, two pistols, and hand grenades. Somehow all four of them had lived through the night.

Just as the first hint of dawn began to illuminate the eastern sky, a large force of foot soldiers rushed the position. The overwhelming number of Japanese would surely have overrun the Lt. Kliewer and his men. But the enemy soldiers had exposed themselves in front of a .50 cal. machine gun that was sandbagged at the western end of the air strip. Just as the soldiers rushed Kliewer the .50 cal. gun opened up, leaving piles of dead Japanese in the sand and sending the living scrambling for cover.

Kliewer knew that the huge enemy force would regroup and return soon. As daylight began to reveal the enemy positions on the island, Kliewer could see Japanese battle flags all around him, including positions farther inland. His position was encircled, so Kliewer decided that it was time to blow the airstrip. He tried to start the generator that was wired to the explosive charges, but try as he would the generator refused to crank.

First light on the morning of December 23 exposed a startling view of the battle to many of the Marine positions. Enemy troops had infiltrated the area between Hanna's gun and the gun batteries at Peacock Point. Where these troops came from is still unclear. The Japanese commanders would later tell of landing on the beach in that area with the objective of silencing the Peacock batteries; however, there were no barges left to show for such a landing. These troops might have come from one of the beached Patrol Craft. Whatever their origin, enemy troops were encroaching upon the area at the east end of the airstrip where the command post and the hospitals were located in the converted magazines. The Japanese were less than one thousand yards from Dick Darden.

Battery E, on the lagoon side of the island and just north of the airfield, began to come under mortar and machine gun fire. The enemy had progressed much of the way across the widest part of Wake Island and was inching ever closer to the concrete domes. Battery A at Peacock Point was coming under even more intense mortar and rifle fire.

Reports came into Major Devereux's command post that a large group of enemy troops was massing in the area between Peacock Point and the eastern end of the airstrip. Apparently the enemy had left a small force to take Hanna's gun while most of the soldiers were being organized to mount a thrust toward Peacock Point and the eastern leg of the Wake Island wishbone. The situation around the hospital became more and more threatening.

Commander Cunningham knew, without any doubt, that the defenders were completely on their own against the Japanese invasion force. The relief task force was well over five hundred miles away, sailing erratically with no specific orders to proceed to the vicinity of Wake Island. From his position on Peale Island Commander Cunningham could look across at Wake and Wilkes Islands. The first glimmers of sunlight allowed him to see dozens of Japanese flags. By 5:00 a.m. he had sent a message to Adm. Pye saying "Enemy on Island—Issue in Doubt."

It was light enough that Wiley Sloman could look out of his position on Wilkes and see the ocean clearly. He was shaken by what he saw. The sea seemed to be covered by enemy warships. There were dozens of them. On the island, however, the Marines were holding their own.

A few minutes after 5:00 a.m. Captain Platt decided to take advantage of the fact that so many Japanese were massed together at Battery F on Wilkes Island. He elected to go on the offensive, ordering Sgt. Raymond Coulson to gather a small group of defenders and .30 cal. machine guns from the western end of Wilkes in the Kuku Point area. They were to join Platt at Gun 10.

Just a few minutes after 5:30 Sgt. Coulson returned to Gun 10 with two machine gun crews and eight riflemen. Platt was planning to attack the enemy at Battery F by positioning a machine gun on each side of the battery. Then the riflemen would charge the position while they were covered and supported by the machine

guns. The operation became especially dangerous as the ever-increasing daylight began to reveal the movements of the defenders. Even so, they were able to get within fifty yards of Battery F and set up the machine guns without being observed by the cluster of Jap troops.

Meanwhile, about four hundred yards to the east near the new channel on Wilkes, Lt. McAlister and Gunner McKinstry had assembled a group of twenty-five Marines and were proceeding toward Battery F to join Platt. They encountered several Japanese soldiers along the beach, killing several while chasing the others back to the coral reef. The Marines pressed their attack against the Japs who had sought refuge under the reef, killing all of them.

Captain Platt gave the order to begin the attack at Battery F. The machine guns opened up on the Japanese troops as the eight riflemen began their charge. Even though the Japanese outnumbered their assailants nearly ten to one, they panicked and scattered, scrambling for cover. A group of about thirty sought safety under the truck which carried the 60" searchlight. As they crouched under the negligible protection of the truck they were wiped out to the last man.

During the fight, Platt's group was joined by McAlister and his men. Ten Marines were assigned to mop up the enemy around the 3" gun while the others searched the island for any remaining enemy soldiers. Wiley Sloman was fighting near the 3" gun when the Japanese were pushed out of the position. He worked his way to

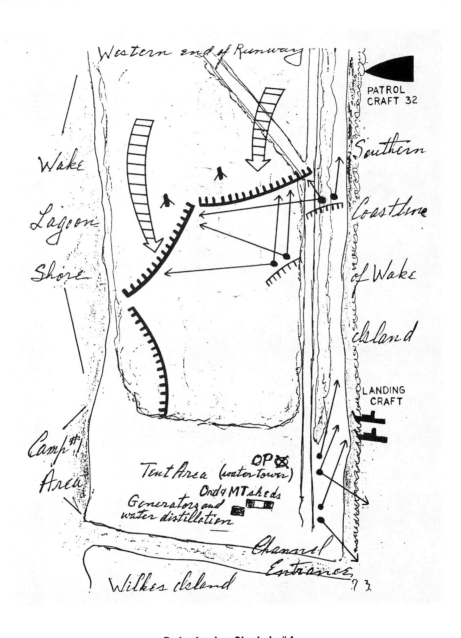

Poindexter Sketch #4
Lt. Poindexter's position at 3:30 a. m. The Marines are moving toward their machine guns near Wilkes Channel

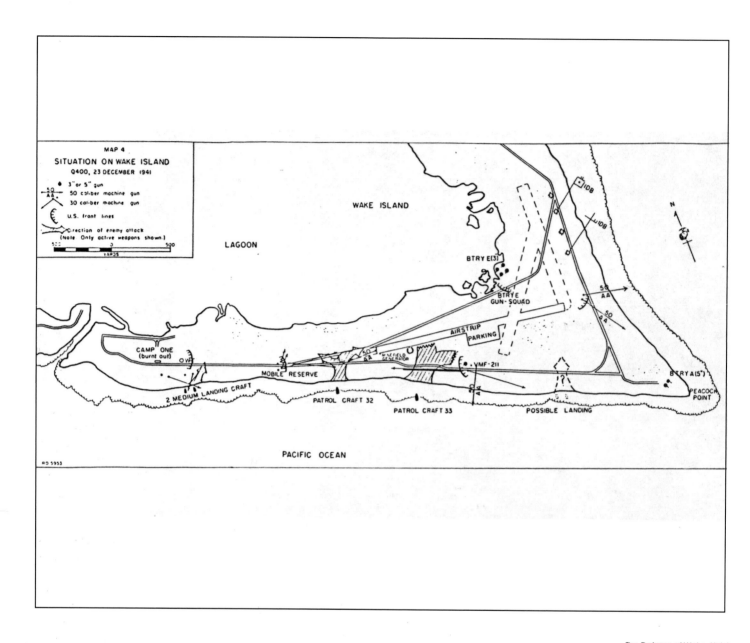

The Defense of Wake- Heinl

At 4:00 A.M. the morning of December 23, 1941, this map shows three, and possibly four, locations where Japanese have come ashore. Lt. Poindexter's mobile reservists are shown defending the confluence of the beach and airport roads from Patrol Craft 32, while the airmen from VMF-211 are shown defending Hanna's 3-inch gun from troops coming from Patrol Craft 33.

a point near the gun, close enough that he could see it clearly. The enemy had already been pushed farther inland, and two Marines were using the 3" gun as a shield against machine gun fire from the retreating Jap unit.

Lt. McKinstry was in command of Sloman's unit, and he was just behind Sloman yelling instructions for the men to move forward. Sloman did just that, finding marginal cover from the incoming fire behind a piece of coral just a few feet from the 3" gun. McKinstry was a big man and he surely made a good target. Even though he was armed only with a .45 cal. pistol, he continued to press forward and rarely took cover. For all the risks he took during the battle, he never was wounded or even received a scratch.

Sloman found himself pinned down behind the small coral boulder. The Japanese machine gun was chewing up the small mound of coral, causing chunks of rock to fly in all directions. Sloman's only protection was rapidly being whittled away. He stayed as low as he could behind the rock as hundreds of bullets came toward him. Sloman couldn't even look around the edges of the rock, and for the moment he was in a very dangerous position.

Sloman could hear Lt. McKinstry behind him yelling, "Come on, move forward. Move forward or I'll shoot you in the ass." Sloman was perplexed at the threatening order, since he was pinned down and could not move anywhere. He thought, "Look, you S.O.B., I can't walk into that machine gun fire. Give me some time before you start shooting at me." He later learned that McKinstry was not shouting at him. Three Marines were in a bomb crater just behind Sloman, and McKinstry was trying to roust them out so they would come forward and give Sloman support.

140

Sloman decided to lie still for a few minutes and see if the Jap machine gunner would pick a different target. Usually if enemy gunners saw no motion at a position for a short period of time they would direct their fire elsewhere toward a position showing signs of life. The machine gun was only about seventy-five yards away, and he knew that if he tried to move toward the gun over the open ground in front of him it would be tantamount to suicide.

Finally the gun directed its fire elsewhere. Sloman took the opportunity moved forward, leaving the protection of the coral rock. Quickly the Japanese gunners pulled the weapon back around and sprayed him with a burst of fire. One of the rounds caught him on the right side of his head. He stood straight up and then fell forward into the sand.

Sloman was not yet unconscious, so he instinctively fired the round that was already in the chamber of his Springfield rifle. He operated the bolt on the rifle, ejecting the spent cartridge and pushing another round forward into firing position. Then he tried to move his left arm forward to aim the rifle. Nothing happened, and suddenly he realized that he was paralyzed. The wound on the right side of his head had rendered the left side of his body useless.

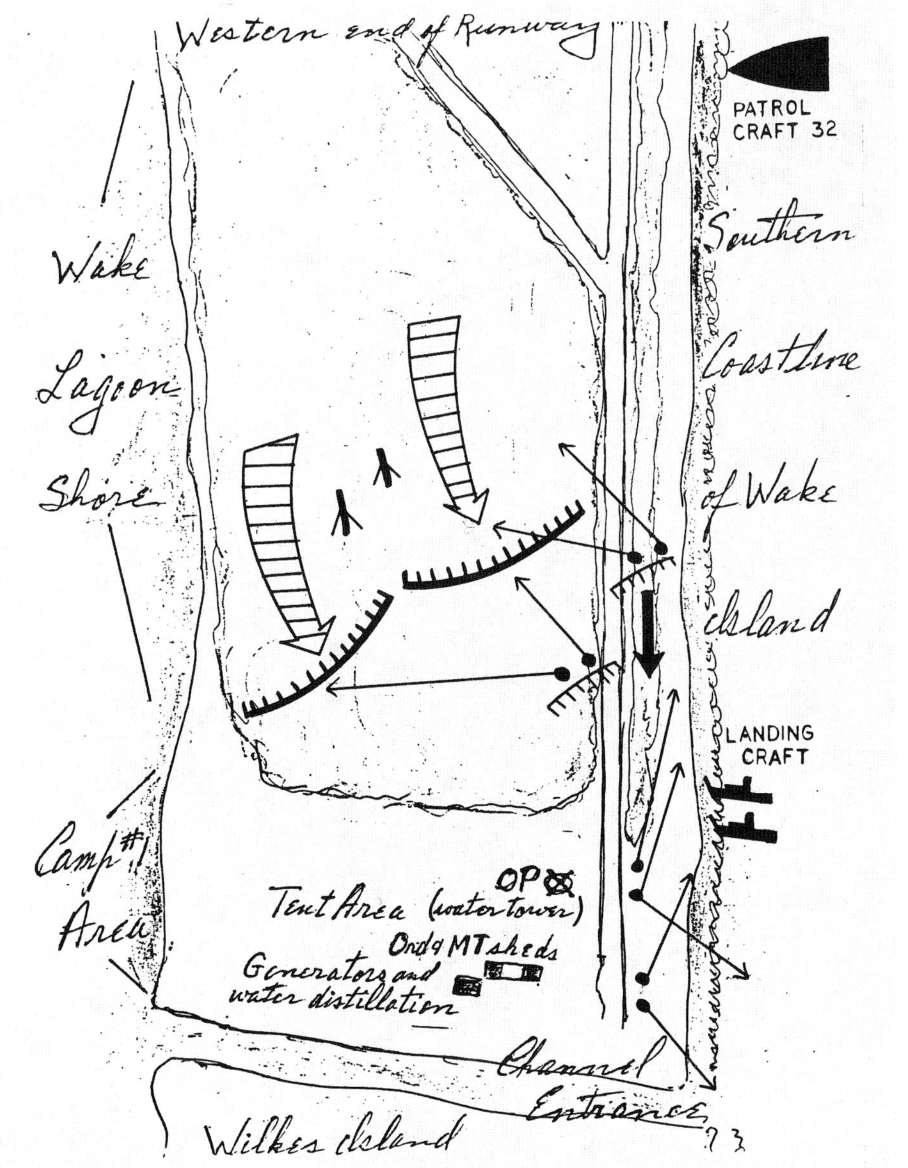

Sloman could see Japanese troops running around everywhere in front of him. There were targets all around him, but he was unable to aim and shoot his gun. The bullet had actually gone inside his skull, exiting about four inches behind the point of entry. The hot bullet had burned brain tissue as it passed through, and as a result his brain was rapidly beginning to swell.

Sloman's head went down onto his rifle. He was still conscious enough to hear what was going on around him. Lt. McKinstry still was armed only with the Colt .45 pistol and he had been complaining that he didn't have a rifle. Sloman heard some one yell, "Hey Mac, you can have Sloman's rifle. He got his." That was the last thing Sloman remembered as he blacked out. He was in and out of consciousness during the remainder of the battle.

The Japanese machine gun position was overrun and the Marines began moving toward the center of the island looking for any remaining enemy troops. None were found as the Marines swept the island, except for two who were found alive. They had apparently avoided being killed by "playing possum." Ninety-four Japanese corpses lay on Wilkes Island, nearly the entire complement of "picked men" from the Takano company. Four were missing and unaccounted for. Japanese flags littered Wilkes Island, presumably left by the enemy units to indicate their locations so fighter planes could avoid them on bombing and strafing runs. Even though the enemy had been wiped out on Wilkes, Commander Cunningham could see the Jap flags from his command post across the lagoon on Peale Island. He made the logical, but completely inaccurate, assumption, based on the absence of communications and placement of the enemy position flags, that Capt. Platt's unit and Wilkes Island had fallen to the enemy forces.

At 5:30 Major Potter's defensive line just south of the bunkers was reinforced by nearly all of the remaining men from

Poindexter Sketch #5

Marines continue at 4:30 a. m. to move toward Camp #1 while Japanese troops advance toward them through the scrubby undergrowth

141

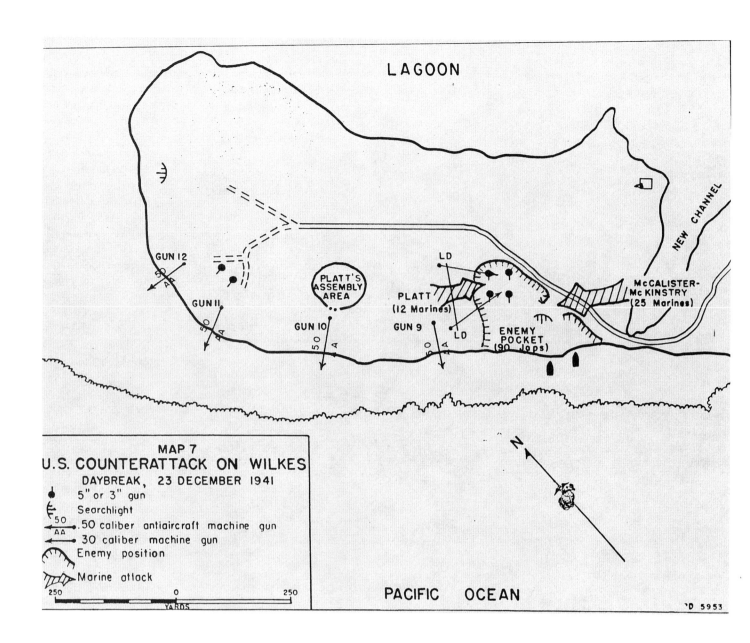

MAP 7
U.S. COUNTERATTACK ON WILKES
DAYBREAK, 23 DECEMBER 1941

● 5" or 3" gun
Ͷ Searchlight
←50 .50 caliber antiaircraft machine gun
   AA
←● .30 caliber machine gun
⌒⌒⌒ Enemy position
〰️▶ Marine attack

250   0   250
        YARDS

PACIFIC   OCEAN

Peale Island. As they dug in with the first daylight they could see enemy ships completely encircling the atoll. One excited Marine gunner reported over the telephone network that he could count thirty-six enemy ships, although the actual number was probably closer to thirty. The ships waited just out of range of the 5" guns. There was nothing the defenders could do but watch and wait for the enemy to rush them again.

Daybreak did not expose any enemy troops in front of Jim Cox's machine gun position. He could not see any of the enemy, but he could hear the fighting as it raged nearby. Lt. Poindexter was still moving his riflemen back toward the defensive line across the island. He could hear Nips moving in the underbrush on the north side of the road, and there was quite a bit of gunfire there as well. He could actually hear Japanese voices, so he was sure that there was a significant enemy force just a short distance across the road in the undergrowth.

A large Japanese force had indeed come ashore during the night and crossed the island. They had come from the Patrol Craft near Hanna's gun and from the smaller landing craft near Jim Cox's machine gun. These enemy troops were massed very near, and in front of, Poindexter's men. They had assembled their units across the road near the end of the airstrip, and by this time they filled the woods on the north side of the beach road. By daybreak they were organized and were ready to confront the defenders in their isolated pockets of resistance.

When all of his men had reached the area around Camp 1, Lt. Poindexter realized that the absence of underbrush there afforded him a good view of the surrounding area. Since there was a clear

142

field of fire all the way across the island, he decided to use the line of machine guns as his defensive position. He would make his stand there, with a line of machine gun nests that were facing to the east and stretched from the lagoon to the beach.

It had taken most of the night to hopscotch his men back to Camp 1, but by 6:00 a.m. Lt. Poindexter had all of his men behind the safety line created by the machine guns. He was completing his preparations at the defensive line and was preparing to face the enemy. Lt. Poindexter positioned his gunners along the line and gathered all remaining personnel on the west end of Wake Island to defend the line as riflemen. He had about seventy men at his disposal, including the thirty who had returned from the foray up the beach road, and the thirty-five to forty who had remained in the machine gun line all night. including Jim Cox. Poindexter's men prepared for what was about to come.

The early morning light had not exposed Japanese troops to Jim Cox, but the situation was much different down the beach at Lt. Hanna's 3" gun. Daylight allowed Hanna and Holewinski to see Japanese soldiers maneuvering all around them. Ammunition was in very short supply, so the men fighting from under the gun had to make every round count. Skee had only three shells left. It began to look very bad.

Dick Darden lay in the hospital—immobile, anxious, apprehensive, and scared of whatever fate lay ahead of him. Everyone in the hospital was awake as the battle began early on the morning of December 23. Even though the men in the hospital were in one of the most bombproof buildings on the island, there was intense anxiety. They lay defenseless in the face of a full-scale enemy invasion, and the front lines of the fighting were less than one half mile from them.

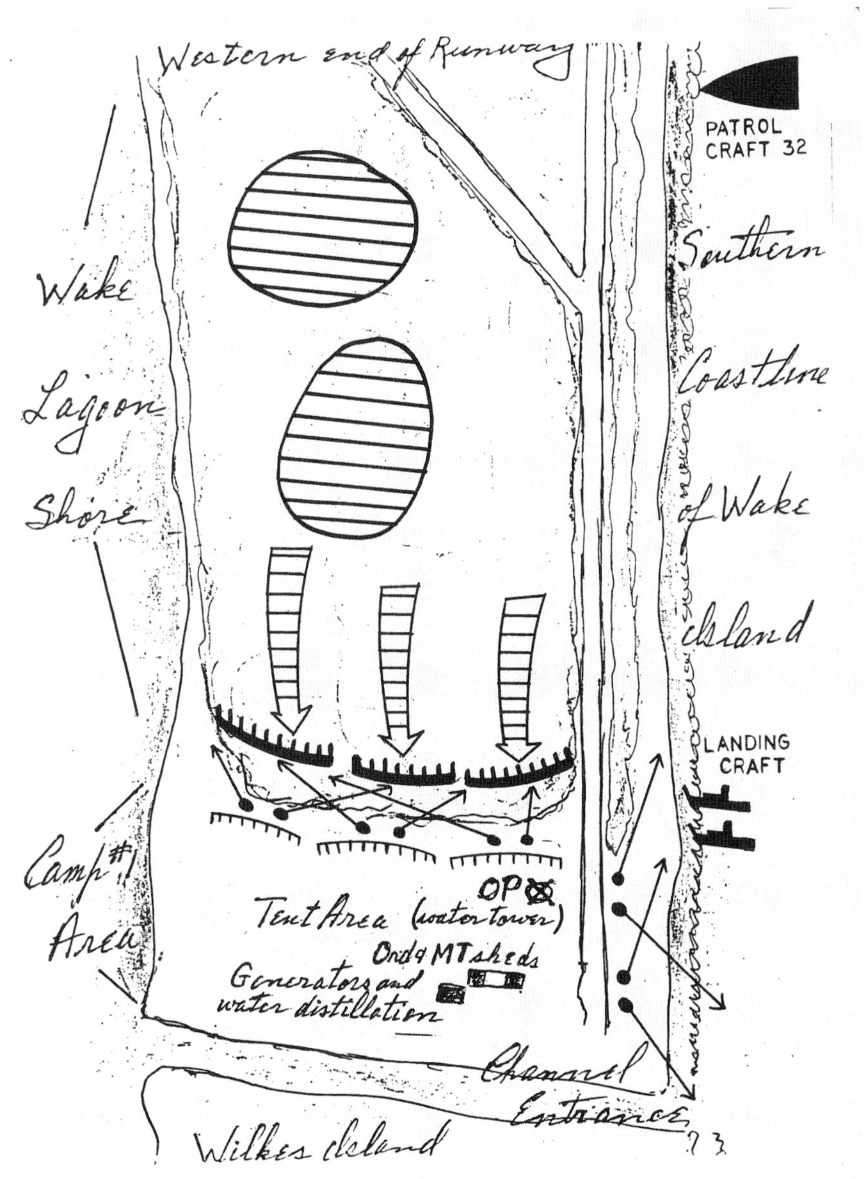

The enemy was advancing toward the bunker hospitals, and a precariously small band of defenders was left to stop them from overrunning the entire eastern end of Wake Island. In fact, the Marine ground forces all over the island was vastly outnumbered by the onrushing enemy. If one subtracted the artillery battery crews and support personnel from the original complement of defenders at the outset of the battle, there were only about forty-five machine gunners and even fewer infantrymen to do battle with over one thousand enemy troops.

To make matters worse, many of the Marines had been killed or wounded, while others like Hanna and Holewinski were pinned down and heavily outnumbered by the enemy. As daylight allowed the remaining positions to see the vast numbers of enemy troops around them, many of the men became preoccupied only with self-preservation. The enemy forces were simply overpowering.

At several positions the battle was raging and much of the fighting was hand to hand, Samurai sword against bayonet, man against man on the beaches and in the foxholes of the coral atoll. At Hanna's gun near the beach the grisly carnage continued.

Poindexter Sketch #6

At 6:30 a.m. Japanese forces are advancing toward Marine gunners at Camp #1 Lt. Poindexter has consolidated his forces in a line across the Island.

143

Holewinski saw two men as they were killed next to him. Captain Elrod stood up to throw a grenade and was killed. He would later be the only man to be awarded the Medal of Honor for his efforts during the defense of Wake Island. Major Putnam was nearby. He had been shot through the face and neck, and was bleeding profusely from the throat.

Lt. Uchida had led his men against the Marines at Hanna's gun throughout the battle. While fighting against Putnam and the VMF-211 flyers, Uchida was shot through the head and killed. In all, sixty-two Japanese soldiers would die trying to overrun Hanna's 3" gun position.

More and more of the battle stations reporting to Major Devereux and Commander Cunningham on the telephone line went silent. To the American commanders it appeared that the situation was steadily deteriorating. The wounded men lay in the hospital, knowing that hundreds of Japanese were on the island and wondering how close they were to the hospital.

While Lt. Poindexter and his mobile force had been moving around during the night Jim Cox had remained at his .30 cal. gun on the beach. Cox fired his gun throughout the night at the shadowy figures that he knew were Japanese soldiers in the nearby woods. But Cox never actually saw an enemy soldier clearly during the battle. He could hear them constantly as they came through the underbrush, but by firing into the darkness toward the sounds he managed to keep them from rushing his position.

Cox could actually hear the Japanese talking just a few feet away. He would later remember that they "sounded like a bunch of goddam monkeys jabbering away out in the brush." Cox would fire in their direction and they would become quiet, only to reposition themselves and start talking again a few minutes later.

By 6:00 a.m. Lt. Poindexter had all five of his machine gun sections (each section had two guns and two crews) in position and was ready to defend the western end of Wake Island. Some called this Mobile Reserve unit the "awkward squad" since the sailors, bakers, clerks, cooks, and other special duty personnel had much less experience at firing guns than the other Marines. But during the fighting of the early morning hours they had proven to have considerable mettle. They had fought courageously, and under Lt. Poindexter's able leadership they had killed a number of enemy soldiers while suffering only a small number of casualties themselves.

National Archives

Marine Captain Henry Elrod - Medal of Honor Winner

Jim Cox proved to be quite effective with his .30 cal. gun, keeping the large number of enemy troops massing nearby at bay all night. Before enlisting in the Navy he had spent two summers in the Civilian Military Training Corp in Fort Custer, Michigan, where he had learned how to operate similar .30 cal. machine guns. As the battle raged all around him that night, his proficiency with the gun probably saved his life.

As daylight brought clarity to the situation Poindexter's men faced their sternest test yet. The large enemy force massed in the woods was pressing nearer, and it appeared that a direct confrontation between the two opposing forces was imminent.

144

Chapter 29
DAYBREAK AT THE HOSPITAL

The battle had been raging for over three hours when daybreak finally came to Wake Island. Suddenly the wounded men in the bunker hospital could hear voices through the ventilation tube protruding through the top of the concrete dome. The voices of the men moving about on top of the sand-covered dome of the hospital were Japanese. Everyone knew what that meant. The Japanese had taken this portion of the island.

The men in the hospital knew they were in real peril! They knew that the ventilation tube that protruded through the sand to the outside would tip off the Japs that something was below. What would the Japanese do to them? Did they know that a hospital was beneath them?

Dick Darden had a more immediate concern. He lay directly below the opening of the air vent. If the Japanese thought that there was a bunker beneath them, they would storm it. Probably the first part of the assault would involve dropping grenades down the air shaft. If they did, the grenades would land in Dick's bed, blowing him and everyone around him to pieces. The atmosphere became extremely tense, with no one knowing what would happen next. The men in the hospital seemed to be completely at the mercy of the enemy troops outside the bunker.

For what seemed an eternity, the men lay in the hospital with no idea what fate would befall them. They would soon have answers to all of their questions. The Japanese did not know who or what was inside the bunker. They found the air vent and the large metal doors that sealed the one-time magazine. Dr. Kahn told one of the men to lash two broom handles together and tie a bedsheet to it. Once the white flag had been made he instructed the man to open the heavy steel doors just enough to push the flag outside. This was done with great caution, since the enemy troops were thought to be just outside the door.

As soon as the white flag was hung through the crack just above the doors, Dick and his buddies in the hospital could hear the soldiers jabbering in Japanese just outside the door, apparently underneath the white flag. The tension in the air magnified itself as the wounded men prayed that the enemy troops understood the message.

The Japanese soldiers apparently did not accept the surrender flag as sincere, and they decided to storm the building. An officer burst through the doors. He was wearing a billed cap and was heavily armed, holding a pistol in one hand. Several troops with rifles came through the doors right behind him. All of their guns were at the ready, the officer holding his pistol upward at a forty-five degree angle, but ready to fire at any provocation.

At first the Japanese did not seem to realize that the concrete bunker was being used as a hospital. Several of the wounded men were already on the floor, and apparently someone flinched near the back of the room. The flicker of movement must have frightened the officer, causing him to fire his pistol into the domed ceiling. The bullet ricochetted wildly off the domed ceiling, striking a civilian patient in the head. He doubled over in pain with a severe wound. A few seconds later more Japanese soldiers rushed in and the hospital was taken.

There was unimaginable tension inside the bunker. Electricity permeated the air. Men looked up to stare into the eyes of the enemy. Enemy rifles and bayonets were trained on everyone, and they were cocked and ready to fire. Dick thought that he was about to die.

Enemy troops filled the hospital. They took everyone who was able to walk and marched them outside where they were bound with communication wire. Only Dick and six other men, all of whom were unable to walk, were left inside the hospital.

The Japanese warships that ringed the atoll were understandably cautious about venturing too close to the Marine's 5" guns. They well remembered the events of December 11. Nevertheless, with Wilkes Island appearing to have been overrun, three destroyers began to move toward the western end of the island. What the ships did not consider was that they had entered the range of a 5" gun commanded by Lt. Woodrow Kessler in Battery B across the lagoon on Peale Island. Peale had not been invaded and the seacoast guns were still operative and in the hands of the Marines.

At 6:45 a.m. the two guns in Battery B on Wilkes Island were tracking the three destroyers, which were closing on the island near Kuku Point. The 5" guns opened fire with their first salvo aimed at the MUTSUKI, the lead destroyer. Projectiles from one of the first three salvos crashed into her, causing the ship to begin to smoke and turn away. Then the big gun began firing toward the other two ships, which likewise retreated. Defenders on Wilkes believed that the MUTSUKI was sunk, while the Japanese would only admit later that she had been damaged.

The Japanese aircraft carriers were now close enough to launch their warplanes toward Wake Island. By 7:00 a.m. thirty-four bombers, known as Vals, and sixteen Zero fighters arrived and pounded any position on the island that was not flying a Japanese flag. Many of these planes and pilots had taken part in the raid on Pearl Harbor only fifteen days earlier. The remaining positions still held by the Wake defenders got a dose of the same Pearl Harbor medicine.

By 7:15 a.m. the enemy had advanced past the Marine hospital igloo and was beginning to put pressure on Potter's line. Major Devereux ordered all available men from the gun batteries on Peale Island to join Major Potter. Capt. Bryghte D. Godbold and Lt. Robert Greeley arrived with several men and joined in the defense of Potter's line. This brought the strength of Major Potter's unit to about forty men.

It appeared that the last stand of the defenders on the eastern end of Wake Island would be at Major Potter's line. This was of little consequence to Dick Darden and the other men in the Marine hospital, however, since Potter's line was north of them, between the second and third magazines. Dick was in the first and southernmost igloo, which had been left unprotected and had already been overrun.

The enemy ground forces continued to apply constant pressure. Devereux ordered McAnally to fall back from his position near the runway to Potter's line. As Potter's men came under fire just south of the command post, Devereux knew that the enemy was only the length of a football field away from him. Furthermore, they had taken the area between Potter's men and the remaining Marine gun position at Peacock Point. That position, commanded by Lt. Barninger, was now fighting with its back to the sea.

Admiral Pye met with his staff at Pearl Harbor. A decision had to be made and made quickly. The scanty radio reports from Wake were all bad. Pye knew that the enemy had invaded the island and that the Marines were in real trouble. Pye and his men considered every plausible option. Should they engage the invading enemy with Task Force 14 or should they direct the SARATOGA to a position that would place Wake within range of the warplanes on her deck? Should they send the transport TANGIER into the tempest alone and let her try to evacuate the sixteen hundred men on the island or should they abandon Wake and avoid a confrontation with the enemy altogether?

Pye's decision was not an easy one. Were the men on Wake of such value that Task Force 14 should press forward with the relief operation while risking a naval disaster on the heels of the Pearl Harbor catastrophe? Even more precarious would be the security of Hawaii and the west coast of the mainland if Task Force 14 were lost from our Pacific defenses before we had time to recuperate from Pearl Harbor.

Admiral Pye made his decision. He would not risk sending the relief ships to Wake Island, and he ordered Task Force 14 to turn back. The entire relief operation was scuttled and the task force was ordered to retire on Midway Island. The Marines and sailors who were poised at sea to come to the aid of their brothers were outraged.

Admiral Stark in Washington was made aware of the withdrawal and the news was relayed to President Roosevelt. When the President heard of the withdrawal he was extremely disappointed, not unlike many of the Marines and Naval personnel taking part in the relief effort, who were furious.

Major Devereux, in his command bunker near the hospital, and Commander Cunningham, still at his command post on Peale Island, conferred by telephone at 7:30 a.m. Neither could effectively communicate with the men who were fighting the battle, much less see the battle to survey the situation, but both knew that the situation was bleak. It appeared that most of the island had fallen. The two leaders were not in contact with the remaining pockets of resistance, so they assumed that nearly all of the positions had been overrun.

Even though the communication lines had been cut and Major Devereux could not coordinate his men, several positions were still fiercely repelling the enemy. In some cases

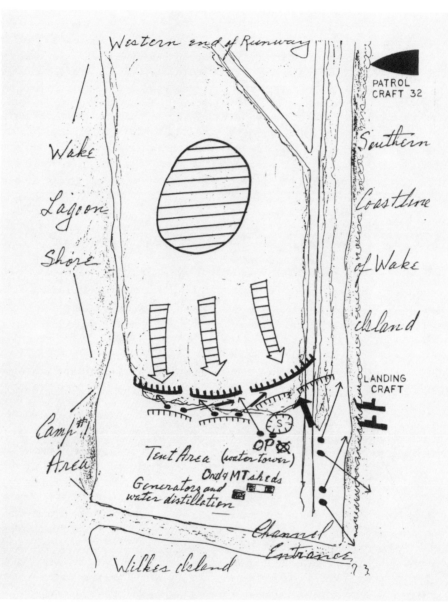

Lt. Poindexter counterattacks with three combat squads against the Japanese positions along the beach road, leaving his remaining machine gunners to defend Camp 1 (About 7:00 AM, December 23, 1941). Poindexter sketch #7

146

they were even going on the offensive. One such position was being commanded by Lt. Poindexter near the west end of Wake's south beach. Poindexter had held his defensive line of .30 cal. machine guns. This line extended all the way across the island at a point east of Camp 1 and west of the end of the airstrip.

Lt. Poindexter had his five machine gun sections, each with two guns, positioned to repel an assault by the Japanese assembled in the wooded area just to the east. Each pair of machine guns was supported by several riflemen armed with the old 1903 Springfields. Japanese troops had moved toward the boat channel and a large number were poised in the scrubby underbrush. The enemy troops had reinforced their positions immediately in front of Poindexter's machine gun line. They were being held at bay by the scorching fire of the Mobile Reserve guns and were unable to press their attack further toward Camp 1.

Lt. Poindexter positioned his ragtag corps of riflemen along the defensive line, ready to engage the enemy if they charged the line. Jim Cox remained at his machine gun position near the beach on this defensive line. Lt. Poindexter gathered all of the men at his disposal, Marines, sailors, and civilians, to protect the defensive line with his machine gunners.

At that point Lt. Poindexter made a courageous decision. He could hear the fighting just a mile to the east toward Peacock Point. This was probably the skirmish that was going on at Hanna's 3" gun, where Putnam's flyers had joined Hanna and Holewinski and were fighting to the death. From the sounds of the battle Poindexter could tell that more Marines were alive and fighting not far away.

Lt. Poindexter decided to initiate an offensive action and attack the enemy, hoping to catch them off guard and ultimately to join forces with the defenders that he knew were battling just a short distance down the beach. He thought that his men could join the other Marines that he knew were on the beach, and then perhaps mount an offensive that would defeat the enemy. It was an extraordinarily courageous decision on Poindexter's part, forsaking the relative security of the strong defensive line in favor of launching an offensive into the ranks of the enemy.

Soon after 7:00 Lt. Poindexter gave the order to go on the offensive, in effect taking control of the battle. He correctly believed that he had adequate men and fire power to launch a counter attack, even though he was seriously underestimating the size of the enemy force that was massed nearby.

Poindexter organized three squads of about ten men each. One was to be a support squad, while the other two were assault squads. The Lieutenant commanded one of the assault squads, positioning himself in the center of the formation so that he could direct and control all three of the squads. The three groups were in a triangular formation, with the support squad protecting the left flank of the other two squads.

The two assault squads would advance alternately, leap frogging their way toward the east and covering each other's movements as they went. The tactic was nearly the reverse of that which Poindexter had used in his movement back down the beach road to Camp 1 during the night.

As the counterattack began, the line of machine guns could offer additional protection by firing on the Japanese in the brush on the north side of the road. If the effort was not successful Poindexter planned to retreat to the original position under the cover of machine gun fire. But he and his men successfully began fighting their way back toward the east along the beach road. By 7:30 the thirty men in Poindexter's three squads had reclaimed over a quarter mile of ground from the enemy along the shoreline, the beach road, and a short distance into the underbrush. Poindexter's force was simply too small to extend the assault across the entire island. Moreover, the thick underbrush just to the north of the road was virtually impenetrable, making it nearly impossible to maintain control of ground gained there. Poindexter was vastly outnumbered by the enemy forces which were poised just beyond the tree line. Had he pushed across the road and toward the airport to the north, he would have run headlong into the enemy's strength. But, by remaining near the beach on the south side of the island, he was able to push the enemy out of the craters and sand dunes. He was constantly making progress, but at the same time he and his men were moving farther and farther away from the protective cover of the machine gunners near camp 1.

In the command posts the situation was beginning to look bleak. Major Devereux was in his bunker between the hospitals on Wake, and Commander Cunningham was on Peale. So many things had to be considered. Could the battle be won? Where was the relief force, and could it possibly reach the island in time to save the defenders there? How many American boys would lose their lives if the battle continued? The unspeakable word for a Marine—surrender—would have to be considered.

Walter Cook spoke with Commander Cunningham at a time when tough, gut-wrenching decisions were being made. The Commander seemed weary and withdrawn. Marines just do not surrender, they don't give up, and they never run from a fight. But the Japanese were swarming the island now in overwhelming numbers. Continued fighting now, it seemed, could only result in the defenders spilling their blood needlessly.

Spending lives now seemed futile, for it could only buy time while waiting for a relief force that had already turned toward home. Cunningham knew that Task Force 14 was over four hundred miles to the northeast and was not steaming toward the Wake defenders to offer assistance. Both Devereux and Cunningham thought that most of their positions on Wake and Wilkes Islands had fallen. It appeared that only carnage remained for the defenders who were still alive if they continued to fight against overwhelming odds.

The two American leaders were faced with nothing but bad choices. Should they fight on and watch their boys die at the hands of this bloodthirsty enemy, or should they order their men to give up? At best, surrender would be humiliating. The worst consequence would occur if the enemy, known to have an abhorrence of those who fail to fight to the death and then surrender, committed an atrocity by executing them all. Cunningham and Devereux discussed the strength of the enemy force, but their options seemed to be rapidly running out.

By this time the Japanese had a significant invasion force ashore on Wake Island. In addition, carrier-based planes were bombing and strafing the island at will. If this were not enough, over a dozen warships sat just offshore within easy range of everything on the island, ready to pulverize any unfriendly target on a moments notice if the Japanese Admiral issued the order. The pressure on Commander Cunningham and Major Devereux was tremendous.

147

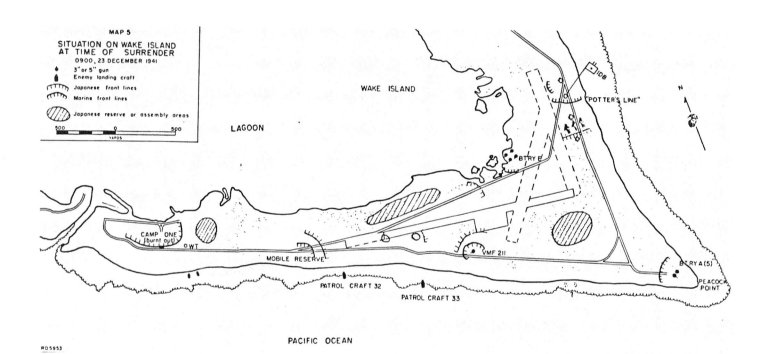

MAP 5

SITUATION ON WAKE ISLAND
AT TIME OF SURRENDER
0900, 23 DECEMBER 1941

◦ 3" or 5" gun
◦ Enemy landing craft
⊓⊓⊓⊓ Japanese front lines
⊓⊓⊓⊓ Marine front lines
▨ Japanese reserve or assembly areas

500   0   500
YARDS

WAKE ISLAND

LAGOON

"POTTER'S LINE"

IDB

N

BTRY E

CAMP ONE
(burnt out)

○ WT

MOBILE RESERVE

VMF 211

BTRY A (5)

PEACOCK
POINT

PATROL CRAFT 32

PATROL CRAFT 33

PACIFIC OCEAN

RD 5953

Chapter 30
SURRENDER

It appeared that to continue the battle could only result in needless bloodshed for the remaining defenders. Major Devereux argued that the fight should be prolonged for a time in hopes that the relief force might arrive. The only valid reason for continuing the fight now would be to hold out for reinforcements, since the situation on the ground was rapidly deteriorating. However, with the relief force in retreat, Commander Cunningham was facing the toughest decision of his life. At this point he revealed to Major Devereux that there was no relief force within one day's sailing time of Wake Island.

Both leaders could see the options clearly, and they knew what had to be done. There seemed to be agreement between Cunningham and Devereux that the only humane option they had was to surrender. Commander Cunningham made the decision, and Major Devereux began to execute the order. The word began to spread to the disbelieving Leathernecks. Wake Island would be surrendered.

At 8:00 a.m. the surrender had begun. Major Devereux alerted all units still on the telephone system to cease fire. The men knew they must prepare their positions for surrender to the approaching Japanese troops. It was a horrible feeling, one that few of the Marines were prepared to handle. They were trained to be winners, to be victorious at all costs. Now they must surrender to the enemy they despised.

Charles Holmes described his feelings as simply being numb. The defenders of Wake who had gotten the message to surrender were psychologically distraught and confused about what was happening and what was to come. This was compounded by their physical condition. Sixteen days of fighting in the sand and grit of Wake Island, moving heavy guns by night, being constantly attacked by bombers from the air, and eating irregularly from the limited field rations had put them in a state of mind that none had ever experienced before.

The defenders of Wake responded to these circumstances in a variety of ways. Some were enraged, while others walked around in a daze. Some simply sat with a perplexed look about them, while others broke down and cried. They had been prepared to fight to the end, be it victory or be it death, but this turn of events had left them with a horribly empty feeling. Even during this stage of the battle most of the men knew they must not tarry. The enemy was closing in on all positions on Wake and the weapons had to be prepared for the surrender.

Major Devereux had instructed all positions remaining on the telephone network to destroy their weapons before surrendering. This was done in a variety of ways. Charles Holmes was intent upon damaging his prized 3" gun to the point that he could be sure that it would never be used to kill American boys. The crew stuffed blankets down the barrel and poured sand in on top of the wadding. They elevated the guns to the point that they could expect maximum damage and then dropped hand grenades down the barrels.

Satisfied that this had rendered the guns useless, they turned their attention to the other equipment. The firing pins from the guns were thrown into the ocean just off Peacock Point. The fire control equipment and electronic gear that Holmes had been so proud of, and that had worked so well against the enemy planes, was smashed. Holmes fired his .45 cal. automatic pistol into the sophisticated equipment and then turned on it with a sledge hammer in order to destroy it completely. He didn't stop until he was sure it was useless to the enemy.

After everything was double checked to be sure that it had been destroyed beyond repair, Lt. Wally Lewis ordered Holmes and the other members of the gun battery to fall into formation. With a white skivvy shirt tied to a stick they marched up the road to encounter the victorious enemy. Holmes had no idea what fate might befall him when his group met the enemy. The answer was not long in coming. Very quickly the Marines were spotted by a group of Japanese troops.

Holmes was a bit surprised to see large husky Jap soldiers instead of the small men, slight of build, that he had expected. The Japanese were members of the Special Naval Landing Force and appeared a bit more formidable than had been anticipated. They were armed with rifles and had fixed bayonets. They ordered the Marines to line up in single file and take off their clothes.

Tom Kennedy had listened as someone in the hospital bunker took the call and was told of the surrender. The men in the hospital began the excruciating wait to see what the Japanese would do with them. It would seem like an eternity before they would find out. The tension was immense as Dick and the other men waited. Would they live or would they die? The wounded men could only lie and wait.

The men aboard the relief vessels were still several hundred miles east of Wake atoll. They reacted predictably to the news that they were being called home without a chance to help the defenders on Wake. There was disbelief among many of the Marines and naval crewmen on the ships. Many were angry, and there was talk of ignoring the order and continuing with the relief effort.

Admiral Fletcher wisely dismissed such talk. It would have been disastrous to make a run to the island because the fleet would have run headlong into the enemy cruisers east of Wake and then the full task force around the island. On December 23 the American relief force began steaming toward Midway Island.

Meanwhile, most of the Wake defenders had been notified of the surrender and had begun to comply with the order. However, the defenders at several positions did not have the benefit of a functional telephone and were unaware of the decision to surrender. Indeed, some were still on the offensive. Lt. Poindexter was counterattacking the enemy with elements of his Mobile Reserve, having broken out of Camp 1 and driven the enemy back toward the airfield.

On Wilkes Island Captain Wesley Platt and his band of about fifty Marines, along with Lt. McAlister and Lt. McKinstry and their two dozen men, were firmly in control. They had killed ninety-eight of the one hundred Japanese who had landed there, and had

This is the High Explosive Ammunition igloo used at Maj. Devereux's command post in December 1941 – 1988 Photo.

captured the remaining two. Both Platt, on Wilkes, and Poindexter, on Wake, were unaware of the surrender. To the contrary, they thought the American forces were winning the Battle for Wake Island.

Commander Cunningham was still at his command post on Peale Island, about four miles from Devereux's command bunker and the hospitals on Wake. Cunningham had already given the order to surrender, so he disarmed himself and drove his pickup truck across the bridge onto Wake and on to his cottage. He had time to clean up a bit, shave, and put on a fresh uniform. He then drove south to surrender to the enemy.

As the word of surrender spread through the ranks of the defenders their emotions intensified. Some joked about their predicament, while others were firmly against a Marine ever surrendering. Some battery commanders wisely instructed their men to eat as much of their food as they could. They were anticipating with remarkable accuracy the treatment their men would receive at the hands of the Japanese captors.

Major Devereux attempted to call the Marine hospital on the telephone hookup. He was concerned about his wounded men there because they were three hundred yards south of his command bunker. He knew that Potter's line was positioned less than one hundred yards south of his position, and this meant that the hospital was either in "no man's land" or in enemy hands. He attempted to get through to Dr. Kahn, but could not get an answer on the line.

Major Devereux had not made contact with the enemy yet, but decided to risk a venture into their midst in order to determine the status of the helpless men in the hospital. The telephone lines had apparently been severed, so Devereux made a white flag by tying a white rag to a mop handle.

Devereux began walking along the coral road southward toward the hospital, ordering each of the Marines that he passed to cease fire. Sgt. Donald Malleck, a Marine radioman, accompanied him and carried the white flag. The men could still hear gunfire about the island, so they knew that to expose themselves was very dangerous.

As the two unarmed men walked southward they spotted a Japanese soldier, who cautiously walked toward them with his rifle and bayonet at the ready. Then several more Japanese soldiers moved into the open. One was an officer who was brandishing a long Samurai sword. The Japanese officer ordered Devereux and Malleck to disarm themselves. They did, placing their weapons and helmets on the coral roadway.

Suddenly a rifle shot rang out. Apparently a Marine in the vicinity, probably part of Potter's defense line, had not gotten the cease-fire order or had ignored it. The marksmanship of the Marine rifleman was perfect, as one of the Japanese soldiers fell to the roadway dead. Devereux screamed at the man to obey the cease-fire order. He and Malleck stood defenseless on the road.

There was, by this time, a host of Japanese soldiers near them, rifles at the ready. A tense situation ensued, but not one of the Jap soldiers made an effort to shoot at the two Marines. The Japs displayed surprisingly little emotion when their comrade was shot. They took no retaliatory action at all against the two Marines who stood fully exposed before them.

Major Devereux learned quickly that the sword-wielding Japanese officer was fluent in English; in fact, he had been educated at UCLA. The three men began walking down the road to the hospital with Malleck still holding the white flag. Major Devereux realized that the hospital had already been taken when he saw a group of Americans, some with fresh wounds, on the ground beside the road. They were under Japanese guard and were bound with telephone wire.

The hands of the men along the road were tied behind their backs and were cinched up with wire that was looped around their necks. The wire was tied in such a way that they could not move their arms without tightening the nooses around their necks to the point of making breathing difficult.

At least one of the patients in the hospital had been killed when the Japanese troops entered the building. Dick Darden and the six other men who were wounded badly enough to prevent them from walking still lay just inside the metal doors to the concrete igloo.

The English-speaking Japanese officer sent for the commander of the invasion force, Captain Itaya. When he arrived he explained that his surrender terms were unconditional. The Japanese would be in complete control of Wake Island.

Just as Devereux reached the entrance to the hospital he encountered a Japanese officer and began to converse with him. Moments later there was a commotion a short distance back up the road. Commander Cunningham had driven past the first three bunker magazines and his truck had been stopped within sight of the fourth, the Marine hospital. He had been captured and was being brought toward the hospital. Upon arrival there Commander Cunningham was searched and allowed to join Major Devereux. Then the American commanding officers accepted the terms of the enemy and made the surrender official.

The sounds of gunfire elsewhere on the island indicated that there was fighting in progress even while the leaders were meeting and agreeing to surrender. It was decided that Commander Cunningham would remain with the Japanese officer to discuss the conditions of the surrender while Major Devereux, escorted by a party of Japanese troops, would attempt to notify the defenders who had not been notified of the surrender and who apparently were continuing the fight. The discussion between Commander Cunningham and the Japanese concerning the terms of the surrender was in progress just outside the hospital bunker where Dick was anxiously awaiting his fate.

Major Devereux was instructed to visit each American position and implement the surrender with every remaining pocket of resistance. Commander Cunningham was placed in the back of the pickup truck and driven away. The Japanese took him northward, back up the road in the direction from which he had come. It was half past nine in the morning.

Major Devereux, along with Sgt. Malleck and about twenty Japanese troops, began walking away from the hospital along the road that ran parallel to Wake's south beach. He had the unenviable and dangerous task of trying to persuade each remaining pocket of defenders to lay down their arms and surrender to the Japanese. Their first objective was to notify the VFM-211 unit which was fighting at Hanna's 3" gun, about one mile away.

Charles Holmes and the other Marines from Battery E had been stripped down to their shoes. They had been bound with the telephone wire using the hand-to-neck method, and the nooses were becoming extremely uncomfortable. They waited tensely to see what would happen next. As they stood naked and bound by the roadway the Japs loaded machine guns and aimed them at the column of men. Holmes began to fear the worst. He had heard of how the Japanese had done the very same thing to prisoners in China, only to mow them down in mass executions. Holmes felt that death was very near, just minutes away at best. A morbid uneasiness fell over the group as they waited. They all felt that death was close at hand.

By this time Major Devereux and the surrender party had begun walking westward along the beach road facilitating

THIS MAGAZINE WAS THE MARINE HOSPITAL AFTER THEIR ORIGINAL ONE WAS DESTROYED BY BOMBING. THE JAPS CAPTURED IT 23 DEC. 1941 ONLY KILLING ONE MAN AND WOUNDED ANOTHER. HERE COMDR. CUNNINGHAM. THE ISLAND COMDR. JOINED MAJOR DEVEREUX TO COMPLETE THE SURRENDER. DEVEREUX STARTED FROM HERE AT 0930 WITH A JAP GUARD OF 20 VISITING ALL MARINE STRONG POINTS ALONG THE SOUTHERN PART OF WAKE AND ON WILKES TO ORDER THEM TO CEASE RESISTANCE.

This wooden sign stood at the hospital bunker in 1951

the surrender, Lt. Poindexter was advancing eastward against the enemy along the same road. Poindexter was heading toward

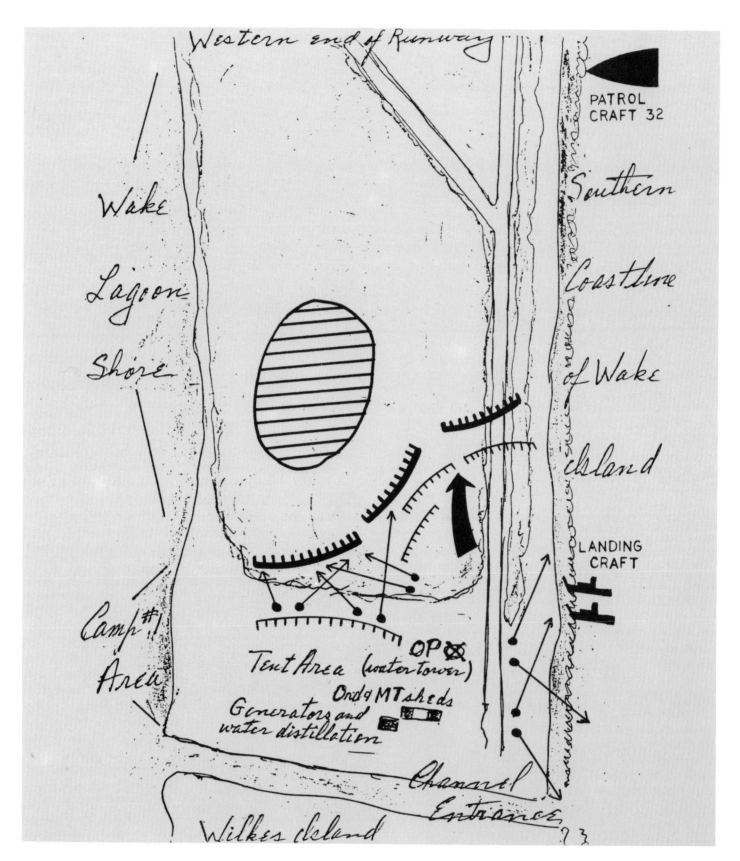

Western end of Runway

Wake

Lagoon

Shore

PATROL
CRAFT 32

Southern

Coastline

of Wake

Island

LANDING
CRAFT

Camp #1

Area

OP

Tent Area (water tower)

Ordg MT sheds

Generators and
water distillation

Channel
Entrance

Wilkes Island

Arthur Poindexter

Lt. Poindexter and his three assault squads attack to the east and take ground along the beach road while Gunnery Sgt. John Cemeris and the rear eschelon hold Camp 1. The Japanese are massing on the Lagoon side of the road at 9:00 AM

Devereux, battling his way into the enemy army which was vastly superior to his in numbers. Amazingly, Lt. Poindexter was successfully pushing the enemy back, winning position after position in one of the most daring attacks and under some of the toughest conditions of the entire battle.

While Gunnery Sgt. John Cemeris maintained command of the rear echelon of the Mobile Reserve defending Camp 1, Lt. Poindexter was lashing out at the Japanese that held the ground between him and the defenders who were fighting farther up the beach. Lt. Poindexter was, for all of his courage and valiant effort, placing himself in a more precarious position all the time. As he advanced against one enemy position after another, he further distanced himself from the support of the machine gun line to his rear.

Poindexter had made one tactical move in an effort to minimize the separation of his men from the support of the machine gun line. He had instructed Sgt. "Q. T." Wade to follow the assault with a section of .30 cal. machine guns. This would protect the counterattack to some extent by protecting the exposed left flank and the rear. Wade followed his orders to the letter, exposing himself without the benefit of supporting riflemen to follow just behind the rear assault squad.

As Lt. Poindexter moved his men farther up the beach road he increased the likelihood that the enemy would move in behind him and occupy the ever widening space between the thirty Marines in the assault squads and the machine gun line at Camp 1. The Japanese could have attempted to drive a wedge between Poindexter and Camp 1, cutting him off from his rear support, if they had decided to press such an offensive.

Had the Japanese decided on such a move they would have greatly outnumbered Poindexter's men and might have boxed them in from three sides with the ocean to their backs. Despite the fact that they were vastly outnumbered, Poindexter's men continued to make progress up the beach road, rooting out enemy positions and pushing them back. One nugget of wisdom ingrained in Poindexter's philosophy was that, in all situations, both in battle and otherwise, one should always take care to cover his rear. Nevertheless, despite the protection offered them by Sgt. Wade's machine gun section and the support squad on the left flank, the threat to Poindexter's flank and rear was steadily increasing.

Between 9:00 and 10:00 a.m. the Japanese had called in air support. Carrier-based fighters began strafing the American positions that continued to hold out. One dive bomber came over and picked Hanna's 3" gun as its target. The plane made an immediate 180 degree turn just after it flew past and headed back toward the four men, still huddled partially under the corrugated steel platform, for the kill.

Hanna tried to take cover under one side of the perforated steel gun deck while Holewinski was able to get partially underneath the other side. The two civilians, Gay and Bryan, were lying on the exposed ground beside Holewinski. Ski was covered up to the waist by the steel platform, his head and chest completely exposed.

As the plane made its return run the rear gunner sprayed the entire area with machine gun fire. A heavy spray of bullets peppered the entire gun position. Gay and Bryan were each hit by several rounds. Gay was lying next to Holewinski, who saw Gay's body perforated by so many bullets and with such force that his chest was

slammed downward and then bounced upward off the ground. There was no sound or movement from the two men. Both of the civilians had been killed instantly.

Holewinski took a bullet in each leg. The bullets felt like a hot knife going through his flesh. Both legs were opened up and began to bleed profusely. Holewinski tried in vain to get his entire body under the gun deck, but without success. The plane passed over again, spraying more deadly bullets into the 3" gun emplacement. The plane circled and Ski felt another bullet as it cut through his leg. The plane came over again, lower this time, and put still another bullet into Ski's bleeding legs.

Holewinski had thought that the steel platform would offer some degree of protection. Ironically, he was wounded in both of his legs, which had been under the assumed protection of the steel platform. Not one of the bullets had found its mark in the exposed upper half of Skee's body. The bullets from the strafing plane hit the platform, sounding like a hard rain and easily penetrated the thick steel. It was a stroke of luck that Skee was lying exactly where he was.

Hanna and Putnam were under the opposite side of the gun, just a few feet from Holewinski. Both had been wounded. The plane circled again and headed in for yet another strafing run. It was so low that Holewinski could clearly see the pilot in the cockpit. As the plane roared directly over the gun pit, Ski could look through the pilot's goggles and see the whites of his eyes.

The plane seemed intent upon killing everyone at the gun. Skee remained absolutely still during the next pass, hoping that by "playing possum" he could make the enemy pilot think that everyone at the gun was dead. This time the strafing started just beyond the gun and missed everything. The plane left for more lively targets and did not return. Perhaps playing dead saved the remaining five lives at Hanna's gun.

In the chaos of the strafing runs, a Japanese rifle grenade had been lobbed into the gun pit and had detonated on the gun platform. The explosion had torn a gaping hole in the heavy sheet of perforated metal just above Holewinski. He had been hit so many times, and was bleeding from so many wounds, that he would not recollect the grenade exploding and wounding him during the chaotic melee. However, the after effects of the grenade would be long lasting.

Holewinski felt something wet running down his back, and he knew there was no water in the area. Sure enough, when he felt his back, his hand was covered with blood. The grenade had blown through the metal platform above Holewinski, and fragments of the deadly device had torn a hole in his back at the beltline, gouging out a large handful of flesh.

By 10:30 Lt. Poindexter's assault squads had progressed over a mile down the beach. He began to encounter more determined resistance but continued to press forward through enemy positions. All of the men in the three assault squads were riflemen except for Sgt. Wade. The ever-reliable Wade had complied with his orders and moved forward with his section of .30 cal. machine guns to support Poindexter's attack.

Poindexter signaled to Wade, pointing to a position near the road. Sgt. Wade set up his machine gun there. From that position he began firing to protect the increasingly perilous left flank and rear of Poindexter's attacking force.

Holewinski was the only man alive on his side of the gun. He lay in the sand bleeding from more wounds than he could count. He prayed that his blood would begin to clot. Cries for help from other wounded men in the vicinity could be heard, but there were no corpsmen to offer assistance. These Marines were in the middle of the tempest.

The Japanese soldiers had kept a modest distance during the strafing runs, but had become brazen with confidence when the planes had finished scorching the gun pit with their machine gun fire. They thought they had conquered the 3" gun. Enemy bullets flew wildly into the position, and Skee knew that if he raised his head off the sandy ground he could expect to be hit immediately. More than two hundred enemy soldiers were poised near Hanna's gun, ready to overrun the position when the order was given.

The Japanese troops continued to gain courage and Ski knew that they were coming toward him. He looked down at his three remaining 30-06 cartridges, slipping one into the breach of his Springfield rifle and sliding the bolt forward. An enemy soldier stood up directly in front of him as if to inquisitively stare into the gun pit. Holewinski fired his weapon at point blank range and watched the soldier fall. Another Jap soldier came into view beside the first. He fired again with the same result.

Skee placed his last round into the rifle and slid the bolt forward. He knew that within seconds he would be completely out of ammunition and defenseless, entirely at the mercy of the advancing enemy. Holewinski aimed his Springfield toward the top of the pit where the next Jap was likely to rush him. He braced himself for what was about to happen.

Moments later, just after 12:00 noon, Major Devereux and Cpl. Malleck appeared as they walked out of the brush shouting for all to surrender. Holewinski had a clear view of Devereux, but could not see the other defenders who were under the other side of the gun. Skee could see the crowd of Japanese soldiers around Devereux and their white flags.

A voice called out to Devereux with a warning, "Look out Major, there are Japs all around you!" Skee thought, "Yeah, they are all around you all right. They have been all around us all night." Holewinski recognized the voice that was shouting to Major Devereux from just behind him as Major Putnam's. Devereux ordered the men to disarm themselves, which they did. Putnam, Hanna, and those who were able stood up to accept the perplexing turn of events.

Holewinski pulled the bolt back on his rifle and watched the extractor slide his last shell out of the chamber. He stared at it for a moment. He then took out the bolt, wanting to throw it so that the Japs could not put the gun back into working order, but without the strength to do so. He simply pushed the bolt down into the sand beside him.

A total of twenty-six men had defended Hanna's 3" gun position during the night. They included Hanna, Holewinski, the civilians Gay, Bryan, and Lehtola, along with Putnam, Elrod, Tharin and the VMF-211 flyers. The 3" gun had hit and seriously damaged both troop ships as they came ashore. The defenders had engaged the enemy for several hours of combat at close quarters, killing so many Japanese that more than sixty of their corpses littered the area just outside the gun pit.

At the time of surrender only a handful of men, among them Hanna, Putnam, Tharin, were able to walk away from the gun. Holewinski was too seriously wounded to stand. Captain Tharin was the only one of the ten survivors at this position who did not have a serious wound. Major Putnam's wounds were serious enough that Captain Tharin had taken over command of the unit.

Putnam had been shot in the face. So much blood was draining from his cheek and down his neck that he appeared to have a terrible neck wound. Hanna had received only one direct bullet wound, but had several additional wounds from bullets that had ricocheted off the metal gun during the strafing.

The VMF-211 unit, along with Lt. Hanna, Corporal Holewinski, and the civilians, had been defending the 3" gun for over six hours. They had steadfastly resisted each of the enemy advances even though sixteen of the twenty-six men had been killed and twenty-five of the twenty-six had been wounded. In the final stages of the battle the enemy had dedicated a force to taking the position, while the defenders were bloodied and virtually out of ammunition. Had Major Devereux been a few minutes later in reaching the gun, the fate of the ten remaining defenders almost surely would have been grim.

Major Devereux saw that Holewinski was immobile and asked the Japanese through an interpreter to help him. Two Japs pulled him out from under the gun and carried him to the road just a short distance away. Ski quickly learned that the Japanese word for water was "mizu," and pointed toward the canteen that one Jap soldier had on his belt. At first they were hesitant, but then a Japanese lieutenant ordered one of the men to give him his canteen as Skee uttered "Meezoo, meezoo." Ski tasted his first Japanese water.

Skee lay on the road in the hot sun. Major Putnam, along with about a half dozen American prisoners and several Japanese soldiers, was nearby. Suddenly a Japanese plane flew very low over the road. It drew fire from a defender who was still active just a short distance down the road. Everyone on the road scrambled into the bushes. Someone grabbed Skee and dragged him into the woods.

The plane circled and came back, strafing the position down the road. Skee could tell that the defender was still fighting back because of the difference in the sounds of the guns. The plane and the machine gunner on the ground were firing at each other. The Japs had planted their flags in the area around Skee to show the planes that they had taken that area. Even so, everyone had hit the deck, including the Japs. A Japanese lieutenant began to jabber on his radio, apparently calling off the aircraft. It did not return. Soon there was no more firing, so Devereux must have reached the gunner.

Major Devereux reached Lt. Kliewer's position at the generator near the west end of the airstrip. Kliewer and three men remained dug in at this position. After Devereux informed them of the surrender and instructed them to come out, the men reluctantly complied. The two machine gun crews farther down at the end of the airstrip were next. They likewise surrendered.

Skee was laid on the hard coral runway at the airstrip, which was being used as a collection area for captured Americans. Already a large group of defenders had been brought there, and most had been bound, arms to neck, with communications wire. The Japanese troops stripped off Skee's clothes, except for his underwear, including his shoes. It would be almost four years before

154

Holewinski would have another pair of shoes that fit him properly.

Bandages were applied to Skee's bleeding legs. The gaping wounds were pulled back together and tightly bandaged. Skee was weary to the bone and as he lay in the sea of misery, he began to get drowsy. Someone advised Skee not to go to sleep, fearing that he might need to be awake for whatever was about to happen. Skee fought for over an hour to stay awake as more and more prisoners were brought to the airstrip. Finally he could hold his eyes open no longer and fell into an uncomfortable slumber.

Major Devereux could hear gunfire farther to the west toward the boat channel and Camp 1. This was probably the advancing assault squads of Lt. Poindexter, which were still fighting their way eastward along the beach road. During the action that Lt. Poindexter had taken during the morning, his assault squads had killed approximately eighty of the enemy. So successful had this group been that they felt they were winning the battle for Wake Island.

Poindexter's men had continued to move eastward and they were approaching the intersection of the beach road and the road that ran north of the airfield. This was very near the position they had established at 1:30 a.m. By this time their only contact with the defensive line at Camp 1 was by runners who were used to carry messages. Despite ever stiffening resistance, Lt. Poindexter and his counterattacking unit continued to push through the pockets of Japanese resistance along the beach road.

By 12:30 p.m. Lt. Poindexter and his men had fought their way back to the confluence of the two roads at the west end of the airstrip, and they were still on the offensive. Poindexter knew that a significant number of enemy troops was on his flank in the underbrush, but he was not aware that there was such a large force. He and his small band of fighters were outnumbered by a huge margin, but they were not aware of the extreme danger at their position. They began to encounter even stiffer opposition.

Lt. Poindexter's unit slowed considerably when they encountered a skirmish line that a large number of enemy troops had formed across the island in front of them. Poindexter and his men were facing the stiffest resistance yet, but they felt that if they could just push the enemy back a little farther they could join up with other Marines they knew were in the area of the airstrip. Poindexter was as optimistic as ever, believing that this larger force of defenders could then push the Japanese back toward Peacock Point, and eventually defeat them by clearing the enemy from the southern shoreline.

Despite the heavy enemy resistance facing him, Poindexter was encouraged by his successful offensive drive during the morning. He felt, as a good Marine would, that his continued efforts might turn the tide of battle. He was intent upon pressing further to the east to join the Marines who were still fighting there.

At this point in the battle Lt. Poindexter was truly optimistic about the chances of the defenders being able to turn the tide of the Battle for Wake Island. He was not aware of the numerical difference between his small thirty-man squad and the force of several hundred Japanese troops who had stopped his forward movement. Several large groups of enemy soldiers had, by this time, assembled in the dense undergrowth just to his left and rear. Despite all of this he was ready to press forward toward Peacock Point.

Walter Cook and the weathermen in their dugout could see trucks running back and forth along the nearby road. They were flying small white flags with red dots in the center, so Cook knew they were Japanese. They were picking up men who appeared to be American and carrying them toward the airfield. It appeared that a surrender was in progress. Cook and his friends did not want to risk being rousted out of their shelter by a hand grenade or machine gun fire, so they agreed to approach the Japanese on the roadway.

They did not have a suitable white flag for surrendering, so they cut a branch off of a tree and tied a skivvie shirt to it. The men then marched in column toward the road. The next truck coming down the road spotted them and stopped. A Japanese assault Marine, wearing a white cap, jumped off the truck and began to frisk the men. He smiled at his new prisoners, offered them a cigarette, and motioned them into the truck.

At about the same time that Lt. Poindexter was starting his next offensive maneuver against the enemy, Major Devereux's party was approaching the back side of the same Japanese skirmish line. Understandably there was confusion, during which some of the Japanese who were involved in the fire fight against Poindexter's advance turned and began shooting toward Devereux's surrender party.

One of Lt. Poindexter's riflemen was in position so that he could see a good distance down the road. Suddenly he noticed movement. He shouted, "Lieutenant, there's a bunch of Nips coming down the road with a white flag." Poindexter looked down the road and, sure enough, he saw a large number of enemy troops coming toward him with a surrender flag. He thought that the enemy was surrendering to him. He was a bit surprised, since the resistance had become intense. Nevertheless, it appeared that the Japanese unit was giving up.

Lt. Poindexter told the men in his skirmish line to cover him. He made his way out of the scrub brush and onto the road, walking toward the surrender party. He was fully armed, taking no chances in case the enemy ploy was a trick. Grenades were clipped across the front of his shirt, a pistol clung to his belt, and he carried a rifle at the ready position. All he could see as he approached the group were armed Japanese troops.

Poindexter walked toward the group until they were only seventy-five yards apart. He still could not see Major Devereux. Since the Major was a diminutive man, measuring only 5'4" in height, he blended in perfectly with the Japanese. Devereux could see Poindexter, but not vice versa. Devereux was walking in the middle of the pack and was almost completely obscured.

Then Devereux shouted to Poindexter, "Drop your rifle." Poindexter recognized his superior's voice and suddenly realized what was happening. He was stunned. In an instant his situation degenerated from victor to vanquished. He did as ordered, allowing his rifle to fall onto the coral road as he then spotted Devereux in the midst of the large group of fifty to one hundred enemy soldiers. He continued to walk toward the enemy troops until he was just a few feet away from them.

As the Lieutenant approached the group of Japanese began to part, some of them scattering to the sides of the road, as if Poindexter was some sort of demon. Indeed, he did present an imposing figure to the smaller Japanese. As he walked into the group he still wore his pistol and had hand grenades hanging from his chest. He wore the grime of twelve hours of combat. He later would learn that the Japanese expected suicide from soldiers who were captured by the enemy. Many in the group probably thought that he was about to commit hara-kiri with the grenades.

Some of the armed troops stared at Poindexter while others scattered and took cover. As his stare penetrated them his image was fierce indeed. His face was smeared with a black ointment that had been used on the facial burns he had sustained from fighting fires during the night at Camp 1. He had a fierce look about him, somewhat like a football player with anti-glare compound smeared under his eyes and smudged all over his face. He could tell the Japs thought he was a mean SOB.

Major Devereux ordered him to disarm, which he did. He unbuckled his pistol belt, allowing it to fall onto the road. As the nervous Japs looked on he carefully took the hand grenades off of his shirt and laid them, one by one, on the ground, each with its safety pin still inserted.

Devereux then ordered him to go back to his men and instruct them to stand up, throw down their rifles, take off their helmets, and put their hands behind their heads. Poindexter reluctantly went about the task. At this point he was terribly disillusioned. A few minutes before he had been leading a successful counterattack against a retreating enemy. Now he was laying down his weapons at their feet.

Poindexter's men were shocked when they learned that Major Devereux had ordered them to lay down their weapons and surrender to the enemy. Just as they stood and disarmed themselves a large number of the Japs in the main group began running toward Poindexter's men. They appeared to be on the verge of thrusting their bayonets into the helpless prisoners. The thought of an atrocity instantly flashed through Poindexter's mind. He feared that the enemy troops were making a bonzai charge and were about to run his men through with their long bayonets.

Holmes Collection

A 3-inch gun of the type used on Wake. It was used by the defenders at Hanna's gun for protection. Note the Perforated steel platform.

Just as quickly as the charge had begun a Japanese officer stepped between the two groups and called off his men. Poindexter felt a huge relief. All twenty-five to thirty men in his three squads were now completely disarmed and at the mercy of the enemy.

After Poindexter's men had surrendered, Devereux's party continued westward along the beach road. Devereux asked

Poindexter to join him and assist in disarming his men in the machine gun positions farther down the beach. This would turn out to be a significant stroke of luck for the young lieutenant, for the treatment afforded Major Devereux and his officers would be significantly better than that of the captured men who were being hustled off to the airstrip.

As the surrender party walked down the beach road toward Camp 1, they could see enemy troops coming out of the brush and organizing into platoons and companies all along the roadway. It quickly became apparent how vastly outnumbered Poindexter's small group of riflemen had been. He was amazed at the number of troops that had come ashore during the assault. Each platoon had thirty-five to fifty men, and three platoons formed a company. The surrender party passed group after group of enemy soldiers along the roadside, some appearing to number over two hundred men.

Lt. Poindexter suddenly realized how precarious his position had been during the early morning push down the island. Hundreds of the enemy had been just beyond his left flank as he charged down the beach side of the island. He realized that during his counterattack he and his men had pushed right past hundreds of enemy troops who probably could have wiped out his small band of defenders if they had turned and charged him. He realized that he had led his men into a serpent's lair, unwittingly responding to a desperate situation with the boldest of actions.

The surrender party approached the line of machine guns that Lt. Poindexter had set up across the island near the boat channel at Camp 1. One by one the positions were ordered to surrender, which they did without question. As the surrender party walked through the burned-out remains of Camp 1 they reached the water tower. The American flag still flew from its top, so two Nip soldiers started climbing up the side of the tower to tear it down.

As the two Japanese soldiers prepared to rip down the Stars and Stripes Sgt. Dave Rush, in a defensive position which had not yet surrendered and was still fully armed, drew a bead with his rifle on one of the Japs who was scaling the tower. Just as the enemy soldier filled Rush's sights and he was about to fire, Major Devereux saw him and shouted to him, admonishing him to stay calm and not do anything foolish. There was great tension within the surrender party. Again Poindexter felt that he had come very near being in a blood bath.

Jim Cox had a clear view of Major Devereux, Malleck, Poindexter, and the party of Japanese soldiers as they came down the road toward the boat channel. Suddenly, just as everyone seemed to become aware of the circumstances, someone very close to Jim Cox fired his rifle toward the surrender party and one of the Japs fell dead. The group never slowed down or broke stride, seemingly unconcerned that one of their number had been struck down.

Major Devereux shouted to the men in Cox's position to lay down their arms, which they did. A group of Japanese soldiers approached them and appeared on the verge of bayonetting the defenseless soldiers, but a Japanese officer shouted an order that stopped them just before they reached Cox. The Jap soldiers disarmed Cox's group and made them strip down to their underwear as they stood on the beach road. Then they were ordered to march toward the airstrip.

Suddenly a Japanese observation plane, a low-performance pontoon craft that had probably been launched from a cruiser offshore, flew over the men on the road at low altitude. Gunnery Sgt. John Cemeris was still manning his machine gun at another position which had not seen the surrender party. Cemeris was about one hundred yards from the channel and just a short distance in front of Devereux's group. He aimed his gun at the slow aircraft and squeezed off several bursts, using just the proper amount of lead to score a perfect bullseye. As his machine gun roared, the spray of bullets ripped into the Japanese aircraft.

The plane began to emit black smoke as its engine caught fire. It headed out to sea, losing altitude as it flew toward its mother ship. Once again Lt. Poindexter thought that his goose had been cooked. The surrender party was momentarily shaken, but regained its composure and Cemeris' position was surrendered. The group continued to walk toward the boat channel.

The machine gun fire from Sgt. Cemeris toward the observation plane was probably the last defiant act of the Wake Island defenders against the enemy. It marked the end of the American opposition to the invasion of Wake. Only the American detachment on Wilkes Island remained involved in the defense of the island.

Having not heard from Captain Platt across the boat channel on Wilkes for hours, Major Devereux assumed that the island had fallen. He was amazed when he was ordered by the Japanese to go across to Wilkes to arrange a surrender of the defenders there.

Captain Platt had begun the battle with only seventy men to defend Wilkes Island. Even though they were outnumbered by the Japanese, Platt's men had successfully defended their ground all night in close hand-to-hand combat. Platt even mounted counterattacks against the enemy, and these surges had decimated the entire Japanese force that had landed on Wilkes Island.

Wiley Sloman was lapsing into and out of consciousness, and the extent of his head wound had become obvious to his Marine buddies on Wilkes. He remembered corpsman Bill Raymond, who was part of his artillery unit, yelling to another corpsman, "Hey, Sloman's still alive." Raymond and corpsman Ernest Valle placed Sloman on a stretcher, but they had to leave him lying in the hot sun in an exposed area. They were in the midst of a battle, and there was no way to move Sloman to the hospital on Wake.

At noon Captain Platt had been preparing for another invasion from the ships and landing craft that his men had sighted just offshore. Platt's men could see the troop transports coming toward them, by this time barely two miles offshore. The accompanying destroyers and cruisers had begun to bombard the island. In addition to this the carrier-based aircraft were bombing and strafing Wilkes.

Platt ordered his men to engage the ships with the 5" seacoast guns, but since they had been stationary during the sixteen days of aerial attacks they had been the targets of the bombers too often. They were not operational, damaged beyond further participation in the battle.

Capt. Platt personally inspected the seacoast guns. Seeing that they were inoperable, he went to Battery F to see if the 3" guns there could be used. Amid the corpses of the Japanese troops who had died at Battery F Captain Platt determined that these guns, as well, would be of no use to the defenders for fighting at close quarters. He instructed his men to take the two .30 cal. machine guns, along with all available riflemen, and move toward the old

157

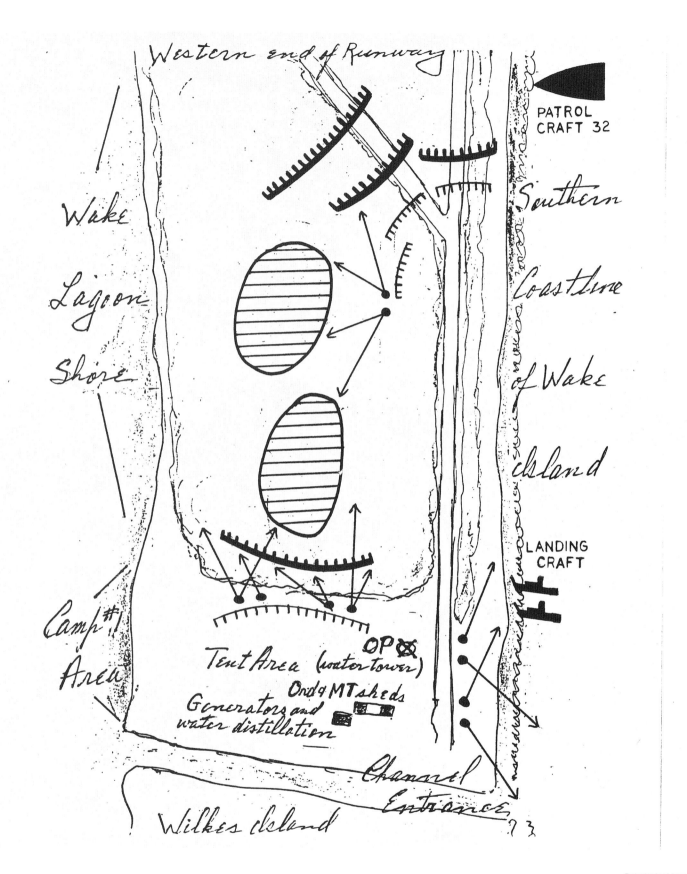

Western end of Runway

Wake

Lagoon

Shore

Camp #1

Area

Wilkes Island

Tent Area (water tower)

OP ⊗

Ord & MT sheds

Generators and
water distillation

Channel

Entrance

? 3

PATROL
CRAFT 32

Southern

Coastline

of Wake

Island

LANDING
CRAFT

Poindexter Sketch #9

This was the position of Lt. Poindexter's Mobile Reserve when the surrender party was sighted about 12:30 PM.
Poindexter and his men have taken the enemy positions at the confluence of the roads near the end of the runway,

channel, where he would continue to battle with the arms at his disposal.

The movement of the Marines on Wilkes toward the channel became extremely dangerous. A Japanese destroyer had closed to just a mile offshore and had begun shelling the men. The warplanes continued to blast any resistance they could detect on the island. One of the planes scored a direct hit on part of the group, killing one Marine.

Major Devereux and his surrender party did not reach the boat channel until 1:00 p.m. They had to wait for a launch to take them across to Wilkes. Just before 1:30 p.m. the surrender party had made its way across the channel and was ready to advance toward Kuku Point. This was extremely dangerous, since Capt. Platt and his men expected an attack and were preparing to engage the enemy near the channel. To make matters worse, the Jap destroyer was moving closer to the island and firing in the general direction of the surrender party, which by this time numbered more than thirty men. A Japanese soldier signaled to the ship and the firing ceased. The surrender party carefully made its way down the island.

At about 1:30 p.m. Platt's men spotted a small group of enemy soldiers coming toward them. They reported this information to Platt, who ordered his men to converge on a point near the channel and attempt to catch the enemy in a crossfire. Lt. Poindexter and Major Devereux were in the middle of the group of Japanese when they saw Platt's men coming toward them. The Marines were armed to the teeth and appeared to be advancing with the intent to repel a landing by the enemy. As Poindexter watched the approaching men he again feared a bloodbath.

Platt, however, spotted the white flag and stopped his men in time, thus avoiding a skirmish. He noticed two figures clad in Marine khaki along with a host of the enemy in dirty green. Platt recognized Devereux and moved closer. Then Devereux delivered an order that caught Platt completely offguard. He informed Platt that the island had been surrendered. The victorious Capt. Platt was shocked, but he complied with the order from his commander.

Platt had been victorious in fighting against overwhelming odds for nearly eleven hours, and had killed nearly all of the more than one hundred Japanese soldiers on the island. Only two prisoners, both of whom had been wounded, remained from the Japanese assault force that had landed on Wilkes Island. Platt's men seemed astonished when Major Devereux yelled the order for the men to put down their arms.

Capt. Platt heard the surrender order and understood it. He ordered his men to obey Major Devereux's command. He knew also that he had upheld every expectation of the Marine Corps in his conduct on Wilkes Island. His tactical moves had outwitted the numerically superior enemy and his bravery was beyond question. In describing the Japanese effort on Wilkes Island, Captain Koyama of the Imperial Japanese Navy would later be quoted as saying, "In general, that part of the operation was not successful."

Platt's men had thrown down their weapons and had their hands behind their heads by the time the surrender party reached them. Lt. Poindexter watched as the Japanese prisoners were liberated. The two prisoners had been tied up with communications wire. When they were untied they began smiling, saluting, and bowing profusely. When this group of Americans was disarmed, the last resistance on the atoll was removed.

The Japanese immediately took full control of Wilkes Island and sent out details to collect their dead. They found Sloman and threw him off the stretcher so they could use it to carry the corpses of their slain comrades. He was barely conscious, and found himself sitting in the stubble that remained of the burned undergrowth.

Several Japanese soldiers began jabbering and yelling at Sloman, pointing their guns at him and motioning as if they were ordering him to come out of the burned thicket. But Sloman was still immobile and could not move. He feared that he was about to be shot. Then, just in the nick of time, Sloman heard Lt. McAlister shouting at the Jap soldiers. He was finally successful in convincing the trigger-happy troops that Sloman was wounded and could not come out of the brush.

McAlister and two of the Japanese came in to get Sloman. The Japs immediately stopped when they got close to him. They noticed that he had hand grenades hanging from both of his shirt pockets, and two more bulged from his pants pockets. The Japs stepped back, obviously frightened by the grenades regardless of the condition of the Marine wearing them. They motioned for McAlister to take off Sloman's shirt and trousers, not wanting to handle the grenades themselves.

Initially, all that the Japanese wanted to do with Sloman was disarm him. They were deathly afraid of hand grenades. After all of Sloman's weapons had been taken, Lt. McAlister was ordered elsewhere and Sloman was left lying in the sand. Not long afterwards, Sloman would remember that two American civilians came, placed him on a stretcher, and moved him to the area near the channel. There they laid him on the ground near a dragline where he would be out of the direct sunlight. There were dead Japs all around him.

Lt. Poindexter and a Japanese officer began looking for survivors on Wilkes Island. Each man was looking for survivors from his own side. There seemed to be countless corpses, mostly Japanese. Poindexter turned over body after body, hoping to find some of the Marines alive. He did not. Most of the corpses were left where they were for the moment. However, when the men came across the body of the Japanese company commander, they picked it up and carried it toward the road.

As Poindexter walked with the legs of the dead officer under one arm, he noticed an open, half-eaten can of peaches in the sand. He was so hungry that he reached down and picked up the can before continuing toward the road. A flatbed truck was on the road, so the two men slung the body up onto it.

It was extremely hot and Lt. Poindexter had been many hours without food or water. He and the Japanese officer sat down on the bed of the truck and shared the half-consumed can of peaches. After the two had finished eating the fruit the Jap officer pulled out his cigarettes and offered one to Poindexter. The two enjoyed a smoke amid their grisly surroundings.

After a brief rest the two went back about the job of searching through the corpses for any signs of life. They were followed by a wounded Japanese soldier as they walked from position to position looking for survivors. As they rolled one dead body over the wounded soldier behind them let out a howl of anguish. The Jap officer told Poindexter that the body was the young soldier's brother. Poindexter felt sorry for the young boy who sobbed with grief for his fallen sibling.

Chapter 31
THE PRISONERS ARE COLLECTED

By the time Lt. Poindexter and the Japanese got back to the channel the Americans had been herded together and were being marched back to Wake. Wiley Sloman saw everyone leaving and tried to yell to them, wanting to be taken with them. But, the paralysis had gotten worse and he could not make a sound. He tried to whistle, but he could not pucker his lips. No one realized that they were leaving Sloman behind. He watched as the last man marched away.

Suddenly Sloman realized that he was alone on Wilkes Island, accompanied only by the dead bodies that littered the area around him. He began to go in and out of consciousness, losing track of time and not knowing how long he had been by the dragline. His gaping head wound was throbbing. He would wake up and endure the pain as long as he could before blacking out again.

The Battle of Wake Island was over. All positions had been notified of the surrender and there were no hostile positions remaining. The Japanese were in complete control of the island.

Kayoshi Ibushi, a Japanese war correspondent, described the event by saying that "... the capture of Wake Island... was so heroic that even the gods wept."

The American prisoners from all over Wake and Wilkes Islands were taken to the beach road as they surrendered. There they were stripped to there underwear, and after a certain number were collected, they were taken to the airstrip. Some men marched while others were picked up by trucks. John Blandy was one of the Marines who was marched to the runway, where an ever-increasing throng of nearly naked men was being guarded.

As Blandy was marched along the road toward the airstrip he could see the horror of the battle everywhere. He could look down into several of the gun emplacements as he walked. Each one was strewn with corpses, both Japanese and American. He noticed one gruesome fact about many of the American bodies. They all had bayonet wounds under their chins. He quickly surmised that, after the Japs overran each position and killed the defenders, they would

Japanese war painting entitled "Landing Operation at Wake Island" by Japanese artist Matsuzaka Yasu, 1941, shows Japanese troops rounding up American prisoners and moving them to the airstrip.

160

make sure none of their enemies was still alive, and they didn't waste any ammunition in doing it. They apparently had thrust their bayonets up into the heads of each casualty through the soft area under their chins.

The men in the hospital realized that they were prisoners of the enemy. Dr. Kahn was still with the men, some of whom had been wounded again during the assault on the hospital. Others, like Dick Darden, had come through the hospital assault with no additional wounds. Warren Connors, the Marine who had manned a machine gun on the beach and killed dozens of Japanese soldiers coming down the sides of the landing vessels during the December 23rd invasion, was brought into the hospital. He had been behind his machine gun all night during the battle. Connors now lay wounded in the hospital on the cot beside Dick.

Dick was one of the seven men who remained in the bunker hospital. The others included Tom Kennedy, Slick Sloman, Warren Connors, Jim Hesson, and Spider Webb. The fact that Dick was left in the hospital proved to be a stroke of luck, for as he learned later, those who were taken outside were placed with the other captured men on the airstrip, where their treatment for the next several days would be harsh.

By the time Jim Cox had been marched to the airstrip, most of the hundreds of men there had been stripped and placed in lines with machine guns in front of and behind them. Cox thought that this was surely the end for him. The prisoners were stripped down to their skivvies and tied with telephone wire in the same manner that Holmes had been tied. Their hands were tied behind their backs and fastened tightly to a cord around their necks. Any relaxation of their aching arms would tighten the wire around their necks and constrict their air passages.

If the men relaxed their arms even slightly the weight of their hands would cause the wire around their neck to choke them. They leaned against each other, trying to find the most comfortable position. Some lay on their sides, naked on the hard rocks of coral, trying to take the weight off their arms and the tension of the strangling wires off their necks.

The Japanese guards would leave these men in the blistering sun on the airstrip over twenty-four hours before the wires around their necks would be removed, and over two days before they were taken to shelter in the remains of Camp 2. They left no doubt about who was in full control of the island. Many of the men who sat bound on the coral runway were certain that they were about to be executed.

Indeed, the Japanese guards set up machine guns all around the men and traversed the guns from side to side to be sure that their arcs would meet and afford them a clear shot at every prisoner. It appeared they had been set up for a massacre. The prisoners knew the Japanese did not want to take prisoners, thinking of them as the most shamed and valueless animals on earth.

The hours began to seem longer and longer to the men on the airstrip. Glenn Tripp was a redhead, and his skin burned to a crisp as he sat in the tropical sun. At night just the opposite was true, as Wake Island was much like a desert. The prisoners felt as if they were freezing when the cool ocean winds swept over their bare, burned bodies. As the wires began to choke some of the men, they searched for any position which might take the pressure off of their aching arms.

The plight of the men on the hard coral airfield was miserable, but for many of the defenders of Wake Island the fighting had ended. There would be no further humiliation for the 124 American lads who lay dead from the sixteen-day battle. Some lay in common graves, while others had been buried where they had fallen. Another fifty, including Dick Darden, had been wounded so seriously that their lives hung by precarious threads. The number of Americans captured by the Japanese on Wake was 1603. This included 453 members of the military and 1150 civilians.

Japanese casualties for the sixteen-day action have never been determined with accuracy. Estimates of the enemy losses, including those men lost at sea when the troop transports were sunk, range from seven hundred to seven thousand. The actual number will never be precisely known. American forces are, however, given credit for sinking one Japanese submarine and four surface vessels. Eight other ships were damaged, the extent of which is unknown.

Is is estimated by authoritative sources that 1,153 Japanese men were killed or wounded during the battle. American warplanes and anti-aircraft gunners were credited with shooting down twenty-two Japanese planes, and at least eleven more were damaged and left the vicinity trailing smoke. Their fate is unknown.

The bravery and steadfastness of the American fighters on Wake was a beam of sunlight to a country which was completely immersed in the dark clouds of war. Journalists grasped the opportunity, comparing the men on Wake to those of such colorful episodes in American history as Bunker Hill, Chateau Thiery, and Belleau Woods.

The Japanese, even in victory, had felt the deadly sting of the defenders on Wake Island. Even though the Americans had surrendered, the state of greatest shame in Bushido tradition, the victorious Japanese soldiers seemed to have respect for the men who had fought so tenaciously. The Americans boys, even in their despair and great discomfort, seemed to cling to the will to live and, in the end, the will to ultimately become victorious.

Chapter 32
JAPS IN THE HOSPITAL

At about 12:00 noon, the Japanese began to bring their wounded into the hospital. Japanese and American fighting men, deadly enemies just minutes before, lay side by side in the makeshift bunker. To make room for more of their wounded the Japanese pushed the wounded Americans to the back of the room with cots packed tightly together.

After the Japanese had taken nearly all of the wounded Americans who could walk outside, they began bringing their own wounded into the hospital. Several of the wounded Japanese troops still carried all of their battle gear, including rifles, bayonets, and hand grenades. As one Japanese soldier raised himself up to look around, his rifle at his fingertips, he spied Warren Connors. With a look in his eyes that would kill he said, "You are the one who shot me!"

Connors was caught by surprise, finding himself completely defenseless and facing the prospect of retaliation by an incensed Japanese soldier. Dick was petrified with fear as he lay next to Connors and again sensed the tension that felt like electricity in the air. He knew that a crazed Japanese fighter could level a spray of bullets at Connors with a flick of the wrist, and would probably kill both of them if he did. "No, not me, it wasn't me," insisted Connors. Finally, after some tense moments, Connors convinced the soldier that someone else had shot him.

The Japs segregated the wounded men in the tiny hospital, packing the cots holding the Americans into a small area of the room. While the Japanese doctors attended to their own wounded with great care, they ignored the Americans. They provided no food and they made no effort to care for the wounds of the Americans. The American civilian who had been struck in the head by the officer's pistol shot during the storming of the hospital moaned and groaned all night. After fifteen hours of agony he died the next morning.

The Japanese were collecting American prisoners from all over the three islands. Men bound with telephone wire were everywhere. The 1200 civilians were scattered in every conceivable hiding place on the islands. Everyone was being collected and brought to the airfield, stripped to their skivvies, bound with telephone wire, and put on the hard coral runway in front of the machine guns.

On Peale Island two civilians hiding in the bushes were watching the movement of the Japanese soldiers as they collected the prisoners. They were Logan Kay and Fred J. Stevens, workers for the construction crew that was building the airport. They had taken cover in the scant forest on Peale when the fighting began in earnest. Since Wake had no high ground it had no caves to offer for cover. There were no coconut palms or other tall forest plants to offer adequate cover. Kay and Stevens had simply found the best shelter that they could in the scrubby undergrowth, sand, and coral.

During the sixteen day seige they had monitored the battle as best they could. They had seen the Pan Am Building destroyed and were aware of the destruction of the Wildcat fighters. The two had hid out separately at first, meeting on the second day of the war,

December 9, when they both used the same sewer pipe as a hiding place. Logan Kay kept a diary during the subsequent days that vividly detailed the events the two saw and heard about on Wake while the Marines and defenders were holding out against the Japanese invaders.

On December 23 Kay and Stevens were still on Peale Island. They knew that the Japanese fleet was moving in, so they took cover as best they could. The two men crawled into a hole in the coral sand and rode out the battle. By 11:30 in the morning they knew they were in trouble because the Japs were rounding up men everywhere and herding them toward the the airport.

Kay wrote in his diary that he looked out of his hiding place and "will never forget the sight. About 500 of our men were being herded past, stripped to nothing but shorts,...It looked like a brick wall for them." Both Kay and Stevens were convinced that there was about to be a mass execution. They wanted no part of it, so they decided to stay in their hiding place and elude the enemy troops as long as possible.

Charles Holmes sat on the coral runway hour after hour, staring down the barrels of the machine guns and convinced that he was about to be executed. The Jap gunners had locked, loaded, and pointed machine guns directly at the group of tense, uncomfortable, tightly bound prisoners. Some of the frightened prisoners saw a Japanese officer pull his sword as if he was about to give an order. About that time a light rain squall blew across the island and the gunners were quickly ordered to cover up their machine guns.

Most of the prisoners felt that the rain had given them a reprieve, but that ended minutes later when the squall passed and the covers came off the guns. Again the gunners appeared ready to fire. Then two Jap officers began arguing in Japanese. The Americans could not understand anything being said, but they felt that their wellbeing was the topic of discussion. Just as Holmes was about to give up all hope, a Japanese boat landed on the nearby beach and a high ranking naval officer and his staff came ashore.

The officer approached the runway and observed the huge group of prisoners. Then he walked over to the machine gunners and spoke to them. Again the conversation was in Japanese, so Holmes could not tell if the gunners were being given the order to fire, but he expected the worst. It appeared that the moment of truth had arrived. The Jap gunners, to the great relief of the prisoners, then proceeded to unload the guns. The prisoners breathed a collective sigh and thanked their maker. Holmes began to think that his life might persist, at least a while longer.

It was between 1:00 and 2:00 in the afternoon when all of the prisoners had been brought together. The naval officer and his men came up to the large group of prisoners near where Holmes sat and began to conduct a victory ceremony. This included raising the Japanese flag and throwing the American flag to the ground. Wake Island was officially renamed OTORI SHIMA, "Island of the Birds."

The throng of nearly 1500 Marines and civilians was

addressed by the Japanese officers. This included nearly everyone on the island except the severely wounded men in the hospitals. All Americans, including the civilian prisoners and military men on Wake Island, with the exception of Kay and Stevens, were prisoners of the Japanese.

The group also included Mr. Heavenor, the government auditor left behind by the PBY, and Chief Thompson, the submariner who had been brought ashore under cover of darkness to have his appendectomy. The Jap officer began speaking to the assembled prisoners. He informed them that they were going to be "guests of the Imperial Japanese Navy."

Later during the day of December 23, the Japanese began to move their wounded out of the hospital area. Where they went, either to another hospital area on the island or back onto the ships that encircled the atoll, was a mystery to the wounded Americans. When all the Japanese were gone and the Americans were left by themselves, Connors told Dick with a grin, "It WAS me that shot that son-of-a-bitch."

Then the waiting began. It seemed like an eternity. The men in the hospital did not know what would happen next. Later a Japanese officer and several troops came to the hospital and made all of the remaining prisoners who could walk go outside and step across the road. A Marine prisoner named Manning was already there along with a Chinese fellow who had been working with the civilian contractor before the war.

Tom Kennedy was also in the group, and he began to sense the worst as he was taken across the roadway. His arm was still in a straight splint from the wounds he suffered on the first day of the war. The men were ordered to kneel on the road in a straight line.

At that point Kennedy noticed that two machine guns had been set up across the road, pointing directly at the line of men. He prayed as he looked at the gunners, thinking for sure that his end was near. He was certain that the prisoners were about to be executed by the machine guns.

Then a rough, tough Japanese sargent who looked just like a bulldog noticed the Chinese fellow, who was kneeling between Kennedy and Manning. The Jap officer ran over to the Chinaman and went into a tirade. The sargent became more livid by the second as he screamed into the Chinaman's face. He grabbed the man by the hair on his head and began to shake him furiously as he jabbered on and on. He was apparently infuriated by the fact that an oriental "brother" had sided with the Caucasian devils in a war against Japan.

The sargent moved back a step and reached for his samurai sword, unsheathing the wicked instrument in front of the prisoner. Kennedy was more than impressed as the gleaming blade slid from its scabbard. He began inching to his right, away from the Chinaman. Kennedy wanted no part of the sword, nor did he want to be close to a chopping blow, which appeared to be imminent.

Tom Kennedy had seen pictures of the horrors and ghastly torture to which the Japanese had subjected the Chinese during their war on the mainland. Kennedy had no doubt that he was about to witness a beheading, and to make matters worse, he was only inches away from the victim. The young American Marine was nearly scared out of his wits.

Then, just as quickly as the episode had begun, it seemed to end. The sargent stepped away from the horrified Chinaman and resheathed his sword. He had decided to let the man live. As he walked away from the line of prisoners he turned and looked at Kennedy, motioning with his hand as if to wave hello. Kennedy did not know that such a motion of the hand in Japan means "come here." Not knowing what the sargent wanted, Kennedy waved back as if to return the hello wave.

The Jap saw absolutely no humor in his gesture and thundered toward him. Kennedy almost died of fright as the sargent grabbed him by his good arm and pulled him back into the bunker. He had merely wanted to put Kennedy back in the hospital with the other wounded men. The language barrier could have cost Kennedy his life.

Later a Japanese officer came into the hospital with an American lieutenant. The two were looking for medical supplies which they thought had been stored in the hospital bunker. They urgently needed medical supplies for the wounded men like Holewinski who were still at the airstrip. The Jap officer started jabbering loudly at the foot of Kennedy's cot, seemingly angered at him. Kennedy had no idea what the Jap was saying, but he did know that he did not like the officer pointing his fixed bayonet at him. Kennedy tried to point to his splinted arm and the drain hole in the dressing, which had become quite messy. The officer only seemed to become more upset.

The officer continued to shout at Kennedy in Japanese, thrusting his bayonet closer and closer. He would jabber a few sentences in Japanese and then thrust, each time coming closer to Kennedy's body. Finally a thrust stopped barely two inches from Kennedy's pounding chest. Once again Kennedy thought his time had come. He tried to prepare himself for the worst, wishing all the while that he could have his .45 automatic pistol under the sheet and respond to the Japanese officer in the way he really wanted.

Just as the Jap was about to thrust again at Kennedy an officer of higher rank walked in through the metal doors. He shouted to the man with the bayonet, causing him to snap to attention. Kennedy did not understand anything that the man had shouted to him, but he was convinced that he was about to be impaled. Then the two officers quickly turned and walked out the door, not to be seen again.

On the airstrip hundreds of men continued to suffer. Holewinski was luckier than most. A Japanese interpreter was acting as a guard near Skee. The interpreter began talking with a Marine prisoner and they discovered in the course of their conversation that both were from Chicago. Unlike many of the guards who treated the men as brutally as possible, this guard actually exchanged pleasantries with his fellow Chicagoan and also began to extend special favors to his new Marine friend.

Holewinski had developed a case of diarrhea. The guard allowed the Marine to take Skee to the woods. Most of the guards did not even allow the men to speak, much less visit the woods. They had to sit in one place regardless of their circumstances. While Skee was in the woods he found a can of condensed milk. Having been severely wounded and not having had anything to eat in nearly two days, the milk was a life saver. Skee was the only man, as far as he knew, who received any nourishment during the two days at the airstrip.

The choking wires stayed on the men on the airstrip until the second day, December 24. Each man tried to come to grips with the unpleasant set of circumstances. There was the physical discomfort of bare skin against the hard coral, the burning sun, and the chilling winds. There was the humiliation of surrendering to the enemy. There was the frightening thought that this hostile enemy could execute the throng of men en masse with the fixed machine guns any time the Japanese commander gave the order. There was the question of the whereabouts of the relief force. There was great apprehension about the future. The captives wondered just what the enemy had in store for them.

The defenders of Wake Island had taken a tremendous beating, but at the same time they had thoroughly bloodied the nose of the Japanese. At least four enemy warships had been sunk and several more had sustained serious damage, America's first such response to the Japanese after Pearl Harbor. Twenty-one Japanese aircraft had been shot down and about a dozen more had begun the long trip home trailing smoke. Over fifty planes had been damaged by the Wake defenders.

All of this had been accomplished by a small garrison of men, only half the prescribed number for such a defense, who were vastly outnumbered by their enemy. They had no radar to warn them of approaching aircraft, and they had precious few planes of their own. Their communication system was crude and ineffective during much of the battle, and many of their larger weapons did not have equipment to aim them. Indeed, several of the big guns did not even have crews to operate them.

Even though the men had an uncertain future in captivity at the hands of the Japanese, they could take pride in their actions during December of 1941. While inflicting hundreds, perhaps over 1000, casualties on the Japanese invasion forces, the gutsy Americans sustained far fewer losses. Forty-nine Marines and three sailors had been killed. The American civilians work force on the island fared worse, counting seventy dead and many more wounded during the seige.

This arithmetic, however, was of little consolation to the uncomfortable men on the airstrip. Hour after hour they baked in the sun. Anyone who uttered a word to anyone around him was hit from behind with a rifle butt by one of the guards. Holewinski's splintered legs lay on the hard surface of the coral airstrip, contact with the firm ground causing his multiple wounds to be all the more painful.

A young lad who was a native of Guam and who had been an employee at the Pan Am base lay near Skee. He had been severely wounded on his back side, having had most of his tail bone shot away. He, too, was experiencing additional pain because of the hard ground.

A cot was brought to the air field to be used by one of the wounded. The two doctors tried to make a decision on who to put on the cot, Holewinski or the young Guamanian. The decision favored Holewinski. He was lifted onto the cot and immediately experienced great relief. It was Christmas Eve, and Skee thought of what a wonderful Christmas present the comforting cot had been.

On December 24 Admiral Kajioka came ashore to claim Wake Island for his Emperor. The man who held the fate of the captured Americans in his hands approached the throng assembled at the airfield. The Admiral appeared in a crisp white uniform with a generous array of medals adorning his chest, and he wore a dress sword by his side.

Jim Cox watched the Admiral closely as a ceremony was held to raise the Japanese flag. The Admiral began to address the prisoners, telling them that they would not be killed as long as they did exactly what they were told and showed no hostility. If they did this, he told them, "your lives will be spared." He read a long list of instructions to the men which made it clear that they would be executed for the slightest disobedient act or infraction of the rules.

Then the Admiral began berating President Roosevelt, implying that he was a warmonger. Kajioka painted a picture of a peace-loving Japanese people who were simply reacting to the belligerence of the hated American President. The Admiral concluded by telling the throng of over 1000 prisoners that all of the Americans on the island had become, "guests of the Emperor."

Wiley Sloman was still lying exposed on the battlefield on Wilkes Island. He was still alone, and for two days he had been awakening and then slipping back into unconsciousness. His head wound was draining and his scalp was matted with blood. He was delirious much of the time and had all sorts of unusual dreams. During the time he was awake his head throbbed until the pain was so great he would again become unconscious.

Sloman knew he needed medical attention, but he could not move from the spot near the dragline. He began hallucinating. He dreamed that his mother arrived to help him and brought with her an

THE HONOLULU ADVERTISER,

THURSDAY MORNING, DECEMBER 25, 1941.

WAKE FALLS

AFTER GALLANT FIGHT

Two Enemy Warships Sunk In Last Attack

WASHINGTON, Dec. 24 (UP)—Two Japanese destroyers were lost in final landing operations carried out on Wake Island in the mid-Pacific, the Navy announced today in its 17th war communique.

Wake apparently fell today after heroic resistance of the Marine garrison against 14 Japanese attacks over a period of 16 days.

Capture of Wake cost the Japanese four warships and several planes.

The Navy's communique also said that in the eastern Pacific the SS Larry Doheny was shelled by an enemy submarine but reached port safely.

Press reports of the sinking of the SS Montebello were confirmed, according to the Navy's announcement.

"In the central Pacific radio communication with Wake was severed and capture of the island is probable," the communique said. "Two enemy destroyers were lost in the final landing operations."

The communique also disclosed that Palmyra and Johnston islands were shelled by enemy submarines, but damage was negligible and there were no casualties.

The Hawaiian area was described as quiet while in the far east there were "no new developments."

Midway Island, between Hawaii and Wake, is still holding out. The Navy assumed that severance of radio communications with Wake indicated that the 14th Japanese assault there was successful.

Wake is valuable as an air base.

JAPANESE ADMIT WAKE WAS TOUGH

NEW YORK, Dec. 24 (UP)—Official Japanese broadcasts from Tokyo heard here by the United Press said today that 300 American Marines defended Wake Island, which was described as a formidable stronghold.

"The Marines put up a strong fight," the Japanese admitted, "and a Japanese landing was not an easy task since the island is naturally protected against landing by a strong surf and American coastal batteries and planes did their utmost to disturb a landing

Wake Garrison Fights to End
1941

Handful of US Marines Holds Out to Last Gun

WASHINGTON, Dec. 24 (UP) —Wake Island's heroic defenders—a garrison of 13 Marine officers, 365 Marines, a naval medical officer and six naval medical ratings—took a toll of four enemy warships and several planes before falling at the end of a 16-day siege, the Navy disclosed tonight.

The U. S. Marines on Wake continued to fight even when they were left only one battery of four three-inch guns.

Equipment of the Wake garrison, according to the Navy, included originally 12 fighter planes, six five-inch guns, 12 three-inch anti-aircraft guns, 18 .50 caliber anti-aircraft guns and 30 .30 caliber anti-aircraft machine guns.

"Finally Dec. 23 (Wake time) the island fell into enemy hands," the Navy said, "but only after the enemy lost four warships and several planes.

"The final prelude came Dec. 21 when heavy bombs knocked out vital defenses and equipment. The garrison fought on, but next came another heavy air attack while several warships and a transport moved in. There was a landing attempt in great force, but the defenders sank two destroyers.

"Finally the enemy landed on the fourteenth attack.

"Commander of the Wake garrison was Maj. James Patrick Devereux, who rose from a pri-te."

old family doctor. The doctor had been dead for many years, but Sloman dreamed that he was being cared for by the old family friend. Many wild dreams and fantasies went through his mind as he lay waiting for help to come.

Dick and his six buddies lay in the concrete bunker hospital for two days. No one came to the bunker, so the wounded men did not know what was happening on the island. They didn't know if they had been left for dead, or if the Japanese would return. They didn't know if they would be killed, or held as prisoners of war.

By late in the day on Christmas Eve the Japanese must have thought they had rounded up all the Americans on the island. But, there were at least two men who had other ideas. Kay and Stevens, the two construction workers, were holding out. A couple of hours before dark they had nearly been caught by a Japanese sentry who was still patrolling. They decided they would try to hold out until dark and then move deeper into the bushes, hoping to find better cover. They were still convinced that a bullet was waiting for the captured men, so they were firmly of the opinion that they would resist the enemy.

In Kay's diary he indicated, "We will not give up without a fight, as we think the other boys were stripped for a firing squad." The two men had been able to find some of the food that had been scattered throughout the scrub-covered parts of the island. "Food is scattered all over the island. Water is our problem once out of the woods."

Kay and Stevens felt that American forces surely were coming to liberate the island, so they were firm in their resolve that they would hold out until friendly forces returned to Wake and freed them. That, they felt, surely could not be long. So, they would not give up to the Jap intruders on the island.

Chapter 33
CHRISTMAS DAY –1941

Christmas day, December 25th, 1941, arrived for the men in the bunker hospital. It was nothing like their Christmases past. They had no food or water, did not know if they would live or die, and did not know what had happened to the other defenders on the island. They were completely isolated in the concrete bunker and had not seen anyone for nearly two days.

Late in the afternoon of Christmas Day, 1945, someone was heard moving around outside the hospital bunker. A voice called out, "Is anyone in there?" "Yes," was the reply. An American prisoner, accompanied by an armed Japanese guard, entered the bunker and took control. They had the wounded men gather their meager possessions and medical supplies, and announced that they would be moved to another hospital.

Later in the day all seven wounded men were moved. Most were taken to the compound where the civilians had previously been quartered at Camp 2. A temporary hospital had been set up there in one of the wooden buildings. Dr. Shank, the civilian doctor, was in charge, and he was joined by Dr. Kahn in caring for all of the wounded men.

Spider Webb was moved to another hospital nearby. Most of the men in this hospital were Japanese, and the doctors were as well. The Japanese doctors kept Webb's wounds wrapped with wet dressings which contained some type of disinfectant. They told him that this was what they used on wounds to fight tropical diseases. At least this medication would be better than what he received in the bunker hospital, which had been out of nearly all medical supplies.

Several times a day the doctors changed Webb's dressings. They would use iodine on the deep wounds every time they changed the bandages. The foot wound where he had lost three toes was becoming especially messy. Webb's condition had improved enough that he was mentally alert, and he began talking with the Japanese who spoke English.

One of the Japanese doctors spoke perfect English. He seemed to be a likeable fellow, and he began to tell Webb about his family back home. The doctors surprised Spider when he told him that he was a U. S. citizen. He had been teaching school in California and just before the war broke out he had gone back to Japan to visit his family. He had been drafted into the Japanese air force and was not allowed to go back to the United States.

The Japanese Admiral questioned several of the prisoners on the airstrip, asking them over and over again, "Where are your buried guns?" So confusing had been the movement of the 3" guns during the battle by Major Devereux, and so destructive had the 5" guns been when used during the battle against the enemy, that the Japanese leader was convinced that there were larger guns on the island which had been buried. He did not believe that 5" guns could sink his warships. He looked in vain for several days for buried 6" or 8" guns, which, of course, had never been on Wake.

On the afternoon of Christmas Day the men on the airstrip began their third day of captivity, and the exposure was beginning to take its toll. Still no food had been provided, only a small quantity of oil-laced water. The water was served from fifty-five gallon metal

National Archives

The Japanese hoist the rising sun over Wake Island

166

drums that had been used near the runway to store aviation fuel. The oily residues had not been rinsed out before water was put into the barrels, so the water was heavily laced with petroleum. Some of the men vomited when they tried to drink it. Most tried hard to stomach the foul mixture, since they had been in the hot sun for two days without food or water and were in desperate need of something to drink.

It was late on Christmas day, more than two days after the surrender, when the first food and was brought to the men on the airstrip. The guards gave them chunks of bread and more of the putrid petroleum-laced water. The hungry men devoured the bread and retched on the water to get it down.

After dark Holewinski and several of the severely wounded prisoners were loaded onto a truck and taken to the barracks where the Japanese wounded were being treated. This was located in the wooden building where the civilian workers had bunked before the battle. Skee would remain in this hospital for about two weeks.

Dr. Shank came into the hospital building and was walking around with a Japanese interpreter. He stepped aside for a moment and said to Skee, "You were not on the beach, no one was on the beach." Skee took this to mean that, if questioned, they should not tell the Japanese that they were at their position at the 3" gun during the battle. Later he learned that only two Japanese soldiers out of thirty-one who came off the beached ship toward their position had lived through the battle.

The Japanese had great respect for their own warriors who fought valiantly and lived through such a battle. They were rewarded after the battle by being given "soft jobs." In this case they had been given the job of guarding the wounded American prisoners in this hospital. Skee did not want the two guards to know that he was one of the men at the gun position who had helped to kill twenty-nine of their buddies.

The Christmas season of 1941 was not a happy one on Wake Island or back in the United States. The country began to realize that it was in a serious war, and gloom replaced the usual festive holiday spirit. Restrictions on the use of electricity curtailed the usual colorful displays of Christmas lights. Eva Bell Darden worried about where her son was and what had happened to him. Millions of Americans were aware of the situation on Wake Island and prayed for the fighting men who were defending it against America's enemies. Wake had become a rallying point for the morale of the country. Dick was one of the lucky ones who lived through the battle, but his future could not be more in doubt this Christmas day. Perhaps it was best that his mother did not know.

Back in North Carolina, particularly at 307 McKoy Street, in Clinton, there was little joy or cause for celebration. Dick's mother listened to scanty reports from the Pacific and worried terribly about her son. Newspapers described the plight of the men on Wake Island as best they could with very limited information. Kirke Simpson described the Christmas mood well as he wrote for THE GREENSBORO DAILY NEWS. "American eyes turn anxiously to peer beyond the sunset this Christmas day, sinister with a war that mocks at the season of peace and good will on earth. That western sky is darkened by grave portents from far away war zones where Americans and gallant comrades-in-arms are giving battle to a treacherous and powerful foe."

"Yet already," continued Simpson, "the defenders of freedom all about the China sea—American, British, Dutch, Filipino, and Chinese—have given the enemy pause on many fronts. And out in the mid-Pacific a handful of American Marines have written an epic tale of valor, holding tiny Wake Island against all attacks for fourteen days. The price paid is out of all proportion to its value to the enemy. But to Americans and their comrades-in-arms that valorous stand on Wake, like the bitter-end British defense of Hong Kong against all odds, is an unforgettable incident of war; a sure symbol of what the future holds in store for the foe."

Kirke Simpson's article continued to accurately describe the mood of the season in America. "Wherever Americans gather in Christmas cheer-making, a salute to the defenders of Wake is in order. They have bravely pointed the way to victory for their countrymen, kept the covenant of their 'always faithful' motto to the death. What men could do, they did. They deserve the 'well done' that good and faithful servants of the flag merit of the nation, and neither that nor vengeance will be denied them.

By their heroism Wake already goes down in the books of this war as an American victory, not a defeat. Ultimate Japanese capture was foredoomed. The odds were too great for it to be otherwise. It is a puzzling facet of Japanese strategy that so much effort and blood was spent upon so small an objective, unless it was to save face.

That is a controlling force in the Japanese psychology. The hara-kiri method of dramatized self-destruction in case of failure illustrates it graphically. And now fully committed to capture of both Singapore and Manila, the Japanese military caste that projected the nation into this war at Hitler's behest cannot turn back."

This brief glimpse into the mind of the Japanese military leaders was frighteningly correct. An attitude hell-bent upon victory at all costs, placing little value on a soldier's life and replacing rational thought with butchery and atrocity, pervaded military thinking at the highest levels in Tokyo. Each of the millions of men in the Japanese military knew that failure to kill the Americans and take what was his meant death. The fanatic commitment was made, and death in battle or at one's own hand was the only alternative to victory for the Japanese. It was with this attitude of minimal value placed on human life that the prisoners were confronted by their captors.

The American media showed respect for the strength and cunning of the Japanese enemy. This position was well taken, for it would take years of savage fighting before the enemy would be defeated and Dick Darden would be freed. America and Japan were beyond the point of negotiation or reconciliation. Dick was in the midst of a tempest, a world war that would not be won until both sides committed themselves to fight to the death if necessary in order to be victorious.

Finally the prisoners on the runway at Wake Island were moved to Camp 2, the civilian camp, where they would be held in the area around the civilian barracks. Some men had the luxury of getting a dry place to sleep in one of the wooden buildings. Jim Cox found himself living out in the open. He had a bullet wound in his upper leg that he received during the final invasion on December 23.

When rain squalls hit the island the men would take the only cover available by crawling underneath the wooden barracks. They would remain there, cohabiting with the rats, hermit crabs,

The Wake of History

National Archives

Victorious Japanese examine a wrecked F4F-3 in its revetment. The white clad naval officer in taking a photograph of the war trophies

birds, and multitudes of insects. Before this time there had been no mosquitoes. But in the discomfort of the situation it seemed that the Japanese had brought some aboard ship from Kwajalein, for soon the mosquitoes also became a nuisance and added to the misery.

The Japanese on Wake had sent out very few patrols into the bush before the Admiral came ashore. Then, on December 26, the Japanese asked for volunteers to go on patrol and collect the bodies. They began inspecting the island very carefully, taking note of their battle trophies. Most of the guns and equipment had been rendered useless by the Marines before the surrender, but some equipment was found to be in working order or repairable. The Japanese carefully studied the wrecked Wildcat fighters, but all were beyond repair and would never fly again. They also took photographs of the planes that remained in their protective revetments.

Glenn Tripp volunteered for patrol duty and was one of the first to see the aftermath of the battle. The prisoners, under armed guard, were taken by truck to each island where they retrieved the bodies of their fellow defenders who had fallen in combat. The bodies were taken to a large cooling facility, which was being powered by an emergency generator. The bodies were cooled because the men knew it would be several days before all of the bodies could be collected and given a mass burial.

The men on the patrol detail came upon sights that were difficult to believe. Tripp found a Japanese soldier and an American Marine, Corporal Paul Tokrymas, who had killed each other with their bayonets. They were in the undergrowth on their knees, both still in a thrust position. Each had his bayonet solidly planted into his dead adversary just inches in front of him.

One of the patrols found Wiley Sloman on the battlefield, where he had lain for three days. Capt. Platt and another Marine found him and realized he was still alive. Sloman mumbled something to them about it being Christmas Eve, thinking that only one day had passed since the battle ended. Capt. Platt surprised him by responding, "God, you sure lost some time. We won't ever see this Christmas again."

Sloman was carried back across the channel and placed in a panel truck. The Japanese navy captain driving the truck spoke English, so the men talked as they drove toward the hospital at Camp 2. When they drove past the hospital building housing the wounded Americans, Capt. Platt asked the driver why he didn't stop. "We are going to the Japanese hospital," he responded. "We have better medical facilities." So Sloman, like Spider Webb, found himself in the building with the Japanese doctors.

Sloman was a curiosity to the Japanese in the hospital. They would come to his bed in groups and stare at him. Some would hold up and feel his paralyzed arm. Sloman did not like the Japanese food, so the Jap doctor ordered that he be fed the same food as the men in the American hospital. American cooks came over and fed him food from the stockpiles left on the island before the battle. There was nothing fancy on the menu, but he got three meals a day and they were quite adequate. Sloman would soon learn that three meals a day of canned American food was a real luxury.

One of the Japanese doctors spoke, as his second language, German. An American corpsman named Unger was assigned to attend to the men in the building, and he also spoke German. He became preoccupied with conversing with the Japanese doctor in German, often allowing his patients to go unattended. Some lay for periods of time in their own excrement while Unger chatted in German with the doctor. Sloman and the other Americans in the Japanese hospital began to curse Unger, despising the care that he was giving them.

169

One thing that Sloman learned very quickly in the Japanese hospital was that you didn't brag about being on Wilkes Island. In fact, it was best not to mention it. It was a real no no to let the Japanese patients or doctors know that you had any part in wiping out their landing party there. It had become a real sore point for them.

Sloman began talking with one of the guards who spoke broken English. The man claimed that he had been aboard a troop ship on December 11. The ship had been preparing for a landing, and had been just beyond the warships which had been caught by surprise by the Marines' cunning trap. The guard said that somehow one of the American guns had landed a shell on his ship causing severe damage.

Sloman did not tell the guard that his 5" gun on Wilkes Island had hit a troop ship just after sinking the HAYATE. The guard said that his unit was in a room below decks, and that the ship was damaged so badly it almost sank. In fact, he claimed that the water level where he was rose up to the necks of the men. Somehow the ship managed to stay afloat and limped back out to the open sea. The ship had barely made it back to Kwajalein, but the troops survived and were back at Wake for the invasion of December 23.

A few days later Dr. Shank came to see Sloman, asking about the care he was receiving at the hands of the Japanese doctors. Shank offered to move him to the other hospital. At first Sloman asked only that another corpsman, Navy Pharmacist Mate 3C Ernest Valle, be sent over to replace Unger. Then he accepted the offer and was moved to the hospital where the other Americans were being cared for.

Another American named Robert Manning had also received a head wound similar to Sloman's. He had been wearing one of the thin WWI "doughboy" helmets and the bullet grazed his head in such a way that he could lay his finger in the crease in his skull. The bullet had not cut into the flesh, but had only bent the skull inward. Amazingly, the man was walking around and helping other wounded men during the cleanup operation.

The Japanese guards would allow some of the men to "sneak" out and look for canned food they knew was hidden in the bunkers on the island. Then the guards would "catch" them and take them back to the prison compound. This was allowed as long as the prisoners shared the canned rations with the guards. One of their favorites was canned peaches.

The able-bodied men were taken out on work patrols and did anything they could to confuse the enemy or make their occupation of the island more difficult. Some of the .50 cal. machine guns were found to be still operable. Several of the American prisoners were ordered to give the Japanese soldiers instructions on the operation of the guns. They were taken out to the guns and, when the Japs were not looking, removed the firing pins from the weapons. On the march back to camp them tossed the pins into the underbrush. The Japanese became irate when they realized what had happened, but they couldn't remember which Americans had been involved, so no one was punished.

Dr. Shank made daily visits to the hospital and did what he could for the men with the limited supplies that were available to him. He would change the bandages and give the men as much encouragement as he could. Holewinski's wounds were draining heavily, and his sheets would usually be covered with blood within

an hour after Dr. Shank left.

One burly prisoner in the hospital was named Charles Tramposh. Tramposh had been a Marine machine gunner at one of Lt. Poindexter's .30 cal. positions. He had caught a fragment of shrapnel from a mortar shell in the stomach, disfiguring his entire abdomen. The shrapnel existed the side of his body and left a wound resembling a limp pouch. Nevertheless, he did everything he could to help keep fresh bandages on Holewinski's wounds. Even though he had been severely wounded, Tramposh was known as one of the most helpful men in the hospital, doing anything he could to make his fellow prisoners more comfortable.

After Dr. Shank had attended to the wounds and changed the sheets in the hospital he would leave to help other men outside. Within an hour Skee's sheets would be bloody again from the draining wounds. The laundry was back in operation and there was no excuse for allowing the men to lie in the bloody mess. But the corpsman in charge of this was lazy and often did not clean the men as he should have.

Tramposh would become irate and yell at the corpsmen to change the sheets of patients like Ralph Holewinski when their bedding became bloody. Flies would have such a good place to breed in the bloody bedding, so the wounded men understood the necessity of keeping their injuries as clean as possible. Holewinski took his bandages off one day to clean his wounds and found maggots writhing in the bloody, smelly mess. A Japanese pharmacist's mate attending Skee told him not to worry because the maggots were eating the dead flesh and would die when it was gone. Not convinced, Skee asked Dr. Shank to look at the wound. He promptly washed it out and put a clean bandage on it.

Holewinski had a great deal of trouble lying on his cot at first since one of his legs had been opened up in the front and the other shot open from behind. He had to lie on his side or prop one leg up with a pillow. He constantly moved around in his bed trying to relieve the pain in both legs while not starting the pain in his back wound. His legs were bandaged in such a way that the torn flesh had been pulled back together. There was no suture material on the island, so the doctors could not sew him up. He found that the skin would grow at 1/2" to 1" per month. It would take five months for the leg wounds to close.

Some of the men were able to shave themselves, while others could not. One of the Japanese wanted to shave those who needed it with his straight razor. Holewinski was afraid that he just wanted to have a slip of the hand and cut his throat. Tramposh had to do some smooth talking to convince Holewinski to let the Jap soldier put the blade on his neck, but not before he had watched Sloman get a shave first.

By December 31 the two civilians, Kay and Stevens, had spent over a week on the lam in the bushes. They had managed to elude the enemy and avoid being executed. But since none of the hundreds of prisoners had been shot, their fear of the Japs had subsided somewhat. Still, they had no plans to surrender, even though the past week had been quite uncomfortable.

"Foliage is thick and ground wet, and flies about as bad as the Japs," wrote Kay in his diary. "Found water enough last night to last us a month. The United States should have this place back by then," he continued. The two American civilians were still certain that American forces were on the way and would kick the Japs off the island. They planned to hold out, no matter how long it took, for the liberating American forces to arrive.

As the year ended there was considerable activity by the Japs on the island. A large number of Nip planes had landed and many troops had arrived. The Jap soldiers very conspicuous to Kay and Stevens as they scurried about the small islands. They were busy about the task of preparing to defend the island against the American forces that they, too, felt would be along soon.

"We're as snug as two rabbits with 4000 hounds after us," wrote Kay. "One more day of the year, and soon Congress will return from its vacation and do more talking about fighting. What a bunch we've been paying all these years....."

Chapter 34
JANUARY, 1942 – POW's ON WAKE ISLAND

The new year brought heartache and uncertainty to the hundreds of American prisoners on Wake Island. Dick Darden lay in a small wooden building in the hospital compound, a 100 foot square area around which a high wire fence had been erected, topped with barbed wire. The wounded men talked and waited, nursed their wounds, and hoped that the American task force was on its way to free them.

There were about twenty wounded American prisoners in the makeshift hospital, most still in serious condition. Along with Dick were Ralph Holewinski, Wiley Sloman, Captain Henry Wilson, Byrdine Boyd, "Spider" Webb, Warren Connors, Kirby Lugwig, Tom Kennedy, Charles Tramposh, Jim Hesson, Dick Reid, and Edwin Ackley.

It was in the hospital that Dick first met Ralph Holewinski. Skee was still in very bad condition, suffering from multiple wounds. Both of the leg wounds that he suffered during the strafing on the final day of the battle were still in very poor condition. Ski's right leg had been torn wide open, and his left leg was split on the front side so that the shin bone stuck out. There had been maggots in the leg wounds eating his flesh.

Skee also had a neck wound, and the Japanese grenade that had exploded on the gun platform just above him had blown away a large piece of flesh from his back just above the belt line. This back wound was beginning to fester badly, and the back wound and the leg wounds were beginning to drain profusely.

As the two young men, each barely into his twenties, suffered together in the hospital under great adversity they became friends. Dick would bring books from the remains of the "library" for Skee to read. The two would play acey-deucy, cribbage, and other card games together to pass the time.

Skee remembered seeing a seriously wounded sailor in blood-soaked white bellbottoms being carried from the runway area on the first day of the war. He was curious to find out whether Dick had been that sailor. One day as the two men lay in the hospital Skee asked Dick if he was the sailor, but he really never got an answer from Dick. The chaos of the first day, and the trauma of the bombing and the injuries, had blurred Dick's memory. If it had been Dick that Skee had seen, Dick would have been unconscious when he was taken to the field hospital. He could only remember passing out in the bushes and then waking up at the aid station.

In addition to several pieces of shrapnel still embedded in his backside, Skee was carrying a bullet in his buttock. Even after a month had passed, Holewinski's legs were still splinted in a straight stiff-legged position, and he was virtually unable to move. Bandages were in very short supply, so Skee had to find his own and then boil and wash them. He either found or traded personal items for first aid kits, each of which

contained one 2"x 3" compress. The other POW's helped him find bandages and attend to the wounds. Skee was all too aware that cleanliness and keeping the bandages changed regularly was his only prayer of avoiding gangrene and the horrors that it would bring.

Wiley Sloman's gunshot wound to the head was very slow to start healing. By January he was experiencing severe headaches. His skull appeared to be creased inward all the way down the right side of his head. The bullet had actually gone inside the skull and burned his brain, leaving bone fragments inside the skull against the brain tissue. The swelling of the brain had made the wound extremely uncomfortable.

Sloman's wound continued to drain, leaving his head covered with blood and drainage fluids all the time. His hair became a matted mess, so Dr. Shank got some clippers and cut all of Sloman's hair off. This helped greatly to reduce the matting and aid in the cleaning of the wound, but since Sloman had previously enjoyed a full head of black hair the change in his appearance was rather drastic. He now had almost no hair and his head looked shiny. In an effort to try and lighten the situation, the other guys in the hospital began calling him "Slick."

Slick Sloman's headaches continued to be persistent, and even seemed to be getting progressively worse. Dr. Shank told him that aspirin would do no good and the supply of narcotic pain killers was very limited. He also told Sloman that even if he had plenty of the narcotics he could not prescribe them. He knew that if Sloman took enough of them to relieve the constant pain he would quickly become an addict. He told Sloman that he would simply have to learn to bear the pain. Slick Sloman began to learn to deal with severe and persistent head pain.

The realization of what had happened on Wake Island weighed heavily on the minds of many Americans back home in the States. The valiant fight waged by the defenders of Wake had provided a glimmer of sunshine in an otherwise gloomy period in American history. The men on Wake had fought heroically. They had given the entire nation's morale a boost by defeating the enemy in battle on December 11. But then, after the long siege and stubborn defense by the American combatants, defeat came.

The White House was quick to respond to the valor of the men on Wake. On January 5, 1942, President Franklin D. Roosevelt issued a citation to the Marine 1st Defense Battalion, under Major Devereux, and the VMF 211 Marine Fighter Squadron, under Major Putnam. This Presidential Citation read as follows:

"The courageous conduct of the officers and men of these units, who defended Wake Island against an overwhelming superiority of enemy air, sea, and land attacks from

December 8 to 22, 1941, has been noted with admiration by their fellow countrymen and the civilized world, and will not be forgotten so long as gallantry and heroism are respected and honored. These units are commended for their devotion to duty and splendid conduct at their battle stations under most adverse conditions.

With limited defensive means against attacks in great force, they manned their shore installations and flew their aircraft so well that five enemy warships were either sunk or severely damaged, many hostile planes shot down, and an unknown number of land troops destroyed."

Americans knew that the enemy now held their heroes captive, but they still found inspiration in their valiant effort. The entire country was thinking about the boys on Wake. They had no word on the numbers killed or captured. The families of the Wake defenders waited anxiously for word, but the Japanese were in no hurry to release the names of those who had been captured and were still alive, or those who had been killed in action. Those at home could only wait and worry, hoping that the dreaded telegram would not come.

In the United States the valiant fight put up by the boys on Wake quickly became a rallying point. The slogan "Remember Wake Island" was on the lips of millions. It joined other famous battle cries, such as "Remember the Maine," "Remember Pearl Harbor," and "Remember the Alamo." Cartoons, songs, poems, and even a movie used the Battle of Wake Island to bolster the confidence of a nation which had been so severely shaken at Pearl Harbor.

The pride generated by the Wake defenders was evident on January 6 when President Roosevelt delivered his State of the Union address to Congress and the American people. He said, "There were only some four hundred United States Marines who, in the heroic and historic defense of Wake Island, inflicted such great losses on the enemy. Some of these men were killed in action, and others are now prisoners of war. When the survivors of that great fight are liberated and restored to their homes, they will learn that 130 million of their fellow citizens have been inspired to render their own full share of service and sacrifice."

Dick's leg wound was becoming messy, to say the least. He had been attending to the wound daily with the only medicine that was available, chlorine tablets that were used for water purification. He would take several of the tablets and dissolve them in water, then pour the chlorine water over the dressing that covered the wound. Several times daily this was applied as a sterilant. Knotty protrusions were visible around the wound, evidence that the cotton twine that had been used as suture material was holding the muscles and tendons together deep in the thigh. The wound constantly dripped fluids which looked and smelled terrible.

The cots in the hospital were paired, two to a bay. The bays were divided by five-foot-high partitions. Two men shared each of these semi-private areas and a small dresser at the end. Holewinski was paired with Captain Wilson. Wilson had a severe case of dysentery and required considerable attention from the two corpsmen who had been left to care for the wounded. Each day the corpsmen were instructed to heat some of the rainwater that had been collected for bathing and give each wounded man a sponge bath. For whatever reason, Ski did not want the corpsman assigned to him to touch him, much less give him sponge baths.

The POW's in the hospital compound had the luxury of eating relatively well during the initial phase of their captivity on Wake Island. During the bombing by Japanese planes prior to their taking the island, much of the Marine's food supply had been blasted away or strewn about the island. Cans could be found in the vicinity where their storage buildings once stood. Some of the civilian cooks searched the rubble and retrieved enough canned food to feed the prisoners during the months in the hospital compound. The menu consisted of such delicacies as canned liver stew, corned beef, and soup.

One of the civilians in particular was a great help to the men in the hospital. He was a tall young man from San Francisco named Hofmeister. Everyone just called him "Babe." Somehow Babe Hofmeister was able to supplement with bland food served in the hospital. He could even manage to get many of the items that the Japanese kept under lock and key and were normally impossible to get, such as cigarettes and medicines.

As it turned out, Babe Hofmeister was a master thief. He had an uncanny ability to steal almost anything he wanted from the Japanese. Babe was a civilian construction worker and a roofer by trade. He was always working on buildings for the Japanese, and if any building contained something that Babe wanted, it would immediately have some sort of damage that needed repair. The Japanese were only too happy to allow him to make the repairs.

After manufacturing a reason to work on a particular building, Babe would simply leave a loose nail or two in the wall or roof so he could go back anytime and gain easy entry. Soon thereafter he would have anything he wanted from the contents inside. He became as slick as a cat, able to loosen just one or two nails and create an invisible opening that no one knew about but him. He would come back at night and be inside the building in seconds.

First and foremost, Babe stole for his own gain. Babe was an alcoholic, and the real reason he took the job on Wake was to get away from alcohol. Even though the civilians were not allowed to have alcohol, Babe's craving was too great. After the surrender of the island he would steal whatever the Japanese pilots wanted and trade the goods to them for their sake ration. His craftiness as a thief and black market friendships with the enemy put him in a position to get things for the men in the hospital. Babe went out of his way to help the wounded Americans and they genuinely appreciated it.

None of the prisoners on Wake would dare take the chances with the Japanese that Babe seemed to consider routine. His ability to steal was complimented by the fact that he was a huge man. Several men agreed that he was over seven feet tall. He intimidated the short Japanese guards, and even though they were armed they wanted no part of him.

Once Hofmeister was seen in a confrontation with

Roosevelt Cites Wake Defenders

Two More Enemy Warships Added To Toll Taken By Marine Forces

WASHINGTON, Jan. 8.—(INS)—The navy tonight announced that a lone United States submarine in far eastern waters of the Pacific has sunk an enemy transport and sent three 10,000-ton cargo vessels to the bottom.

The smashing foray was disclosed in a terse one paragraph navy announcement, which also revealed that the heroic marine garrison at Wake Island destroyed a total of seven Japanese warships before being overwhelmed on December 22. The final count gave the 378 gallant defenders two more ships than originally credited to them.

Wake Heroes Cited.

Initial reports said that the Japanese lost five warships in their conquest of Wake, including a cruiser, a submarine and three destroyers. Latest information received by the navy showed that the Wake defenders also bagged another destroyer and a gunboat.

A citation by President Roosevelt extolling the heroic defense of the tiny Pacific outpost was attached to tonight's navy communique.

In addition to destroying seven enemy warships, the garrison also brought down at least nine Japanese bombers, of the Dornier two-engine type. Three more bombers may have been shot down. The marines also bagged a four-engine flying boat.

Up to December 20, two days before the island finally fell to the Japanese, 28 members of the garrison's air force were killed and six wounded.

Fate Unknown.

There was no information regarding the fate of the remainder of the military and civilian force on the island. There were 1,000 civilian workers at Wake. 365 marines and 13 officers. The garrison composed of the first defense battalion under command of Maj. James P. S. Devereux. The Japanese announced subsequently that 1,400 were taken in the capture of the island.

In his citation of the Wake defenders, led by Major Devereux and Maj. Paul A. Putnam, commandant of the marine fighting squadron 211 of the marine aircraft group 21, the President stated:

"The courageous conduct of the officers and men of these units, who defended Wake island against an overwhelming superiority of enemy air, sea, and land attacks from December 8 to 22, 1941, has been noted with admiration by their fellow countrymen and the civilized world, and will not be forgotten so long as gallantry and heroism are respected and honored. These units are commended for their devotion to duty and splendid conduct at their battle stations under most adverse conditions. With limited defensive means against attacks in great force, they manned their shore installations

---

several guards. One had his rifle pointed at Babe with the bayonet touching his stomach. Most of the men would have been rigid with fear, but not Babe. He simply reached down, thrust the sharp blade aside, and turned to walk away. Most of the prisoners agreed that they would not dream of taking such a chance, for they had already seen how brutal the guards could be. Most of the Japs were simply scared of the towering American, and he somehow knew when he could take such chances and get away with it.

Babe Hofmeister brought a tremendous amount of supplies and food to the wounded men in the hospital. When medical supplies were needed and the Japanese would not give them to Dr. Shank, Babe was contacted. He was very generous with the patients in the hospital in particular, befriending many during the early part of 1942. The men especially appreciated the medicines he brought, but also the food and cigarettes.

Fresh water was in short supply since the only source was the collection of rainwater. There was none available for bathing except to wash hands and faces. The doctors and corpsmen did what they could to clean the wounds regularly, but the lack of water hampered their efforts to keep the wounded men clean.

After over a month without a bath, Ralph Holewinski consented to have a civilian nurse, Milt Dryer from Iowa, give him a sponge bath. He still had blood on several parts of his body from the original wounds. Dryer took some rainwater from a barrel where it had gotten very hot in the sunshine. He gave Holewinski a thorough sponge bath, which made Skee feel good for the first time since being wounded. After the warm bath Skee began to feel as if he might actually get well and back on his feet again.

One by one the wounded men in the hospital on Wake were able to get up onto their feet during the next few weeks. Some could walk, while others like Dick had to use crutches to hobble about. He walked on the crutches for the first three months of 1942. Those who were mobile enough to move around were assigned the job of collecting hand grenades that the Marines had left booby-trapped around the island.

The American grenades had a pin in the top, which could be pulled to allow a metal attachment to be lifted. A few seconds later the grenade would detonate. The Marines had pulled the pins on hundreds of grenades, but left them lying in such a way that the detonation bar was still down.

The Japanese soldiers who were first assigned to clean up the grenades did not know how they worked, so they picked up the bombs with a "look what I found" attitude. The grenades would go off in their faces, and several Japanese were killed. They decided to let the prisoners have the job. The mobile POW's went on grenade patrols and found quite a few. They would pick up the devices while carefully holding the detonation bar down. Then they threw the grenades into the lagoon, allowing them to detonate harmlessly.

While walking in the fenced area around the hospital, Dick and other prisoners noticed tiny silver specks high in the sky, and knew they were reconnaissance planes sent by the Navy to photograph the island. The wily POW's decided to try to communicate with their comrades back at Pearl Harbor. A communications specialist among them devised a scheme to put the men's blankets on the fence around the compound and spell, in Morse code, the letters P-O-W. The accomplishment of this fete would later prove to be an ingenious lifesaver.

The Japanese guards heard that a plane had been seen but did not know which prisoners had made the sighting. They lined up the men and demanded to know of each, "Did you see an airplane?" Dick answered, "No," and convinced the guard that he had no knowledge of any airplane over Wake. Each man did the same, until the guard intensely interrogated one POW. "I didn't see a plane, but Darden did," said the frightened prisoner to the Japanese guard. Immediately the guards came to where Dick was standing and began to shout in his face and ask what he knew about the airplane.

The guards had been particularly brutal on several occasions, so Dick Darden wanted no part of what the guards might do to someone they thought was a liar. He insisted, time and time again as the intense guards demanded information, that he had seen no plane. The guards became livid and were about to take him away for more intense interrogation, when they were called away by their superiors. They never asked about the airplanes again. Another close call had come and gone.

Jim Cox and Kirby Ludwig, two of the sailors from the boat crew, discussed their situation as they lay on the sandy ground in a pen under a barracks building at Camp 2.

They were being held there with a large number of the Marines who had been captured during the surrender.

Cox and Ludwig did not like any of their options. Both had minor wounds, and they found themselves stranded in the middle of the Pacific Ocean under the thumb of an oppressive enemy who liked to see American blood. To remain there would mean that they would be the target of their own American guns and in the middle of another battle when the Yanks came back to take the island. To be shipped to the Japanese homeland would be even worse. They tried their best to come up with another plan because there seemed to be little for them to lose.

Both of the Navy men were trained on the small boats and they were comfortable on them in the ocean around Wake Island. They knew that one of the twenty-six foot skiffs was still in running order. They decided to steal the boat at night and rig a mast, hoping to sail the small vessel across the Pacific to the nearest Allied island. They thought they could sneak away from the guards at night and get to the boat which was moored at a nearby dock.

Cox and Ludwig were not too concerned about food, feeling that they could catch enough fish to sustain them while they crossed the 1800 miles to Hawaii. They reasoned that the Polynesians had sailed from island to island in small craft, so they could do the same. If they died at sea it would be better than being killed by the Japanese on Wake Island or in Japan, which seemed to be the only other options they had. They really didn't know where they would go if they were lucky enough to make it off the island in the boat. They just wanted to get off of Wake Island.

In the end Cox and Ludwig decided not to try the escape for two reasons. If they were lucky enough to make it to the boat, get it in the water, get out of sight of the island, rig a sail, and catch enough fish to eat, they still had two seemingly unsurmountable problems.

First, they had no fresh water to take with them. Second, if it rained and they were lucky enough to have the chance to collect some water, they had nothing to store it in. Weeks or months at sea without water would certainly mean an excruciating death. They scrapped their plans, but several of their friends knew of their idea, and rumors would circulate several months later that they had left the island by boat.

By January 11 the war had been going on for thirty-five days, and Kay and Stevens had been hiding out for twenty days. They had had several close calls, so they had moved about and covered their tracks well. They were literally living among the 3000 heavily armed enemy soldiers who were swarming about the few square miles of Wake atoll. Even though they had effectively camouflaged their tiny camp a Japanese soldier had "looked right at us......must have had his eyes on something nearer."

The two men were tired of lying in the gritty coral sand all day under cover, and they hoped more than ever that the Americans would come quickly and liberate the island. "Our eleven inch guns will be music," Kay dreamed in his diary. Conditions had become even more uncomfortable for the two men. While they did have food aplenty, they had to eat it cold. We "do not dare light fire; maybe later when it gets stormy. Cloudy tonight, will set paper to catch rainwater." The two had a piece of tar-paper roofing material which served as their means of catching water.

After several additional close calls with the enemy Kay and Stevens decided to move their camp, feeling that if they didn't they would surely be captured. They waited until darkness and moved along the lagoon on the inside of the island, moving to the east and into the inside of the "V" on Wake Island. Finally they found a spot near the lagoon about half way down the eastern leg of Wake, and there they set up yet another hideout. Still, the enemy was all around them. "There are just too many people on Wake for such a small spot."

There had been a series of close calls, any one of which could easily have been the end of Kay and Stevens' fugitive status. Once the Japs had actually "knocked on the door" of the primitive hideout. We "thought we were caught finally." But for some reason the soldier had turned away. Later, however, the enemy had come back and "raided us, and took what few trinkets we had gathered."

Chapter 35
THE VOYAGE OF THE NITTA MARU

On January 12, 1942, less than three weeks after the Japanese victory on Wake Island, most of the prisoners who could travel, including Major Devereux and Commander Cunningham, were taken to a large ship that was waiting just offshore, the NITTA MARU. This large group of men was to be taken first to Japan, and then on to prison camps at Woosung and Kiangwan in Japanese occupied China. There they would remain as prisoners of war in the work camps for the indefinite future.

It was decided that a small group of the American military men would be allowed to remain on Wake, but only until their wounds had healed adequately for them to travel. About twenty men in the wooden hospital building who had serious wounds would remain, including Darden and Holewinski. About a hundred civilian workers remained, and with the group was the American civilian doctor, Dr. Lawton Shank.

Soon after the NITTA MARU arrived, Ralph Holewinski was lying on a stretcher just outside the hospital door. Dr. Shank, accompanied by several Japanese officers, walked up to the small wooden building. They were discussing whether or not the wounded men should be shipped to Japan on the NITTA MARU with the other prisoners. The men walked through the hospital where the wounded

men lay. The officers told Dr. Shank to take Skee inside with the other wounded prisoners so that he would not hear the discussion. The officers and the doctor went outside, still discussing the question at hand.

Dr. Shank later came into the hospital and told the men that the Japanese had allowed him to make the decision about their movement. He knew there would be little room on the ship for wounded men, so he decided that they should remain on the island for now. "I think you are better off here than on that ship, because the officer told me there is no room on the ship for sick people," he told them. The doctor had wisely detected during the discussions with the Japanese that conditions on the NITTA MARU would be stark at best.

Knowing the propensity of the Japanese toward harsh treatment of conquered people, Dr. Shank correctly decided that the situation on the NITTA MARU would be intolerable for the group of wounded men. This would have been especially true for Ralph Holewinski, who was the only patient still in a completely immobile condition. Dr. Shank told the Japanese that there was no way the men could travel in their condition. They would have to remain on the island for a period of time before they could be moved. The

Japanese Photo – U. S. Marine Corps

American civilian workers are marched form a construction site to their prison accommodations on Wake

decision almost surely saved Skee's life.

The wounded men were dejected about staying on Wake Island. They had already seen the potential for very rough times for prisoners if they stayed behind. They felt that their best chance for survival was to remain with the large group of prisoners. But they could not know how good the doctor's decision had been for them. They would later learn of the horrid treatment to which the men aboard the NITTA MARU would be subjected, treatment that would almost certainly have cost many of these wounded men their lives.

The Japanese decided to keep the twenty wounded Americans on the island until a later date when they would be moved to Japan. About one hundred of the American civilians would also to be kept on the island indefinitely to work on the airstrip. The Japanese intended to use Wake Island as a refueling point for their planes that would be used to do battle with the Americans to the east toward Hawaii.

The thought of moving to Japan, the enemy homeland, was not particularly appealing to the wounded men. Such a move would mean that they would surely have to wait out the entire war in prison. At least Wake Island might be retaken by the Allies before the war ended. Neither of the two options, to remain on Wake or be shipped to Japan, appeared good. Of the two, most men in the hospital favored leaving with the others, because they knew they didn't want to be left behind. The decision had, however, already been made. They would remain on Wake.

Dr. Shank gathered the twenty patients in the hospital at the end of Holewinski's cot. "I just wanted you to know that it was my decision to keep you here," he told them. "If anything happens you can blame me." The doctor was trying to console the men, but with little success. It was about 3:00 in the afternoon. The three corpsmen helped everyone back to their beds. There was no movement and very little conversation for the rest of the afternoon.

The mood in the hospital was somber. The distraught men lay on their cots and stared here and there, trying to untangle this turn of events. Was it best for them, or was it a dangerous decision? They feared being on an isolated enemy outpost where poor treatment was likely and military action was probable. Even Capt. Wilson, known for his exuberance and gift of gab, lay uncharacteristically silent until the dinner meal was served at 6:00.

Some of the men in the hospital became extremely depressed because they were being left behind. All were confused, but most felt that it would be best to go with the main group. There were a couple of civilians in the hospital who had been injured in the bombing raids. They wanted to go with their 1100 buddies who were about to be moved. They decided to "get well" in a hurry. Wounded or not, they got their personal effects together and joined the group of civilians that were about to be shipped out.

Holewinski felt the same way. He was openly afraid of what might happen to the men who stayed on the island. He also would have pulled off his bandages and "gotten well" if his injuries had not been so severe. But with his leg wounds not healed and his back wound still draining profusely, it was simply not possible for him to join the defenders as they prepared to board the transport ship.

The healthy men would be trucked back to the Marine camp, Camp 1, and then taken out to the transport ship on Japanese landing craft that had been used in the battle. The NITTA MARU had been a luxury passenger liner before the war, but had been converted into a Japanese troop transport.

The time came for the prisoners to board the NITTA MARU. They were transported through the breaking surf and out to the ship in several of the small boats and landing craft. When Jim Cox's boat reached the NITTA MARU he was ordered to climb up a cargo net which had been draped over the ship's side. He was searched and then made to run toward a hatch which led down into the ship's hold. For about forty feet the ship's crew lined both sides of the passageway, and they were armed with tools, bamboo sticks, and various bat-like instruments. As each prisoner ran the gauntlet toward the open hatch the guards "beat the hell" out of him with their sticks, poles, and handles.

Some of the prisoners received serious wounds and broken bones when they ran the gauntlet. One prisoner, Marine Corporal Bob Cooper, took a blow from a ball bat that broke the end of his tail bone. Despite the painful injury he kept on running the gauntlet until he reached the safety of the hatch. The injury would be painful for the rest of his life.

Once Jim Cox reached the inside of the ship he was able to see the spartan accommodations he would have to endure for the next twelve days. The hold of the ship was a large, bare metal box with nothing in it but crowded prisoners, many bruised and bleeding from running the gauntlet.

Walter Cook also had to undergo a search as he boarded the NITTA MARU. A Japanese guard ordered him to "empty pockets, empty pockets, everything, everything." Cook had a small New Testament in his hip pocket. He laid it down on a table along with everything else that he had in his pockets. "You get it back, you get it back," garbled one of the Jap guards. Cook was never to see any of his possessions again. He was then shoved roughly across the deck toward the large open hatch. He, too, met with the double line of Japanese crewmen wielding sticks and poles.

Glenn Tripp was one of the last of the prisoners to be put aboard the NITTA MARU. On the way out to the ship the Japanese coxswain lost control of his boat when the rudder cable broke. The landing craft was dead in the water and drifting quickly in the swift current. The prisoners and three Japanese guards aboard the boat drifted on the fast current over the horizon and completely out of sight of the NITTA MARU and Wake Island. For a while all aboard feared they would be lost at sea, but finally the Japanese coxswain repaired the rudder cable and was able to head back toward the ship. He arrived just in time to get the men aboard as the ship was preparing to leave.

As Tripp climbed up the jacob's ladder on the side of the ship, he was wearing his high school class ring. He put the ring and his watch into a pocket of his coveralls, hoping to be able to hide the jewelry, especially the ring, and keep it out of the hands of the enemy. The captain of the ship, Captain Toshio Saito, was having each of the prisoners searched as they came aboard, and he was taking what he wanted of their valuables.

Tripp was searched by one of Captain Saito's guards, who tore the pocket off of the coveralls, causing the ring to fall out on the deck. The Captain grunted something in Japanese that Tripp did not understand and then picked up the ring and put it in his pocket. The ring was gold with a red ruby inset. Around the ruby was inscribed "NBHS," (New Bloomfield High School), "1938". There was a misprint in the initials, which read "GRT" instead of "GET."

"NITTA MARU," a woodcut by Maj. James R. Brown depicts a POW being beaten while hanging by his thumbs in the hold of the NITTA MARU in January 1942, while enroute to Japan.

After being searched Tripp was given a strong shove by one of the guards, which caused him to start moving into a passageway which led across the ship. All of the men who had thusfar boarded the ship had been pushed across the deck and through the gauntlet. As the Japanese sailors swung freely the prisoners got a good taste of the type of treatment what was to become a way of life for years to come. The Japs would, from this time on, use harsh treatment and beatings to assert their authority over the defenseless POW's.

Each of the prisoners got the same treatment as he went below. As each man ran toward the opening into the ship's hold he was severely beaten by the men with the sticks. Each of the Jap seaman, probably half a dozen on each side, would take his best shot, hitting the prisoner with his weapon and then shouting "ush" as he pushed the slumping man on to the next guard. The gruesome sounds coming from the passageway were clearly audible to the men being searched on deck.

By the time Tripp got to the end of the gauntlet he was bruised and bleeding. He was instructed to climb down a ladder into the hold of the ship, where he joined a large number of his fellow prisoners, nearly all of whom were nursing wounds and injuries from the beatings they had just been given. They found themselves crowded into a large, bare metal chamber, where they settled down on the cold, dirty steel floor.

One blanket was issued to each prisoner. Each man laid the folded blanket on the cold steel floor to reserve his sleeping spot. Some were unlucky enough to reserve a spot near the five-gallon buckets in each corner. Soon after entering the metal chamber Walter Cook noticed two things that added to his discomfort. First

was the heat. There was no ventilation in the ship's hold and the tropical sun of Wake Island was beating down on the ship causing her hold to be stifling. Secondly was the odor; already the stench of human wastes and body odor in the hold was nauseating.

The guards gave the men orders not to cause any commotion in the ship's hold, or even talk to each other. A written list of regulations was issued to the men. It indicated that almost any minor infraction of the rules would be punishable by immediate death. The regulations stated that the death sentence would be given for the following:

1. disobeying orders and instructions;
2. showing any signs of opposition to the Japanese;
3. talking without permission;
4. raising loud voices;
5. walking or moving without orders;
6. carrying unnecessary baggage;
7. touching any of the ship's wiring or mechanisms;
8. climbing the ladder without permission;
9. attempting to run away;
10. trying to take more food than was served;
11. using more than two blankets.

Four days into the journey one of the guards was looking down through the hatch above the men and saw Glenn Tripp whispering to one of the other prisoners. The guard, a Third Class Petty Officer known to the men only as "Square Jaw," immediately came down into the hold and ordered Tripp to stand at attention.

Tripp did exactly as he was told, for by now the men knew, in no uncertain terms, that the guards meant business. Square Jaw proceeded to give the helpless POW a severe beating with his fists.

The ship got underway and within a couple of days the temperature seemed to become a bit more bearable. Rumors began to circulate among the prisoners. Some said the civilians were being quartered one deck below. Another rumor, which caused the men to worry, was that the American aircraft carrier SARATOGA was operating in the area. "Sara" would surely have escorts, which would include submarines.

The NITTA MARU was a transport, so it would be a juicy target for our boys down under who might mistake it for an enemy troop ship. But if a torpedo were to sink the NITTA MARU it would kill over one thousand Americans. Concerns permeated the thick putrid air in the hold when the throb of the NITTA MARU's engines seemed to increase or decrease as if she was trying to move faster or change speed. Thankfully for the men there was no encounter with a submarine. No one wanted to tangle with an American U-boat because they knew that a direct hit from a torpedo would almost surely turn the ships sealed hold into a mass grave.

It took two or three days after the departure of the NITTA MARU for the mood of the men left behind in the hospital on Wake to improve. Their spirits began to brighten up and the morale of the men became visibly better. The men began talking about Wake Island being retaken by American forces. This would mean freedom for the wounded men long before those in Japan would be liberated, assuming that they lived through the battle. Perhaps they would be bait for some sort of prisoner trade. They conjured up dozens of scenarios, all illustrating how their situation was better by being left behind. The men got more optimistic as the days wore on.

Lt. Poindexter was locked in the NITTA MARU's mail room along with most of the other officers. The food and sanitary conditions were bad, but nothing to compare with the grim conditions in the hold. The officers were occasionally roughed up but not abused like the enlisted men below. They were confined in the small room with just enough space for each man to stretch out on the floor. This presented problems because some of the men, including Capt. Tharin and Lt. Frueler, had serious wounds.

Dr. Kahn was with the men on the ship, but could do little since he had no supplies. Frueler had been shot in the shoulder and was seriously wounded. During the voyage his wounds began to smell terrible. Some of the men feared that he had developed gangrene.

One of the Japanese guards always wore a mean look on his face and a long Samurai sword. Occasionally he would pull the gleaming blade from its scabbard so the prisoners would have a greater appreciation of its potential. His antics with the sword earned him the name "Sword Happy" among the prisoners.

Inspections became a nightly ordeal in the hold. About 6:00 p.m. a petty officer would come into the hold and instruct the men on exactly what formation and physical position they were to assume for the upcoming inspection. They had to take the position immediately, and the positions became uncomfortable in just a few minutes.

"Sword Happy" had a funny look in his eyes as if he might enjoy using the sword on one of the Americans. One evening early in the voyage he came down into the hold as part of the inspection party. Usually no one provoked him in the slightest for fear that he might use his big blade. However, on this evening three POW's did not stand exactly as ordered during the shakedown that preceded the inspection. A group of guards jumped on the two Marines and one sailor and, using martial arts techniques, beat them severely and slammed them to the deck. The men were beaten until they were not able to get up, and several bruises were visible on their nearly naked bodies. Luckily for the prisoners "Sword Happy" did not get into the fray.

Often the men were forced to stand at attention while they waited for the inspection to take place. Usually Captain Saito did not enter the hold for the inspection until about 9:00 p.m., so the pain of holding the uncomfortable position became excruciating. If any man fell out of position due to fatigue or dizziness, he would be beaten.

Conditions in the hold of the ship became increasingly horrid. Two hundred and seventy-nine men were confined to the cramped hold and were forced to sleep on the cold steel floor with very little clothing and no cover over their bare skin. The men were not given any water for bathing during the entire twelve day voyage. Indeed, precious little water was provided for drinking. Twice a day each man was given a cup of water and a cup of barley gruel. The "sloppy crap" was terrible, mostly rice and water with a few kernels of barley or some similar grain. It was lowered down into the hold in a bucket with a rope.

Many of the men became weak and sick from the lack of food, and diarrhea became commonplace. The men's throats begged for water, and they called out frequently to the guards to get some, but to no avail. Most of the time the hatches were battened down and the men were completely isolated in the hold. There was no way for the men to get out. The diarrhea began to spread.

The epidemic of diarrhea was soon complicated by another problem, the lack of toilet facilities. The only accommodation for the men's physical wastes were five-gallon metal cans which had had the tops cut out and were placed in each corner of the room. The guards would allow the prisoners to empty the cans only once a day. Two POW's would be allowed to go up through the hatch and drop a rope down into the hold. The wastes of 279 men far exceeded the 20 gallon capacity of the four cans and were already overflowing onto the floor of the hold and the men around them.

The buckets were tied to ropes and the two men topside would pull the slurry of vomit, urine, and feces up out of the hold onto the deck. Invariably the contents of the overflowing buckets would slosh and spill as they were being hoisted up, sending the acrid filth back down on top of the men who were crowded into the hold below. The material dried on the men and the deck, but no one was allowed to clean up either the room or themselves. The men topside would dump the remainder of the wastes over the side of the ship.

Conditions in the hold quickly became unbearable and remained so for the duration of the trip. The men were compelled to live in their own filth. This situation was further complicated by the fact that only rarely would the Japanese open the hatch to the hold that was located directly over the men. This caused the unbearable stench and humidity to be held in the metal chamber without the benefit of ventilation.

During the voyage the Japanese gave the POW's questionnaires and instructed them to fill out the forms. The men were questioned about their specialties in the service and many other things. They were told to be specific and that they would be punished if they lied. Glenn Tripp filled out the forms along with all of his buddies. He indicated that he was merely a yeoman and knew nothing of importance.

Two of the men sitting next to Tripp, Seaman First Class John William Lambert and Seaman First Class Roy J. Gonzales, were Glenn's close friends. Both were aviation machinist mates on Wake Island who had eaten in the same mess tent with Tripp before the war broke out. Since they knew each other they stuck together when they became prisoners. They were in the same hold together on the NITTA MARU.

After a week at sea the NITTA MARU docked in Yokohama, near Tokyo. The Japanese proudly announced the arrival of their prisoners in a radio broadcast which was monitored by the Associated Press and relayed to the United States. AP reported from Tokyo on January 19 that 1235 prisoners were aboard the NITTA MARU. This included thirty officers, 423 enlisted men, and 782 civilians.

Soon after the ship arrived in Yokohama all aviation and radio men were instructed to leave the ship. Glenn Tripp, Lambert, and Gonzales were sitting in a circle together in the crowded ship's hold. Suddenly guards came down into the hold and ordered Lambert and Gonzales to come topside with them. Tripp surmised that they were being taken away for questioning, since radiomen were thought to know secret codes and the Japanese were frantically trying to decode American radio messages. The two men climbed out of the hold and disappeared from view.

The following day both Lambert and Gonzales came back down into the ship's hold. They appeared to be frightened and very nervous. They had been ordered to come back into the hold and get their shoes and a blanket. When the guards were not looking, the two men told Tripp that they had been caught lying on their interrogation forms. Apparently they had admitted being radiomen on the second form, but had tried to conceal this fact on the first by saying they were cooks. The Japanese had noticed the discrepancy and told them they were going to make examples out of them and severely punish them for lying about their specialties.

Before they could tell Tripp more about their predicament, the scared men gathered their blankets and shoes, and the guards came to get them. They were taken from the hold immediately. Tripp began to worry about his friends. Even though they had spoken to him only briefly, he sensed fear in their voices. As they left the hold one of them told Tripp he did not think they would be back.

A couple of days later, after the NITTA MARU had left the port of Yokohama, a Japanese Warrant Officer came down in the hold of the ship for a routine inspection. He did not seem as brutal as some of the others, so Glenn Tripp approached him and asked about his two friends. The Warrant Officer shocked him by saying that five prisoners had been taken up on the deck of the ship and beheaded in a ritualistic ceremony. "Some of your comrades were beheaded for lying," he told Tripp. He said that the POW's had been gathered on the deck and blindfolded. They were encircled by a ring of officers, one of whom read them their death warrant. The readings were done in Japanese, which they did not understand, and informed them that they were to be executed for the crime of lying.

This heinous act on Captain Saito's part was not intended to scare or control the prisoners, since none of them was brought up to witness the execution and report back to the men below. To the contrary, only the group of Japanese officers were present. It was probably a Bushido ritual intended to be symbolic retribution for the Imperial troops who were killed during the invasion and capture of Wake Island.

The Warrant Officer told Tripp that he had been ordered to behead one of the prisoners. He told the Captain that he did not want to do it. Then he balked at the second order, at which time the Captain told him that if he did not behead the man that he would be made to kneel and the Captain would behead him. With this choice before him the Warrant Officer told Tripp that he walked over to the kneeling man, drew his officer's sword, and raised it into the air. He closed his eyes and brought the razor-sharp Samurai blade down on the back of the kneeling man's neck, chopping as hard as he could. He told Tripp that he had immediately turned and run to his stateroom, not knowing if he had completely beheaded the man. "To this day I don't know if I beheaded the man or not," he insisted.

(It must be said at this point, in the interest of complete accuracy on this very delicate matter, that while Glenn Tripp steadfastly stands by his story, other credible participants who were in the same hold on the NITTA MARU have questioned the fact that any of the prisoners were told of the executions. They did not hear such a story and doubt that a Japanese officer came into the hold and told of the beheadings. Their doubt stems from the belief that, if anyone had been told the gruesome truth about the killings, the news would have spread like electricity through the scared and nervous group of tightly packed men. Regardless of which account of the happenings below decks is accurate, it is true that the five beheadings did occur, are documentable, and the account of what happened on the deck of the ship is factual.)

After eight days at sea the NITTA MARU docked at the Woo Sung Docks in Shanghai, China. Tripp was still looking for his friends and hoping that the bizarre story told by the Japanese Warrant Officer was not true. When the prisoners were brought up out of the hold they were segregated on the docks for a count. There had been 279 men put in Tripp's hold at Wake Island. Only 277 came out onto the docks in Woo Sung. Gonzales and Lambert were gone.

Captain Saito came out and, through an interpreter, addressed the cold, weak men as they stood at attention. The Captain told the men that he was honored to be the captain of the first prison ship. He said that he was sorry to have to part company with the men, but that the Japanese Army would probably be able to feed them better.

Glenn Tripp continued to look for his buddies on the eight mile walk to the prison camp. No one, even from the other holds on the ship, had seen them. The two were never seen again.

The men in the hospital on Wake had been extremely apprehensive about the decision to separate them from the main body of prisoners and leave them on the island. They were terribly depressed when the NITTA MARU sailed away and left them behind. As the days passed, however, their morale improved. They settled into the daily routine in the hospital and began to adjust to the discomfort from their wounds. Much of their time was spent talking to each other and changing the bandages on their wounds. They had become isolated, both from friendly American forces and from their fellow POW's.

One night as Dick slept on his cot in the hospital he was awakened by a bright light shining in his eyes. As his eyes popped wide open and his heart pounded he looked up into the face of a Japanese guard just behind the flashlight. The guard was crouched over him with his face very close to Dick as if he were looking for something. Dick could tell that the Jap soldier had been drinking because he could feel the hot breath of the man as he teetered from side to side. His breath had a heavy smell of alcohol.

The guard was holding the flashlight very near Dick's face, virtually blinding him. But the flashlight was not his greatest concern. In his other hand the guard held a Nambu pistol, a side arm similar to the German luger. The drunk soldier was pointing the gun directly at Dick's head, and he was moving from side to side as he struggled to stay on his feet. Dick's heart raced faster as he realized that the Jap had a pistol pointed at his face at close quarters and was so inebriated that he had little control over what he was doing. Why was he doing this, and what could he want?

Dick was horrified. Any slip by the soldier and the gun could discharge in Dick's face. He tried to show no emotion as he looked down the barrel of the gun, not even letting the drunk Jap know that he was awake. Seconds seemed like hours as the man remained for several minutes over Dick, the gun held just inches from his head.

Then, as quickly as the episode had started, the guard turned and staggered away. As sweat sprang from Dick's body he breathed a huge sigh of relief. His heart still pumped wildly as he wondered what had caused the incident. His question was never answered. The man never came back into the hospital and Dick never knew why he had come so near death in the middle of the night.

During late January, Kay and Stevens were still on the run. Since there were so many Japs all around, the close calls continued and it was miraculous that they were not found. Once the Japs "missed us by fifteen feet...Guess we will have to put up signs, 'Private Property, Keep Out.'"

The two men had spent over a month undercover, lying motionless all day in a tiny camouflaged hole. At night they would eat cold food while sitting in the hot, bug-infested sand, and then sleep on the hard coral. Their physical condition was declining, and the ordeal of waiting for American forces to liberate the island was taking its toll. They needed food and exercise soon in order to get back into reasonable physical shape. We "were out two hours last night and got a little exercise, which we really needed. Been lying down so long we get dizzy when we stand."

The food supply available to the two fugitives was rapidly becoming depleted. They had to find ways to eat the creatures living around them. While their diet was not to be envied, their resolve in holding out and their methods of procuring food were nothing short of amazing.

"Went out early today and found two by six tongue and groove which I will make into a crossbow. Will hunt some nails for ammunition. (Scotty eventually was able to kill rats at twenty yards.)" Their ability to live off the land became even more important shortly thereafter when they had "bad news, last night the Japs found two-thirds of all our food supply and took it away....These Japs are regular bloodhounds."

There was intense activity going on around the hideout much of the time. On January 20 Kay wrote that he "spent the day in hideout No. 4. No light, no food, no flies, no room, but no Japs." Kay and Stevens admired the energy with which the Japanese worked at transforming Wake into their own fortress. "These Japs have done more work on the island in thirty-seven days than the United States did in nine months."

Hideout No. 4 was on the lagoon just a short distance over water from the airfield. The fugitives watched the constant construction and air traffic in the bustling area of the island. There were people working all around the hideout. From inside their hole the two men could hear voices outside. Most were Japanese, but some were American. The two mistook these for English-speaking Japanese, and Kay wrote that "some talk English to each other." He would later learn that these were actually American prisoners on work details.

Ever the optimist, Kay had counted the days since he had come to Wake, and still envisioned being freed any day. "Arrived on this island three months ago—my $30.00 bonus will start Sunday. I am burying this book, will start a new one so as not to lose my record if anything slips."

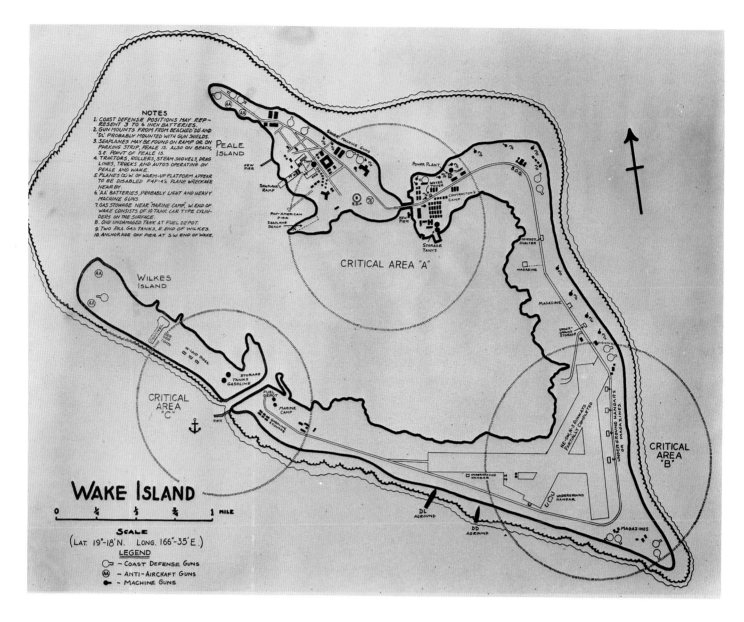

American reconnaisance map of Japanese occupied Wake Island, February 1942. Destroyers (Patrol Craft) and troop landing craft are shown aground on south beach. POW's were in Critical Area 'A'.

Chapter 36
FEBRUARY, 1942 – YANKS SHELL WAKE

The Japanese occupation force on Wake Island feared reprisal bombings from American forces that were thought to be in the area from time to time, and they knew that the reconnaissance planes had gotten detailed photographs of their fortifications on the island. The Japanese ordered some of the American civilians to use their heavy equipment and dig out a hole inside the prisoner's compound, and then they constructed a crude wooden shelter. This was covered with coral sand, thus providing a makeshift bomb shelter. The Japanese probably intended to use the shelter themselves.

Kay and Stevens were still in a sandy hole of their own. Still near the lagoon side of Wake, they had become accustomed to the discomforts of living underground. February 2, Groundhog Day, fostered entries in Kay's diary that showed he still had his sense of humor. "We are two ground hogs, and today is Ground Hog Day. Sun's shining, so I guess we will stay in our holes for six weeks more unless the Japs smoke us out."

Fred Stevens became excited and optimistic. Help had to be coming soon. As the two men lay together in their hole and watched lizards crawl across their bodies catching flies, they discussed Stevens' hunch that help was on the way. It needed to come soon, since the health of the two middle-aged men was seriously declining. "Haven't tasted bread in six weeks, and won't, I guess. My eyes are okay. Lost my glasses when the Japs landed, but found a good enough pair."

Help came for Kay and Stevens on Lincoln's Birthday, February 12, when they found a ten-day supply of food. The stash included "seven cans of artichokes, three cans of milk, a gallon of lima beans and a gallon of water." The men enjoyed their newly found rations and began to notice that the Japanese were intensifying their training and preparations. "The Japs seem to be getting ready. Much machine gun practice...." This fed their speculation that something was about to happen. We "can feel excitement in the wind," read Kay's diary. "Planes are coming and going, staying hardly an hour. We're all set to have the Star Spangled Banner played on 14" guns. Will stand up and cheer, or even climb a tree....."

By mid-February information was trickling back to the United States about the action on Wake Island. On February 19 the Charlotte Observer printed a story which named a number of North Carolinians who had been taken prisoner on Wake and Guam. Among them was Seaman First Class James B. Darden. The story indicated that over a thousand Navy and Marine officers and men had been captured in the Pacific in the ten weeks since the bombing of Pearl Harbor, which already was far more than the fifteen Navy men taken prisoner by the Germans in all of World War I. It was already apparent that this war would place a far greater burden on the young men of America than World War I.

Several days later, on February 22 (Washington's Birthday), Kay and Stevens were still waiting patiently for a big event to take place on Wake, perhaps a landing by American forces that would free them. But, no liberating force had visited Wake by George Washington's birthday. "Happy Birthday, George," wrote Kay. We "have not had hot food or a fire for seventy-seven days. The bottoms of my feet are as soft as my hands from disuse."

On February 24, 1942, an American naval task force approached Wake Island. The task force was built around the aircraft carrier ENTERPRISE. In an ironic twist of fate, it was this same ship which, less than three months earlier, had visited the vicinity of Wake to deliver the twelve F4F-3 Wildcat fighters for the defense of the island. The February visit would be considerably different. This time the American forces were approaching the island with the intent of attacking the atoll, both by aerial bombing and naval bombardment. The objective this time was destruction. Unfortunately, Dick Darden would be a resident of the island during both of the visits of the ENTERPRISE.

In addition to the ENTERPRISE, the task force included three cruisers and nine destroyers. Even though the ships were over the horizon, several miles out of sight of the men on Wake and never seen by them, they bombarded the island with amazing accuracy. The Navy gunners could not see the island when they laid down a "rolling barrage" of 5",6", and 8" shells, starting on the beach on one end of the island and moving systematically to the other end. The bombardment caused the destruction of several buildings on the island and set fire to a dredge that was in the lagoon.

Kay and Stevens were elated when the attack began on February 24. This was evident from Kay's diary. The "shooting started all over the island at 5:30 a.m. and continued until 7...Our planes shot down two little Jap scouts first thing. This is the sweetest symphony I ever heard. Our shells whistle in and seem like bursts of Roman candles. Fred and I spent one-third of our time in a tree, one-third climbing up and down, and one-third in a dugout.....I'd not miss it for anything."

"Boy, how our big shells whistle before they land—and do our little planes sound sweet when they dive! When the Japs dive, they shut off their motors and drift down. But, our boys step on the gas and come in like wasps. Soon they'll come in flocks."

The carrier-based planes swarmed down onto the island with a vengeance, bombing targets on both Wake and Wilkes Islands. They destroyed several of the large fuel tanks located on both sides of the Wilkes channel. The American planes also shot down three of the large Japanese four-engine sea planes which had taken off from the island during the bombardment. When the attack was over, many of the buildings and fuel tanks on the island were in flames.

A Japanese patrol ship had the misfortune of being just a few miles off Heel Point, the northeastern tip of Wake Island. Several of the ships fired their guns at the craft, and the planes emptied their magazines into her as they returned to the ENTERPRISE from their bombing runs. When last seen the ship was sinking.

The prisoners in the hospital on Wake would never know if the spelling of the letters P-O-W on the fence had been photo-

More Than 2,200 Americans Held As Prisoners By The Japanese

James Bizzell Darden, Seaman 1st Class, of Clinton, Who Was Serving on Wake Island in December Among Those Listed as "Likely" to Be a War Prisoner

WASHINGTON, Feb. 19 (AP) — The Navy Department released today a list of 1,010 Navy and Marine Corps officers and enlisted men presumed to have been taken prisoner by the Japanese on the Islands of Wake and Guam and at Peiping, Tientsin and Shanghai, China.

Lieut. Comdr. John T. Tuthill, Jr., Public Relations Officer of the Third Naval District, also made public a roster of 1,200 civilians who were employed in defense construction work on the two Pacific islands and who also are presumed to be prisoners of war.

Among the Navy officers serving at Guam when the islands was captured by the Japanese on Dec. 12 were the Governor, Captain George Johnson McMillan of Youngstown, Ohio; Capt. William Taylor Lineberry, Colerain, N. C., and Commander Donald Theodore Giles, Annapolis, Md.

Heading the 11 officers and 63 men serving at Wake were commander Winfield Scott Cunningham, Long Beach, Calif., and Commander Campbell Keene, Naval Air Station, San Diego, Calif.

Commander Leo Cromwell Thyson, Washington, D. C., was one of four officers and 11 men stationed at Peiping; Lieut. (JG) William Thomas Foley, Flushing, N. Y., and five enlisted men were serving at Tientsin, and three Lieutenants Junior Grade were serving at Shanghai. They were George Theodore Ferguson, Wausau, Wis.; Robert W. CcElrath, Murray, Ky., and James Stephen O'Rourke, Washington, D. C.

The Marine garrison of 413 at Wake Island was commanded by Major James Patrick S. Devereux, New York, and included three majors in the Marine Corps aviation branch — George Hubbard Potter and Henry T. Elrod of Honolulu, and Paul Albert Putnam, Coronado, Calif.

Lieut. Col. William Kirk MacNulty of San Francisco was in command of the seven Marine officers and 147 men serving at Guam. Major Ronald Spicer, Coronado, Calif., also was stationed at Guam.

Among the seven officers and 132 men serving at Peiping were Colonel William S. Ashburst, San Diego, Calif., and Major Edwin P. McCaulley, Ontario, Calif. At Tientsin the three officers and 53 men included Major Luther A. Brown, Auburn, Pa., and Captain John A. White, Dayton, O.

Navy personnel who were serving at Wake Island and are deemed likely to be prisoners of the Japanese, include:

Darden, James Bizzell, Seaman 1st Class, 307 McCoy Street, Clinton, N. C.

Navy personnel who were serving at Guam and are deemed likely to be prisoners of the Japanese, include:

Captain William Taylor Lineberry, U. S. N., Colerain, N. C.

Enlisted men who were serving at Guam and are deemed likely to be prisoners of the Japanese, include:

Bryan Webster Berry, Pharmacist's Mate 3rd Class, Engelhard, N. C.

Leroy Wilson Bowman, R. F. D. No. 1 Sanford, N. C.

graphed and understood. If, however, that was not the case, then surely a miracle happened during the American bombardment that day. The systematic shelling approached the compound and then, as if the American gunners several miles away on the ships knew that their buddies lay wounded before them, stopped just short of the compound fence. Moments later the blasts began again just on the other side. Only a couple of errant shells landed inside the fence, doing little damage while just outside the fence everything was devastated.

When the shelling had begun, all of the men inside the hospital compound who were able to move had scrambled for the sand-covered bomb shelter. Sloman could only creep along, but he could move. His gunshot in the head had fouled up his equilibrium, so he would frequently fall forward right on his face. Dr. Shank was holding the door, beckoning the men to move out. He helped one of the men out the door and toward the protection of the shelter, leaving only Dick and Skee in the building as the shells began exploding just a few feet outside the compound.

Dick was near the door and about to limp out onto the porch when he looked to his left and saw Skee, who was immobile but had somehow managed to pull himself upright and was standing at the end of his cot. There was no mistaking the scared look on Skee's face, and Dick made an instant decision. He knew that he simply could not leave his helpless friend. He knew that if he left Skee in the small wooden building that he probably would not see him alive again.

As the earthshaking explosions came closer and closer to the building Dick swung around to the end of the bed where Skee was standing. The deafening blasts of the naval artillery shells seemed to be right outside the hospital and Darden and Holewinski realized that they faced almost certain death if they did not get out of the building quickly. The systematic wave of shells had almost reached the hospital.

Dick hobbled to the end of Holewinski's bed. Skee's splinted legs were holding him in a stiff-legged position on the end of the cot. The men looked eye to eye for a split second, and the look on Holewinski's face was unmistakable. Dick knew that his friend couldn't make it to the safety of the shelter on his own, and he also knew that he could not leave Skee behind. He looked at the immobile Marine and said, "Come on, get on." Skee did just that, painfully crawling aboard Dick's back in piggyback fashion.

Dick began the struggle to reach the door. Moving through the door, he started down a ramp outside which led to the bomb shelter. He moved as fast as he could, feeling all the while the burning and snapping in the leg wound as the weight of the two men strained it to the limit. Just as one of the shells landed next to the

National Archives

American planes prepare to take off from the flight deck of the USS ENTERPRISE in February, 1942, for an attack on Wake Island.

The USS SALT LAKE CITY fires on Wake Island February 24, 1942. A Curtis SOC Seagull observation plane is in the foreground

fence a few feet away, Dick fell forward into the earthen shelter, throwing both men into its safety. Both screamed with pain, but both were still alive. Somehow the throbbing leg had held together well enough to carry both men to safety.

The other wounded prisoners were already in the bunker. They sat and waited. Were the American forces that were just over the horizon softening up the island for an invasion? Were the prisoners about to be liberated? Was there about to be a battle? If so, would one side or the other kill the prisoners during the battle? Would there be another shelling? They were scared, having no idea what to do next, or what was about to happen to them.

Within a few minutes the wave of shells had passed over the hospital compound and, for the moment, the men seemed to have been spared. They wondered if their "POW" message on the fence had been seen and understood when the American plane had photographed the island. The consensus of the group was that it must have been. What they knew for sure was that, for the moment, their lives had been spared.

There was no food or water in the sandy bunker and nothing to do but wait. Captain Wilson told stories to break the monotony. The corny tales helped divert Dick's attention from the frightening situation, but did little for Skee since he had bunked in the same bay as Wilson and had already heard all of his stories.

The hours passed slowly as the men sat quietly in the bunker. They hoped that the shelling by American forces signaled that there was about to be an amphibious landing by the American forces. They knew that Americans were just a few miles away, and they wanted their buddies on the ships to kick the Japs off of Wake atoll.

No one seemed to be worried about the possibility that

there might be reprisals by the victorious Japs against their defenseless group of prisoners if a landing did occur. But, as they would soon learn, the shelling had just been part of a hit-and-run exercise. There would be no Yanks coming to rescue these men. It would be years before they would see the faces of the American troops who would eventually liberate them.

Finally, late that night and long after the shelling had stopped, Dr. Shanks felt that it was safe for the wounded men to be moved back inside the hospital building. The doctors, corpsmen, and the wounded men who were mobile began helping carry Dick, Skee, and the other immobile men back inside what was left of the hospital. Most of the men were able to spend the rest of the night on their bunks.

During the bombardment there were five shells which fell near the hospital compound. One exploded very close, sending shrapnel through the side of the wooden building. The metal fragments went through several beds, sending feathers throughout the room. Holewinski's bed had been cut in half. Had he remained in the hospital on the bed he would have surely been killed by the flying metal. Several of the able-bodied men began cleaning up the feathery mess in the building as the wounded men again settled onto their cots.

Kay and Stevens, still hiding out in their hole, had avoided the destruction on the island and felt that the liberating force had finally arrived. The fact that the attack ended and the American forces seemed to leave was taken in stride. The excited men rationalized that this was a normal preliminary part of such an invasion operation.

"Uncle Sam seems to have left his calling card," wrote Kay. "But we expected this, as Uncle was just getting pictures." The two

186

fugitives did not know that the American force was leaving the waters around Wake, and that the "flocks" of planes would not be back to liberate them.

There were eighty-five of the American artillery shells that did not explode when they crashed into the island during the bombardment. A considerable number of the projectiles that were made in American plants during this time were defective and they did not detonate upon impact. The shells could go off at any time, and the Japs did not want to handle them. But they had to be cleaned up, lest there be live explosives lying around on the island in the way of whatever construction projects that the Japs had planned.

The Japs came to the hospital and ordered eight or nine of the patients who could walk to go on a cleanup detail. Both Dick and Skee were thankful that they were unable to take part. A civilian drove a truck around the island while the POW's loaded the shells on the back end. The men held their breath during the operation, but luckily none of the shells went off.

Later in the month an American torpedo washed up on the reef just off Wake Island. It had either missed its mark or, like the artillery shells, had failed to go off. Even though it had failed in its attempt to rendezvous with the enemy, it was heartening for the men to see evidence that Americans were, or had been, in the area.

When the American aircraft carriers had launched the air strikes, the planes had encountered heavy anti-aircraft fire from Japanese positions on the island. Although not as effective as the American gunners had been during the siege, Jap anti-aircraft fire hit one of the planes from the ENTERPRISE. The plane went down and the two flyers aboard, the pilot and his tail gunner, parachuted safely into the ocean. They managed to survive and floated on the ocean current, which luckily brought them to the island during the night.

The next morning a civilian work detail saw the two and began talking with them. They learned that the pilot's name was Winchester. They talked for about a half hour, yearning to hear all of the latest news about the war. Finally the Japanese guards decided that something fishy was going on. There were two new faces in the group, and on top of that, they were wearing flyers' outfits. They grabbed the two men and took them off to the brig for questioning.

Holewinski never saw either of the two men again. They were taken off the island and put aboard a ship shortly after being captured, presumably for interrogation. Later Skee asked a Japanese guard if he knew their whereabouts. He was told that they were killed when their ship was sunk near Yokohama. The story did not sound plausible, since Holewinski knew that American forces were not working the seas near the Japanese homeland in early 1942.

Skee looked into the matter after the war since he had known the pilot Winchester from an earlier assignment. He wanted to advise Winchester's family that he had been shot down near Wake and what had happened to him. In searching postwar records he found that the Allies took no credit for sinking a Japanese ship near Yokohama during that period. Winchester and his tail gunner never made it to Japan. What happened to them is still not known, but Holewinski is sure that they never got off of a ship alive in Japan.

Tom Kennedy was also among the group that remained on Wake. His arm wound was still draining heavily and giving off a horrible odor, so it was put into an "airplane splint" so that a drain tube could be inserted. This type of splint fixed the arm in a waving position over Tom's head. For six weeks his arm remained in the waving position.

Tom Kennedy received constant ribbing from his roommates who took every opportunity to face him, raise their own arms, click their heels, and address him with a crisp "Heil, Hitler." The good natured ribbing got old and began to hurt Kennedy's feeling, but the pain was much greater when the airplane splint was removed and the arm was allowed down for the first time in weeks. The pain was intense, but the arm had drained well and was healing.

During the early part of 1942 most of the men in the hospital on Wake began to mend and move around. Most were able to walk outside the building. Dick became pretty good at moving about on his crutches. Breakfast was served every day at 8:00 a.m., after which most of the men would stay close to the compound and read until lunch. They were still eating canned American food that had been stashed on the island during the siege in December. During the afternoons the men would move outside to get some sun. The nearby laundry was in operation, so several walked to and from it for exercise. Overall, the conditions were improving.

During the early part of 1942, a representative from the Navy visited the campus of Davidson College, near Charlotte, N.C., and presented seniors at the all-male school a new program called the V-7 plan. The Navy needed high caliber men to become officers. They offered to give seniors with high academic averages several months to finish school without being drafted. The young men could finish school and get their degrees, and then go straight into Midshipman School, tantamount to Officer's Candidate School, to be trained as a Naval officer.

One young man at Davidson who accepted this call to arms was Rufus Geddie Herring. Like Dick Darden, Geddie Herring was from Sampson County, hailing from the small town of Roseboro. Geddie had the academic qualifications, so he took the Navy up on their offer. While Dick lay wounded in the prisoners' hospital on Wake Island, Geddie was finishing his senior year in college and preparing to dive headlong into the defense of his country.

Chapter 37
MARCH, 1942 – "BABE" HOFMEISTER

Days turned into weeks as the men in the makeshift prison waited for the freedom which would not come for another three years. Each 7-10 days a glimmer of hope would raise their spirits as another reconnaissance plane would come over, seen only as a speck of silver miles up in the tropical sky with a contrail following behind.

Though conditions for the prisoners in the hospital were bleak, the "library" did offer a diversion to the realities of the present. This was a small collection of books and reading material that Pan Am had maintained in the hotel for its travelers before the battle. Dick Darden read and waited as his leg continued to heal. He read THE GRAPES OF WRATH, THE JOURNEYMEN, TOBACCO ROAD, and several other books. How he wished that he could be back home on Tobacco Road in North Carolina.

The Japanese soldiers in the occupation force were clearly not experienced with equipment of the type that the American soldiers and civilian workers had on Wake Island. They attempted to become familiar with the equipment, but frequently had major problems in doing so. Once a Japanese soldier was driving a truck loaded with guards along the road on Wake Island when he attempted to take a curve at a high rate of speed. The truck overturned, killing several of the Nip soldiers.

Another time a Japanese soldier was attempting to operate a crane when his inexperience with the piece of heavy equipment caused a gruesome scene. The Jap soldier was in the cab playing with the levers to see if he could figure out how the complex gadgets worked. About two dozen of his fellow soldiers were milling around under the boom inspecting their trophy of war. The "driver" in the cab hit the wrong lever, or, as some of Dick's friends would later say, "the right lever," and the bucket of the crane fell into the midst of the group of soldiers. Several Japs were crushed to death instantly.

The Japanese commander on the island was able to establish his authority firmly over the prisoners by employing barbaric methods of mind control and discipline. The troops who guarded the POW's became more and more brutal. One Sunday the Japanese leaders were apparently looking for a reason to levy "severe punishment" upon one of the prisoners to make the others think twice before disobeying any orders. They found their man, and it was none other than Babe Hofmeister.

Babe had left a hole in the roof of one of the storage buildings. Later he had gone back to steal a box of cigarettes. Just as he had closed his hole in the roof and started down a ladder to make his escape he saw that the Japs were waiting for him on the ground. They locked him up and then gave him a rather farcical trial in which he was not allowed to offer a defense. He was found guilty of stealing cigarettes, and the sentence was death by decapitation.

Later in the morning everyone in the hospital knew that something was going on, because several hundred of the Jap soldiers were gathering in the lumber yard and taking seats on the stacks of wood in grandstand fashion. Dick and several of the wounded men were standing outside the hospital building. They knew that something out of the ordinary was happening but had no idea what

it was. Their curiosity would soon be quelled.

A Japanese sergeant came into the hospital compound and immediately ordered everyone who could walk to come to the lumber yard. About fifteen POW's were in the yard and began to comply with the order. Dick was one of the men who immediately began to move toward the piles of wood, now teeming with excited Japanese troops. As the men were hurried along by the guard they sensed a serious, "all business" tone in the soldier's directives.

Slick Sloman was unable to walk outside, so he remained inside the hospital building. He watched as two Japanese soldiers brought Hofmeister around the side of the hospital compound and took him toward the assembly in the lumber yard. They stopped about 100 feet from the hospital building, and Sloman could see enough to know that something was about to happen to Babe.

Holewinski's injuries were still so severe that he could not walk, so he also remained behind in the hospital. He, too, got a funny feeling as he realized that most of the patients from the hospital had been taken out of the compound, apparently to watch some sort of spectacle. Skee could only wait and listen as the commotion across the fence in the lumber piles seemed to intensify.

When the prisoners reached the lumber yard there was a large throng of spectators watching as Hofmeister was being forced to dig a large hole in the coral sand at the center of the yard. When the hole was finished, Babe's hands were tied behind his back and he was ordered to kneel with his head out over the open void. A Japanese officer approached him and unsheathed his Samurai sword.

The executioner positioned himself beside Hofmeister and began to waggle, much like a golfer trying to assume the most comfortable position over a target, with the razor-sharp blade just above the accused's neck. The officer went through several warm-up motions, being sure that his positioning was exactly as he wanted it.

The officer raised the sword one last time and then he brought the blade down with all of his might on the back of Babe Hofmeister's neck. To the horror of the American witnesses, Babe's head was severed cleanly from his trembling body. The coral sand turned red. Dick could not believe what he had seen. The entire event had occurred right in front of him. Could the horror of the moment be real?

Skee was looking out through a window but the crowd of soldiers prevented him from seeing the atrocity. He could only see the blade as it rose into the air and then quickly disappeared from sight. Sloman was not so lucky. As Babe's head parted his body, the entire throng of Japanese soldiers spoke as one voice with a deafening roar of "Bonzai!" The Japanese seemed excited to see American blood. But, more importantly, it is traditional for the Japanese to show their approval of the executioner if he carefully and cleanly carries out his grisly task. This one did, and the response was unmistakable.

Hofmeister's body writhed forward and, as blood spewed

forth from the stump, the thrashing torso seemed to jump into the hole and attempt to rejoin its head. Sand was then thrown on the body until the grave was completely filled. The Japanese had made their point in crystal clear terms. The prisoners made their way back into the hospital, and Skee knew that something horrible had happened because all the men were very quiet and had shocked looks on their faces.

Soon everyone knew what had happened. This ghastly moment would flash into Dick's mind a hundred times over the coming years when he would have the choice of stealing food or starving. The guards suddenly became the objects of great respect, and obedience became the rule. They threatened even the mildest offenses, such as talking with each other at certain times, with "severe punishment," which could range from a simple beating or torture to the ultimate penalty. The prisoners knew now what could happen to them for virtually any offense, and this stress would hang over them at every waking moment for years to come. Babe Hofmeister's fate would be burned into Dick's memory for the rest of his life.

During the next three years, Dick Darden would have to steal many times in order to survive. Each time he reached for the contraband that would prolong his own life, thoughts of the beheading raced vividly through his mind. The Japanese had etched a message clearly into his thought processes that would be indelible for as long as he lived.

Kay and Stevens apparently were not aware of the beheading. To the contrary, Kay's diary implied that the two fugitives were actually losing some of their fear of the enemy. In March Kay wrote, "The Japs almost stepped on us again. I've lost some of the terror I felt of them at first."

Time was drawing short for the two holdouts. According to the journal they were "very weak, and growing more so each day." I "am not sick, but legs are very thin and arms are only half the normal size, and my knees won't control. I just stumble around." Over two months of living in a small hole, inadequate exercise and food, and constant fear were taking their toll on the men.

Food for the two was becoming extremely scarce. On March 9 the men "ate three booby bird's entrails for breakfast—our first hot food in seventy-seven days. Found our first egg last night, but Fred broke it. Fred is impatient and left-handed." The spring season was arriving on Wake, and the two men noted that new flowers were coming on the trees and the booby birds were beginning to lay eggs all around them. Perhaps there would be more to eat.

The nightly foraging for food was becoming more difficult since the two men were in such bad physical condition. "Last night I was so weak and tired I could hardly get back to camp," said Kay. "Now hear voices, and must hug the ground."

The next afternoon, March 10, Scotty made his last entry in the diary. The two men, ragged, filthy, and bearded, discussed their conditions and decided to give themselves up. They were no longer afraid of being shot by the Japanese. "I have no fear of the Japs even if they catch us now, seeing how the other boys have been treated."

Soon after the discussion Kay walked almost into the arms of a POW named Ted Hensel who was working as a carpenter. "You can't be living men," exclaimed a shocked Hensel. "You're already identified as dead and buried."

189

Chapter 38
APRIL, 1942 – BENI KATSUMI

Time wore on, but ever so slowly. Dick Darden continued to heal, finally to the point that he could walk without his crutches. His limp was severe and the leg was stiff, but he could hobble about without assistance. He was greatly relieved, since it seemed at this point that the danger of gangrene and the possibility of losing the leg seemed to be diminishing.

The Japanese continued to have trouble with the American equipment. One of the 3" anti-aircraft guns had jammed in the down, or firing, position. Such guns would recoil when fired, and then two springs, housed in two cylinders that were located on the sides of the barrel, would push the barrel back to its original position. The Japanese wanted to put the guns back into working order to use them for their own defense of the island.

Unable to repair the jammed gun, the Japanese lined the men up in the yard and asked each if he could repair such artillery pieces. When they came to Dick Darden a guard shouted, "Come and fix this gun!" He responded that he could not. When asked why, he insisted that he had just joined the Navy a few months before being captured, and that he had not ever been to artillery school. Further, he insisted, his job in the Navy was to operate a motor launch, and that was all that he could do.

Just a couple of spaces down the line from Dick stood an artillery specialist, who could have easily put the gun back into working order. When the guards questioned him, he pointed to Darden saying that he was also a boat operator, and had no idea how to fix the 3" gun. The guard was irate. He ordered one of his Japanese ordnance specialists to try to repair the gun.

The man walked over to the gun and began tinkering with it. He pushed his hand deep inside the open recoil cylinder and tried to feel the damaged spring mechanism. He apparently put his hand on the hung mechanism and, when he did, the spring came loose, and the gun barrel jumped back into the normal firing position. In the process of returning to its original position the breach instantly flew forward and caught the Jap's arm in the powerful spring cylinder. The heavy barrel mechanism cleanly severed the man's arm just above the elbow, throwing the bloody appendage through the cylinder and over one hundred feet out in front of the gun.

One guard, whose name was Beni Katsumi, was particularly brutal, frequently beating the prisoners. When the beatings would occur, an armed guard was always standing close behind the guard who was delivering the beating. If the prisoner did not stand at attention and take the beating, or if he showed any signs of fighting back, a bullet or bayonet was waiting just a step away, always at the ready.

One day Beni Katsumi, apparently in a depressed or lonely state, ordered Dick to join him and talk. To Dick's great surprise, Katsumi told him that he once lived in eastern North Carolina, less than one hundred miles from Clinton. Indeed, he still had a wife and two children in the "sandhills" part of the state. This meant the area near Pinehurst, probably no more than seventy-five miles from the home Darden longed for so much.

Then Katsumi made another surprising statement. He told

Dick that when the war ended, he planned to move back to North Carolina and settle down. What irony. On this speck of coral in the middle of the largest ocean on earth, two men in opposing armies who were different in every way longed to be in the very same part of North Carolina, USA.

Dick was completely cut off from the events of the outside world. He was not aware that in April of 1942, Col. Jimmy Doolittle had flown deep into the heart of the Japanese homeland, bombing several targets and sending the Nips a message that we, too, were capable of a surprise air raid.

Americans were hungry to know more about the war, and to see and hear what their fighting men were experiencing on the battlefields around the world. There was little good news to tell them, but the stiff resistance of the defenders on Wake Island, and the victory scored over the enemy on December 11, were vivid in the memory of America. Hollywood could wait no longer to place the war on the silver screen. The glimmer of hope offered by the men on Wake Island was the logical place to start. Paramount Pictures seized the opportunity first, starting production on the movie "WAKE ISLAND."

In Late April, 1942, Paramount began filming the movie. An effort was made to authenticate the film's portrayal of the actual events, but several problems made this difficult. One was that no Americans, including those in Hollywood, knew exactly what had happened on Wake. In fact, they did not even know where the remaining defenders were. No communications between Japan and the United States had officially indicated the number of casualties or prisoners taken. Had the valiant garrison defending Wake fought to the death? The film producers did not have all of the answers. Even so, filming began.

The Hollywood film crews ventured to California's Salton Sea trying to find a site which would be similar to Wake Island with its desolate sand dunes. Paramount employed some of the same companies who had taken part in the civilian construction on Wake prior to the war to build sets in the sandy desert. Men who had actually participated in construction projects on the Pacific islands did their best to build sets that were similar to the actual circumstances on Wake. Even though the war effort was consuming virtually all of the explosives and fighting equipment in the country, the military cooperated with the producers by providing materials. Rifles, machine guns, uniforms, and even a few F4F-3 fighter planes and several tons of explosives were made available.

Everyone seemed to realize the potential for putting the story on the screen in 1942. While the names of the actual participants of the battle were changed, there was little doubt as to the identity of several of the characters. Brian Donlevy's portrayal of the mustachioed, all-business Marine major could be none other than Maj. James P. S. Devereux. The get-the-job-done, to-hell-with-the-military-brass chief of the civilian construction force had to be Dan Teters.

Two of the fighting Marines in the trenches were played by Robert Preston and William Bendix. Others in the cast of Hollywood notables included McDonald Carey, Albert Dekker, Walter Abel, and Rod Cameron. The project began in earnest during late spring, 1942.

Chapter 39
MAY, 1942 – THE ASAMA MARU

Early in May, 1942, Ralph Holewinski tried for the first time to walk. Even then movement was extremely difficult because he had been shot in both legs and still had an open wound in the right one. Without skin grafting, a procedure which was impossible under the circumstances, he had to wait until the open wounds healed over. This was very time consuming since the right leg was open to the bone, and the left one was almost as bad.

Dr. Shank had told Skee that he could try to walk whenever he was ready. He was too scared to try at first, but finally decided to give it his best shot. He tried to take the first step, but stopped. It just didn't feel well enough to push it. The next day he tried again, and this time he moved several steps. On the third day he did a little better, and each day he progressed until finally he could move all the way outside to the porch by himself.

As the prisoners entered their fifth month of captivity on Wake, the supply of American food that the Japanese had captured began to dwindle. There was more and more rice in their diets, and the canned American meats were noticeably absent. The men began to worry because they did not like the bland food eaten by the Japanese, not to mention the fact that the smaller Japanese were not given full portions by American standards. Their days of eating American food in reasonable amounts were about to end.

Shortly after Skee began moving around, a Japanese officer came into the hospital and asked, "Can everybody be moved now?" Dr. Shank answered, "Yes." Apparently the Japanese had made plans to move all of the remaining military prisoners in the hospital to mainland Japan.

A few days later, on May 15, 1942, a large Japanese ocean liner appeared just off the island's coral reef. Its name was the ASAMA MARU, and it was one of Japan's finest luxury liners. The big ship was normally used by wealthy Japanese to travel the world in comfort, but with the outbreak of the war it had been conscripted into service by the Imperial Japanese Navy. It was about to carry Dick Darden deeper into the empire of Japan.

The ASAMA MARU had been in Los Angeles in November, 1941. It had been unable to unload its cargo of silk, and the passengers, many of whom had been coming from Japan to the U.S., had been "convinced" not to leave the ship in California. The ship had raised its anchor and sailed down the South American coast and then toward Australia and the south Pacific. By the time the ASAMA MARU reached Wake Island in May, 1942, many of the Japanese citizens on board had been at sea for over seven months.

The ASAMA MARU was the first exchange ship used to bring diplomats, including Ambassador Grew, back to the United States from Japan after the war had started. The prisoners were hoping that they, too, would be allowed to go home since their injuries were severe and they would be unable to fight. They hoped that the Japanese would consider them a liability, but these hopes would soon be dashed.

The men in the hospital on Wake were told to prepare to be transported to Japan, the motherland of the enemy. For the twenty wounded prisoners in the hospital this was a very ominous move. Japan itself would be the last enemy territory to fall when the war was over. It meant that the men would be in captivity for the duration of the war. The men were apprehensive about their futures, as well they should have been. Every inch that they moved toward Japan carried them farther from their own homeland and freedom.

For more than three years to come, this last vestige of the fighting men on Wake Island would be slaves under the thumb of Japanese tyranny, and they would be reminded daily that they were nothing more than the property of the Imperial Japanese war machine. If they were to live through the coming years they would have to put their backs to the wheel of the warring Japanese economy. The word was given for all remaining prisoners to board the ship. There was no choice to be made, no alternative that appeared to be a good one. Preparations began for the men to leave Wake Island.

CHAPTER 40
FROM WAKE ISLAND TO JAPAN

The prisoners were ordered to board the ASAMA MARU. The men gathered their meager possessions and were allowed to pick through the clothing left behind on Wake by the Marines. Not knowing when clothing would be available again, Dick donned a pair of blue Marine slacks with a red stripe down the legs, a khaki Marine shirt, and a lime green civilian sport coat. What would the Japs think of an enemy who dressed like this?

The men were taken by motor launch to the waiting ocean liner. The first thing Spider Webb noticed was that anti-aircraft guns had been mounted on the deck of the luxury liner. The ship was crowded with Japanese civilians who had been picked up from all over the Pacific. When the war started there were Japanese all over the hemisphere, and when a means became available to return to the homeland many jumped at the chance. There were military men and civilians, women and children, families and soldiers, all sorts of people on the ship.

The swimming pool of the ASAMA MARU had been nearly drained, leaving only enough water to fight a small fire. If the ship were to be hit by an American torpedo the passengers would fight fires in a bucket brigade. This was of little consolation to the prisoners, most of whom were to be housed during the voyage on the concrete and tile area immediately around the pool. The sleek new ship got underway, and a fast one she was. The ASAMA MARU was capable of sustaining a brisk twenty-four knots. At that speed she would be in Japan in four days.

One bare light bulb hung from the high ceiling by a single electrical cord over the pool. It produced only a dim light, but this was adequate for the men to be able to see their way around after dark. The men slept with only a thin blanket over the hard tile floor. Spider Webb swore that this was the hardest bed he had ever slept on. He would have to change positions constantly in order to keep his wounds from hurting. The men were not crowded, and there were restroom facilities provided nearby. These were of the oriental type which required the used to squat.

Ralph Holewinski still had open wounds and had to be carried aboard the ship. He was taken directly to the sick quarters, which was a small room elsewhere on the ship. There the guards tried to block his view from the room so that he could not see what was happening outside by placing curtains over his window. When the guards were not looking he would sneak a peak outside and see Japanese men, women, and children who were equally interested in looking in to see him.

As the Japanese travelers peered into the pool area, they got their first look at war prisoners. This made the prisoners more aware than ever of their predicament and made them even more uneasy. They knew that they were 2300 miles west of Pearl Harbor, 600 miles north of the Marshal Islands, and 1800 miles east of Japan. And they knew one other thing. This ship was steaming away from Wake in the wrong direction.

Japanese guards were posted at the pool around the clock. They were armed and there was no doubt that they would use their weapons at the slightest provocation. However, there was no brutality, and compared to the "Hell Ships" on which the Japanese would bring American prisoners from the Philippines, this mode of transportation was relatively comfortable. The men were allowed to come out one at a time to go to the toilet, and a guard accompanied them on each trip. The men were fed once each day with a rice ball which was about the size of a softball. Sometimes they would receive one or two dicons, a bland tasting raddish-like vegetable with green leaves on top.

Soon after the ship had departed from Wake Island, the Japanese officers began to take one prisoner at a time out of the pool area and into a conference room below decks for questioning. The Japanese interrogators spoke excellent English, since nearly all of them had attended college in the United States. The session began with friendly gestures by the soldiers, intended to make the prisoner feel comfortable and possibly give more information.

There was a table in front of Dick with cigarettes, chocolate bars, and Coca-Cola. Dick was offered anything that he wanted on the table. He could drink, eat, or smoke as much as he wanted. Dick didn't smoke, but he had not seen such luxuries as candy or soft drinks since December, nearly five months earlier. The Coke and candy looked awfully good, so he grabbed a handful of candy and began drinking a Coca-Cola. Perhaps this wouldn't be so bad. Dick began to think that his situation might actually improve.

The interrogators began with pleasantries and asked meaningless questions, which Dick answered. They asked about his background, family, religion, and business or vocational trade back home before entering the service. Then they turned the conversation to his military service. They asked his rank, length of time in service, and what ships he had served on. They wanted to know where he had been stationed while in the Navy.

It quickly became apparent that the interrogators were leading to questions that could be damaging to the United States. Dick soon realized that he was dealing with a very skillful, cunning enemy. One slip of the tongue, or one errant reference to a place or weapon that the enemy wanted to know about, and Dick knew he was in for trouble.

Soon the questions became more specific and military in nature. The interrogators were very good at dropping loaded questions which would tell them if the prisoners knew anything they wanted to find out. They were particularly interested in military facilities and installations on Midway and in the Oregon and Washington areas of the northwestern continental United States. Very quickly it became clear to Dick that to fall into their traps would mean big trouble.

Dick pointed out that he had just joined the Navy before being shipped to Pearl Harbor and that he had never been on Midway or in Washington state or Oregon. He tried to convince the officers that all he knew how to do was operate a motor boat. He made himself appear to be too ignorant, so the officers began to use increasingly forceful tactics.

The questioners began to raise their voices as they delivered the questions so that the tension in the room changed noticeably. One of the men took his Samurai sword out of its sheath and laid it on the table in front of Dick, the sharp point at the end of the blade almost touching his stomach. Despite the increasing tension in the air, the young sailor's story remained the same. Seeing that they were getting nowhere, the other interrogator pulled his Japanese luger-style Nambu pistol, cocked it, and laid it on the table, pointing it directly at Dick's midsection. His patience had run out, and he was calling Dick's bluff.

The Japanese began barking questions in a threatening tone of voice. "Tell me about the oil reserves on Midway Island," he demanded. Despite the increasing pressure to cooperate, Dick maintained his ignorance. One of the interrogators began fingering the trigger of the Nambu. He was running his finger around and around the trigger guard. The officer looked Dick in the eye and said, "You know, this pistol has a hair trigger." "I don't doubt that one bit," Dick countered, continuing to maintain that he was just an innocent seaman who drove motor boats.

Finally, after over an hour of harsh interrogation, the officers were convinced that Dick was of no use to them. He was marched back to the swimming pool to join the other prisoners. Apparently some of the men knew information useful to the enemy. One or two of the men who were led into the interrogation room did not return, and were not seen or heard from again by the POW's in the pool area.

The prisoners around the pool were under strict orders not to talk with the Japanese civilians. Holewinski, however, was in the sick bay and did converse with some of the ship's crew. The ship's purser would bring him sweetened condensed milk to put on his rice ball so he could get the bland white mush down.

The purser told Ski that he could not understand why America had started a war with Japan. He had enjoyed working with Americans on the ship before the war and appreciated their "big tips." He had just begun to make good money and suddenly there was Pearl Harbor. He liked Americans and just could not understand why they wanted to fight his people. He had already been thoroughly indoctrinated by the Japanese propaganda he had heard over the ship's radio.

In May of 1942, while Dick Darden was being shipped to Japan as an enemy prisoner, Geddie Herring was graduating from Davidson College. With his diploma in hand he was ready to enter the Navy's officer training program. In his four years at Davidson he had watched the international situation degenerate from a relatively peaceful world in 1938 to global war in 1942. Since America had been plunged into the conflict at Pearl Harbor just five months prior to graduation, the young man from Roseboro correctly anticipated that he would soon be a part of the fight. He was ready and willing to go to the aid of his country. Geddie Herring was about to follow Dick Darden into the dangerous waters of the Pacific.

PART 4—THE WAR YEARS

Chapter 41
IN THE LAND OF THE ENEMY

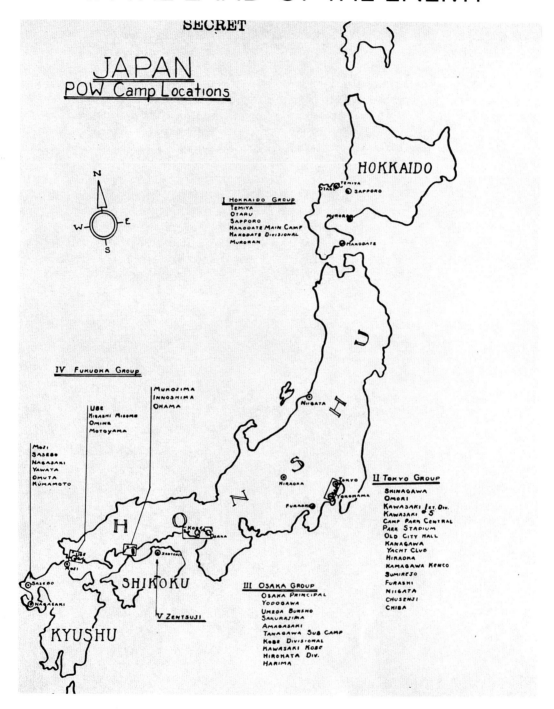

SECRET

JAPAN
POW Camp Locations

N
W E
S

HOKKAIDO

OTARU TEMIYA
SAPPORO

MURORAN

HAKODATE

I HOKKAIDO GROUP
TEMIYA
OTARU
SAPPORO
HAKODATE MAIN CAMP
HAKODATE DIVISIONAL
MURORAN

IV FUKUOKA GROUP

MUROJIMA
INNOSHIMA
OHAMA

UBE
HIGASHI MISOME
OMINE
MOTOYAMA

MOJI
SASEBO
NAGASAKI
YAWATA
OMUTA
KUMAMOTO

NIIGATA

HIRAOKA

TOKYO
YOKOHAMA

FURASHI

II TOKYO GROUP
SHINAGAWA
OMORI
KAWASAKI 1st. DIV.
KAWASAKI #5
CAMP PARK CENTRAL
PARK STADIUM
OLD CITY HALL
KANAGAWA
YACHT CLUB
HIRAOKA
KAMAGAWA KENCO
SUMIREJO
FURASHI
NIIGATA
CHUSENJI
CHIBA

KOBE
OSAKA

ZENTSUJI

SHIKOKU

V ZENTSUJI

SASEBO

NAGASAKI

KYUSHU

III OSAKA GROUP
OSAKA PRINCIPAL
YODOGAWA
UMEDA BUNSHO
SAKURAJIMA
AMAGASAKI
TANAGAWA SUB CAMP
KOBE DIVISIONAL
KAWASAKI KOBE
HIROHATA DIV.
HARIMA

HONSHU

US Navy

American intelligence map of Japanese prisons holding American POW's.

Late in May of 1942, on the fourth day after leaving Wake Island, the ASAMA MARU docked at the port of Yokohama on the main island of Honshu in Japan. What an uneasy feeling it was for Dick Darden to make port in a country that was in such a violent world war with his countrymen. What possible good could the future bring? How long before friendly forces would come to liberate him? Even if American troops came to liberate the prisoners, Dick wondered what type of battle would be required to defeat the Japanese and he wondered if he would be in the middle of that battle.

The prisoners were taken off the ASAMA MARU and put on a tug boat for the short trip ashore. As the boat began to head for the Yokohama docks, the prisoners were blindfolded. The Jap in charge of the tug began asking the men, "Do you know where you are now?" When the boat reached to dock the men were taken off and went ashore. They were ordered to get onto the back end of open flatbed trucks.

Once everyone was aboard the truck the men were ordered to remove their blindfolds. As they squinted to allow their eyes to adjust to the bright sunlight they could look out into the bay and see the ASAMA MARU. There was no secret about where they had come from or where they were sitting. They realized that the Japanese were simply playing games with the blindfolds, apparently trying to intimidate them.

After the prisoners had been taken off the ASAMA MARU, the luxury liner was sent to pick up American diplomats and their dependents who would be included in an exchange of non-military personnel. The ship would go on to South America, where it would meet an American ship and the exchange would take place.

The prisoners on the dock noticed that there was a large group of civilians on the dock looking at them. Most of the spectators appeared to be Japanese, but amazingly there seemed to be some blond-haired Caucasians mixed into the crowd. The prisoners would later learn that there were several Swedes present that day. All of the people on the docks appeared to be well dressed, and the displaying of the American prisoners began to take on a theatrical atmosphere.

Shortly after the blindfolds were removed the guards searched each man. Spider Webb had forgotten that he still had a Japanese coin in his pocket. While he had been in the hospital with the Japanese on Wake a wounded pilot had given him the coin. He had placed the coin in the inside pocket of the swim suit he was using as underwear. When the Japanese found the coin they were none too happy.

It wasn't long before the men were loaded onto flatbed trucks, which began to move through the streets of Yokohama. There were crowds waiting all along the route, apparently hoping to get a glimpse of a prisoner of war. The men were slowly driven all over the city of Yokohama and shown off as the prize catches of great Japanese victories.

Thousands of Japanese men, women, and children stared at the Americans as the trucks rolled slowly through the streets. For many it was their first look at a Caucasian. Many of the civilians taunted the POW's or shouted "Horeo," the Japanese word for "Prisoner," as the truck crept through the city's crowded streets.

The humiliating experience of being shown off to the Japanese civilians made Dick feel as though he had become the subject of ridicule of an entire people. Many of the Japanese civilians in the throngs that lined the streets jeered or spat at the men on the trucks, while others simply looked on curiously. For hours the men were driven through the streets in a carnival atmosphere, unwittingly becoming part of the Japanese propaganda machine.

Later that afternoon the prisoners were taken to a train station where they were made to stand on a raised wooden platform so that all could see them. Dick was decked out in parts of Marine and Navy uniforms, the lime-green civilian sport coat, and a jungle hat. In just a few minutes a crowd of several thousand Japanese people had gathered to stare at these evil enemies of the Emperor.

Finally a train arrived, and the group of prisoners were ordered to get on board. They were isolated in one car, and the window curtains were drawn tightly so they could only see glimpses of commotion outside. The train got underway, moving out of the congested city and into the open countryside.

About fifteen minutes after the train pulled out of the station it suddenly began to stop. When it had come to a complete halt the names of six of the men were called and they were ordered to follow the guards off the train immediately. Those called were Ralph Holewinski, Spider Webb, Slick Sloman, Berdyne Boyd, Charles Tramposh, and Henry Wilson. A faint glimmer of hope crossed Ski's mind. The men were all badly wounded, so could it be that they being taken to a real hospital? Better still, could it be that they were going to be repatriated, part of a prisoner swap.

The answer to these questions was quickly forthcoming. There were about a dozen guards, several of them nearly six feet tall and quite large by Japanese standards. They grabbed the six Americans, several still showing outward signs of severe wounds, and began to rough them up as they jerked them off the train. Holewinski immediately realized that they were not going to a country club. He had barely progressed to the point that he was gingerly taking a few steps a week. To be roughed up by the guards would be excruciatingly painful and probably would damage some of the tender tissue that had begun to heal.

As the guards grabbed Holewinski, Tramposh came to his defense even though he had wounds of his own. Tramposh had several broken ribs from the wound that had disfigured his lower chest and abdomen. But, he was a big, tough Marine who did not like seeing his friends treated harshly. One of the guards quickly hit him with his rifle butt and got the message across in no uncertain terms: there would be no helping one's buddies today.

Tramposh had a feeling that all the wounded men were going to be shot anyway, so he took a big chance. He remained at Skee's side and pulled up his shirt so that the guards could see several of Skee's wounds, including the draining hole in his back. The guards quickly showed their displeasure at seeing the grotesque flesh, and they allowed Tramposh to assist Skee off the train. Tramposh took Skee's arm and helped him take the painful steps out the door.

The six men were marched to a camp called Ofuna, which turned out to be an interrogation camp of the Japanese Navy. When they arrived they were told by a Japanese warrant officer that they had not yet been reported as prisoners of war. They were still considered to be fighting men, and the Japanese were not going to report them unless they cooperated by answering all questions put to them. In other words, they could be killed and simply disappear.

The interrogators told the six men that the Japanese would not be responsible for the lives of prisoners at Ofuna. They said that they knew the answers to most of the questions that they would pose to the prisoners, and if they were given incorrect answers the prisoners would be punished. It was made clear that the penalty for lying would be severe.

The American prisoners at Ofuna were very surprised at the size of the Japanese guards. The Yanks were accustomed to Japanese men who were much shorter than Caucasians. The guards at Ofuna were specially picked men from the Japanese navy who were unusually large and mean looking. Men with these characteristics were picked in an effort to intimidate the prisoners being interrogated.

When Slick Sloman was taken in to be questioned he was surprised by the perfect English spoken by the Japanese interrogators. They had apparently spent a good bit of time in the United States. They were extremely well-dressed, wearing the finest suits that Sloman had ever seen. He could tell right away that they were very intelligent and well-trained men, and he would really have to be careful when he answered their questions.

When Sloman was first interrogated he was taken into a small room, where he sat by himself for over a half hour. The desk in front of him was covered with maps and papers, which he could easily see. In the center of the desk was a very detailed map of Midway Island. It was apparent that the Japs wanted any information they could get on the tiny American base northwest of Wake.

The Japanese came into the room and began to ask Sloman simple questions. They were cordial at first, and one asked Slick, "What do you think of President Roosevelt?" "He is my commander and chief," answered Sloman, "and a good one at that." "Well, what do the people think of him?" was the next question. "He has been elected three times by the people in free elections, so they must like him," answered Sloman. The Japanese were not amused.

Then came the questions on Midway. Sloman told the interrogators only what he felt they already knew, based on the map in front of him. They would ask him what he knew about Sand Island and Eastern Island, both tiny sand spits at Midway. They knew which unit Sloman was in, and they knew his unit had been stationed on Midway in 1941. He insisted that his unit had been stationed on Sand Island. After a few more questions about Midway they would change the subject, asking about Hollywood movie stars to loosen Sloman up a bit.

The casual conversation was short lived, however, and soon the questions again centered on Midway Island. The Japs continued to question Sloman about Eastern Island. Finally, after many more questions on the subject, Sloman convinced the Japanese that he was just a PFC who had a battle station on Sand Island, and had never been on Eastern Island, which they seemed to be greatly interested in learning about.

The fact was that Slick Sloman had been on Eastern Island on several occasions during his stay on Midway, and he knew a considerable amount about the American presence there. The 300 men in his battalion had been all over the American base at Midway. But, once the Japs started the questioning about Midway by saying, "We know you were on Midway," and he had responded that his unit was on Sand Island, he knew he had to stick with that story. He knew that if he changed his story during the interrogation, the Japanese would have coaxed him into admitting a lie, and he knew how harshly they dealt with liars. He was able to stick to his story until they finished the questioning.

Dick and the other prisoners who had remained on the train outside Yokohama would learn later that their train ride had taken them to Tokyo and on to a port on the Inland Sea of Japan. From there they were taken aboard a barge and ferried to an island in the Inland Sea called Shikoku. There the men were taken by truck to Zentsuji…their first prison camp in Japan.

196

Chapter 42:
ZENTSUJI PRISON

At Zentsuji there were American prisoners from Wake, Guam, China, and all over the Orient, along with prisoners of several other nationalities. There were Englishmen, Australians, and Philippinos. Some even said that a dozen countries were represented in the prison population.

One of the prisoners in Zentsuji was a nineteen year old Englishman named George Williams. Williams was the governor of Butariteri, a tiny speck of land located at the northern end of the Gilbert Islands. Williams had governed these islands by sailboating from island to island. He was known for his prowess at butterfly catching, and perhaps one of his greatest contribution was his collection of the south Pacific insects.

The men were subjected to relatively little brutality from the guards at Zentsuji because most of the prisoners there were officers and the Japanese respected the higher ranking military men. Another reason for the humane treatment at Zentsuji was the fact that the commander of the prison was Major General Mizuhara. He was an old professional, a line officer who seemed to have a great deal of respect for military men of all nationalities. If the prisoners bowed or saluted like professional military men when they came in contact with the General, they seemed to maintain his respect.

However, the one thing that the Japanese guards did seem to enjoy was standing the tall Caucasian prisoners at attention and slapping them hard in the face. The prisoners could see over the fence at Zentsuji into the next compound which consisted of Japanese army barracks. They could watch such slapping exercises being levied upon Jap soldiers by their superiors, so it was not hard to understand why the soldiers passed such treatment on to the prisoners. It seemed to be part of their training to stand erect and be slapped silly.

The six men who had been taken off of the train were not as lucky as those who went to Zentsuji. After they were taken to Ofuna they learned that it was known to be one of the worst prisons in Japan. Ofuna was more dungeon than prison. It was used by the Japanese as an interrogation prison. Holewinski apparently had been singled out to go there because he had been on Johnston, Palmyra, and Wake Islands, and presumably would be able to tell the Japs about the

fortifications on each.

Japanese photo of Dick Darden as POW at Zentsuji prison, summer, 1942.
Darden Collection

Life for Ralph Holewinski in Ofuna quickly became a test of endurance at the hands of the Japanese guards. The menu consisted of a small bowl of very watery soup in the morning. At night there would be a small bowl of rice, about the size of a tea cup, and another bowl of the watery soup. Occasionally there would be a small piece of green onion top in the broth.

The men were placed two to a cell at Ofuna. No talking was allowed between the prisoners at any time. The guards would patrol very quietly outside the cells hoping to catch the men talking so they could punish them. The Japanese believed in exercising the prisoners, so each day they would throw lots of nails into the yards and make the prisoners go out and pick them up.

Many of the prisoners in Ofuna prison were officers. Several naval officers, both British and American, who had survived the sinking of their ships, were brought to Ofuna for interrogation. Among the men there with the Wake Islanders were officers from the USS HOUSTON and the submarine USS POPE. Both of these ships had been sunk.

It would have been very difficult for the six men from Wake Island to survive for long in Ofuna in their physical condition. There were almost no medical supplies or facilities at Ofuna, and Skee was having problems with the bullet he was carrying in his buttock. With no way to kill the pain, and no X-ray equipment to locate the bullet, an American doctor cut into Skee's buttock, where he found and removed the slug. Just over a month after arriving at Ofuna, the six men from Wake Island were taken to Zentsuji.

Skee was very happy when he was moved from Ofuna to Zentsuji. He soon became aware that some of his old buddies from Wake Island were already there. He and Dick lived in the same wooden barracks, but they were in different rooms and were not able to socialize. There was some consolation in knowing that old friends were nearby.

At Zentsuji the men, including Dick and Skee, were served two meals each day. These consisted of a ball of steamed rice about the size of a softball along with some thin soup. Occasionally a small piece of the radish-like vegetable called a dicon was included in the

Darden Collection

Henry G. "Spider" Webb, in official Japanese POW photo, Zentsuji prison, summer 1942. Webb was a native of Oxford, N.C.

thin watery substance. The men were always hungry. Always!!

There were 600 men who were being held prisoners at Zentsuji. While none of the officers was required to work, the entire enlisted population of the camp was made to work at hard labor. By this time Dick was walking without crutches, so he was forced to join the other men in their daily duty as laborers.

The first job that befell the men was working the soil on a small mountain about five miles from the camp. Early each morning the men were marched to the top of the mountain approximately 2000 feet above Zentsuji. They began at the top of the mountain and cleared all of the undergrowth from the soil, roots and all. All of the clearing was done with hand implements, such as rakes, hoes, and shovels.

About 90% of the plants in the undergrowth were azaleas, very similar to the "Formosa" variety that was grown back in North Carolina. Ironically, this very variety of azalea, which was growing wild here in its ancestral Japanese home, was one of the most popular landscape plants back home in Clinton. For over 100 years it had been one of the predominant landscape plants throughout the South, exploding into its magenta coat during the blooming season each spring.

Here in Japan the prisoners were ripping out these undesirable "weeds" to clear the land for a more important purpose, presumably to make tillable land on which the Japanese peasants

could grow food. The azaleas were in full bloom as they were chopped out of the earth and burned in large piles.

The men had to be careful on the mountain because of the scorpions which lived in profusion under the logs, rocks, and undergrowth. As the prisoners tore up the hillside they destroyed the scorpions' homes, a fact that the pesky little critters were none too happy about. One prisoner reportedly had one crawl up his pant leg, which resulted in a rather violent dance on his part to shake the varmint out. When a scorpion was spotted he was killed on the spot.

Every ten to fifteen feet down the mountain the men were ordered to build a wall three or four feet high with the rocks they excavated. After the wall had been built they pulled the remaining topsoil over the area between the walls to a depth of about three inches. These terrace gardens would be leveled and planted, using every available square inch of soil to produce food for the Japanese war effort. The work was slow and difficult, but over a period of weeks the men worked their way down the side of the mountain.

Eva Bell Darden received notification of Dick's imprisonment via a telegram from a Provost Marshall General in the Navy Department which indicated that he was a prisoner in Japan. This was the first word that Eva Bell had received about her son in the six months since the fall of Wake. While earlier preliminary reports indicated that it was thought that Dick was a prisoner, this was the first confirmation.

As horrid as the prospects were of having a son in an enemy prison, at least Eva Bell was relieved that her son was alive. This was the first time that she had been assured that Dick had not been among those Americans who were killed in action during the Japanese

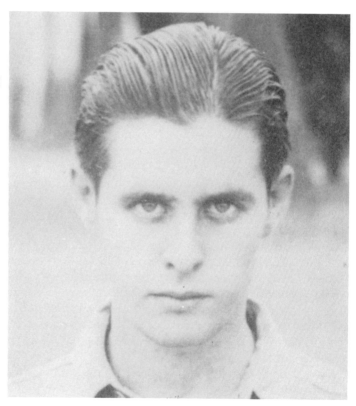

Darden Collection

Wiley "Slick" Sloman in Japanese POW photo, Zentsuji prison, summer, 1942.

invasion of Wake Island. Dick's picture was run in the newspapers under the headline "Jap Prisoner." The caption indicated that he was in Zentsuji Prison.

Dick Darden spent between six and eight weeks at Zentsuji. About the first of July, 1942, he and approximately 150 other POW's were told that they would be moved. By the time Dick left Zentsuji the Japanese had vegetables growing in the newly constructed terrace gardens on the mountain, so the men who were to remain in Zentsuji hoped the daily food rations would increase. Dick was apprehensive about moving to a different prison, but the move would prove to be a stroke of luck that would probably save his life.

Other prisoners would be taken to toil in zinc mines, lead mines, steel foundries, and salt mines. In such work camps there was no chance to steal food, so death by starvation was common. Dick's group was being sent to the waterfront in Osaka to work as stevedores. Holewinski was not among the group, so for a time he would remain in Zentsuji prison.

The treatment that the men received at Zentsuji had been, relatively speaking, pretty good. The captured officers experienced very little brutality from the Japanese guards. Beatings were administered to the enlisted men, but were infrequent. The food, however, left much to be desired for everyone. Feeding continued to come twice daily, once early in the morning before work and then again after the men returned from work at night.

Dick was wearing a worn out Japanese army uniform which would have properly fit the average Japanese soldier who stood about five feet tall. Dick's 6'3" frame could barely be forced into the uniform, with the long sleeves extending just beyond his elbows, and the pants ending just below his knees.

The men were loaded onto trucks at Zentsuji and taken back to the port which was located on the Inland Sea. There they boarded a barge and were transported across to the main island of Honshu. Such barges were commonly used to bring freight into the shallower waters of the Inland Sea from ocean-going ships that had to remain in the deep water ports along the coast, such as Osaka and Yokohama.

Upon reaching Honshu, the men boarded a train for the journey to Osaka. There were a number of POW camps in the Osaka area. Dick Darden, along with about 600 other prisoners, would be housed at the main camp, called Osaka 1 (also called Honshu 1). In this camp there were POW's representing thirteen nationalities.

While Dick was spending the late spring and early summer of 1942 in Zentsuji prison, American forces in the Pacific were taking the first steps toward rebounding from the Pearl Harbor attack and slowing the westward expansion of the Japanese empire. By the middle of 1942 the Imperial Japanese Navy ruled vast expanses of the western Pacific Ocean. In addition, the Japanese empire had swallowed up huge land masses on the Asian mainland, including Burma, Thailand, French Indo-China, Korea, and a large portion of eastern China. The empire reached northward to Attu in the Aleutian Islands, and south to include the Gilbert and Marshall Islands.

The Japanese-dominated lands also included virtually all of the islands north of Australia, thus placing the great island continent down under at great peril. The Solomon Islands, Java, Sumatra, Borneo, and much of New Guinea had fallen to the Japanese. Deep in the center of the Emperor's vast holdings were the Caroline Islands, the Marianas, and the Philippines.

Having been transported to the Japanese homeland itself, Dick and his buddies found themselves deep inside the empire, thousands of miles from friendly forces. The frightful truth was that hundreds of enemy bases and hundreds of thousands of enemy troops were on the many Pacific islands between Dick and the American forces on Midway and Hawaii which might set him free. The situation was depressing, for it was obvious that there would be no quick settlement of the differences between Japan and the United States. The Japanese empire had grown to its greatest geographic size ever, and the enemy appeared to be virtually impregnable in the western Pacific. Dick feared that his stay in Japan would not end soon.

As Dick Darden was being consumed deep inside the belly of the Japanese monster, it seemed that the tentacles of the beast were spreading farther outward than ever. Japan was usurping more foreign lands, crushing any domestic or colonial resistance, and broadening its influence throughout the Pacific. hemisphere. With each expansion of the Empire it became more unlikely that Allied forces would soon be able to liberate the prisoners in Japan. As the monster became more swollen, the likelihood of freedom for Dick became remote. The possibility of a lengthy imprisonment was becoming more likely with each Japanese victory.

Darden Collection

Ralph Holewinski in Japanese POW photo at Zentsuji prison, summer, 1942. His message written to Dick Darden on the photo reads, "Too a wonderful "Buddy", Skee."

As bleak as the outlook had become for Dick, the first American initiatives on the long road toward the defeat of Japan were beginning during the middle of 1942. At about the same time Dick was being shipped from Wake Island to Japan, during early May of 1942, Japanese and American warships fought a naval battle in the Coral Sea, off the northeastern coast of Australia and south of New Guinea and the Solomon Islands. Even though this engagement was nearly 3000 miles south of the Japanese mainland, it would have a profound effect on Dick's future.

Of great importance to the men at Zentsuji was the fact that, for the first time since Pearl Harbor, the Japanese aggression was stopped in the Battle of the Coral Sea. Neither side could claim a clear victory, but Japan had her first bloody nose of the war. There was not yet an American rescue party close on Dick's heels trying to rescue him, but for the first time friendly forces were not in retreat. The tentacles of the monster had been frozen.

In the Battle of the Coral Sea not one ship on either side fired its guns at the enemy. This sea battle marked the first to be conducted between aircraft carriers in the history of the world. Never before had enemy armadas battled without the ships actually seeing each other. For this reason the fight in the Coral Sea was called a "blind battle."

Both sides launched between seventy and one hundred warplanes from mighty aircraft carriers in an effort to destroy the other. Swarms of American planes descended upon the Japanese warships, making the SHOHO the first carrier to be sunk during the war.

The Japanese were attempting to take Port Moresby on the southern coast of New Guinea. This strategic location, less than 300 miles from the northern coast of Australia, would have allowed the Japanese to control the Coral Sea and the waters on the northern and eastern coasts of Australia. It could have been used as a staging area and springboard for an invasion of the Australian continent. The three aircraft carriers in the Japanese task force had their first test against American naval forces. The American carriers LEXINGTON, YORKTOWN, ENTERPRISE, and HORNET met the Japanese challenge.

Although the Japs lost their carrier SHOHO, the Emperor's fliers extracted their revenge on the Americans by sinking the LEXINGTON and damaging several other ships in the American fleet. The Japanese carriers SHOKAKU and ZAIKAKU were damaged so badly that they were forced to head for friendly ports where they could undergo extensive repairs. The ramifications of this would be dramatic a month later at Midway Island, where the absence of these two carriers would seriously affect the Japanese effort during their next scrap with the Americans.

Maj. James R. Brown

"Mt. Fuji Project," by Major James R. Brown. Allied POW's carry soil to make earthen mounds using only primitive hand tools and rail cars, always under the haunting glare of armed guards.

"Enroute to Fuji," by Major James R. Brown. American POW's are being marched to work by strict Japanese guards, one whose rifle has a fixed bayonet, and another brandishing his unsheathed Samurai sword.

After the standoff in the Coral Sea both the United States and Japan licked their wounds and turned their attention toward the next confrontation. Since the fall of Wake Island the American base on Midway Island was the closest Allied base to Japan. If the Japanese could take Midway they could press their empire even farther to the west. They would be within range of the prized Hawaiian Islands, and ultimately California and the mainland United States. Suddenly all eyes in the Pacific focused on tiny Midway Island.

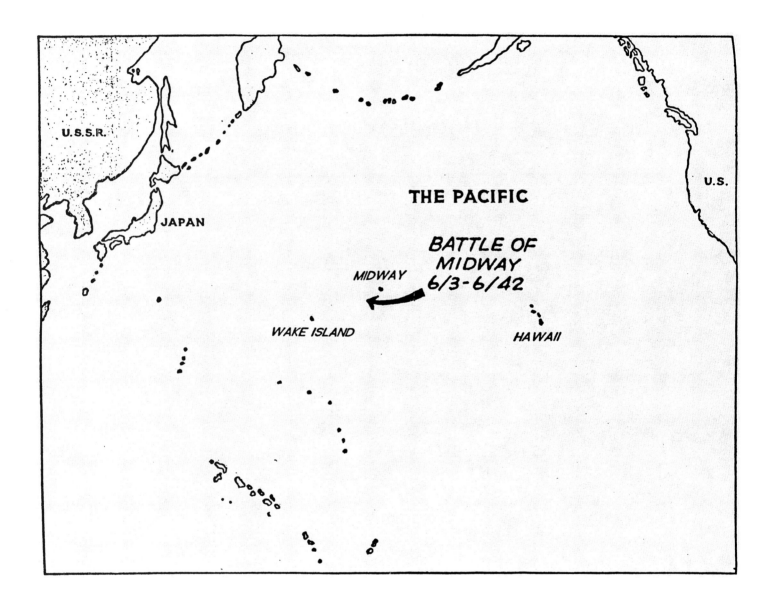

THE PACIFIC

BATTLE OF
MIDWAY
6/3-6/42

MIDWAY

WAKE ISLAND

HAWAII

U.S.S.R.

JAPAN

U.S.

US Army

202

Chapter 43
Midway—The War Turns Toward Japan

A damaged Japanese cruiser after tangling with American pilots at Midway.

The Japanese planners in Tokyo hoped to lure what remained of the U. S. Pacific Fleet into a great sea battle near Midway Island. There they could finish the job they started with the sneak attack at Pearl Harbor. If the Imperial Japanese Navy could wipe out the American fleet and gain superiority over the entire Pacific, the west coast of the United States, including Alaska and the Pacific Northwest, plus the Panama Canal, would be in extreme danger.

The Japanese assembled one of the mightiest armadas in the history of the world for the battle at Midway. No fewer than eight Japanese aircraft carriers would be involved, bringing the maximum number of available Japanese warplanes to over 700. Over 150 Japanese ships, from aircraft carriers and battleships to submarines and transports, would be thrown into this glorious effort to expand the Emperor's realm.

The Japanese strategy called first for an attack on the American base at Dutch Harbor far to the north in the Aleutians. This diversion, it was hoped in Tokyo, would cause the Americans to think that the major Japanese attack was coming from the north. Meanwhile, the Japanese ships, divided into two powerful fleets, would approach Midway Island. Carrier planes would neutralize Midway's coastal defense positions, and then 5000 amphibious troops would storm the island.

The trap was set, and Tokyo hoped that the American Pacific fleet would take the fatal step of committing itself fully in the defense of Midway. The Japs wanted to annihilate the fleet and remove the last naval opposition to their conquest of the entire Pacific Ocean.

With Pearl Harbor still less than six months past, American forces had not been able to replace the ships lost on December 7, 1941. The American position since that action had been extremely precarious, since the enemy admittedly had gained the upper hand. When U. S. intelligence became aware that Midway was the next target, nearly all of the remaining warships in the Pacific, including the damaged YORKTOWN from the Coral Sea, were assembled at Pearl Harbor. The stage was set for the American fleet to take the bait at Midway.

On June 3, 1942, both of the enemy fleets were in place. One fleet, carrying the large Japanese occupation force, was approximately 370 miles southwest of Midway, while the huge striking force, with five aircraft carriers, was a mere 260 miles to the northwest. Two smaller American task forces had secretly rendezvoused the day before at a point some 350 miles north northwest of the island. Combined, the American force had only three aircraft carriers—the YORKTOWN, ENTERPRISE, and HORNET. With the Japanese strike force and the American fleet barely 400 miles apart, the stage was set.

Just after 9:00 a.m. on June 3 an American PBY patrol plane sighted the enemy fleet southwest of Midway. By that afternoon American B-17's were bombing the enemy ships. The next morning both sides launched their planes toward the other. From the airfield on Midway, and from aircraft carriers on both sides, fighter planes, torpedo planes, and bombers took to the skies. American planes were seeking out the two Japanese fleets, while the Japanese were bombing both the American fleet and the air base on the island. The battle was intense.

For three days the two sides did everything within their power to wipe out the other. Both sides lost ships and men. The Japanese Navy had not lost a sea battle in 350 years. It was numerically superior in this battle and fully expected to be victorious again. The Americans, on the other hand, knew that their backs would be to the wall if they lost at Midway. The American pilots fought with great courage against overwhelming odds. One American torpedo squadron from the carrier HORNET was wiped out to the very last plane by the faster Japanese fighter planes.

The ships never actually came within sight of each other. Each side battled its enemy in the air. Several Japanese carriers, heavy cruisers, and destroyers were sunk or seriously damaged. Two American ships, the carrier YORKTOWN and the destroyer HAMMANN, were lost. But the tenacity of the men of the U. S. Navy prevailed and the tide of the battle began to turn.

The enemy fleets broke away in retreat after sustaining heavy losses, only to be chased for two days by planes from the ENTERPRISE and HORNET. During these raids four Japanese cruisers and one destroyer were damaged. With the Emperor's fleet in retirement and obscured by bad weather, the battle ended—a decisive victory for the American forces.

For the first time the tentacles of the monster were being pulled back toward the body. Japanese expansion and visions of world conquest ended at Midway. American forces had inflicted a serious blow to the enemy, killing an estimated 4800 men. The tide was turned, and Allied forces were ready to begin the march toward Japan. For the POW's in the Japanese homeland the distance to freedom would begin to shorten with each of the ensuing battles in the Pacific.

It was during June of 1942 at Midway that the United States scored its first clear victory over the Japanese in the Pacific. Dick was completely unaware that American forces had outfoxed Japanese naval forces at Midway, but that event was the beginning of the end for the Empire of Japan. The tide of the war had turned toward the home islands of the Japanese people.

Dick knew that he was being put to hard labor in the heartland of the enemy's home, and that the road to freedom for him and his fellow prisoners would be a long and difficult ordeal. What he did not know was that, at Midway, American forces had taken the first step down that road. Every step of the trail to Japan would be an excruciating one and would be strewn with the bodies of many young American boys. But after the battle of Midway, plans were laid for a great Pacific campaign that would ultimately lead American forces to the shores of the Japanese homeland.

In late June of 1942 U. S. Army bombers from Hawaii staged a daring raid on the Japanese occupation force on Wake Island. Hawaii was 2000 nautical miles from Wake, making a bombing raid risky at best. To complicate matters, the raid was planned to be a night bombing run. The Associated Press wire reports of the raid quoted several participants who gave great credit to the navigators of the bombers. The men who charted the courses of the planes were able to fly over the 2000 miles of black ocean without the benefit of any geographical markers and score a bullseye on the island. Their accuracy was compared to "picking up a handkerchief in the ocean."

Despite overcast weather all the way from Hawaii, the bombers found Wake sparkling under perfectly clear moonlight. One flyer, Col. Art Meeham, described the approach to Wake by saying, "When we came over the island it was the most beautiful sight I ever saw." The bombers hit all of their targets, setting the main buildings on fire as they "leveled everything on the surface." Col. Meeham, a former quarterback at West Point, was further quoted as saying that the raid had "crippled this Japanese stepping stone in the Pacific," indicating that the ability of the Japanese to use Wake's air facility for any air strikes toward the east had, at least temporarily, been reduced.

The raid was a complete success. In addition to the great damage done to the Japs, there were no American casualties and only one plane received minor damage from fragments of an anti-aircraft shell that exploded a bit too close. Three Jap planes tried to get airborne to challenge the bombers. One never made it off the ground, and only one of the other two even approached the American planes. The lone Japanese plane tailed the formation of bombers for some time but decided not to engage them.

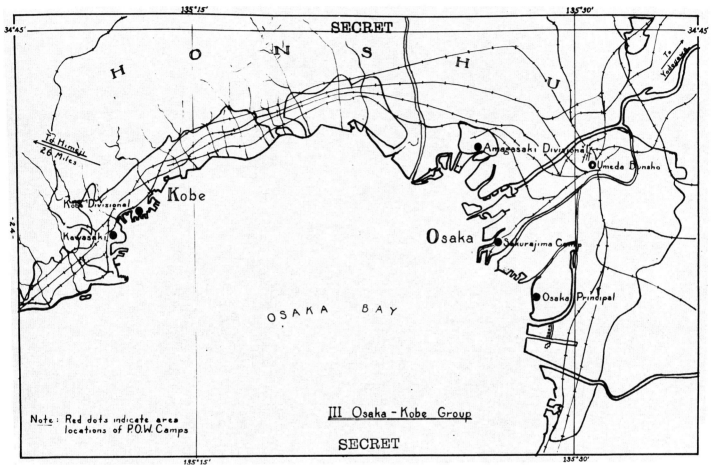

American intelligence map of POW camps in Osaka. Dick Darden was in "Osaka 1," also called "Osaka Principal," camp near the waterfront.

Chapter 44

Osaka 1—1942

Osaka 1 was a relatively small prison compound. It was also known as Osaka Principal because it was the location of the offices of the Commander of all POW camps in the area, Colonel Akami. It was rumored that Col. Akami had been serving with his troops during the invasion of China, but had gone mad during a battle and had been returned to the homeland for the less stressful assignment of guarding prisoners. He was particularly brutal in his treatment of the men and was executed after the war for his atrocities. The Colonel controlled more than 10,000 POW's in the Osaka group of camps.

Dick Darden would spend almost three years in Osaka, from July of 1942 until he was moved in June of 1945. He would survive this hellish three years at hard slave labor only by stealing

US Army - Institute of Pathology

A dormitory at Nihama Prison, sleeping shelves similar to Osaka 1.

daily and risking severe punishment or execution in order to get enough food to sustain life. For the most part he would do stevedore work in and around Osaka, unloading ships and barges of every imaginable type of cargo. The hard labor and scant diet would cause nearly 100 pounds to drop from his lanky 6'3" frame.

Osaka was a very large city to Dick, especially since he came from a small southern country town. Clinton had a population of less than four thousand, while Osaka was overflowing with more than five million inhabitants. The prisoners were made to work in a variety of locations, including lumber yards, junk yards, iron foundries, steel mills, cement factories, warehouses, docks, barges, sampans, and ships. Most of the work, however, was stevedoring on the waterfront, a job that most of the men liked best because the opportunity to steal food was frequent.

The bunks used for sleeping in the barracks were made of rough cut lumber and were stacked in threes. These "shelves" were nothing more than rough board slats covered with a thin straw mat. The mat provided only a small degree of comfort for the weary bodies on the hard boards. Personal belongings went on a narrow wooden ledge on the wall just behind the sleeping shelves.

The men at Osaka 1 were housed in eight crowded wooden buildings, each approximately 18' wide and 33' long. The camp was surrounded by a tall wooden fence. Each building housed about 75 prisoners. Water was provided by outside spigots at wooden wash tables.

Down at the docks where the prisoners toiled on the ships and barges the work conditions were filthy at best. The barges were huge, measuring from 100 feet to 200 feet in length, and often in excess of 50 feet wide. They typically carried 300 to 500 tons of cargo. Each barge was captained by a man who lived in a small wooden cabin or box, which was located below the deck of the barge and somewhere near the stern.

In the one-room cubicle on the barge there might also live several additional people if the captain was married, including his wife and children, and sometimes several in-laws as well. It was estimated that one million people lived on the barges in the bay between Osaka and Kobe. This made the barges floating slums and the bay a huge receptacle for wastes and sewage.

The problem of cleanliness on the barges was compounded by some of the customs and habits of the Japanese civilians, which seemed very crude to Dick in comparison to his Anglo-Saxon upbringing. The men were always on the lookout for one particular Japanese custom when working barges. There were no toilet facilities on board the barges for sanitation, so when one of the family members felt the "call of nature" he would simply hang his naked posterior over the side railing and let fly. Osaka harbor was

US Army - Institute of Pathology
A POW carries cargo in typical Japanese fashion.

literally a cesspool for multitudes of people. Only rarely would a warning cry be issued to whomever might by working on the docks below.

One day Dick was working at the waterfront and the tide was in, thus causing the barges to rise high above the cement docks. A Japanese woman approached the rail above Dick. She was bare chested, as was the custom of the women who lived on the barges. Some one yelled "lookout" as she threw up her skirt and revealed her bare bottom hanging directly above Dick's work station.

Dick and his mates bolted for cover just in time. It was not uncommon for the boat people to have diarrhea, and this woman had a fine case indeed. As the POW's sprinted out of the way she sprayed the entire area. Dick learned to always be acutely aware of everything that was going on around him.

Daily life was predictably grueling for the prisoners. The Japanese told them when to get up, what they would eat, where they were going to work, how long they would work, and everything else about the daily routine. The Japanese had them completely under their control, while providing the men with only a few of the necessities of life.

The 600 men were forced to rise early in the morning and be in line by six o'clock. Japanese companies, such as Mitsubishi and Sumitomo, would send representatives to the prison to buy POW labor from the military (guards). They would usually ask for three to fifty men to use that day. With each ten prisoners there had to be one armed soldier and one civilian guard supplied by the company.

The company men were truly unpredictable, some being passive and reasonable while others were vicious, stick-wielding thugs. Some company men liked to show off for the women on the docks by slapping or fisting the prisoners, or by smashing them with their bamboo sticks. The military guards never did anything to help the POW's during such abuse. Some of the local workers and honchos, however, were more humane and would even converse with the prisoners.

The entire compound at Osaka 1 prison was probably less than one acre. The wooden wall around the camp had barbed wire on top and there was a guard house at the front gate which housed about a dozen Japanese guards. The guards were regular army, and were assigned guard duty on a rotating basis, usually drawing the assignment for one to two weeks. The rough treatment, beatings, and brutality the prisoners received usually depended upon the nature of the guards on duty. Some of the guards were reasonably humane, while others made an effort to be particularly brutal. The prisoners never knew what sort of detail would arrive next.

There were two rows of barracks, the front row having four buildings, and the second row having five. The center building in the second row was a storage building, which contained food and supplies the Japanese had for the POW's. Directly behind the dormitories was a latrine building. It was essentially a covering for an open pit which had a vile odor and was swarming with flies.

Beside the latrine was a platform which had several spigots for washing up and cleaning clothes. Beside the platform was was a small wooden kitchen. Directly in front of the kitchen was an alleyway which contained a boiler. There was also a bath house, which had the only tub that was available to the 600 men for bathing. The tub was made of 2" x 12" wooden boards, and measured 4' square and 3' deep.

On weekends the prisoners would have bath night, and as many as two hundred men would line up to bathe in the large wooden tub. This was their only opportunity to get hot water, which went through a coil of metal tubing in the boiler to be heated and then to the wash house. The sick men were bathed first. On the rare occasions that the men were able to find space in the tub, the water was well used, usually having scum an inch deep on top.

Each day brought work, work, and more work. The prisoners would load or unload ships, load or unload barges, load or unload train cars, or work in lumber yards day after day after day. They never knew what cargo they would be moving until they arrived at the site. Foodstuffs were always the favorite cargo. They loaded and unloaded shipments of peanuts, soybeans, rice, corn, dried bananas, powdered milk, and sugar. Sometimes the cargo was tin cans. Those which especially excited the men were canned tangerines or pineapples.

The men would begin before daybreak in the morning and work until after dark in the evenings. They would be given one or two days off each month, thus working twenty-eight or twenty-nine days out of each thirty. The days off usually came on Sundays.

All types of inedible materials also came into Osaka on the ships and were off-loaded by the POW's. Metal cargo came in many different forms, some of it processed but much in the form of scrap metal. This including lamp posts ripped from the streets of cities all over Asia where the Japanese had conquered and raped the land. The metal was melted down and forged into war materials by the Japanese.

Several ships came into port loaded with money in the form of coins. Metal coins of all types, including copper, aluminum, and alloys, had been stolen from the conquered lands of "liberated" Asian countries and were brought to Japan to feed the war machine. Sometimes the holds of the ships were full of straw sacks filled with coins and weighing between 100 to 200 pounds. The men had to lift the sacks onto their backs and walk them ashore. It was common for the heavy bags to tear and for money to spill all over the floor. Sometimes the men worked in money that was ankle deep. The Japanese would bring in groups of old women to re-bag the money.

In August of 1942 the movie WAKE ISLAND was released in the United States. The movie's first audience was made up of Marines at their base in Quantico, Virginia. Predictably, it got a resounding response. As the movie was shown around the country it undoubtedly helped the United States to arouse the young men who were needed to fight the war. The movie became very popular and was nominated for several Oscars.

w   Late in August an encouraging message was forwarded to Eva Bell Darden in Clinton about her son in Japan. The Japanese were apparently looking for any propaganda which might divert the world's attention from their ruthless invasions all over the Pacific and shed a positive light on their treatment of prisoners. About once a month they would ask the POW's to write a message, exactly fifty or one hundred words, to be sent to parents or relatives back home.

The Japanese censors would study the letters closely, and they would select several to be sent to the families in the United States. They would then pick those letters which they felt served their purposes best and release them. If a message was picked for transmittal the prisoner who authored it was instructed to provide one hundred copies in his own handwriting.

Occasionally the Japanese would allow the POW's messages to be read on a broadcast via shortwave radio. On August 27 the SAMPSON NEWS reported that Eva Bell had received such a message. On August 17 a short wave message from Japan had been intercepted on the west coast and forwarded to the Navy Department. The office of the Provost Marshal General in turn contacted Eva Bell. Even though the message was very short and nothing specific was discussed, it did allow the first indirect contact between Dick and his mother concerning his whereabouts and physical condition.

The text of the message was the following:
"Dear Mother,

I am held in a Japanese prison camp in southern Japan. I am in good health, and hope that you and the rest of the family are the same. Please try and not worry. If you need anything I have or have coming be sure and use it.

J. B. Darden
Seaman 1C" U. S. Navy

The message was exactly fifty words in length. The War Department indicated that it could not verify the contents of the message, nor could it assume that Dick was not under duress when he provided the message. Eva Bell was assured that any further news concerning Dick would be forwarded to her at once.

In addition to the information that came from the War Department, Eva Bell received two post cards from citizens in California. Mrs. R. Washburn, of Washington Park, and Mrs. R. L. West, of Long Beach, each monitored the broadcast from Japan and sent the text of the message, as best they could transcribe it, to her, hoping that the fragments of the message would be of some comfort.

One morning Dick and his labor crew were working on the docks in Osaka unloading cargo from a ship for the Sumitomo Company. Materials were being off-loaded from the ship with a huge boom that was mounted on a tall pole, similar to a telephone pole. The huge wooden pole was anchored deeply into the cement of the dock, and rose several stories above the ships moored nearby.

The long boom mounted on the pole would swing out over the ships, and a winch would be used to raise cargo from deep in the holds of the ships. This mechanism offered one of the few instances in which the men were spared the many trips walking back and forth from the hold of the ship to the dock with heavy materials on their backs, usually over narrow rickety wooden gangways.

Dick was awaiting his turn on the dock to lift the heavy cargo onto his back and carry it into a warehouse. A rope hung from the boom and mounted on it were eighteen metal hooks, on each one of which hung a one hundred kilo (220 pound) bag of rice. As the boom swung toward the docks with nearly a ton of rice dangling from the rope, Dick looked up to see the boom directly above him.

Suddenly there was a loud "crack" caused by the snapping of the metal cables that supported the boom. The bags of rice, along with the rope and metal hooks, came crashing down onto the dock. In the split second that it took him to glance upward Dick instinctively lunged backward. As he did a large piece of the wooden boom smashed down onto the cement just in front of him, raking across his forehead as it passed his head. He was spun wildly by the blow and knocked unconscious.

The jagged piece of wood dug deeply into Dick's forehead, shearing out flesh as it went. Had he not lunged backward immediately upon hearing the boom snap, the piece of wood would surely have caught him squarely in the head, probably smashing his skull and killing him instantly. Dick had again averted death by the narrowest of margins.

The Japanese guards had little sympathy for injured men. Less than an hour later Dick was revived, and they put him back to work carrying the 220 pound sacks of rice on his back. Blood still oozed from the grooves across his face. Still groggy and listless, he stumbled along under the heavy weight in a semi-conscious state.

Dick bore scars on his forehead for years as evidence of this mishap. However, the greatest pain to befall him was the continued incarceration at hard labor. Perhaps worse than the daily drudgery of laboring in the filth of Osaka was knowing that his current conditions were likely to continue for a considerable period of time. Dick prepared himself mentally for a long stay, knowing that his endurance would be tested during the months to come.

American forces elsewhere in the world were not sitting idly by during August of 1942. It was clear to the Navy, Marine, and Army strategists that Japan had intended to push its empire farther south, perhaps to Australia and New Zealand. This was evident because transport ships had been in the Jap fleet which was stopped in the Coral Sea. They had planned to land and capture more territory on the islands near Australia, or perhaps on the subcontinent itself.

It was decided that American forces would begin a campaign at the bottom of a long chain of Pacific islands, most held and fortified by the Japanese. The ultimate objective was to reach the Japanese homeland, driving to the heart of the evil monster and killing it. At the bottom of this long succession of islands, nearly 2800 miles from Japan itself, was an island called Guadalcanal.

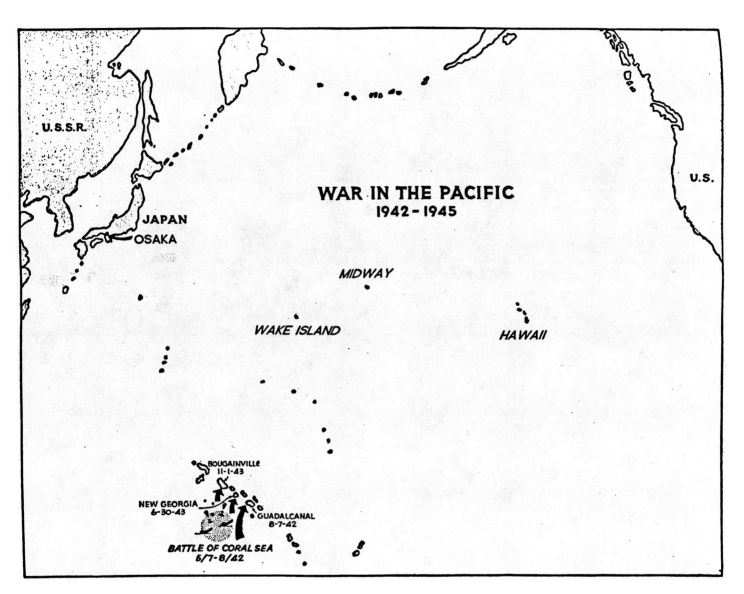

U.S. Army -Modified

Chapter 45

Guadalcanal

Guadalcanal is a large island in the South Pacific, one of the Solomon Island group located about 1000 miles northeast of Australia. It measures eighty miles long and thirty miles wide. The Marines who landed there in August of 1942 had to ask themselves a number of troubling questions. Would they be able to engage and defeat an enemy on his home turf in the hellish filth and disease-ridden conditions of these South Pacific jungles? Would the Americans be able to overcome the Japanese warriors, who had been portrayed as tough, vicious soldiers? The Emperor's men were said to be crazed by the Samurai traditions of victory at all costs. Were these crack units of the Japanese army invincible?

If the assault on Guadalcanal had failed, there might not have been an island-hopping march to Japan. Much had to be proven by American fighting men. Since the Japanese success at Pearl Harbor, many Americans were skeptical about the ability of Allied forces to beat the Japanese in the Pacific. This had to be done while American boys were also needed in the European theater, where the Germans were nearer to the American homeland and thought by many to be a greater threat than the Japanese. Even though the strength of America's military had been spread thinly around the world in two great theaters of war, the attack upon the Japanese began during the summer of 1942.

On August 7 units of the First Marine Division made simultaneous landings on Guadalcanal, and across the Sealark Channel on the islands of Tulagi, Gavutu, and Tanambogo. This marked the first offensive action by American troops against the Japanese in the war. Fighting became bitter on all fronts. The enemy had many miles of well-fortified defensive lines. On Guadalcanal itself the Marines landed near Lunga Point, with their objective being the airbase at Henderson Field.

The two opposing sides each received an education at Guadalcanal. The Americans learned many of the tactics and much of the determination of this new enemy. Many young American boys spilled their blood learning that the Japanese soldier was, indeed, a formidable opponent. Respect for, and an understanding of, this oriental enemy reached a new high.

The American troops in the Pacific also learned that they could be victorious over the best Japanese troops. They learned that the Japanese soldier would fight to the death for his Emperor, even when the odds were heavily stacked against him and when his positions were meaningless. Small Japanese units would stage frontal assaults against much larger American forces in actions certain to be suicidal.

The Marines on Guadalcanal did not always understand such unusual tactics, but they began to understand their enemy more than before. For over four months the two adversaries fought in the jungles and on the beaches. Finally the Japanese were beaten and Guadalcanal was taken. Australia and New Zealand had been saved from the enemy. American fighting men had proven themselves against the Japanese.

New tactics were developed that would enable our forces to be successful against this enemy in the future. Despite the courage of the Japanese soldier, Americans had begun the march toward Japan and would not be turned back short of total victory. Many a Jap-infested island lay between Guadalcanal and Osaka, and these islands would be covered with the blood of men from both sides in the three long years that were yet to come. Dick Darden was still thousands of miles from friendly forces, but after Guadalcanal, though he did not know it, help was on the way.

Dick began to draw a variety of work assignments in the dock area of Osaka. Occasionally he would be assigned to work in an Army lumber yard. It covered a huge area, having four sides that measured over a mile each in length. Prison labor was used to unload the rough-cut wood from barges and move it into the lumber yard. Then the men would have to move it from place to place within the yard. All of the rough, splintery materials had to be moved on the backs of the laborers.

The most common type of wood in the lumber yard was the type that the Japanese used for weatherboarding on the sides of their houses. These boards were thin, less than one inch thick, and measured 6" wide and up to 20' long. Each man was required to be loaded with ten or twelve of these long, rough, heavy boards on his back. When a man positioned such a load on his shoulder the flexing boards would nearly touch the ground in his front and rear.

In order to carry the heavy load of wood without having his shoulder chewed to pieces by the rough cut boards, each man had to develop a rhythm or method of walking which worked in cadence with the motion of the wood. As a man walked across the yard, the wood would bow down almost to the ground and then flex back up into a straight position.

To get out of step with the flexing wood usually resulted in the front end grinding into the ground, jolting the carrier and scraping hard on the skin of his shoulder. Dick quickly learned the dance of the timbers, which allowed him to work in harmony with his heavy loads.

If no wood came in on the barges or railroad cars on a day when the prison laborers were working at the lumber yard, the guards made the men move lumber anyway. The men would be forced to carry the heavy loads from one corner of the yard to the opposite corner, often a walk of nearly a mile, just to keep busy. The men were ordered to take wood from one stack, make the meaningless walk to the far side of the yard, and then restack the wood there. For twelve long hours a day the men toiled under their heavy burdens, carrying the lumber across the huge yard.

There was tall grass growing in much of the lumber yard, and sometimes the men would find long green grass snakes slithering between the stacks of lumber. If the Japanese guards saw the snake first they would kill it and hold it up yelling "Horeo, horeo," indicating "Prisoner, prisoner." The POW's would gladly come over and get the snake. These snakes in the lumber yard provided the men with a few rare opportunities to add meat to their diets. The protein-starved prisoners were glad to see the dangling reptiles.

Since the underfed men suffered from the pangs of continual hunger, those days when Dick and the other prisoners found a big juicy snake in the lumber yard were lucky days indeed. The men were always on the lookout for the green grass snakes, especially in the tall grass in out of the way parts of the lumber yard where they might be hiding. Some of these snakes were five or six feet long.

The prisoners would take the captured reptiles over to the cook, who was busy boiling water over an open fire. He would skin and clean the snake, gutting it and cutting it into 6" plugs. These snake plugs would be dropped into the boiling water, without the benefit of salt or other seasonings. They would be cooked until the meat could be sucked off the backbone.

To starving men at hard labor, the boiled snake plugs weren't bad. Dick would remember that, "It tasted a lot like chicken necks." The Japanese guards were amused to watch the commotion over the snakes, and sometimes killed snakes for the men just to watch them devour the remains. Before this ordeal in Japan was over the men would eat many new foods, including crow, dog, and cat, in order to survive.

One prisoner, usually the sickest man on the detail, was allowed to build a fire and boil water for the men to drink. Since human wastes were used for fertilizer all along the creeks from which the men drank, the water was not fit for human consumption without being boiled.

Ralph Holewinski had such an assignment with his work crew. Skee was being held at another camp in the Osaka area known as Umeda Bunsho. He still ad an open wound from his injuries on Wake Island, and he was still having drainage from the wounds over two years after receiving them. For this reason he frequently drew the relatively easy assignment of cook.

Holewinski was able to handle the physical tasks of cooking without major problems. Normally the duties of the water man included building a fire, boiling the water, and occasionally cooking food that the men brought back from the job. Sometimes other problems associated with this job were harder to deal with. For instance, he had to be especially careful when ladeling out the rice for the men, for they always watched him carefully to be sure that he gave them a full, or at least equal, serving.

The starving men knew that only a certain amount of food was available and Skee could only give them a certain amount. But they were so hungry that sometimes they actually counted the grains of rice in their pan. One of the easiest ways to start a violent argument was to cut a starving man short on his food ration. More than once fights erupted among the hungry men over a few meager grains of rice or morsels of food.

There was a Japanese officer's camp a short distance up the dirt road outside the front gate of Osaka 1. There the officers were fed fish which arrived in their camp in five gallon buckets. Occasionally there was more than the men would want to eat, and some of the fish would be left in the buckets until they spoiled. When this happened the old fish would be sent down the road to Osaka 1 prison. This would often be the only source of meat in the diet of the prisoners.

Sometimes when the buckets of rotting fish arrived in camp Dick could see that they were in a watery solution with an inch of maggots floating on top. The cooks at Osaka 1 would pour this in the dicon soup and many of the men considered it one of the best meals that

they received since there was actually a small amount of meat in the rancid slurry. The fishy, watery mess was cooked until there was no meat visible. The only evidence of meat or fish in the brew was the strong odor. Some of the men ate the maggots that floated on top, glad to get the protein and insisting that they had been cooked to the point that they were no longer filthy.

The fish soup was the only food that Dick received that he could not eat. The smell was so nauseating that he simply could not hold it down. One prisoner, however, was different. He was a Pharmacist's Mate named Squeegee Harrod. Squeegee went to great lengths to get the basic nutrients that he knew his body needed. His training had given him a good idea about the basic nutrients needed in order to stay reasonably healthy.

Squeegee would get fish heads out of the fish soup, boil them and eat them by sucking any remaining meat out of the heads. Even though it may have been a revolting practice to many, Squeegee knew that the proteins and oils in the fish heads would keep him alive. He was always on the lookout for a snake or any green vegetable that he could find. As hungry as the prisoners were, most stopped a bit short of Squeegee's health food cuisine. He was one of the few, however, who remained "in the pink of condition" throughout his stay in Osaka.

Several of Dick Darden's fellow prisoners at Osaka became close friends and helped him endure his bleak existence. Dick slept on the end of the top shelf near a window in the end of the barracks building. His bunkmates on the top shelf were a New Zealander named Jim Muller, and James C. (Jimmy) Muldrow of Florence, South Carolina. On the top shelf across the narrow aisle on the other wall of the building were Walter J. Cook, from Crisfield, Maryland, Squeegee Harrod, and Odie O'Neal. Cook had been with Darden on Wake Island, and would be with him in Osaka 1 for the entire three years he was imprisoned there.

Another friend was Jack Leaming. Leaming had been a radio-man on a dive bomber. His plane had been on a raid in the Marshall Islands when the pilot became lost. They could not find their way back home, nor could they break radio silence to ask for help. The pilot had flown around looking for a familiar landmark in the many islands below until he ran out of fuel. They decided to pick an island that appeared to be the least inhabited and ditch the plane there. As soon as they hit the water, it seemed that Jap boats converged from all directions, and they were taken prisoner.

Dick became a good friend of the New Zealander, Jim Muller. Muller bunked next to Dick and often at night the men would lie on their top shelf and talk of home. The New Zealander was amazed by even the commonplace occurrences that he heard from the Americans about life back home. He simply would not believe that in America a family could drive 100 miles in one day in their automobile.

Apparently there were few cars in New Zealand, and most family outings were taken by bicycle. In fact, a long trip for the New Zealander's family would be the fifteen mile bike ride to a nearby state park. They would pedal there one day, spend the night, and pedal back the next. So, when Dick told of his family riding sixty miles to Raleigh AND BACK in the same day, a total of 120 miles, the fellow could simply not grasp the idea.

Another good friend of Dick's was Mack Williams. Williams slept near Dick, and often was heard running to the latrine in the middle of the night with diarrhea. It seemed that most of the men who worked the barges by day had to supplement their diets with loose soy beans that they found rolling around on the filthy floors inside the barges. The nasty beans were as hard as a rock, but an invaluable source of protein which helped to keep some of the men alive.

The men would pick them up and hold them in their mouths until the warmth and saliva softened them enough to be chewed. Eventually the soybeans would become palatable and the men could swallow them. Williams, like the other prisoners, ate the beans every time he worked a ship where they could be found.

It seemed that Williams, unlike most of the men, had a gastric reaction to raw soybeans. When he ate them they would tear up his bowels, causing him to have the "runs." Every night after he had worked on a soybean ship, he could be heard climbing down from his shelf and sprinting toward the latrine building. Usually he did not make it, and was frequently heard cursing at himself after failing to cover the distance before his time ran out.

Some of the men found Williams' nightly race with nature funny, wondering during the actual event if he would make it to the john. What irritated Williams most was the fact that he was sleeping in his only set of clothes. The POW's worked and slept in the only shirt and pair of pants that they owned. When Williams would foul his clothing he would have to take them off, clean himself as best he could, and then go outside to the only water outlet and wash out his clothes, sometimes in frigid weather. Then, two or three hours later, he would have to put the cold clothes back on and head out on a work detail. Everyone felt sorry for Williams and his soybean reaction.

Jimmy Muldrow, one of Dick's bunkmates, along with another friend named Norman Searls, had been put on the gun crew of an American merchant ship. Such crews were put on transport ships to offer a small degree of protection in case of trouble at sea. The Germans had sent out ships called German raiders, which looked like the combination of a passenger ship with a cargo ship. These ships would fly the flag of a neutral nation, but when allowed to come along side an American ship they could quickly raise hydraulic walls on the sides to expose 6" or 8" guns.

Such a German raider steamed past Muldrow's ship and did just that, sinking their ship before Muldrow and Searles could get off even a single shot. The sinking occurred in the Atlantic and both men were captured. They were then taken around the world on the German ship, their labor to be traded to the Japanese for Indonesian oil.

There were three cooks, all Americans, who prepared the scant rations for the 600 men. Except when the buckets of rancid fish came into camp, the cooks usually prepared five-gallon buckets of weak soup for the evening meal to supplement the rice balls. Sometimes a five-gallon bucket of dicon soup would be made to serve seventy-five men in one of the barracks.

Malnutrition caused a variety of ailments in the prison population. Boils, carbuncles, night blindness, scurvy, and "electric foot" were but a few. The men knew that certain foods, if they could be stolen, would help tremendously in alleviating medical problems. Among these were fish oil, fresh fish, onions, garlic, fresh greens, any citrus fruits, and any vegetables.

Dicon soup was simple to make. Two buckets of the leafy, turnip-like dicon tops would be chopped up into five gallons of water and heated over a fire to become what was called soup. It was actually just warm water with an occasional speck of green leaf floating in it after it had been split seventy-five ways. The "soup" had virtually no nutritional value at all. The prisoners' diet was far from adequate, both in quantity and quality, and left the men in a chronic state of hunger and starvation.

The lack of vitamins and oils in the bland food would cause the skin at the arm pits, navel, and groin to become painfully raw. Teeth became loose due to the lack of vitamin C. If one can of citrus fruit could be stolen and eaten the skin and gums would improve dramatically. The rawness would clear up and the bleeding of the gums would stop for two or three weeks.

The men were faced with two choices: They could die of starvation, or they could risk death at the hands of the Japanese guards if they were caught stealing food. The best choice seemed to be to steal food and hope that you didn't get caught. Some of the prisoners became master thieves, devising brilliant methods for stealing food and returning it to camp.

Some work details in the warehouses provided opportunities to steal various types of food. The thefts were usually group activities, since guards were posted and there was a much better chance of success if someone could create a diversion for the guards. More than one prisoner got a bloody nose fighting with a fellow POW at one end of a warehouse while another POW was stealing food for him at the other end. Some of the men became masters at faking fights. They would appear to be killing each other, knowing all the while that they were earning a morsel of food or a can of tangerines.

Life for Dick was becoming bleaker as time passed. Everything was in short supply and virtually all of life's basic necessities, not just food, had to be stolen. Towels were very difficult to get and brought a high price when bartered. The men were wearing rag-tag clothes and took whatever they could get their hands on to cover their withering bodies. This presented an obvious problem. If a prisoner stole clothing and wore it, the guards would see the contraband articles. If they asked where the clothes came from, a good answer had to be forthcoming.

The prisoners came up with ingenious methods for masking the true origins of stolen clothing. A POW from New Zealand who had been captured in the Gilbert Islands received a package from home which contained several white dress shirts. The men took the labels out of the shirts and sewed them into stolen clothing, mostly warm wool sweaters that were stolen from the belongings of citizens being shipped out of the cities.

When the Japanese guards asked the origin of the new clothes, it was easy to convince them that they were from abroad by showing them the non-Japanese labels. Towel labels were also used to camouflage stolen clothes. The Japs must have felt that the Cannon Company made a pretty good copy of a Japanese sweater, since many of the sweaters worn by the POW's bore that label.

Dick was able to steal some cloth while aboard a ship one day. He devised a way of tying the cloth into a G-string which he wore between his legs in the crotch of his pants. Occasionally Dick would be able to steal a can of food from broken boxes in the warehouses and he would hide it in the G-string until he could eat it later that evening. The baggy pants and shirt tails worn outside would cover any tell-tale bulges, and he could hide stolen food for the trip back into camp at night.

The only place that the guards were not constantly watching the men was in the open latrine. The men ate all kinds of stolen food with their hands while sitting over the foul-smelling dung pots, glad to eat the sparse nourishment even in such acrid conditions.

If a private moment could be found during the work day on the docks, Dick would wolf down stolen food on the spot. If evidence of such thefts were found by the guards, there would be severe

Umeda docks, not at Osaka 1 camp, but on the waterfront nearby.

punishment for all of the men, so wrappers or cans had to be disposed of without a trace. If Dick ate the contents of a can, he would cut out both the top and bottom, and then crush the can and lids flat. Then he would tighten up the rope which served as a belt for the baggy, crumpled pants he was wearing and slip the flattened can into the waistline under the rope.

On his next trip across the rickety board, which spanned the distance from the dock to the ship's deck, Dick would eye the guards carefully to be sure that none was watching him. Then, as he walked across the board over the water, he would suck in his belly and allow the can to drop down his pants leg and into the bay. The evidence was gone forever to the bottom of Osaka harbor.

Back in Clinton, Dick's mother was frantically trying to get more information about her imprisoned son. She tried every avenue imaginable to get through to him. With the help of Howard Hubbard, a young lawyer in Clinton and friend of the family, she hounded the congressmen in Washington who represented her district, trying to get information about Dick.

Eva Bell had heard that the Catholic Church still maintained relations with Japan, so she contacted Rev. Fr. John Renehan at the Catholic Church in the nearby town of Newton Grove and asked that he request information about Dick through the Church. He did so, asking for help through the Vatican. The Pope had set up a War Prisoner Information Bureau in Washington, and was able to relay information about some of the boys held in Japan. But this turned out to be a dead end for Eva Bell, as the church was unable to get a message to Dick in Japan.

The ranks of Camp Osaka 1 swelled as time passed, finally reaching nearly 600 prisoners. The men worked from early in the morning until after dark unloading the ships and barges in the port of Osaka. Since Osaka was not a deep water port and had little dock space, often the larger ships would have to be off-loaded their cargo onto barges outside the bay. These barges would then bring the materials to the docks for the POW stevedores to unload. Long lines of POW's would form on the gangplanks of the barges, waiting to take a load of the cargo on their backs from the barge to warehouses or railroad cars on shore.

Much of the cargo that the men unloaded was in bags, such as the ever popular soybeans that were a staple of the Japanese diet. Soybeans would arrive in 100 kilo bags made of burlap and straw. The bags weighed 220 American pounds. Two men lifted the heavy bags with cargo hooks, singing a Japanese chant to help them coordinate the swinging of the heavy sack. They would swing the sack over a laborer's head, resting it on his shoulders. He would make his way some distance to the warehouse ashore. Failure to complete the work task expeditiously could result in a beating or worse.

The weight loss problem for the prisoners became more serious with the advent of the heavy labor. The rice balls that the men were fed each morning and evening were far from adequate. As the war took its toll on Japanese food resources, the balls of rice diminished from the size of a softball to that of a baseball, or even smaller. Food became a prized possession.

Luckily for Dick Darden, much of the cargo that he unloaded was edible, and stealing food became necessary for survival. The bags of soybeans were unloaded with metal hooks, similar to ice tongs. Each time a man reached to pull a bag up out of the ship's hold, he could give an extra jerk and rip the bag enough to free several beans. When the guards were not looking he could reach down and collect a few of the precious rations.

The prisoners had no choice but to steal food whenever possible. Even so, Dick Darden's weight continued to drop. Many of the men got scurvy because of the absence of vitamin C in their diets. There was almost no citrus fruit to provide the much needed vitamins. Many of the men could move their loosened teeth with their fingers, and their gums bled constantly. Some of the prisoners had gums that were in such poor condition that eating even the soft mushy rice each day would make their gums bleed.

The men were especially interested in unloading ships laden with bags of fruit, since a scrap of citrus could mean almost instant relief from some of the discomforts of POW life. Even if the fruits, like the soybeans, had wallowed in the filth of the floor in the ship's hold, they were prized.

Stealing food became a true art for many of the POW's. Since the penalty for stealing could be anything from a beating to beheading, each man tried to devise the best way possible to hide contraband and get it back into camp. Several tied socks to their legs inside their pants to hide the stolen articles. One prisoner was caught with a sock full of rock salt under his pants. The Japanese guards promptly took him out and beat him to death with the salt-laden sock. But, the choice for the remaining prisoners was to steal food or wither up and die of starvation, so the stealing continued regardless of the penalties for being caught.

The Osaka 1 camp was located about one block from the waterfront. Most of this area near the docks was actually below sea level, with the sea held back by retaining walls. Once a tidal wave, caused by a typhoon, hit the city. As the tidal wave smashed into the retaining wall it sent a wall of water several feet high rolling about three blocks into the city, including the Osaka 1 prison. The wooden buildings had been built several feet above ground level, and Dick watched the approaching water as he peered out through his window from his top shelf. The water came into the building and rose up to the level of the bottom shelf, which was about five feet above the ground outside.

Once the water had found its way inside the retaining walls it became trapped in the city. All of the toilets in the Japanese homes overflowed causing a great stench. Pumps were set up to move the water back over the walls and into the sea, a job which took several weeks to complete. For several days the docks were covered with water so there was no stevedore work for the men. Some of the hungry men were assigned to work in the lumber yard, which was farther inland, while others simply waited in the barracks.

Near the end of 1942 the cold Arctic winds came howling into Osaka, and Dick Darden began to experience the onset of his first Japanese winter. This new discomfort, on top of all of the others, was most unwelcome to say the least. By this time Dick, and all of the enlisted men who were compelled to perform hard labor for the Japanese, were poorly clothed and in steadily declining physical condition. The chronic malnutrition and uninterrupted succession of long days doing gut-wrenching labor in the filth of the Japanese harbor district was beginning to take its toll. The coming of the cold weather was another serious problem for the men.

Since the American officers in the prison were not required to work like the enlisted men, most still enjoyed the marginal warmth of their original uniforms. The tattered and worn clothing of the POW's who labored was another matter. Having adjusted to the intense heat of the summer, Dick was wearing shorts, sandals, and a lightweight shirt.

Dick was not accustomed to the cold weather of Osaka. Back home in North Carolina Dick lived only sixty miles from the port of Wilmington, close enough to the Atlantic that Clinton received the warming effects of the sea breezes coming off the ocean. In addition to this, just another sixty miles or so offshore was the balmy Gulf Stream. This current is a river of warm Caribbean water, sparkling clear and teeming with tropical life, which comes up the eastern coast of the United States and provides a warming effect to the entire southeastern coastal region. Due to the effects of the gulf stream it was a rarity to see farm ponds back home frozen over hard, even during the harshest winters. Temperatures rarely fell below +10 degrees, and subzero cold was felt but once a century.

But Osaka was different. While the salt water in Osaka Bay did not freeze over, the many canals that penetrated deep into the city with their brackish waters did freeze over completely during cold weather. Dick did not know what to expect from the Japanese winter, and he went into the cold season unprepared. As the weather got colder in late 1942 the prison laborers began to search for warmer clothing as they worked on the barges and ships.

The barracks at Osaka 1 became excruciatingly cold at night as the depths of winter fell upon the city. Each man was issued one lightweight Japanese army blanket. Dick's lanky frame could not be adequately covered by his blanket. This was true of many of the men, so they had to cast modesty aside and sleep in pairs so that they could share blankets and body heat.

The prisoners would come in from work, often after dark, and bathe from a pan of water if one was available. Then they would slide onto their sleeping shelves for a few hours of rest before the next morning's wakeup call began the labor cycle over again. They would get as close together as they could, back to back, and roll up in their pair of blankets on the hard grass mat. Dick dreaded the long nights of shivering in the cold drafty buildings. However, there was nowhere to go for help against the cold, nothing to do but endure the misery brought on by it.

Dick managed to steal a large pair of British army pants while working on one of the ships. The waist measured over 50", far too large for Dick's shrinking mid-section. Though comical by western standards, the pants could be overlapped in front and tied with a rope belt to resemble the baggy pants worn by many of the native Japanese coolies. Dick took advantage of this situation by sewing a secret pocket into the crotch of his G-string. When the situation arose he would steal food and store it in his crotch pocket for the rest of the day until he could get it into camp that night. The secret pocket worked, helped him to avoid starvation, and was never found by the guards.

The guards would come through the camp after the men had put in a long grueling twelve hour day and select men for beatings. They would order the men to go outside and while one watched with his weapon at the ready, another would administer the punishment. The prisoner would have to stand at attention while the smaller guard beat the living hell out of him. This was a dreaded nightly activity.

Taking these beatings was the hardest thing that Dick had to endure during his entire imprisonment in Japan. His blood boiled as the shorter Japanese guards beat him, knowing that since he was larger, stronger, and better coordinated he could whip the hell out of both guards if he was given a fair chance. Nevertheless, none of the POW's wanted to go up against the rifles and bayonets of the guards. So they stood erect and took the punishment and humiliation. Time after time the guard's slaps would sting and fists would put the prisoner on his rear, after which he was ordered to jump back up for more.

All the time the guards were hoping that the prisoner would fight back. To Dick's recollection, no one was ever fool enough to do that. A bullet or bayonet in the gut would be the probable result, and most of the men had the attitude that they had gotten this far alive and they were not going to blow it now. They would tough it out, bleed some if need be, and return home alive, just as long as they did not betray their country or fellow prisoners.

On one occasion betrayal became an issue. A ship arrived loaded with munitions which obviously would be used in the war effort against the United States. The men chose not to betray their country, and refused to work the ship. The Japanese gave in on this issue and assigned the men to another job, unloading the ship with Japanese men.

A few days later another ship arrived which was loaded with necessary materials other than munitions. The POW's decided not to push their luck, but to use slowdown tactics, dragging along unloading the ship at half speed. The Japanese brought in a "goon squad" with bamboo sticks about the size of baseball bats. Any man thought to be moving slower than the desired pace was beaten unmercifully with the sticks. Things got back to normal in a hurry.

The work schedule set for the prisoners was relentless, so the men relished the one day off that they were given each month. In December of 1942 the entire camp was given Christmas Day off. In an effort to boost the morale of the men and make the best of a bad situation, the ranking American officers decided to put on a talent show. The men took turns singing songs, dancing, and telling stories. One crusty seaman was even able to salvage some chuckles from the situation when he began telling stories and reciting poems. Though his verses were filthy by most standards, they didn't seem to be out of place in the quagmire of the labor camp.

On December 13, 1942, about six months after Dick Darden had arrived in Japan, a new Japanese commander was assigned to Wake Island. Shigimatsu Sakaibara, an Admiral in the Imperial Japanese Navy, took command of the occupation force. Almost immediately he began to feel the tightening noose of Allied forces around the island. American naval forces were rapidly gaining control of the seas in the area, and in so doing began to severely restrict Japanese shipping which supplied the island.

Admiral Sakaibara began to increase the size of the occupation force, ultimately reaching a population of over 4000. This was nearly ten times the size of the contingent of American Marines who had defended the island in 1941. The senior Army officer on Wake was Colonel Shigeharu Chikamori.

National Archives

Admiral Sakaibara (left) with an assistant on Wake Island.

215

Chapter 46

OSAKA 1—1943

The year 1943 would be an agonizing one for Dick Darden. The slave labor was constant, unrelenting, almost every day filled with hour after hour of grueling physical exertion. The food was far from adequate, barely enough to stave off starvation, and supplemented only with the sweepings from the floors of filthy ships or by the occasional contraband that would have cost so dearly

Dick also continued to use the hidden pockets that he had sewn into the crotch of his trousers to hide bits of food that he found on the job. To have been caught in such an act would have meant severe punishment, but to take no such chances would have meant subsistence on the meager rice ball and dicon soup diet. Dick knew that if he tried to work long hours every day under the existing

Holmes Collection

American prisoners endure the unsanitary conditions of a Japanese prison.

had the starving men been found out. The weight loss continued, and with it went the strength that was so necessary for the daily toil.

The grossly oversized British army pants which Dick had stolen on one of the ships looked more and more ridiculous as his lanky frame became more emaciated. But the fact that the guards accepted such baggy attire as normal on the prisoners worked to Dick's advantage. The crotch of the huge pants hung down to Dick's knees, and he continued to move considerable amounts of contraband loot in his G-string. When goods could be stolen on the barges he usually brought them back into camp inside the baggy pants.

conditions without somehow stealing food, he would surely experience an even more dramatic weight loss. All of the men in the camp had agonizing decisions to make.

As the months wore on, the men working out of Osaka 1 prison came in contact with almost every imaginable cargo to be unloaded from the barges. In addition to soybeans, they unloaded bags of rock salt, corn, scrap metal, iron ingots, and coal to fuel the war effort in Japan. The coal was not bagged, but came in loose in the ships. Each man was issued a large straw basket with two looping handles. The basket was worn like a jacket on the man's back, with an arm through each of the straw handles. The only protection between the man and the heavy basket of coal was a woven straw pad which he could place under the basket.

A long line of men would wind out of the barge, down the gangplank, and onto the docks. The front man in line would be deep in the bowels of the barge, where he would have the loose coal shoveled into the basket on his back. When full he would start the long walk back to the dock and through the warehouse, bending under the weight of the heavy load of coal.

When each man reached the dumping point, he would bend over in a forward position and allow the coal to pour over the back of his head into a gondola car. Though the weight was removed from his aching shoulders, the back of his head would be covered with coal dust. At night the men would return to the barracks filthy from the black coal powder. Some would have a chance to rinse under the spigots, while others would not.

One day Dick and a group of prisoners were working for Osaka Koe, one of the favorite details since there were frequent opportunities in the warehouses of this company to steal food. This day they were moving sacks of bran, a powdery form of grain similar to chicken feed.

It was a very hot day and the powder seeped from the large sacks onto the sweaty men toiling beneath them. The men became covered with the powder to the point that the only thing white about them was their eyes. Their bodies were caked with the pasty substance. The powder caused many of the men to break out in a rash and itch intensely. They begged the guards to let them go somewhere to wash it off.

Finally the guards agreed, and they marched the men down to the waterfront. They ordered the men to jump into the bay, but one look at the water told the men that the itching might be better. A scum of oil and chemicals covered the filthy water. Several dead animals were visible, and it was not uncommon to see human corpses floating by the docks.

Thousands of Japanese lived on the barges and the bay was their toilet facility. They were frequently seen defecating or urinating over the sides into the murky waters. As excruciating as the powder had become on the prisoner's skin, the thought of jumping into the slurry of the bay sickened them. The men vetoed the guard's idea of getting into the filthy water, deciding that it might be better to endure the increasingly unbearable itch. They continued to beg the guards for clean water.

About one block from the waterfront, Osaka Koe had a tall office building. The building was a modern structure some ten to twelve stories high and made of steel and glass. It covered an entire city block. However, in sharp contrast to the modern structure, there was a concrete vat of water on the street just in front of the building that was used to water oxen and other animals which passed by.

The watering trough measured three feet square and was about four feet deep. A spigot and hose were used to fill it when the water got low. Finally the guards offered the men a chance to clean themselves in the vat. The offer was instantly accepted. The guards marched the men up the street through the teeming masses of Japanese people toward the Osaka Koe building.

Since it was a sweltering day the men were clad only in G-strings. They peeled off these scant clothes and began to wash away the itching powder. The cool water of the ox trough, along with the spray of the hose, rinsed away the bran and began to soothe their painful rashes.

The prisoners were more than willing to forego their modesty and bath naked while thousands of Japanese walked and biked along just a few feet away. They soon began to notice giggles coming from the many open windows of the Osaka Koe building. The prisoners looked up to see what appeared to be a thousand people standing at the glass windows and watching the naked Americans bathe in the animal trough.

Many of the spectators were young girls on summer vacation working for the company as their part in the war effort. The sight of naked men was apparently a first for many of them, and they took in the whole show. Soon hundreds of people, both in the building and in the streets below, had stopped what they were doing to watch the spectacle. The throngs of people became so large that it reminded Dick of an audience with the Pope.

The prisoners were so happy to be enjoying a few minutes frolicking in the water and spraying each other with the hose that their attitude was, "Oh hell, let them watch if they want to." In a few minutes a group of Japanese coolies who had been working on the docks with them came along. Seeing the POW's enjoying the water, they too stripped naked and began to cavort about in the water. Some of the older male executives could be overheard making sly comparisons of the naked men's anatomy to the giggling girls. They would point to the Japanese coolie's genitalia and say "Chesi," (little) and then point to the larger Americans and say "Oki," meaning "Big."

Bathing in the vat became a daily custom for the men when they worked ships carrying coal, bran, grains, or other cargo that made them filthy. After a few days the masses of people moved briskly past the vat attending to their daily business and paying little attention to the prisoners bathing in the vat.

On several of the work days in 1943 the prisoners again unloaded bags of money from the ships. They noticed that the coins bore names of countries all over the Orient. The treasuries of these countries had been plundered by the conquering Japanese forces and the metal brought back to the motherland to provide hardware and precious metals for the war effort. A few days after each shipment of coins would arrive, the men would load ingots of the metal back on another ship to be taken elsewhere. It was obvious that the coins had been taken to a smelter and melted down, since the ingots would still have a menagerie of foreign coins visible and protruding from their bottoms.

When New Year's Day, 1943, arrived, Ralph Holewinski found himself still imprisoned at Zentsuji. Zentsuji was an officer's camp, however, and in January of 1943 a group of Army officers who had been captured in the Philippines were brought in. As a result, several of the enlisted Marines and sailors from Guam and Wake had to be moved to another camp. Skee was among the group sent to the prison at Tanagawa.

Tanagawa was in a rural area away from the larger urban centers. The prisoners from Zentsuji had heard that Tanagawa was a rough camp, so they presented themselves in the strongest possible way when they arrived. They marched into the camp four abreast in perfect step. Their heads were held high and they tried to prepare themselves for what was to come.

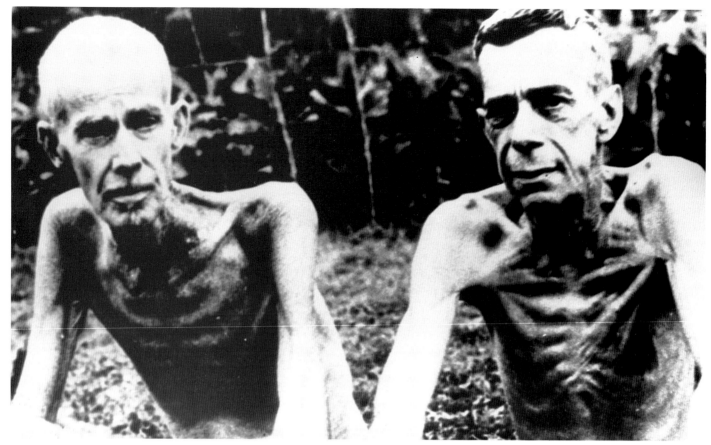

POW's in the Philippines suffered through even harsher camps in which men could not steal food to supplement the prison diet.

The camp at Tanagawa had just been opened in December of 1942 and the population when Holewinski arrived was six hundred. The prisoners were mostly from the Philippines, so their condition was generally not good. Many had been on the Bataan death march, and nearly all had been subjected to constant brutality and starvation. At the beginning the death rate was three men per day. Each day there was a burial detail which had to take the corpses about one and a half miles away to be cremated. It was a horrible detail to be assigned. The odor of burning American flesh was unforgettable.

Navy Boatswain's Mate 1st Class Jim Hesson took charge of the group from Zentsuji. He was well-liked by the Marines and sailors in his group and eventually became well liked by the men from the Philippines. Holewinski was in the camp hospital since he was still having considerable drainage from the deep wound in his back. He was one of over one hundred men in the hospital. Most of the men around him suffered from dysentery, malaria, or malnutrition. There was no medicine to give to them.

The prisoners from the Philippines had been through even more brutal treatment at the hands of their Japanese captors than those from Wake and Guam who had come from Zentsuji, so Hesson and his group did a lot to raise their morale. When the group had left Zentsuji they were given a Red Cross package for each two men. Hesson asked each of the ex-Zentsuji POW's to donate his powdered milk and cheese to the men in the hospital, and the prized cans of corn

to the kitchen so that a stew could be made for all of the men.

The men from the Philippines were near starvation and couldn't believe that the hungry strangers would share their food with them. But the deed was done and everyone enjoyed a meal with a small amount of beef in it. Chief Myers, a corpsman from Guam, took all of the milk and cheese to the hospital and within a week the death rate dropped to less than one man per day.

The Japanese saw what the Americans had done and how the health and morale of the men had improved. Afterwards they made a token effort to improve things by serving a small portion of fish once a week. They justified the small increase in food by putting the men to work. At first Skee was forced to work in a dry dock where the Japanese were going to build miniature submarines. The POW's were made to dig with picks and shovels and load the soil onto wheelbarrows. The harassment and beatings never stopped. Every man, to the last POW at Tanagawa, was beaten at one time or another.

It was at Tanagawa that the war nearly ended for Ralph Holewinski. His wounds were still giving him a considerable amount of trouble. The grenade wound to his back was still open and draining, and he was in a seriously weakened condition.

One day all of the prisoners were assembled in the prison yard. A letter was read by a Japanese colonel who then proceeded to give a speech on how great the Japanese were and how well the war was going for them. Holewinski stood for the oration as long as he could, but finally became dizzy and passed out. The Japanese officer's speech continued as Holewinski slumped to the ground. Two POW's tried to pick him up and hold him, but three guards came over and began beating the two. They let Skee fall to the ground until the speech was over.

After the speech they beat the two again for helping Holewinski. Then they marched Skee into the colonel's office. Through an interpreter he was told that he had insulted the officer by not listening to his speech. The Japs wanted to make an example of someone, and Skee was to be the unlucky choice. He began to fear the worst.

The three guards had their rifles, and two others were told to get their weapons. Firing squads usually were made up of five gunmen. As they began to load their rifles Holewinski tried vainly to explain that he was very weak and had just fainted. As he spoke one of the guards caught him across the head with his rifle butt, sending Skee across the room and knocking him out again.

When Skee came to he saw that Chief Myers was in the office. He had pulled Skee's pants down enough to show the Japanese the messy wound that he still carried on his back. He was trying to explain to the Colonel that Skee was weak and sickly from his wounds and had not intentionally insulted him.

Sometimes the Japs would show respect for wounded men, and this time the Colonel had mercy on the wounded man. He ordered Holewinski to go back to his barracks. Chief Myers had taken a huge risk in coming to Skee's defense. As Holewinski was taken away the guards began beating Myers. He spent several days in bed afterwards recuperating from the beating, but he had saved Skee's life.

The labor of the POW's in Osaka 1 prison were being sold more frequently to Japanese companies, which needed cheap labor more than ever. Osaka Koe, Mitsubishi, Sumitomo, and several other companies would rent the men, taking them on a variety of work details. Sometimes only a few men were taken, while on other occasions several dozen would be needed. Once while working in the warehouses along the docks in Osaka, Dick was stacking 500-pound bales of cloth. The big bales were being lifted with winches and placed on top of wooden crates. Dick was up with the bales trying to jockey them into position, often having to hang out over the edge of the high platform and use his body weight to maneuver the sluggish bales where he wanted them to fall. He decided to try to jump onto the edge of the wooden surface, push his weight against the bale to stop it, and then hop out of its path as it settled down.

One bale began moving toward Dick faster than he anticipated, settling down before he could move out of its path. It pressed his foot down between two of the wooden crates, causing the toe to come back up and touch his shin. As the weight of the bale settled on his foot Dick heard a loud "pop." Pain shot up his leg and the crushed ankle began to throb. The swelling began immediately, finally pushing the ankle to several times its normal size. He tried

Americans are severely beaten with sticks before beheading, Cabanatuan, Philippines.

to limp away but could only drag the injured foot behind him.

There was no medical attention to be had when Dick arrived back at camp. The guards gave him five days off from work, but then ordered him to resume a normal work load carrying heavy cargo from the barges on the broken ankle. The foot would bother Dick for the rest of his life. His left leg still bore the scars of having been blown open on Wake Island, and now the same leg had been crushed on the docks of Osaka.

One morning Dick was lined up with the other men to await the daily work assignment. His labor for the day was purchased by a company which needed a cargo of pigiron ingots unloaded. These rough bars of cast iron were about three feet long and weighed about 150 pounds. Dick did not look forward to working all day with the heavy metal. The work be difficult, but even worse, he would have no opportunity to steal food.

Dick and two other prisoners, along with a guard and a company stickman, went down to a railroad yard where a row of railroad cars sat near a platform. There they were ordered to wait. Before long a group of old Japanese women, most appearing to be sixty to eighty years old, were brought by the guards to join the prisoners. The guards had gone into the small homes along the docks and ordered the women to come and work. Most were dressed in their ragged kimonos, and had been caring for children while their parents were working elsewhere.

The women were lined up between the railroad cars and the platform. The prisoners were told to load the heavy iron ingots onto the backs of the old women, who were ordered to carry them from the platform into the railroad cars where one of the POW's waited to stack the metal. After about thirty minutes the thin cloth on the backs of the women had worn through, and most were bleeding across the shoulders from the scraping of the rough iron.

Even the prisoners felt sorry for the poor women, who were made to work all day carrying the heavy bars. If one of them fell, the guards would kick and beat her until she got back up or proved to be unconscious. Several stumbled back into line to shoulder the next ingot while bleeding profusely from the beatings as well as the scrapes on their backs.

Mild earthquakes seemed to be almost a daily occurrence in Japan. They were easy to detect if Dick was sitting on his top shelf in the barracks because the single light bulb that dangled from the ceiling would begin to swing from side to side. The Japanese were accustomed to the mild tremors, but the POW's were usually startled when the motion began and the buildings started to sway.

One day the men were working along the waterfront on reclaimed land just at the edge of the water. Dirt had been dredged from the bottom of the harbor and used as fill dirt behind a retaining wall to provide a storage area for metal barrels. The fifty-five gallon drums were filled with an unknown cargo and were being unloaded from railroad cars. They were being stacked on the ground, some piles reaching fifteen feet in height.

Suddenly a severe earthquake began. The ground seemed to come at Dick in waves and then run right out from under him. A huge crack opened in the earth about fifty yards away. There was chaos as everyone, Japanese and POW laborers along with civilians from buildings in the vicinity, began running for the nearby railroad. Dick was puzzled to see the bizarre conduct of the civilians, but he did likewise and ran to hold onto the tracks.

As the crack opened wider the barrels began to roll in, and soon over half of the huge shipment had disappeared into the earth. Dick watched in amazement as the crack in the earth seemed to come back together, as if swallowing up the hundreds of barrels that had fallen in. When the crevasse came together steam belched out and moist gray silt bubbled up out of the hole. The ash colored mud spread for several feet on both sides of the crack.

It seemed that thousands of civilians ran out of the buildings and quickly ran to the railroad tracks, clutching them tightly. Dick later learned that people did this so that if the earth opened beneath them they could hang on to the suspended tracks. He wondered if all the people who were holding the tracks would have been electrocuted if high tension electric wires had fallen onto the metal rails.

In May of 1943 the Japanese decided to separate the Army POW's from the Navy and Marine internees at Tanagawa. This was a stroke of luck for Ralph Holewinski because a man in his condition would certainly face a very bleak and desperate situation if he were to be confined under such harsh conditions for the remainder of the war. Only four months after arriving at Tanagawa, Skee was transferred to a prison in the heart of the city of Osaka.

Dick Darden and Ralph Holewinski were in the same Japanese city but in different prison camps. Skee was confined to a camp called Umeda Bunsho. It housed about 300 men, including fifteen U.S. Army officers and two Army enlisted men. The remaining prisoners were Marines and sailors. Most of the men in Umeda Bunsho had been captured in the Philippines. Some had been in China and were transferred to the Philippines before the war started. Some were sailors whose ships had been sunk near the Philippines at the beginning of the war.

Umeda Bunsho was a work camp and the men labored in the freight yards. They did have the opportunity to steal foodstuffs when such was found in the materials they were moving. This proved to be a life saver for Skee, who was still on the mend from his Wake Island wounds but was able to get stolen food from his friends. Most of Skee's friends in Umeda Bunsho were only 40-60 pounds underweight, as compared to the Army men in Tanagawa who had been reduced to living skeletons in the Philippines.

On April 12, 1943, American naval forces launched a bombing attack on the Marshall Island, causing serious damage to the Japanese base at Kwajalein. On May 10 an attack was made on Wake Island, with the bombers again causing significant damage. American forces made Admiral Sakaibara's first summer on Wake Island as uncomfortable as possible. Frequent raids on the island from Midway, coupled with everpresent submarine patrols in the area, made the island virtually inaccessible. The Japanese army and navy personnel on the island began to feel the squeeze brought on by the blockade. The men were forced to live underground because of the American bombers and their food supplies began to dwindle.

A 10,000 ton merchant vessel, the SUWA MARU, attempted to run the blockade and bring critically needed supplies to the Japanese garrison. She made her way safely to within sight of the island and to her moorings off the south beach. An American submarine skipper found the SUWA MARU in his sights, however, and fired two torpedoes. Both ripped ferociously into the helpless freighter.

One torpedo exploded into the SUWA MARU's side,

The Suwa Maru still clings to the reef on Wake's south beach in this 1951 photo.

while the other blasted into her stern. The captain of the SUWA MARU realized that his ship was sinking, so in desperation he ordered that she be headed toward the island just a short distance away. The ship plowed up onto the reef, making a deafening grinding roar as the metal scraped and buckled over the hard coral ridge. The reef carved out a gaping hole in her bow as the SUWA MARU become a permanent resident of Wake Island.

With her bow resting high and dry, the stern of the ship sank into the deep water beyond the reef. It appeared as if she were clinging to the rim of the island. That is, in fact, exactly what she was doing, teetering on the edge of this tropical mountaintop. The ship and its precious cargo was in danger of sliding backwards off the edge of the mountaintop and being swallowed up by the depths of the Pacific.

The crew of the SUWA MARU was decimated when she was torpedoed and then ran aground. Twenty men were killed, and another thirty crewmen were wounded. The SUWA MARU joined the two nearby Patrol Craft that had been used in the invasion of December 23, 1941, as shipwrecks on the south beach of Wake Island.

The fate of the SUWA MARU was typical of Allied treatment of the enemy on Wake Island during 1943. Virtually all aboveground buildings were bombed and destroyed. Nearly all of equipment and vehicles captured by the Japanese were destroyed by the incessant bombings. Probably fewer than a dozen vehicles remained in working order on the island. The lagoon became choked with the remains of barges, tugboats, and PT boats that had been destroyed and sunk by the Allied bombings.

In August of 1943 Eva Bell received two written messages from Dick. On the second of August a card arrived through the Red Cross. It was the first message that had gotten through from Dick since the radio broadcast of a year earlier. This message gave Dick's prison address. The text of this message was as follows:

"Imperial Nipponese Army. I am interned in Osaka prison of war camp. My health is usual. I am working for pay. Please see that your health is taken care of. My love to you.

Dick"

A story about the receipt of the message was published in the local Newspapers in Clinton. It described Eva Bell as "delighted that she had a direct message from her son." As least she knew where Dick was imprisoned and that he was still alive.

One Saturday night the men in Osaka 1 were told that they would not work the following day, so they looked forward to one of their infrequent days of rest. To Dick's surprise, the next morning at 5:00 a.m. all 600 men were rousted out of their shelves and assembled in the street in front of the camp. They were never given advance notice when they would be moved to another camp, so during such assemblies they carried everything of value with them.

Metal cans which had held one pound of Klem brand powdered milk in the Red Cross packages were used to carry supplies on such occasions. With their blankets on their backs and

Klem cans clanging from their belts, the men were marched away from camp, not knowing if they would ever return.

To their surprise the prisoners were marched only a short distance across the road to an old stadium that had been used for the Asian Olympics. There waiting for them was Colonel Akami, standing ramrod straight on a platform in his full dress uniform with ribbons, medals, sword and all appropriate regalia. What fate the crazy colonel had in store for them they did not know. The prisoners were divided into squads of twenty and were ordered to march around the track. One Japanese private was assigned to lead each group, marching with the prisoners around the track in strict military fashion. Around and around they went, lap after lap after lap.

When each squad circled the track and approached the platform on which Col. Akami stood at attention, the Japanese soldier with the group would shout "hashida magee," which meant "eyes right." Everyone would snap their eyes toward the Colonel and the squad leader would salute. If the Colonel liked the crispness of the salute he would yell "Uroshi, uroshi," which meant "Good, good."

After about a dozen laps around the track it was decided that the Japanese soldiers needed a rest, so a prisoner was put in charge of each group. The POW put in charge of Dick's squad was a Second Class Navy cook, the most foul-mouthed man Dick had ever known. On and on the thirty squads marched, holding all of their gear and saluting the Colonel at the end of each lap.

Fatigue began to set in, but the men still didn't know what game the Colonel was playing, so on they marched. Were they going to be moved to another camp? Were they going to be shot? Finally the Navy cook leading Dick's squad began to get irritated at the saluting. "All right, get ready fellows," he said as they approached Colonel Akami.

When the time came for the squad leader to give the men their command to look toward Akami, he stunned the men by snapping his head toward the Colonel and shouting as loud as he could yell "You old son-of-a-bitch." The men didn't know whether to be horrified or to explode with laughter. The Colonel, who did not know a word of English, roared "Uroshi, uroshi." Soon every squad was saluting the Colonel with a hearty "You old son-of-a-bitch" each time they passed the reviewing stand. Apparently thinking that the men were getting excited about showing their respect for him, Col. Akami was giving everyone long loud "Uroshi's."

On the men marched, hour after hour, mile after mile around the track. Finally Captain Wilson had had enough. Wilson was an irritable sort anyway. He and his team of five Army radiomen had been on Wake Island to put in a radio station. When he found himself in the Japanese prisons he continued to enjoy his lofty rank by insisting that fellow POW's of lower rank continue to salute him when they passed by. This annoyed the men, since it made a bad situation even worse. Often they would salute him with their middle finger. Wilson despised the gesture and would threaten to have them court maritaled when they returned to the States.

But, on this day Wilson's anger was aimed toward Col. Akami for the senseless marching, which was becoming more painful with each lap. Wilson, addressing the Colonel, said that he refused to march any farther, and he began to recite a part of the

Geneva Convention. A loud "whap" was heard through the ranks as the Japanese private in charge of his group knocked Wilson to the ground. He rose and continued the recitation. Again there was a "whap," and again Wilson hit the ground. When he arose for the third time he addressed the Colonel by saying "Where do you want me to go?"

On the men marched, now hungry and thirsty and increasingly fatigued. The Klem cans and water bottles clattered together on their belts, and the blankets and other materials tied on their backs got heavier and heavier. Legs became weary and the men, emaciated as they were from the many months of malnutrition, neared exhaustion.

Finally, at about 3:00 p.m., after marching for over eight hours, the parade stopped. The men were instructed to line up in one long line, which extended nearly all the way around the stadium. One of the Japanese guards said, "It is customary in Japan to bow as well as salute. I will show you how, and you can practice. If Colonel Akami thinks that you know how to do it well, he will tell you." The guards thought the Americans would always be slaves to the Japanese, so they should learn the proper etiquette.

The bow practicing began, with the men instructed to

✚ **American Red Cross**

Form 1631-P
Feb. 1942

STANDARD PACKAGE NO. 8
for
PRISONER OF WAR
FOOD
CONTENTS

Evaporated Milk, irradiated	1	14½ oz. can
Lunch Biscuit (hard-tack)	1	8 oz. package
Cheese	1	8 oz. package
Instant Cocoa	1	8 oz. tin
Sardines	1	15 oz. tin
Oleomargarine (Vitamin A)	1	1 lb. tin
Corned Beef	1	12 oz. tin
Sweet Chocolate	2	5½ oz. bars
Sugar, Granulated	1	2 oz. package
Powdered orange concentrate (Vitamin C)	2	3½ oz. packages
Soup (dehydrated)	2	2½ oz. packages
Prunes	1	16 oz. package
Instant Coffee	1	4 oz. tin
Cigarettes	2	20's
Smoking Tobacco	1	2¼ oz. package

Glenn Tripp Collection

This list of foodstuffs came from one of Glenn Tripp's

222

stand at attention with arms straight and bow to the Colonel at just the right angle. One at a time, the men were brought in front the the Colonel to bow. He would respond to their bowing with a "Uroshi" if he thought it was done well, or a "Tomina, tomina," if it was "Bad, bad." Those who bowed properly to the Colonel went into one group, while those who got a "tomina" went to the back of the line and started over.

Some of the POW's were sufficiently maddened by the strain of the long ridiculous march that they purposely antagonized the Colonel by bowing improperly. Finally, at 6:00 p.m., the Colonel became tired of the exercise and allowed all of the men to return to their barracks. After over twelve hours of non-stop marching and bowing, some of the prisoners refused to the end to bow correctly to the Colonel.

Various theories emerged concerning the mystifying day in the stadium. The most plausible theory was that Colonel Akami had become confused and, thinking that he was still in command of the regular army troops in China, he had decided to review his troops.

A number of maladies began to take their toll on the men, who lacked any medical supplies. Diseases such as scurvy, wet and dry beriberi, tuberculosis, and pneumonia made their way into the prison population. One Marine corpsman from Texas, Larry Atwood, had been on Wake Island attached to Lt. Poindexter's unit. While in prison at Osaka 1, he contracted TB, but did not die until after he had returned to the States at the end of the war.

Many other discomforts existed in Osaka 1. Since the men lay almost body to body in the cramped sleeping quarters, insects spread freely throughout the general population. Lice were a problem and fleas sometimes turned men's legs nearly black. The body lice were called "seam squirrels," since they inhabited the men's tattered clothes. Men were often seen pulling off their shirts and "popping seam squirrels." Everyone had them in his clothes and "they could bite like hell."

About the middle of 1943 a trickle of letters from home began to come into Osaka 1 prison. Also, a shipment of Red Cross parcels arrived. They were not given out, but were stored in a locked room in one of the wooden buildings in the camp. Even though these parcels contained items that would have brought the men some small pleasures, they were not distributed. Guards could be seen going into the storage room only to emerge smoking Camels or Lucky Strikes, or eating chocolate bars. The men knew what was happening to the boxes from home.

The temptation to take some of the boxes was great, but the

National Archives

An American pilot prepares to drop his explosives on Japanese positions on Wake while his machine gunner watches for enemy planes.

Big American naval guns roar, sending destruction to the Japanese occupation force on Wake Island, October 5, 1943.

Results – The American bombardment of Wake October 5 set fire to a boat in the Wilkes Channel

224

The 98 Rock - inscribed"U. S., P. W. 5-10-43."

fear of severe punishment kept the men from taking the chance. Dick had seen men punished for minor offenses by being forced to kneel onto hard ground where small wooden strips or metal bars had been placed under their knees. Then they were given ten-quart buckets of water, one in each hand, which they were forced to hold directly out in front of their chests with their arms fully extended. Some had to do this for hours on end. They tried not to waver, but they always were pushed so far into pain that they did. The guards were waiting, hoping the prisoners would falter, so they could go to work on the men with bamboo sticks.

By the latter part of 1943 Slick Sloman noticed that the severe headaches he suffered from the headwound sustained on Wake were beginning to subside. Very gradually the headache got better, so much so that occasionally the pain would almost completely disappear. Sometimes the headache would come back and be intense, but the improvement allowed Sloman an occasional day without pain. He had suffered constant head pain for nearly two years while in the Japanese prisons.

Slick Sloman learned quite a bit about pain while in Japan. He learned that pain reaches an apex, or threshold, at which time the sufferer knows that the severity of the pain can become no greater. Some of the men were actually glad to reach the zenith of their pain, because they would black out and get away from it for a time. Sloman had a high tolerance for pain and could withstand a tremendous amount of it. His head pain was unbearable, but he bore it.

Ironically, Sloman would learn later in life that eating chocolate would give him a terrible headache. On those rare occasions when he got a Red Cross package in the Japanese prisons he would crave the chocolate bar inside and he would trade for as much chocolate as he could get. Soon after eating the chocolates he would have terrible seizures and headaches, but he did not link the two. Finally, one day late in 1943, Slick Sloman woke up to find that his headache was completely gone.

The Red Cross boxes were nutritional to be sure, but their greatest effect on the prison population was the tremendous boost in morale that they caused among the men. When the boxes were distributed they set off "the biggest bartering session west of Wall Street," according to Slick Sloman. The men enjoyed seeing how much they could trade for, and they enjoyed having tangible items from home. Even though every one of the men needed foodstuffs more than anything, some would trade all of their food for cigarettes.

Some of the men were master traders. They knew which men had cravings for certain items, such as chocolates or cigarettes. They would approach various men with proposals for trades, each time improving the value of their own box. Within a couple of days some of the better traders would have the equivalent of two or three Red Cross boxes.

The English "Limeys" were good to trade with, since they had different tastes than the Americans. The Brits did not like coffee, but they had a craving for cheese. Even though the small bar of cheese was moldy, they would gladly give up their entire coffee allotment for a bar of American cheese. Some of the Englishmen did not smoke, so they would give up the two packs of cigarettes in their box for 1/4 pound of cheese. Since cigarettes could be used almost like currency, the Americans were always glad to trade for them.

In 1943 the NITTA MARU was still serving the Emperor in the Pacific, but not by ferrying passengers. The ship which had taken most of the men from Wake Island to China in January, 1942, had been commissioned a warship later in that year and she was converted into an aircraft carrier. The name "NITTA" means "sailfish" in Japanese, and "MARU" means "ship." So the name NITTA MARU actually means "sailfish ship." In 1943 the NITTA MARU was sunk by an American submarine. Ironically, the name of the submarine was the U.S.S. SAILFISH.

While Dick Darden was enduring wretched captivity at the hands of the Japanese in 1943, there had been a pronounced turn of events on Wake Island. American naval forces had replaced the Imperial Japanese Navy as the dominant force in the central Pacific. The island lay in waters controlled by the U. S. Navy, but no attempt had been made to invade and reoccupy the atoll by American troops. The Japanese forces who occupied the island had been subjected to more devastating bombings at the hands of American pilots in order to curtail the activities of Japanese patrol bombers, which were based at the renovated airstrip on Wake.

On October 5 and 6, 1943, a force of six American aircraft carriers, the LEXINGTON, YORKTOWN, ESSEX, BELLEAU WOOD, INDEPENDENCE, and COWPENS, launched their planes near Wake. In less than forty-eight hours more than 600 tons of high explosives, and more than one half million rounds of .50 caliber machine gun ammunition were used to scorch the island in what could be termed a mauling.

The bombing raids damaged the Japanese installation so badly that it was unable to function for quite some time. A number of raids, both by carrier-based planes and by naval bombardment, ensued and virtually all of the enemy's ability to fight back was stamped out. The Associated Press indicated that Admiral Chester Nimitz had reported the results of the attack, saying that over 60 Japanese planes had been destroyed. Thirty of the planes had been airborne when they were destroyed, indicating a ferocious air battle in the skies over Wake.

Admiral Nimitz also said that over thirty planes had been destroyed before they ever had a chance to leave the ground. The price that the American forces paid for the destruction of more than sixty enemy planes was the loss of thirteen planes in combat.

In addition to the destruction of the enemy's aviation unit, other targets on the ground were subjected to intense bombing and shelling. Defensive positions, barracks, shops, and the area around the airfield were shattered. It was thought that this attack, from the aerial bombing and the naval bombardment, represented the largest amount of explosives dropped on the Japanese in a single action in the Pacific thus far in the war.

When the bombing ended, many of the barracks, storage areas, and other buildings on the island were in flames. Two small ships, one of which had been loaded with gasoline, were in flames as well. The response to the bombers by the Japanese antiaircraft positions was weak and ineffective.

The bombings and naval bombardment against the Japanese occupation force on Wake extracted a heavy toll. By the end of the war it was estimated that between 700 and 1000 Japanese troops had been killed by the American planes and ships. Since American ships controlled the seas around the island, the only supply ships to make it to the island were submarines. Their limited capacity to act as supply vessels caused the replenishment of vital materials to slow to a trickle. It was estimated that, due to the extremely short food supplies on Wake, over 2000 Japanese died from starvation during the war.

Since Admiral Sakaibara had taken command of the occupation force on Wake in December of 1942, the situation had continually worsened. By the fall of 1943 he was helpless as he watched the devastation of the island at the hands of the U. S. Navy. Casualties among his ranks were high, and with supply lines cut the island was virtually out of food.

Sakaibara's troops, faced with starvation, began eating the birds and rats that inhabited the island. In fact, the voracious rats, which had been such a nuisance, and which had seemed to be all over the island in copious numbers before the war, were strangely missing, seemingly extinct, by the end of the war.

With the circumstances of the Japanese on the island being so bleak, the ninety-eight American civilian laborers who remained there became an unfortunate liability. There was little need for their labor since American bombardment had neutralized any chance of a Japanese air base on Wake. In addition to this, and of greater importance to the Japanese occupation force on the island, the presence of the American men on the island represented a threat to the meager food rations of the hungry Japanese soldiers.

Admiral Sakaibara decided to solve this dilemma in a particularly brutal and heinous manner. In order to justify the events that were about to unfold, Admiral Sakaibara concocted a ludicrous charge against the civilians. He accused them of secretly communicating with the Allies and helping to direct the bombing of the island. The charges were tantamount to treason, and since the laborers were American civilians they were not afforded the status of prisoners of war.

In October of 1943 there were actually only ninety-seven American civilians left on Wake. It was later learned that during July of that year one of the civilians had been executed for an unspecified charge. In July Admiral Sakaibara had assembled a group of men from his command, ordered that the civilian be brought forward, and ordered an Ensign Nonaka to execute the man. Nonaka did so, beheading the American with his sword.

On October 7, 1943, Admiral Sakaibara ordered that the 97 remaining civilians be marched to the beach on the north side of Wake Island. This group included Dr. Shank, who had helped to repair Dick's leg wound after the initial bombing on the first day of the war. Admiral Sakaibara ordered that the American civilians be executed by machine gun.

The men were taken to the north beach in three groups by a squad of Japanese commanded by Lt. Kiroku Horie, Imperial Japanese Navy. Horie took five or six men from his platoon to carry out the atrocity. The first group of prisoners was thought to number about twenty-five men. They were placed in one long line and machine guns were positioned in front of them. The men were blindfolded and their hands tied behind their backs. They were given no trial.

Lt. Commander Soichi Tachibana was the senior officer present at the execution. Lt. Horie assigned one of his non-commissioned officers to each of the two machine guns. Then, when the order was given by Horie, Tetsuo Okura at one gun and Hideichi Komori at the other, began mowing down the doomed men. In short order all of the innocent civilian workers had been shot to death in a mass execution. A trench was dug in the coral sand with a bulldozer and the bodies were thrown into a mass grave.

Another group of about thirty-one men was brought forward

and received the same fate. The final group of about forty men was treated likewise. In all 96 Americans were murdered by the machine gunners on the north beach of Wake Island on October 7. Admiral Sakaibara no longer had the problem of having to feed American laborers.

The choice of Lt. Horie to carry out the killings was, very possibly, not an accident. Horie had previous experience with atrocity. Horie apprehended an American civilian prisoner in July of 1942 in a Japanese canteen. The man was accused of stealing food and cigarettes, and drinking saki. He also was accused of "signalling" with a flashlight. Horie delivered the man to headquarters.

A day or two later Lt. Somin Ogawa informed Horie that he was to execute the prisoner. Horie took the doomed man at the prescribed hour to the place of execution. There assembled were Lt. Ogawa, Captain Susumu Kawasaki, and Commander Hikaru Cho, along with a group of Japanese and 20-30 American civilians to witness the execution. Ogawa read a statement to the condemned man which presumably made him aware of the charges against him. Ogawa then ordered Horie to perform the execution. Horie beheaded the man.

One final problem had to be dealt with concerning the Americans. During the killing frenzy one American civilian managed to escape. However, he was later apprehended, and one week later, on or about October 15, the man was brought before several of the personnel under Admiral Sakaibara's command. There, in front of the assembled men, Sakaibara drew his sword and personally executed the prisoner by beheading. The cruel Admiral had closed the final chapter of the story of the American civilians captured on Wake Island.

Unfortunately, this atrocity was not uncommon behavior for the Japanese commanders throughout the Pacific during the war. Captured Americans, and prisoners of many other nationalities who were unfortunate enough to fall into the grasp of the Japanese butchers, were tortured and executed by the Japanese using a variety of insidious methods. In addition to the ritualistic beheadings, the Japanese shot, stabbed, and beat many prisoners to death. Some were tied to posts and used for bayonet practice.

The Japanese devised a number of sadistic torture methods. Some injected their victims intravenously with solutions such as coconut juice. Others threw boiling water into the faces of their victims. If they did not wish to kill their prisoners with fixed bayonets they occasionally used sharpened bamboo spears. Some Americans were beaten with clubs and rifle butts and then forced to stand at attention for forty-eight hours.

Other American servicemen were burned to death, subjected to electrical shocks, or injected with virulent bacteria. Some were killed by strangulation; others were killed by dynamite explosions. The fate of many Americans taken prisoner by the Japanese in the Pacific was particularly grisly.

In addition to the atrocities on Wake Island, similar bizarre and barbaric behavior was reported on a considerable number of the Pacific islands which were occupied by the Japanese. Torture and killings of POW's, missionaries, and native civilians occurred on Wake, Truk, Chichi Jima, several of the islands in Kwajalein atoll, and of course, in the Philippines.

Perhaps the most bizarre behavior by the Japanese was cannibalism. This was reported on several islands, including Wake and Chichi Jima. Two Japanese soldiers, both in the Imperial Japanese Navy, were suspected of cannibalism on Wake during 1943. After the war they were not interned.

Chapter 47

TARAWA—2700 MILES FROM JAPAN

By the fall of 1943 the American Joint Chiefs of Staff had decided that its conduit to Japan and victory in the Pacific would be through the chain of islands that stretched from the Solomons to the Gilberts to the Marshalls, and then on to the Carolines, Iwo Jima, and Okinawa. After the battles of the Coral Sea and Guadalcanal, the next link in the chain was the Gilberts.

Two islands in the Gilberts, Tarawa and Makin, were targeted. Amphibious assaults by the U. S. Marines would be the method of attack used to overrun the chain of Pacific islands which had been heavily fortified by the Japanese. Victories on their sandy atolls would press the war toward the Japanese homeland.

Unlike Guadalcanal, where it took several months to obtain victory, the battle at Tarawa would have to be much shorter. There was a tremendous amount of Japanese firepower in the region which could be directed to Tarawa in just a matter of days to join in the enemy's defense of the island. There was a potent Japanese fleet in the region whose guns and planes were numerically equal to the Americans.

In addition to these potential obstacles to a protracted battle at Tarawa, there were numerous air bases in the Marshalls from which the Japanese could launch air raids toward the Gilberts. Clearly, the battle for Tarawa had to be carried out swiftly if the wrath of additional enemy reinforcements was to be avoided.

On Makin the enemy was thought to have fewer than 1000 troops. Tarawa was another matter. One small island in the Tarawa atoll, Betio, had been made into a fortress by the Japanese. Over 4800 Japanese troops manned the gun pits and trenches, pill boxes, and heavily reinforced positions near the all-important airport. The Japanese felt that the island was impregnable and could not be overrun by American forces.

As would be the case so often in the Pacific island-hopping campaign, a coral reef provided an additional obstacle to landing troops on Tarawa. Research was conducted on various types of landing craft, and modifications were made in the American strategy that were commensurate with the findings. It was decided that amphibious tractors would be used as landing craft to traverse the dangerous reef. This was a major advancement in the evolution of the American strategy that would win the war in the Pacific.

On the morning of November 20, 1943, after the most intense naval bombardment and aerial bombings yet delivered anywhere in the Pacific, waves of assault troops were loaded onto amphibious tractors and landing craft. They made their way over the reef and onto the beach at Tarawa. The Japanese grudgingly gave ground, only enough the first day of the battle for the Marines to establish a precarious beachhead. On the second day more Marines came ashore to expand the existing beachhead and solidify the American foothold on the island.

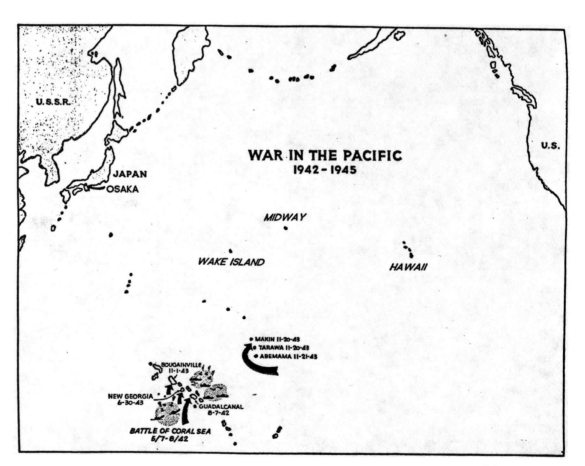

U. S. Army – Modified

The well-entrenched enemy put up a stinging defense, extracting American blood for every foot of ground that they gave up. On the fourth day of the Battle of Tarawa the Americans virtually wiped the enemy off the island. Tarawa was taken at a cost of nearly 1000 American lives. The enemy, once again, had fought nearly to the last man. Out of an original force of 4836 men, the enemy lost 4690 during the battle. Only 146 Japanese survived the battle.

The American forces continued to learn more of the fine points of amphibious warfare. Tactical changes were made in the plans for future assaults, and strategies were put in place which would help earn additional victories during the coming drive to Japan. Having taken Tarawa, American forces were closer than ever to Osaka and mainland Japan. Dick Darden was 2700 miles from the liberation forces, and the gap was narrowing much more rapidly now than before.

On Christmas Day, 1943, Dick and his fellow POW's at Osaka 1 prison were given a rare day off. In fact, it began to appear that the Japanese guards were going to actually do something nice for them when they set up long tables in the yard outside the barracks and began to cover the tables with all types of food and necessities for the men. There were several types of fruit piled high on the tables, along with candy, shoes, socks, and many other items that the men had long needed.

Reporters with newsreel cameras positioned themselves at the end of the table, and the prisoners were brought out and lined up. As the cameras began to click the men went down the line and the guards gave them some of each and every commodity. By the time they reached the end of the table both arms were full, with the goods piled so high that some of their faces were hidden. From there they walked around behind a wooden fence and out of sight of the still-clicking cameras.

As they rounded the fence they immediately became aware of the farce that was going on in the yard. Behind the fence the Japs had another table and they were taking everything back. The whole event was staged for the media and the world would be led to believe that the deprived, half-starved men were being treated kindly by their captors. For a few moments the men had thought that the guards might actually have changed their tune about their treatment. Without the camera clicking, however, it was business as usual and the men ended up getting absolutely nothing out of the piles of basic materials they needed so badly.

By the end of 1943 the plight of supply ships coming from Japan to Wake Island had become extremely perilous. The last such ship to reach the island probably came in December of that year. After that time only submarines could actually make physical contact with the island and avoid the near certainty of being sunk. From the end of 1943 until the end of the war only five such submarines, acting as transports, were able to reach Wake with supplies. These submarines were filled to capacity with supplies, mainly food and ammunition. Some even had rice sealed in rubber waterproof bags which were lashed to their decks.

Even though the end of 1943 signaled the beginning of severe hardships for the Japanese occupation force on Wake, enough supply ships had landed there during the previous two years to bring the materials needed to transform the atoll into a fortress. The Japanese, with the help of the unfortunate civilian workers and their equipment, had prepared the island for attack from the Allies.

Along the entire perimeter of the island a deep ditch had been dug to act as a tank trap. The rock and coral coming out of this ditch had been piled on the land side of the crevasse to form a high berm. This would further deter tanks from landing during an amphibious invasion. Behind the mounds were miles of connecting trenches, dotted with rifle pits, pill boxes, and bunkers. Barbed wire was spread thickly along the beaches to ensnare any troops who might come ashore. If this did not stop them, thickly sown land mines almost surely would.

In the ensuing months and years the ocean salt took its toll on the barbed wire along the beach. When it rusted into uselessness the Japanese sharpened wooden stakes and planted them in the beach sand, angled toward the sea. These, like the land mines behind them, could have been lethal to Marines landing on the beach in an invasion attempt. No more Americans would die here, however, as the thrust toward Japan was far to the west.

The interior of Wake Island was transformed into a maze of military fortifications. Concrete magazines, command centers, and bombproof buildings were constructed in great numbers. There were an estimated 200 pill boxes made of concrete and coral. Defensive positions covered the landscape. For Allied forces to retake the island from the Japanese would surely require an extended period of bloody fighting from one ditch or underground fortification to the next.

In the heavily fortified perimeter of the island, the Japanese had inserted a number of large guns that were to be used as anti-ship guns. These included 4.7", 5", 6", and even 8" guns. Not only did the Japanese have larger guns than the Americans defenders had used in 1941, they also had considerably more of them. Some of the Marine 3" and 5" guns, perhaps as many as half of the original number, were used by the enemy. The large guns being used by the Japanese to defend Wake Island represented a real hodgepodge of armaments. In addition to the Japanese and American guns, there were thought to be some British guns that were captured by the Japs when they overran Singapore.

Unlike the Marine gun positions of 1941, the Japanese built coral revetments to protect their artillery from all but direct hits. In addition, they also had thirty-six field artillery pieces (37mm and 75mm), and twenty-four light tanks. Movement of these guns was infinitely easier than the backbreaking task of manually moving the equipment that had been endured by the Marines.

The Japanese seemed to fortify everything. Revetments were built for the large seaplanes. Petroleum was stored in concrete blockhouses and then buried in the sand, usually only ten to sixteen barrels per hill. The bombing raids could destroy some of the fuel reserves, but not all. This was a distinct improvement over the large vulnerable fuel storage tanks used by the defenders in 1941.

Underground living quarters for the Japanese troops were constructed just above the water table. Even the remaining vehicles were stored in revetments to minimize damage during the bombings. Admiral Sakaibara had a three-level concrete command post constructed, much of it underground.

By late 1943 there were more than 4000 Japanese defenders on Wake Island. The ground was literally full of soldiers, ready to defend the island to the death. The Japanese had intended for Wake to be a forward base of operations, to be used as a staging area for expanding their military control farther to the east. It had become, however, an isolated fortress behind enemy lines.

The United States took the most expedient course of action concerning the enemy occupation of Wake Island. The plan was to avoid the great loss of life that surely would result from an amphibious landing. The Allies simply maintained a tight blockade on the island and bombed it into submission from the air while also bombarding it from the sea. The pressure was kept on the Japanese to such an extent that they were forced to remain underground much of the time. They were not able to construct the air field and naval base they had planned, nor were they able to launch attacks eastward toward Hawaii.

The Japanese on Wake were simply forced to remain underground and starve. The Allies decided to play a waiting game, hoping to retake the island without significant losses. In the end, the strategy worked exactly as planned. Not a single drop of American blood would spill when Wake Island was reoccupied by American forces.

National Archives

Bodies of American men litter the beaches on Tarawa, 11-22-43, a costly toll paid on the march to Japan.

Chapter 48

OSAKA 1—1944

"Kwang Wong" by Maj. James R. Brown. Emaciated American prisoners peer with hollow eyes through the barbed wire fence of a Japanese prison. Another POW hangs from the fence while the ever present guards watch from behind.

About eighteen months after Dick was moved to Japan, the Red Cross got word to his family in Clinton that he was alive in a Japanese prisoner of war camp. The family would write letters and Dick would receive several at a time. What a wonderful thing it was for Dick to have letters from home to brighten his otherwise drab existence.

Dick's mother began to send him packages, most of which never made it to him. Packages bearing Dick Darden's name were found in the storeroom by other POW's on work details, but their contents had been stolen by the guards. One package made it to him and contained, among other things, several double-edged razor blades. Dick shaved with them until they got terribly dull. Then he would put a blade inside a glass and, with two fingers on the center of the blade, move it back and forth until the blade assumed a small degree of sharpness. At one point three men used one of the blades for three months.

Brutality continued to be a constant companion. The men never knew who would be beaten next. Some of the more brutal guards enjoyed the beatings and would react at the least provocation by taking a POW outside the barracks at night and bloodying him up. Even so the men continued to take great risks and steal food whenever the opportunity was provided.

Edward M. Ackley was the radar specialist who had been waiting on Wake Island to set up the new radar equipment when the island was seized. He had been a radio specialist in the Navy and was one of only twelve men sent to Canada to a special school to learn about radar. The new phenomenon would allow men on the ground to detect incoming planes at a considerable distance, and would be a remarkable asset for any military unit being attacked by aircraft.

Ackley worked with Dick on hundreds of labor details while in Osaka, and he was constantly fearful that the Japanese would find out that he was a radar specialist. Had they known of Ackley's training they would surely have spared none of their gruesome methods to extract the technology from him.

Several of the men who had been on Wake knew of Ackley's training, and he was afraid that one of the "rats" the Japs had among the POW's would tell them in return for favors. He knew that if they found out about his knowledge of this sensitive new equipment, it would mean they would torture him until they were convinced they had all of the information out of him. Luckily for Ackley the Japs never found out. He told Dick that Wake Island had been sent a garbage truck instead of the radar unit that was so crucial to the defense of the island.

One night early in 1944 several of the men decided they had better get some of the food in the Red Cross packages before all of it had been stolen by the guards. The boxes were stored in a locked wooden building located next to the barracks. The men knew where the boxes were located because they could see them through a window at the rear of the building. Dick was among the seven or eight who set out one evening after dark in search of food.

A guard on foot patrol was always walking around the perimeter of the camp just inside the fence. It would take him about five minutes to make a round, and his route took him near the rear of the storage building within sight of the back window. The prisoners stationed one man on each corner of the building so one of them could always see the guard. One could see the guard when he was coming toward the area, and the other could keep an eye on him

as he walked away. The rest of the group went into the darkness behind the building to the window.

One of the men took a knife and gently worked one of the glass panes out of the window. Another man named Bradshaw had become so skinny he could fit through the hole where the pane had been removed. Two of the men picked him up and slid him through the hole into the building. Just as he got inside the building, one of the lookouts motioned that the guard was coming.

The men quickly replaced the glass pane in the window and then scampered into the bathroom building, located immediately behind the storage building. This latrine area consisted of nothing more than a wooden floor which was built high enough above the ground so that large clay urns could be pushed underneath. Holes had been cut in the wooden floor for the men to use, and these were inadequately small causing the area to be generally covered with feces and urine.

Two or three times a week Japanese civilians would come and empty the vats of the human excrement and carry it away. This was accomplished by using small doors built into the outside wall of the building. These allowed them to go under the wooden floor and retrieve the honey pots. They would take the excrement to collection boats called "honey barges." The Japanese civilians were in great need of fertilizer for their tiny home gardens, upon which many relied for much of their daily foodstuffs. The contents of the latrine vats were very important to them.

The crude facilities in the latrine building resulted in a stench that would cause one to gag. No matter this night though, as the bathroom offered a safe hiding place. If the guard happened to step into the bathroom, they could tell him they all had to go.

After the guard had passed by, the men quickly went back to the window. Bradshaw handed 15-20 boxes out through the

U.S. Army – Institute of Pathology

Concealed medicine in a POW's hiding place under the flooring .

window so that each man had two or three of the precious parcels. Just as it was time for the guard to pass by again, the men hid the boxes in the bathroom until it was safe to come out. They knew their theft would be detected if they did not leave the window exactly as it had been before they removed it. So, this time the guard made his rounds they set about the task of replacing the glass pane.

The man who had removed the glass pane had handed it to another of the conspirators. He asked the man where the pane was. "Oh, I threw it into the binjo," he responded, indicating that he had thrown the pane into the sewage pit. "Well, go and get it," snapped the first man. Everyone knew what this meant. The man who had tossed the glass pane into the urn went back into the bathroom, reached down into the full urn and felt around until he located the missing glass pane. He quickly rinsed it off and another man took off his shirt and dried it. The pane was gently placed back into position and secured just seconds before the guard made his next pass.

The men made their way back to the barracks in the darkness. Dick carried one of the Red Cross boxes under one arm as he made his way back onto his shelf. He had a hiding place that he had used for several months to conceal items stolen while he was at work. The other POW's knew about it, but the Japanese guards had never detected it. Dick was not afraid of his fellow prisoners taking his goods. There was an unwritten law that, no matter how hungry you became, you never touched anything another man had risked his life to steal and bring back into the camp.

Dick had loosened a board in the floor of the building near his sleeping shelf. He could remove it and stash materials under-neath the floor in the ground. He had also hollowed out an area under the floor in the dirt as far as his arm would reach. The Japs would probably never find it since their arms were much shorter than his. Out of sight under the floor he had stored a supply of stolen sugar, salt, rice, and soybeans.

Dick also had another storage area in the wall behind his upper sleeping shelf for stolen contraband. The walls were of similar construction to wooden buildings everywhere, consisting of vertical framing timbers onto which siding boards had been nailed. There was an area of just over one foot between the vertical framework boards in the wall. Horizontal boards were nailed between these vertical boards to give the wall stability. This amounted to a small shelf inside the wall.

Dick had a removable siding board in the wall that allowed him access to the inside of the wall. He could reach down and feel the cross board in the wall upon which stored a variety of goods, most of which had been stolen on the ships or from the warehouses along the docks. At one time he had fifteen bars of soap, the only soap in the camp, hidden in the wall. This was used to barter for more important materials and foodstuffs as needed.

A set of notes was also stored in Dick's upper hiding place. He had stolen paper and a pencil, and had been writing a description of the conditions in the camp and the daily events there in diary fashion. This set of notes was not nearly as important as the life sustaining food that Dick placed in the wall from time to time. But, Dick hoped that he would be able to keep an accurate record of the behavior of the Japanese and somehow get this back home to properly document his years in the POW camps.

Chapter 49

During late 1943 American strategists in the Pacific theater were deciding how and where to continue the island hopping campaign toward Japan. It was decided that the Marshall Islands would be next. The Marshalls are made up of 37 atolls and islands of varying sizes covering a considerable geographic area. The Japanese were well entrenched, particularly on Kwajalein Atoll, where they had numerous bases and air fields. Japanese fortifications included Kwajalein, Roi-Namur, Wotje, and Eniwetok, which were used to bomb Wake Island at the beginning of the war.

It was decided that the Kwajalein, Roi/Namur, and Eniwetok islands would be the primary targets of the American forces. First would come Kwajalein, a roughly bean-shaped string of islands measuring 68 miles long and 20 miles across at the widest point. The Japanese had large bases on Kwajalein Island at the southern tip of the atoll, and on the twin islands of Roi and Namur on the northeastern corner.

A huge American naval fleet, one thought to be large enough to defeat the Japanese Pacific fleet, was assembled. The American armada boasted six large aircraft carriers, including the SARATOGA, five small aircraft carriers, and two escort carriers. Several of the great battleships reported for duty with their huge

guns, including the IOWA, NEW JERSEY, and NORTH CARO-LINA. There were also seventeen cruisers and fifty destroyers. The fleet was truly impressive.

During January, while the assault force was assembling on the west coast and in Hawaii, planes from the American carriers constantly bombed and strafed the Japanese bases throughout the Marshalls. After four weeks, on January 30, all of the invasion forces were ready to throw themselves at the battered enemy. Hundreds of American warplanes, plus the thundering naval guns of the big ships, began to reduce the enemy installations to heaps of debris. The Japanese took a tremendous beating from the bombardments, losing countless men in the process.

It was in the Marshall Islands that Geddie Herring, the young graduate of Davidson College and native of Dick Darden's home county in North Carolina, would get his first taste of battle. By January of 1944 Geddie Herring had been in the Navy over a year and had been trained extensively on troop landing craft. He had been promoted to the rank of Ensign and was assigned to a 125' long LCI(G) (Landing Craft Infantry-Gunboat) on the west coast. Herring was a junior officer who assisted the captain of the ship.

Ensign Herring's LCI(G) was ordered first to San Diego,

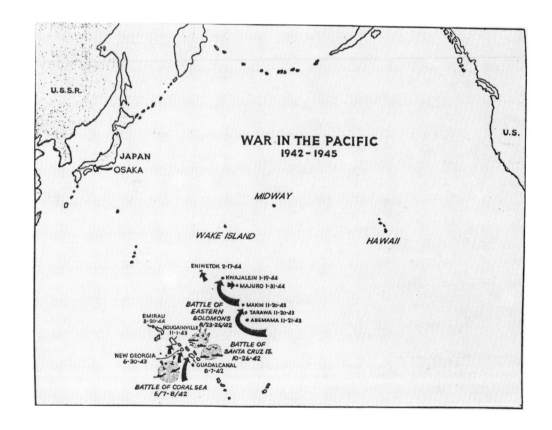

US Army- modified

then on to Pearl Harbor. After a short stay there Herring's ship had headed farther out into the Pacific, its destination being the battle for the Marshall Islands. His landing craft would be involved in the amphibious landings on Roi and Namur Islands in Kwajalein atoll. The landing craft on which Geddie Herring served joined the "Island Hopping" campaign which saw thousands of Marines hitting the beaches on remote islands, each time defeating the fight-to-the-death enemy occupation force and thereby moving one step closer to Japan.

Geddie Herring's LCI(G) played several roles during the battle for control of the Marshall Islands. The primary duty of the ship was to be a gunboat, and a potent one it was. The ship was armed with 20mm and 40mm guns, plus rockets. Sometimes the function of the LCI would be to cover the men going ashore by pouring fire into the enemy positions on the beaches. Herring called this "pecking the paint off of the pill boxes."

The job of covering the troops as they went ashore was dangerous, to say the least. The big ships offshore would heavily bombard the enemy's beach positions prior to a landing attempt. Then, as the landing craft moved toward the beach, the big guns would have to cease fire and allow the landing craft to hit the beach. There was a lull of about five minutes during which the troops going ashore were extremely vulnerable to any enemy position which had survived the bombardment, or to which the Jap troops could scramble and set up their machine guns to quickly return fire at the Marines.

Sometimes the job of the heavily armed gunboats was to move into the dangerous area near shore and direct fire into the enemy positions to protect the landing troops. During that critical span of minutes after the big naval guns had been silenced and while the landing craft were maneuvering back out to the mother ships for more troops, the first men who had hit the beaches were almost naked against enemy machine gun nests, pill boxes, and riflemen in trenches. This first wave of Marines to hit the beaches would be cut to ribbons without some cover from the water.

Geddie Herring's gunboat would spew all possible fire from its guns and rockets into the enemy positions to protect the boys on the beach. The rockets were especially deadly during the landing operations, because they produced vicious explosions which sprayed shrapnel into the trenches filled with enemy soldiers. The rockets could silence large numbers of the enemy troops before they had a chance to cut down the American boys coming across the beaches.

Herring's boat was called upon to render another very hazardous service. Since most of the Pacific Islands were atolls much like Wake Island, they consisted of volcanic mountain tops with very deep water just offshore and usually had a coral reef just off the beach. Landing craft had a difficult time getting their cargo of soldiers across this obstacle as they approached the beaches. Navy frogmen trained in underwater demolition had devised methods of setting explosive charges in the reefs and blowing holes in them, thus allowing the landing craft to pass through freely and hit the beaches quickly.

The usual methods of accomplishing this was for the ships offshore to try to pin down the enemy positions with a bombardment while motor boats would take the frogmen in toward the beaches. They would roll off the sides of the boats, which were moving at high speeds, and quickly disappear underwater near the reefs. Naturally, the Japanese were not happy to see holes blown in the reefs that protected them, so they took great pains to stop the frogmen from approaching the coral barriers. Everyone involved in these operations was in great danger.

After adequate time had been given for the explosive charges to be set, someone had to go in and pick up the frogmen, who were bobbing in the water near the enemy's beach positions. Geddie Herring's LCI frequently got the order, and proceeded into the jaws of the monster to retrieve the divers. As the enemy did all that they could with their machine guns and artillery to stop the demolition activity, the LCI's would speed toward the beach, under cover of the naval bombardment, and pick up the frogmen. With their 20mm and 40mm machine guns blaring, the LCI's successfully recovered the Navy divers time after time. Then the reefs would be blown open for landings and the Marines were ferried through the alleyways to meet the enemy face to face.

On February 1 simultaneous landings occurred on Kwajalein, Roi-Namur, and several other islands in Kwajalein atoll. Geddie Herring's gunboat was one of eight which slipped between Roi and Namur islands and approached the Japanese stronghold from the lagoon side. There were reefs on both the ocean side and the inner lagoon of the islands, so amtracks had to be used. They were precariously slow and depended upon heavy support from the gunboats.

Huge guns on the American battleships unleashed massive bombardments which "softened up" the islands prior to troop landings. The bombardments left the islands pockmarked with blast craters and denuded of much of the tropical flora. Many of the buildings on the enemy bases were leveled and tremendous damage was done to the Japs' defensive abilities. Even so, those enemy troops who were not killed by the bombardments clung to their resolve and waited for the chance to die for their Emperor.

When the big naval guns stopped firing, the gunboats cut loose with their 20mm and 40mm guns, plus their deadly rockets. The LCI's were positioned about 600 yards off the beaches and were no more than 200 yards apart. Their cover allowed the landing craft to ferry the men ashore without feeling the full brunt of the Japanese guns. By nightfall on February 1 there were over 11,000 American troops ashore on Kwajalein.

The American invasion force fought brilliantly on Kwajalein. With tactics and strategies that had been well refined during the previous amphibious landings of the Pacific campaign, and with great confidence that the huge American force would be victorious again, the enemy troops who had survived the long bombardment were butchered. American casualties totaled less than 1000, including fewer than 175 killed or missing. The Japanese, on the other hand, suffered unimaginably. Of the 4700 enemy on Kwajalein, 4650 were killed and only fifty captured.

By February 4 Kwajalein was secured by the American forces. The victorious Americans came upon gruesome sights. Whole trenches of enemy soldiers lay dead and rotting in the tropical sun. The stench of death permeated the air over the islands. Thousands of human bodies were decomposing rapidly and being cleaned of flesh by carnivorous animals.

Truk, the great Japanese base in the Caroline Islands from which Admiral Inouye had ordered the attack on Wake Island on

A Japanese pillbox on Kwajalein after the American bombardment.

December 8, 1941, was called "Japan's Gibraltar of the Pacific." It received a devastating attack from American forces on February 17.

The Japanese paid a dreadful price at Kwajalein Atoll, only to lose in the end. On February 21 Eniwetok Atoll, some 285 miles northeast of Kwajalein, was taken by the surging American force. With Kwajalein firmly in American hands, Dick Darden was within 2200 miles of the American fleet. Serious opposition still stood between Dick and the liberating forces, but by February of 1944 the American forces in the Pacific were gaining strength and confidence, and they were steaming directly toward Japan.

During the early months of 1944 the Japanese occupation force on Wake Island continued to endure the constant pounding from American bombers and warships. Between January and May of that year American planes flew 996 sorties against the island, dropping over 1000 tons of bombs. American ships offshore poured many tons of high explosive artillery shells into the island. Over 7000 five-inch and six-inch shells were fired at Wake by the United States Navy. The blockade cut off virtually all supplies coming to the island. The Japanese soldiers were literally starving to death.

At first the majority of the bombing of Wake was done by Army B-24's based on Midway. This began on July 8, 1943, when eight B-24's made the first land-based strike on Wake. When the Japanese bases on Kwajalein and Eniwetok were captured early in 1944, this provided three American air bases within striking distance of Wake Island. Wake Island was too far east to be involved in the island-hopping American campaign. It would never be subjected to an assault by an American Marine landing force. It did, however, harbor enough men and aircraft to be a problem to the backside of the American drive toward Japan. The Japanese occupation force, therefore, began to take a terrific pounding from aerial bombings at regular intervals.

The Japanese ships that had originally attacked Wake Island were not faring much better than the garrison which was still occupying the island. On April 27, 1944, the YUBARI was sunk in the Philippine Sea. Just over two weeks later, on May 13, 1944, the TATSUTA was sunk by a submarine while off the Japanese coast near Yokohama. Prior to these actions, the TENRYU had been sunk on December 18, 1942, in the Bismarck Sea, also by submarine attack.

The work parties of prison laborers from Osaka 1 prison frequently encountered memorable situations as they were being marched to and from work. The groups ranged from two or three men in small details to several dozen men used on some of the larger job sites. The earthquake tremors came to be accepted as one of the perils of being in Japan. One day the earth began to rumble as a group of POW's were marching back toward Osaka 1 after a day's work. The formation of men was in front of a public bathhouse which was packed with men, women, and children. When the tremor hit, the naked bathers came running hysterically out of the building. They began running in all directions, jabbering frantically as they went.

In a matter of moments the prisoners watched the street fill with naked people. The earthquake caused the walls of the wooden bathhouse to pitch at a forty-five degree angle. The next day as the men were being marched along the same street to another work site they noticed that the bathhouse walls had been jacked back up into the original position, and business was booming just as it had been

American landing craft, probably including Lt. Geddie Herring's LCI, approach Roi and Namur Islands from the lagoon.

before.

The POW laborers were paid at the rate of "ten sen" per day, which was virtually no money at all. It would take months to save enough to buy a morsel of food. Eggs sold for the equivalent of $1.00 each in Japan, and meat simply was not in Dick's diet. He had eaten no meat or poultry for months.

Japanese street vendors sold shish-ka-bobs that were made by skewering onions, potatoes, blubber, and several other types of mystery meat. If a prisoner could save enough money, he might be lucky enough to persuade one of his friendly Japanese coolie co-workers to sneak out into the street and purchase a shish-ka-bob for him. This was considered to be a real delicacy to the prisoners.

There was an old Japanese man who often worked as a coolie with Dick's work crew. The old man was very much against the war and was willing to help the POW's whenever he could. Most of the work details, however, were aboard ships and were strictly regulated. There was little opportunity for anyone, the Japanese coolies included, to get ashore and purchase food. The opportunities to send someone in to the markets or street vendors was rare indeed, so food purchases were virtually impossible.

One evening Dick was among a group of sixteen prisoners who were being marched back to camp after a day's labor. There were four rows of prisoners, marching four abreast. They were coming through a residential area where most of the small Japanese homes had a few square feet of garden space and small livestock such as chickens. Suddenly, as the men were marching along, a chicken darted out of a house and ran into the formation. The unfortunate fowl had run into one side of the formation, but failed to exit from the other. One of the men had grabbed the chicken, quickly choked it to death to avoid any noises, and stuffed the bird into his knapsack.

The old Japanese man who owned the chicken had seen his valuable fowl run into the group of men and knew that one of the men had it, but he did not know which man was guilty. The old man ran ahead of the POW's who continued to march toward the prison about three blocks down the street. There he told the officer of the day what had happened and angrily jabbered that he wanted his bird back. The men were standing in four rows and the chicken was somewhere in the second. The old man, two guards, and the Duty Officer began searching each man thoroughly, starting with the front row.

The four were so attentive of each man they searched that they ignored all of the others. As they were feverishly searching a man in the front row, a POW on the third row gently reached forward and took the knapsack from the man's shoulder in the second row and slipped it onto his own shoulder. The chicken was successfully moved back one row and away from the next row to be searched.

When the old man and the guards searched the actual culprit in the second row, they found nothing and went on down the line, focusing all of their angry attentions on the next man. The conspirator on the third row then slowly slipped the napsack back onto the shoulder of the man in the second row. All of the men were thoroughly searched, but no chicken was ever found.

Americans take cover in a bomb crater on Roi and fire their M1 Carbines at the Japanese.

Japanese machine gun position on Namur wiped out by artillery fire.

The Japanese Duty Officer then became irritated at the old man for falsely accusing the prisoners of such a serious offense and then he proceeded to chew the civilian out in no uncertain terms. The POW's were ordered to go on into camp, an order they quickly followed. Once inside, they told the three American cooks of their prize. The cooks told them to dress the bird and carefully hide all of the evidence. They did this, but were then faced with the problem of disposing of the feathers, feet, head, and the few inedible entrails.

The men went to the edge of the yard outside the barracks and stationed lookouts at each end of the building to tell them when the two guards marching around the compound were getting close. When the time was right they cut a 12" square of sod from the ground and took enough dirt out beneath it to bury the chicken parts. When the sod was replaced it was virtually impossible to tell that anything was amiss. The extra soil was taken to the wall and innocently tossed over the top into the dirt street outside.

About 4:45 the next morning, fifteen minutes before the normal wakeup call, someone nudged Dick as he slept on his top shelf and quietly told him to "go to the galley." All sixteen men who had taken part in the theft were there with their Klem cans ready for what they expected to be a meager ball of rice for breakfast. Instead they were grandly surprised to find that the cooks had prepared a tasty chicken and rice soup, and each man got a Klem can full. Dick took his back to the barracks and climbed back up onto his shelf to savor the delicacy. He slid back against the wall and slowly sipped the soup. It was such a wonderful deviation from the normally bland

An M1 Garand marks a fallen Marine on Eniwetok.

Dead Japanese soldiers in a ditch on Kwajalein.

Landing strips were soon repaired and American planes took off from Eniwetok.

rice that he would remember the taste of that bowl of chicken and rice soup for the rest of his life.

The theft of the chicken could have easily been detected by the Japanese guards and would probably have been dealt with severely. But since the men were being fed only two small rice balls each day, and since some had already lost nearly 100 pounds during the years of toiling at hard labor, such risks became acceptable. Certain chances had to be taken if they were to avoid starving to death. As the war progressed and American naval activity around the island nation intensified, the flow of food into Japan and Osaka 1 Prison slowed to a trickle.

By the middle of 1944 the horrid war seemed to be endless to Dick and the prisoners in Osaka 1 prison. Very little information, much of it rumors or propaganda, reached the men about the progress of the war outside Japan. The bits of news that reached them indicated that American forces were pressing ever closer to the island country. Little did they know that earlier that year the island hopping Marine, Army, and Navy forces had decided that the time had come to thrust themselves deep inside the defensive perimeter to which the Japanese military had withdrawn.

The Japanese had to guess where the next offensive might come. Would it be their big bases in the Carolines at Truk. Would it be at their strategic air bases in the Marianas at Guam, Tinian, and Saipan? Would it be the Philippines? The Japanese began pouring their defensive forces into the Carolines and Marianas.

"Chow Down" by Maj. James R. Brown. American POW's in Japanese prison sit on wooden sleeping shelves with their bowls as a kneeling man ladels out the daily ration of thin rice soup.

Chapter 50
SAIPAN, TINIAN, and GUAM –
1200 MILES FROM JAPAN

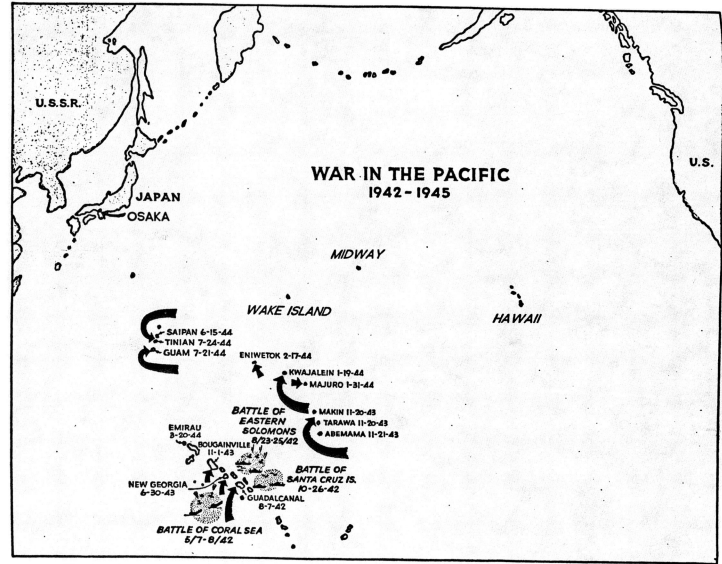

WAR IN THE PACIFIC
1942 – 1945

U.S.S.R.

JAPAN
OSAKA

MIDWAY

WAKE ISLAND

HAWAII

U.S.

SAIPAN 6-15-44
TINIAN 7-24-44
GUAM 7-21-44   ENIWETOK 2-17-44

KWAJALEIN 1-19-44
MAJURO 1-31-44

BATTLE OF
EASTERN
SOLOMONS
8/23-25/42

MAKIN 11-20-43
TARAWA 11-20-43
ABEMAMA 11-21-43

EMIRAU
3-20-44
BOUGAINVILLE
11-1-43

BATTLE OF
SANTA CRUZ IS.
10-26-42

NEW GEORGIA
6-30-43

GUADALCANAL
8-7-42

BATTLE OF CORAL SEA
5/7-8/42

The American military hierarchy decided that the next thrust would be to the Marianas. A victory there would give the Allies control of numerous air bases from which long range B-29 bombers could reach the Japanese motherland. A victory there would also breach the enemy's lines of supply and communication with bases farther to south. The move by the Americans was bold, and would carry them almost a thousand miles closer to the Japanese mainland. By mid-July of 1944 the Americans were poised and ready for the assaults on three Japanese occupied islands in the Marianas…Guam, Tinian, and Saipan.

Strategy for the attack on the Marianas would incorporate many of the techniques learned in the previous atoll battles, but there would be new concerns. The Mariana Islands had considerably more land mass to be conquered and the topography was more difficult to overcome than the flat sandy atolls. In the Marianas there were mountains, thus offering the enemy high vantage points and the protection of caves. There were steamy tropical jungles, adding to the discomfort of the American soldiers and providing ideal defensive obstacles which would have to be overcome. But there were also plains, and it was there that the prized airfields were to be had.

A huge American force was gathered. More than 700 naval ships were massed to form a potent fleet. Included were aircraft carriers, which brought the available number of aircraft to over 2000, battleships for bombardment with their massive guns, and every other conceivable type of ship. Over 300,000 men from the Marines, Army, and Navy would be involved. About half of these were amphibious troops, many of whom had cut their teeth during the previous battles.

They were tough, battle tested men, well trained, experienced, and confident. The date was set. Saipan would be invaded on June 15, 1944, with the other two islands to be hit soon afterwards.

The Japanese on Saipan numbered 30,000 men. They were approaching the point of having their backs to their homeland, so everyone knew that they would fight to the bitter end. A large number of warplanes were stationed on the airfields of the islands, but many fell victim to the incessant naval bombardment and air strikes that occurred during the month before the landing.

On June 15 American forces went ashore on Saipan. They were met at the beach by Japanese troops who offered stubborn resistance. Fighting was bitter and progress was slow. In three weeks of tough, bloody fighting, the landing force pushed the enemy back into the northern tip of the island. A vicious counterattack was conducted by 1500 tough Japanese troops who penetrated the Marine's front lines in bloody fighting before being killed to the last man. With this victory secured, the battle for Saipan was essentially over. By July 9 Saipan was completely in American hands.

The planned attacks on Guam and Tinian had been held up for several reasons. The intense resistance by the Japanese on Saipan had not been expected. In addition to this, a large Japanese naval fleet had sortied from the Philippines toward the Marianas. It had been met and soundly defeated by the American Fifth Fleet in the Battle of the Philippine Sea on June 19-22. In what became known as the "Saipan Turkey Shoot," the enemy had lost over 400 planes.

With the situation on Saipan under control and the Japanese fleet repulsed in the Philippine Sea, the American force turned its attention to Guam. Geddie Herring had been the junior officer on his LCI since the landing on Kwajalein in early 1944. Thusfar he had come through the campaign without injury. During preparations for the American landing on Guam his ship was called upon to encounter the enemy, and while in harm's way Herring had his first close call.

Prior to the invasion of Guam, steps had to be taken to penetrate the protective reef that surrounded the island. Herring's LCI was ordered to approach the shore at Guam and provide cover for ten Marine frogmen who were attempting to blow a hole in the reef. The underwater demolition specialists had been dropped from the speed boats and were setting the charges that would open the door in the reef for the invasion. Herring's boat was to provide cover for the operation and then pick up the frogmen after the explosives had been put in place.

While Herring's gunboat picked up the first eight divers it began to take fierce fire from the Japanese shore positions. A Jap wasp's nest had been irritated and Herring was beginning to feel the sting. The LCI was forced to wait for the last two frogmen. Needless to say, Herring was in a terribly vulnerable position and wanted to steer his boat back out into safer waters.

Finally the last two divers came aboard. It was learned that they had actually gone beyond the reef and onto the enemy beach. They had left the eight divers to set the charges and had risked their lives in the face of the Japanese machine guns to run onto the beach and plant a sign in the sand that would greet the invasion force soon afterwards. The sign read, "Welcome Army to Guam." It was signed "The United State Marines." The gutsy divers had taken one-upmanship to the extreme.

On July 21 the landing on Guam was made. A fierce effort by the enemy held the Marines at their beachhead for nearly a week. By August 10 the island had been taken, but the large land area and variety of terrain offered the enemy numerous hiding places. Thousands of enemy soldiers were still at large on the island with no idea of giving up. In the next five days over 6000 Japanese were killed.

The landing on the island of Tinian began on July 24. Tinian had three airfields, and was therefore prized by both sides. After several days of fighting the Japanese made their last stand near the southern end of the island. There they were defeated, and by August 1 the American forces were in control of the island and the air bases. Work began shortly thereafter to place the air bases back into working order.

The victory in the Marianas was expensive and bloody. American forces suffered 25,000 casualties, including 5000 killed or missing in action. However, the carnage to the Japanese was staggering. The Emperor lost 48,000 men defending Saipan, Tinian, and Guam. Very few Japanese troops elected to endure the disgrace of surrender. Many committed suicide, firing their rifles into their mouths with their toes, rather than be captured alive by the Americans. The war had come to the very shores of the Japanese homeland.

With the air facilities in the Marianas securely in American hands, the Japanese fate was virtually sealed. Saipan and Tinian became home for hundreds of B-29 superfortresses, big bombers which could easily negotiate the 1200 mile distance to Japan. Soon the bombing of the heart of the Japanese empire would begin. Though Dick Darden was not aware of the happenings in the Marianas, he would soon be only too aware of the proximity of American bases. The big American bombers would soon be dropping thousands of their calling cards on the enemy homeland, some directly on top of Dick Darden.

During the fall of 1944 the Japanese unleashed a new weapon which would terrorize many an American sailor. It was called the Kamikaze. For the first time in history, airplanes would be packed with explosives and flown directly into enemy ships by pilots who were eager to commit suicide for their Emperor. During the final year of the war hundreds of Japanese planes and pilots would meet their demise in such a manner, bringing death and tremendous damage to the Allied forces.

On October 25, 1944, Japan introduced its first kamikaze to American forces. Several of these manned bombs flew from Japan toward the Philippines where they encountered an American carrier force just off Leyte. The aircraft carrier ST. LOUIS was sunk and three other ships seriously damaged by the kamikazes. The death planes introduced a new element to naval warfare which brought fear and uncertainty to the men aboard our fleets plying the waters of the Pacific and inching ever closer to the Japanese islands.

America was not without new weapons of mass destruction of her own. These new weapons would figure much more prominently in deciding the outcome of the war with Japan than the kamikaze. One such weapon was the B-29 bomber. The B-29 was a vast improvement over the B-17, which had proven itself so well as a workhorse over Europe. Boeing built these great new silver birds to be nearly 100 feet long, with a wingspan of over 140 feet. The B-29 was truly a vehicle for spreading carnage and death on a massive scale.

There were twelve .50 cal. machine guns mounted on these

A Kamikaze crashes into the USS MISSOURI as helmeted artillerymen strain to see where the impact will be.

great four-engine bombers, and there was a 20mm cannon mounted in her tail. The huge planes could cruise at 350 miles per hour at an altitude of over five miles. They could carry 8000 pounds of bombs over a range of 3500 miles. Relative to any aircraft ever built for the purpose of war, in 1944 the B-29 could only be described as awesome. The Japanese people were about to feel the sting of this potent fighting machine.

In order to effectively neutralize the will of the Japanese people and the enemy war machine itself, the B-29's needed bases near their targets that could be efficiently supplied. In the fall of 1944 General Curtis Lemay was assigned to fly the B-29's on raids over Japan from Chengtu, China. There he learned the capabilities of the B-29, along with its strengths and weaknesses. The bombing runs were relatively long, and the supply routes were inefficient.

Bases in China had to be supplied by American transport planes which carried fuel, bombs, and many other necessary materials over the "hump," or Himalaya Mountains, from India. This was cumbersome and inefficient. The massive bombing raids that were needed to bring Japan to her knees would be difficult to conduct from China. When the American forces took control of the critical air bases in the Marianas in late 1944, the conduct of the war would take on a new appearance. The B-29's would find a home at Guam and Tinian, only 1400 miles from Japan and with easy access to American-controlled shipping lanes.

The industrial cities, such as Osaka and nearby Kobe, became targets for destruction. The great American bombers would attempt to cripple the Japanese war effort by shutting down the factories. The POW's in those cities were, unfortunately, in the direct path of a wave of American destruction.

The men in Osaka 1 prison were still getting two rice balls each day. However, the rice balls were no longer as large as softballs, as they had been in the beginning. By late 1944 they were smaller than baseballs. Small dried cubes of the turnip-like dicons were occasionally chopped and thrown in with the rice, and a few of the green leafy tops would be boiled in water to make a thin soup for the 600 prisoners. A lucky man would find a few green bits of leaf in his soup.

After years of such an austere diet Dick made a pact with himself. He promised himself that, if he ever got out of Osaka 1 and made it home alive, he would NEVER allow himself to go hungry again. Dick had suffered through years of starvation, saved from death only by the theft of dirty scraps of food from the floors of the barges. He dreamed about food while the pangs of hunger shot through his belly. If he ever found his way out of this Japanese monster, he promised himself, he would never be denied again.

At the onset of cold weather in 1944 Dick and his mates in Osaka 1 were much thinner and in poorer health than had been the case during any of their previous winters in Japan. There was real concern as to whether they would have the stamina to endure another harsh Japanese winter. As the physical condition of the prisoners deteriorated and their work conditions and food supply steadily worsened, everyone prayed that the war would soon end.

By late 1944 the emaciated, weakened men had lost so much weight that their resistance to cold temperatures had become extremely low. Their ragged clothes and thin blankets would be no match for the frigid temperatures they knew were about to settle into the city. At least this winter, their third in the Japanese prison, they knew what to expect as the cold season encroached on the city.

In the fall of 1944 Henry Franklin Darden, Dick's brother "Pete," was drafted into the U. S. Army. He had not taken his older brother's suggestion to join the Navy, so he found himself at Camp Croft, South Carolina, in basic training learning to be a foot soldier. This suited Pete just fine, however, since he relished the thought of being in the infantry and fighting against the Japanese. As cold weather approached Pete hoped that his unit would be assigned to the Pacific where he could fight against the Japanese who were holding his only brother.

The men at Osaka Principal again began their practice of sleeping in pairs in order to fend off the freezing temperatures. Now, more than ever, they had no choice. Dick would bundle up under his half of the two blankets and hope that the body heat that he shared with his bunkmate would be enough to keep the two alive through the night. The practice had worked many times before. Perhaps it would work again.

But, late in 1944, even this ploy was not enough to ward off the cold. The combination of the life at hard labor, inadequate food, constant hunger, and bitter cold proved too much for Dick's bunkmate. When Dick awoke one morning there was a strange coldness to his shelf. When he reached over to feel for his partner he found a cold, firm corpse. The man had given in to the austere conditions and was dead.

Dick's buddy was hard and had turned dark blue in color. He had apparently died early the evening before. Dick was momentarily shocked, but quickly realized that he must not give in to the same fate. He promised himself, even more determinedly than

Darden Collection

Private Henry Franklin "Pete" Darden was drafted during the fall of 1944 into the Army.

ever before, that he was going to outlive the slanty-eyed bastards that were doing this to him. Only those men with such an attitude, with a real commitment to survive, would be able to endure much more.

Since the general physical condition of the prisoner population had deteriorated into the critical phase, it had become almost accepted in Osaka 1 prison for the day to begin with the disposal of the dead prisoners' bodies. This time the corpse happened to be in the same bed with Dick. The Japanese method of getting rid of bodies was cremation. A crew of prisoners was chosen and sent out the cremate the body.

A few days after the incident in Dick's bed, another prisoner died and Dick was assigned to the cremation detail. He would never forget it. First, the men took the body to a nearby field. Then they were told to collect scrap lumber from the general area and make a pile over the body. A can of gasoline was poured over the pile and it was set on fire.

Some of the men would become nauseated as the body began to burn. First the body would swell and the belly would pop. The prisoners would have to continue to add wood to the fire for several hours before the ghastly job was done, all the while retching from the unbearable stench of the burning corpse.

Finally there would be nothing left but the skull and some bones. A few of the ashes and bones were placed in a small white box to be sent back home. The worst part for the prisoners was watching the burning body and wondering if they would end up going home in one of the white boxes. Some wondered to themselves if the dead were not really the victors, having been freed from the agony and misery of living year after year in Osaka 1 prison.

By the end of 1944 Jim Hesson had talked the guards at Umeda Bunsho into allowing Ralph Holewinski go out on work details. His draining back wound had finally healed to the point that a small amount of work was possible, and Hesson knew that Skee had to get out of camp and steal some food if he was going to survive.

Since each work detail needed a water boy who would boil water for the men, and since this job usually went to a man who was sick or otherwise unable to work at hard labor with the other men, Skee certainly fit the job description. In fact, the water boy was really a cook who would take some of the food stolen during the morning shift and prepare it in the boiling water so that the men could have some type of soupy meal at midday.

Each work detail of prisoners at Umeda Bunsho formed a strong union, each man looking out for his fellow POW. The prisoners made the rules to a great extent as long as they functioned together as a unit. If food rations were cut, so too was the amount of work done by the team. The group could go from its normal speed into very slow gear, and a job which might have taken a half hour to complete would become a half day operation.

The company men who were furnished to guard the prisoners never complained to the soldiers or company officials about incidents at work because they knew that if they did something would probably happen to them. Sometimes heavy objects would mysteriously fall on uncooperative company men in the warehouses. Accidents did happen, and the Jap honchos did not want one to happen to them. The prisoners had precious little power to control the situations around them, but they had learned many tricks about being imprisoned and making things happen.

One day the Japanese soldiers and company officials

decided to rearrange the groups of men and work schedules in order to break up these unions. The water boys were ordered not to cook any food, only to provide the men with water. Within two days the POW's had reorganized and it was business as usual. The company men were interested only in getting their materials loaded or unloaded, and they knew that hungry prisoners would not, and could not, function very well. The company men told the POW's privately not to tell the guards that they were cooking food on the job.

The Japanese population was getting cracked corn mixed into their rice as a filler since there was not enough rice to feed them. When no one was looking the POW's could steal raw rice and take it back to Holewinski who would boil it for them. He learned to sprinkle cracked corn on top of the cook pot so that it would appear that the men were eating corn, not the Jap's precious rice. If it had not been for the ingenuity of the prisoners in locating, stealing, and preparing food on the job there would surely have been a lot of American POW's who would never have seen home again.

Some of the POW details worked yards where beer and sake came into Japan. Many a prisoner got his fill of liquor on the job. Bribery was common, and occasionally a Japanese company man would "forget" to seal the door properly to a railroad car full of beer. After the prisoners had taken their fill they would seal the car properly and no one would be the wiser. For a kickback of ten pounds of stolen beans or rice a car would be left conveniently open for the prisoners. Most of the workers in the Japanese breweries were Korean children 12 to 15 years old who worked at forced labor while receiving even less food than the American POW's.

Japanese coolies also learned how to play the game. They were some of the poorest people in Japan and needed food almost as bad as the prisoners. There was usually one coolie working with each three or four POW's. They, too, liked to work on details that unloaded beer or sake cars.

The varieties of foodstuffs coming through the freight yard were seasonal. During the fall there would be lots of sweet potatoes and tangerines. Cases of these foods frequently broke apart and the men would eat what they could wolf down without being seen. They would eat skins and all to avoid leaving telltale garbage behind that the guards might find. From February until August there were few fresh foods. Usually only dried beans and rice came through. Occasionally during the cool season the men might find some onions or dicons.

After Guam was taken by American forces on July 21, and Tinian was taken three days later, Geddie Herring and his LCI were stationed eight miles away on the newly conquered island of Saipan. There they would await the next move by the American forces in the island-hopping campaign. Herring and his men waited on Saipan throughout the fall of 1944 to see where the next battle would be.

It was decided that the invasion forces would not cross the vast expanses of the Pacific to Hawaii or California to await the next battle orders. Even though the ships might be safer in waters closer to the continental United States, it was thought that the wear and tear on the engines of the ship during such long trips could not be justified. During the assignment in Saipan in the fall of 1944, Geddie Herring became skipper of his LCI. When the next battle in the trek toward Japan came, Lt. Herring would be in command.

Herring's first assignment as commander of the ship was to assist several meteorologists in atmospheric tests in the area around Saipan. The military had problems with their radar units because it had not been determined exactly how to bend radar waves around the horizon. The meteorologists wanted to know the air temperature at 500 feet, 700 feet, 900 feet, and so on. They were trying to see if radar could be built that would take advantage of varying temperatures and corresponding densities in the strata of air to bend radar waves around the horizon of the earth, thus alerting them of enemy planes which were below the horizon and out of sight.

In order to conduct these tests Lt. Herring would mount a steel cable to the fantail of his boat. This cable was connected to a large kite. When the ship was moving at five knots the kite could be adjusted to different altitudes and the scientists would take their readings. During August and September Herring's LCI conducted the atmospheric tests almost daily.

When the meteorologists left, Lt. Herring's ship was given another assignment. It became a mail boat. Each day the ship would carry the mail across the four mile channel between Saipan and Tinian. This was important because Tinian had become a major airbase. From runways in the Marianas hundreds of B-29's were launched to carry out bombing raids on Japan. A reliable courier service between the islands was very important to the bombing effort over the enemy homeland.

As the Christmas season of 1944 drew near for the people in Clinton, Eva Bell had one son in a Japanese prison camp and another preparing to go to the Pacific and join the fight. Pete was nearing the end of his basic training in South Carolina. No word had been received from Dick in sixteen months. Then, less than a week before Christmas day, a letter arrived from Japan. The text of the letter was printed in the local newspaper, and Eva Bell was described as "elated." The dark shadow over her Christmas season would not be quite as gloomy as before.

Dick had anticipated that the letter would take many weeks to deliver. He had written the message on September 17, over three months before Christmas. Nonetheless, he wrote, "If you get this in time, Merry Christmas." Dick finished the letter by saying, "Pray this mess is over soon. It can't be too soon for me and I know you are tired of it, but keep smiling." The letter was exactly 100 words in length.

At about the same time, during the Christmas season of 1944, another message was broadcast over Radio Tokyo from Dick to his mother. This one, like the previous message, was monitored by Americans on the west coast and in Hawaii. Luckily for Eva Bell a young man named R. D. Pridgen was a Seaman First Class in the Navy stationed in Hawaii. Pridgen had lived in Clinton for several months in 1940 when he was employed by Carolina Power and Light Company. As he listened to the broadcast from Radio Tokyo he heard Clinton mentioned and hurried to write down as much of the message as he could. While he could not get the entire text of the message on paper, he was able to quote small parts of it and summarize the broadcast.

Seaman Pridgen wrote a letter to Eva Bell immediately after hearing the message over the radio. In his letter he relayed Dick's message that he was in good health and receiving good treatment. Dick would have had to say such nonsense in order to be selected for broadcast by the propaganda-hungry Japanese censors. Even so, the words surely brightened Eva Bell's Christmas. Pridgen quoted Dick directly in the letter, saying, "Although I cannot see you this Christmas I hope to be with you next."

Seaman Pridgen followed this quote with one of his own which made his feelings about the Japanese clear. "That I promise you, Mrs. Darden," he said. "All of us in the Pacific will never rest until our friends and loved ones have been liberated and the Japanese Imperialists have been made to pay for every ounce of American blood they have caused to be spilled." With that he asked Eva Bell to pass his regards along to Dr. Turlington and his family, with whom Pridgen had lived in Clinton, and he ended the letter with "Aloha, Rufus D. Pridgen."

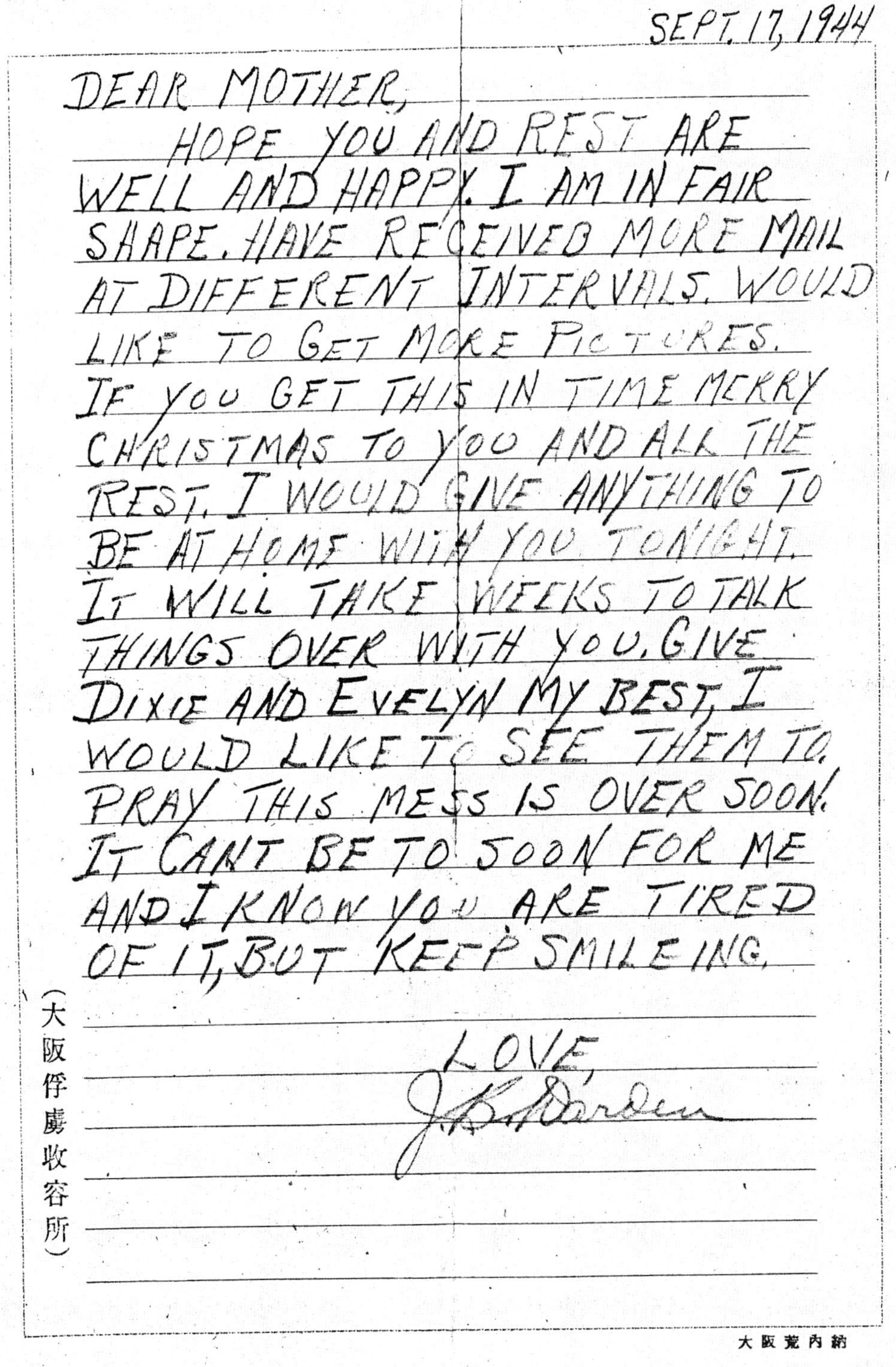

SEPT. 17, 1944

DEAR MOTHER,
HOPE YOU AND REST ARE WELL AND HAPPY. I AM IN FAIR SHAPE. HAVE RECEIVED MORE MAIL AT DIFFERENT INTERVALS. WOULD LIKE TO GET MORE PICTURES. IF YOU GET THIS IN TIME MERRY CHRISTMAS TO YOU AND ALL THE REST. I WOULD GIVE ANYTHING TO BE AT HOME WITH YOU TONIGHT. IT WILL TAKE WEEKS TO TALK THINGS OVER WITH YOU. GIVE DIXIE AND EVELYN MY BEST, I WOULD LIKE TO SEE THEM TO. PRAY THIS MESS IS OVER SOON. IT CANT BE TO SOON FOR ME AND I KNOW YOU ARE TIRED OF IT, BUT KEEP SMILEING.

LOVE
J.B. Darden

（大阪俘虜收容所）

大阪荒内納

"The Long Dark" by Major James R. Brown depicts an emaciated American POW, his face showing the hellish agony of years in a Japanese prison, restrained by barbed wire. The entangled man behind him symbolizes the futility of the situation.

Chapter 51
OSAKA 1—1945

National Archives

America's weapon of mass destruction, the Boeing B-29, bristles with bombs, machine guns, and cannons

By early 1945 Dick Darden had been a Japanese prisoner of war for more than three full years. The effects were obvious, as he had lost over 100 pounds. Dick had entered the Navy weighing 220 pounds. When he was taken from Wake Island to Japan in early 1942, after spending five months in the prisoners' hospital on Wake recovering from his wounds, his weight had dropped by forty pounds to 180. By mid-1944 his official weight, kept accurately by the Japanese, was 51.2 kilos, or 112 pounds.

Dick maintained his weight at about 112 pounds for the final year of his Japanese captivity. There simply was nothing left to lose on his lanky frame. As emaciated as he was, Dick could still lift and carry the 100 kilo (220 pound) bags of rice and soybeans on the barges and carry them on his back for considerable distances to the warehouses on the docks. While many of the other men finally gave up and died, Dick made a pact with himself. He decided that, come hell or high water, he simply was not going to let these Jap SOB's kill him.

As the war moved into its final stages there were noticeable changes in the POW camps in Japan. There were indications that the war was moving closer to the Japanese homeland, and this was good news for the prisoners because it implied that the end of their imprisonment was getting nearer. Fewer and fewer ships were coming into port, and of the ones making it through, many were blown to pieces and barely afloat. Seeing the damaged ships tickled the hell out of the POW's because it told them that America was winning the war and friendly forces were getting close to Japan. The fact that American submarines and planes were taking a heavy toll on Japanese shipping fostered encouragement and optimism in the POW camps.

When the bombing by land-based planes began, the POW's knew that Allied forces were within a few hundred miles of Japan. Since the Allies had taken the Japanese bases on Guam and Saipan, American bombers were able to operate within range of the Japanese homeland. The long-range flying fortresses flew wave after wave of bombing attacks, dropping millions of tons of high explosives on the enemy.

Osaka was about nine or ten miles across the harbor from the city of Kobe. Kobe was usually visible in the distance to the men working the docks in Osaka because it was positioned on a mountainside that faced toward Osaka. Kobe was both a port city and an industrial center, so it was one of the first areas to become a prime target of Allied bombing raids.

The POW's working the waterfront area in Osaka could look up and see the waves of American bombers as they came directly over Osaka in formations heading toward Kobe. The men watched as the B-29's seemed to release their bombs directly over Osaka, and they could follow the deadly projectiles as they fell through the air toward Kobe. Wave after wave of the bombers would come over. The men could see the bombs landing in Kobe, eventually leveling much of that city. City blocks appeared to be lifted off the ground by the bombs, only to settle back into piles of rubble. The prisoners, happy to see fellow Americans so close, would cheer as each block went down.

Soon after the raid on Kobe, the formations of American bombers turned their attention to the city of Osaka. The American strategy seemed to call for the bombers to alternate between the two cities until both were obliterated. Dick watched the first air raid on Osaka from his bunk at Osaka 1 prison. It was a night raid, and since his shelf was in a top corner by a window facing the waterfront he could see the fence and sky outside the barracks. Dick watched the sky all night, from 11:00 p.m. until 5:00 a.m., as wave after wave of American planes came directly overhead. Such sights would become commonplace in the weeks and months ahead, as American bombers would bring massive amounts of explosives to the area, alternating between Kobe and Osaka as their primary targets.

On February 4 representatives of the "Big Three" Allied powers met near Yalta, a Russian resort city on the Black Sea in the Crimea. With Germany reeling under intense pressure on both the eastern and western fronts in Europe, an Allied victory appeared certain. The Yalta conference was held to firm up Allied strategies for the final phases of the war.

President Franklin D. Roosevelt represented the United States at Yalta, while Prime Minister Winston Churchill represented the British. Premier Joseph Stalin was the Russian representative. One of the topics to be discussed was the involvement of Russia in the war in the Pacific. When the Allied powers met in Yalta Russia had not yet declared war on Japan and was not assisting the Allies in theirs effort to defeat Japan.

At the Yalta Conference Premier Stalin promised that he would enter the war with Japan after hostilities ceased in the European theater. A time schedule was placed on the promise. Russia agreed to commence hostilities against Japan within three months after the surrender of Nazi Germany. In return for the much-needed assistance, the Allies conceded that Russia would get the Kuril Islands and the southern part of Sakhalin Island, along with other concessions of war.

Smokestacks rise from the ruins of industrial Kobe, Japan, completely destroyed during the spring of 1945.

Chapter 52
IWO JIMA – 700 MILES FROM JAPAN

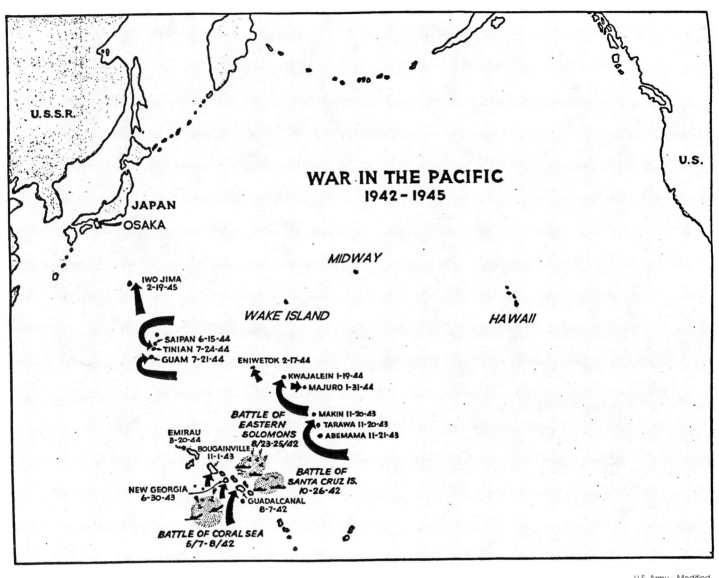

WAR IN THE PACIFIC
1942 – 1945

U.S.S.R.

U.S.

JAPAN
OSAKA

MIDWAY

IWO JIMA
2-19-45

WAKE ISLAND

HAWAII

SAIPAN 6-15-44
TINIAN 7-24-44
GUAM 7-21-44   ENIWETOK 2-17-44

KWAJALEIN 1-19-44
MAJURO 1-31-44

BATTLE OF
EASTERN
SOLOMONS
8/23-25/42

MAKIN 11-20-43
TARAWA 11-20-43
ABEMAMA 11-21-43

EMIRAU
3-20-44
BOUGAINVILLE
11-1-43

BATTLE OF
SANTA CRUZ IS.
10-26-42

NEW GEORGIA
6-30-43

GUADALCANAL
8-7-42

BATTLE OF CORAL SEA
5/7-8/42

U.S. Army – Modified

The island-hopping American forces had reached a point just 700 miles due south of Tokyo by February of 1945. They had kicked the Japs off of island after island along a bloody 2000 mile path across the Pacific Ocean. The next Japanese base that lay in their way was on a small island named Iwo Jima. As had been the case on Kwajalein, Saipan, Guam, and Tinian, Geddie Herring's LCI would take part in the invasion of Iwo Jima. With Mt. Suribachi looming in the background, Lt. Herring received his orders and prepared for the battle. Iwo Jima was impregnated with mile after mile of underground fortifications, and hundreds of hidden gun emplacements.

For weeks before the assault on Iwo Jima, U.S. Army bombers attacked the island relentlessly. So complete was their bombing that the island was said to look like a moonscape covered with craters. For several days prior to the landing, American naval forces bombarded the island, laying down rolling barrages similar to that which Dick had experienced on Wake but much more extensive. Despite the thousands of tons of explosives that were hurled at the island, the Japanese defenders, numbering 24,000 first-rate troops, lay in waiting.

The enemy had prepared well for the attackers from the sea, having hidden hundreds of artillery pieces in camouflaged positions throughout the island. Each rocky crack, each trench in the gray powdery volcanic sand, was well-fortified and manned by well-trained Japanese troops. They would give the 60,000 U. S. Marines their stiffest resistance thus far in the Pacific campaign.

The Japanese on Iwo Jima were fanatics, willing to fight to the very last man in order to stop the Americans short of their homeland. The Americans were facing an enemy with its back to the wall. Lt. Herring's assignment would be his most dangerous of the war. He was to take his ship into the dangerous waters near the island on February 17, two days before the February 19 D-Day for the invasion. He would approach the reef just offshore and assist in blowing an opening in the reef as was customary just prior to an invasion. The operation would place him and his men immediately in front of a massive amount of enemy fire power.

To make matters even more perilous for Herring, the American 7th Fleet was in the vicinity enroute to Tokyo and had stopped to help the invasion attempt by shelling the island. The battleships, cruisers, and destroyers of the Fleet were an imposing naval force as they sat offshore and fired their big projectiles into the Japanese fortifications on the island. The Navy gunboats began moving toward the island. Lt. Herring headed his boat toward the reef, one of twelve LCI's involved in the forward wave.

The Japanese mistook the smaller flotilla for the entire fleet. When the group of gunboats reached a point about a half mile offshore, the enemy opened up with their heavy artillery. The Japs thought this was the full invasion force, and Geddie Herring's LCI was caught in the middle of the fury. Shells began crashing into the surf all around Herring's boat, and he realized that he was in the midst of a battle.

The Japanese knew that there were only two places where the invasion force would likely come ashore. In preparation for this they had aimed a number of large guns at these spots from a considerable distance away. Lt. Herring's LCI was one of nine American craft that were heading directly into one of these areas when the Japs began firing with their 5" and 8" guns.

The demolition operation got underway, and Herring eased the bow of his LCI onto the reef and began covering the divers. Just as he ordered his machine guns and rocket launchers to open up on the enemy shore positions, the entire flotilla began to take a tremendous beating from the enemy artillery. The Japanese shells began exploding all around the ships, and the situation became a fire storm.

Suddenly a 5" shell blew the 40mm machine gun off of the bow of Herring's vessel, killing the sailors who were manning it. Then another 5" shell crashed into the ship amidships, just below his conning tower, destroying the other 40mm gun and cutting the electrical lines to the rocket launchers. This second shell had hit the wheelhouse, killing or immobilizing all of the men there.

Herring's ship had lost its largest guns, but still had the 20mm guns and small arms. The explosion from the second blast had sent shrapnel through the steel floor of the bridge, ripping into Herring boot's and breaking his foot. Even so, Herring ordered his men to sustain their fire with the remaining guns to cover the operation.

Then one of the enemy's largest guns found its mark. The conning tower of Lt. Herring's LCI took a direct hit from an 8" projectile. A tremendous blast swept through the steel compartment. Seven men were in the room at the time, including Herring, three other Navy men, two reporters, and one photographer. The other six men were killed instantly. Only Geddie Herring remained alive, and he had sustained severe injuries.

When the 8" shell had smashed into the ship's steel conning tower, Herring's executive officer had the misfortune of standing directly between Herring and the brunt of the blast. He was hit so badly, and by so many fragments of shrapnel, that afterwards his remains had to be gathered with a shovel for burial. Enough shrapnel went through this officer to inflict severe wounds on Lt. Herring, breaking his arm and shoulder.

Geddie Herring, with a broken foot, broken shoulder, and broken arm, looked up dazed to see his shoulder laid open. He could see a large half-moon shaped piece of shrapnel clearly visible and lodged between the bones of his shoulder. Everyone on the upper level of the boat, both fore and aft, was either killed or maimed. No one remained alive on the deck below. Herring knew that he had to do something to save the boat and the remaining men. He tried to pull himself together.

Herring reached across with his good arm and pulled on the piece of steel that protruded from his bleeding shoulder. He managed to remove the shrapnel, only to accidentally drop it onto the steel deck below the tower. He had the presence of mind to attempt to place the piece of steel into his pocket and save it for a souvenir, but cursed as he watched it hit the deck and roll over the side of the ship and into the ocean.

There was no one left in the wheelhouse one deck below Lt. Herring to steer the ship, and the enemy artillery rounds continued to explode all around. Nearly three dozen men were still alive and trying to operate the vessel below deck, and their lives were in serious jeopardy. The crippled boat was a juicy target for the enemy guns. One well placed round and the boat could be sunk with a loss of all hands. Herring knew that he had to somehow summons enough energy from his mangled body to save his men.

The enemy projectiles began coming more relentlessly than ever as the LCI sat dead in the water, a sitting duck. Despite his wounds Lt. Herring righted himself. With one arm hanging limp by his side and with one foot mangled and broken, he made his way down the ladder one level to the ship's pilot house. He took the ship's wheel with his one good arm and ordered the ship to full speed astern. He looked down on the deck and noticed two of his life-jacketed men who were still alive but on fire. He grabbed a fire hose with his good arm and began spraying them down, dousing the flames.

Geddie Herring was still groggy from the blast, but he remembered that his orders called for him to pull out of the line of fire if his ship became disabled so that one of the three reserve LCI's could take his place. He grabbed the telephone in the wheelhouse and found that the circuit was still in working order. He was able to give instructions to the men in the engine room below decks. He quickly issued orders for the ship to assume flank speed astern.

Herring began trying to steer the vessel out toward the protection of the fleet and away from the hostile area around the reef. But, in the confusion of putting out the fires on the burning men and moving to the wheelhouse, Herring had not noticed that the bow of his boat had actually been turned outward by the waves. He had ordered that the ship move in reverse, trying to back away from the intense fire near the shoreline. Instead, he was backing in closer to the beach and the deadly artillery barrage.

Enemy shells were still landing near Herring's LCI as he changed his orders to flank speed ahead. The ship began moving forward and out toward the larger ships. Herring propped himself up against a steel door and some ammunition cans. He was rapidly losing his strength due to the loss of a considerable amount of blood. Some of the men below had begun to trickle up on deck, so Herring ordered a boatswain's mate to take over the helm. He began to issue instructions to the sailor so that he could navigate the ship out toward safer waters. Even so, the ship was flooding in the hold and was on fire below deck near the magazine. The boat was still in great danger as it maneuvered out toward the fleet.

The warships just a short distance farther out were returning the enemy fire with their broadside guns, firing their projectiles at almost point blank range and just over Herring's boat. As Lt. Herring's crippled vessel limped toward safety he requested permission from the closest ship to bring his burning boat alongside. Permission was granted by the ship using flag signals, but as he moved closer he realized that he was coming in directly under the broadside guns on the ship.

The ship was the USS ARKANSAS, and it was in full engagement with its monstrous 14" guns. When the ship roared again with a salvo from the huge guns, the muzzle blasts blew out over 150 yards, almost striking Herring's boat as the projectiles whistled right over his head. He realized the danger of this position, and quickly navigated away from the line of fire. He knew that he must quickly get medical aid for his men, so he steered the ship through the dangerous waters and toward a mine sweeper he had spotted a short distance away.

Permission was requested and granted for Herring's boat to come alongside the mine sweeper. The wounded men were taken aboard by a crane and medics aboard the ship began to administer medical attention. There had been 54 men under Lt. Geddie Herring's command on the LCI. During the attempt to blow the reef off Iwo Jima 21 had been killed and another 19, Herring included, had been seriously wounded.

Geddie Herring's heroic response under intense fire that day almost surely saved the lives of the 33 men on his ship who lived through the holocaust. The wounded men were cared for on the mine sweeper and the dead were buried at sea at sundown. Of the 450 American men who took their ships toward the reef off Iwo Jima that day, 225 were killed by the Japanese. The war was over for Lt. Geddie Herring, but the island-hopping American troops pressed onward toward Japan.

Two days later, on February 19, the landing on Iwo Jima began. At 9:00 a.m. two Marine divisions landed on the beaches just below Mt. Suribachi. The Japanese opened up on them with every weapon available, from large coastal defense guns down to rockets, mortars, and machine guns. The landing beach became a hell on volcanic sand, and the assault began to bog down. Landing boats were hit in the surf by artillery fire, and enemy projectiles began falling onto the beach as it was cluttered with American men and equipment.

The Japanese had divulged many of their most important gun positions two days earlier when they fired on Lt. Geddie Herring and the gunboats just off the southeast coast of Iwo Jima. If that had not happened, the assault on February 19 would have surely cost many more American lives. Having seen many of the camouflaged guns in action, American naval guns were able to neutralize them prior to the invasion. Otherwise, the beachhead established on the 19th might have been a bloodbath.

Marines continued to hit the beaches on Iwo Jima until finally, by nightfall, there were 30,000 men ashore. They widened their beachhead and pressed the battle inland. The battle raged for several days and progress made in the ashen sands was measured in yards per day. Fighting was bitter, often hand to hand, as Marines had to use deadly frontal assaults to overrun foxhole after cave after ditch. Bayonets, hand grenades, flame throwers, and small arms became the weapons of the day.

Finally, on the fifth day of the battle, the American flag was raised on top of Mt. Suribachi. Still progress northward on the island was slow and treacherous. The enemy was dug in well and gave ground grudgingly. The Japanese retreated and massed near the northeast coast of the island. Continued artillery barrages could not blast the enemy into submission. By March 16, almost a month after the invasion had begun, the enemy was backed into a small area near Kitano Point at the northern tip of the island. By nightfall enemy resistance had been wiped out and the island was in American hands.

Immediately American B-29's started using the airfields on Iwo Jima, one damaged plane crash landing even before hostilities had actually ended. Before the war ended it was estimated that almost 2900 planes would land on Iwo rather than crash land into the ocean. Each had a crew of ten men, so it can be accurately said that by successfully invading and securing the island and its air facilities, the American forces saved a great number of the 2900 airmen who were forced to stop there.

But, the price for Iwo Jima was staggering. There were almost 21,000 American casualties. Of these, nearly 5000 men were killed. The carnage to the Japanese defensive forces was almost complete. Having paid the price of victory on Iwo Jima, the American campaign in the Pacific seemed unstoppable, heading northward toward the Japanese home islands. Victory over Japan, and freedom for Dick Darden, was less than 700 miles away.

Due to the severe injuries suffered at Iwo Jima, the war was over for Lt. Geddie Herring. This was not the case for Dick Darden's brother Pete, who had finished boot camp at Camp Croft, South Carolina, and had immediately been shipped to the west coast. Soon he was ordered farther west to Hawaii, where he got orders to join the fight near Japan. He was happy and eager to join the war in the Pacific, hoping to help drive the American campaign through the Japanese defenses and to Japan itself, where he could help his brother.

From Hawaii, Pete went first to Leyte in the Philippines. He corresponded with his mother, telling her that he was going to help liberate Dick. He made it clear that he was anxious to go and fight the Japanese. They had held his brother for more than three years, and it was time to bring Dick back home.

Since the fall of Iwo Jima the battle lines had been pushed closer to the enemy's home islands. With just a few hundred miles separating Pete from the Japanese main islands, the young Army private hoped for the opportunity to set foot on Japanese soil. It surely must have been exhilarating for the young soldier, who had just months before been a senior at Clinton High, to be able to participate in the battles to conquer the Japanese enemies who had imprisoned his brother for so long.

In Osaka 1 prison early in 1945 Dick Darden took part in a theft which was his greatest risk of the entire forty-five month

Death on the deck of an LCI at Iwo Jima. American sailors die at their gun positions after taking enemy artillery rounds.

imprisonment in Japan. Stolen goods, especially food, could be used in many ways other than just to gain nourishment. If men could steal more than enough to satisfy their immediate needs, the surplus was very valuable. Extra food was often shared with fellow prisoners who were sick and had no opportunity to steal for themselves. In addition, the contraband goods provided a means of bartering for other needed items. So when the chance to steal quantities of food presented itself, the temptation was great.

While working in a warehouse along the docks one day, Dick came upon stacks of boxes filled with canned tangerines. Each case contained forty-eight tin cans. Dick knew how valuable the tangerines would be since they were full of the vitamin C that so many of the sick men needed. It would be dangerous, but Dick enlisted the services of two other POW's in an effort to steal an entire case of the tangerines and get them back into camp. The three

managed to steal the case of tangerines and hide their valuable contraband under some other materials in the warehouse.

For several days they tried to think of a scheme that would allow them to get the materials into camp with a relative degree of safety. They knew how badly needed their stolen goods were to the men inside the camp, but they also knew that the punishment would likely be extreme if they were caught in the act. Stealing from the Japanese people during these austere times could be punishable by death. Dick did not want to take any foolish risks, but he knew how important it was to get the tangerines into the prison compound.

If the men were working a coal ship sometimes they would be allowed to clean up some of the coal on the floor and take it back to burn in the outdoor incinerator which was the only source of hot water available for bathing. The guards would allow this during winter because the frigid cold was severe, sometimes well below zero, and the men had no way to cleanse themselves of the irritants they encountered on the grain and coal ships unless they could bath occasionally in the camp.

The men decided that their best chance was to hide the tangerines in a sack of coal, which the guards probably would allow them to take back to camp. Their plan was to place the cans of tangerines deep inside a sack of coal and simply walk into camp with the seemingly innocent bag of fuel on Dick's shoulder. The first problem, however, was that they were not working any coal ships, so they would have to somehow come up with a bag of coal, and then get permission to bring it into camp.

The men went about the task, and within a few days had located some coal aboard a freight train they were loading. They stole a 100 pound bag of coal from the train that morning and hid it in a warehouse. During their lunch break, with the two other prisoners acting as lookouts, Dick retrieved the case of tangerines. The men hid behind stacks of materials in the warehouse as they removed most of the coal from the sack and carefully placed the entire contents of the box, forty-eight cans in all, in the middle of the coal sack.

Then coal was placed along the sides and over the top of the precious cans of citrus. They would carry this back to camp that night and tell the guards that a supervisor at work had given them permission to take the bag of coal. The sack looked innocent enough, just like a sack of scrap coal should look, with no cans visible. Under normal conditions the sack would be given a modest inspection at the prison gate and would be permitted inside. Everything appeared normal at this point, and the three expected the theft to be pulled off without a hitch.

Then trouble developed. The Japanese civilian supervisor found out that the three POW's had stolen the bag of coal. Dick and his buddies had expected to get his permission to carry the coal back into camp by telling him that they had cleaned it up off of the floors. But the supervisor had somehow found out about the theft. The first problem in this dangerous operation had arisen, and the three did not know what their fate would be. If they were reported to the military guards, they would be in real trouble.

Rather than having the men severely punished, as he could have done, the civilian supervisor approached them and said, "I hear that you have some coal, and I need some." This was the best thing that could have happened at this point, since it meant that the supervisor wanted a cut out of the coal and in return he would not report the theft. But he did not know that a far more serious theft had also taken place and that the stolen goods were in the coal sack.

Dick knew that he couldn't let the man get a bucket of coal out of the sack or he would find the tangerines. This would surely result in severe punishment. The supervisor stared at the sack, expecting his share immediately. The civilians were experiencing shortages of fuel, and the supervisor thought that he had found the perfect way to get heating fuel that he would take home to his family.

Dick had to think quickly and somehow keep the supervisor out of the sack. The only answer was for Dick to transfer the coal from the sack to the supervisor's bucket himself. Dick volunteered instantly, reaching for the supervisor's coal bucket.

"Yes, of course, let me get you some," Dick responded, still cool and collected. He knew that he had to maintain his composure or he was probably dead. He took the small bucket that the man had

National Archives

The invasion of Iwo Jima by thousands of American troops

U.S. Navy

The first American B-29 lands on IwoJima, March 5, 1945
This photo is autographed by Gen. Harry Schmidt.

given him and filled it to just over half full with coal. "More, this is not enough," insisted the supervisor. Dick had almost uncovered the cans, but he managed to get enough coal out to satisfy the man without exposing the tangerines.

A complex set of circumstances existed which made the chances of getting the cans into the camp look pretty good. The supervisor had taken part in the theft by skimming some of the booty off the top, and he didn't know about the tangerines, so he probably would not expose the caper. The Japanese guard, who had been watching the entire transaction, didn't know about the tangerines, but he did know about the dishonest supervisor.

Even so, since the Jap guard had not reported the theft to a higher authority, he too could be punished if his military superiors found out about the coal theft. He was under orders to report any such theft, and he had not. So both of the Japanese, either of which would probably have the three POW's executed had they known about the tangerines, would now allow the sack of coal to go back into the camp that night. Dick breathed a sigh of relief.

The men started back toward Osaka 1 with Dick carrying the heavy sack of coal on his back. Now there was only a thin veneer of coal, about one inch, concealing the tangerines since so much had been taken out to pay off the supervisor. As they turned the final corner before reaching camp Dick was greeted by a sight that made his heart stop. Not only were there about 500 prisoners standing at attention and being individually searched as they passed through the camp gate, but the Japanese duty officer at the gate was the most brutal of them all.

Another fact made the situation even worse than it might

already seem. The duty officer had just recently lost his entire family during an American bombing raid on the city. His wife, children, and in-laws were all killed when an American bomb had turned their house into an inferno and it had caved in on top of them. The brutal officer had been seething for several days, and was taking every opportunity to exert severe punishment on any American that he could.

Dick trembled as the thought of Babe Hofmeister, the man he had seen beheaded on Wake Island, flashed through his mind. Electricity seemed to shoot through his body and the flow of adrenaline caused his heart to pound as he sensed the severity of the situation he was about to put himself into. He continued to walk toward the prison.

As Dick neared the camp gate he prayed that he would not have to explain the origin of the coal sack. The worst thing right now would be for the officer to search him. He knew that if he looked nervous and showed the anxiety that now billowed inside of him that it would tip off the guards. He would try to walk right into the camp without stopping and without showing any emotions. He thought of the forty-eight cans and Babe Hofmeister.

Dick realized that he would have to fall into line like the other men, since none were being allowed to pass through the gate without being searched. He took his position, checking to see that the duty officer was at the other end of the line. Then the worst possible thing happened: the large sack over Dick's shoulder caught the Japanese officer's attention. He immediately came toward Dick in a trot. Dick snapped to attention with the heavy sack on his shoulder as the officer approached. His heart pounded as the officer

256

Japanese cities become infernos after air raids by American planes

pulled his samurai sword from its scabbard.

The Japanese duty officer glared at Dick, looking for him to break in the slightest. He seemed to be hoping for the slightest reaction that might indicate that something was wrong. The officer walked to the side and slid the cold steel blade into the sack, probing the contents but not striking the tangerine cans. The officer was toying with the thin layer of coal just inside the bag with the tip of his sword. Dick's heart beat wildly, but he managed to maintain a countenance that gave no clue of wrongdoing.

Dick could feel the guard glaring at him from the side as if electricity was piercing the air between them. He dared not look back. Then the officer walked to the rear and again Dick could feel him pierce the sack with his sword. Around to the other side he stepped, probing the coal all the while but amazingly not finding the cans. For what seemed several minutes Dick stood horrified while the officer toyed with him. He had absolutely no doubt that if the officer found the stolen goods on his shoulder he would be beheaded.

The Japanese guard was now getting nervous himself, since he had accompanied the prisoners back to camp with a large sack of coal. Since the guard was in charge of the work detail, he knew that the explanation for the origin of the coal would be his responsibility. Just as the duty officer was beginning to probe deeper into the bag with his sword, the guard spoke up, now covering for himself and with no regard for Dick. He explained that the men were given permission by a supervisor at the warehouse to pick up the coal to burn in their boiler so the men could have a bath. The guard's reasoning had justified Dick's having the coal in a way that Dick probably never could.

The officer stared back toward Dick again, and then slowly put his sword back into its scabbard. "Eroshi," he shouted, motioning toward the steps of the barracks. Dick didn't need a second order, and moved out at once. The incident was over, and still none of the Japanese knew about the tangerines.

Once inside the barracks Dick distributed the tangerines as quickly as possible. He wanted to hide as much evidence as possible in case the officer came to check the sack again. The other two conspirators got twelve cans each, and twelve cans went to sick men. Dick kept twelve cans for himself, hiding them in his secret spot under the floor of the building. He kept these citrus fruits until the next time his gums began to bleed, indicating a need for vitamin C. Then he would eat a can of tangerines to firm up his gums and stop the bleeding.

Other POW's learned that the citrus fruit was in the warehouse, and they began to steal cans and eat them in large quantities. So many of the cans were removed that it eroded the support at the base of the tall column of boxes. Finally the entire stack fell over onto the floor of the warehouse. The Japanese were enraged and accused their own people of stealing, to the amusement of the guilty prisoners. The POW's played innocent, suggesting to the guards, "We didn't think your folks would do something like that, with the war going on and all."

Most of the other prisoners hoarded their canned goods, just as Dick did. Everyone placed great value on anything that was not perishable. It was amazing to watch as some of the men tried to prolong the rare opportunities they had to eat meat. One man had gotten a container of canned meat (Spam) in his Red Cross package. Having had almost no protein for many months he wanted to enjoy the meat for as long as possible. He opened the can, but shaved off

257

only a paper-thin layer to eat. This he placed on his tongue, wallowed it around without chewing, and then laid back on his shelf to relax and allow the meat to slowly dissolve in his mouth.

He would then bend the tin lid of the can back over the lump of meat and place it back into his Red Cross box. The next night he did the same thing again, savoring the meat just as long as possible. After about ten days the meat in the can turned green. Not to be denied his Spam, the man continued to eat a thin piece each night until the entire contents of the can were gone.

Dick knew that the Japs had him under their thumbs, and they could beat him and starve him and make him work like a slave all day every day. But he also knew that if he lived to see America win the war, and if he lived to go home to his family, despite everything that the Japs could do to him, he would have beaten the Japanese. Dick Darden decided that he would damn well do just that. The ability to survive the hellish conditions of the POW camps lay squarely in Dick's mind. It was much more a struggle with the mental than the physical. Dick's stubborn streak won out and undoubtedly saved his life.

By the spring of 1945 the Manhattan Project was close to making the atomic bomb a reality. At Hanford, Washington, the man-made element plutonium was being created. The technology and the ingredients for an atomic bomb were becoming a reality. More importantly for Dick Darden and Americans throughout the world, the new weapon was materializing in the minds and the hands of American, not Japanese or German, scientists.

Two bomb designs were being implemented in the United States. One was long and slender, shaped much like a traditional bomb or torpedo, and using uranium 235 as its explosive material. It was nicknamed "The Thin Man" for President Roosevelt. After minor modifications were made to the bomb's design, it was re-nicknamed "The Little Boy." It was known that enemy agents occasionally intercepted top secret communications. It had been hoped that, by using a nickname which appeared to refer to the President, the eavesdroppers would misinterpret any references to the atomic weapons.

The other atomic bomb was shorter and more oval, or bulbous, in shape. Its thicker design gained it the name "The Fat Man." It was hoped that some would interpret this reference as Winston Churchill. The Fat Man was more powerful than The Little Boy, and it used plutonium as its nuclear ingredient. The scientists were less confident that The Fat Man would actually work, so a test firing was planned later in the spring of 1945 at a site in the New Mexico desert.

The Allied bombing of Wake Island continued unmercifully, and the Japanese occupation force took a horrible beating. Very few days passed when there was not some type of mission by American planes over the island. They could be photography or reconnaissance missions, but more often they were full scale bombing raids. A Japanese diary was later captured that described the 268 days from April, 1944, until March of 1945. The diary indicated that, during that period, American aircraft were spotted over the island 243 times.

In a strange twist of fate the Japanese on Wake were faced with conditions so austere that they were very similar to those endured by Dick in Japan. The Japanese men had their rations cut to two small meals a day for their final two years on Wake. They ate virtually all of the rats on the island, and after eating the birds' eggs they nearly depleted the island's avian population. They planted tiny gardens in unlikely spots, enriching the coral sand with the

Japanese cities are reduced to rubble by U. S. bombing. Note the bomb craters and 'PW' in the lower left

contents of their privies. Even the noxious morning glory vine on Wake became a vegetable.

Fishing the lagoon or ocean around the atoll was extremely dangerous since any boat visible from the air represented a new target for American pilots, who had just about exhausted their supply of discernible objectives on the island to bomb. The troops of the occupation force began dying in large numbers. It was estimated that nearly 1300 perished from starvation.

At Osaka 1 prison there was one particularly brutal Japanese civilian supervisor who was sometimes in charge of Dick's work group. The POW's hated him, and had given him the nickname "Scatterbrain." As a supervisor of the civilian guards, each morning he gave the men their work instructions. Just before the men were moved from the Osaka 1 camp, Scatterbrain surprised several prisoners by saying in Japanese, "Japan is going to lose this war, and I want someone to teach me English." Apparently he wanted to prepare himself to converse with the American troops when they took over Japan. The Navy cook with the foulest of tongues was chosen to teach Scatterbrain English. Each morning he gave Scatterbrain an English lesson, and the Japanese supervisor could be seen walking around the grounds practicing the new words.

The Navy cook taught Scatterbrain that, whereas the Japanese would greet someone by walking up to them and bowing, a good American would walk up, shake hands, and say, "Kiss my ass, you son-of-a-bitch." He taught the supervisor every vile curseword and bit of tawdriness that he had in his extensive vocabulary of vulgarities, and he convinced Scatterbrain that all of the actual meanings were very proper. Scatterbrain would walk around practicing the words, and could be overheard saying, "Kiss my ass, you son-of-a bitch, kiss my ass, you son-of-a-bitch," over and over again.

The cook taught Scatterbrain that, if he ever was introduced to a white woman, he should properly introduce himself by saying, "Baby, I want to yodel up your canyon of love." Dick said he would be willing to give a month's pay to be around when Scatterbrain ran up to the first Marine sergeant to arrive in camp and recited, "Kiss my ass, you son-of-a-bitch."

In January of 1945 Gen. Curtis Lemay had been reassigned from China to Guam, where he took command of the B-29's there. He was given the responsibility of neutralizing the industrial might of the major Japanese cities with scores of these massive new bombing machines. During the first few weeks of his command the big bombers used standard tactics and met with limited success. Having learned a great deal during his first few weeks on Guam about the weapons at his disposal and the enemy in Japan, Lemay changed his tactics and embarked upon a new strategy which would use the B-29 to its fullest potential over Japan.

On March 9 Lemay conducted a new type of bombing raid over a target which had long been thought impregnable to enemy attack because of its tremendous defenses. The target was none other than Tokyo itself, the capital of the Japanese empire. The operation was code named MEETINGHOUSE, and it would be radically different from previous high-altitude raids. The B-29's would come in over the city at low altitudes, sometimes barely a mile above the ground, for peak accuracy. The attack would be at night in order to neutralize much of the anti-aircraft fire and reduce the response of the Japanese fighter planes.

Much of this bombing raid would be conducted using incendiary bombs. These would set massive fires in the wooden homes and buildings that were tightly packed into one of the most densely populated areas of humanity in the world. On the evening of March 9, over 300 B-29's rose from the runways on Guam heading north over the ocean toward Tokyo.

The first planes to reach the target were "pathfinders." It was their job to drop various incendiaries, such as napalm canisters, so that the bombing zone below would be marked by fires clearly visible from the air. The main body of the attacking formations would follow soon afterwards to drop their bombs on the area marked for destruction by the pathfinders.

As the hundreds of B-29's sped over Tokyo that night and dropped their incendiary bombs over the city, thousands of fires erupted. Multitudes of horrified civilians, many of whom manned the plants and factories of the Japanese war machine, fled into the streets in a chaotic effort to flee the hellish fires. Many small fires became walls of flame as they were whipped by the brisk winds.

So massive and intense were the fires in Tokyo that night that the heat rose in chimney-like fashion into the heavens with such force that violent updrafts pounded the planes as they continued to arrive over the bombing zones. The huge conflagration was unimaginable. Thousands of homes, buildings, and factories disappeared in the flames. Countless Japanese citizens burned to death, while untold numbers more suffocated from the lack of oxygen that was caused when the monstrous fires sucked the air into their upward-rushing columns of flame.

The sight was spectacular from the B-29's in the sky over the city, and a horrifying hell to those unlucky enough to be on the ground below. American flyers looked on in amazement as the Japanese war machine was being reduced to ashes before their eyes. They realized that they were curbing the enemy's ability to kill American boys, and ultimately they were hastening the end of the war. A large portion of Tokyo was in ruins after the MEETINGHOUSE raid. In places the temperature on the ground was said to have exceeded one thousand degrees, and the charred bodies of the dead littered more than a dozen square miles of the city.

As predicted, the defenses of the city had been inept. Only fourteen of the 300+ B-29's were lost. General Lemay immediately began planning similar bombing raids on other industrial cities which were cogs in the Japanese war machine. Osaka and nearby Kobe were high on the list.

It was impossible to bomb Japan without endangering the lives of American POW's. There were over 10,000 prisoners in Osaka alone. In many cases the labor of the prisoners powered the steel mills and factories so essential to the Japanese economy and war effort. These facilities were clustered in the urban areas of Japan and were seen as the most desirable targets for the American bombers. In order to devastate these industrial centers, the American planes had no choice but to bomb areas which were known to be near POW camps. Perhaps the most dangerous phase of the long war was about to be endured by Dick Darden.

During the early part of 1945 Dick got to see the big beautiful, but dreaded, American bombers on a number of occasions. The frightened Japanese civilians would shout "Bi-Ni-Gi-Ku" when they spotted the big bombers overhead, meaning "B-29."

Kobe and Osaka were being hit on alternate days. Kobe, too, was an important port which had to be neutralized to slow the movement of Japanese military supplies. The first bombing of Osaka began on the night of March 17, 1945.

The prisoners in Osaka 1 watched as U.S. "pathfinders" flew over dropping flares which marked the drop zone. Luckily for Dick, that night they began one block up the street from the Osaka 1 camp, including much of the city in a huge bombing zone. During that night seven square miles of the city were burned to the ground. No bombs came closer than a block from the camp, but this was sheer luck since the Allies did not know that the camp was there.

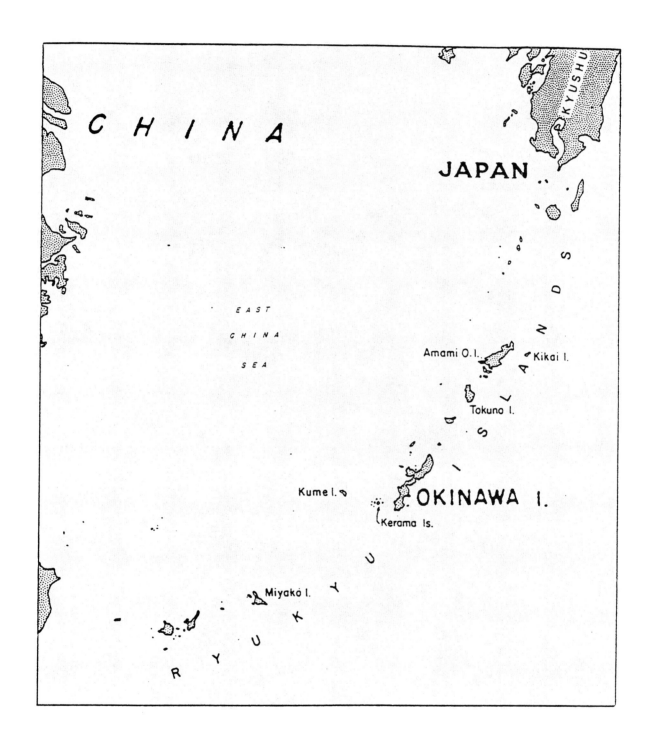

US Army – Modified

Chapter 53
OKINAWA—150 MILES FROM JAPAN

Near the end of March, 1945, the American soldiers of the Pacific campaign planned to launch the final major amphibious invasion of the war against the Japanese. This time the objective was not a small atoll far out in the Pacific from the homeland. The landing was to be on Okinawa, a sixty-mile-long island in the Ryukyu chain, which was due south of the homeland itself. Okinawa is located just over 150 miles from Kyushu, the southernmost of the major Japanese islands. Clearly, if the American forces could score a victory here they would be knocking on the door of the enemy.

If the Americans could use Okinawa as a staging area for bombing raids and a jumping off spot for the ultimate invasion, the Japanese knew that their vulnerability would be much greater than ever before. Control of Okinawa and its many airfields would win American planes easy access to the skies over Japan. Furthermore, control of the port cities on Okinawa would provide the American fleet with a home close enough to Japan to block all the shipping and supply routes coming through the East China Sea.

Both sides, the Americans and the Japanese, knew how important a victory at Okinawa would be. If the Americans were not stopped at Okinawa, their next landing would be on mainland Japan. The Japanese were well aware of the magnitude of their situation, and they responded accordingly with a massive defensive effort on Okinawa. General Mitsuru Ushijima commanded the Japanese defense of Okinawa. He watched, but did not respond in force, when American forces took the lightly defended Kerama atolls just offshore in late March.

On March 26, just a few days prior to the landing of American troops on Okinawa, Pete Darden's outfit was assigned to occupy a small island in the vicinity named Zamami Shima. The island had already been taken, but scattered resistance was still being encountered and Pete was part of a unit assigned to the "mopping up" operation. As his unit was routing out the remaining Japanese holdouts, it came under sniper fire. One of his buddies, a medic, was hit and lay helpless in a small clearing. As Pete and his buddies took cover in the trees near the clearing, they could see that the medic was not dead.

The medic was screaming for help as the snipers continued to fire at him. Pete could see sand jump up near the man as the bullets smashed into the ground. Everyone knew that the snipers were sure to hit their immobile target shortly. Pete made the decision to help, and he jumped from behind his cover and ran out into the clearing to pull his friend to safety.

As Pete reached the medic and began to assist him, a sniper's bullet found its mark. Pete Darden fell dead. The reports said later that he died courageously while helping a fellow soldier. It also said that he died quickly and did not suffer. Pete would never set foot on the big Japanese islands with the forces that would be victorious over Japan. His effort was stopped just a few hundred miles short of the enemy land in which he hoped to find and free his brother.

On April 1 both Marine and Army divisions began landing on Okinawa's western shore. They met little resistance, quickly gaining a beachhead eight miles long. But as they would learn, it was not the Japanese strategy to meet them on the beach. Some of the bitterest fighting of the war lay ahead of them. As the Americans pressed inland they encountered some of the most savage fighting they had seen.

On April 2 a letter was mailed to Eva Bell Darden in Clinton from the officer in charge of the Casualty Notification Section of the Navy Department. Somehow the mutilated letter from Dick had become undeliverable and ended up in Washington. The Navy Department was able to study the remains of the letter and determine where it should be forwarded. It arrived in Clinton eleven months after being written in Osaka on May 2, 1944.

This letter was another in the 100 word format (actually Dick has squeezed 102 words into this one). He indicated that a personal parcel, a cable, and several letters had made it through to him in Osaka. The long years of incarceration and hard labor had clearly taken a toll on Dick. Dick told his Mother in the letter that he hoped "this mess ends and I can see you all soon."

In early April the great Japanese battleship YAMATO, the most powerful battleship in the world, displacing nearly 73,000 tons, set out from the inland sea of Japan for Okinawa. The YAMATO, along with two cruisers and six destroyers, plowed through the seas at 22 knots on what amounted to a suicide mission.

The YAMATO was going after American carriers in the area, but was sighted and attacked by American planes. After several hours of continual attack, a succession of blasts caused the great ship to list heavily. On April 7 the YAMATO and four other enemy ships went down, the remaining four warships running for home. The Japanese had thrown their finest offensive naval forces at the encroaching Americans, but to no avail.

On April 12, 1945, the world was shocked to learn of the death of the American President, Franklin D. Roosevelt. The President had died at his vacation home in Warm Springs, Georgia. Harry Truman was immediately sworn in as President of the United States. Suddenly he had to shoulder the burden of conducting the final stages of the great global war. Even though the war would soon be over, Truman had to make a number of courageous decisions, some of which would result in the deaths of thousands of people. President Truman went about his duties in earnest, proceeding with the war in Europe as well as the other war in the Pacific.

By April 19 the American forces had secured nearly the entire northern half of the island of Okinawa. They learned that the enemy forces were concentrated in two places: on the Motobu Peninsula, a protuberance jutting off of the northwestern side of the island, and near Naha, the capital city, located near the southern tip of the island. The enemy troops on Okinawa were determined to resist, and the fight for the island began to be a protracted battle which would ultimately require eighty-two days of bloody fighting before the island was secure.

The Marines had to adjust their strategy for fighting in hilly terrain instead of the flat coral islands that had provided their battlefields since 1942. Ferocious frontal assaults were necessary to pry the enemy from fortified positions on, and even in tunnels beneath, the Okinawan hills. Sugar Loaf Hill, a strategic high point near Naha, was assaulted eleven times before being captured by the Americans.

ndependent

per In North Carolina.

1, 1945

$2.00 PER YEAR IN ADVANCE

Ivanhoe Soldier On Philippines

Cpl. John F. Fisler Writes of His Experiences; Is With Paratroop Group

Mr. and Mrs. G. E. Fisler, of Ivanhoe, recently received a letter from their son, Cpl. John F. Fisler, in the Philippines, describing his mission on Leyte as a paratrooper. He relates:

"The days in the Leyete mountains were rugged but we learned much of the Jap that is helping us now. The trails up there were so narrow, undefined and slippery that you would never believe men could possibly make it. Some places were so steep that we used ropes and had to pull each other up. Many times the mud was knee deep right along up the highest trails. We always had rain, got so we didn't feel right if we were dry.

"Our food was always dropped to us, that is, when they could find us. Some days we were without food—some units went a week without any. In those times we resorted to camotes (sweet potatoes), green corn, cocoanuts, papaya or anything else we could get. And the bed we had to sleep in—we rolled up in a poncho and tried to keep our heads above water. You'd be surprised how cold it got at night up there; we were plenty miserable but very fortunate in other ways.

"Now I must apologize for giving you all the bad side of our Leyete campaign, but when they lifted cen-

Killed In Pacific

Pvt. Henry Franklin (Pete) Darden, son of Mrs. Eva Bell Darden, of Clinton, who was killed in action in the Pacific war theater on March 26, 1945.

Variety Program Rotary Meeting

"Open Night" Program Proved Most Interestig; Austin Talked About Bonds

An "open night" prgoram presented at the weekly meeting of the Clinton Rotary club last Thursday

Crops Damaged By Hail Storm

Destructive Hail Struck in Three Townships, Wiping Out Crops, Saturday Night

One of the most devastating hail and rain storms ever to strike in Sampson county played havoc with growing crops in parts of Dismal, Honeycutt and Mingo townships around 11 o'clock last Saturday night. Crops were practically wiped out in many instances. The scope of the hail storm was about one mile wide and it ranged for a distance of 12 or 15 miles in length.

The hail was accompanied by an unusually heavy rainfall and the lands were washed badly in some places. Some farmers in the path of the storm planned to replant their crops, it was stated.

Much of the hail still lay on the ground Monday. L. H. Matthews, who lives on route 2 from Roseboro, brought a lump of the hail 27 inches long, 17 inches wide and 5 inches thick to Clinton Monday afternoon. The stones were not that large, of course, but it was an accumulation of the hail that fell. The hail was said to have been several feet deep in the ditches and ravines in some localities. One farmer reported that several of his hogs were killed by the hail storm.

Good rains were reported in most sections of the county Saturday and Sunday. Only a "good season" of rain fell in and around Clinton.

During April the city of Osaka was subjected to intensive air raids. The prisoners at Umeda Bunsho went to the second and third story windows of their barracks and watched as Osaka began to burn during one particularly devastating bombing raid. Japanese searchlights lit up the sky so that the bombers were clearly visible. Bombs could be seen falling from their bays. It was quite a sight to watch the bombs explode and the fires erupt, sending flames high into the heavens. During this raid alone, over 40% of the city was destroyed.

There were no work details outside the camp for two days after the big raid. When the work parties did go out again they could see the unbelievable damage that had been done by the bombers. For miles and miles all of the homes and buildings had been burned to the ground. Afterwards, when the work parties went out of camp the Japanese civilians would shake their fists at the POW's and spit at them, shouting "Bi-Ni-Gi-Ku," (B-29).

As the spring wore on the bombings came almost daily. Some of the smaller American carrier planes knocked out most of the Japanese searchlights. This made it difficult for the "one pound" anti-aircraft gun that the Nips had mounted on top of several buildings to be effective. With few lights to help illuminate the heavens, the gunners would have to wait until they could hear the drone of the B-29's.

During the raids there seemed to be hundreds of B-29's raining down their fire bombs. It was an awesome sight as the whole city seemed to be exploding into a blazing inferno. Dick and the men at Osaka 1 knew that a massive bombing of the waterfront was coming. It was just a matter of time.

Thousands of Japanese civilians no doubt were killed in the massive fires that followed the raids. The families usually dug a hole under their houses to act as a bomb shelter. When the fire bombs hit they burned the shacks down right on top of them. The entire city seemed to be leveled the next morning. The men in Osaka 1 did not leave camp for a couple of days after the first big raid. The Japanese seemed to be cleaning up as best they could and adjusting to the catastrophe.

After the bombing started in Osaka it was obvious that the Allied forces had fought their way to within range of the B-29 bombers, a distance probably less than 1000 miles. The men in Osaka 1 knew that the fight was very close and coming their way. The guards at Osaka 1 realized that an invasion of their homeland could actually happen. It was unthinkable, unbelievable to them that such a thing could happen to the invincible Emperor's people on their home islands. They began to think about the inevitable.

The desperate Japanese military had formulated a defense plan for the main islands called KETSU-GO. Should Americans invade Kyushu, Honshu, or Shikoku, this plan would go into effect. It called for an all out last ditch defense of the homeland. Enough guns, equipment, and planes had been hidden throughout the country to mount a potent final defense. Every man, every gun, and every resource would be thrown into the effort.

Several things could be expected to happen if KETSU-GO was initiated. There were over 5000 aircraft which would make one-way Kamikaze flights toward the invasion front. In Osaka 1 it was understood that, when the guards left for the front, any Americans left behind the Japanese lines would be a military liability.

This last savage battle would not be a battle to defeat the Americans. It would be a battle calculated explicitly to kill the greatest number of invading troops possible in the faint hope that the price paid in blood would be so staggering that pressures would come to bear on the Americans and they would stop the invasion short of total victory, opting to negotiate rather than conquer. The Japanese had not lost a major battle defending their home soil in more than 2000 years. It was hoped that KETSU-GO would keep that record intact.

Dick and several of his buddies noticed one day that machine gun positions were being installed all around the prison compound. These had not been used before, and they made the prisoners wonder what was happening. The machine guns were not yet in place, but their supports were. It was clear that the guns could be employed very quickly.

Dick and his friends asked the Japanese duty officer about the new gun positions. The officer told them in no uncertain terms that if American forces landed on any of the main islands, particularly Honshu where the city of Osaka was located, all of the POW's were to be executed immediately. Machine guns were to be used to perform the executions.

The Jap officer explained that if a landing were to occur, all troops throughout the entire island would be called to face the enemy. This would include the guards at all of the prisons. They could not leave American prisoners to run freely behind their lines, especially since there were over 10,000 in Osaka alone. So, the order had been given to execute them before the troops moved out to the front.

Dick understood the grim orders. He knew that if the guards left the area unsecured he and his mates would destroy everything they could. They would sabotage any ships, barges, warehouses, or military materials they could find in support of the invasion effort.

The future began to look bleak. No one could imagine anything short of an invasion that would root out and defeat the never-say-die Japs. What could possibly happen to avert an invasion? It appeared certain that the Japs would not give up their homeland without a fight to the death. The prisoners were equally sure that the Americans could not conquer the island nation without first landing troops and then driving the enemy back.

Dick and his buddies began to face the grim reality. An invasion seemed almost certain. The orders had been given for Dick's execution when it began. It appeared that the American bombers might hit the camp and kill the men even before the invasion scenario was played out with its almost certain atrocity to follow. Dick knew of no means that the United States had in its arsenal for ending the war quickly and averting a horrible end for the thousands of prisoners in the camps.

The men in Osaka 1 began to plan for the worst scenario. They knew of nothing that could save them. Each man had a knife of some fashion, either stolen or homemade. It was decided that if the machine guns were put into position and a mass execution appeared imminent, the prisoners would fight to the death. Their crude knives would be little help against the machine guns of the Japanese guards, but the men fully intended to make an effort to defend themselves. They might all be killed, but the prisoners decided that they would take some of the slanty-eyed bastards with them.

On May 8, 1945, less than one month after the death of President Roosevelt, General Dwight D. Eisenhower informed President Truman that the Germans had surrendered and the war was over in Europe. The long awaited V-E day had finally come. President Truman could turn his full attention to ending the war in the Pacific, and finally bring to a close the most devastating war in the history of the world.

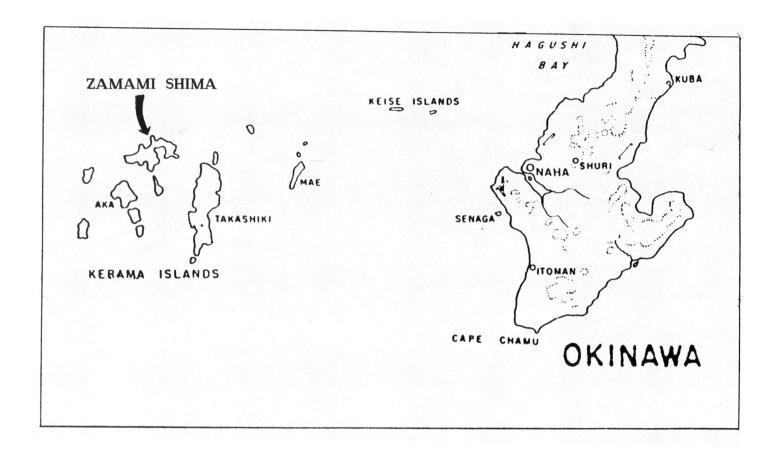

During late May most of the men at Umeda Bunsho were shipped out to camps in northern Japan. A group of about fifteen men, including Ralph Holewinski, remained at Umeda for a short time and then was transferred to Osaka 1. During the short train ride between camps Skee took some satisfaction in seeing several miles of Osaka that had been leveled, burned to the ground by the bombings. "The bombers have done their work well," he thought. In one 3-5 mile area he could see only two buildings over one story tall that remained standing. Although they were of concrete construction and the walls were still standing, even they were only burned-out shells.

Skee and the men from Umeda reached Osaka 1 prison, and for the first time since they had lived in the same barracks at Zentsuji during the summer of 1942, Skee saw Dick. Even if for only a few minutes under very adverse conditions, it was good to see an old buddy. The two men talked briefly before moving quickly to their work assignments.

Osaka had become one of the primary targets of the massive American bombing raids. The city was one of Japan's most densely populated, having more than 3.25 million people. There were 45,000 people per square mile in Osaka. The city was one of the most highly industrialized cities in Japan, and was one of the most vital centers for the production of war materials. The American bombers had levied massive bombing raids against Osaka, hitting the city three times during the last eight days of May.

Osaka was not the only Japanese city suffering the wrath of the B-29 Superfortresses. In a single week the great bombers dropped 8500 tons of incendiary bombs during two raids on Tokyo, and another 3200 tons of explosives on Yokohama. Over eighty square miles of heavily industrialized Japanese cities had been bombed and burned to the ground. Even so, the Japanese persisted and their will to fight the Americans had not been broken.

Just before the first of June, Osaka had been hit by a huge raid. Interference for the bombers had been run by 150 Mustang fighters from Iwo Jima. They swept in over the city and neutralized the feeble attempts of a few Japanese pilots to offer token resistance. Then an estimated 300 B-29's followed unescorted, dropping 2000 tons of explosives onto the city. Much of Osaka burned, but still Osaka 1 prison was spared. Smoke reached over five miles into the heavens from the thousands of fires below.

The ability of Osaka's factories to feed the war machine of the Emperor lay virtually in ashes. The shipyards, factories, steel mills, and anything else unfortunate enough to be in the path of the great bombers was burning out of control. The remaining Japanese cities lay vulnerable, completely at the mercy of the American B-29's.

On the first of June flares were dropped and the 600 men in Osaka 1 found themselves, for the first time, inside the bombing zone. The camp was squarely in the path of the "friendly" bombers. It was a bittersweet time for the POW's, who had waited these long years for freedom and could now see help coming so close, but who would have to escape the hellish rain of bombs in order to live and take advantage of it.

Osaka 1 prison was near the waterfront, which was one of the primary targets of the June 1 raid. Also targeted for destruction was the Sumitomo factory, which manufactured sheet metal and airplane propellors. Other targets included electrical equipment plants, power stations, and the main railroad station, which was the center of Osaka's communications system.

The prisoners had dug a small bomb shelter in the compound,

May 2, 1944
Osaka, Japan

Dear Mother,

I pray that you are all well. I am in fair shape. Received a hundred letters, a personal parcel and one cable so far. Keep them coming. They are God sends. "Spider" Webb is a good friend of mine. I impatiently await another parcel from you, hope it is chow. Dont forget to give my best to Dixie and Evelyn. I thought of you as well as both of them, when I heard a song the other day. Title was "I'll Be Around," Mills Brothers singing. Hope this mess ends and I can see you all soon.

Love to all,

J. B. Warden

but it would not accommodate all of the men. All were assembled in the compound so they would not be trapped in burning barracks. All the men who could got into the shelter. Then came the waves of bombers and fire bombs plummeted to earth all around the terrified men.

The raid started at about 9:00 a.m. Japanese air resistance was so low by that point that the raids were carried out in full daylight. As Mustangs crossed the city they found virtually no resistance. The American flyers referred to such an easy attack as a milk run. Both the prison camp and the waterfront were hit hard. Bombs came precariously close to some of the men on work details at the docks. Some were severely burned, but luckily none were killed.

A fire bomb scored a direct hit on the compound and the barracks were immediately ablaze. The prisoners began fighting the fires with buckets of sand and beaters soaked with water. Each time a wave of bombs would rain down, the men would hit the deck, only to jump up after the explosion and begin fighting the fires again. Within fifteen minutes it was obvious that they were fighting a losing battle. The guards opened the gates and the men spilled into the street as the camp burned to the ground before their eyes.

The situation was no better outside the camp. Fires raged everywhere. In the chaos that ensued several Japanese guards ran up to the group and announced that a building down the street was ablaze, and its contents included the rice rations for the camp for the next 90 days. The men were told that if they wanted to eat at all they had better come and save the rice.

With guards lining the street the men ran to the burning warehouse. Food was so precious that, without hesitation, the men darted into the burning structure and retrieved the sacks of grain. Men came stumbling out of the fire with the 220 pound sacks on their backs and took them across the street to a lot where a house had already been burned to the ground. Bombs were still falling all around the men. When the screaming bombs could be heard close overhead the men would throw the sacks of rice down into the street and try to get as far underneath as possible for protection.

The adrenalin was flowing freely as terror gripped the prisoners. Many weighed less than 100 pounds, and yet they tossed the heavy sacks of rice onto their backs, ran across the street out of the fire, dropped the sacks into piles, and then raced back for more. POW rice was that which had been swept up from the warehouse floors and was often filled with filth and rocks. And yet it was so valuable that the men risked their lives without hesitation for it. Not a single bag was lost to the fire.

During the chaos of the air raid Chief Pharmacist's Mate Lonnie Merritt noticed a Japanese woman who had been badly injured by shrapnel from one of the bombs and was lying in the street. First he noticed that both of her legs had been blown off above the knees. Then he noticed in the bloody mess that she was in the late stages of pregnancy. Merritt stayed with the woman and delivered the baby. The woman died, but miraculously the baby lived.

Osaka Principal prison, Dick's home for three long agonizing years, was almost completely destroyed. That night the prisoners slept along the Osaka waterfront, some in the open and others under freight shelters. During the night Dick ran to an area near the docks where Holewinski's group was sleeping. He told the men that part of one of the barracks was still standing and could be used for shelter. Skee was glad to see Dick again, but there was little time to talk. Dick moved on quickly to another group.

With nowhere in the vicinity of the docks to go for shelter,

and the remains of the bombed out barracks at Osaka 1 uninhabitable, the men would have to be moved. The following day they were taken to another part of Osaka which had also been bombed in one of the previous raids but did still offer crude shelter. The air raids kept coming incessantly, day and night, and the city of Osaka was leveled, section by section. Soon there was no place left to go. The prisoners would have to be moved out of the city.

Other Wake Islanders were being moved in early June as well. Many of the 1100+ civilians and the 400+ military men who had participated in the defense of Wake Island in December of 1941 were among the group taken from the island on the NITTA MARU in January, 1942. They had been taken to camps near Shanghai, China, and had spent over three years in prisons on the Chinese mainland.

In May, 1945, as the Japanese empire crumbled under increased pressure from virtually all sides, the many of the Wake defenders in China were moved 800 miles north to Feng Tai. On June 19, 1945, they were moved by rail to Pusan, Korea, and then placed on ships and taken to the island of Hokkaido in the Japanese homeland. The Japanese were pulling back to their home islands and they were taking their slave labor with them.

In early June the Japanese were also trying to find a new camp for the POW's in Osaka. Dick Darden had no idea that American forces were fighting viciously just a few hundred miles to the south, attempting to defeat the enemy at Okinawa and thereby breach the last defensive line before reaching the main Japanese islands.

The American forces on Okinawa were smelling victory. They were pushing the stubborn enemy back, and for the first time large numbers of the Japanese troops were surrendering. Ultimately over 7000 Japanese would surrender on Okinawa rather than commit suicide or endure the consequences of trying to hold out against the advancing Americans and suffer the inevitable. Finally there seemed to be a crack in the code of the Japanese warrior.

On June 18th the commander of the Tenth Army on Okinawa was Gen. Simon Bolivar Buckner. General Buckner was the son of a Confederate Lt. General by the same name who had served the Confederacy just eighty years earlier. The elder Gen. Buckner had graduated from West Point before joining the Southern cause. He surrendered his army to General Ulysses S. Grant in 1865. Later he became Governor of Kentucky in 1887 and was a candidate for Vice President of the United States in 1896.

While on Okinawa the younger Gen. Buckner had led his forces to the brink of victory. During the final stages of the battle General Buckner came to the front lines to observe his troops. A Japanese artillery shell exploded near him, the blast propelling a chunk of coral rock into Buckner's chest. He died before the day had ended. Though he had courageously led his men so near the final objective, he would not live to see the defeat of the Japanese or the liberation of the thousands of American prisoners. Gen. Buckner became one of thousands of American fighting men who spilled his blood during the march to Japan.

Three days after Gen. Buckner's death, Japanese Gen. Ushijima emerged from his bunker deep beneath hill #89 on Okinawa. Knowing that he had failed his Emperor by allowing the Americans to defeat him on Okinawa, the General knelt and, upon his order, a subordinate beheaded him. With the death of General Ushijima the battle of Okinawa was over. The last remnants of organized resistance were crushed, and the Americans were in complete control of the island.

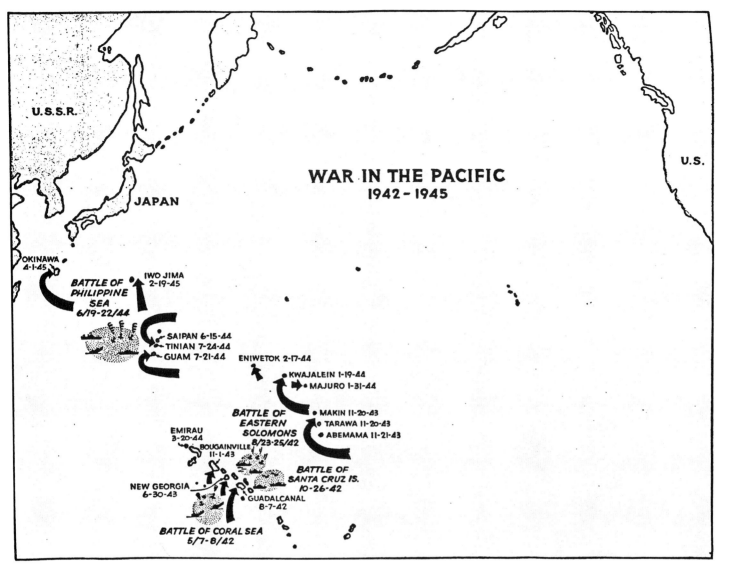

WAR IN THE PACIFIC
1942-1945

US ARMY – Modified

The last defenses short of the Japanese homeland had been split, and the Allied forces began to plan the ultimate attack on the Japanese mainland. The remaining factories and vital centers on the island nation were easy prey to short American bombing runs. Both sides began to calculate their next move. The Japanese last ditch strategy became a distinct reality, along with its ominous implications for the prisoners held in the motherland.

On Okinawa 12,000 American and 100,000 Japanese men died. The casualty lists were staggering. Having paid such a horrible price, the Japanese were reeling in retreat and the Americans held land closer than ever to Japan. From the air bases on Okinawa the American planes had to cross only 350 miles of ocean to reach the main Japanese islands. The entire island nation lay vulnerable to American bombing raids.

American leaders began planning for the invasion of the major Japanese islands which would be the death blow, a thrust to the heart of the enemy. But everyone knew the Japanese would put up a horrid fight on their home soil to make one last attempt to save their pride, their homeland, and their Emperor. They would fight to the death, taking thousands of American boys with them. Plans were drawn for the invasion. The carnage would be unprecedented to the

armies on both sides. For Japan, and perhaps for the American POW's in Japan, time was about to run out.

Even as late as the middle of June, President Truman instructed the Joint Chiefs of Staff to proceed with the invasion plan. The possible use of the atomic weapons, which were so close to reality, had not been given the go-ahead as an option for ending the war with Japan and avoiding the inevitable bloody invasion. However, some high ranking American military decision-makers were already thinking in terms of attempting to reduce the number of casualties that was sure to result from an invasion of Japan. Rather than use force, they were content to consider something less than unconditional surrender from the Japanese government. Clearly, all options were being aired, including negotiating and accepting something less than victory, in order to avoid the annihilation of so many men in an invasion.

With the coming of summer in 1945 the naval and air forces of the Emperor of Japan had been, for the most part, brought under control by Allied forces. The army, on the other hand, was a completely different matter. There were more than four million men in the Japanese Army, more than ever before. If the previous battles fought in the Pacific by the soldiers of the Emperor were any indication

National Archives

Marines on Okinawa burn the enemy out of caves in the hilly terrain.

of the ferocity with which these men would fight, it could logically be expected that they would fight to the last man before giving up their homeland.

The stage appeared set for the inevitable confrontation. The battle for Japan would be catastrophic, and would surely result in the deaths of millions of Japanese people, both military and civilian. In addition, untold thousands of Americans would surely die while waging the final battles. The carnage which appeared certain to follow loomed as a nightmare for all sides.

What could happen, what cataclysmic event could occur, which might cause the Japanese to capitulate without the massive carnage that would surely result from a battle for the home islands? What could happen that would stop an American invasion of the Japanese islands and prevent the executions of the many thousands of POW's who were being held there?

Both sides calculated and recalculated all of the options. Surely the Allies would have to invade to win the war, and surely the Japanese would defend. There seemed to be no answer to these questions, no way to circumvent a bloody slaughter, one which would probably begin with the POW's in Japan. What could possibly happen to avoid the unthinkable loss of life? Surrender appeared to be out of the question for the Japanese, even though the war was obviously lost. There seemed to be no way to avoid the inevitable carnage and butchery that would soon come.

As plans were being drawn for the invasion of Japan, the destruction of her industrial centers was stepped up. Massive bombings became commonplace. The newly acquired American air bases on Okinawa, Iwo Jima, Guam, and Tinian were bustling with

hundreds of planes and thousands of tons of high explosives.

Osaka 1 prison, like most of the city of Osaka and other POW camps in the area, had been completely destroyed by the American bombing. The Japanese knew that the prisoners would have to be moved to another part of the country. About the middle of June, 1945, half of the 600 men at Osaka 1, including Dick Darden, were put on a train and shipped out. They were transported to a small camp on the north shore of Japan called Fusiki. Fusiki prison was located near the south end of Toyama Bay, about four miles from the city of Toyama.

At Fusiki the men were immediately put to work, spending long days at hard labor in the dock area on Toyama bay. The men again toiled as stevedores, doing much the same type of work that they had had been forced to do in Osaka. Each morning at daybreak the men marched the four miles into town to their work assignments. Then at dusk, after a full day of hard work, they marched the distance back to Fusiki prison.

The Japanese had built piers along the edge of Toyama Bay so that rail lines could extend out over the water. The prisoners unloaded ships and sampans onto the piers, while others reloaded the cargo into the rail cars. Few large ships came into Toyama Bay from long distances away, providing ample evidence of the effectiveness of American submarines. Most of the ships came from Korea.

A variety of materials were coming into Japan from Korea. Most of the ships carried rice, and many also brought salt which had been taken from mines by other POW's in Korea and China. Soybean meal cakes were also common. The soy beans had been molded into large disks, about three feet across and a foot thick. The size, shape, and weight of the soybean disks reminded Dick of millstones he had

Ruins of Umeda prison after American B-29's bombed the city of Osaka.

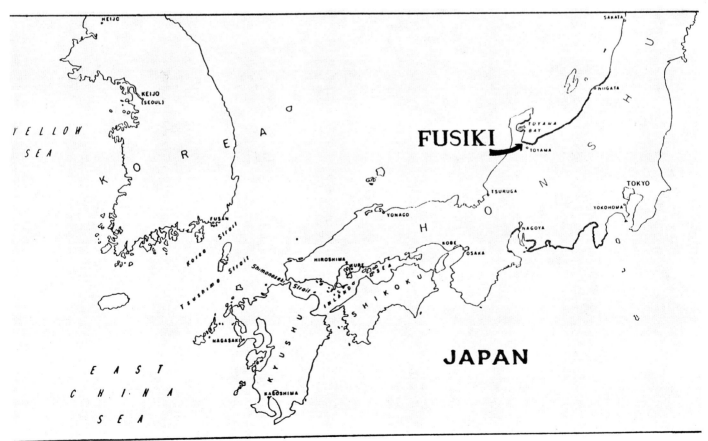

seen back home.

Plans for the invasion of the Japanese mainland were being laid by American strategists. Operation Olympic would begin in about four months, on or about the first of November, 1945. This would involve more than a dozen American divisions which would land on the southernmost of the major islands—Kyushu. The beaches at Kagoshima and Araike would be the main invasion fronts. Japan would be stormed by force. Unless something unprecedented occurred during the 150 day interim period, the American plans would go into effect. Perhaps more forebodingly for the POW's in Japan, so would the Japanese plans.

It was understood that the conquest of Japan would not only be costly in lives, but it would also be a protracted battle. The second part of the invasion, Operation Coronet, was not scheduled to begin until March of 1946. A huge army of 25 divisions would stab at the heart of the empire, invading the main island of Honshu and attacking Tokyo itself. As the bombings and bombardment continued, preparations were being made for the invasion to begin.

Everyone in Fusiki prison was aware that extraordinary things were happening near Japan. American warplanes were flying across the sky over Toyama Bay, so surely the war was closing in on Japan. The prisoners were concerned about their safety. The end of the war had to be near, but the POW's in Fusiki wondered just how it would end for them.

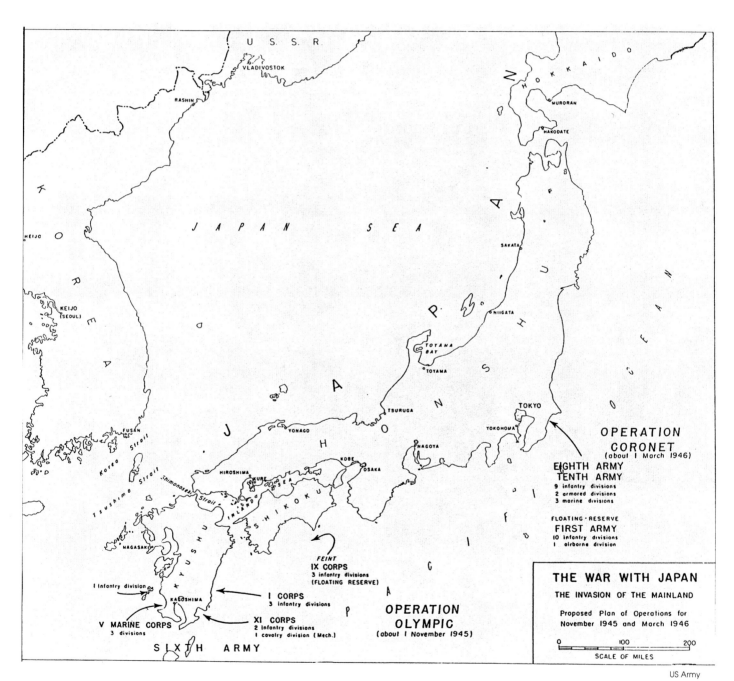

US Army

Operation Olympic and Operation Coronet – The American plans for the invasion of Japan

Maj James R. Brown

A collage of woodcuts by Maj. James R. Brown dipicting the hardships and horrors of the years spent in Japan as a POW.

Chapter 54
THE PRISON AT FUSIKI

During the summer of 1945 Dick and many of his fellow POW's in Fusiki prison toiled at hard labor in the area around Toyoma Bay. Ralph Holewinski had also been moved from Osaka to Fusiki. During late June, 1945, he had entered the camp, but never knew that Dick was among the 300 men there. This was probably because the weather was cold and rainy in Fusiki, so the men went out on work details each morning more interested in finding food and keeping warm than socializing.

When the men got back to camp at night after the long walk from the docks they usually went straight to their barracks where they ate their rice ration and tried to stay warm. Rarely did they move around into other barracks to visit or look for old friends. Skee never saw Dick while living in Fusiki prison or working the docks near Toyoma.

The long years of captivity, deprivation, neglect, and intense labor had long affected the men, both mentally and physically. Physically, many of the men had become little more than skin and bones. Holewinski was beginning to have nightmares. One night he woke up in a cold sweat, dreaming that rats were eating his toes off. Two men were holding him down so that he would not fall off of his top bunk.

The bits and pieces of information gleaned by the prisoners indicated that the battle lines were coming closer and closer to Japan. Word began to leak in to the prisoners from the general population that Japan was losing the war. The Japanese military attempted to cover up the fact that they were taking a horrible beating at the hands of the advancing American forces by launching ridiculous propaganda efforts. As long as the Japanese people believed they were winning, they would continue to support the war effort.

The prisoners had access to Japanese newspapers in Fusiki and, while most of the prisoners did not read Japanese, much could be gained from looking at the photos. One full-page spread praised a young Japanese pilot for apparent heroism. One of the POW's who could decipher the Japanese characters read the amazing story to the men. It indicated that the pilot had been on a bombing raid, and after he expended all his bombs and ammunition he headed toward home. He met an American plane which was going in the opposite direction and was also returning to its home base after a mission.

The story went on to say that the Japanese pilot took a rice ball out of his lunch pail, slipped the cowling back on his plane and threw the rice ball through an open window in the cockpit of the American plane, striking the pilot in the head. The American then lost control of his plane and crashed. The Japanese pilot was credited with a "kill," and the pictures of him and his plane were all over the newspaper. The prisoners got a good chuckle from the article, since they knew what would happen to a rice ball thrown from an open cockpit 20,000 feet above the ground at 200 miles per hour. The Japs must be losing badly if they had to conjure up wild stories like that.

Having been bombed out of Osaka, the men as Fusiki attempted to communicate with Allied planes to avoid being bombed there as well. They would tell the Japanese that they wanted to air out their bedding, and spell "POW" in morse code with their blankets. Later the prisoners spelled "POW" on the roofs of their buildings with white paint. The messages apparently were detected because American B-29's avoided the camp when they bombed Fusiki.

Spider Webb was still in prison at Zentsuji, and he was also in danger of being killed by American bombers. The men interned there knew that the war was coming to Japan. They had access to a Japanese newspaper which was printed in English. They knew that the paper was full of bull, easily recognizable to them as propaganda intended for the Japanese population.

One of Spider's friends had studied Japanese in Tokyo before the war, and he spoke fluent Japanese. He would read Japanese newspapers and then compare the stories to the English-speaking version. One day the English-speaking paper stated that one hundred American bombers had attacked Rabaul. The other paper, written for the Japanese population, said that the "intrepid Japanese soldiers" had shot down 101 enemy planes. The stories obviously did not corroborate, so it was clear that the Japanese people were being fed a line of propaganda that the government wanted them to hear.

According to the Japanese newspapers, the Jap navy was continually sinking the American navy, seemingly ridding the Pacific of the entire fleet several times a year. The men quickly learned not to believe the Japanese version of events. The best source of accurate information was from new arrivals. A Navy pilot who had been shot down over Rabaul came into camp. He was severely wounded, having lost a leg, but he recovered and filled the men in on the progress of the war. He was able to give the men information on the last twenty-four months of the war, and his story was quite different from the stories published in the Japanese newspapers.

One problem at Zentsuji gave Spider Webb and his friends plenty to worry about. Zentsuji was more than a prison camp. It was also a military base and was therefore a prime target for American bombers. There were several bombing raids in the vicinity during the spring and summer of 1945. When the B-29's came over the camp, Webb could look up into the sky and barely see the great planes. When the sun reflected off their fuselages they would almost sparkle. Even when they were difficult to see, the drone of their engines could be heard on the ground. Luckily for Spider Webb, no bombs ever landed inside Zentsuji prison while he was there.

On June 24, 1945, Spider Webb and many of the prisoners at Zentsuji were moved. They walked several miles to a ferry, which took them from Shikoku Island in the inland sea to the main island of Honshu. Once on Honshu they went to a railroad station where they spent the night. They were taken down into the station, which was two stories underground. Spider was glad to be in a protected area because that night there was a bombing attack going on up above.

The next day the men were loaded aboard a train and the blinds on the windows of their car were tightly shut. By peering through small cracks in the blinds they could see the devastation as they went through Osaka and Kobe. Then they turned northward and traveled another 100 miles. Finally they reached their destination and got off the train. They were marched over ten miles in the dark of night up into a small mountain range. Their new home was Rokuroshi prison.

The first and only time that Dick was caught stealing food was in Fusiki prison during August of 1945. Dick was on a work detail which had been taken several miles out into the countryside. Most of the men had been able to steal small quantities of rice and soybeans, which they had in their pockets. The guards searched them and found the grain, so they decided that punishment was in order. Dick immediately thought about one man who had been severely beaten for being caught with five soybeans in his pocket.

About ten men, including Dick, were caught with soybeans. They were taken back to camp, ordered to strip naked, and placed into a tiny room which measured about three feet wide by seven feet long. They were jammed into the small space so they could not sit down. They could only lean on each other. A single light bulb dangled from the ceiling and was left on all night so that it would draw thousands of the ferocious mosquitoes that infested the area. The men stood for one long miserable night sweating, scratching, and splattering the bloody insects on themselves and each other. The next morning they were given their clothes back and were sent on a work detail as usual. Nothing else was ever said about the stolen food.

The daily work details continued all summer, even though the men continued to hear bits and pieces of information from the Japanese civilians that an American victory was imminent. The Japanese newspapers began to give thinly veiled versions of the truth, even though they continued to attempt a cover-up of the fact that Japan was losing the war. They told of retreating Japanese forces but indicated that the military brains had simply consolidated forces elsewhere or regrouped for another offensive.

But to the POW's the gist of the geographical movements was clear. American forces had driven the Japs out of Guadalcanal, Borneo, Saipan, and then the Philippines. The "strategic withdrawals" and "regroupings" were steadily moving northward, step by step moving closer to the island homeland.

The bombing was getting closer and closer to Fusiki. The Americans had not yet hit Fusiki, but were in the area. American PBY's would come in on cloudy nights and drop mines by parachute into the water just outside the bay. The next incoming tide would then bring them into the bay. The Japanese had to patrol the mouth of the harbor constantly with small minesweepers. Even so, some of the mines got through and made it to the harbor area.

One day at Fusiki while Walter Cook's crew was working on the docks they took a break and sat on some cargo where they could look out over the harbor. Suddenly a sampan just a short distance across the channel struck a mine. There was a huge explosion and the boat was lifted out of the water in two pieces. Cook saw men flying end over end through the air. It was too close for comfort, so from then on when a minesweeper patrolled the channel or when a civilian boat was near, the work crew of prisoners would move back a safe distance until it had passed.

Then came the night in August when the POW's in Fusiki prison watched hundreds of American bombers as they wiped out Toyama. Massive amounts of fire bombs and explosives literally burned the city to the ground. Again, as in Osaka, thousands of Japanese families crawled into the dugout shelters under their homes only to have the wooden structures burn down on top of them. Toyoma was a prime target because there was an airfield alongside the town. Thousands of the small wooden houses were burned to the ground with a staggering loss of life. The prisoners at Fusiki did not go to work the following day since so many of the Japanese dock workers who lived in Toyoma had been killed.

At the same time, back on Wake Island, the Japanese occupation force was being subjected to the same type of relentless bombing. In August of 1945 the island was visited by yet another carrier task force. While most of the enemy anti-aircraft guns had been destroyed, the few that remained had become, with years of practice under their belts, pretty good shots with their relatively crude equipment. Several American planes were lost over Wake during the raids.

Dick was a veritable skeleton by the summer of 1945, carrying barely half the weight he had when he joined the Navy in 1940. But now there was hope in Fusiki prison. Everyone could tell that the end, in one form or another, had to be near.

A number of POW's, weakened mentally and physically by years of starvation, disease, neglect, and hard labor, died in the Fusiki prison. When the head count was made each morning it was not uncommon for one or two men to be dead in their bunks. One morning Dick was assigned duty on the detail that took the corpses out into a nearby field and cremated them. He recalled the ghastly cremation detail the previous years at Osaka 1 prison. He would never forget the smell of the burning human flesh.

Nuclear weapon known as the "Little Boy", the kind detonated over Hiroshima, Japan in World War II. The bomb is 28 inches in diameter and 120 inches long. The first nuclear weapon ever detonated, it weighted 9,000 pounds and had a yield equivalent to approximately 20,000 tons of high explosive.

Nuclear weapon of the "Fat Man" type, the kind that detonated over Nagasaka, Japan in World War II. The bomb is 60 inches in diameter and 128 inches long. The second nuclear weapon to be detonated, it weighed about 10,000 pounds and had a yield of about 20,000 tons of high explosives.

Chapter 55
THE FAT MAN AND THE LITTLE BOY

The year 1945 wore on for Dick, his fourth in captivity. During the summer of that year, however, events were happening in and near Japan which would cause his imprisonment to come to its conclusion, either for better or worse. With Allied planes bombing all around Fusiki and planting mines in the harbor, it was apparent that something big was about to happen. But the magnitude of the events that were about to unfold could not even be imagined by the prisoners at Fusiki prison.

On July 17 President Harry Truman had gone to Potsdam, a city in occupied Germany near Berlin, to meet with the British and the Russians to discuss ending the war with Japan and dividing the spoils. Winston Churchill represented England, but he would be replaced later in the month by Clement Atlee, the new British Prime Minister. Joseph Stalin represented the Soviets.

The western allies were having trouble dealing with the Russians, who had not yet declared war on the Japanese. Even so, they were ready to step in and share in the booty when the Japanese empire was divided. It had been more than two months since V-E day, but the Soviets appeared no closer to helping with the war against Japan. A serious division emerged between Stalin and the western Allies.

In addition to failing to enter the war against the Japanese, the Russians had begun setting up communist governments in the eastern European countries they had liberated from the Germans. They also took Manchuria and North Korea, strengthening their position all the while. Stalin and the Soviets were setting the stage for world conflict and the cold war which would last for over four decades to come.

Averell Harriman, the U. S. Ambassador in Moscow, realized that the Kremlin leaders were dragging their feet on the question of entering the war to defeat Japan. They were spilling none of their own blood, but were waiting in the wings to claim a victor's share of the Pacific. Harriman urged Truman to be firm with the Russians, to put pressure on them to join in the fray and help bring a speedy end to the war.

It was while President Truman was in Potsdam that he received word of an accomplishment by American scientists which might have been the single most important event to occur concerning the future of mankind on the planet Earth. On July 16, 1945, the United States exploded the first atomic bomb in a New Mexico desert. A plutonium bomb, similar in design to the "Fat Man," had been exploded, the light from which was visible over 100 miles away in Las Vegas, Nevada. The blinding light of the explosion, its shock wave, and its overall magnitude exceeded the expectations of those who observed the blast, including General Groves, the project commander, and Robert Julius Oppenheimer. The news of this event cast a completely new light on the talks at Potsdam.

Both Truman and Secretary of War Henry Stimson were elated at the news of the new weapon, because they knew that the successful test meant that America had the technology to build a weapon that might end the war with Japan without the slaughter of thousands, perhaps millions, of lives. It also meant that the Russians and their military help would not be needed. Suddenly America carried the biggest stick in the world. Neither Russia, nor Britain, and certainly not Japan, could equal the new American might.

Could it be that this new advancement, only a theoretical dream in the realm of science fiction for years, could help America avoid the invasion of Japan, and indirectly, save Dick Darden from execution? Work began immediately to assemble and ship the bombs with which to confront the government which had killed over 2000 of our boys at Pearl Harbor and then thousands more throughout the Pacific.

At Potsdam the Americans began to negotiate from a noticeably stronger position. No longer was Russia needed, so the pressure for them to enter the war subsided. This put President Truman in an uncomfortable position. He knew that the Russians would not be crucial to victory over Japan. But both sides would be bound to the Yalta agreement, and since the Soviets had agreed to declare war against Japan, they had every right to do so. At that point they had not, electing to play their cards cautiously and wait. Stalin would wait to enter the war until he was able to maximize the Russian gains while minimizing their risk.

On July 25 the components of atomic bombs were taken ashore on Tinian in the Mariana Islands from the cruiser USS INDIANAPOLIS. Two special B-29 crews had already been stationed there. They had trained in the United States, as well as in the Pacific and over Japan, for one special mission. They were prepared to deliver these bombs of unknown proportions to Japan if so ordered. The three B-29's, named ENOLA GAY, THE GREAT ARTIST and BOCK'S CAR, were preparing for the most significant bombing run in the history of aviation.

As the Potsdam Conference was ending on July 26 an ultimatum was issued to the Japanese government. The Potsdam Proclamation offered Emperor Hirohito and his government two choices. They could surrender unconditionally or face "prompt and utter destruction." Since the Japanese were not aware of the catastrophic power of the atomic bomb, they could very well have interpreted the phrase "prompt and utter destruction" as a continuation of the massive conventional bombing raids or an invasion of the islands. Not feeling the urgency of an atomic confrontaton, they delayed making a decision.

It was virtually certain that many of the Japanese people would prefer death to a future without their Emperor, whom they worshipped as a god. This provoked further controversy in American thinking. Should the United States insist upon an end to the Emperor's 2600 year dynasty? This was certainly an option well within the power of the only player in the game holding atomic weapons. Such a move would surely galvanize many Japanese against any form of surrender. Another option open to the Allies was to concede the continuation of the rule of Hirohito, at least in title. That strategy could save untold thousands of lives if it was perceived by the Japanese as a softening the American position so that surrender might be somewhat more acceptable to them. The ultimatum was worded in such a way that, for the moment, the decision had not been made about Hirohito's future.

The Japanese cabinet delayed making the dreaded decision. After all, destruction or surrender was equally horrid and unacceptable to them. As the cabinet polarized and the hard liners in Tokyo quarreled with those favoring a speedy end to the killing, none of the Japanese leaders could envision the magnitude of the "utter destruction" that the "Little Boy" and the "Fat Man" on Tinian were prepared to bring to them.

During the first week of August, less than three weeks after the test firing of the first atom bomb in Utah, the special B-29 crews on Tinian were given their first detailed briefing on the weapon itself. They watched a film of the Utah detonation, and for the first time they understood the peculiar training procedures they had been learning. They understood why the steep turns immediately after release of the bomb would be required, a procedure intended to get their plane as far away as possible before the immense, blinding fireball brought "complete and utter destruction" to the unlucky victims below.

On August 6, 1945, the B-29 named ENOLA GAY took off from Tinian with the Little Boy, the uranium bomb, inside her. After several hours over the Pacific Ocean and southern Japan she reached her destination—the city of Hiroshima. Hiroshima lay just 250 miles southwest of Fusiki prison and Dick Darden. Just after 8:00 a.m. her bomb bay doors opened and the Little Boy fell from her belly toward the unsuspecting city and its quarter-million inhabitants. The bomb, which weighed just under 10,000 pounds, fell until it reached a point in the sky about 1/3 of a mile above the ground. There the bomb detonated exactly as planned.

Inside the bomb an explosive device fired one mass of uranium toward another like a bullet. When the two smashed together, atoms were split and released inconceivable amounts of energy. The bright light of the sunny morning over Hiroshima became pale by comparison. "Complete and utter destruction" took on a new definition for the people of Hiroshima and everyone on the planet. Horror filled the floor of the earth beneath the ENOLA GAY as hell burned brightly and thousands were consumed in it.

President Truman was aboard the cruiser USS AUGUSTA in the Atlantic steaming home from Germany and the Potsdam Conference when he was informed of the successful bombing mission. Much of the city of Hiroshima had been annihilated, reduced to rubble, twisted steel, and charred bodies. Over 60,000 human beings were dead, or filled with amounts of radiation which would allow a few hours or days of wretched agony before death would thankfully come. The first atomic bombs to be used on human beings in time of war had worked perfectly.

Americans rationalized that the carnage brought to Hiroshima by the Little Boy was preferable to the loss of hundreds of thousands of American lives, perhaps millions on both sides, which would almost surely be lost in a protracted invasion of Japan using conventional means. By using the atomic bomb, it was thought that perhaps Japan would see the futility of their situation and accept surrender. Then legions of young American men in the landing forces, the millions of Japanese who were poised to defend to the death, and the many thousands of POW's in Japan might live.

The prisoners at Fusiki received no word of the cataclysmic

new bomb. At Rokuroshi, however, the news was handled differently. The Japanese commander came into the camp where Spider Webb was being held and told the American officers that the Americans were using an inhumane weapon. He ordered that the American prisoners there be punished by working at hard labor.

Everyone at Rokuroshi was very weak and virtually starved during the summer of 1945. Spider Webb weighed only 100 pounds, sixty less than in 1941. Everyone, however, even the sickest man in camp, was ordered to go out on the mountain and work at hard labor. The men were made to dig into the rocks and thin layer of soil on the mountain. They were told that they were being punished for the American atomic bomb dropped on Hiroshima.

The Japanese cabinet members who formed the War Council began to scramble into action, and their quarreling became intense. Their two choices, surrender unconditionally or suffer the horrors of the nuclear bomb, had become even grimmer than before. The pressure on the enemy hierarchy became crushing, but their expedience in the matter was even more urgent than they knew. This was because the "Fat Man" was being prepared on Tinian. More "complete and utter destruction" would soon fall on Japan if surrender was not immediate.

It was decided that the target for the Fat Man would be Kokura, a Japanese city about 350 miles southwest of Fusiki. The plutonium bomb was considerably more potent than the uranium device in the Little Boy. It was loaded aboard BOCK'S CAR, and the great silver B-29 prepared for the flight to Japan. Bad weather between Tinian and Japan had become a concern. Despite this and problems with the fuel system on the big bomber, the decision was made to proceed with the mission. Early on the morning of July 9, 1945, BOCK'S CAR struggled to lift its heavy cargo into the air over Tinian. It then slowly ascended into the dark sky and sped away toward its Japanese enemy.

When BOCK'S CAR reached Kokura, it prowled the sky over the city, unable to see through the clouds well enough to get a precise fix on the landmarks below that were being used as targets. The crew was under orders not to drop the bomb unless they could be certain of their accuracy. Nervous men strained to see familiar structures below. As they spent more and more time above the city, the Japanese anti-aircraft fire and fighter planes began rising to meet the intruders.

The bombardier tried again to find the precise drop point without success. Flak from the exploding anti-aircraft shells came precariously close to the big silver bird. Having enough fuel for the return trip was rapidly becoming a problem. A critical time in the mission arrived and the decision was made—there would be no drop over Kokura. BOCK'S CAR broke away and headed southwest toward home, hoping for better conditions for a drop over the alternative city. That city was Nagasaki.

Nagasaki, like Kokura, could be easily justified as a military target. Among its population were thousands of workers who labored for the war machine. Mitsubishi had factories there which built weapons for the war effort.

The morning wore on, and BOCK'S CAR was losing precious minutes. By the time it reached Nagasaki the fuel situation was critical. There was not enough left to reach Tinian. The bomber would have to land on Okinawa to refuel. By 11:00 the city of Nagasaki was visible beneath BOCK'S CAR. For the people on the

No life remains in this part of the scorched city of Nagasaki, September 12, 1945. Only a Japanese shrine remains standing amid the rubble.

ground below, the plane appeared to be a tiny silver speck, moving slowly across the sky over five miles above the city.

The bomb bay doors were opened as the plane approached the drop site. There was no time to make additional passes over the city. If the bomb was not dropped it would have to be jettisoned into the ocean or carried back to a friendly air field. No one wanted to risk a dangerous landing with a heavy plane that was low on fuel at an American air base while carrying the largest bomb ever built in the history of the world.

Fatigue and nervousness began to take their toll on the crew. As BOCK'S CAR moved across the sky over Nagasaki it's crew sighted the required landmarks on the ground and the bomb was armed. At the prescribed moment the Fat Man dropped from the belly of the plane. When it reached an altitude just under 1/3 of a mile above the ground, a sophisticated arrangement of electrical devices set off the bomb. An unprecedented blinding flash erupted over the city, and a blast wave raced out in every direction with the speed of a typhoon and heat of the sun.

Every human being in a large area under the bomb was immediately charred or evaporated. The entire valley that cradled Nagasaki was enveloped in an incredible fireball and its concentric blast wave. Fires began to erupt even at high altitudes on the sloping sides of the great valley around the city. As Nagasaki writhed below, BOCK'S CAR had turned southward and headed for Okinawa and a refueling stop that would prevent it from having to ditch into the sea. The B-29 that carried the Fat Man to Japan would return safely to Tinian.

Early on August 10, less than a day after the second atomic blast had ruined a Japanese city, the war cabinet met with Emperor Hirohito in Tokyo to wrestle with the grim options. They had an additional problem to contend with. Russia had declared war on Japan, but not until after the first bomb had been dropped. The Soviets were seizing Manchuria and North Korea, parts of the far east not agreed upon in Potsdam. With minimum participation in the Japanese defeat, the Russians were grabbing a disproportionate land area, setting the stage for later conflict with the Allies.

The Japanese leaders were clearly divided into two groups, the hardline militants who favored continuation of the war, and the peace faction who favored surrender. They entered into an intense debate. Several of the ministers argued in favor of accepting the unconditional terms of the surrender as outlined in the Potsdam ultimatum. But those who were intent upon mounting one last all-out frantic battle to defend the homeland felt that there were enough men, guns, and materials to be victorious. They argued vehemently to continue the fight.

Finally, after the debate had raged for some time, it was realized that no course of action would be agreed upon. With a consensus of the group impossible, Premier Kantaro Suzuki tactfully turned the decision over to the Emperor himself. Hirohito addressed the group in his quiet, soft-spoken manner. It quickly became clear that he deplored the unbearable suffering that his subjects were enduring.

The Emperor hinted to the military strong men that they had been unable to stop the advancing Americans, and that they were unprepared to do so even as the enemy armies approached the very shores of the home islands. The Emperor regretfully accepted the conditions of the Potsdam ultimatum, and then the 124th Emperor of Japan, the direct descendent of Amaterasu, the Goddess of the Sun, turned quickly and left the room.

The Japanese people who came in contact with the POW's in Fusiki became very disturbed when news came of a massive new American weapon that had been used to destroy the city of Nagasaki. Dick and the other POW's in the Fusiki prison got a Japanese newspaper every day, and several of the men had gotten pretty good at reading them. However, nothing was said about the new bomb, and everyone was curiously ignorant of exactly what had happened in the city where the bomb had been used. The government had put a lid on things there by sealing off the city of Nagasaki so that news of the catastrophe would not become common knowledge.

Even so, the people knew of the horrible new bomb. Slick Sloman had been moved to Zentsuji where he worked with Japanese civilians each day outside the camp. They told him that a horrendous new weapon had been dropped on Hiroshima. The prisoners quickly learned that something extraordinary had happened. The word coming from the civilians was that this new and dreaded bomb was small, but it had done massive damage beyond comprehension.

The prisoners at Zentsuji did not pay a great deal of attention to the Japanese civilians at first. After all, they were fed a steady diet of propaganda, and they might be simply repeating a story fed to them by the government. In addition, when it suited their purpose they would lie to the Americans to get something they wanted. Some of the prisoners rationalized that news of such a monstrous new weapon sounded like something the government would feed the people in order to justify a surrender, which otherwise would have been incomprehensible.

The prisoners in Zentsuji were unsure about the rumors of the new bomb, but they were certain that an American fleet was offshore not far from Japan. For several weeks there had been American carrier-based planes flying over Zentsuji. There was much talk in the prison about the end of the war being close at hand. Spirits were high because of the possibility of freedom, but this was tempered by apprehension about the methods that the Japanese would use for dealing with the prisoners in the case of an American invasion.

On the morning of August 10 President Truman met with his top advisors to discuss the Japanese acceptance of the Potsdam conditions, which had been received by radio from Tokyo. The Japanese government accepted the conditions of the surrender with one reservation. The Japanese insisted that the preservation of the reign of the Emperor must be accepted by the Allies. They would surrender only if the royal dynasty, which had been intact for over 2600 years, was left in place.

The American war council realized that many of the Japanese would be loyal to the Emperor and would never waver from their devotion to him under any conditions. They would fight to a suicidal death for him if necessary to show their obedience. After considering the possibility of continued fighting and bloodshed, and with a great deal of concern for the health and safety of the POW's

US Navy

The aftermath of the atomic bomb at Nagasaki as seen in august 1945 cannot begin to mirror the inconceivable horror of the blast.

still being held by the Japanese, the council generally agreed that the Emperor should be allowed to retain his title.

The problems associated with the surrender of an empire and the return of thousands of prisoners began to be discussed. On August 12 an American communique reached Japan which neither confirmed nor denied that the Emperor would remain. It merely indicated that the Supreme Allied Commander would have the ultimate authority in Japan, and that, in the final analysis, the Japanese people would choose their own form of government democratically. There was still no clear message to Japan about their Emperor. This led to continued resistance to the surrender from the hardliners.

On August 13 the hardline militants in the Japanese armed forces planned a coup that would overthrow the government the following day. They would take over the surrendering government and forge onward with the fight to preserve Japan. High ranking military leaders were being approached and asked to join the rebellion. Those who refused place their lives in danger.

Also on the 13th, American forces were notified that peace was possible within a short time. They were advised not to take any offensive action until the enemy had time to respond to the peace (surrender) initiative. American planes were poised and ready to carry out more massive bombing raids over the enemy homeland, but they remained silent as everyone waited and hoped for peace.

The next day, August 14, Emperor Hirohito met with his war council and listened once again to the arguments for and against the acceptance of the Allied peace conditions. Militants voiced a strong argument against the Emperor's previous request for surrender, but in the end, Hirohito would rule. He made his position clear. In order to spare lives and further suffering, he made a direct and highly emotional request to everyone, both military and civilian, to support his position and honor the terms of the surrender agreement.

With that, the Emperor left the room. Japan's top leaders began to experience the shock and grief of the moment. The unimaginable had happened. Japan had lost. The Emperor had decided to surrender the homeland to an enemy army. Everyone in the meeting knew that the end had come.

As word of the Emperor's decision shot through their ranks, isolated segments of the military began efforts to stage a revolution. There were some who were simply incapable of surrender. Their code of honor called for one of two courses—either fight to the death or commit suicide. Radicals in the military went into action, killing several leaders who would not support the insurrection.

Even Premier Suzuki was not immune from danger. He had supported the Emperor completely, thus becoming the highest ranking member of the government to favor surrender. Radicals searched for him in vain, feeling that his support for the Emperor's plan was tantamount to treason. When the radicals went to his home to kill him, the Premier had fled. They burned his house to the ground.

On August 15 President Truman announced to an exuberant American public that the Emperor had accepted the terms of the Potsdam Declaration. As Americans enjoyed their victory and partied until dawn, the Japanese were sobbing in defeat and attempting to bring the radical factions under control. There was still considerable danger lurking in Japan for the POW's. American advance teams began to consider the methods that would be used to land and take control of Japan.

The greatest danger to the POW's in Japan was from the hardline zealots who had vowed never to surrender despite Emperor Hirohito's clear instructions. A frenzy of killing began at isolated locations in Japan by some of the radical groups. One group of captured B-29 airmen had been beheaded or chopped to death by swordsmen near Fukuoka on August 11. Several of the top political and military leaders were assassinated by those who felt they were not taking the proper stance against the surrender.

Slick Sloman was on a work detail several miles from Zentsuji prison. He and the other men were making up trains by pushing cars together on the tracks with their bare shoulders. Suddenly several extra guards showed up. Everyone knew something was up. The guards ordered the men to drop what they were doing and not to lift another thing. They instructed the prisoners to go back to camp immediately. The men headed for a depot where they were to catch a train back to camp.

When they arrived at the train station the guards seemed intent upon getting the men back to camp the quickest possible way. They argued with the station master, insisting that the men be put aboard a train without delay. "There isn't one running right now," he insisted. "You will just have to wait until another train arrives."

The men were taken into the station where they waited. When the first train arrived, they were quickly herded aboard. The prisoners tried their best to figure out what was happening. They were concerned that a landing by American forces might have taken place. Some men feared what the Japanese might do when they got all the men back together in the camp. When they reached the camp they were told to go to their barracks and take a rest. The men complied with their orders, returning to their barracks where they anxiously waited for an indication of what was happening.

While most Japanese followed their Emperor's directives to the letter, some were still bent upon revenge against the Americans. Many of the prisoners found themselves at the mercy of the radicals. Clearly, the danger had not subsided for the men who were still being held in Japanese prisons. Knowing that such reprisals were a possibility, the victorious American forces wanted to get their rescue personnel to the camps as quickly as possible.

At noon on August 15, 1945, Emperor Hirohito delivered a radio address to his people. This was the first time they had ever been allowed to hear their ruler's voice. In the unprecedented broadcast he told his unsuspecting subjects of the surrender terms that had been offered by the Allied powers. The entire population was shocked. Many sobbed uncontrollably. They could not believe what they were hearing. Could it be that the beloved homeland would be surrendered by the Emperor himself?

Hirohito worded his message carefully, portraying Japan's initiation of the war as a patriotic effort to protect the country's national interests. He also indicated that his country had gone to war in order to bring stability to all of southeast Asia. He indicated that Japan was not simply trying to usurp the lands of the other nations.

The Emperor attempted to rationalize the surrender of his country by describing the deterioration of the international situation to the disfavor of Japan. The efforts of the Allied powers had become so overwhelming and dangerous that it was in the best interest of Japan to cease its war efforts. Then the Emperor made reference to the real reason for surrender. He indicated that the Allies had produced a new weapon capable of bringing "incalculable" death and suffering to his subjects. He implied that only surrender could save millions from the fury of the new bomb.

The Emperor finished his radio message by thanking his subjects for the work, bloodshed, suffering, and lost lives that they had endured during the war. The general reaction of the Japanese people to the broadcast was shock and disbelief, but the range of individual responses to the speech was more diverse. While most obeyed their Emperor explicitly, others committed hara-kiri, and still others vowed to continue the fight. More captured American prisoners in isolated parts of the country were executed by swordsmen. There was still great danger for all of the American prisoners in Japan.

The day after the Emperor's address, the guards at Zentsuji told Slick Sloman and the other men that a surrender had occurred, but they indicated that they did not know if it would be valid. The men waited, and as they did they noticed that each day their rice ration was noticeably reduced. They had been getting laborers rations, but since the work stopped they were given non-laborers rations, which was about half as much. The prisoners were anxious to find out what was happening and were getting irritable about the food situation.

The next day the Japanese camp commander surprised everyone when he turned over the supply room keys to an American warrant officer. The Americans took all of the rifles, pistols, and ammunition. They began to wait, and they wondered what would happen to them next. One of the prisoners had been trained in the Navy as a radioman. He went into the nearby town and came back with a radio. The first broadcast that the men listened to was from American forces on Saipan. The announcer said that there had been an unconditional surrender of all Japanese forces, and that all POW's were to take charge of their camps and stay put. American units would be coming to liberate the prisons, but the safest way to facilitate the removal of the prisoners was for them to stay where they were.

Within a few days American B-29's began dropping food and supplies to the men in the camps. Only 109 prisoners remained in Zentsuji, but enough material was parachuted into the camp for several hundred men. Over 500 parachutes were gathered by the men. Most of the supplies came down in metal barrels which weighed 250-350 pounds. In the containers the men found clothing, medical supplies, shoes, and every type of food from C-rations to candy bars to canned peaches.

Some of the heavy metal containers tore loose from their parachute lines before they hit the ground. They became deadly projectiles as they slammed into the fields and buildings below. One hit a Japanese shrine across the street from Zentsuji prison, almost completely destroying it. Others ripped through the roofs of buildings, killing or injuring people inside. Six Japs were killed at one time when a double-sized drum smashed through the roof of their wooden shack.

The Japanese realized that the war was over and that they should treat the Americans as well as possible. Some of them came to the camp with carts loaded with fruits, vegetables, and beer. Only two guards remained in Zentsuji prison. Most guards had abused the men, so they left immediately when the surrender was announced in order to avoid reprisals.

The two guards who remained at Zentsuji had actually been friendly with the Americans before the surrender. They had been dealing in black market goods for some time, and they had nothing to fear from the prisoners. They actually reaped the benefits of the surplus goods that had been parachuted into the camp. They were able to carry on a brisk black market business while the POW's were waiting to be liberated.

At Rokuroshi prison the camp commander had left, apparently going to get official word of the surrender. He ordered that the men be put to hard labor while he was gone. After Spider Webb had been on the rock pile for several days the commander returned. First, the Jap officer dismissed all of the guards and told them to leave. Then he announced to the Americans that the war was over. He became very friendly, offering to do anything he could to help the men.

The first thing on the minds of the prisoners was food. The Japanese commander ordered the local people to bring bags of rice to the prisoners, even though the civilians were starving themselves. He also provided the men with a radio. They listened as American broadcasters told them, "Stay where you are. We are coming to get you. Put the letters 'PW' on the tops of your buildings, and we will find you."

Due to clouds and rainy weather, it took over a week for American planes to spot the camp at Rokuroshi. When the first B-29's came over they were only 200 feet above the amazed men. They had not seen the huge new planes that close before. The planes turned around and came back over the camp, this time at an altitude of about 500 feet. They began to drop metal barrels of supplies by parachute. C-rations and K-rations were everywhere, more than the men could eat. One steel canister went through the roof of a kitchen nearby, breaking a Jap cook's arm.

General Douglas MacArthur was the Supreme Allied Commander in the Pacific. He would represent the United States, England, Russia, China, and all other countries aligned against Japan during the transfer of power. General MacArthur had many urgent matters to consider and act upon, but at the top of his list were the orderly occupation of Japan and the earliest possible removal of the POW's from enemy camps. Americans went into action on many fronts to locate and liberate captured Americans.

During the early stages of the surrender process, messages darted back and forth between the American victors and the surrendering Japanese. Attempts were made to arrange a face to face meeting between representatives of each side in order to begin the formalities of surrendering an empire. Finally, on August 19, the Japanese were able to sidestep a myriad of internal problems and assemble a delegation. The reluctant Japanese delegates flew to Manila where they began the painful ordeal of giving up their country in defeat.

The implementation of the surrender, indeed the acceptance of its reality by Japanese forces throughout the empire, was still dangerously cloudy in the minds of the Emperor's military men. Surrender was a crushing blow to them, but the prospect of occupation by their dreaded enemy was even worse. The Americans wanted to land at the Atsugi air base near Tokyo in just four days to begin the occupation. The Japanese balked at this suggestion, knowing that considerable resistance still existed in the homeland. Finally the two sides agreed—Americans would land in Japan on August 28.

When word reached Japan that American military forces would land within a few days, tension among the militant holdouts reached a critical point. The Japanese military machine, including millions of patriotic soldiers and civilian laborers, still had the potential to be a very potent force. Pockets of resistance to the surrender began to surface. Even Atsugi air field, the site of the proposed American landing, was controlled by a cadre of troops resistant to the surrender.

Soon after the Emperor radioed his peace message to the Japanese people, efforts were begun by Allied forces to provide relief to the American POW's throughout Japan. American bombers dropped food and supplies

US Army Institute of Pathology

Evacuating POWs from Rokanoshi Prison by Truck.

by parachute to dozens of prison camps all over the country. While former prisoners of war waited anxiously for their liberation, teams of American military personnel worked feverishly to prepare for their evacuation. But first, the zealots who resisted the surrender had to be silenced.

Col. Charles Tench was assigned the dangerous job of being the first American to set foot on Japanese soil. He landed in an American C-47 cargo plane at Atsugi air base on August 28. He was aware that his was a perilous assignment, and that such a landing into the midst of the enemy just a few days before would have been suicidal. Even so, he was not aware that Atsugi was rife with militant Japanese soldiers who still questioned the validity of the surrender. Even though the surrender had already taken place, Col. Tench's mission at Atsugi was fraught with danger.

A large number of Japanese troops were positioned near the landing area at Atsugi, ordered to protect the Americans from other Japanese. The tension was extraordinary as the plane touched down and a reception committee met the deplaning Americans. Americans and Japanese were finally face to face on Japanese soil. As Tench and a Japanese General first spoke to each other they stood rigidly at attention, each man with a piercing stare directed at the other and assessing the circumstances of the dangerous situation.

Then Colonel Tench courageously began to walk across the airfield through what amounted to enemy territory. He could have been shot at any moment by one of the bitter hardliners who remained in the area. He and the Japanese general made their way to a secure area where they began to discuss the occupation. More C-47's began to land. The Americans were moving in.

In the days following Colonel Tench's landing, a large number of American planes and men came in Japan. The occupation

began in earnest as American ships entered Tokyo Bay and thousands of American troops and hundreds of ships and planes came into the country. Japan became more firmly under the control of the Allies with each successive hour. Only a few scattered pockets of resistance remained in the Tokyo area.

Gen. Douglas MacArthur landed at Atsugi within a couple of days. This part of Japan was thought to be secure enough for the leader of the Allied forces to be present. The great world war was over, and the United States was victorious. Americans reveled in merriment around the globe, but not in Fusiki prison. There Dick Darden and nearly 300 fellow prisoners waited patiently, still apprehensive enough about the dangerous situation that they preferred to wait for American forces to come to them rather than venture out into the unsettled population.

The days at Fusiki prison, several hundred miles north of Tokyo, passed ever so slowly for Dick Darden. By September 1, two full weeks after the surrender, no Americans had come to liberate the men at Fusiki. The men continued to wait, but their patience became strained. They began to ask questions. Where were the Americans? Because of the air drops they knew that Americans were aware of the prison at Fusiki. What was going on? What was the delay? The prisoners had waited more than forty-four months for the war to be over. They wanted to leave Fusiki and leave Japan. Where were the American liberators?

A contingent of troops from the American 8th Army made its way up the road in the mountains near Rokuroshi. Spider Webb watched as the officers, medics, and nurses arrived in camp. They treated the men and then began loading them on trucks which would

281

take them down to the town and its railroad station. Spider Webb was free at last.

The train took Spider Webb to Yokohama. There Gen. Eichelburger shook hands with the gaunt men as they got off the train. The General had a band behind him playing "California, Here I Come." It was great, such a good feeling!! It was just great!! Just great!! Spider Webb knew he was going home.

By September 1 General MacArthur was in firm control of most of Japan, and the transition of power had been relatively peaceful. Most of the POW's had been contacted, liberated, and moved. They were either receiving medical attention or had been allowed to leave the country. While the men in Fusiki waited to start the long trip home, the final touches were being applied to the formal surrender documents. Emperor Hirohito instructed Gen. Yoshijiro Umezu to represent Japan at the formal surrender ceremonies the following day. The stage was set for the surrender of the Japanese empire.

Japanese surrender signatories arrive aboard the USS MISSOURI, September 1, 1945, to participate in the surrender ceremony.

Allied POWs at Aomori prison camp near Yokohama cheer US Navy rescuers, August 29, 1945.

CHAPTER 56
THE WAR IS OVER

On September 2, 1945, the Japanese delegation was taken by a destroyer to the USS MISSOURI waiting in Tokyo Bay. Aboard the American battleship were General MacArthur and an assemblage of American and Allied military leaders who would witness the surrender. Along with the admirals and generals present that day were many sailors who sat informally watching the historic events with their legs dangling across the barrels of the MISSOURI's big 16" guns. When the documents were formally signed by all parties, the collapse of the Japanese empire became official.

Slick Sloman and the men at Zentsuji were still waiting to be liberated. They had been going into the nearby town and getting the supplies they needed, but they did not abuse or steal from the Japanese people in any way. The Americans were able to trade their surplus supplies from the air drops to the hungry Japanese for whatever they wanted. They compensated the civilians for everything they took back to camp.

Finally, a contingent of Americans made their way to Zentsuji prison. They arrived in a charcoal-burning Japanese truck. The group included a major, a sergeant, and a nurse. The group made arrangements for the prisoners to be taken out of the camp on trucks. Slick Sloman realized that he was a free man. He had overcome serious wounds and forty-four months of brutality. He had lived through the Japanese ordeal.

U. S. Marine Corps

A Japanese officer salutes Marine Colonel Walter L. J. Bayler, "The last man off Wake Island," as he makes history by being the first American to set foot on Wake after the Japanese surrender, September, 1945.

U.S. Marine Corps

Japanese Adm. Shigematsu Sakaibara, far left, on the front row and Japanese Navy and Army officers under his command stand at attention during the reading of a proclamation transferring control of Wake Island to American Forces.

The prisoners at Fusiki had not been given any word of the surrender and were unaware of the events that were transpiring some 300 miles to the south in Tokyo Bay. Then one morning, about the 4 of September, 1945, an old Japanese woman who worked for the Japanese officer in charge told some of the prisoners that the war was over. Coincidentally, the guards did not come to make the men go to work that morning. They mysteriously stayed in the guardhouse.

The highest ranking American enlisted man in camp was Philip Sanders. Sanders was a Navy Boatswain's Mate who was called "Sandy" for short and was well-liked by nearly everyone. Sanders represented the men in Fusiki prison whenever it was necessary to have a spokesman. Soon after the men realized that the guards were remaining in their guardhouse and something was going on, the Japanese duty officer called Sanders to his office and said, "I've got some good news for you. The war is over." Sanders had been waiting for nearly four years to hear those words.

Sandy responded to the Japanese officer by saying, in a concerned and suspicious voice, "Are you sure?" "Yes," replied the officer. "If this is true, tell all of your men to come into this room and put their weapons on this table," Sandy instructed him. To everyone's surprise, the guards did exactly that. Could it be that after forty-four months of this hellish ordeal it was finally over?

As the POW's began to realize what was happening they took control of the camp but did not immediately know what to do about leaving. One prisoner from Mississippi named John Smith had allowed his hair and beard to grow down to his shoulders. His tattered Japanese uniform was many sizes too small. He was truly a pitiful sight to see. Sandy ordered Smith to take a rifle and go to the gate and stand guard duty. As Smith did, the Japanese civilians who walked by the gate stared at him intensely, as if to say, "What could be happening with guards who look like this?"

Sandy looked at his emaciated comrade and immediately gave the Japanese officer another order. "I want you to get a quarter of beef for these men," he instructed. "There is no beef in Japan," responded the officer. Sandy called in a Marine POW and handed him a watch. Then he took a pistol from the pile of weapons on the table and gave this to the Marine as well.

Sandy's orders to the Marine were short and terse. "Take this man anywhere he wants to go, but if he had not found a side of beef in thirty minutes, SHOOT HIM." This particular guard, who normally had a very poor command of the English language while working with the prisoners, suddenly understood the English orders explicitly, and the two were off.

In fifteen minutes the men were back. They had gone only a half mile down the road to a Japanese officer's camp, and with them they brought back a quarter of prime Australian beef. Sandy ordered the 300 men to plunder the tiny Japanese gardens that were found everywhere across the countryside. The men did just that, ravaging the gardens like a plague of locusts. For starving men the prospects of their first good meal in several years was exhilarating.

Soon the men returned with buckets of vegetables. Potatoes, carrots, cabbage, snapped and shelled beans, and several other vegetables were peeled, cleaned, and put into three large rice pots. Then the entire quarter of beef was cut up and put into the pots. The most glorious stew that Dick Darden had ever seen began to simmer. The stew became so thick that it couldn't be stirred with a paddle. Soon the aroma of this delicacy permeated the air, and the men began to eat.

All night long Klem cans could he heard clattering as the men ate. They had been starved for so long that many tried to make up for lost time by gorging themselves. Some had gastric problems and diarrhea from devouring the rich food so quickly. Not Dick! He filled his Klem can and ate a belly full every three or four hours throughout the night and into the next day, and he never got sick. Finally the gut- wrenching pain of starvation was abated.

Dick had never eaten so much stew in his life, and he had never eaten any that tasted better. In the forty months that Dick had been a prisoner in Japan the sum total of meat that he had been given by the Japanese would fit into the palm of his hand. Now the rich beef stew was his for the taking, and all he wanted of it at that. He would never forget the delicious beef stew at Fusiki prison.

Several days passed and nothing happened at Fusiki prison. There was no contact from the liberating American forces. The Japanese guards at Fusiki made no moves at all, remaining in their guard shack. On Wake Island, however, major changes were unfolding. Just after daybreak on Saturday, September 4, American ships approached Wake. They closed to within 1000 yards of Wilkes Channel. Admiral Sakaibara was aware that the war had ended and had been instructed on the methods to be used for surrendering the island by leaflets that had been dropped from American planes. The Admiral was ready and willing to cooperate in the surrendering of the island.

Sakaibara and several of his officers came out to the ships on an American motor launch, one which had probably been used by Dick Darden in 1941, and boarded the destroyer escort USS LEVY where they met Marine Brig. Gen. L. H. M. Sanderson. No one shook Admiral Sakaibara's hand. The details of the transfer of power on Wake were agreed upon and the surrender documents were formally signed. Admiral Sakaibara left the ship at 10:00 a.m. About twenty minutes afterwards Marines went ashore in the agreed upon manner and the surrender began.

A note of irony had preceded the actual surrender ceremony. Col. Walter Bayler had earlier been given the title of "The Last Man Off Wake Island" when he rode the last PBY out on December 21, 1941. He would later author a book by that same title. Col. Bayler was given the privilege of being the first American to step on the island after it was surrendered, thus giving him the distinction of being the last American off Wake Island and the first to return. Moments after he set foot on the dock, a contingent of Marines followed him onto the island and began an inspection.

A preliminary inspection of the airstrip was made by vehicle, after which the entire length of the mile-long runway was inspected. Men on foot formed a scouting line and inspected the entire landing area. When the men were satisfied that it was free of land mines and other obstructions, the airfield was pronounced ready for aircraft to land. The first American plane, however, did not land on the runway. It was a PBM flying boat from Eniwetok in the Marshall Islands. It splashed down on the lagoon at 11:30 a.m.

At 1:30 that afternoon a ceremony was held at the boat landing to transfer power from the occupation force to the American delegation. Men from both sides watched as a flag raising ceremony was conducted. The Marines at the ceremony carried only small arms, but they received control of the island in an orderly fashion just as had been agreed upon earlier that morning. Wake Island was retaken without firing a shot or spilling a drop of blood from either side.

In great contrast to the bloody landings of the four preceding years on the Pacific islands in which nearly all Japanese combatants were either killed or committed suicide, Admiral Sakaibara handed over his Samurai sword and surrendered Wake

National Archives

Captured Japanese on Wake Island line up for medical assistance, September 20, 1945. Some are extremely emaciated from years of starvation due to the American blockade of the Island.

Island without a fight. The Jap's heavy coastal guns and extensive fortifications were not used against the American forces that reclaimed the island. Wake Island once again became American territory.

While the forty-five month ordeal in Japan had been an extended period of extreme hardship for Dick Darden, so too had the duration of the war been severe for the Japanese occupation force, especially the enlisted men, on Wake Island. Some of the troops who had landed with the invasion force on December 23, 1941, were still on the island when it was surrendered on September 7, 1945. Many of them, like American POW's in Japan, had the thin, gaunt, emaciated look of severely malnourished men.

Chapter 57
THE POW'S AT FUSIKI SEEK FREEDOM

National Archives

American, British, and Dutch POWs cheer U.S. Navy Rescuers at Aomori Prison Camp near Yokohama, August 29, 1945.

Dick and the other men at Fusiki knew that the war must have ended. One reason was that they were not working, and they knew how critical their labor was to the Japanese war effort. When American B-29's flew over and dropped food and supplies to the men by parachute, the men rejoiced in the fact that their four-year struggle to survive the oppression of their Japanese enemy had come to an end. The men began to realize that the war really was over and that they, not the Japanese, were the victors.

The regular Japanese guards were replaced by a fresh group of unarmed soldiers. The POW's wondered if the previous guards, some of whom had been brutal to the men, had asked their superiors for permission to leave so that the freed prisoners would not kill them for revenge. Dick had never seen any of these guards before. They waited on the POW's, trying to make them comfortable and attending to their needs. They were quite the opposite of the guards Dick had known for the past four years.

The new guards would sit in the guardhouse and help the prisoners, sometimes appearing puzzled about exactly what they should be doing. Indeed, a miraculous change had come over the Japanese. Their normally angry temperament and the beatings had ceased completely, and now they were saying "Yes sir" and "No sir" to the POW's. They were actually bowing to the prisoners. Since the POW's were holding the firearms, they didn't mind the guards staying around.

Still, since there had been no contact with Allied forces except the air drops, no one knew exactly what was going on between Japanese and American forces outside the camp. The men decided that it would be best to sit tight and wait, since the mental state of the defeated Japanese people, especially the soldiers who were still armed, was still unclear.

The big B-29 Flying Fortresses dropped materials by parachutes only once to the men in Fusiki prison. Some of the materials were so damaged by the impact with the ground that they were not usable. Most, however, survived the parachute experience in reasonably good condition.

The Japanese people, most completely without materials to make clothing, made dresses and shirts from the parachutes. They were willing to use any of the parachuted goods that were not wanted by the POW's. They became very efficient at scavenging goods from the drop zones, which sometimes were not precisely on target. Several Japanese families in the area had special delivery packages to come crashing through their roofs.

The Japanese officer who was supervisor of the guards had been particularly brutal before surrendering to the POW's. Before he had given up control of the camp, he had been the man who gave orders to the guards, and he had always spoken only Japanese. He never gave the slightest hint that he spoke or understood English. All of the prisoners assumed that he did not understand them when they spoke in English, so they called him every name in the book, even when he was in easy earshot of their conversations.

Just as the Americans were preparing to leave Fusiki, the officer walked up to Dick and a group of his friends and, in crystal clear English, said, "Well, I hope that you fellows have a good trip home." The men were shocked when they realized he spoke fluent English. They all wondered how many of their curses and insults he had heard and understood.

Three long weeks passed and still no word or contact came from the Allied forces. The men began to get restless. Finally a large group, Dick included, decided they had waited long enough and maybe they had been forgotten. They were free and they longed to be at home with their loved ones. About 300 yards from the gates of Fusiki prison was a train station. The men noticed there were still trains running along this line. They convinced Sandy to allow them to take a train toward Tokyo in search of the Allied forces they hoped would be in the area.

The men decided to ask the POW's in a nearby camp if they wanted to join them in taking a train out of the area. The camp, about a half mile away, had been in a steel foundry. The men had worked for the Japanese making metal barrels. At one time there had been over 400 men in this camp. They were housed inside the foundry where they worked and never left the building. After work in the filthy building they were made to live and sleep on the cold damp cinder floor of the foundry. Conditions there had been terrible. To make matters infinitely worse, these men never had the opportunity to steal food.

When Dick first saw the men from the foundry he was amazed at their horrible physical condition. Even though his frame was 100 pounds lighter than he had been on Wake Island, he was in much better condition than many of these men. He realized that the stark conditions that he had survived for the past forty-five months could have been even worse. Over one hundred of the men in the foundry, Dick later learned, had died in the previous year from starvation and malnutrition. A man was sent to the foundry to tell the POW's that a train was going to take the men to Tokyo, and they could go if they wanted. Some did, while many others were simply too weak to move.

The first train to arrive in the station had about a dozen passenger cars. Sandy called the train's conductor out and told him what he wanted to do. "We are taking over this train, and we are going to Tokyo," he said. "Can't do it, can't do it," responded the engineer in broken English, refusing to transport the prisoners on his train.

Sandy calmly pulled his Japanese pistol from its holster, placed it to the man's head, and cocked it. "Then I'm going to shoot you," he warned. Immediately the attitude of the conductor became more positive, and he was happy to take the men to Tokyo. Another man with a pistol encouraged all of the Japanese civilians to get off the train at once. They complied with great haste.

There were nearly 600 men in the two camps. At Fusiki prison 295 men remained out of the 300 who were moved from Osaka. Only 250-300 men remained alive in the foundry. All of the men who were able to travel headed for the train station. As the men went out the gates of their camps, they were each given a box of the C-rations which had been dropped by the B-29's. Each box was supposed to feed three men for one day. All of the remaining Japanese on the train were chased away, and the former prisoners piled into the cars. When the train pulled out of the station at about 6:00 p.m., the spirits of the men were high and the prospects of liberation gave the event a festive atmosphere.

Sandy ordered Smith into the cab of the train with the Japanese fireman and engineer. He told them that the men wanted passage to Tokyo. "If they don't keep this thing running, shoot them," Sandy instructed. Suddenly it seemed that every Jap to come in contact with the men understood English. The fireman and engineer clearly understood Sandy's orders and went about following them to the letter.

The conductor went into the station and made a telephone call, after which he returned to the train and said the tracks were being cleared all the way to Tokyo. This was all the train load of Americans wanted to hear. Shortly thereafter the journey to freedom began. The train pulled out of the station at about 6:00 p.m.

John Smith looked like a wild man in his ill-fitting clothes and long uncombed gray mane. He almost scared the Japanese fireman and engineer to death. They had no doubt that if they didn't get the train to Tokyo, Smith would put a bullet through them. In fact, this man who was fresh from a horrible forty-five month ordeal and who was now taking an exhilarating ride to freedom, probably would have done just that if the two Japanese had not done their job properly. The fireman threw the coal to the engine like never before. It was said that he shoveled coal until he was blue in the face. The train bolted down the tracks, fireballing southward.

Dick ate the entire contents of his food box during the night, as did most of the excited and still hungry men. As they flew down the tracks there was a continuous clatter of tin cans hitting the rails. Over 500 men ate and ate and ate. They left a trail of paper cartons, tin cans, and food wrappers the entire length of the journey. By first light the next morning the train had crossed Japan and reached the southern coast. It then turned eastward and traveled along tracks perched high on the sides of steep mountains. Dick looked just outside his window to see the mountain drop off sharply into the ocean far below.

The magnificent scenery was of only passing interest to the men as they yearned for freedom more than ever. Then the train came over a small hill and someone yelled, "Look, down there!" It was the view everyone had been waiting for. There in the bay far below the train were American ships, including several destroyers and a hospital ship, lying at anchor. Dick had never seen a more beautiful sight. The American flags flying on the ships were a spectacular sight to see.

The train continued down the mountainside and then began to slow down as it approached a barricade. The tracks had been blocked at the bottom of the hill so the train would be forced to stop. American sailors in their crisp white uniforms knew the POW train was coming, and they were stopping it to help the men find their way to the processing center. At last the ordeal of slave labor in Japan was over, really over. Dick was back in friendly hands at last.

Messages from POWs adorn the rooftops of prison camps along the Tokyo waterfront. Bomb craters pock-mark the landscape just beyond the buildings. Signs say "Yorktown, nice going! Thanks, milk, sugar, coffee," and "Take us home."

A POW suffering from malnutrition at Niiyama Prison.

American soldier find sharpened bamboo torture poles used by the Japanese at TSUMORI prison.

A freed American POW assembles his meager belongings as he sits in rubble and prepares to leave a Japanese POW camp. Of primary importance is the food box before him.

Yank Magazine

Prisoners pour out the gate at Fusiki prison to board the freedom train. Under their arms and on their shoulders they carry food boxes that were parachuted in from American planes

Freed POWs enroute to Yokohama enjoyed the luxuries of eating, smoking and reading magazines.

US Army Institute of Pathology

PART 5 – THE RETURN HOME
Chapter 58 – IN FRIENDLY HANDS AT LAST

Dick and the other men at Fusiki knew that the war must have ended. One reason was that they were not working, and they knew how critical their labor was to the Japanese war effort. When American B-29's flew over and dropped food and supplies to the men by parachute, the men rejoiced in the fact that their four-year struggle to survive the oppression of their Japanese enemy had come to an end. The men began to realize that the war really was over and that they, not the Japanese, were the victors.

The regular Japanese guards were replaced by a fresh group of unarmed soldiers. The POW's wondered if the previous guards, some of whom had been brutal to the men, had asked their superiors for permission to leave so that the freed prisoners would not kill them for revenge. Dick had never seen any of these guards before. They waited on the POW's, trying to make them comfortable and attending to their needs. They were quite the opposite of the guards Dick had known for the past four years.

The new guards would sit in the guardhouse and help the prisoners, sometimes appearing puzzled about exactly what they should be doing. Indeed, a miraculous change had come over the Japanese. Their normally angry temperament and the beatings had ceased completely, and now they were saying "Yes sir" and "No sir" to the POW's. They were actually bowing to the prisoners. Since the POW's were holding the firearms, they didn't mind the guards staying around.

Still, since there had been no contact with Allied forces except the air drops, no one knew exactly what was going on between Japanese and American forces outside the camp. The men decided that it would be best to sit tight and wait, since the mental state of the defeated Japanese people, especially the soldiers who were still armed, was still unclear.

The big B-29 Flying Fortresses dropped materials by parachutes only once to the men in Fusiki prison. Some of the materials were so damaged by the impact with the ground that they were not usable. Most, however, survived the parachute experience in reasonably good condition.

The Japanese people, most completely without materials to make clothing, made dresses and shirts from the parachutes. They were willing to use any of the parachuted goods that were not wanted by the POW's. They became very efficient at scavenging goods from the drop zones, which sometimes were not precisely on target. Several Japanese families in the area had special delivery packages to come crashing through their roofs.

The Japanese officer who was supervisor of the guards had been particularly brutal before surrendering to the POW's. Before he had given up control of the camp, he had been the man who gave orders to the guards, and he had always spoken only Japanese. He never gave the slightest hint that he spoke or understood

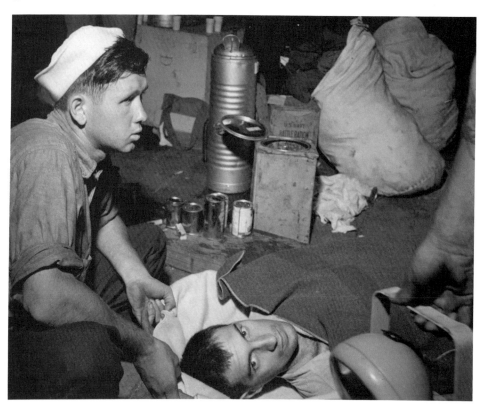

An Allied POW, emaciated and too weak to walk due to malnutrition, is carried aboard a hospital ship in Tokyo Bay, August 30, 1945. Emergency food and medical supplies are in cans at left.

National Archives

A litter patient boarding the USS MARIGOLD, a hospital ship.

English. All of the prisoners assumed that he did not understand them when they spoke in English, so they called him every name in the book, even when he was in easy earshot of their conversations.

Just as the Americans were preparing to leave Fusiki, the officer walked up to Dick and a group of his friends and, in crystal clear English, said, "Well, I hope that you fellows have a good trip home." The men were shocked when they realized he spoke fluent English. They all wondered how many of their curses and insults he had heard and understood.

Three long weeks passed and still no word or contact came from the Allied forces. The men began to get restless. Finally a large group, Dick included, decided they had waited long enough and maybe they had been forgotten. They were free and they longed to be at home with their loved ones. About 300 yards from the gates of Fusiki prison was a train station. The men noticed there were still trains running along this line. They convinced Sandy to allow them to take a train toward Tokyo in search of the Allied forces they hoped would be in the area.

The men decided to ask the POW's in a nearby camp if they wanted to join them in taking a train out of the area. The camp, about a half mile away, had been in a steel foundry. The men had worked for the Japanese making metal barrels. At one time there had been over 400 men in this camp. They were housed inside the foundry where they worked and never left the building. After work in the filthy building they were made to live and sleep on the cold damp cinder floor of the foundry. Conditions there had been terrible. To make matters infinitely worse, these men never had the opportunity to steal food.

When Dick first saw the men from the foundry he was amazed at their horrible physical condition. Even though his frame was 100 pounds lighter than he had been on Wake Island, he was in much better condition than many of these men. He realized that the stark conditions that he had survived for the past forty-five months could have been even worse. Over one hundred of the men in the foundry, Dick later learned, had died in the previous year from starvation and malnutrition. A man was sent to the foundry to tell the POW's that a train was going to take the men to Tokyo, and they

Lt. Col. James P. S. Devereux arrives at Honolulu Naval Air Station on his way back to the United States, September 20, 1945

could go if they wanted. Some did, while many others were simply too weak to move.

The first train to arrive in the station had about a dozen passenger cars. Sandy called the train's conductor out and told him what he wanted to do. "We are taking over this train, and we are going to Tokyo," he said. "Can't do it, can't do it," responded the engineer in broken English, refusing to transport the prisoners on his train.

Sandy calmly pulled his Japanese pistol from its holster, placed it to the man's head, and cocked it. "Then I'm going to shoot you," he warned. Immediately the attitude of the conductor became more positive, and he was happy to take the men to Tokyo. Another man with a pistol encouraged all of the Japanese civilians to get off the train at once. They complied with great haste.

There were nearly 600 men in the two camps. At Fusiki prison 295 men remained out of the 300 who were moved from Osaka. Only 250-300 men remained alive in the foundry. All of the men who were able to travel headed for the train station. As the men went out the gates of their camps, they were each given a box of the C-rations which had been dropped by the B-29's. Each box was supposed to feed three men for one day. All of the remaining Japanese on the train were chased away, and the former prisoners piled into the cars. When the train pulled out of the station at about 6:00 p.m., the spirits of the men were high and the prospects of liberation gave the event a festive atmosphere.

Sandy ordered Smith into the cab of the train with the Japanese fireman and engineer. He told them that the men wanted passage to Tokyo. "If they don't keep this thing running, shoot them," Sandy instructed. Suddenly it seemed that every Jap to come in contact with the men understood English. The fireman and engineer clearly understood Sandy's orders and went about following them to the letter.

The conductor went into the station and made a telephone call, after which he returned to the train and said the tracks were being cleared all the way to Tokyo. This was all the train load of Americans wanted to hear. Shortly thereafter the journey to freedom began. The train pulled out of the station at about 6:00 p.m.

John Smith looked like a wild man in his ill-fitting clothes and long uncombed gray mane. He almost scared the Japanese fireman and engineer to death. They had no doubt that if they didn't get the train to Tokyo, Smith would put a bullet through them. In fact, this man who was fresh from a horrible forty-five month ordeal and who was now taking an exhilarating ride to freedom, probably would have done just that if the two Japanese had not done their job properly. The fireman threw the coal to the engine like never before. It was said that he shoveled coal until he was blue in the face. The train bolted down the tracks, fireballing southward.

Dick ate the entire contents of his food box during the night, as did most of the excited and still hungry men. As they flew down the tracks there was a continuous clatter of tin cans hitting the rails. Over 500 men ate and ate and ate. They left a trail of paper cartons, tin cans, and food wrappers the entire length of the journey. By first light the next morning the train had crossed Japan and reached the southern coast. It then turned eastward and traveled along tracks perched high on the sides of steep mountains. Dick looked just outside his window to see the mountain drop off sharply into the ocean far below.

The magnificent scenery was of only passing interest to the men as they yearned for freedom more than ever. Then the train came over a small hill and someone yelled, "Look, down there!" It was the view everyone had been waiting for. There in the bay far below the train were American ships, including several destroyers and a hospital ship, lying at anchor. Dick had never seen a more beautiful sight. The American flags flying on the ships were a spectacular sight to see.

The train continued down the mountainside and then began to slow down as it approached a barricade. The tracks had been blocked at the bottom of the hill so the train would be forced to stop. American sailors in their crisp white uniforms knew the POW train was coming, and they were stopping it to help the men find their way to the processing center. At last the ordeal of slave labor in Japan was over, really over. Dick was back in friendly hands at last.

Chapter 59
BACK ON AMERICAN SOIL

After Dick's brief stay in Hawaii it was on to Oakland, California, and Oak Knoll Naval Hospital, where he arrived on September 13. The former POW's received a thorough physical examination at the Oak Knoll. Amazingly, when Dick was examined by a dentist at Oak Knoll, he had only two cavities to show for forty-five months of neglect in the Japanese prisons.

While Dick was in Oakland he bumped into Nick Waller, an old buddy from Clinton. Nick had also been in the Navy serving in the Pacific. He had not been a POW, so he was able to fill Dick in on much of the news he had missed during the past four years. Nick and Dick had grown up just a short distance from each other, and Dick eagerly listened as he was told about the events of the war and about what had been happening back home. Reality was beginning to set in. Dick had made his first link with home, and he was beginning to truly feel that he was free.

It was from Oakland that Dick was able to make his first telephone call home. After two days of trying to get a call through, Dick heard the sweet voice of his mother. Talking with her made him feel even more that he really was near home at last. He told her he was in California and would be home just as fast as he could get there. The Navy had a few plans for him first. A local newspaper got word that Dick was back in the States and suggested an "appropriate homecoming" for the hero who had been gone for so long. The town began to plan for an event through which it could show its appreciation.

Dick remained in the Oak Knoll Hospital for one week. All thirty-six of the former POW's that were with him on the plane were assigned to the top floor of the back wing of the hospital. They were told to blow off some steam during their stay there, giving the doctors time to evaluate their conditions and assess their readiness to leave the hospital. There was a kitchen on the ward which was always stocked, and Dick satisfied his craving for vitamin C by drinking fruit juices almost nonstop.

There were two nurses assigned to the ward at all times. The first night one of the girls brought a record player and the music did not stop all night long. The men had not seen a pretty girl they could touch in almost four years, and they were ready to party. As soon as each dance would finish, one sailor would sit down and another would be ready to go. The nurses were really troopers, dancing all night long with any and every sailor who cared to join them. Dick wondered how they could hold out as long as they did on the dance floor. The nurses administered a type of medicine to their patients that the doctors were unable to provide.

Dick's family and friends in Clinton were concerned about his adjustment to freedom. The comforts of being at home would be so vastly different from what he had known for the past four years. On the day before Dick had been liberated in Japan, a hometown friend, a young attorney and family friend named Howard Hubbard, was trying to contact him by letter. Hubbard felt that, since so much time had elapsed since the Japanese surrender, surely all of the POW's had been evacuated and were enroute back to the States.

Hubbard wrote a long and poignant letter to Dick on September 4, hoping that it would intercept Dick while he was in California. In it he tried to describe the happiness that Dick's mother had felt since the POW's had been released, and how much she looked forward to his returning home. Hubbard also filled Dick in on some of the happenings in Clinton during the war, and what had happened to many of Dick's friends who had gone away to fight.

The main reason that Hubbard wrote to Dick, however, was to soften the blow that he knew Dick would feel when he heard the news about his brother Pete. Hubbard and Dick's mother did not want him to have his homecoming, an event which should have been wonderfully therapeutic for him, shattered by the news of Pete's death. Hubbard attempted to break the news to Dick in the letter in a straightforward but eloquent manner.

"Your mother has asked me to tell you about Pete," he wrote. "He was killed on 26 March on Zamami Shima, a little island off the coast of lower Japan. She got the news of his death in May and took it like the good soldier she is. Pete was killed by a sniper while helping rescue a 'medic.' He died instantly and did not suffer at all. He wanted to go to the Pacific and was happy to be in the Army.......She is happy to know that he was an excellent soldier and did not suffer at all. She wanted to write you this, but thought it best that I do so."

Hubbard wanted his letter to reach Dick so that by the time he came home the initial grief for Pete would be over. He continued, "Dick, do not let this dim your happiness. Pete would not want it to do so, nor does your mother. We are telling you now, so that there will be nothing to cloud the happiness your homecoming is going to bring your mother and family, all of whom are well."

Howard Hubbard mailed his letter to Dick, addressing it to the Liberated Personnel Section in San Francisco. It was returned to Hubbard as undeliverable, foiling his attempts to make a preliminary contact. Clearly the family in Clinton was uneasy, not knowing what Dick's condition would be, plus having to tell him about Pete. Even so, they could not wait for him to return home.

Every POW was allowed to draw as much money as he wanted against his back pay while at Oak Knoll. Each man was given a pass with A-1 priority. No one would stop them if they wanted to leave the hospital, day or night. Dick did not have a whole uniform yet. He was sporting parts of a Navy uniform along with a Marine shirt. As Dick approached the front gate on his way out the first time the sentry asked, "What in the hell kind of a uniform is that?" "The best kind," he retorted.

"Where are you going?" questioned the sentry. "I'm going to town," he replied, flipping out his priority pass. "In that outfit?" questioned the guard. "In this!" was his firm answer. No one had his thumb on Dick Darden now, and he was free to go anywhere he wanted. It was time to spread his wings and fly like an eagle, a victorious American eagle, free to enjoy life again.

4 September 1945

Dear Dick:

As yet, no official word has come that you are safe, but
your mother expects to hear the good news any moment now.
She is the happiest person I know. Her spirits and faith,
which have never failed her, were given a tremendous boost
this morning when she got a letter from you which was
written in January. That was the first direct word she
had received in many months. She is in excellent health
and a picture of happiness. Everyone in town is rejoicing
with her and we are all looking forward to seeing you
soon.

That part of your letter in which you said you hated to
come home with no higher rating than first class seaman
gave us a good laugh. Of course, you do not know it,
but the admirals take a back seat in the public's mind
as far as you boys from Wake are concerned.

I know you are anxious for news from home and will try
to give you a little. I know of no better place to
start than to try to tell you how wonderful your mother
has been through-out the whole war. She has been an excellent
soldier. Her faith has never dimmed and her morale has been
high. During the long months when she did not hear from
you, she was a marvel to everyone, a perfect example
of the old saying "keep your chin up and carry on".
She did just that. How she managed it, no one knows, but
the important thing is that she did. She is an expert
on the war with Japan and knows every inch of the road to
Osaka.

Your mother has asked me to tell you about "Pete". He was
killed on 26 March on Zamami Shima, a little island off
the coast of lower Japan. She got the news of his death
in May and took it like the good soldier she is. Pete was
killed by a sniper while helping rescue a "medic". He
died instantly and did not suffer at all. He wanted to
go to the Pacific and was happy to be in the Army. He
was rejected for service first because of his arm, but
later passed and was delighted. After taking his training
at Camp Croft, S.C., he was shipped to California. From
there, he went to Hiawaii by way of Oregon. He arrived in
Hiawaii last summer -- and from there went to Leyte, P.I.
Mrs. Darden has had many letters giving her the details
of his death. These have helped her a lot, and she is
happy to know that he was an excellent soldier and did
not suffer at all. She wanted to write you this, but

thought it best that I do so. Dick, do not let this
dim your happiness. Pete would not want it to do so,
nor does your mother. We are telling you now, so that
there will be nothing to cloud the happiness your
homecoming is going to bring your mother and family,
all of whom are well.

Clinton, as a whole, was most fortunate in the war. We
lost Pete, A.B.Butler, and Hal Teachey. A.B. and Hal
were killed in Europe. A.B. was a gunner on a B-24
and was lost over the Adriatic Sea. Hal was killed in
France. Fortunately, we have no seriously wounded boys.
My brother Jim was hit in February and is still in a
hospital. He, however, is going to be alright. I will
try to give you a bit of news from some of the other boys.
Jay Stewart is a pilot and made his missions over France.
He is back in this country now and married to Dot Starling.
Kenneth Smith was in the Army for a while, but received
a discharge. C.C.Tart is a pilot and is in the Pacific.
"Lang" is in the medical corps of the Army and is assigned
to a hospital ship. The two Turlington boys are in the
air corps, but have not been shipped overseas. Lang and
Nina are married. Hal Stewart has been with the Air Corps
in England, but is back in this country and is engaged to
Doris Butler. Bud Wellman and Norman Hurwitz are both
instructors in the Air Corps and have been on duty in
this country. John Thomas Ashford, Roland Jones and
Stephen Jones are all pilots and have been in Europe, but
are in the States now. Dick Kerr has been in France with
a tank outfit. Purcell Jones is in training for the Naval
Air Corps. He, too, is married. Joe Royal is in the
Navy. He married a Philadelphia girl, a very nice one, too.
David Stone Jackson is an ensign, somewhere in the Pacific.
So is George Williams. Believe George, however, is a Lieutenant
now. Chubby Kerr has been in the Pacific, but is home on
leave. Charles Kerr got back in the Navy with the Seabees,
but was released some months ago. Bobby Hargrove is in
the Army and back in this country after a long tour in
Iceland. His brother is in Italy. As you see, practically
all the boys are in service. To name all of them would
be impossible. Other than missing the boys, the town is
the same. The war had little effect on this country, other
than the rationing of a few items, which became scarce, such
as gasoline, tires, cars, sugar, etc.

We are hoping that you are coming out in good physical
condition. Your letter gives up more hope with respect
to this than we have had. In case, you are to be assigned
to a hospital, see if you can not get assigned to the Naval
Hospital at Camp Lejeune. Camp Lejeune is a large Marine
base which has been built at Jacksonville, N.C., and is just

298

fifty five miles from here. Hope you will not need
anything more than some meat on your bones, and, if
that is all, hurry home and your mother will have you
fat in a short time, if chicken, country ham and
good food is what you need.

It is impossible to tell you how glad we all are that
you are on your way home. Be sure to let your mother
know your condition at the earliest possible moment --
she is living to hear that you are all right.

With best wishes, I am,

Sincerely yours,

Howard H. Hubbard

Several of the men drew $1000.00 or $1500.00 and headed for the first bar past the front gate of the hospital. Several simply burst into a tavern and shouted, "Drinks on the house," setting up the drinks for everyone. Some were so happy to be home they partied all night again, blowing three or four years pay in so many days. When Dick returned to the hospital that night, he found that two of his buddies had bought a suitcase, filled it with liquor, and brought it back into the ward.

The nurses were there dancing all night again. They never stopped dancing or even complained about being tired. They just kept dancing and frolicking with any of the servicemen who seemed to need their company. The girls realized that this was a really special event. As soon as one man would get tired, another would take his place on the dance floor.

The men ate and drank whatever they wanted from the hospital kitchen. They could come and go as they wished, either day or night, as long as the doctors did not have a test planned for them. At the end of the week Dick was pronounced fit. He was ready to go home to Clinton by the fastest method he could find.

The first available means of transportation for Dick out of California was a mail plane, which was heading eastward with a load of mail and a few seats for passengers. The men had been given A-1 priority passes to go home, so Dick and a buddy who was also a former POW decided to try to hop aboard the mail plane.

When the two reached the gate at the airport, they told the attendant they wanted to go to Norfolk, Virginia. "There is a plane warming up right now but its full," he said. "Will this help?" Dick asked, flipping out the priority pass. The clerk whistled to another attendant. "This is the first one of these I've seen," he said. "Go bump two off that plane. These two men have got to go."

A few minutes later two grumbling officers, one a Navy Lt. Commander and the other a Marine Major, hopped off the plane and headed back toward the terminal. Dick and his buddy passed them on their way across the tarmac toward the plane. "Is that what bumped us off?" one asked the other, eyeing the two enlisted men still clad in ill-fitting uniforms. "I guess so," muttered the other. Dick and his buddy were the only two enlisted men on the plane.

The plane took off and headed eastward, dropping off mail at Oakland and Bakersfield, California; Alberquerque, New Mexico; Amarillo, Texas; Columbus, Ohio; and finally Norfolk, Virginia. A fast checkup at the Norfolk Navy Base showed Dick to be in reasonably good condition, so a 30 day pass was granted, starting the next day. This time he did not call home, wanting to savor the joy of surprising his family. He caught the first available bus, arriving in Fayetteville, N.C., at 11:00 p.m. Even though Dick was only thirty-five miles from home, the reunion with his family that he wanted so badly would have to wait. The last bus of the evening had already pulled out.

Dick spent the night in the Fayetteville bus station, happy to be a free man who could do anything he wanted to do. The next morning he boarded the first bus heading eastward out of

Dick Darden Is Back In States

SEPT. 20 - 1945

Had Been Prisoner of Japan For 45 Months Prior to Liberation September 5

Mrs. Eva Bell Darden is the happiest woman in Clinton, and rightfully so.

Her son, J. B. (Dick) Darden, who had been a prisoner of the Japs for 45 months, called Saturday afternoon from Oakland, Calif., advising that he had arrived there by plane from Tokyo on September 13. He was two days getting the phone call through. A telegram filed before he reached the states was delayed and reached Mrs. Darden after he had gotten the phone call through.

Mrs. Darden received a letter mailed from Oakland Tuesday afternoon. Dick wrote that he flew on a B-29 from Tokyo to Oakland,

He wrote that he was okey, except being underweight. He stated, however, that he had gained 20 pounds in 10 days, or since he was liberated and had been in American hands. That was on September 5. "I need to gain 20 more pounds before I reach normal," he said. He also told of the destruction wrought in Japan by the B-29 Superfortress raids. The Osaka camp, where he was stationed, was bombed six times from June 1 to June 19, he wrote, and the entire camp was burned. He escaped injury, however.

Mrs. Darden received a telegram from her son early this morning, in which he stated that Nick Waller, of the U. S. Navy, and a son of Mrs. Ethel Waller, of Clinton, spent several hours with him Tuesday of this week. Dick is in a Naval hospital at Oakland, but will be flown to Portsmouth, Va., as soon as his physical check-up is completed.

"Dick," as he is best known locally, enlisted in the U. S. Navy on June 11, 1940. He was seaman, first class, when he was captured by the Japs on Wake Island, December 24, 1941. He was a prisoner of the Japs for 45 month. His mother had received word from him several times, but she had not had any direct word for some time before the call Saturday. He expects to get home in a short time, and Mrs. Darden is looking forward with keen anticipation to that occasion.

Fayetteville. As it rumbled over the bridges that crossed Coharie Creek just outside town, Dick sensed the smell of the swamp, remembering the many afternoons when he was a boy fishing there with his dad. Coharie swamp had never smelled so sweet. All of his senses began to tell Dick that he was nearly home at last.

300

Chapter 60
AT HOME AGAIN IN CLINTON, N.C.

By 6:30 a.m. Dick was walking down McKoy Street in Clinton, North Carolina, U.S.A., safe at home at last. The reunion was ever so sweet. The local newspaper covered the event and described Dick and his mother as the happiest man and woman in town.

News spread over the town like wildfire. All day long there was a steady stream of visitors. Everyone expressed their best wishes at his return, but Dick knew that many just wanted to see what an ex-Japanese POW looked like. His weight was back up to 140 pounds, but this was still eighty pounds lighter than he had been when he left in 1940. Dick spent the month at home eating, visiting with old friends, eating, catching up on the news of the war, eating, enjoying his family, and, of course, eating. He would gain forty pounds during the thirty days that he spent at home, savoring Mama's cooking all day every day.

After the thirty-day leave at home with his family in Clinton, Dick's weight loss was becoming less and less apparent. Mama's home cooking seemed to be a never ending source of nourishment and comfort for him. Chicken and dumplings, hush puppies, country ham, and Mama's special chocolate layer cake had never tasted so good. Dick began to regain his strength and he soon tipped the scales at 180 pounds for the first time since 1942.

Dick went back to the Navy base in Norfolk, Virginia, on the appointed day. There he was granted an additional sixty day leave and a promotion. He came back home where he continued to enjoy his Mom's good cooking. The town

planned a parade and special event honoring Dick and Medal of Honor recipient Geddie Herring. On November 12 the two heroes were given a parade through town in their honor. Dick rode with his mother and Geddie rode in another car with his family. At a reception both men were honored and given a beautiful silver wine bucket as a symbol of their town's appreciation.

Dick enjoyed the fall of 1945, living at home with his family and eating his fill of foods he had dreamed about for the previous four years. With the pay he received at his new rank, he could afford an automobile. He purchased a used 1939 Chevrolet, the first car ever owned by anyone in his family. It was also in the fall of 1945 that Dick met Edythe Taylor. One of Dick's friends, Fatty Collins, had introduced the two at a get-together just a few weeks after Dick had returned home from Japan. Edythe was a school teacher, the daughter of a well-known school principal in the local school system. She was teaching at Clinton High and was, by all accounts, a dark-haired beauty who was one of the prettiest girls in the county. She and Dick hit it off and began seeing each other on a regular basis.

Late in 1945 when he had exhausted all of his official leave time, Dick received orders to report to Cherry Point Marine Air Station in Havelock, N.C. This meant he would be stationed only 100 miles from home, so Dick was elated about his assignment there. By that time Dick had been promoted again to Chief Boatswain's Mate. The pay was good, the uniform was smart, and Dick began to enjoy the privileges afforded to a former POW and war hero.

Dick would be under the command of a Marine Major, and was stationed at Cherry Point. His assignment would be to operate a crash boat out of Morehead City, N.C.

SEPT. 20 - 1945

FROM THE EDITOR'S DESK
DICK DARDEN

Dick Darden, the Clinton sailor who was captured by the Japanese on Christmas Eve, 1941, telephoned a very happy mother in Clinton Saturday that he was back in the United States, had gained 20 pounds, needed 20 more, and that he was o. k.

Dick's mother, Mrs. Eva Bell Darden, has patiently waited these years, listening to radios to the wee hours of many mornings hoping to pick up some broadcast which might contain a message from her son. Dick sent her a wire message before he left Tokyo for Oakland, Calif., where he landed Sept. 15 in one of the Army's huge C-54.

Uninjured except for constant hunger, Dick said the Osaka prison camp where he was interned was raided six times by B-29's within a period of three weeks, that it was burned completely but that he managed to escape.

A telegram Wednesday told Mrs. Darden that Dick had talked with Nick Waller, also of the Navy, son of Mrs. Ethel Waller, of Clinton. Dick's in a hospital at Oakland, and expects to be transferred to Portsmouth, Va., within a few days.

For a man like Dick Darden, and for a courageous mother such as his, The News this week suggests the town of Clinton plan an appropriate homecoming. Gen. Wainwright was welcomed home, and he suffered no more than did Dick.

Certainly Clinton's hero is deserving, and the occasion could well be dedicated to the memory of all those Sampsonians who paid the Supreme Sacrifice that Freedom should not perish.

Dick Darden Is At Home Today

Arrived This Morning After Spending 45 Months in a Jap Prison Camp

The people of Clinton are happy today—happy to have J. B. (Dick) Darden back home after an absence of more than five years, 45 months of which was spent as a prisoner of the Japs. He arrived in Clinton at 6:30 this (Wednesday) morning and went immediately to the home of his mother, Mrs. Eva Bell Darden, McCoy street. Quiet naturally, she is the happiest woman in Clinton today, and just as naturally, Dick is the happiest man.

Mr. Darden came to Clinton from a Naval hospital in Portsmouth, Va., where he had arrived by plane from Oakland, Calif., last Saturday. His only stop between Oakland and Portsmouth was in Washington, D. C. He made the entire trip from Japan to Portsmouth by plane, having been liberated from the Jap prison camp on September 5, this year. He gained 20 pounds in 10 days after getting into American hands and has continued to gain. He looks well, considering his experiences. His last visit home was in August, 1940.

As has been stated in The Sampson Independent, "Dick," as he is familiarly known to his friends, was captured by the Japs when Wake Island fell on December 24, 1941. He was in the regular Navy, having enlisted in June, 1940. He was seaman, first class, when captured. He was taken to Japan and for some time had been in the Osaka war prison camp. This camp was bombed by American Superfortress planes six times from June 1 to June 19, this year. The entire camp was completely burned by the raiders, but Dick escaped unharmed.

Mr. Darden will be at home for 10 days and then return to Portsmouth for a few days, after which he will get another 90-days leave.

Dick with the first car ever owned in his family, His 1939 Chevrolet, in the fall of 1945.

This suited Dick just fine, and when 1946 rolled around he was skippering a powerful PT boat in the waters between Bogue Sound and Cape Lookout. Just after the New Year's holiday Dick wrote a letter of appreciation to the newspaper in Clinton, thanking the town for the honors it had presented to him on his return home. Clearly, Dick had enjoyed the fall of 1945, savoring the warmth given to him by his family, his hometown, and his new girlfriend.

The Marines had a bombing range just off Morehead City, so Dick's usual assignment was to operate just outside the limits of the range and be prepared to lend assistance in case a problem occurred with the planes that were practicing their bombing and strafing in the range. Should any pilots have to bail out of their aircraft, Dick was nearby to pick them up. His boat would "lie to" just out of danger and be ready if needed. Actually many of his days were spent carrying V.I.P.'s from Washington, "inspectors" as they were called officially, out 100 miles into the Gulf Stream on fishing jaunts.

Later in the spring of 1946 Dick was reassigned to the Coast Guard Station near Fort Macon, the old Confederate fort at the inlet on Bogue Sound across from Morehead City. This was another good assignment, since the Coast Guard station was located near the quaint old fishing village of Beaufort, where Dick had relatives, and Atlantic Beach. Bogue Sound is a twenty mile long stretch of shallow water on the land side of Bogue Banks, and just through the inlet on the other side is the Atlantic Ocean. Dick could take his boat from the Coast Guard Station through the inlet and into the ocean in ten minutes. During the spring of 1946 Dick was told to report to the Major's office at the Cherry Point Marine Air Station in Havelock. As he walked into a long quonset hut and approached the major's office, Dick noticed a man standing near the other end of the building. "I know that guy," Dick thought to himself. The two men had spotted each other and stood about fifty feet apart, each eyeballing the other.

Then each man recognized the other. Marine Colonel Henry G. "Spider" Webb still limped because of the missing toes which had been shot off at Wake Island. Even so, the two men ran toward each other. The two men embraced, Dick hugging the old friend who had spent time with him in the bunker hospital on Wake during the Japanese invasion.

The reunion was quite a spectacle, a Marine Colonel hugging a Navy Chief Boatswain's Mate. The breach of protocol caused several Marines nearby to stop and stare. The two men could not care less what anyone around them thought since the younger Marines, for all their toughness and training, could not possibly understand the bond between these two men. Dick and Spider talked for a while and then agreed to keep in touch. Spider was stationed at Cherry Point, and he visited Dick in Morehead City several times in the weeks that followed.

Dick remained in the Navy and assigned to the Coast Guard station until his discharge in July 1946. Good job opportunities were plentiful for the young war hero in the post-war 1940's. Wedding plans quickly bloomed for Dick and Edythe, and the two were married in September. Clinton was more than willing to offer one of its favorite sons a good job in local government. The possibility of running for public office surfaced. Dick decided to leave the Navy and settle down in his hometown. The future looked rosy indeed for Dick Darden as he approached his 27th birthday.

Darden Collection

Dick with Edythe Taylor, the pretty school teacher he met in the fall of 1945.

Dick sits on the stern of his crash boat as it zips across the water.

First Class Boatswains Mate J. B. Darden during the fall of 1946.

Chapter 61
THE AFTERMATH

Shortly after the American forces reoccupied Wake Island, in September of 1945, work began to make the airstrip ready for air traffic. By mid-September the runway was ready for planes to land, and by late September members of the 85th Naval Construction Battalion began to arrive on the island. Their mission was to construct a naval air base. About the same time that the SeaBees began work on the island, the 1242 Japanese were preparing to leave Wake for home. Over 700 boarded the transport TACHIBANA MARU on October 4, 1945, and the remaining 519 boarded the HIKAWA MARU on November 1.

Sixteen Japanese were held on Wake Island when the HIKAWA MARU sailed for Japan. These included Admiral Sakaibara, his Adjutant, Lt. Col. Soichi Tachibana, and others who were suspected of war crimes in connection with the disappearance of the 98 American civilians from Wake in late 1943. These sixteen men were taken to Kwajalein in the Marshall Islands on November 5 aboard the destroyer SOLEY. This ended the Japanese occupation of Wake Island.

After the surrender of Wake, no Americans were found alive on the island. Admiral Sakaibara and the other officers were questioned concerning the 98 American civilians who had been left on the island when the final group of wounded American military men, including Dick Darden, had been taken off the island in May of 1942. During the interrogations several of the Japanese gave identical stories about the demise of the 98 men, suggesting that the Japanese officers on Wake had jointly prepared a fictitious story they thought would be the most acceptable reason for the disappearance of the civilian work force.

The Japanese stated that during the aerial bombing and naval bombardment of the island on October 6-7, 1943, all of the 98 men were in two bomb shelters. One of the shelters took a direct hit from an American bomb, killing all inside. That night the remainder of the American group, housed in the other shelter, overpowered and killed their guard. They took two rifles and escaped to the beach on the north side of Wake Island. There the men were cornered by the Japanese, refused to surrender, put up a fight (presumably with the two rifles), and were wiped out to the very last man.

The idea that such a group of civilians would put up any fight at all, armed with two shoulder weapons against hundreds of heavily armed Japanese troops with machine guns, and then refuse to surrender in the face of death in the classical Japanese style, surely sounded ridiculous to the Marine interrogators. They continued to

National Archives

The wreckage of this Japanese Zero litters the beach on Wake Island, September 20, 1945

The bombed out remains of the Pan Am Hotel on Wake Island, September 20, 1945

pursue the truth.

The trial of Admiral Sakaibara and the other suspected war criminals was held on Kwajalein. One of the defendants, Lt. Commander Torashi Ito, committed suicide while awaiting trial in prison. He left a statement behind that implicated Admiral Sakaibara. The Admiral was confronted with the signed document, at which time he confessed to ordering the execution of the 98 Americans.

Admiral Sakaibara admitted that during the bombardment of October 6-7, 1943, he feared that the island was about to be invaded by American forces. He prepared his men for such an invasion, but was concerned that he would have the 98 Americans at his rear if an invasion were to occur. His barbaric remedy for the problem followed shortly thereafter. He had the 98 men taken from their barracks to the northern shore of Wake Island near the channel. There he had the men bound and blindfolded, and made them face the sea. Japanese soldiers took positions on the beach behind the helpless men. The Japanese gunners opened fire with rifles and machine guns, executing all of the men by shooting them in their backs.

The bodies of the 98 civilians were buried in a crude mass grave at the sight of the execution. Some twenty-two months later, when it became apparent that the island would be surrendered to American forces, the remains of the 98 bodies were exhumed and reinterred at the American cemetery near the end of the airstrip and Peacock Point. Later the remains were again unearthed by Americans who wanted to bury the men properly in the American cemetery. After weeks of sorting, the job of identifying bones and matching bodies proved to be impossible. The remains were interred for a third time. On that occasion they were given a proper memorial service.

The town of Clinton was proud of its native sons who served their country during World War II. Dick Darden was welcomed home and shortly after his return in the fall of 1946 he was nominated as the Democratic candidate for Sheriff. The Democrats produced a strong slate of candidates, most young veterans of the war. Geddie Herring was on the ticket, running for Clerk of Superior Court. When the election was held on November 5, Dick lost to the Republican candidate Perry Lockerman.

Dick's hometown offered him a job working with the local city government. Before long he had worked his way up the ladder to become City Manager of Clinton, and soon the title of Civil Defense Director became his as well.

Dick and Edythe had their first child in 1947. Jim was born in September and the future appeared rosy indeed for the popular couple. By 1950 a second child was on the way, and son Steve was born in April, 1951. Dick and Edythe began thinking about building a new home, and plans for more children were in the works. Edythe continued to teach home economics at the local high school.

In 1951 the position of Postmaster in Clinton became available. The persons scoring highest on the Civil Service exam would have the best chance at the job and veterans would have first priority. Dick decided to pursue the job and became Postmaster late in the year. He was confirmed by President Harry Truman as one of his last acts before turning over the Presidency to Dwight D. Eisenhower the following year. Dick would hold the position of

Postmaster in Clinton for seven years.

In the years after his return to Clinton, Dick was asked to present programs to numerous civic clubs concerning his war experiences. He addressed the local Rotary, Grange, and Jaycee chapters. Walter Moore was a young Jaycee when Dick was the speaker for the Clinton chapter. Forty-seven years later Moore would still vividly remember that meeting. He would recall that there was a charged atmosphere at the meeting in which "you could hear a pin drop" as Dick recounted his experiences on Wake Island and in the Japanese prisons to the young men.

Dick and Edythe's family continued to grow during the early 1950's. Their third son, Ron, was born in September of 1952. Not to be denied a daughter, the couple had their fourth child in November of 1953. A fine daughter, Denise, was born, and construction began on the new house. The following year Dick and Edythe moved into their new home, a spacious brick duplex on Blount Street that they shared with Dick's aunt, Frances Wright.

In the late 1950's Dick Darden left his position as Postmaster in Clinton, divorced his wife Edythe, and moved to the nearby city of Fayetteville. There he served as a deputy sheriff for several years and ultimately became a detective in the Cumberland County Sheriff's Department. Dick later became a Magistrate in the Cumberland County court system, and served the public for the final fifteen years of his career in that capacity.

During his tenure with the Sheriff's Department, Dick met and married his second wife, Sally W. Vann. Dick and Sally settled several miles north of Fayetteville and live there today. Sally, a nurse, and Dick both retired in the early 1980's and went into the nursery/greenhouse business. For several years they enjoyed a good plant brokerage and growing business.

Sally became very adept at growing indoor plants, and Dick made frequent trips in his truck to Florida to buy plants for resale in North Carolina. The couple built a successful business and constructed five greenhouses before selling the business and retiring in 1985. They are currently enjoying their retirement, fishing in their three-acre pond, loafing, traveling to Wake Island Defender's reunions, and corresponding with POW buddies.

Edythe Taylor Darden also remarried and lives near Fayetteville, N.C. Her second husband is Ernest West, a fine man and prominent resident of the Linden community. Both are now retired and are active in community affairs, especially their church. Both are teachers in their Sunday School, and Ernest is well known as an outstanding lay preacher.

Dick is active in local POW organizations. On several occasions he has addressed the graduating class of the U. S. Army Special Warfare School at Fort Bragg. The topic of his talks to the young Army officers is the plight of prisoners of war. He describes his years in the Japanese prisons and offers suggestions for surviving such an ordeal. Dick has also addressed gatherings of veterans during Veteran's Day ceremonies.

Dick and Sally Darden now live peacefully near Interstate 95 just north of Fayetteville. Dick occupies himself by fishing in his pond, playing with his nine grandchildren, watching television, and corresponding with his fellow Wake Islanders. When they get

Darden Collection

Dick proudly wears his Chiefs uniform, Spring 1946.

Darden Collection

Dick and Edythe just before their marriage in September, 1946.

HERE'S LUCK FOR SAMPSON'S DEMOCRATIC VETERANS.

. . . if luck is any factor, Sampson County's slate of veterans stands a good chance to defeat Republican county officials in the coming general election. Here, State Auditor George Ross Pou, at right, hands out rabbit's feet to Stewart B. Warren of Clinton, Sampson Democratic chairman; James B. Darden of Clinton, candidate for sheriff; and R. Geddie Herring of Roseboro, candidate for clerk of court. Herring won the Congressional medal of honor, and Darden was a prisoner of the Japs for 45 months. Both served in the Navy.

together, as they frequently do now, they always enjoy the conversation, good food and drink, and friendship so common whenever there is a meeting of true friends. That which is unique to this group, however, is the fact that rarely is their an encounter among these friends when there is not a mention of the days gone by when they were "Guests of the Emperor."

Darden Collection

Dick Darden as City Manager of Clinton during the early 1950's

Darden Collection

Dick and Edythe with their first child, James B. Darden III, late in 1947.

Chapter 62
THE WIG–WAG – AN EPILOGUE

Dick Darden, Jim Cox and Ralph Holewinski pose by a Confederate mortor at Battery Park in Charleston across form Fort Sumpter, October, 1988

The Wake Defenders are extremely proud of their "continuing camaraderie." They currently have an active association which publishes a newsletter, the WIG-WAG, and has a reunion each year at various sites throughout the United States. Occasionally the Wake Defenders in various geographical regions of the country will also have semi-annual mini-reunions.

The friendships that are formed by men who go into battle together are unlike any other. An outsider senses very quickly that these men possess a common thread which cannot be seen or understood by the rest of us. They have fought together and bled together. They are brothers in the awful experiences of Wake Island and the Japanese prisons. They have seen their friends die under horrible conditions. The quotation on the cover sheet of their newsletter perhaps explains it best: "Destiny forged inextricable bonds of friendship."

Despite the intensity of the friendships within this group of men, it was not until the mid-1980's, forty years after returning from Wake Island and the POW camps, that Dick Darden was ready to rejoin his buddies. He began to receive and faithfully read THE WIG-WAG, and correspond with his former buddies in the Wake Defenders organization. He was contacted by several of his old military acquaintances, including Ralph Holewinski and Jim Cox, who invited him to join them at the annual Wake Defenders reunion. Finally, in 1987, the reunion was held in New Orleans, Louisiana.

Dick attended the emotional four-day affair, accompanied by his second wife, Sally, and oldest son, Jim. Once again Dick saw and spoke with James P. S. Devereux, by this time a retired General in failing health.

Again in 1988, when the reunion was held in Charleston, South Carolina, Dick, Sally, and son Jim attended. Evidence of the intensity of the friendships between the men was easy to see. At this meeting Dick enjoyed the company of Ralph Holewinski, Jim Cox, Glenn Tripp, Charles Holmes, Robert Hanna, Arthur Poindexter, and others. Most of the men are now in their late sixties or older. Even so, they still snap to attention when they see their nation's colors, and have little compassion for those who do not have the same pride in their country.

These men seem amazingly young and fun-loving. Many have gone on to enjoy prestigious careers while others have not. Some still show physical evidence of their time in battle, and others have physiques that offer no hint of the pain they have endured. All are still embraced by their "inextricable bonds," however, and all still have the vivid memories.

Most of the former POW's seem to harbor little ill feeling toward the Japanese, and some openly admire their culture and work ethic. However, all vividly remember the events that occurred between 1941 and 1945. Nearly all of these men hated their Japanese captors during their imprisonment, but most now seem to have mellowed, at least to the point that they will tolerate the Japanese. Some even drive Toyota and Nissan automobiles, and are reluctant to criticize the current economic takeover by the Japanese of American businesses and large amounts of American real estate.

When one digs deeply enough, however, the old scars are still there, and some of the Wake defenders despise the Japanese people, or specific Japanese individuals, to this day. One Wake Defender insisted that he holds no grudge against the Japanese people in general, but commented that he would never go back to Japan. "There are a few people," he said as he remembered the brutal treatment he received nearly fifty years ago, "who, if I came face to face with, I would kill on the spot."

Some Wake Islanders wonder aloud just how well the current generation is handling the burden that every American carries on his shoulders, the duty to defend our freedom. Some wonder if today's youth, having never been hungry or lived through a depression, would be willing and able to fight to defend America as the men of World War II did. Interestingly, some of the Wake Islanders feel that we are better prepared today than ever before. They feel that today's young people would be quite accountable if freedom were threatened.

Whichever the case might be, the Wake Defenders seem comfortable with their current state of affairs. They are proud that they carried their nation's flag and never gave in to the harsh oppression of the Japanese government. Perhaps these men are so relaxed now because they know that they have fought their last battle. They have passed the torch of freedom to the next generation.

They won their war, and they will never have to fight again.

In November, 1985, Ralph Holewinski and Arthur Poindexter were among thirty former Marines who participated in a return visit to Wake Island. The men flew to Hawaii and then on across the Pacific to Wake. Upon touching down they were allowed to tour the island, visiting many of the positions from which they fought. They found much of the old Wake Island still remaining, but they also found that many changes had been made.

One man who had been a Marine on Wake, Corporal "Swede" Pearsall, took along a metal detector so that he could look for a safe that he contended he had buried in the coral of Wake just before the Japanese takeover. He claimed to have filled it with a considerable amount of money, but after carefully scanning the sands of Wake atoll, he was unable to find the forty-four year old treasure. There are far more bones of dead men on Wake today than pieces of treasure. In addition to the Americans who are buried on Wake, hundreds of Japanese troops died at their battle stations and were buried nearby in the coral sand.

Ralph Holewinski remembered Wake as a forbidding place with only scrubby trees and undergrowth for vegetation. To his surprise, the island now supports a much greater variety of vegetation. Contractors and landscapers have introduced palm trees and beautiful flower gardens.

The military base on Wake now has an impressive airport and several large modern administration buildings. Most of the building and changes on the island since the war have come as a result of the airplane. These changes date back to the early postwar days.

In late November, 1945, a plane arrived on the island with Pan Am officials who would survey the remains of the airline's

Darden Collection

Dick Darden poses with General Devereux at the New Orleans reunion in 1987. General Devereux passed away a few months later.

This January, 1956 photo of Wake shows both Peale and Wilkes Islands as heavily foliated, and the three parts of the airport are finished. There is no sign of the Sewa Maru. It apparently has slipped into the depths of the ocean.

facilities. They found that the Pan Am Hotel had been completely destroyed during the many Japanese and American bombing raids of the past four years. In the months immediately after the war there was a world-wide shortage of vessels for shipping, so Pan Am had considerable difficulty in having supplies and materials shipped to the island for rebuilding their facilities. Despite these difficulties, on March 26, 1946, Pan American World Airways resumed flights across the Pacific Ocean using Wake Island as a refueling point.

The coming of the long range jetliner with the capability of holding enough fuel to complete a trans-Pacific flight without landing to refuel made the Wake Island stop unnecessary. Pan Am discontinued service to Wake on December 7, 1971, thirty years to the day after the bombing of Pearl Harbor.

While few travelers visit the island now, the military garrison there enjoys the beauty of a remote desert isle wrapped around a magnificent blue lagoon. The rusty hulks of cannons, along with the small museum and a few remains of bunkers and pill boxes, offer scant evidence of the carnage and suffering that happened here nearly a half century ago.

Between the airport and the site of the old Camp #2 are the ruins of several homes that appear to have been very nice accommodations at one time. They were built during the Korean conflict and were used until the Vietnam War. The ships that ground ashore during the battle on Wake's south beach, and during the Japanese occupation of the island, have long since slipped off the reef and into the unseen depths just offshore.

The men who returned to Wake noticed a difference in the fauna as well as the flora. They saw none of the peculiar rats which had been omnipresent during their pre-war occupation of the island. The rodents had apparently been killed to extinction by the hungry Japanese troops during the late phases of the war.

Gone also were many of the birds which had been too numerous to count in the early days. The flightless rail, a peculiar wading bird which had bright red tail feathers and resembled a small Kiwi, had been one of Skee's favorites on the island. Some of the Marines had used the long red feathers for decorations. None of these birds were seen when Skee returned in 1985. They, too, were apparently victims of the war and the appetites of the starving Japanese troops.

During the war in Vietnam, Wake Island became very active as a refueling stop for aircraft going to and from southeast Asia. During the later stages of the war Vietnamese refugees were flown to Wake. They remained on Wake for some time while officials tussled with the decision about what to do with them.

Apparently no one wanted to issue the order to fly the refugees to the United States, so they stayed on Wake until finally they demanded to be taken on to the U.S.A. They gave the officials on Wake an ultimatum-take us to the United States or else. As they became more disgruntled they vandalized the houses in which they were living, smashing doors and windows so that the structures became uninhabitable.

Along with the new administration buildings on Wake, Holewinski saw a night club and a post office. Another "first" for Skee was seeing several women among the nearly 200 military personnel stationed on Wake. The garrison on Wake now maintains the base primarily as a fuel depot, to be used in the event that the Philippines some day might be taken over by unfriendly forces and the United States would lose Clark Field and other bases that provide a jumping-off point toward Asia. In 1985 the entire population of Wake Island was less than 200, including the American servicemen and women, and the Filipino civilian workers.

Several of the Marines who returned to Wake Island in 1985 scoured the sand dunes for evidence of the extraordinary events of December, 1941. Skee found a couple of the old bunkers, and he located the area where he fought so valiantly on the morning of December 23. He found some old rusted metal that he thought was the remains of the 3" gun where he and Lt. Hanna had been. Several of the men found .50 cal. machine gun shells in the coral sand where they had taken part in the battle. Just a couple of weeks before the men arrived on Wake, a Filipino worker had found what remained of a .50 cal. machine gun. It had been stored with other artifacts that will eventually be put in a museum on the island.

Ironically, a Korean salvage firm had been contracted to pick up the scrap metal that littered the island, some of World War II vintage, but also some from the Korean and Vietnamese wars. The firm gathered all sorts of twisted steel and threw it into piles before mysteriously ceasing the operation. The mounds of artifacts now sit and rust in Wake's salty trade winds.

President Ronald Reagan paid tribute to the defenders of Wake Island in 1985 by stating: "In December, 1941, Americans held their breath as a heroic band of Marines and civilian workers defended Wake Island against overwhelming forces. More than forty years later, forty years after the final victory, we continue to be inspired by your magnificent valor and moved by the sufferings you endured. There are no words to express the magnitude of your sacrifice for America and for the cause of freedom. But I do want you to know that all Americans are grateful and that we shall never forget what you and your departed comrades did and how much we owe you."

Again in June of 1988 a group of Wake Island defenders visited the island. This time they were taking part in a service honoring the civilians and their contributions on Wake. Charles Holmes, along with a dozen Marine defenders and one sailor, took part in a service for the 98 civilians who were murdered by the Japanese occupation force in 1943. Over 170 men, mostly from the group of civilian contractors who were captured on Wake and spent the war in Japanese POW camps, were present during the 1988 trip.

While on Wake, Holmes also participated in a service honoring the memory of the Marines who gave their lives defending Wake. This time the Marines were dressed in Bermuda shorts and sneakers instead of battle gear and combat boots. They carried cameras instead of Springfields on this visit to Wake Island.

Today a monument has been erected to honor those who fought and died on the island. It has bronze plaques on the four sides of the base, and a Marine crest on the top. According to Charles Holmes, even in the harsh salt spray of the island, corrosion has not been allowed to tarnish the metal at the memorial. Marines frequently visit the site, shining and oiling the plaques and crest that honor their fallen brothers. The bonds between the new and old Marines also seem to be "inextricable."

Chapter 63
THE PARTICIPANTS – THE PATHES THEY TOOK

CMDR. WINFIELD SCOTT CUNNINGHAM...A graduate of the Naval Academy at Annapolis, Maryland, Commander Cunningham was the highest ranking American officer on Wake Island during December, 1941. He was ultimately responsible for the American defense of the island, and for its surrender. Cmdr. Cunningham was taken prisoner on Wake and spent forty-five months in Japanese prisons during the war in China. During his captivity, he escaped twice and was recaptured both times.

When the war ended, Cmdr. Cunningham was still in prison in China. After being liberated, he was flown to a U. S. Army hospital in Kunming, China, for a complete physical examination. Then he was flown over the "hump" to Calcutta, India, and on to Egypt. After flying around the southern shore of the Mediterranean and across the Atlantic he arrived in Newfoundland. Finally, on September 7, 1945, he arrived at LaGuardia Airport in New York, and within hours he was flown to Washington where he was united with his wife.

The official versions of the Wake Island saga offered the American public little information about Cmdr. Cunningham's involvement in the defense of the island. In fact, his very presence on the island was questioned by some. Most of the accounts of the action on Wake give little or no credit to the Navy Officer who commanded the Marines there. Cmdr. Cunningham's wife spent much of her time during the war attempting to see to it that her husband was given the accolades that he deserved.

After the war, Cmdr. Cunningham was awarded the Navy Cross for his valiant on Wake Island. He remained in the Navy stationed at Memphis Naval Air Station until 1950, at which time he held the rank of Rear Admiral. He retired in 1950 and went into private business.

Cmdr. Cunningham spent years making continued efforts to gain recognition as the commander of the American forces on Wake Island. In 1986, President Gerald Ford wrote to Admiral Cunningham and acknowledged his part in the defense of Wake Island. Admiral Cuningham died on March 3 of that year. He was survived by his loyal wife and one daughter.

ʹMAJ. JAMES P. S. DEVEREUX...awarded the Navy Cross for his role in the defense of Wake Island in December of 1941. He was liberated from Japanese POW Camp #3, Nishiakibetsu Prison, on Hokkaido Island in September of 1945 and turned over to American forces in Sapporo?. He was accompanied by Lt. Arthur Poindexter, with whom he had been imprisoned, on the long journey back to the United States. The flight made stops in Yokohama, Guam, and Hawaii before reaching Oakland, California.

Holmes Collection

Charles Holmes offers words of rememberence for fallen camrades at the dedication of the USMC Memorial on Wake Island to marines, sailors, and soldiers who defended the island against the Japanese in December 1941.

Devereux was promoted to Lt. Colonel after his return and remained in the Marine Corps until his retirement in 1948. His highest rank was Brigadier General.

General Devereux ran for Congress in 1950 as a Republican in Maryland's 2nd District. He was elected and served as a Representative from 1951 until 1959. He then left the House of Representatives to run for Governor of Maryland. He lost that race to J. Millard Tawes.

While serving in the United States Congress, General Devereux had the opportunity to make an official visit to Japan. At a reception for the congressmen one of his Japanese hosts asked if he had ever been to Japan before. He was said to have momentarily silenced the group around him by responding, "Yes, I was a guest of your Emperor at one time."

General Devereux died of pneumonia on August 5, 1988, at the age of 85. He is survived by his wife, Edna, three sons, four stepchildren, and twelve grandchildren. He was buried at Arlington National Cemetery in Arlington, Virginia.

CAPT. HENRY T. ELROD......one of the true heroes of World War II. The man who found Dick Darden wounded in the woods near the airstrip on Wake Island on December 8, 1941, shot down several enemy planes

The sleek guided missile frigate USS HENRY T. ELROD, at its commissioning July 5, 1985 in Brunswick, GA. It was named for Capt. Henry Elrod, the first Marine airman to receive the Medal of Honor in World War II and the man who found a wounded Dick Darden near the runway on Wake Island and assisted him to an aid station after the first bombing attack on Wake.

as he patrolled the skies around Wake, usually vastly outnumbered by the Japanese raiders. He was the first American to sink a Japanese warship using small caliber bombs from a fighter aircraft during WWII.

When all of the aircraft on Wake Island had been damaged beyond repair, Captain Elrod organized ground troops into a beach defense line in front of the 3" gun manned by Lt. Hanna and Corporal Holewinski. He fought through several hours of intense hand-to-hand combat during the early morning of December 23, 1941. While gallantly defending his position against overwhelming odds, he raised to throw a hand grenade and was shot to death.

Capt. Henry Elrod was the only man to be awarded the Congressional Medal of Honor for his efforts in the defense of Wake Island. The medal was presented posthumously to his widow in November of 1946. In 1986 a U. S. Navy guided missile frigate was named in his honor, the USS ELROD. Dick Darden, along with his wife, Sally, Ralph Holewinski and his wife Edith, Glenn Tripp and his wife, Dorothy, and Tom Kennedy attended the christening of the ship in Brunswick, Georgia.

At the commissioning of the USS ELROD, a young man gave a speech welcoming the crowd to south Georgia. He was an aide to Lindsay Thomas, the congressman representing Brunswick and the district in the U.S. House of Representatives. The young man was Milton Woodside, son of Milton Henry Woodside, who survived the Bataan Death March and spent four years in Japanese prisons. Young Woodside met Tom Kennedy, who had lived in

Umeda Bunsho prison with his father for most of the war. Kennedy and Woodside had been in the prison just a few miles from Osaka 1 prison and Dick Darden.

LT. RUFUS GEDDIE HERRING—After being severely wounded in the landing effort on Iwo Jima in February, 1945, Geddie Herring was brought back to the United States to recuperate. While in the hospital in Quantico, Virginia, he met Virginia Lee Higgs, a Navy nurse from West Virginia. They were later married and settled near Lt. Herring's childhood home of Roseboro, North Carolina, nine miles from Dick Darden's home in Clinton.

In October of 1945, for his courageous efforts in the preparations for the landing on Iwo Jima, and for saving his crew under heavy fire while seriously wounded, Lt. R. Geddie Herring became one of only nineteen North Carolinians to be awarded the Congressional Medal of Honor. He retired from the Navy in April, 1947.

Geddie and Virginia Herring returned to North Carolina where he went into the feed mill and egg hatching business. He operated the business until he retired in 1982. In his retirement he continues to be active in dozens of civic and church activities. The Herrings live today in a spacious colonial home located on the edge of the quiet hamlet of Roseboro and shaded by dozens of tall loblolly pine trees.

CORPORAL RALPH HOLEWINSKI—released on September 8, 1945, after forty-five months of incarceration at the hands of the Japanese. He was granted a 90 day leave, and then went to

314

Great Lakes Hospital where he remained until March, 1946. Skee was still carrying several pieces of Japanese hand grenade in his buttocks. Even though five Japanese doctors had examined him during the war and pronounced him unfit to work except as a water boy at a time when they hungered for his labor, the U. S. Veteran's Administration Compensation Board ruled him only 10% disabled.

Ralph Holewinski's severely injured legs have left him unable to run a step in the nearly fifty years since he ran to help man the 3" gun on Wake Island's south beach on December 23, 1941. His injuries have caused him problems anytime he has attempted to lift objects weighing over twenty pounds since the wounds were sustained. Even so, the Veteran's Administration pronounced him 90% able to go to work.

Ralph Holewinski's home town of Gaylord, Michigan, however, felt differently. Holewinski ran for Sheriff of Otsego County and was elected the youngest sheriff in the state of Michigan. He never lost an election and served as sheriff for thirty-four years before retiring from the job. He was then elected as a County Commissioner.

Ralph Holewinski and his wife, Edith, a former Army nurse who served in India and China during World War II, raised eight children who now live throughout the United States from Boston to California. The Holewinski's live in Gaylord, Michigan, two blocks from a new Veteran's Administration clinic, where Skee is a regular visitor.

SGT. CHARLES HOLMES…remained in the service of his country in the Marine Corps until his retirement in 1964. He served in Yokosuka, Japan, in 1951. One day while eating in the mess hall Holmes spotted a Japanese civilian woman working there that he remembered from the war. When he was a POW this woman had risked her life to bring food to the hungry prisoners. Holmes talked with the woman, and during the conversation each thanked the other. From then on when he visited the mess hall the woman served him as if he were a king.

Charles Holmes also served in Pusan, Korea, in 1953. There he served with the 1st 90mm Anti-aircraft Artillery Battalion. Afterwards he served at various Marine posts across the United States from Indiana to Pennsylvania to Virginia. Holmes is currently the historian for the Wake Island Defenders Association, and was very helpful to the author in compiling materials and photographs for this publication.

Charles Holmes enjoys calligraphy and is active in his hometown church. He is married to Alice Suttie Holmes, and they live on Pecan Street in Bonham, Texas.

LOGAN KAY and FRED J. (SCOTTY) STEVENS…the two civilians who hid for seventy-seven days after the Japanese captured Wake Island. They were transported to Japan in September, 1942, and spent the remainder of the war in Japanese prisons.

First, Kay and Stevens were interned at Sasebo Dam where they endured eighteen months of beatings, starvation, and hard labor. One fifth of the 265 American prisoners in that camp died. In the spring of 1944 they were sent to Camp #23 on the island of Kyushu. They were still there when they were finally liberated after the war.

Logan Kay and Fred Stevens lived through the POW experience and returned home to their families (both were married and had children) in the United States. Logan Kay returned to Clearlake Park, California, and Fred Stevens went back to Sioux City, Iowa.

SGT. TOM KENNEDY—Marine radio specialist. Kennedy was wounded in the first air raid on Wake Island. He spent time in the hospitals on Wake with Dick Darden and Ralph Holewinski before being taken to Japan, where he spent the entire war as a POW. He was in virtually all of the same prisons where Darden and Holewinski were held.

Kennedy joined the Marines in 1934 and almost left the service after his first hitch was up. He had been told, however, that if a Marine pulled twenty years he could retire and be guaranteed a pension for life of $60.00 per month. This was considerably more than he was making at the time, so he decided to stay in until he could retire and claim the exorbitant pension.

Kennedy knew he wanted to go home to Orange Cove, California, and farm like his father. His Dad had forty acres, twenty of it in oranges. His dad made him a deal. The elder would hold the forty acres for Tom until he finished his twenty years with the Marines. He would then allow him to buy out the farm, making one payment each year.

Tom Kennedy retired on schedule in 1954. He returned home and took over the farm, planting the other twenty acres in oranges. He grew oranges until 1982 when he sold out his entire farm, then totaling over 150 acres of orange groves. Tom and his wife, Adina, had one daughter, Donna. They are now retired (on more than $60.00 per month), "just traveling and having a good time."

On the current Japanese expansion in the United States, Kennedy holds no resentment for the Japanese and their purchasing power. He feels that he fought to make America a free country. If the Japanese are willing to work, says Kennedy, its OK for them to buy things with their money. He remembers the Japanese who settled in California before the war as good people who did not interfere with others, taking English classes on Saturdays so that they could fit into American society. He holds some contempt, however, for the emigrants who are moving into southern California now and bringing their language with them, forcing it on English-speaking Americans. Kennedy thinks that the Japanese-Americans who were resettled in detention camps during World War II "got a raw deal."

ADMIRAL HUSBAND E. KIMMEL…became Commander of the Pacific Fleet of the United States Navy in February, 1941, and held that post during the Japanese attack at Pearl Harbor. He was relieved of his command on December 16, 1941, after which he was forced into an early retirement. Adm. Kimmel was court-martialed after the war for his performance during the Pearl Harbor attack.

LT. ARTHUR A. POINDEXTER…Commander of the Mobile Reserve unit during the Battle of Wake Island. Arthur Poindexter was cited for his valor and heroism on Wake Island, and he was held prisoner by the Japanese for forty-four months during the war. He remained in the Marine Corps, serving his country again in Korea. He served as a Marine for twenty-six years, retiring as a Colonel in 1963. After World War II he served in numerous locations around the world, including China, Korea, Taiwan, and Guam.

Colonel Poindexter also taught at the (Nationalist) Chinese Naval War College in Taiwan. He was senior advisor to the

Commandant of the Korean Marine Corps.

After leaving the Marine Corps, Colonel Poindexter enrolled in graduate school and simultaneously coached football at Pomona College in California, having played football in the late 1930's at Kansas University. He went on to become a college professor, teaching political science and international relations. His first teaching assignment was at the University of California at Santa Barbara. Later he taught for twelve years at California State University at Long Beach.

Five of the twenty wounded Wake Island defenders who remainded on Wake Island in January, 1942 attended the Detroit Reunion September 16, 1989. They are L-R: Tom Kennedy, Dick Darden, Spider Webb, Ralph Holewinski, and Slick Sloman

men, numbering fewer than one hundred, maintained control of the island throughout the battle, killing all Japanese troops who landed there except two who were taken prisoner. He surrendered only when ordered personally by Major Devereux to do so. Captain Platt was killed in Korea.

MAJ. PAUL PUTNAM…commanding officer of VMF-211, the Marine fighter squadron on Wake Island. Major Putnam was awarded the Navy Cross for his heroism on Wake Island, and retired from the Marine Corps as a Brigadier General. He died in 1985.

Colonel Poindexter does not seem overly concerned that the Japanese are purchasing large amounts of American real estate. He feels that Japanese competition is good for America, but he feels that their economy has a tremendous advantage over ours since very little of their gross national product goes into defense. He cites a case in point—recent events in the Persian Gulf. The Japanese get the vast majority of their oil, the lifeblood of their economy, from that region. The U. S. is spending billions of dollars keeping the sea lanes open and safe from Iranian terrorism, thus allowing middle-eastern oil to continue flowing into the burgeoning Japanese economy.

Colonel Poindexter gives the Japanese credit for being a people who are willing to work. But they, like the West Germans, do not have an economy that is encumbered by maintaining a large military establishment to preserve their freedom to conduct business. All of their resources can go into the civilian economy.

Poindexter thinks that the Korean economy is even more of a miracle than that of the Japanese. South Korea must maintain one of the largest military establishments of any country its size in the world in order to protect itself from the communists in North Korea. Even though the South Koreans have been on a wartime footing for the last 40 years, they still have an extraordinarily productive economy.

Colonel Poindexter has numerous interests, including scuba diving, writing, lecturing, and even spelunking. He now lives with his wife, Patricia Ann, formerly a nurse, in Huntington Beach, California. The Poindexters have two daughters, one an elementary school teacher and the other an attorney at law.

CAPT. WESLEY PLATT…commanding American officer on Wilkes Island during the final attack on Wake Island. His

CAPTAIN TOSHIO SAITO…the Japanese captain of the NITTA MARU, the ship which transported most of the Americans from Wake Island to Shanghai in January, 1942. Saito ordered and supervised the beheadings of the five Americans on the deck of his ship during the voyage. He was never apprehended after the war to be tried for his crimes. He might be alive today.

ADM. SHIGEMATSU SAKAIBARA…Imperial Japanese Navy—Commandant of Japanese forces on Wake Island during World War II from December, 1942, until the surrender of the island in September, 1945. He was the commanding officer responsible for ordering the mass execution of 96 American civilian laborers on the north beach of the island on October 7, 1943.

In addition to these 96 murders, Admiral Sakaibara personally executed the only civilian who escaped the mass killing. This lone civilian was apprehended and executed one week later on or about October 15, 1943. This execution was carried out by Admiral Sakaibara before an assemblage of officers under his command. Admiral Sakaibara personally beheaded the civilian with his Samurai sword.

Prior to these executions, in July of 1943, Admiral Sakaibara ordered the execution of an American civilian who was being held prisoner on Wake Island. The offense committed by the civilian is not known. Admiral Sakaibara ordered Ensign Nonaka to execute the civilian by beheading the man with a sword. Nonaka carried out the execution in the manner prescribed by Admiral Sakaibara.

Admiral Sakaibara was apprehended by the American forces who occupied Wake Island after the war. His official apprehension date was November 6, 1945. He was taken to Guam where he was tried in a court of law, a luxury not afforded to the 98 unarmed and defenseless civilians who were murdered on Wake. The trial lasted for three days, December 21-24, 1945.

Initially Sakaibara persisted in the alleged necessity of killing the civilians for military reasons. However, one of his co-defendants was Lt. Toraji Ito. Ito committed suicide in prison prior to the trial. He left a written confession which described the actual events of the executions, implicating Sakaibara. When confronted with the truth, Admiral Sakaibara confessed to his part in the killings.

Adm. Shigematsu Sakaibara was found guilty of the murders of the American civilians on Wake Island. He was sentenced to death. For his atrocities on Wake Island, Admiral Sakaibara was hanged on Guam on June 19, 1947.

WILEY "SLICK" SLOMAN…returned to his home state of Texas after the war and initially went to work for the city of Texas City. Later he went into the insurance business, ultimately combining that company with a real estate business.

Wiley Sloman married his high school sweetheart, Mildred, soon after returning from World War II. After more than twenty years of marriage, he lost his wife in 1969 to complications resulting from a wasp sting. His second marriage ended in divorce, as did his third. Later he remarried his third wife, Polly, and they continue to live happily together. He is proud of the fact that his fourth marriage is his second marriage to his third wife.

After spending many years living in the Houston area, Wiley Sloman chose a country setting for his retirement. He and Polly live thirty-five miles west of San Antonio on Hwy 90 in a very quite rural area. They are over seven miles from the nearest town.

NATHAN DAN TETERS…head of the civilian construction work force on Wake Island at the outset of World War II. Teters was captured along with all Americans on the island on December 23, 1941. He, along with all but 98 of the civilian workers, was taken with the Wake Island defenders, to China aboard the NITTA MARU. He remained with the officers while on the NITTA MARU and while in Japanese prisons during the war.

Teters and Cmdr. W. S. Cunningham escaped from their Japanese prison in China in 1944. They hoped to make their way down the Yangtze River and encounter Chinese who were sympathetic to the Allied cause. Most Chinese were opposed to the brutal Japanese occupation of their homeland and would do whatever they could to assist the Nationalist Chinese or Allied forces. The Japanese tracked the two men down, captured them, and tried them for escaping. Both were found guilty and sentenced to be shot to death. Both men managed to avoid execution and were liberated after the war.

After the war Dan Teters resumed his career in the construction field with Morrison-Knudsen. He was awarded the Bronze Star for service to his country on Wake Island. His world-wide construction projects included building air bases for the government of France in French Morocco. For his efforts there France bestowed upon him the rank of Knight in the National Order of the Legion of Honor.

Dan Teters died at his home Friday in Harbor, Washington, on July 25, 1960.

CAPT. FRANK C. THARIN…Marine pilot in VMF-211 on Wake Island. He is thought by Dick Darden to be one of the two officers who found him after the bombing of the airstrip on December 8, 1941, and saved his life by facilitating his removal to the field hospital.

Captain Tharin remained in the Marine Corps after the war. He attended Marine Corps schools at Quantico, Virginia, and the National War College in Washington, D. C. He commanded several Marine air wings based at El Toro, California, and he served as Deputy Commander, Fleet Marine Force, Pacific.

Frank Tharin served in the Marine Corps until his retirement in 1970. Before leaving the service he attained the highest rank that any Marine aviator had ever attained, Lieutenant General.

Gen. Tharin and his wife Betty have three sons. They live in Laguna Beach, California. He enjoys traveling and being involved in numerous civic activities, including the Red Cross. In 1985 Gen. Frank Tharin attended the 50th anniversary reunion celebrating the graduation of his class of 1935 at the U. S. Naval Academy at Annapolis, Maryland. General Tharin passed away in eary 1990.

GLENN E. TRIPP…Yeoman to Cmdr. W. S. Cunningham on Wake Island prior to the war. Immediately after the Pearl Harbor attack on December 8, 1941, Yeoman Tripp was assigned to a 5" artillery unit. He served there and at other assignments during the fifteen-day siege and was taken prisoner on December 23, 1941.

Glenn Tripp survived the voyage of the NITTA MARU to Japan and served forty-five months in Japanese POW of war camps in China and Japan. He was liberated in September, 1945, and remained in the U. S. Navy until he retired with the rank of Lt. Commander.

Glenn Tripp and his wife, Dorothy, now live in Springfield, Virginia. They travel extensively throughout North America in their motor home, visiting friends, relatives, children, and old Wake Island buddies. They are very active in the annual Wake Island reunion.

An interesting story links Glenn Tripp to Tochio Saito, captain of the NITTA MARU. After the war Saito was hunted in Japan in an effort to prosecute him for his war crimes, particularly the beheading of the American servicemen on board the NITTA MARU enroute to Japan in January, 1942. It was Captain Saito who took Glenn Tripp's gold high school class ring as the men were boarding the NITTA MARU at Wake Island. During the search of Saito's home after the war a class ring was found in his belongings. Glenn Tripp later identified the ring, which had his identifying initials on the inside. The ring was returned to Tripp, who still has it in his possession today.

VMF-211…the Marine aviation squadron that fought so valiantly in the skies over Wake Island has a long and distinguished history. The unit was formed in 1937 and was based at the San Diego Naval Air Station where it was equipped with Grumman F-3F biplanes. In 1941 the squadron was moved to the Marine Corps Air Station at Ewa, Hawaii, where the biplanes were replaced with Grumman F4F-3 Wildcats.

All twelve of the VMF-211 pilots who were assigned to Wake Island were either killed or captured as a result of the action there. While the captured Marines of Wake's VMF-211 unit were held in Japanese prisons during the remainder of World War II, other VMF-211 pilots distinguished themselves in many of the major battles of the Pacific theater. VMF-211 fought throughout the

Pacific from Bougainville to the Philippines.

In 1952 the squadron was re-named VMA-211. It has continued to serve, participating in the conflicts in Korea and Vietnam. In Vietnam, VMA-211 was equipped with A-4 Skyhawk jet fighters. In 1980 the squadron returned to the United States from an assignment in Japan. It was based at the Marine Corps Air Station at El Toro, California, where it remains today.

HENRY GORHAM "SPIDER" WEBB...pilot of one of the Grumman F4F-3 Wildcat fighters on Wake Island. Webb was one of the twenty wounded men who, along with Dick Darden, remained on Wake Island until May, 1942. He was shipped to Japan on the ASAMA MARU and remained a prisoner of war in Japan until the end of the war.

When the men from Webb's prison camp were liberated they were separated by service affiliation; he remaining with the Marine contingent. They were deloused and allowed to bathe, after which they were issued new khaki clothing. They were taken to the battleship WISCONSIN where they remained for three days.

Major Putnam was the senior officer in Webb's group. He, Webb, and the other officers were invited to dine with the captain of the WISCONSIN. Webb was rooming with a pilot who flew one of the catapult planes from the battleship. He found a supply of medical alcohol which was called "torpedo juice" and brought it to Spider. The strong spirits were mixed with orange juice to make a concoction which gave Webb "a pretty good glow" for the duration of his time on the WISCONSIN.

Spider Webb boarded an American C-54 airplane in Japan for the return trip to the United States. He flew to Guam where he remained for three days and got a complete physical examination. Having been pronounced healthy enough to travel, he flew on to Kwajalein, where the plane stopped briefly for fuel, and then on to Hawaii.

Henry Webb remained in Honolulu for three days. Then he flew on to California. He was offered his choice of Marine hospitals in the United States to complete his recuperation. He chose Camp Lejeune in Jacksonville, North Carolina, so he could be near his family in Oxford.

After recovering his health, Henry Webb was stationed at Cherry Point Air Station in Havelock, N.C. While there he decided to go to law school. He left the Marines Corps in 1946 and attended George Washington Law School. After graduation he was admitted to the bar and began practicing law in Washington, D.C.

Henry Webb became a successful estate lawyer, spending his entire career in the Washington area. His specialty areas are probate law, wills, trusts, and estates. He is now semi-retired. Spider Webb married a beautiful young lady from Salisbury, N.C., while living in Washington. He and Nancy still live in Kensington, Maryland.

GEN. TOMOYUKI YAMASHITA...commander of the Japanese 25th Army, which attacked the Malay Peninsula at the outset of the war and captured Singapore. He was tried in November and early December of 1945 in Manila and executed for his atrocious war crimes.

THE END

Interviews

Glenn Tripp, Springfield, Va., September, 1987. Ralph Holewinski, New Orleans, La., September, 1987. Jim Cox, New Orleans, La., September, 1987. Glenn Tripp, New Orleans, La., September, 1987. Walter Cook, Crisfield, MD, January, 1988. Sil Caruso, Clinton, NC, September, 1988. Ralph Holewinski, Charleston, SC, October, 1988. Walter Kennedy, Charleston, SC, October, 1988. James R. Brown, Charleston, SC, October, 1988. Arthur A. Poindexter, Charleston, SC, October, 1988. Charles Holmes, Charleston, SC, October, 1988. John Blandy, Charleston, SC, October, 1988. R. Geddie Herring, Roseboro, NC, April, 1989. R. Geddie Herring, Roseboro, NC, May, 1989. Wiley Sloman, Detroit, MI, September, 1989. Henry G. Webb, Detroit, MI, September, 1989.

BIBLIOGRAPHY

THE DEFENSE OF WAKE, Peter Andrews, American Heritage, July, 1987.
LAST MAN OFF WAKE ISLAND, Walter J. Bayler, Bobbs Merrill, 1943.
ENEMY ON ISLAND, ISSUE IN DOUBT, Stan Cohen, Pictorial Histories Publishing Co., 1983.
CHRONOLOGICAL REPORT ON NAS WAKE ISLAND, Walter J. Cook.
WAKE ISLAND COMMAND, Winfield S. Cunningham, Little, Brown & Co., 1961.
THE STORY OF WAKE ISLAND, James P. S. Devereux, Pippincott, 1947.
WAKE ISLAND WIG-WAGS, Franklin D. Gross, Published Quarterly.
THE DEFENSE OF WAKE, R. D. Heinl, Jr., U. S. Marine Corps, 1947.
THE RISING SUN IN THE PACIFIC, 1931-April 1942, Samuel Eliot Morison, Little, Brown & Co., 1963.
AMERICA'S BEACH OF BAYONETS, Military, Arthur A. Poindexter, September, 1987, and October, 1987.
WAKE ISLAND, THE HEROIC GALLANT FIGHT, Duane Schultz, St. Martin's Press, 1978.
DEPOSITION CONCERNING TREATMENT OF AMERICAN PERSONNEL ABOARD THE NITTA MARU, Glenn E. Tripp, 1947.
MUSTER ROLL, WAKE ISLAND DEFENDERS, Charles Holmes and Arthur Poindexter, 1988.
WAKE ISLAND MARINE, STILL IN LOVE WITH THE CORPS, by Tom Bartlett, LEATHERNECK, 1988.
WAKE, 1568-1946, by Captain E. A. Junghans, U.S.N., 1946.
WAKE, PACIFIC DIVISION, Pan American Airways.
WAKE ISLAND, by Don DeManche, 1966.
HYDROPONICS AT WAKE, Pan American Weekly New Bulletin, Vol. IV, No. 2, May 3, 1938.
HISTORY OF WAKE FROM MARCH, 1946 TO INACTIVATION, by Captain E. A. Junghans, U.S.N.
INFAMY, by John Toland, Doubleday.
THE FALL OF JAPAN, by William Craig, The Dail Press.
I SAW TOKYO BURNING, by Robert Guillan, Doubleday & Co., 1981.
CORREGIDOR, FROM PARADISE TO HELL, by Ben D. Waldron, Pine Hill Press, 1988.
SURVIVAL AMIDST THE ASHES, by Lyle W. Eads, Stewart Publishing Co., 1985.
THE HISTORY OF WORLD WAR II, by Lt. Colonei Eddy Bauer, The Military Press, 1966.
THE TWENTY MEN LEFT BEHIND ON WAKE ISLAND, a report by Wiley Sloman, 1989.
WAKE REMEMBERED, by Captain Kevin K. Krejcarek, VFM Magazine, September, 1986.
IT BEGAN AT WAKE ISLAND, by Eugene Monihan, Description of lithograph by the same name, 1989.
MILITARY SMALL ARMS OF THE 20TH CENTURY, by Ian V. Hogg, DBI Books, Inc., 1985.
A SPECIAL VALOR, by Richard Wheeler, Harper & Row Publishers, 1983.
FIGHTERS OF WORLD WAR II, Crescent Books, Crown Publishers, 1987.
HISTORY OF PRISONER OF WAR UTILIZATION, by Lt. Col. George G. Lewis, Department of the Army, 1955.
JAPAN'S SECRET WAR, by Robert K. Wilcox, William Morrow and Company, 1985.
JAPAN AT WAR, Time-Life Books, 1980.
THE ROAD TO TOKYO, Time-Life Books, 1979.
THE RISING SUN, Time-Life Books, 1979.

Published by
The Greenhouse Press
P. O. Box 1087
Clinton, N. C. 28328
(919) 592 - 3725
Additional copies of this book are available at this address at
a cost of $20.00 plus $4.00 for packaging and mailing. N.C.
residents include $1.00 sales tax.